MARRIAGES
from
EARLY TENNESSEE
NEWSPAPERS
- 1794-1851 -

Edited By:
The Rev. Silas Emmett Lucas, Jr.

Southern Historical Press, Inc.
Greenville, South Carolina

SOUTHERN HISTORICAL PRESS, INC.
PO BOX 1267
Greenville, SC   29601

ISBN #0-89308-092-6

Printed in the United States of America

Introduction

These Marriage notices from the earliest Tennessee Newspapers had been available to the public in the card file of the Tennessee State Library and Archives in Nashville, and hence were unknown to many people working on families in Tennessee.

The Publisher wishes to thank Miss Kendall J. Cram, Director of the State Library and Archives in Nashville for allowing him to have these thousands of cards xeroxed for use in this book.

The reader will note that these notices cover the entire state of Tennessee for the most part, beginning with the earliest ones in 1794 in the Knoxville Gazette.

CONCERNING AN INDEX: It will be noted that this book has not been indexed and that the book is arranged alphabetically by groom. In transcribing these entries from the cards from the files at the Tennessee State Library and Archives, it was found that two cards were typed for each marriage - one for the groom and one for the bride. Therefore, instead of preparing an Index the Publisher has entered the Bride's name and spouse alphabetically by her maiden name in the section with the groom. Thus if one was looking for instance, the marriage of "Mary Childs", he would look in the "C" section until her name was found together with herspouse who in this case was " Walter Lowrie,Esq." To find the date and other details of their marriage, the reader would then go to the "L" Section and find "Walter Lowrie,Esq." to find the date and other details concerning their marriage.

Aaron, Mr. Wm married in Henry County to Julia Parker.
National Banner & Nashville Daily Advertiser. (Friday, February 8, 1833)

Abbay, Mr. Richard married in Davidson county on the 24th inst., by the
Rev. M. Hume to Miss Mary Ann Compton.
National Banner Nashville Whig (Monday, March 28, 1831)

Abbe, Miss Asenath A. married to Rutland, James B.

Abbey, Mr. Anthony S. married in Davidson county on the 31st January
by the Rev. Wm. Hume to Miss Susan L. Compton.
National Banner Nashville Daily Advertiser. (Friday, Feb. 1, 1833)

Abbott, Miss Elizabeth married to Dr. Pierce.

Abbott, Mr. James T. married in Gibson County to Miss Rebecca C.
Barton.
Nashville Whig (Tuesday, April 21, 1846)

Abbott, Josiah B. Jr., Esq., Editor of the Richmond Whig, married to
Miss Catherine C. Randolph in Richmond.
Nashville Republican and State Gazette. (Aug. 27, 1832, Vol. 8, #46).

Abby, Mr. Richard, Davidson County, married to Miss Mary Ann S. Compton.
Nashville Republican and State Gazette (Saturday, March 26, 1831,
No. 109, Vol 6)

Abernathy, C. C. of Giles married in Rutherford County to Miss Narcissa
A. L. Wright, of Rutherford.
Nashville Whig (Wednesday, Jan. 16, 1839)

Abernathy, Miss Elizabeth, married to Mr. Thomas J. Denty.

Abernathy, of Giles married in Montgomery County to Miss Louise Baxter,
daughter of Robert Baxter, Esq., of the Tennessee Iron Works.
Nashville Whig (Monday, Jan. 14, 1839)

Abner, M. Vaughn, married in Williamson county to Harriet F. Craig.
The Western Weekly Review, Franklin, Tenn (Friday, Feb. 10, 1832)

Abstin, Mr. Merry C. married on the 5th inst., to Miss Mary Ann Douglass,
daughter of James Douglass, all of Sumner County.
National Banner & Nashville Daily Advertiser (Monday, April 9, 1832)

Abston, Mr. Joel L., of the Western District, married in Sumner County,
Tennessee to Miss Eveline A. B. Cage, daughter of Mr. Reuben Cage.
National Banner & Nashville Daily Advertiser (Tuesday, June 24, 1834)

Achey, Mr. P. H. of Nashville, formerly of Dayton, Ohio, married on
Tuesday the 12th inst., by the Rev. Mr. Owen to Miss Rebecca R. Moore,
daughter of Mrs. Susan Moore, of Davidson County.
Nashville Whig, (Saturday, May 16, 1846)

Acklen, Mr. John R. H. married in Madison County, Ala., to Miss Harriet
H. Cash.
National Banner & Nashville Whig (Wed., Oct. 19, 1831)

Ackland, Miss Ann married Mr. Spotswood W. Black.

Acklen, Major William Sen. of Franklin County married in Alabama to Mrs.
Mildred Carroll.
National Banner & Nashville Whig. (Friday Feb. 6, 1835)

Acklin, Mr. Claiborn married in Franklin county to Miss Martha M'Carley.
National Banner & Nashville Whig (Sat., Sept. 9, 1826)

Acock, Miss Mary E., married in Logan County, Ky. to Mr. James Utley.

Acuff, Miss Elizabeth married to Mr. Peter C. Moore.

Ada, Miss Nancy married in Giles County to Mr. Matthews C. Russell

Adam, Rev. Absolom of Nashville married by Mr. T. Tanning on the 23rd to Miss Mary C. Richardson of Rutherford County.
National Banner & Nashville Whig (Friday, Sept. 26, 1834)

Adam, Daniel W., Esq. of Jackson, Miss. married on the 26th ult in Sumner Co., by Rev. J. T. Wheat to Miss Anne Bullus.
Nashville Whig (Tuesday, Oct. 1, 1844)

Adams, Mr. Adam G. married on Tuesday evening last 12th inst., by the Rev. Dr. Lapsley to Miss Susan Porterfield, all of Nashville.
Nashville Whig (Thursday, May 14, 1846)

Adams, Miss Agnes married to Mr. William Mayor.

Adams, Charles Francis, Esq., son of Ex-President Adams, married at Medford, near Boston on the 3rd inst., to Miss Abby Brooks, daughter of Hon. Peter Brook.
National Banner (Sat., Sept. 26, 1829)

Adams, Rev. David married in Sullivan County, Tenn. to Miss Susan Craff.
National Banner & Nashville Whig (Friday, May 8, 1835)

Adams, Eliza S. married to Nathan A. Dazey.

Adams, Geo. W. married in Williamson County to Miss Jane H. Arms.
The Western Weekly Review (Franklin Tenn., Tuesday, Dec. 14, 1832)

Adams, Mr. J. T. married in Scott Co., Ky, to Miss Ann Hutchinson.
National Banner & Nashville Whig (Friday, July 18, 1828)

Adams, James married in Williamson County to Miss Charlotte Ingram.
National Banner & Nashville Daily Advertiser (Monday, March 26, 1832)

(Repeat of above)
The Western Weekly Review (Franklin, Tenn, Fri., March 23, 1832)

Adams, Miss Jane married to Mr. Robert Gibson.

Adams, Mr. John married on Tuesday the 24th inst., by Elder Reddick Dishaugh to Miss Mary Nannally, all of Hardeman County.
National Banner & Nashville Daily Advertiser (Sat., Jan. 4, 1834)

Adams, Miss Margaret married to Mr. Edwin Cabill.

Adams, Miss Matilda married to Dr. James O'Riley.

Adams, Miss Nancy married to Capt. Jesse L. Dortch.

Adams, Miss Nancy married to Mr. John Bates.

Adams, Miss Nancy married to Dr. David Sims.

Adams, Miss Nancy B. married to Mr. John Norsworthy.

Adams, Mr. Nathan married at Springhill, Tenn. on the 13th June by the Rev. Peter R. Bland to Miss Gracy Arrington Howell Stanton, formerly of Columbia, S. C.
National Banner & Nashville Daily Advertiser (Fri., June 21, 1833)

Adams, Miss Rebecca married to Mr. Wm Gibson.

Adams, Robert H. Esq., married at Natchez to Miss Juliana Davidge, daughter of Rezin Davidge, Esq.
National Banner & Nashville Whig (Sat., Jan. 27, 1828)

Adams, Miss S. W. married to Mr. Joseph Martin.

Adams, Mr. Samuel married at Louisville, Ky, to Miss Christiana Wheeler.
National Banner & Nashville Daily Advertiser. (Fri., Aug. 17, 1832)

Adams, Samuel married in Williamson County to Miss Diana Yates.
The Western Weekly Review (Franklin, Tenn, Fri., March 8, 1833)

Adams, Mr. Samuel married on Sunday 18th inst., by Josiah Ferriss, Esq.,
to Miss Mary A. L. Ogburn, all of Nashville.
The Politian and Weekly Nashville Whig (Fri., April 23, 1847)

Adams, Mr. Samuel A. married on Sunday 18th inst., by Josiah Ferris,
Esq., to Miss Mary A. L. Ogburn both of Nashville and both deaf and dumb.
The Christian Record, (Sat., April 24, 1847)

Adams, Miss Susan married to Mr. John Carlton.

Adams, Mr. Thomas P., merchant, married on Thursday last by the Rev. Mr.
Hume to Miss Aron Tennant, both of Nashville.
The Nashville Gazette (Sat., Nov. 20, 1819)

Adkison, Mr. Gilbert B. married in Maury Co., to Miss Nancy Barnett.
National Banner & Nashville Whig (June 1, 1831)

Adrian, Miss Elizabeth E. married to Cha. Genett, Jr.

Ady, Miss Mary married to Mr. Jesse Oliver.

A-ga-lee-ga, married at the Valley Towns by the Rev. E. Jones 12th April
1830 to Ga-lo-nus-gee.
National Banner & Nashville Whig (Mon., July 26, 1830)

Agent, Miss Katherine, married to Mr. Jesse Hinton.
National Banner & Nashville Whig (Mon., March 20, 1835)

Aiken, Mr. Thomas M. married in Giles County to Miss Judith Ann Farmer.
Nashville Whig (Sat., April 11, 1846)

Akin, Miss Evelinn married to Mr. Thomas J. Oliphant.

Akin, John J. married in Maury County to Jone B. English.
National Banner & Nashville Whig. (Wed., Feb. 25, 1835)

Albert, Miss Mary E., married to Mr. Z. H. Tannehill.

Albert, Mr. Samuel married at Louisville, Ky, to Miss Mary Moore.
National Banner & Nashville Whig (Sat., June 14, 1828)

Albright, Mr. Thomas H. married in Sumner County to Miss Amanda Hunter.
National Banner & Nashville Daily Advertiser. (Thurs., March 20, 1834)

Alcock, Miss Lucinda married in Warren County, Ky, to Mr. George Lively.

Alcocke, Miss Lavena married to Mr. Samuel Westbay.

Alderson, Miss Ann married to Mr. Samuel Wantland.

Alderson, Mr. James married at Russellville, Ky to Miss Emily Hall.
National Banner & Nashville Daily Advertiser. (Mon., Jan. 7, 1833)

Alderson, Mr. Josiah, married in Giles County, to Mrs. Walker of Giles.
National Banner (March 24, 1826)

Alderson, Miss Sarah J. married to Capt. Thomas East.

Alderson, Mr. Thomas married on Feb. 28th by the Rev. J. T. Edgar to Miss
Rebecca Compton, daughter of Henry Compton, Esq., of Davidson County.
Nashville Republican (Thurs., March 2, 1837)

(Repeat of preceding)
National Banner & Nashville Whig (Fri., March 3, 1837)

Aldrich, Mr. Jo. A. of Nashville, married on Thursday 4th inst., by Rev.
Jno. B. M'Ferrin to Miss Susan C. Joyce, of Davidson County.
Nashville Republican (Sat., Feb. 6, 1836)

Aldridge, Miss Emily married in Tuscumbia, Ala to Anthony H. Davis, Esq.

Aldridge, Miss Emily married at Florence, Ala to Anthony H. Davis, Esq.

Aldridge, Miss Hannah married to Mr. W. B. B. George.

Aleston, Mr. M. C. Married in Sumner County to Miss Mary Ann Douglass.
National Banner & Nashville Daily Advertiser (Wed., April 18, 1832)

Alexander, Dr. of Athens married in M'Minn County to Miss Salina Moss,
daughter of Mr. John Moss.
National Banner & Nashville Whig (Fri., July 15, 1831)

Alexander, Miss Anges R. married to Rev. Beverly T. Lacy.

Alexander, D., Esq., married at Greenville to Miss Sarah Ann Graham.
National Banner & Nashville Whig (Sat., April 19, 1828)

Alexander, Ebenezer, Esq., married in Knox County, to Miss Margaret Ann
White, daughter of Hon. Hugh L. White.
National Banner (Sat., Oct. 31, 1829)

Alexander, Ebenezer, Esq., of Knoxville, married on the 31st to Miss
Margaret M. McClung, of Knox County.
National Banner & Nashville Daily Advertiser. (Mon., Feb. 11, 1833)

(Repeat of preceding)
Nashville Republican and State Gazette (Mon. Feb. 18, 1833, Vol. 8, #121)

Alexander, Lieut. Edmund B. married at Detroit, to Miss Elizabeth Craig.
National Banner (April 21, 1826)

Alexander, Miss Eleanor, married to Mr. Anadab Arne.

Alexander, Miss Eliza married to Mr. C. Leatherman.

Alexander, Franklin, married to Miss Rachel Leaton, in Williamson County.
The Western Weekly Review (Franklin, Tenn., Fri., Dec. 14, 1832)

Alexander, Frederick G. of Shepherdsville, married in Louisville, Ky, to
Miss Mary Louisa Anderson, daughter of the late Col. R. C. Anderson.
National Banner & Nashville Daily Advertiser (Fri., March 2, 1832)

Alexander, Mr. James married in Russellville, Ky., to Miss B. Robinson.
National Banner & Nashville Daily Advertiser (Tues., June 26, 1832)

Alexander, Miss Jane M married in McMinn County to Mr. James F. Twomey.

Alexander, Miss Jane Maria married to Capt. Green Pryor.

Alexander, Mr. Jefferson in Henry County married to Miss Cynthia Ray.
National Banner and Nashville Advertiser (Thurs., Aug. 16, 1832)

Alexander, Mr. Jefferson in Henry County married to Miss Nancy Leeper.
National Banner and Nashville Advertiser (Wed., Jan. 11, 1832)

Alexander, Mr. John of Washington County married in Sullivan County,
Tenn. to Miss Delila Woods, daughter of Mr. John Woods.
National Banner & Nashville Whig (Fri., March 13, 1835)

Alexander,Miss Margaret married to Mr. Ezekiel Richmond.

Alexander, Miss Martha V., married to Mr. Wm. P. Craig.

Alexander, Mr. Moses at Bath Steuben County, N. Y., married to Miss
Frances Tompkins. Nashville Republican and State Gazette (May 26, 1831)

Alexander, Miss Susan, married to Mr. James G. Haskell.

Alexander, Miss Phebe C., married to Rev. James Park.

Alexander, Miss Tabitha, married to Mr. Horace Lawson.

Alford, Mr. Edward married in Williamson County to Miss Margaret Irvin.
The Western Weekly Review (Franklin,Tenn., Fri., Dec. 2, 1831)

(repeat of preceding)
National Banner and Nashville Whig (Wed., Dec. 7, 1831)

Alford, Mr. John, married in Williamson County to Miss Nancy Irwin.
The Western Weekly Review (Franklin, Tenn., Fri., Dec. 2, 1831)

(repeat of preceding)
National Banner and Nashville Whig (Wed., Dec. 7, 1831)

Allcorn, Miss Emily married William L. Martin, Esq.

Allcorn, Miss Madeline T., married to Maj. Alexander Allison.

Allen, Miss married to Mr. Guy Kinkead.

Allen, Mrs. Alethia, relict of Hon Robert Allen, married Rev. Robert A.
Lapsley, D. D.

Allen, Mr. Andrew A. F. married in Williamson County to Miss Susan H.
Johnson.
National Banner Nashville Daily Advertiser (Mon., May 13, 1833)

Allen, Miss Ann C. married to Mr. John S. Blair.

Allen, Mr. Ben C., married in Lincoln County, Ky., to Miss Susan H.
Warren.
National Banner & Nashville Whig (Sat., Feb. 21, 1829)

Allen, Miss Charlotte married to Mr. Charles Halcum.

Allen, Mr. Daniel in Smith County married to Miss Nancy Buckett.
National Banner and Nashville Advertiser (Fri., Jan. 27, 1832)

Allen, Mr. David married in Williamson County to Miss Susan Brooks.
National Banner and Nashville Whig (Mon., Nov. 14, 1831)

(repeat of preceding)
The Western Weekly Review (Franklin, Tenn, Fri., Nov. 11, 1831)

Allen, Mr. Davis, married in Smith County to Miss Susan Saunders.
National Banner & Nashville Daily Advertiser (Thurs., March 20, 1834)

Allen, Dixon, Esq., of Smith County, member of the House of Representatives of Tennessee, married in Davidson County, last evening, to Mrs.
Louisa A. Brown, widow of the late William L. Brown, Esq., and daughter
of Gen. George W. Gibbs.
National Banner & Nashville Daily Advertiser. (Fri., March 14, 1832)

Allen, Miss Eliza married to Hon. Samuel Hauston.

Allen, Miss Eliza E. married to Mr. David A. Smith, Esq.

Allen, Miss Elizabeth married to Mr. Claborne Allman both of Dickson Co.

Allen, Miss Elizabeth of Loudon County, Va., married in Decatur, Macon
Co., Illinois on the 24th Aug. to Dr. Thomas H. Read.

Allen, Mr. G. J. married in Williamson County to Miss Nancy Allen.
The Western Weekly Review (Franklin, Tenn., Fri., Dec. 2, 1831)

Allen, Mr. Henry of Nashville married to Miss Elizabeth Young on Thursday last.
Nashville Republican (Sat., Feb. 14, 1835)

Allen, Mr. James married in Henry County to Miss Eliza Travis.
National Banner & Nashville Daily Advertiser. (Fri., Feb. 8, 1833)

Allen, Mr. James H. married in Fayette County, Ky., to Miss Sarah M'Dowell.
National Banner (Sat., Oct. 17, 1829)

Allen, Mr. John married in Danville, Ky., to Miss Harriet Doneghy.
National Banner & Nashville Whig (Sat., Aug. 4, 1827)

Allen, Mr. John H. married in Williamson County to Miss Lucinda Meadow.
The Western Weekly Review (Franklin, Tenn., Fri., March, 23, 1832)

(repeat of preceding)
National Banner & Nashville Daily Advertiser (Mon., March 26, 1832)

Allen, Mr. Joseph W. of Carthage married in Jonesboro on the 4th inst., to Miss Catharine R. Maxwell.
Daily Republican Banner (Fri., April 19, 1839)

Allen, Mr. Joseph W. married in Franklin County, Ky. to Miss Lucindia Anderson.
National Banner (Jan. 20, 1826)

Allen, Miss Margaret married to Mr. Christopher Nichols.

Allen, Miss Margaret married to Dr. Joseph Smith.

Allen, Miss Martha married to Mr. Asa Anderson.

Allen, Miss Mary married to Mr. Geo. A. Lucas.

Allen, Miss Mary married to Major John F. Farley.

Allen, Miss Mary married to Mr. William Thweatt.

Allen, Mrs. Mary married to Mr. Edward Capen.

Allen, Miss Mary Ann married to Mr. Erasmus D. Tansil.

Allen, Miss Mary M. married to Mr. W. G. Hudson.

Allen, Miss Mary T. married to Mr. Benjamin Holland.

Allen, Miss Nancy married in Williamson County to Mr. G. J. Allen.

(repeat of preceding)
National Banner & Nashville Whig (Wed., Dec. 7, 1831)

Allen, Miss Nancy married in Williamson County to Mr. Hugh Dempsev.

Allen, Miss Nancy L. married to Mr. John Robertson.

Allen, Miss Nancy L. to Mr. John Robinson.

Allen, Nathaniel H., Esq., attorney at law, married in Montgomery to Miss Lucy Ann Neblett, daughter of Sterling Neblett, Esq.
The Nashville Whig and Tenn. Advertiser (Nov. 10, 1817)

Allen, Miss Polly married to Mr. William Allen.

Allen, Miss Rebecca married to Mr. Waller B. Redd.

Allen, Mr. Richard married in Fayette County, to Miss Rosey Ann Kav.
National Banner & Nashville Whig (Sat., Jan. 17, 1829)

Allen, Mr. Richard married in Henry County to Miss Elizabeth Parker.
National Banner and Nashville Whig (Fri., Nov. 18, 1831)

Allen, Mr. Robert J. married in Blount County, Tenn. to Miss Eleanor
Harmon.
National Banner & Nashville Whig (Fri., Jan. 9, 1835)

Allen, Miss S. H. married to Mr. Benjamin Townsent.

Allen, Miss Sarah Ann married to Mr. Philip H. Mitchell.

Allen, Mrs. Tabitha A. G. married to Mr. Cornelius Boyle.

Allen, Mr. Thomas J. married in Davidson County to Miss Jane D. Hart on
the 4th inst.
Nashville Republican and State Gazette (Thurs., Sept. 11, 1834)

Allen, Mr. Walter C., married in Smith County to Miss Mary E. Bridgewater.
National Banner and Nashville Whig (Fri., Nov. 11, 1831)

Allen, Mr. William of Carthage married to Miss Polly Allen of Smith
County on Thursday 1th inst.
Impartial Review and Cumberland Repository (Nashville, Sat., Jan. 10,
1807)

Allen, Capt. William married in Todd County, Ky to Miss Tabitha A. G.
Barry, daughter of Mr. William L. Barry of Gallatin, Ten.
National Banner & Nashville Daily Advertiser (Tues., June 11, 1833)

Allen, Mr. Wm. D. married in Woodville, Miss., to Miss Martha S. Landrum.
National Banner & Nashville Whig (Sat., March 17, 1827)

Allen, Mr. Wm. H. married in Shelbyville, Ky., to Miss Susan D. Owen.
National Banner & Nashville Whig (Sat., Sept. 30, 1826)

Allen, Mr. William W., married on the 22nd inst., by Rev. J. W. Hannah
to Miss Mary Ann Elizabeth, daughter of J. H. Sadler, both of Nashville.
Daily Republican Banner (Tues., Dec. 29, 1840)

Allensworth, Elizabeth M., married to Nimrod E. Kav.

Allensworth, Mr. Phillip married in Logan Co., Ky. to Miss Eliza A. Cook.
National Banner & Nashville Whig (Mon., Jan. 17, 1831)

Alley, Mr. Henry married in Nashville on the 12th inst., by the Rev. Mr.
Green to Miss Elizabeth Speece.
National Banner & Nashville Whig (Fri., Feb. 13, 1835)

Alley, Mr. Isam P., married in Knox County, to Miss Mary C. Grills.
National Banner (Nashville, April 14, 1826)

Alley, Miss Jane married to Francis A. L. Dean.

Alling, Miss Helen M. married Hon. Joseph C. Mayes.

Allison, Mr. Alexander, married in Maury County to Miss Sarah Bryant.
National Banner & Nashville Whig (Fri., April 16, 1830)

Allison, Maj. Alexander of Carthage married to Miss Madeline T. Allcorn
in Wilson County.
National Banner and Nashville Advertiser (Wed., June 13, 1832)

Allison, Mr. F. S. married in Russellville, Ky., May 12th to Miss M. L.
Emmit both of Russellville, Ky.
Daily Republican Banner (Tues., May 21, 1839)

Aper, Mr. married in Logan County to Mrs. Rutherford.
National Banner & Nashville Whig (Sat., March 10, 1827)

Allison, Miss Frances married to Mr. Charles Wilson.

Allison, Mr. James of Louisville married in Clarksville to Miss Elizabeth Garrett.
National Banner & Nashville Whig (Thurs., Sept. 23, 1830)

Allison, Miss Nancy married to General John Brown.

Allison, Miss Prudence married to Mr. Joseph P. Thompson.

Allison, Dr. R. P. of Lebanon married on the 24th by the Rev. George Donnell to Miss Alethia Saunders, daughter of the late James Saunders of Sumner County.
Daily Republican Banner (Sat., July 27, 1839)

Allison, Miss Sarah A., married to Mr. Warren Jordan.

Allman, Mr. Claborne, married on 30th to Miss Elizabeth Allen, both of Dickson County.
Nashville Republican. (Tues., Jan. 19, 1836)

Alman, Mr. Richard married in Williamson County to Miss Elizabeth Hill.
National Banner (Sat., Aug. 15, 1829) Mr. Alman of Murfreesboro.

Aloway, Miss Elizabeth married to Dr. John S. M'Nairy.

Alsobrook, Lunsford, L., Esq., of Tuscumbia, Ala., married in Warren County, N. C. to Miss Temperence Eaton.
National Banner & Nashville Whig (Sat., July 22, 1826)

Alston, Miss Eliza married in Madison County to Mr. Oliver Pegee.

Alston, Mr. James, of the Western District, married in Davidson County last evening by Rev. Mr. Hume to Miss Jane Johnson, daughter of Maj. Johnson.
National Banner & Nashville Whig (Wed., Oct. 26, 1831)

Alston, Miss Mary S., married to Mr. David Harding.

Alston, Miss Temperance S. married to Mr. John Johnson.

Alvord, Mr. Joseph H. married in Detroit on the 11th inst., by the Rev. Mr. Wells to Miss Sarah M'Farland.
National Banner & Nashville Daily Advertiser (Wed., April 4, 1832)

Ambress, Miss Evelinia married to Mr. Thomas J. Haile.

Ament, Mr. Thomas W. married in this town on the 10th inst. by Rev. Mr. Rowe to Miss Melinda Gholson.
National Banner & Nashville Whig (Sat., April 19, 1828)

Ames, Daniel, Esq., married in White County to Miss Oela Fisk.
National Banner & Nashville Whig (Sat., June 16, 1827)

Amos, Miss Adeline married to Mr. Wm. Edwards.

Anderson, Miss married to Mr. David Deadrick.

Anderson, Mr. Alexander M. married at Cincinnati, to Miss Sarah Bakewell of Louisville, Mr. Anderson of Hopkinsville.
National Banner, (April 14, 1826)

Anderson, Mr. Andrew married in Lexington, Ky to Miss Eliza Woodruff.
National Banner & Nashville Whig (Sat., Aug. 30, 1828)

Anderson, Miss Ann Eliza married to Mr. James Bibb.

Anderson, Mr. Asa of Madison County married on the 12th inst., to Miss Martha Allen. (from Louisville Journal)
Nashville Republican (Tues., March 1, 1836)

Anderson, Miss Augusta married to Thomas Shewell, Esq.

Anderson, Miss Caroline M. married to Dr. Henry F. Washington.

Anderson, Miss Caroline P. married to Maj. Thomas P. Taul.

Anderson, Mr. David married in Jefferson County to Miss Sarah Dobbins.
National Banner & Nashville Whig (Mon., April 25, 1831)

Anderson, Mr. E., Jr., married in Hickman County on the 30th by William
B. Cook, Esq., to Miss Mariah Durring, daughter of Maj. Lewis Durring,
all of Hickman County.
Nashville Republican (Tues., April 6, 1837)

Anderson, Dr. Edmund of Bolivar married in Henry County to Miss Evelina
A. B. Peyton of Gallatin.
National Banner & Nashville Whig (Sat., June 16, 1827)

Anderson, Miss Eleline at Jonesborough married to Mr. Joseph Deaderich.

Anderson, Miss Elizabeth married to Mr. William Donelson.

Anderson, Miss Elizabeth married to Mr. Robert Dickey.

Anderson, Miss Emeline, married to Mr. Joseph Deaderick.

Anderson, Miss Emily C. married to Mr. M. McDonald.

Anderson, Miss Frances R., married to Mr. Wm. K. McAlister.

Anderson, Miss Harriet married to Mr. Wm. Watkins Jr.

Anderson, Mrs. Harriet R., married to Mr. Wm. H. Avery.

Anderson, Miss Isabel Berryhill married to Col. Beverly W. White.

Anderson, Mr. James married in Knox County to Miss Mary Simpson.
National Banner & Nashville Whig (Mon., Jan. 2, 1832)

Anderson, Mr. James B. married at Louisville, Ky., to Miss Mary Ann
Robertson.
National Banner & Nashville Whig (Sat., Jan. 10, 1829

Anderson, Miss Jane, Esq., married to William S. Wisdom, Esq.

Anderson, Miss Jane A. married to Mr. James A. Potts.

Anderson, Miss Jemima M. married to Mr. James D. Nooman

Anderson, John of Louisville, Ky., married in Nashville on the 24th Feb.
by John Wright, Esq., to Miss Mary Marshall, of Nashville.
National Banner & Nashville Whig (Fri., Feb. 27, 1835)

Anderson, John Esq., of Nashville, Tenn., married to Mrs. F. Donaldson
of Nashville on Thursday last.
Impartial Review and Cumberland Repository (Nashville, Thurs., Aug 11,
1808)

Anderson, Mr. John married in Lincoln County, Tenn. to Margaret Kid.
National Banner & Nashville Whig (Mon., April 20, 1835)

Anderson, Mr. John, married on the 13th inst., by the Rev. Dr. Lopsley
to Miss A. McClain of Wilson County.
Nashville Whig (Thurs., Oct. 15, 1846)

Anderson, Mr. John V., married in Madison County, Tenn. to Miss Elizabeth
Freeling.
National Banner & Nashville Whig (Wed., Aug. 17, 1831)

Anderson, Miss Letitia married to Mr. John A. M'Cord.

Anderson, Miss Lucindia married to Mr. Joseph W. Allen.

Anderson, Mr. M. married in Bowling Green, Ky., to Miss Ann Ruland.
National Banner & Nashville Daily Advertiser (Mon., June 30, 1834)

Anderson, Miss Malinda, married to Mr. Amos A. Edwards.

Anderson, Miss Martha married to Mr. James T. Leath.

Anderson, Martha J. married to William Donelson.

Anderson, Miss Mary married to Mr. Layton Sullivan.

Anderson, Miss Mary married to Mr. Benjamin Wallace.

Anderson, Miss Mary A. married to Mr. John Morrison.

Anderson, Miss Mary C. married to Col. Jacob Perkins.

Anderson, Miss Mary Louisa, married to Frederick G. Alexander, Esq.

Anderson, Miss Mary T. married to G. W. Jones, Esq.

Anderson, Miss Melinda, married to Mr. Amos A. Edwards.

Anderson, Miss Nancy married to A. L. Gammons.

Anderson, Miss Nancy C. married to Mr. Duncan Campbell.

Anderson, Miss Nancy W. married to Mr. Samuel C. Hughes.

Anderson, Mr. Nehemiah married to Mrs. Catherine Duncan, both of Nashville, on Sunday the 31st by the Rev. Mr. M'Ferrin.
Nashville Republican (Tues., Feb. 2, 1836)

Anderson, Miss Pamelia, married to Mr. Bantley M. Clark.

Anderson, Miss Phoebe, married to Mr. Robert Rochelle.

Anderson, Richard, Esq., married in Giles County to Miss Sally Faris.
National Banner & Nashville Whig (Sat., Nov. 29, 1828)

Anderson, Miss Sa. L. married to Mr. James H. M'Elwee.

Anderson, Miss Sarah B. married to Mr. Charles Yarborough.

Anderson, Miss Sarah J. married to James Price, Esq.

Anderson, Miss Susan, married to Mr. A. H. Dudley.

Anderson, Rev. Thomas C. married to Miss Rachel A. M'Murry, in Wilson
County. Rev. Anderson of Nashville.
National Banner & Nashville Daily Advertiser. (Tues., June 24, 1834)

Anderson, Thos M. married in Williamson County to Minerva A. T. Neal.
The Western Weekly Review (Franklin, Tenn., Fri., Feb. 10, 1832)

Anderson, Mr. Thomas P. in Lebanon married to Miss Mary S. Johnson.
Nashville Republican and State Gazette (Tues., Aug. 5, 1834)

Anderson, Mr. Thompson P. married in Wilson County, Tenn. to Miss Mary
S. Johnson, daughter of Joseph Johnson, Esq.
National Banner & Nashville Daily Advertiser (Tues., Aug. 5, 1834)

Anderson, Mr. W. J. of Trenton, Va., married in Winchester Tenn., on
Thursday 3d inst., to Miss Anne E. Young, of Winchester.
The Western Weekly Review (Franklin Tenn., Fri., Nov. 9, 1832)

(repeat of preceding)
<u>National Banner & Nashville Daily Advertiser</u> (Tues., Nov. 13, 1832)

Anderson, Rev. William married to Miss Sarah Bigly at Columbia.
<u>National Banner</u>, (Sat., Nov. 14, 1829)

Anderson, Mr. William L. married to Miss Amanda Vick in Jackson.
<u>Nashville Whig</u> (Tues., May 5, 1846)

Andres, Mr. Anderson married to Miss Mary Ann Stephens in Green Co.
<u>National Banner Nashville Daily Advertiser</u> (Mon., June 30, 1834)

Andrew, Rev. James O., Bishop of the Methodist Church, married in the
Methodist Church at Greensborough, Ga., on the 12th ult by the Rev.
Wesley P. Arnold to Mrs. Ann L. Greenwood of Greensborough.
<u>Nashville Whig</u> (Sat., Feb. 10, 1844)

Andrew, Miss Olivia F. married to Edwin R. Glascock.

Andrews, Miss Alice Jane married to Mr. John M'Call.

Andrews, Miss Elizabeth married to Mr. Eaton Parrish.

Andrews, Miss Evelina married to Mr. David L. Derryberry.

Andrews, Mr. Gray of Davidson County married to Miss Rebecca Walker of
Davidson on Wed. last.
<u>Impartial Review and Cumberland Repository</u> (Nashville, Sat., Mar. 21,
1807)

Andrews, James married in Giles County to Jane Hastings.
<u>National Banner & Nashville Daily Advertiser</u>. (Thurs., Jan. 17, 1833)

Andrews, Miss Jane married to Mr. Allen Asher.

Andrews, John Esq., married to Miss Harriet Carter at St. Louis.
<u>National Banner & Nashville Daily Advertiser</u> (Mon., Sept. 17, 1832)

Andrews, Mr. John W. married to Miss Elizabeth Cole at Tuscaloosa, Ala.
<u>National Banner & Nashville Whig</u> (Sat., Nov. 17, 1827)

Andrews, Miss Lydia married in Williamson County to Horatio H. Smithson.
<u>The Western Weekly Review</u> (Franklin, Tenn., Fri., Dec. 14, 1832)

Andrews, Miss Martha married to J. E. M'Cord.

Andrews, Miss Mary married to Mr. Henry R. Crampton.

Andrews, Miss Mary married to Mr. James Livingston.

Andrews, Miss Nancy married to Mr. James Watson.

Andrews, Miss Nancy W. married to George W. Johnston, Esq.

Andrews, Mrs. Olivia F., married to Mr. Edwin R. Glasscock.

Andrews, Maj. Patrick married to Miss Harriet Asher in Florence, Ala.
<u>Nashville Republican and State Gazette</u> (Sat., June 4, 1831)

Andrews, Mr. Wm married in this town on Thursday by Rev. Mr. Fall, to
Miss Olivia F. Reed.
<u>National Banner</u> (Sept. 26, 1829)

Angling, Philip married in Williamson County to Miss Betsy Watkins.
<u>The Western Weekly Review</u> (Franklin Tenn., Fri., Dec. 14, 1832)

Anthony, Miss Ann Eliza, married to Dr. Austin M. Hamner.

12

Anthony, Mr. Jacob in Bedford County married to Miss Phoebe Landers.
Nashville Republican and State Gazette (Wed., Dec. 12, 1832)

Anthony, Dr. James W. married in Madison County to Miss Cynthia Johnson.
National Banner & Nashville Whig (Thurs., June 17, 1830)

Anthony, Miss Lucretia married to Mr. Benjamin Manning.

Anthony, Miss Margaret married to Mr. Levi Kimbro.

Anthony, Miss Polly married to Mr. Franklin M. Brown.

Anthony, Mr. Wm. S., married to Miss Tailda A. Gowen in Williamson County.
National Banner & Nashville Whig. (Wed., Dec. 7, 1831)

Appleby, Miss Carolina married to Mr. Frederick Hurst.

Applewhite, Miss Martha married to Mr. Sterling Davis.

Arcambal, Miss Henrietta married to Mr. Joseph Gibbs.

Archer, Miss Prudence married to Mr. John Walker.

Arguish, Miss Angeline married to Mr. Francis H. Wilkinson.

Armistead, Mr. William B., of the House of Yeatman and Armistead, married
at Westwood in the vicinity on the 22d inst., by Rev. Dr. Edgar to Miss
Robina Woods, daughter of the late Robert Woods, Esq.
Nashville Whig (Sat., Feb. 25, 1843)

Armorer, Miss Matilda married to Mr. William Martin.

Armour, Mr. David of Paris, married in Jackson to Miss Ann Cromwell, of
Baltimore.
National Banner & Nashville Whig (Sat., June 7, 1828)

Arms, Miss Harriet W., married to Mr. Turner G. Hill.

Arms, Miss Jane H. married to Geo. W. Adams.

Armstrong, Miss Arabella married to Mr. Samuel M. McCurdy.

Armstrong, Miss Eleanor N. A. married to Joseph Vaulx, Esq.

Armstrong, Miss Elizabeth married to Mr. John Campbell.

Armstrong, Miss Elizabeth M. married to Mr. William Flournoy.

Armstrong, Major Francis W. married to Miss Elizabeth Aylett of Cahawba.
Major Armstrong of Mobile.
Nashville Whig (Feb. 19, 1823)

Armstrong, Maj. Francis W. of Alabama married at Washington City to Miss
Ann M. Millard, daughter of Mr. Joshua Millard.
National Banner & Nashville Whig (Mon., April 25, 1831)

Armstrong, Mr. George C. married in Bedford Co., Tenn, to Miss Mary
Cathey.
National Banner & Nashville Whig (Wed., Dec. 17, 1834)

Armstrong, Gen. Hugh C., senator from Overton County, married at the
residence of Mrs. Shirely on the 18th inst., by Rev. R. B. C. Howell, to
Mrs. Sarah Wilson of Nashville.
Nashville Union (Thurs., March 22, 1838)

(repeat of preceding)
Nashville Whig (Wed., March 21, 1838)

(repeat of preceding)
Daily Republican Banner (Wed., March 19, 1838)

Armstrong, Mr. James married in Mecklenburgh Co., Ky., to Miss Narcissa
M. Moore, daughter of Mr. Maurice Moore.
National Banner & Nashville Daily Advertiser. (Sat., March 30, 1833)

Armstrong, Mr. John married at Natchez to Miss Christina Lape.
National Banner (May 27, 1826)

Armstrong, Mr. John B. married to Miss Nancy Turner, Smith County, on
Thurs. Oct. 24 inst.
Impartial Review & Cumberland Repository (Nashville, Oct. 8, 1807)

Armstrong, Mr. Joseph R. married in Kingsport to Miss Margaret W. Netherland.
Nashville Whig (Wed., Oct. 7, 1840)

Armstrong, Mrs. M. M. married in Rutherford County to Dr. M. W. Armstrong.

Armstrong, Doctor M. W. married to Mrs. M. M. Armstrong, in Rutherford
Rutherford County on the 24th inst., by Rev. J. Alexander.
National Banner & Nashville Whig (Fri., Oct. 3, 1834)

(repeat of preceding)
Nashville Republican & State Gazette (Sat., Oct. 4, 1834)

Armstrong, Miss Mary married to Thomas Notgrass.

Armstrong, Col. Pleasant M. married to Miss Polly Cullum by James R.
Copeland, Esq. in Overton County on 22d May, all of the town of Livings-
ton.
The Union (Sat., June 16, 1836)

Armstrong, Capt. Robert married to Miss Mary L. Bass in Madison County.
National Banner (Sat., April 18, 1829)

Armstrong, Mr. Samuel married to Miss Minerva Doran on the 4th inst.,
in Rutherford County by Rev. Jesse Alexander.
National Banner & Nashville Whig (Fri., Jan. 14, 1831)

Armstrong, Miss Sophia married to Mr. George Shaw.

Armstrong, Miss Susan married to Lieut. A. Harris, 7th U. S. Infantry.

Armstrong, Mr. Thos in Giles county married to Miss Mary Ann H. Jones.
Nashville Republican & State Gazette. (June 16, 1831)

Armstrong, Mr. Thomas H. married to Miss Elizabeth Perrine in Louisville,
Ky.
National Banner & Nashville Whig (Sat., Oct. 6, 1827)

Armstrong, Mr. Thomas T., of N. C. married in Giles County to Miss Mary
Ann H. Jones, daughter of E. D. Jones, Esq.
National Banner & Nashville Whig (Fri., June 17, 1831)

Armstrong, Captain William of Tuscaloosa, married to Miss Nancy Irwin,
daughter of Mr. David Irwin of this town.
Nashville Whig (July 7, 1823)

Armstrong, Mr. Wm. C. married in Knox County to Miss Hannah Lucas.
National Banner (Jan. 27, 1826)

Arne, Mr. Anadab married in Henry County to Miss Eleanor Alexander.
National Banner & Nashville Daily Advertiser (Wed., Jan. 11, 1832)

Arnett, Mr. George married to Miss Nancy Watkinson in Henry Co., Tenn.
National Banner & Nashville Whig (Fri., May 1, 1835)

Arnett, Mr. Granville married in Franklin Co., Tenn. to Miss Nancy Hatchett, daughter of Archibald Hatchett.
National Banner & Nashville Daily Advertiser (Sat., Feb. 22, 1834)

Arnett, Mr. Richard married in Franklin County, on the 12th inst., to Miss Martha Woods, daughter of James Woods, Esq.
National Banner (Sat., Nov. 21, 1829)

Arnold, Miss Abigail M. married to Mr. Bird S. Jones in Madison County.
National Banner & Nashville Whig (Fri., Nov. 18, 1831)

Arnold, Mr. Diodate L. married to Miss Ellen Charles in Louisville, Ky.
National Banner & Nashville Whig (Fri., March 13, 1835)

Arnold, Mr. John of Madison County married in Tipton County to Miss Mary Stokes, daughter of J. G. Stokes, Esq.
National Banner & Nashville Whig (Fri., Nov. 18, 1831)

Arnold, Miss Mary married to Mr. Thomas Pollard.

Arnold, Miss Sarah P. married to Mr. Samcel Odell.

Arnold, Hon. Thomas D. of Knoxville married to Miss Luritta Rose at Tazewell on the 27th ult.
National Banner & Nashville Advertiser (Mon. Aug. 6, 1832)

Arpo, Mr. John married at New Orleans to Miss Mary Ann Payer.
National Banner & Nashville Whig (Sat., Dec. 23, 1826)

Arthur, Mr. William in Henry County Tenn., married to Miss Susan Peters.
Nashville Republican & State Gazette (Thurs., Oct. 6, 1831)

Arwine, Miss Rachel married in Campbell County to Mr. John R. Hackney.
National Banner & Nashville Daily Advertiser (Fri., May 10, 1833)

Aryes, Miss Solina married to Mr. Harris D. Thorp.

Asaley, Mr. Wm. married to Mrs. Eleanor Robberts, in Russellville, Ky.
National Banner (Jan. 13, 1826)

Asburn, Miss Martha married in Williamson County to Henry Pritchett.
The Western Weekly Review (Franklin, Tenn., Fri., March 8, 1833)

Ash, Henry married in Maury County to Miss Polly Hicks.
National Banner & Nashville Whig (Mon., Aug. 8, 1831)

Ashbridge, Rev. G. W. of Tuscumbia married in Franklin Co., Ala., to Miss Christiana Mitchell.
National Banner & Nashville Whig (Fri., July 25, 1828)

Ashburn, Mr. Hiram W. married in Todd Co., Ky., to Miss Carolina Bristow.
National Banner & Nashville Whig (Sat., March 10, 1827)

Ashby, Miss Nancy married to Mr. Thomas Duke.

Ashe, Mr. John B. of Haywood county, married to Miss Melissa Jefferson in Madison County by A. F. Driskill.
National Banner & Nashville Daily Advertiser (Wed., Aug. 14, 1833)

Asher, Mr. Allen married to Miss Jane Andrews, daughter of Maj. P. Andrews at Florence.
National Banner & Nashville Whig (Fri., July 29, 1831)

Asher, Miss Eliza married to Mr. E. F. Wills.

Asher, Miss Harriet married to Maj. Patrick Andrews.

Ashley, Miss Amanda married to Mr. Joseph N. Love.

Ashlock, Miss Sarah J. married to Mr. Eli Mourfield.

Askew, Mr. D. O. married in Henry Co., Tenn to Miss Emily Morgan.
National Banner & Nashville Daily Advertiser (Wed., April 4, 1832)

Askew, Dr. Eli married in Maury County to Miss Alice Cathey, daughter
of Alexander Cathey, Esq.
National Banner & Nashville Daily Advertiser (Thurs., Feb. 23, 1832)

Aston, Mr. Isaac C. married on the 11th Aug at Woodland Cottage, Jackson Co., Ohio, by Rev. Mr. Ferguson, to Miss Ellen R. Ferree, daughter
of the late Rev. John Ferree.
The Politician and Weekly Nashville Whig (Wed., Sept. 8, 1847)

Aston, Mr. Jas. married on Feb. 16th by the Rev. Thos. J. Neely to Miss
Sarah R. Hardin, daughter of William Hardin, Esq., all of Hardeman Co.
Nashville Republican (Thurs., March 2, 1837)

(repeat of preceding)
National Banner & Nashville Whig (Fri., March 3, 1837)

Atcheson, Mr. James L. married in Shelby County to Miss Levina Stanley.
National Banner & Nashville Whig (Sat., Nov. 17, 1827)

Atchinson, Mr. Robert of Madison married in Carroll County to Miss
Sarah M'Mullen.
National Banner & Nashville Whig (Thurs., June 3, 1830)

Atchison, Miss Catharine C. married to Mr. Nathaniel A. Davis.

Atchison, Mr. Hamilton married in Warren Co., Ky. to Miss Hannah Burch.
National Banner & Nashville Whig (Thurs., Oct. 14, 1830)

Atchison, Mr. Hamilton Sr. aged between 60 and 70 married in Favette
Co., Ky. on the 23d of May by the Rev. John Hudson to Miss Kitty Harri-
son, aged between 50 and 60.
National Banner & Nashville Whig (Mon., June 7, 1830)

Atchison, Samuel Esq., married in Yazoo Co., Miss. to Miss Martha J.
Winn.
National Banner & Nashville Daily Advertiser (Mon., March 11, 1833)

Atchison, Samuel A., Esq., Editor of the Bowling Green Advertiser,
married to Miss Octavia Morehead.
National Banner (Sat., Nov. 7, 1829)

Atchison, Miss Zurrah N., married to Mr. Alexander Frazer.

Athey, Mr. Samuel W. married at Louisville, Ky. to Miss Susan Steward.
National Banner & Nashville Whig (Mon., Nov. 5, 1832)

Atkerson, Mr. Dorsey married on Tues. evening 17th ult. by the Rev. Dr.
Hardin to Miss Mary Patton, daughter of Maj. I. Patton.
The Western Weekly Review (Franklin, Tenn. Fri., Jan. 4, 1833)

Atkieson, Mr. Howell married in Nashville on Thurs. evening last, by
the Rev. Mr. Robinson to Miss Charlotte White, formerly of Lexington,
Ky.
National Banner & Nahsville Daily Advertiser (Tues., Sept. 3, 1833)

Atkin, Mr. Charles married in Knoxville to Miss Harriet Gill.
National Banner & Nashville Whig (Sat., Sept. 9, 1826)

Atkins, Miss Elvira married in Henry Co., to Mr. H. H. Govin.

Atkins, Mr. James H. F. married in Henry Co., to Lucy A. Dabney.
National Banner & Nashville Advertiser (Mon., April 23, 1832)

Atkins, Martha married to Mr. Richmond G. Kindall.

Atkins, Miss Mary married to Mr. John Fulbright.

Atkins, Miss Mary Ann married to Rev. O. D. Street.

Atkins, Mr. Samuel J. married in Calhoun to Miss Martha L. Brown.
National Banner (May 20, 1826)

Atkins, Miss Sarah C. married to Mr. W. G. Winns.

Atkinson, Mr. Dorzey, married in Williamson County to Miss Mary Patton.
National Banner & Nashville Daily Advertiser (Mon., Jan. 7, 1833)

Atkinson, Francis (sic) L. married to William R. Hodge.

Atkinson, Gen. Henry of the U. S. Army married at Louisville, Ky. to
Miss Mary Ann Bullitt, daughter of the late Thomas Bullitt, Esq.
National Banner (Jan. 27, 1826)

Atkinson, Mr. Jesse B. married on Thursday last in Williamson County
to Miss Margaret Patton, by Rev. Mr. Hardin.
The Western Weekly Review (Fri., Oct. 28, 1831)

Atkinson, Mr. John C. married to Miss Susan B. Fleming in Lexington, Ky.
National Banner & Nashville Whig. (Mon., Oct. 11, 1836)

Atkinson, Mary married to Jas. Berryman.

Atkinson, Miss Mary A. married to Mr. Fountain B. Carter.

Atkinson, Miss Nancy B. married to James Hodge.

Atkinson, Mr. Quintus of Dover, married on the 17th inst., by the Rev.
Mr. Parrish to Miss Arabella C. West, daughter of Col. Robert C. West,
of Dickson County.
National Banner & Nashville Whig (Wed., Dec. 23, 1835)

Atkinson, William married in Williamson County to Miss Mary C. Hobbs.
The Western Weekly Review, (Franklin Tenn., Fri., Dec. 14, 1832)

Atwater, Miss Susan M. married on the 15th Oct by the Rev. Dr. Howell,
to Mr. James R. Mershon.

Atwood, Dr. N. B. Married in Tipton Co., to Miss Elizabeth F. LeGrand.
National Banner & Nashville Advertiser (Jan. 11, 1832)

Atwood, Mr. William, Merchant of Huntsville, A. T., married in this
place on Tues. evening last,by the Rev. Mr. Hume to Miss Caroline
Plummer, daughter of Wm. Plummer, deceased.
Nashville Whig and Tenn. Advertiser. (Jan. 31, 1818)

Augustine Mrs. P. married to Doct. John D. Nixon.

Ault, Mr. Henry married in Roane county to Miss Sarah Jones.
National Banner & Nashville Whig (Mon., Aug. 16, 1830)

Austin, Miss Alcenia A., married in this town on the 21st ult., to Mr.
Fountain Hume.

Austin, Miss Amanda M. married to Mr. George W. Green.

Austin, Miss Ann married to Dr. James Brewer.

Austin, Miss Delila married to Mr. Bailey W. Taylor.

Austin, Miss Dorinda W. married to Mr. George Haslope.

Austin, Mr. John married in White County to Miss Mary Bryan.
National Banner & Nashville Whig (Sat., Feb. 14, 1829)

Austin, Miss Lavina married to Mr. Sampson Carper.

Autry, Micajar, Esq. of North Carolina married on Tues. evening the 23d

December to Martha Wilkinson of Haysbobo.
Nashville Whig (Jan. 5, 1824)

Avant, Miss Eveline married to Mr. Beesley.

Avent, Miss Ann D. of Madison County, Ala., married to Mr. Clement W. Nance.

Avent, Miss Epsey B. married to Mr. William Gaston.

Avery, Mr. Charles S. in Clinton, Mass. married on the 29th ult. to Miss Mary Jane Perry, formerly of Pulaski.
Nashville Republican (Dec. 20, 1836)

Avery, John C., Esq., married at Cincinnati to Miss Lydia Robinson.
National Banner (Sat., Nov. 14, 1829)

Avery, Mr. Wm. H. married in Nashville on the 7th by the Rev. Mr. Hume, to Mrs. Harriet R. Anderson, both of New Orleans.
National Banner & Nashville Daily Advertiser. (Wed., May 8, 1833)

(repeat of preceding)
Nashville Republican & State Gazette (Wed., May 8, 1833)

Axley, Miss Lumima married in Monroe County to Mr. William Gibson.

Ayars, Mr. Robert married in Louisville, Ky. to Miss Elizabeth Hikes.
National Banner & Nashville Daily Advertiser. (Wed., June 20, 1832)

Aydelott, Mr. J. D., merchant of Mills Point, Ky., married on Monday . 3d inst., by Rev. A. L. P. Green to Miss Sarah E. Grizzard, daughter of James Grizzard, Esq., of the vicinity of Nashville.
Nashville Whig (Thurs., July 6, 1843)

Ayles, Mr. Preston married in Knox County to Miss Chandler.
National Banner & Nashville Whig (Sat., Jan. 10, 1829)

Aylett, Miss Elizabeth of Cohawba, married on the 12th ult. to Maj. Francis W. Armstrong.

Ayliff, Miss Charlotte married to Mr. Henry Miller.

Ayre, Lt. Thomas Jefferson, of the U. S. Army married on the 19th ult. to Miss Miriam E. Fowler, of Louisiana
Nashville Whig (June 11, 1823)

Ayres, Mr. Alexander D., married in Blount County to Miss Esther D. Johnson.
National Banner (March 24, 1826)

Ayres, Mr. Baker W. married in Lincoln Co., Tenn. to Miss Elizabeth West.
National Banner & Nashville Whig. (Fri., Dec. 6, 1834)

Ayres, Miss Elizabeth, married to Mr. Abraham Bransford.

Babbitt, Miss E. married to Mr. J. Prescott.

Babbitt, Miss Mary J. married to Mr. Robbert J. Lacy.

Babcock, Mary Ann married to Rev. John Breckinridge, D. D.

Bachelar, Littlebury married in Franklin Co., Ky., to Miss Mary Ann Dillon.
National Banner & Nashville Whig (Mon., Dec. 13, 1830)

Bacon, Miss A. P. of Dixon married to R. E. Whitlock.

Bacon, Mr. Edmund A. married in Franklin Co., Ky. to Miss Rebecca Hawkins.
National Banner (Jan. 20, 1826)

Bacon, Mr. Edward married in Christian Co., Ky. to Miss Nancy Henry.
National Banner (Jan. 20, 1826)

Bacon, Miss Elizabeth married to Mr. Gideon Shryock.

Bacon, Dr. James H. married on Thursday 16th inst., by Rev. Mr. Howell to Mrs. Sarah Luster, all of Nashville.
Nashville Whig (Fri., May 17, 1839)

Bacon, Mr. John married in Franklin Co., Ky. to Miss Louisa Montgomery.
National Banner (March 31, 1826)

Badger, Miss Ann married to Jno. W. Wilson.
Badger, Miss Henrietta married at Lexington, Tenn. to Mr. Daniel D. Wilson.

Badgett, Miss Nancy F. married to Mr. Henry Buman.

Badlun, Miss Ann Married to Mr. Irwin Windham.

Baell, O. B. Esq., married in Bardstown, Ky. to Miss Matilda M'Gill.
Nashville Republican (Sat., Jan. 24, 1835)

Baell, O. B. Printer, formerly of Tennessee, married in Bardstown, Ky. to Miss Mechtileis M'Gill.
National Banner & Nashville Whig (Fri., Dec. 12, 1834)

Bagby, Miss Mary married to Mr. Silas Edwards.

Baggett, Mr. William in Montgomery County married to Miss Susannah Davis.
National Banner & Nashville Advertiser (Feb. 11, 1832)

Bagwell, Miss Sinia married to Mr. Richard B. Slaughter, Esq.

Bailey, Mr. David married in Madison Co., Ala., to Miss Louisa Bledsoe.
National Banner & Nashville Whig (Sat, June 2, 1827)

Bailey, Miss Henrieta married to Mr. Ryland W. Woodfin.

Bailey, Mr. James married in Nashville, last evening by the Rev. Mr. Green to Miss Lucinda Brown.
National Banner & Nashville Daily Advertiser (Sat., Sept. 22, 1832)

Bailey, Mr. James in Wilson County married to Miss Lucy Puckett.
National Banner & Nashville Whig (Sat., Dec. 30, 1826)

Bailey, Miss Jane married to Mr. D. R. Lacy.

Bailey, Miss Jane married to Mr. William H. Thomas.

Bailey, Miss Mary married to Mr. John Taylor.

Bailey, Miss Mary Ann Eliza married to James Kay, Esq.

Bailey, Miss Mary W. married to Mr. William B. Bryan.

Bailey, Mr. Philip married in Williamson Co. to Miss Ann Johnson
National Banner & Nashville Daily Advertiser (Thurs., May 1, 1834)

Baileis, Mr. Samuel married in Knoxville to Miss Nancy Lister.
National Banner & Nashville Whig (Sat., March 31, 1827)

Baily, Miss Clarena M. married to James R. Hallum.

Baily, Miss Elizabeth A. married to Mr. Thomas A. James.

Baily, Miss Henrietta married to Mr. Ryland H. Woodfin.

Bain, Miss Harriet Newell married to Mr. Cullen E. Douglass.

Bain, Mr. Jesse married in Lincoln Co., Tenn to Miss Nancy C. McLain.
National Banner & Nashville Whig (Fri., Dec. 6, 1834)

Baird, Mrs. married to Edward W. Dale, Esq.

Baird, Miss Eliza Ann married to Mr. John B. Johnson.

Baird, Miss Elizabeth married to Mr. Alfred H. Russell.

Baird, Mr. John of Nashville, married on Tues. morning last to Miss Julia C. Young, eldest daughter of Evan Young, Esq. of Maury Co., Tenn.
Nashville Whig (Tues., Nov. 19, 1844)

Baird, Miss Mary Jane married to Mr. Samuel W. Paul.

Baird, Mr. Pinckney married in Sumner County to Miss Eleanor Kirk.
National Banner & Nashville Daily Advertiser. (Fri., Aug. 16, 1833)

Baird, Miss Sarah married to Mr. Wm. Hodge.

Baker, Miss Ann married to Mr. William Sewell.

Baker, Miss Brunetta married to Mr. John Gillium.

Baker, Mr. Caleb H. married in Knox county to Miss Mary L. White.
National Banner & Nashville Whig (Mon., Oct. 31, 1831)

Baker, Mr. Christian married in Knox county to Miss Elizabeth Henderson,
on the 6th inst.
National Banner & Nashville Whig (Thurs., May 20, 1830)

Baker, Mrs. Cynthia married in Lincoln County to Mr. Sylvester Rife.
National Banner & Nashville Whig (Sat., Dec. 30, 1826)

Baker, Miss Eliza married in Williamson county, Tenn. to Mr. Henry W.
Reaves.
National Banner & Nashville Whig (Mon., April 13, 1835)

Baker, Miss Elizabeth married to Mr. John Stinson.

Baker, Elizabeth married to Mr. Carrick W. Crozier.

Baker, Mr. Ephraim married in Henry County to Miss Lucretia Daniel.
National Banner & Nashville Whig (Wed., Dec. 28, 1831)

Baker, Dr. German of Davidson County, married in Davidson Co., on Thurs.
the 27th by Rev. Mr. Edgar to Miss Mary Jane Read, daughter of Thomas J.
Read, Esq., of Nashville.
National Banner & Nashville Daily Advertiser (Fri., March 28, 1834)

(repeat of preceding)
Nashville Republican and State Gazette (March 29, 1834)

Baker, Mr. Giles married in Williamson County to Miss Martha Mullin.
National Banner & Nashville Whig (Fri., March 6, 1835)

(repeat of preceding)
National Banner & Nashville Whig (April 13, 1835)

Baker, Mr. Isaac married in Knox County to Miss Sally Hickey.
National Banner & Nashville Daily Advertiser. (Tues. Oct. 30, 1832)

Baker, Isaac L. (Maj.) of Louisiana married on Wed. evening last by
the Rev. Mr. Craighead to Miss Charlotte Lewis, daughter of the late
Maj. William T. Lewis of this vicinity.
The Nashville Gazette (Sat., May 6, 1820)

Baker, Rev. Jarman married on the 24th ult. to Miss Mary Keyser.
National Banner & Nashville Whig (Sat., Jan. 24, 1829)

Baker, Mr. John B. married on Wed. Feb. 26th by Joseph S. Jarrell, Esq.
to Miss Mahala Burgess, all of Davidson County.
Nashville True Whig and Weekly Commercial Register (Fri., March 7, 1851)

Baker, Mr. Leonard D. married in Nashville on the 18th inst. by the Rev.
A. L. P. Green to Miss Lamira D. Garner, daughter of William Garner, Esq.
Nashville Whig (Thurs., Jan. 20, 1842)

Baker, Dr. L. W. married at Knoxville to Miss Susan W. Park.
National Banner (Sat. April 25, 1829)

Baker, Miss Maria J. married to Mr. Albert G. Ward.

Baker, Miss Martha married to Mr. Robert Smtih.

Baker, Miss Martha Ward married to Mr. Berthier Jones.

Baker, Miss Mary married to Mr. Benjamin R. Howard.

Baker, Mrs. Mary married to Mr. G. W. Roister.

Baker, Miss Matilda married to Mr. George Hurt.

Baker, Miss Pauline G. married to Mr. Andrew Couch.

Baker, Rev. Robert of Carroll County married in Madison County to
Miss Charlotte Lynne, daughter of Robert Lynne, Esq.
National Banner (July 11, 1829)

Baker, Miss Rosanna married on the 9th inst., by Joseph L. Jarrell, Esq.
to Mr. James Snider.

Baker, Miss Sarah married to Mr. Sanderson Robert.

Baker, Miss Sarah married to Rev. John Bargo.

Bakewell, Col. John married in Hardeman county to Miss Mary Philpot.
National Banner (Sat., Dec. 19, 1829)

Bakewell, Miss Sarah married to Mr. Alexander M. Anderson.

Bakewell, Miss Selina H. married to Rev. Alexander Campbell.

Bakewell, Mr. William G. married at Louisville, Ky. to Miss Alicia A.
Matthews.
National Banner & Nashville Whig (Sat., Dec. 6, 1828)

Balch, Alfred, Esq. married on Wednesday evening by the Rev. Mr. Hume
to Miss Ann Newnan, both of this place.
Nashville Whig (Sept. 1, 1817)

Balch, Mr. Amos P. married in Warren Co., Ky. to Miss Polly Sawyer.
National Banner (March 10, 1826)

Balch, Mr. James married in Bedford County to Miss Eliza Haslett.
National Banner & Nashville Whig (Sa   Jan. 10, 1829)

Baker, Mr. William married in Huntsville, Ala. to Miss Mary Hebert.
National Banner & Nashville Whig (Sat., Nov. 22, 1828)

Baker, Mr. William married to Miss Drucilla Maginas in Green County.
National Banner & Nashville Whig (Fri., Jan. 29, 1830)

Balch, Miss Jane P., late of Georgetown, D. C., married to Hon.
W. Russell.

Balch, Capt. John K. married at Memphis to Miss Amanda Wheatley.
National Banner (Sat., Oct. 3, 1829)

Balch, Dr. Stephen B. married at Washington City to Miss Elizabeth King.
National Banner & Nashville Whig (Sat., Nov. 22, 1828)

Balch, Rev. Stephen B. of Georgetown, D. C. married at Easton, Md.,
to Miss Jane Parrott
National Banner & Nashville Whig (Mon., Dec. 6, 1830)

Baldridge, Miss Jane B. married in Williamson County to John F.Hughs.
The Western Weekly Review (Franklin, Tenn., Fri., Dec. 14, 1832)

Baldridge, Mr. William H. married in Maury County to Miss Nancy C.
M'Donald.
National Banner & Nashville Whig (Fri., March 26, 1830)

Baldwin, Henry Jun., Esq., married at Hunters Hill, the seat of Col.
E. Ward in Davidson county, on Tuesday evening last by Rev. Mr. Weller
to Miss Mary Flordia Dickson, youngest daughter of the late William
Dickson, Esq.
National Banner & Nashville Whig (Thurs., Nov. 4, 1830)

Baliff, Mr. Thos. married in Smith County to Miss Nancy Bates.
National Banner & Nashville Whig (Tues., Dec. 13, 1831)

Ball, Mr. E. F. married in Cincinnati, O., to Miss Martha Ballon.
National Banner & Nashville Advertiser (Mon., June 9, 1834)

Ball, Miss Martha married in Madison County, Ala to Mr. Martin Weatherly.

Ball, Miss Mary E. married to Maj. William Houston.

Ballard, Miss Elly married to Mr. Robert Cox.

Ballard, Miss Nancy married to Mr. John M'Farland.

Ballard, Mr. Isaac married on the 3d of Nov. to Miss Rebecca Carson,
all of Humphreys county.
National Banner & Nashville Whig (Wed., Nov. 11, 1835)

Ballard, Miss Polly married to Mr. Smith Isaacks.

Ballentine, Miss Margaret married to Mr. Peter Thomas.

Ballon, Miss Martha married to Mr. E. F. Ball.

Bandy, Mr. Richard C. married on the 17th inst., Monday, by the Rev. Mr.
McFerrin to Miss Ann Eliza Grizzard, daughter of James Grizzard, Esq.,
all of Nashville.
Nashville Whig (Wed., May 19, 1841)

Bang, Mr. William F. married in Nashville to Miss Jane R. McJilton, on
Wed. last by the Rev. Mr. Gwinn.
National Banner & Nashville Advertiser (Fri., April 27, 1832)

Banister, Miss Elizabeth married in Louisville Ky to Mr. George Barnett.

Banister, Mr. Nathaniel H. married on 30th June by John Wright, Esq.,
to Mrs. Amelia Stone, both of the Treatre.
National Banner & Nashville Whig (Wed., July 1, 1835)

Bankhead, James married on Tuesday evening 16th inst.,by the Rev. J. T.
Edgar to Miss Elizabeth Flint, all of Nashville.
The Union (Sat., May 27, 1837)

Bankhead, Mr. James, merchant of the firm of Crockett Read & Bankhead,
married by the Rev. J. T. Edgar, D. D. on the 16th May to Miss Elizabeth
Flint.
National Banner & Nashville Whig (Mon., May 29, 1837)

Banks, Miss Amanda married to Mr. Richard N. Harris.

Banks, Miss Eliza married in Shelby county to Mr. William Huntsman.

Banks, Mr. James married to Miss Elizbaeth F. Hendrick in Henderson Co.
National Banner & Nashville Whig (Fri., June 10, 1831)

(repeat of preceding)
Nashville Republican & State Gazette (Thurs., June 9, 1831)

Banks, Maj. Lawrence S. married in Triana, Ala., to Miss Margaret Noble.
National Banner & Nashville Daily Advertiser. (Mon., May 12, 1834)

Banks, Miss Mary married to Mr. Thomas W. Wilson.

Banks, Miss Mernerva married to John J. Ormond, Esq.

Banks, Miss Nancy married to Mr. Thomas W. Spivey.

Banks, Mr. William L. married in Logan Co., Ky. to Miss Mary Haddox.
National Banner & Nashville Daily Advertiser (Mon., May 13, 1833)

Banner, Capt. Sterling M. of the Steam Boat Ellen Kirkman, married in
Nashville this morning at the residence of Capt. Joe Miller to Miss
Jane West.
Nashville Whig (Wed., Aug. 9, 1838)

Barbee, Mr., merchant of Baton Rouge, La., married at Washington, Mi.
to Julia Ann Pike.
National Banner & Nashville Whig (Wed., Sept. 24, 1834)

Barbee, Dr.. Allen J. of Brownsville married in Haywood Co., to Miss
Susan Y. Taylor, daughter of Mr. John Y. Taylor.
National Banner & Nashville Whig (Thurs., June 24, 1830)

Barbee, Miss Amanda married to Mr. Robert Enders.

Barbee, Mr. Thomas married in Mercer Co., Ky., to Miss Nancy Fry.
National Banner & Nashville Whig (Sat., Jan. 3, 1829)

Barbour, Miss Ann Eliza married to Mr. B. W. Ewing.

Barbour, Mr. Jas. M. married at Henderson, Ky. to Miss Lydia Scott.
National Banner & Nashville Daily Advertiser. (Mon., Feb. 18, 1833)

Barbour, Miss Jane P. married to Mr. William D. S. Taylor.

Barby, James G. married in Madison Co., Tenn., to Miss Mirando Burrow,
daughter of the Rev. B. M. Burrow, of Carroll Co.
National Banner & Nashville Whig (Wed., Nov. 26, 1834)

Barclay, Miss Hannah married in Lincoln Co., to Mr. Spruce M'Coy.
National Banner & Nashville Whig (Sat., July 29, 1826)

Barclay, Dr. Joseph married in Warren County, Ky. to Miss Adeline Lapsley.
National Banner & Nashville Whig (Sat., Dec. 30, 1826)

Barclay, Mr. Philander married in Barren Co., Ky. to Miss Elizabeth Garnet.
National Banner & Nashville Whig (Sat., Nov. 22, 1282)

Bard, Rev. Isaac married in Christian Co., Ky. to Miss Matilda Moore.
National Banner & Nashville Whig (Sat., March 31, 1827)

Baresford, Mr. Richard married at Cincinnati to Miss Elizabeth Suttin.
National Banner & Nashville Daily Advertiser (Tues., Aug. 7, 1832)

Barfield, George C., Esq., of Arkansas, married in Madison Co., to Miss
Harriet Smith.
National Banner & Nashville Whig (Sat., Feb. 21, 1829)

Bargo, Rev. John married in Logan Co., Ky. to Miss Sarah Baker.
National Banner & Nashville Whig (Sat., April 7, 1827)

Barham, Mr. Lewis D. married in Henry Co., to Miss Mary J. Robins.
National Banner & Nashville Advertiser (Thurs., Sept. 27, 1832)

Barham, Mr. Tho. J. married in Davidson County to Miss Lovy M'Afae.
Nashville Republican (Tues., Jan. 27, 1835)

Barker, Dr. David married in Yazoo Co., Miss., by Q. D. Gibbs, Esq.,
Mayor of Manchester, to Miss Elizabeth J. Martin, all of Yazoo Co.
Nashville Whig (Wed., Nov. 14, 1838)

Barker, Miss Sarah N. married to Mr. W. H. Hines.

Barker, Mr. Skidmore married in Elizabethton, Carter Co., to Miss
Nancy Folsom.
Nashville Whig (Tues., May 5, 1846)

Barker, Capt. Thomas, a soldier of the battle of Bunkerhill, aged 76,
married at Marble head, Mass. to Miss Grace Swan aged 68.
National Banner & Nashville Whig (Sat., July 15, 1826)

Barkley, Miss Mary married to Mr. S. Perrill.

Barkley, Miss Mary married to Mr. J hn Craine.

Barksdale, Dr. married in Gibson County to Miss Sarah Ann Davis.
National Banner & Nashville Whig (Sat., Aug. 11, 1827)

Barksdale, Miss Ann. G. married to Mr. Robert M. White.

Barksdale, Mr. Harrison married in Rutherford Co., on Tuesday 30th Jan.
to Miss Laura C. Read, daughter of Major Sion S. REad.
Nashville Union (Tues., Feb. 13, 1838)

(repeat of preceding)
Daily Republican Banner (Wed., Feb. 14, 1838)

Barksdale, Miss Susan married in Carroll County to Mr. David Marshall,
Jr.

Barlett, Mr. Thomas H. married in Lexington, Ky. to Miss Lucy Frazer.
National Banner & Nashville Whig (Sat., Aug. 9, 1828)

Barnard, Mr. Joseph married in this vicinity on Thursday evening by the
Rev. A. L. P. Green to Miss Susan Bateman.
National Banner & Nashville Whig (Mon., Nov. 10, 1834)

Barnes, Miss A. G. Married to Mr. A. L. Barnes.

Barnes, Mr. A. L. married in Maury County to Miss A. G. Barnes.
National Banner & Nashville Whig (Dec. 17, 1831)

Barnes, Miss Bulah married to Mr. Thomas Williams.

Barnes, Miss Esther married to Mr. William Murray.

Barnes, Mr. George F. married in Fleming Co., Ky. to Miss Elizabeth Dudley.
National Banner & Nashville Whig (Jan. 20, 1827)

Barnes, Mr. John A. married near Port Gibson to Miss Sarah L. Humphreys.
National Banner & Nashville Whig (Sat., Dec. 9, 1826)

Barnes, Miss Louisa C. married in Lincoln Co. to Henry Beck.

Barnes, Miss Mary married to Mr. Andrew Halfacre.

Barnes, Miss Mary E. married to John R. Higgenbothem.

Barnes, Mr. Robert A. married on the 1st inst. by the Rev. P. P. Neely to Mrs. Ann Eliza Hydes, all of Davidson County.
Nashville Whig (Sat., May 4, 1844)

Barnes, Miss Tabithia married to Mr. James H. Jones.

Barnet, Miss Caroline married to Mr. Daniel Virden.

Barnet, Mr. John M. married in Madison Co., Tenn., to Miss Martha M. Clements.
National Banner & Nashville Whig (Fri., Oct. 17, 1834)

Barnett, Miss married to Mr. Grove.

Barnett, Miss Agnes married to Mr. Chs. Gilkey.

Barnett, Miss Elvira M. married to Mr. Nelson Walkly.

Barnett, Miss Esther married to Mr. D. Ragan.

Barnett, Rev. James G. married in Christian Co., Ky. to Miss Elizabeth H. Usher.
National Banner (Sat., Aug. 8, 1829)

Barnett, Mr. John M. of Madison Co., married to Miss Martha M. Clement.
National Banner & Nashville Whig (Fri., Oct. 3, 1834)

Barnett, Miss Lucinda married in Madison County to Mr. James R. McMillan.

Barnett, Miss Lucy Ann married to Mr. Virgil J. Burke.

Barnett, Miss Nancy married to Mr. Gilbert B. Adkison.

Barnett, Polly married to Mr. Jas. Putnam.

Barnett, Miss Sophronia married to Mr. Thomas S. Sappington.

Barnett, Teresa W. married to Robert S. Riddle.

Barnett, Mr. William G. married to Miss Matilda Carr.

Barnhill, Mr. William married to Miss Lydia Scott at Pittsburgh, Pa.
National Banner (April 28, 1826)

Banott, Rev. Harmon married on Sun. evening 5th inst., to Miss Polly Jones, both of Warren County.
Nashville and Tenn. Advertiser (April 11, 1818)

Barnwell Miss Martha married to Mr. William Shipp.

Barr, Miss Abby married to Mr. Baranrd P. Gash.

Barr, Miss Ibby married Mr. Bernard P. Gash.

Barr, Col. William married in Woodford Co., Ky. to Miss Eliza Jane Bowmar.
National Banner & Nashville Advertiser (Tues., June 26, 1832)

Barrell, Mr. Alexander married in Nashville on Thurs. 27th Sept by the Rev. William Hume to Miss Ann Patterson, all of Nashville.
National Banner & Nashville Daily Advertiser (Fri., Sept. 28, 1832)

Barret, Joseph Esq. married at Tuscaloosa, Ala., to Miss Ruth Moore.
National Banner & Nashville Whig (Sat., Dec. 2, 1826)

Barrett, Miss Elizabeth married to Mr. Samuel Dickey.

Barron, Miss Ann C. married to Mr. Felix Wells.

Barrow, David, Esq., late of Nashville, married in the Parish of Iberville, La., to Miss Lavinia Wilson.
National Banner & Nashville Whig (Fri., Apr. 29, 1831)

(repeat of preceding)
Nashville Republican & State Gazette (Thurs., April 28, 1831)

Barrow, Mr. James married in Sumner County to Miss Anne Boone.
Nashville Republican & State Gazette (Feb. 22, 1831)

(repeat of preceding)
National Banner & Nashville Whig (Mon., Feb. 21, 1831)

Barrow, Miss Jane A. married to Henry Crabb, Esq.

Barrow, Mr. John E. of Louisiana married on the 5th inst., by the Rev. Dr. Wharton to Miss Catherine S. Gringery, daughter of Joseph Gringery, of Davidson County.
Nashville Whig (Sat., Oct. 7, 1843)

Barrow, Miss Louisa married to Granville C. Torbitt.

Barrow, Miss Nancy married to Mr. Merritt Pilcher.

Barrow, Washington, Esq., married in this town to Miss Ann Shelby, daughter of Dr. John Shelby.
National Banner & Nashville Whig (Sat., Oct. 6, 1827)

Barrow, Willie, Esq., of Davidson Co., married to Miss Ann Beck., of Davidson Co., on last Sunday.
Impartial Review & Cumberland Repository (Nashville, Jun.13, 1807)

Barry, Miss Ann married to Samuel L. Childress, Esq.

Barry, Miss Elizbaeth Ann married to Mr. George W. Parker.

Barry, Miss Eudora R. married to Rogers Barton, Esq.

Barry, Miss Maria married to Major M. A. Price.

Barry, Miss Mary Ann married to Mr. William Wallace.

Barry, Miss Mary Ann W., married to Mr. William Wallace.

Barry, Miss Mary H. married to Mr. John Hegan.

Barry, Mr. R. H. married in Nashville, last evening, by the Rev. R. B. C. Howell to Miss Elizabeth J. Haynes.
Nashville Whig (Wed., Oct. 27, 1841)

Barry, Mr. Richard H., merchant of Nashville, married in this county last evening by the Rev. Mr. Hume to Miss Mary L. May.
National Banner & Nashville Whig (Sat., Sept. 15, 1827)

Barry, Miss Sarah G. M. married to Mr. Aaron Haynes.

Barry, Miss Harriet G. married to Mr. William M'Laughlin.

Barry, Miss Sarah G. M. married to Mr. Aaron Haynes.

Barry, Miss Susan married to Mr. James Taylor, Jr.

Barry, Miss Tabitha A. G. married to Capt. William Allen.

Barry, Thomas Esq., married in Sumner County to Miss Sarah Peyton, daughter of Mr. John Peyton.
National Banner & Nashville Whig (Fri., Nov. 26, 1830)

Bartee, Miss Frances A. married to Mr. W. O. Harris.

Bartlett, Edward B., Esq., married to Miss Ann T. Sanders, in Grant Co., Ky.
National Banner & Nashville Daily Advertiser. (Thurs., June 19, 1834)

Bartlett, Miss Lucinda married to Mr. Joseph H. Mckee.

Bartlett, Miss Martha married to Francis E. Goddard, Esq.

Bartley, Mr. W. of Belfast, age 52 years, married at New Orleans, to Miss Anne Robinson, age 15 years.
National Banner & Nashville Daily Advertiser (Wed., March 26, 1833)

Barton, Miss Eliza married in Kaskaskia, Ill., to Mr. Louis A. Benoist.

Barton, Miss Elizabeth married to Mr. Wm. Dickson.

Barton, Miss Louisiana married to Capt. Joseph Kemp.

Barton, Miss Polly Ann married to Mr. George McFarland.

Barton, Miss Rachel married to Mr. Andrew M'Clure.

Barton, Miss Rebecca C. amrried to Mr. James T. Abbott

Barton, Roger Esq. married in Bolivar to Miss Eudora R. Barry, of that place, on the 2d inst.
National Banner & Nashville Advertiser (Mon., May 21, 1832)

Barton, Mr. W. M. of Grainger county married in Jefferson Co., Tenn., to Miss Mariah Donaldson.
National Banner & Nashville Daily Advertiser (Mon., Sept. 9, 1833)

Bartow, Miss Ann married to Mr. David S. Wade, Esq.

Bascom, Rev. H. B., D. D. married in New York to Miss Eliza Van Antwerp, daughter of the late Thos. Van Antwerp of New York City.
Daily Republican Banner (Thurs., March 24, 1839)

Basey, Miss Francis married to Mr. George Wade.

Bass, Miss married to Mr. Arthur Loftin.

Bass, Mrs. Ann married to Mr. John A. Cheatham, Esq.

Bass, Mr. John of Elkton married to Miss Temperance A. Sumner of this county on the 13th inst.
Nashville Republican and State Gazette (Sat., Jan. 15, 1831)

(repeat of preceding)
National Banner & Nashville Whig (Mon., Jan 17, 1831)

Bass, John M. Esq. of St. Louis married in this town on Wed. last 7th inst., by the Rev. Mr. Hume to Miss Malvina C. Grundy, daughter of Felix Grundy, Esq.
National Banner & Nashville Whig (Sat., Jan. 10, 1829)

Bass, Kinchen married on Thursday to Miss Ann Doris of this county.
The Clarion and Tennessee Gazette (Sept. 14, 1813)

Bass, Miss Mary L. married to Capt. Robert B. Armstrong.

Bass, Mr. Richard J. of Athens married in Florence, Ala., on the 28th ult. by the Rev. Jeptha Harrison, D. D. to Eliza Bigger, daughter of Joseph Bigger, Esq.
The Politican and Weekly Nashville Whig (Oct. 15, 1847)

(repeat of preceding)
The Christian Record (Sat., Oct. 16, 1847)

Bass, Miss Sarah Jane married to Mr. Eldred Rawlins.

Bass, Mr. William married to Miss America R. Elam, in Williamson County.
National Banner & Nashville Whig (Mon., Nov. 14, 1831)

(repeat of preceding)
The Western Weekly Review (Franklin, Tenn., Fri., Nov. 11, 1831)

Basset, Dr. John G. in Madison County, Ala., married to Miss Isaphoena P. Thompson.
National Banner & Nashville Whig (Wed., April 27, 1831)

(repeat of preceding)
Nashville Republican & State Gazette (Thurs., April 28, 1831)

Batchelder, Mr. Thomas married in Portsmouth, by the Rev. Mr. Bollaw, to Miss Martha Muchmore.
National Banner & Nashville Whig (Fri., May 6, 1831)

Batchelor, Mr. James married in Maury County to Miss Patsey Patterson.
National Banner & Nashville Advertiser (Thurs., April 5, 1832)

Bateman, Miss Charlotte of Davidson Co., married on Wed. evening last, to Mr. Joel M. Smith.

Bateman, Miss Frances married to Mr. Thos. J. Jagges.

Bateman, Miss Rosa married to Mr. Samuel Wilson.

Bateman, Miss Sarah H. married to Mr. James H. Kendrick.

Bateman, Miss Susan married to Mr. Joseph Barnard.

Bates, Maj. Ambrose of Jefferson County married in Knox Co., To Mrs. Susan Hanner.
National Banner & Nashville Whig (Fri., May 8, 1835)

Bates, Mr. Caleb married in Cincinnati to Miss Elizabeth T. Humphreys.
National Banner & Nashville Whig (Sat., Feb. 16, 1828)

Bates, Mr. Hamlet, Editor and proprietor of the St. Croix Courier, married on Tues. the 21st by the Rev. W. A. Whitwell to Miss Martha Langley of the city of Portland.
National Banner & Nashville Whig (Wed., Jan. 21, 1835)

Bates, James W., Esq., married in Crawford Co., Ark., to Mrs. Elizabeth W. Palmore.
National Banner & Nashville Whig (Sat., Feb. 23, 1828)

Bates, Mr. John married in Fayette Co., Ky. to Miss Nancy Adams.
National Banner & Nashville Whig (Sat., Feb. 23, 1828)

Bates, Miss Nancy married in Smith Co., to Mr. Thos. Baliff.

Batey, Mr. James married in Maury County to Miss Sarah Pitchett.
National Banner & Nashville Whig (Fri., March 26, 1830)

Batte, T., Jr., A. P.M ., at Stewartsboro, Tenn., married in Rutherford Co., Tenn on March 6, by Rev. Martin Clark., to Mrs. Ann D. Hunter. form-
Nashville Union (Mon., March 18, 1839) erly of Brownsville, Tenn.

Batte, Mr. Thomas, A. P. M. Married at Murfreesboro, Tenn., Tues. March 5th by the Rev. Martin Clark, to Mrs. Anne O. Hunter, formerly of Brownsville, Tenn.
Daily Republican Banner (Thurs., March 14, 1839)

Battle, Miss Mary Ann married to Henry W. Collier, Esq.

Battle, Miss Susan L. married to Mr. Benjamin W. Williams.

Batts, Mrs. Susan H. married to Mr. James Coleman.

Batty, Miss Isabella H. married to Mr. James Stephens.

Baucanan, Mr. Jas B. of this county married in Jackson Co., to Miss Letty Robert.
National Banner & Nashville Whig (Sat., May 19, 1827)

Bauchanan, Miss Sarah married to Mr. Thoams Trotter.

Baucom, Miss Nancy married to Mr. Joseph F. Wilson.

Baugh, Mr. John married to Miss Martha Trotter, in Williamson Co.
National Banner & Nashville Whig (Sat., July 15, 1826)

Baugh, Mr. Philip W., married in Williamson Co., to Miss Elizabeth Lemons.
National Banner & Nashville Whig (Mon., Nov. 14, 1831)

(repeat of preceding)
The Western Weekly Review (Franklin, Tenn., Fri., Nov. 11, 1831)

Baughn, Mr. Samuel H. married in Tipton Co., on Tues. Evening the 12th inst. to Miss Nancy Durham, daughter of Maj. Thomas Durham.
National Banner & Nashville Whig (Wed., May 181, 1831)

Baugus, Miss Nancy married to Mr. John Moore.

Baulding, Miss Alexandra married to Mr. Gustavius Burraugh.

Baurland, Mr. Bayles E. married in Lauderdale Co., Ala., to Miss Sarah Brown.
National Banner & Nashville Whig (Sat., March 17, 1827)

Bawls, Miss Mary Ann of Mississippi married to Dr. Paul H. Otey.

Baxter, Miss Ann Rebecca married to Mr. Stephens Cooke.

Baxter, Mr. David married in Rutherford Co., on Thursday last to Miss Frances Elder.
National Banner & Nashville Daily Advertiser (Sat., April 14, 1832)

Baxter, Mr. Jeremiah married at Louisville, Ky. to Miss Elizabeth Jacobs.
National Banner & Nashville Whig (Sat., May 12, 1827)

Baxter, Miss Louisa married to G. L. Abernathy.

Baxter, Miss Louise married to Mr. John Gordon.

Baxter, Miss Margaret married to Henry B. Hawkins, Esq.

Baxter, Miss Mary D. married to Stephen D. Watkins, Esq.

Baxter, Miss Rebecca married to Charles B. McKeirnan.

Baxter, Mr. Robert of Montgomery Co., married on the 8th inst., by the Rev. Robert Williams to Miss Sarah Jane Connell of Robertson Co.
Nashville Whig (Tues., July 21, 1846)

Baxter, William married in Williamson co., to Miss Eleanor Cowen.
The Western Weekly Review (Franklin, Tenn., Fri., Dec. 14, 1832)

Baxton, Dr. James W. of Abingdon, Va., married in Knox Co., to Miss
Martha Rebecca Campbell, daughter of the late Col. Robert Campbell.
National Banner & Nashville Daily Advertiser (Mon., Dec. 10, 1832)

Bayce, Mrs. Margaret J. married to Mr. James H. Cobb.

Bayer, Miss Margaret married to Dr. D. G. Benbrook.

Baylan, Mrs. Priscilla P. married to Judge William T. Brown.

Bayless, Dr. Benjamin M. married in Philadelphia, Monroe Cty., to Miss
Louisa M. Yoakum.
National Baner & Nashville Whig (Mon., Nov. 10, 1834)

Bayless, Mr. William B. married in Louisville, on the 18th by the Rev.
W. L. Breckenridge, to Miss Ann Maria Tannehill, daughter of Wilkins
Tannehill, Esq., both of Nashville.
Daily Republican Banner (Sat., Jan. 27, 1838)

Bayliss, Mr. Henry W., married in Logan Co., Ky., on the 28th ult.. to
Miss Martha V. Williams, of Simpson Co., Ky., daughter of Capt. Richard
Williams.
National Banner & Nashville Daily Advertiser (Sat., Feb. 9, 1833)

Baylor, Miss Mary Jane married to Franklin Wharton, Esq.

Baynes, Mr. Marcus H. of Sumner Co., married on Thursday 18th inst., by
the Rev. T. Fuqua to Miss Mary Ann Rowe of Davidson Co.
Nasvhille Union (Tues., Jan 23, 1838)

Baynton, John Esq., married at China near Natchez to Miss Carolina
Sessions.
NationalBanner (Sat., June 27, 1829)

Bazdell, Miss Elizabeth married in Williamson Co., to John Maupin.
National Banner & Nashville Whig (Fri., Jan. 9, 1835)

Bazzell, Miss Lucy married in Williamson Co., to Mr. William Warren.

Beadles, Mr. Anderson married in Mercer Co., Ky. to Miss Margaret Cooper.
National Banner & Nashville Whig (Sat., March 31, 1827)

Beal, Mr. John, a Revolutionary Soldier, married to Miss Elizabeth
Hargorve, age 18 on Tuesday 1 inst., by Rev. Philip Courtney.
National Banner & Nashville Advertiser (Fri., Jun 1, 1831)

Beale, Miss George Ann married to Mr. Reuben B. Norvell

Beale, Mr. John a soldier in Pulaski legion, married on Tues. evening
1st inst., by the Rev. Philip Courtney, to Miss Elizabeth Hardgrove,
aged 18.
National Banner & Nashville Daily Advertiser (Fri., June 1, 1832)

Bealer, Mr. Geo. married in Fayette. Co., Ky., to Miss Nancy Fitzgerald.
National Banner (Sat., May 2, 1829)

Beall, Mr. James M. married in Robertson Co., to Miss Sarah Y. Bryan.
National Banner & Nashville Whig (Sat., April 21, 1827)

Beams, Miss Ann T. married to Mr. Charles E. Sneed.

Bean, Miss Margaret married to Mr. John Gott.

Beard, Mr. Andrew married in August 1831 to Miss Nancy Edwards.
The Western Weekly Review (Franklin, Tenn., Fri., Sept. 2, 1831)

Beard, Miss Eliza married to Mr. R. S. Craddock.

Beard, Miss Jane married to Mr. James L. Davis.

Beard, Mr. John married in Lincoln Co. to Mrs. Rebecca Turner.
National Banner (May 20, 1826)

Beard, Miss Margaret married to Mr. James G. Smith.

Beard, Mr. Samuel of Indiana married in Claiborne Co., Miss. to Miss
Ophelia Bullock.
National Banner & Nashville Whig (Sat., March 31, 1827)

Beard, Mr. William Married in Cincinnati, Ohio, to Miss Frances H.
Stall.
National Banner & Nashville Daily Advertiser (Mon., April 2, 1832)

Bearden, Mr. John P. married in Knox Co., to Miss Carolina O. R. W. B.
Odell, daughter of Wm. Odell.
National Banner (Sat., Oct.3,   1829)

Bearden, Miss Maria married in Knox Co., to Mr. Seth Lee.
National Banner & Nashville Whig (Mon., April 11, 1831)

Bearden, Mr. Richard Jr., married in Knox Co., to Miss Catherine Scott,
daughter of Mr. Thomas Scott.
National Banner & Nashville Daily Advertiser (Mon., Feb. 13, 1832)

Beasley, Miss Amanda, married in Smith Co., to Mr. Noel Read.

Beasley, Mr. Bennett H. married on the 15th inst.,by the Rev. Mr. Howell
to Miss Susan Carper, both of Nashville.
Nashville Republican (Tues., Oct. 11, 1836)

Beasley, Mr. Henry married in Smith Co., to Miss Lydia Shoemake.
National Banner & Nashville Whig (Tues., Dec. 13, 1831)

Beasley, Miss Louisa married Mr. Joseph Hollowell.

Beasley, Miss Lucretia married Mr. John Price.

Beasley, Miss Massey married to Mr. Thomas Hunter.

Beasley, Mr. Needham married in Rutherford Co., to Miss Louisa Black.
National Banner & Nashville Daily Advertiser (Sat., Feb. 25, 1832)

Beasley, Mr. Wiley married in Williamson Co., to Miss Polly Johnson.
National Banner (Sat., April 25, 1829)

Beasly, Mr. Esau married in Maury Co., to Miss Martha Wilkins, daughter
of Mr. James Wilkins.
National Banner & Nashville Daily Advertiser (Fri., Sept. 6, 1833)

Beasly, Miss Mary A. married to Mr. Riddeck Godwin.

Beasly, Miss Masey married to Mr. Thomas Hunter.

Beatie, Major Robert married in Abington, Va., to Miss Paulina White.
Nashville Whig (Feb. 26, 1823)

Beatty, Miss married to Rev. Clark Mansfield.

Beaty, Miss Narcissa married to Maj.James W. Crenshaw.

Beaty Mr. W. G. W. married in Rutherford Co., to Miss America S. Crockett,
daughter of Overton W. Crockett, Esq.
The Union (Tues., Dec. 20, 1836)

Beauchamp, Miss Elizabeth married to Mr. Jona Brown.

Beaumont, Mr. William of Clarksville, Tenn., married in Logan Co., Ky. to Miss Susan Cook, daughter of the late Rev. V. Cook.
National Banner & Nashville Daily Advertiser (June 20, 1834)

Beaver, Major Jas. married in Henderson Co., on the 2d inst., to Miss Nancy G. Kirk.
National Banner & Nashville Daily Advertiser (Tues., Jan. 21, 1834)

Beavers, Miss Matilda married to Mr. Jesse Overton.

Beaver, Miss Nancy married to Mr. Abner Shindlebower.

Beck, Miss Ann married to Willie Barrow, Esq.

Beck, Miss Georgianna married to John T. Hill.

Beck, Mr. Henry married in Lincoln Co., to Miss Louisa C. Barnes.
Nashville Whig (Tues., March 24, 1846)

Beck, Capt. John of Davidson Co., married to Mrs. Harris of same, on Thurs. last.
Impartial Review & Cumberland Repository (Nashville, Sept. 28, 1808)

Beck, John E., Esq., attorney at law, married to Miss Levinia Robertson Davidson Co., on Sunday last.
Impartial Review & Cumberland Repository (Nashville, Oct, 13, 1808)

Beck, Mrs. Lavina married to Mr. John B. Craighead.

Beck, Mr. Phlegmon, married at Vandalia, Ill to Miss Chancy Luster.
National Banner (May 20, 1826)

. Beckham, Miss Mary married to Mr. John S. Brown.

Beckwith, Miss Mary married to James M. Bucklin, Esq.

Becton, Mr. George W. married in Rutherford Co., to Miss Martha L. Henderson.
National Banner & Nashville Daily Advertiser (Fri., May 3, 1833)

Becton, Mr. John M. Married in Rutherford Co., to Miss Eleanor E. Sharpe.
National Banner & Nashville Whig (Sat., Feb. 3, 1827)

Bedford, Mr. Benjamin W., Merchant, married on Thurs. evening last, to Miss Nancy Whyte, daughter of Robert Whye, all of Nashville.
The Nashville Gazette (Sat., March 3, 1821)

Bedford, Miss Cornelia married to Col. John T. Burtwell.

Bedford, Miss Mary married to Burrel Warren.

Bedford, Dr. Rob. of Tipton married in Haywood Co., to Miss Nancy Turner daughter of the late Simon Turner.
National Banner & Nashville Whig (Sa., June 2, 1827)

Bedford, Dr. Robert married in Haywood Co., on the 22d ult., to Miss Nancy M. J. P. Turner, daughter of the late Simon Turner.
National Banner & Nashville Whig (June 9, 1827)

Bedford, Mr. Sideny married in Fayette Co., Ky., to Miss Susan Price.
National Banner & Nashville Whig (Sat, July 14, 1827)

Bedford, Miss Susan married to Rev. Jacob Creath Jun.

Bee, Mr. James married in Cincinnati to Miss Ellen Bom.
National Banner & Nashville Whig (Sat., June 7, 1828)

Beech, Mr. O. C. of Woodbury, married in Nashville on Thurs. evening last at the residence of Mr. George H. Burton, to Miss Virginia Vaughn.
Nashville Whig (Thurs., April 16, 1846)

Beeman, Philo, Esq., of Louisville, Ky. married on the 23d ult., by
the Rev'd Henry B. Bascom to Miss Martha C. Campbell, of Franklin.
The Nashville Gazette, (Wed., March 15, 1820)

Beers, Mr. David married in Columbua, Ohio, to Miss Mary Ann Parkinson.
National Banner & Nashville Daily Advertiser (Thurs., Feb. 21, 1833)

Beesley, Mr. of Huntsville, Ala., married in Rutherford Co., Tenn.,
to Eveline Avant, of Rutherford.
National Banner & Nashville Whig (Wed., Sept. 24, 1834)

Belew, Capt. Micajah B. in Knox Co., married to Miss Polly Brooks.
National Banner & Nashville Whig (Wed., Aug. 17, 1831)

Belknap, Miss Jane G. of Smithville, Ky., married in Smithville, Ky.
by the Rev. Mr. Willis to Thomas L. Jewett, Esq.

Bell, Miss A. H. married to Mr. William Harvey.

Bell, Mr. A. L. of Wilson Co., married in Sumner Co., to Miss Rhoda M'Call.
National Banner & Nashville Daily Advertiser (Sat., Dec. 8, 1832)

Bell, David D, Editor of the Murfreesborough Telegraph, married in Jackson, to Miss Martha Catharine Gibbs, daughter of Gen. George W. Gibbs.
Nashville Whig (Tues., April 14, 1846)

Bell, Miss Eliza married to Mr. D. Woodruff.

Bell, Miss Elizabeth married to Mr. Skyles.

Bell, Miss Elizabeth married to Rev. Reuben Burrow.

Bell, Miss Elizabeth married to Mr. Miles Warford.

Bell, Miss Fanny M. married to Thomas H. Maney, Esq.

Bell, Mr. Henry C. of Obion Co., Tenn., married in Russellville, Ky. to
Miss Susan J. Cates.
National Banner & Nashville Daily Advertiser (Sat., July 28, 1832)

Bell, Miss Hetty married to Mr. Oliver Hakill.

Bell, Mr. Hugh F. of Nashville married to Miss Sarah Maria Voorhies in
Columbia.
National Banner & Nashville Whig (Thurs., May 27, 1830)

Bell, Mr. James married in Georgetown, Ky., to Miss Eliza Remington.
National Banner (May 10, 1826)

Bell, Mr. James of Nashville married in Rutherford Co., to Miss Mary
Dickinson.
National Banner & Nashville Whig (Sat., Dec. 23, 1826)

Bell, Mr. James G. in Hardeman Co., married to Miss Adelia C. Neely.
Nashville Republican and State Gazette (Thurs., May 5, 1831)

(repeat of preceding)
National Banner & Nashville Whig (Fri., May 6, 1831)

Bell, Miss Jane married to Mr. Peter H. Martin.

Bell, Mr. Jesse married in Wilkinson Co., Miss., to Elizabeth Ann Jones.
National Banner & Nashville Whig (Sat., Feb. 10, 1827)

Bell, Mr. John married in Logan Co., Ky. to Miss Rachel Miller.
National Banner & Nashville Whig (Mon., Aug. 23, 1830)

Bell, John Hon., representative in Congress from this Dist., married in
Nashville on the 25th Oct by the Rev. Dr. Edgar to Mrs. Jane Yeatman,
widow of the late Thomas Yeatman, Esq. Nat'l Banner & Nashville Whig

(Mon., Oct. 26, 1835)

Bell, Capt. Jonas J. married in Tuscumbia on the 6th by the Rev. James Weatherby to Mrs. Harriet H. Carter, all of Tuscumbia.
Nashville Republican (Sat., April 29, 1837)

Bell, Mr. Joseph married in Franklin Co., Ky., to Miss Sarah Ann Taylor.
National Banner & Nashville Whig (Mon., Dec. 13, 1830)

Bell, Dr. Joseph E., married in Green Co., to Miss Mary Ann Farnsworth.
National Banner & Nashville Daily Advertiser (Sat., Feb. 25, 1832)

Bell, Rev. Joshua married in Gibson Co., to Miss Bledsoe.
National Banner & Nashville Daily Advertiser (Mon., Nov. 4, 1833)

Bell, Miss Maria S., married in Columbia, to Dr. George A. Glover.

Bell, Miss Mary married to Mr. William Houston.

Bell, Miss Mary married to Mr. William Hardy.

Bell, Miss Mary A. H. married to Mr. Wm. Harvy.

Bell, Miss Mary Ann married to Mr. Jesse Serginer.

Bell, Miss Mary E. married to Mr. Lyttleton J. Dooly.

Bell, Miss Mary Ann married to Mr. Jacob W. Earie.

Bell, Mr. Monroe married in Nasvhille on the 9th inst., by the Rev. John T. Edgar to Miss E. Fursman.
National Banner and Nashville Whig (Wed., March 11, 1835)

(repeat of preceding)
Nashville Republican (Tues., March 17, 1835)

Bell, Mr. Philip D. married in Knox Co., to Miss Harriet Jane Murphy.
National Banner & Nashville Whig (Sat., Sept. 8, 1827)

Bell, Miss Rebecca married to Capt. James D. Murray.

Bell, Robert H., Esq., married in Hindes Co, Miss. to Miss Susan M'Cain.
National Banner & Nashville Whig (Sat., Jan. 19, 1828)

Bell, Mr. Robert J. in Davidson Co., married to Miss Tyrana Brown,
Nashville Republican & State Gazette (Tues., April 12, 1831)

Bell, Mr. Robert J. married in Davidson Co., on the 7th inst., by H. Blackman to Miss Tyrana Brown.
National Banner & Nashville Whig (Fri., April 15, 1831)

Bellamy, John Esq., in Todd Co., Ky., married to Mrs. Mariah A. H. Smith.
National Banner and Nashville Whig (Mon., April 25, 1831)

Bellessome, Julia married to Mr. James Snell.

Bellitt, Miss Amanthus married to Mr. Geo. Weisinger.

Beloate, Miss Susan married to Mr. Samuel Paschal.

Beltzhoover, Elizabeth married to Mr. William Cox.

Benbridge, Miss Eveline married to Mr. Henry Emerson.

Benbrook, Dr. D. G. married in Hartsville to Miss Margaret Bayer.
National Banner and Nashville Whig (Jan. 5, 1828)

Bender, Miss Betsey married to Mr. Christopher Brooks.

Bender, Mr. Burrell married in Wilson Co., to Miss Elizabeth Smith, daughter of Mr. George Smith.
NationalBanner Nashville Daily Advertiser (Mon., Aug. 20, 1832)

Benderman, Mr. Dickenson married at Louisville, Ky., to Miss Eliza Vance.
National Banner & Nashville Daily Advertiser (Wed., Jan. 4, 1832)

Benford, Mr. John married in Lawrence Co., Ala., to Miss Martha Craig.
National Banner & Nashville Whig (Sat, March 17, 1827)

Benham, Miss Harriet married to Mr. George D. Prentice.

Bennett, Miss married to Mr. Jesse Kirby.

Bennett, Miss Elizabeth P. married to Mr. Jas. Kennedy.

Bennett, Miss F..L. O. A. married to Mr. B. C. Hancock.

Bennett, Miss Lydia married to Mr. George W. Denham.

Bennett, Miss Mary married to Mr. William Cisna.

Bennett, Mr. Moses G. married in Maury Co., Tenn., to Miss Sarah Woollard.
National Banner & Nashville Whig (Wed., Feb. 25, 1835)

Bennett, Mr. Nelson married in Louisville, Ky., to Miss Celina Custer.
National Banner & Nashville Advertiser (Aug. 4, 1832)

Bennett, Miss P. C. married at St. Louis to Mr. Isaac N. Henry

Bennett, Mr. William married in this county on the 20th ult to Miss Mary Sneed.
National Banner (Sat., June 13, 1829)

Bennett, Mr. Willis D. married in Fayette Co., Ky., to Miss Paulina T. Haley.
National Banner & Nashville Whig (Sat., July 8, 1826)

Benoist, Mr. Louis A., of St. Louis, married in Kaskaskia, Ill., to Miss Eliza Bartow.
National Banner & Nashville Whig (Sat., Sept. 2, 1826)

Benoit, Mr. Ernst of this place married on Thurs evening last to Mrs. Fanny Gains of Rutherford co.
The Nashville Whig & Ten. Advertiser. (Nov. 3, 1817)

Bensford, Mr. Robert married in Rutherford Co., to Miss Mary Ann Jarrett.
National Banner & Nashville Whig (Sat., Dec. 30, 1826)

Benson, Mr. Sylvanus E. married on Thurs., Nov. 30th by the Rev. J. T. Wheat to Miss Elizabeth Marshall, all of Nashville.
Nashville Union (Sat., Dec. 2, 1837)

Benson, Mr. Sylvanus E. married in Thurs., Nov. 30th by the Rev. J. T. Wheat to Elizabeth Marshall, dau. of Col. Saml. B. Marshall, all of Nashville.
Daily Republican Banner (Sat., Dec. 2, 1837)

Benthal, Miss Rosanna J. of Giles married to Mr. Spencer Dobson.

Bentley, Miss Ann married to Mr. John Robinson.

Bentley, Mr. Leonidas M. married in Lawrence Co., to Miss Martha A. Moore.
Nashville Whig (Thurs., March 19, 1846)

Bentley, Miss Malinda married to Mr. Richard Fowler.

Bentley, Miss Maria B. married in Madison Co., Ala., to Mr. Daniel B. Friend.

Bentinger, Mr. Jacob married in Jefferson Co., Ky. to Miss Sarah Hoke.
National Banner (Jan. 20, 1826)

Benton, Miss Eliza Preston Carrington married to William Carey Jones.

Berkley, Miss Malinda married to Mr. James W. Thornberry, Esq.

Bernard, James C. married in Christian Co., Ky. to Miss Thyrsa Kav.
National Banner & Nashville Whig (Wed., Oct. 19, 1831)

Bernard, Miss Virginia married to Mr. William Wood.

Berrien, Hon. John Macpherson married in Savanah to Miss Eliza Cecil Hunter on 10th July.
Nashville Republican & State Gazette (Sat., Aug. 3, 1833)

Mrs. Berry married to Robert Wash, Esq.

Berry, Augustus D. Esq., of Nashville, married in Salem, Mass., on the 6th inst.,by the Rev. Dr. Brazer to Miss Mary Farnham, daughter of P. I, Farnham, Esq.
Nashville Whig (Wed., Sept. 22, 1841)

Berry, Miss Barbara Ellen married to Ebenezer J. Hume.

Berry, Miss Clarissa L. married to Mr. James White.

Berry, Mr. Daniel D. married in Hardeman Co., to Miss Olivia Polk, daughter of Wm. Polk, Esq.
National Banner & Nashville Whig (Mon., April 25, 1831)

Berry, Mr. Daniel D. married in Bolivar to Miss Oliva Polk.
Nashville Republican & State Gazette (Thurs., April 21, 1831)

Berry, Mr. John D. married in Knox Co., to Miss Elizabeth Kinnannon, late of Wythe Co., Va.
National Banner & Nashville Whig (Mon., Nov. 15, 1830)

Berry, Miss Margaret married to Mr. James H. Cowan.

Berry, Miss Mary Louisa married to Mr. James M. Hamilton.

Berry, Susan E. married to Mr. Robert K. Woods.

Berry, Mr. W. L. printer of the Yeoman, married in Fayetteville, T., to Miss Nancy G. Wallace.
National Banner & Nashville Daily Advertiser (Mon., May 12, 1834)

Berry, Mr. Wm. married in Fayette Co., Ky., to Miss Martha T. Herndon.
National Banner & Nashville Whig (Sat., Dec. 16, 1826)

Berry, Mr. William T. married in Louisville, Ky. on the 12th inst., to Miss Mary Margaret Tannehill, daughter Wilkins Tannehill.
National Banner & Nashville Daily Advertiser (Thurs., Sept. 19, 1833)

Berry, William W., Esq., married at White Hall, near Nashville by the Rev. John W. Ogden to Miss Jane Eliza White, daughter of Gen. William White, deceased.
Nashville Whig (Wed., March 11, 1840)

Berryhill, Miss Ann married to Mr. James Jackson.

Berryhill, Miss Harriet C., married to Capt. Edward W. B. Nowland.

Berryhill, Miss Mary I. married to Mr. Edward W. Warner.

Berryman, Mr. Charles married in Fayette Co., Ky., to Miss Nancy Hudson.

National Banner (March 3, 1826)

Berryman, Jas. married in Williamson Co., Tenn., to Mary Atkinson.
National Banner & Nashville Daily Advertiser (Mon., Aug. 26, 1833)

Berryman, Miss Mary R. married to Mr. George Boswell.

Bertrand, Miss Arabella Jane married to Mr. Lorenzo N. Clark.

Bertus, Miss Marie Louise Emeline married to Mr. John Carnes.

Mrs. Best married in Harden Co., to Mr. H. G. Waggoner.

Bestkinson, Mr. Jesse married in Franklin to Miss Margaret Patton.
Nashville Republican & State Gazette. (Tues., Nov. 1, 1831)

Bettes, Miss Harriet married to Mr. George R. Snell.

Bettes, Miss Cinderella married to Thomas Stephenson Drew, Esq.

Betty, William H. married in Williamson Co., to Miss Mary Covington.
The Western Weekly Review (Franklin, Tenn., Fri., Dec. 14, 1832)

Beverly, Miss Eglantine Beverly married to Robert B. Randolph.

Beville, Miss Elizabeth married to Mr. James Loller.

Beville, Miss Sarah married to Mr. Charles L. Roberts.

Beynroth, Mr. Charles E. married to Miss Aminta Howard, in Jefferson Co.,
Ky.
National Banner & Nashville Whig (Thurs., Oct. 21, 1830)

Bibb, Miss Fanny May married to William Parker Scott.

Bibb, Miss Frances Ann married to Abbot T. Burnley, Esq.

Bibb, Mr. James married in Logan Co., Ky., to Miss Ann Eliza Anderson.
National Banner & Nashville Daily Advertiser (Thurs., Aug. 23, 1832)

Bibb, Miss Julia Ann married to Col. Jno. N. Wright.

Bibb, Miss Mary married to Mr. Samuel Fitzhugh.

Bibb, Miss Mary married to Mr. Charles Cosswell.

Bibb, Maj. Thos. H. married at Florence, Ala., to Miss Sophia M. Byrn.
National Banner & Nashville Whig (Sat., Aug. 18, 1827)

Bibbs, Miss Frances married in Knox Co., to Mr. Hugh S. Copeland.

Bick, Miss Susannah married to Rev. Robert Paine.

Biddle, Mrs. Eliza married to Mr. John B. Enness.

Biddle, Miss Mary married to Mr. Peter Vandervoort Jun.

Biddle, Miss Sarah S. married to Maj. Whitmell H. Boyd.

Biddle, Miss Sarah S. married to John S. Lytle, Esq.

Bieller, Miss Elizabeth married to Hon. Felix Boswoth.

Bigelow, Elijah, Esq. married to Miss Maria O. Childs, of Nashville, on
Tues. evening last.
National Banner (Fri., Dec. 23, 1825)

Bigger, Eliza married to Mr. Richard J. Bass.

Bigger, Mr. Joseph B. married in Montgomery co., on Tues. last, to Miss Lucy B. B. Slaughter, daughter of Thomas S. Slaughter, Esq., of Russell-ville, Ky.
The Nashville Gazette (Sat., April 8, 1820)

Biggs, Miss Elizabeth married to John Springer, Esq.

Biggs, Miss Nancy married to Mr. Elias Simpson.

Bigham, Mr. Samuel married in Madison Co., Ala., to Miss Ann Maria White.
National Banner & Nashville Whig (Sat., May 26, 1828)

Bigley, Mr. Thomas married on Thursday 14th inst., by the Rev. Mr. Senter of the Convention, to Miss Nancy Patrick, both of Nashville.
National Banner & Nashville Daily Advertiser (Fri., Aug. 15, 1834)

Bigly, Miss Sarah married to Rev. William Anderson.

Bilbo, Miss Barbara married to Maj. E. A. White.

Bilbo, William N. Esq., of Nashville married in Columbus, Miss., on the 28th ult., by the Rev. F. E. Pitts, to Miss Martha W. Fort, of Columbia, Miss.
The Christian Record (Sat., Feb. 20, 1847)

Biles, Miss Sophia married to Mr. Smith Butler.

Biles, Mr. William J. married in Murfreesborough to Miss Sarah Ann Johns.
National Banner & Nashville Daily Advertiser (Fri , Jan. 27, 1832)

Billiard, Mr. Peter of Nashville, Tenn. married at Cincinnati on the 3d inst. to Mrs. Catharine Caburit of Cincinnati.
Nashville True Whig and Weekly Commercial Register (Dec. 20, 1850)

Billings, Mr. John D. married at Chillicothe, O., to Miss Sabra M' Collister.
National Banner (Jan. 27, 1826)

Billingsley, Rev. Samuel of Bledsoe county married in Pikeville to Miss Tennessee Whiteside, daughter of Mr. James Whiteside.
National Banner & Nashville Whig (Fri., July 15, 1831)

Binford, Miss Francis of Limestone Co., Ala., married in Huntsville, Ala., to Mr. Theophilus Lacy.

Bingham, Mr. John J. married to Miss Sarah Riddle at Huntsville, Ala.
National Banner (Feb. 10, 1826)

Binkley, Miss Angelina married to Mr. John B. Fisher.

Birch, Miss Elizabeth married to Mr. Britton P. Powell.

Birch, Mr. Wm. F. married in Mountsterling, Ky., to Miss Harriet Ann Campbell.
National Banner & Nashville Whig (Sat., Oct. 28, 1826)

Birdsall, Maria Louisa married to Mr. E. J. Harker.
National Banner & Nashville Daily Advertiser (Thurs., July 10, 1834)

Birdwell, Mr. married on Wed. the 6th inst., by T. Fanning, Pres. of Franklin College to Miss Elizabeth Harris, all of Davidson Co.
The Politician & Weekly Nashville Whig (Fri., Oct. 15, 1847)

Birdwell, Miss Marilda married to Mr. Neal C. Deavers.

Birk, Mr. Johnson married in Henry Co., Tenn., since the first of Jan. to Miss Jane Ramsey.
National Banner & Nashville Whig (Fri., Feb. 13, 1835)

Bishop, Mr. Harman married in Hardeman county, Tenn to Miss Polly Williams.
National Banner & Nashville Whig (Wed., Oct. 22, 1834)

Bisor, Miss Polly Ann married to Mr. Hatch.

Bissell, Mr. Israel married at Cincinnati, Ohio, to Miss Margaret Clay.
National Banner (Feb. 3, 1826)

Bizzell, Mr. William married in Maury Co., Tenn to Miss Sarah Scott.
National Banner & Nashville Whig (Mon., Jan. 26, 1835)

(repeat of preceding)
Nashville Republican (Tues., Jan. 27, 1835)

Black, Miss Barcinia married in Maury County to Mr. Levi Kitchum.

Black, Mr. George F. married in Anderson county to Miss Nancy Y. Oliver, daughter of Douglas Oliver, Esq.
National Banner & Nashville Daily Advertiser (Tues., July 2, 1833)

Black, Mr. H. of Nashville on 7th inst., married to Miss Elizabeth Morgan, at Kingston, Tenn.
Nashville Republican & State Gazette (Thurs., Oct. 30, 1834)

Black, Mr. Isaac C. married in Williamson County, Tenn. to Miss Elizabeth Jane Cody.
National Banner & Nashville Whig (Mon. April 13, 1835)

Black, Mr. John D. married in Rutherford Co., to Miss Sarah C. Sublett, daughter of Capt. Wm. A. Sublett.
National Banner & Nashville Whig (Fri., Feb. 11, 1831)

Black, Mr. L. P. married in Rutherford County to Martha Ann Nelson.
Nashville Whig (Tues., April 21, 1846)

Black, Miss Letitia married to Zachariah Coleman.

Black, Miss Louisa married to Mr. Needham Beasley.

Black, Miss Margaret married to Mr. Charles Thompson.

Black, Mr. Robert married in Rutherford Co., to Miss Rebecca Miller.
National Banner & Nashville Daily Advertiser (Wed., April 23, 1833)

Black, Mr. Spotswood W. married in Rutherford County to Miss Ann Ackland.
National Banner (Sat., Oct. 16, 1829)

Black, Miss T. married to H. M. Watterson, Esq.

Black, Mr. Thomas J. married in Smith County to Miss Jane Wright, on the 27th of Oct.
Nashville Republican (Tues., Nov. 10, 1835)

Blackberry, Mr. N. married at Sunbury, Mass. by the Rev. Mr. Cranberry to Miss C. Elderberry, daughter of Dr. N. Elderberry of Danberry.
National Banner & Nashville Whig (Mon., Dec. 29, 1834)

Blackburn, Mr. Salathael married in Knox Co., to Miss Betsey Mitchell.
National Banner & Nashville Whig (Sat., Feb. 7, 1829)

Blackburn, Miss married to Dr. Charles W. Todd.

Blackemore, Miss Fanny married to Mr. John Gallegher.

Blackemore, Mr. Willie B. of Gibson Co., married in Rutherford Co., to Miss Catherine V. Tussell.
National Banner & Nashville Whig (July 1, 1826)

Blackimore, Miss Carolina M. married to Mr. William G. Massey.

Blackman, Mr. Hays married in this county to Miss Elizabeth B. Compton.
National Banner (April 28, 1826)

Blackman, Miss Nancy E., married to Col. Blackburn Hays.

Blackman, Mr. Zachariah married in Claiborne Co., Mo., to Miss Rebecca
A. Stout.
National Banner & Nashville Daily Advertiser (Tues., May 20, 1834)

Blackmore, Andrew J., Esq., married on the 26th inst., at the residence
of Mr. John Patton by Rev. Dr. Edgar to Miss Harriet McCorkle, all of
Sumner county.
Nashville Whig (Fri., Jan. 20, 1841)

Blackmore, Miss Catharine married to J. C. Guild, Esq.

Blackmore, Miss Emeline M. married to James H. Hadley, Esq.

Blackmore, Dr. James A. married in Williamson county on the 9th inst.,
by the Rev. Mr. Hume to Miss Evelina Hadley.
National Banner & Nashville Whig (Sat., April 12, 1828)

Blackwell, Miss Elizabeth married to William S. Neely.

Blackwell, Mr. Preston married in Woodford Co., Ky. to Miss Nancy Crutcher.
National Banner (March 31, 1826)

Blackwell, Miss Sarah C. married in Morgan Co., Ala., to Mr. Floyd Minor.

Blain, Margaret married to Parish Hubble.

Blain, Mr. Richard C. married in Henderson county on Thurs. 26th inst.
to Miss Anges Howard.
National Banner & Nashville Daily Advertiser (Wed., Feb. 15, 1832)

Blair, Mr. Alexander of Bedford married in Rutherford Co., to Miss
Melinda Henderson.
National Banner (Sat., Sept. 26, 1829)

Blair, Dr. Colbert married in Miller Co., Ark., to Mrs. Ann Thompson.
National Banner & Nashville Whig (Mon., Nov. 1, 1830)

Blair, E. P. Samuel, Esq., married in St. Augustine to Miss Selena Blair.
National Banner & Nashville Whig (Sat., Dec. 16, 1826)

Blair, Miss Jane married to Mr. J. Poindexter.

Blair, Miss Jane V. married to Mr. John M. Hendrix.

Blair, Mr. John S. married in Limestone Co., Ala., to Miss Ann C. Allen.
National Banner (Sat., April 25, 1829)

Blair, Miss Margery F. married in Grainger Co. to Capt. James Campbe.

Blair, Miss Maria married to Mr. James C. Todd.

Blair, Miss Mariam married to Mr. John Farrar.

Blair, Miss Mary C. married to Mr. Francis Simpson.

Blair, Miss Nancy D. married to Mr. Allen J. Holliday.

Blair, Miss Selena married to E. P. Samuel Blair, Esq.

Blake, Miss Anna T. married to John W. Sanders, Esq.

Blake, Daniel, Esq. married in Nashville on Thurs. evening last, to
Miss Emma P. Rutledge, daughter of Col. Henry M. Rutledge.
National Banner & Nashville Whig (Mon., June 13, 1831)

Blake, Mr. Daniel of South Carolina married to Miss Emma Rutledge on
Thursday.
Nashville Republican & State Gazette (Tues., June 4, 1831)

Blake, Miss Eliza Ann daughter of Mr. N. O. Blake married to Mr. John
Kirk.

Blake, Miss Sally married to Mr. John Marr.

Blake, Mr. William of Fayetteville married in Sumner County to Miss
Carolina Malinda Hall.
National Banner & Nashville Whig (Wed., Nov. 2, 1831)

Blake, Mr. William C. of Fayetteville married in Sumner County to Miss
Carolina Malinda Hall, daughter of Mr. George Hall.
National Banner & Nashville Whig (Wed., Nov. 2, 1831)

Blackburn, Bethenia B married to Thomas W. Davidson.

Blackburn, Miss Jane M. married to Rev. Wm. A King.

Blakey, Miss Clarisaa married to Mr. Ewen Cameron Jr.

Blakey, Miss Eleanor Ann married to Mr. Resin P. Haden.

Blakey, Mr. George D. of Logan Co., Ky. married in Nashville on Tues.
23d inst., by Rev. Mr. Gwin to Miss Lucy Ann Thomas.
National Banner & Nashville Whig (Fri., Feb. 26, 1830)

Blakey, Miss Susan married to Major John Poindexter.
Blakey, Miss Sally married to Mr. James Proctor.
Blancett, Mr. Tiller married in Christian Co., Ky. to Miss Betsy Hill.
National Banner & Nashville Daily Advertiser (Thurs., Oct. 18, 1832)

Blanchard, Mr. Thomas J. married in Knoxville to Miss Martha J. Lea.
Nashville Whig (Sat., April 11, 1846)

Bland, Miss Malinda married to Mr. Joseph Rutherford.

Bland, Miss Mary married to Mr. Samuel Cochran.

Blankenship, Mr. Benjamin married in Rutherford Co., to Miss Mary G.
Butts.
National Banner & Nashville Whig (Sat., Jan. 12, 1828)

Blanton, Miss Sarah Ann married to Major John C. Porter.

Bliss, Col. William Wallace Smith of the U. S. Army married on Tues. the
5th Dec. by the Rev. John Burke, Rector of St. James Church, Baton Rouge,
to Miss Elizabeth Taylor, daughter of Gen. Zachary Taylor, President-
elect.
The Christian Record (Sat., Dec. 23, 1848)

Blocker, Miss Eliza A. M. married to Mr. Theophilus R. Thomas.

Blocker, John R., Esq., of Mobile, Merchant, married in Davidson Co., on
Monday 2nd inst., by the Rev. Dr. Edgar to Ann F. Dunn, daughter of Mi-
chael C. Du n, Esq. of Davidson County.
Nashville Whig (Thurs., Sept. ,5, 1844)

Blood, Mr. Henry of New Orleans married at Fatherland on Monday 18th inst.
by Rev. John T. Wheat, to Miss Caroline Laura Shelby, niece of Dr. John
Shelby.
Nashville Whig (Thurs., Nov. 21, 1844)

Bloodworth, Mr. Alfred of Rutherford County married in Wilson Co., to Miss Lucinda Bloodworth of Wilson.
National Banner & Nashville Daily Advertiser (Sat., April 13, 1833)

Bloodworth, Mr. Joseph in Haywood Co., married to Miss Bridges.
National Banner & Nashville Advertiser (Wed., Jan. 18, 1832)

Bloodworth, Miss Lucinda married to Mr. Alfred Bloodworth.

Bloodworth, Miss Minerva married to Mr. William Cock.

Blount, Dr. Owen C. of La. married in Lexington, Ky. to Miss Maria N. Stedman.
National Banner & Nashville Whig (Sat., Nov. 22, 1828)

Blount, Mr. James married in Conway Co., Ark. to Mrs. Whittington.
National Banner & Nashville Whig (Sat., Aug. 26, 1826)

Blount, Mr. James F. married in Blount county to Miss Caroline F. Custis.
National Banner & Nashville Whig (Wed., Nov. 23, 1831)

Blow, Miss Charlotte, T., married to Mr. Joseph Charless, Jun.

Blythe, Miss Elizabeth married to Mr. Robert G. Douglass.

Blythe, Miss Elizabeth married to Mr. James B. King.

Blythe, Miss Martha married to Mr. Richard Graham.

Blythe, Miss Theodosia married to Mr. Henry McCallen.

Boardman, Mr. E. H. married in Utica, N. Y. to Miss Lucretia Miller.
National Banner & Nashville Whig (Sat., Aug. 5, 1826)

Boardman, Mrs. Frances C. of England married to Franklin Gorin.

Bobbett, Mr. John W., printer, married in Rutherford Co., on Sat. last to Miss Margaret Jane Rose by Benj. Marable, Esq.
Nashville Whig (Aug. 6, 1838)

Bobbit, Mrs. Matilda C. married to Mr. William Montgomery.

Bobbitt, Mrs. Elizabeth married to Mr. John Glenn.

Bobbitt, Miss Maria married to Mr. Abner Jones.

Bobbitt, Miss Mary married to Mr. James Elliot.

Bobbitt, Miss Mary J. married to Mr. Robert J. Lacy.

Bobo, Miss married to Mr. John Duke.

Boddie, Miss Elizabeth B. married to William R. Elliston, Esq.

Bodisco De, Alexander, Envoy Extra-ordinary and Minister to the U. S., married in Georgetown, D. C. Thurs. 9th April by Rev. Mr. Johns to Miss Harriet Williams, daughter of Brook Williams, Esq.
Daily Republican Banner (Sat., April 18, 1840)

Bodley, Miss Ann J., daughter of Gen. Thomas Bodley married to William Henry Hurst, Esq.

Bodley, Mr. Anthony P. married at Cincinnati to Miss Rebecca W. Talbert.
National Banner & Nashville Whig (Sat., Feb. 10, 1827)

Bodley, Miss Maria Innes married to Dr. Edward B. Church.

Bodly, H. I. Esq., married in Lexington, Ky. to Miss Sarah G. Bledsoe.
National Banner & Nashville Whig (Sat., Dec. 2, 1826)

Boehms, Miss Mary Jane married on Tues. last in Franklin by the Rev.
Mr. Poster to Mr. James M. Gault.

Bogardus, Miss Aspasia S. J. married to Mr. J. Bayard Snowden.

Bogardus, Miss L. A. married to Mr. Arthur H. Snowden.

Boggan, Miss Lydia married to Mr. Edmund Grizzard.

Boggs, Miss Catherine married to Mr. Samuel Reader.

Boggs, Miss Emily married to James Irwin, Esq.

Boggs, Miss Jane married to Mr. W. Renish.

Boggs, Miss Julia married to Mr. Seymour Plummer.

Boice, Miss Eliza married to Mr. Wm. Rowan.

Bolden, Miss married to Mr. James Miller.

Bole, Mr. G. G. married to Miss Harriett Payne in Bedford Co.
National Banner & Nashville Whig (Sat., Sept. 30, 1826)

Bolling , Miss Adelener H. married to Mr. Wm. D. Partlow.
National Banner & Nashville Whig (Wed., Oct. 12, 1831)

Bolling, Mr. R. P. of Nashville married on Thurs. the 11th inst. by the
Rev. Mr. Hendrick to Miss Mary A. Wheeler of Clarksville.
Nashville True Whig & Weekly Commercial Register (Fri., April 19, 1850)

Bolton, Miss Leathey Elizabeth married to Mr. Washington H. Simpson.

Bolton, Miss Mary of Smithville married to Capt. Jacob Hunter.

Bom, Miss Ellen married to Mr. James Bee.

Boman, Miss Sarah married to Capt. James Phillip.

Bomar, Miss Louisa married to Mr. Alexander M'Cullough.

Bomar, Miss Lucy married to Mr. E. A. Guthrie.

Bond, Miss Angelina married to Mr. William J. Jones.

Bond, Miss Elizabeth married to Mr. John Goodrum.

Bond, Mr. John married in Henry Co., to Miss Charity Settle.
National Banner & Nashville Daily Advertiser (Thurs., March 22, 1832)

Bond, Miss Mary T. married to Dr. James H. Taylor.

Bond, Mr. N. married in Williamson county to Miss America Shelton.
Nashville Whig (Sat., July 11, 1846)

Bond, Miss Polly B. married to Mr. Wm. P. M'Affry.

Bond, Mr. William married in Hickman county to Miss Clara Maberry.
Nashville Whig (Sat., July 11, 1846)

Bondurant, Mr. Jacob married on Wednesday evening last to Miss Elizabeth
C., daughter of Jones Read Esq. of this county.
Nashville Whig (Nov. 22, 1824)

Bondurant, Miss Martha married to Mr. Graves Pennington.
The Nashville Gazette (Wed., June 14, 1820)

Bonham, Mr. John P. married in Blount County to Miss Sally Jones.
National Banner (March 17, 1826)

Bonner, Mr. John H. married in Lincoln Co., Tenn. to Miss Lucy Phillips.
National Banner & Nashville Whig (Mon., April 20, 1835)

Bonny, Miss Ann Caroline married to Mr. Nathaniel Cross.

Bonnycastle, Mr. Charles married in Loudoun Co., Va., in the University
of Va., to Miss Anne Tutt.
National Banner (Feb. 10, 1826)

Booen, Miss Mary married to Mr. David Hester.

Booker, Mr. Gray married in Maury County to Miss Ellen Smiser.
National Banner & Nashville Whig (Wed., March 4, 1835)

Booker, Mr. James Gray married in Maury Co., to Miss Ellen Smiser.
Nashville Republican (Thurs. March 5, 1835)

Booker, Mr. Lafayette married in Lincoln Co., to Miss Eliza Coffman.
National Banner & Nashville Whig (Mon., Feb. 21, 1831)

Booker, Miss M. A. married in Tipton Co. to Granville D. Searcy.

Booker, Miss Maria J. married in Tipton Co. to Mr. Robert B. Clarkson.

Booker, Miss Mary T. married to Mr. W. Meredith.

Booker, Mr. Peter R., attorney at law, Williamson Co., married to Miss
Susan Gray of Williamson Co., on Wed. evening last.
Impartial Review & Cumberland Repository (Sat., April 26, 1806)

Booker, Peter R. Esq., of Maury Co., married by the Rev. Dr. Stephens
on Wed. the 23d ult., to Mrs. Cynthia Rodes of Giles Co.
National Banner & Nashville Whig (Mon., July 5, 1830)

Booker, Miss Sarah Ann married to Mr. Samuel D. McCulloch.

Booker, Wm. P. Esq. of Murfreesboro, married to Miss Ann Smith on Wed.
evening last. Miss Smith of Rutherford Co.
Nashville Whig (Nov. 15, 1824)

Boon, Lucinda married to Mr. S. A. Jones.

Boone, Miss Ann married to Mr. James Barrow.

Boone, Miss Mary married to Mr. J. L. Moore.

Boone, Col. S. H. married in Todd Co., Ky. to Miss Emily New.
National Banner & Nashville Whig (Sat., Jan. 17, 1829)

Booth, Mr. Thomas married in Franklin Co., to Miss Frances Cox, of
Florence, Ala.
Nashville Republican & State Gazette (Tues., Dec. 13, 1831)

Booth, Col. William A. of Lawrence Co., Ala., formerly of Brunswick Co.,
Va. married on the 13th inst. by the Rev. Lemuel Sanderling, to Miss
Delia Jane Leathers of Haywood Co., Tenn. formerly of Orange Co., N. C.
Nashville Union (Fri., Nov. 29, 1838)

Boots, Miss Elizabeth Ann married to Mr. Samuel Freeburger.

Borex, Capt. James married in Lincoln Co., to Miss Parthena Parks.
National Banner & Nashville Whig (Sat., April 14, 1827)

Borland, Dr. Solon, Editor, of the Western World, married in Memphis on
the 3d July by the Rev. P. W. Alston, to Miss Eliza B. Hart, recently
of Ky.
Daily Republican Banner (Thurs., Aug. 1, 1839)

Borrough, Miss Ann P. married in Limestone Co., to Mr. Wm. Eastland.
National Banner & Nashville Whig (Sat., April 7, 1827)

Bose, Miss Elizabeth married to Mr. Nelson Side.

Bosen, Miss Louisa V. married to Mr. Samuel P. McCorkle.

Boseley, Mr. Charles Jr. married on the 30th ult by Rev. Dr. Edgar
to Miss Martha A. Carden, daughter of Mr. A. D. Carden, of Nashville.
Nashville Whig (Sat., April 2, 1842)

Bosley, Miss Delilah married to Mr. Jeremiah Scales.

Bosley, Miss Elizabeth married to Mr. Harding.

Bosley, Miss Lavinia married to Mr. M'Nairy Newett.

Bosley, Miss M. E. married to Mr. W. S. Cockrill.

Bosley, Miss Margaret married to Mr. Hugh Erwin.

Bosley, Miss Sarah Ann married to Dr. Alexander H. Stothart.

Boss, Miss Lydia married to Mr. Zephaniah H. Judson.

Bostick, Miss Catherine W. married to J. Bentley Holbert, Esq.

Bostick, Miss Christiana married to Mr. John Collart.

Bostick, Mr. James married on the 23d inst. by the Rev. J. B. McFerrin
to Miss Maria L. Smith, daughter of G. S. Smith, all of Davidson County.
Nashville Union (Fri., May 24, 1839)

Boswell, Miss Ann Maria married to Orvill Shelby, Esq.

Boswell, Mr. George married in Lexington, Ky. to Miss Mary R. Berryman.
National Banner & Nashville Whig (Thurs., July 1, 1830)

Bosworth, Mr. Benajah married in Fayette Co. to Miss Eliza Greer.
National Banner & Nashville Whig (Sat., June 7, 1828)

Bosworth, Miss Eliza married to Mr. James H. Wallace.

Bosworth, Miss Eliza Ann married to Mr. James H. Wallace.

Bosworth, Miss Ellen married to David P. Richardson, Esq.

Bosworth, Miss Ellen married to David P. Richardson.

Bosworth, Hon. Felix of Carroll, Louisiana married in Jefferson Co., Mi.,
to Miss Elizabeth Bieller of Concordia.
National Banner & Nashville Daily Advertiser (Sat., Sept. 13, 1834)

(repeat of preceding)
Nashville Republican & State Gazette (Tues., Aug. 26, 1834)

Bosworth, Mr. James married in Knoxville to Miss Julia A. M. Dudley.
National Banner & Nashville Whig (Mon., Aug 9, 1830)

Bosworth, Miss Mary Ann married to Mr. John H. Hart.

Bosworth, Mr. William married in this county on Monday last to Mrs.
Mary Ann Payne.
The Nashville Whig & Tenn. Advertiser (May 9, 1818)

Botts, Mr. William of Flemingsburgh married in Frankford, Ky. to Miss
Jane Isibell Instone.
National Banner & Nashville Whig (Sat., Feb. 23, 1828)

Bouck, Raymond Augustin, Esq., of Vicksburg married on Monday at the
residence of Joseph Woods, Esq., by Rt. Rev. Bishop Miles to Miss Jane
M. West of Nashville.
Nashville Whig (Thurs., Oct. 29, 1846)

Bounds, Miss Ellin married to Mr. James Luttrell.
National Banner & Nashville Whig (Sat., Aug. 19, 1826)

Bovard, Mr. Thomas married in Hinds Co., Miss., to Miss Martha Young.
National Banner & Nashville Whig (Sat., Jan. 6, 1827)

Bowden, Mr. John married in Aug. 1831 to Miss Nancy Fitzgerald.
The Western Weekly Review (Franklin, Tenn., Fri., Sept. 2, 1831)

Bowen, Miss Barbara married in Louisville, Ky., to Mr. Napoleon Schingig.
National Banner & Nashville Whig (Fri., March 13, 1835)

Bowen, Miss Mary married in Smith Co., to J. S. Yerger, Esq. of Nashville.

Boyd, Miss Letitia married to Mr. Simpson Gorham.

Boyd, Miss Martha married to Mr. Ananias Pence.

Boyd, Miss Mary Jane married to Mr. Thoams L. Skeggs.

Boyd, Miss Mary M. married to Mr. John D. Whitehead.

Boyd, Mr. Nicholas H. of the Western District married in Davidson Co.,
on the 12th Nov. inst. by Rev. Edgar to Miss Emeline M. B. Campbell, of
Davidson Co.
National Banner & Nashville Whig (Wed., Nov. 18, 1835)

Boyd, Miss Rachel Douglass married to Robert G. Smiley, Esq.

Boyd, Mrs. Rhoda married to Eliha S. Hall, Esq.

Boyd, Mr. Samuel of Blount married in Knox Co. to Miss Dorcas F. M'Nutt
daughter of Benj. M'Nutt, Esq.
National Banner (Sat., Sept. 19, 1829)

Boyd, Miss Susan married to Mr. Archibald Gresham.

Boyd, Miss Susan Ann married to Dr. Alexander Lowe.

Boyd, Major Whitmell H. married in this town to Miss Sarah S. Biddle.
National Banner & Nashville Whig (Sat., Jan. 10, 1829)

Boyer, Miss Margaret married to Dr. D. G. Benbrook.

Boyer , Wm. D. Esq., married in Logan Co., Ky. to Miss Sally Lewis.
National Banner & Nashville Whig (Sat., June 16, 1827)

Boykin, Miss Mary C. married to Mr. Dillard Hardwick.

Boylan, Mrs. Priscilla B. married to Judge William T. Brown.

Boyle, Mr. Cornelius married on the 30th inst to Mrs. Tabitha A. G. Allen.
Nashville Union (Aug. 31, 1838)

(repeat of preceding)
Nashville Whig (Fri., Aug. 31, 1838)

Boyle, Miss Eleanor married to Mr. Robert Willis.

Boyle, Mr. Erasmus of Garrard Co., Ky. married to Miss Caroline F. Talbott, in Jessamine Co.
National Banner & Nashville Whig (Mon., Oct. 31, 1831)

Boyles, Miss Mary married to Mr. Pezil Nelson.

Bozeman, Mr. Hugh B. married at Courtland, Ala. to Miss Martha A. Hill.
National Banner & Nashville Whig (March 21, 1831)

Bozewell, Miss Sarah married to Geo. W. Morine.

Bozzel, Miss Lucy married to Mr. William Warren.

Bowen, Miss Mary, married to J. S. Yeager, Esq.

Bowen, Miss Mary E. married to J. P. Chase.

Bower, Mrs. Anna M. married to Mr. Mason Picher.

Bowers, Miss Elizabeth married to Mr. William Hurt.

Bowers, Mr. William M. married to Miss Malinda Buie on the 22nd inst.
by John Garrett, Esq., all of Davidson County.
Nashville Union (Fri., Jan. 25, 1839)

Bowie, Langdon, Esq. of Abbeville, S. C. married at Knoxville to Miss
Eliza H. Coffin, daughter of Rev. Charles Coffin, D. D.
National Banner (Sat., Aug. 8, 1829)

Bowls, Mr. John F. married in Madison County, Tenn. married to Miss
Rachel R. Stubbs.
National Banner & Nashville Whig (Wed., Aug. 17, 1831)

Bowls, Miss Susan A. married in Montgomery Co., Tenn to Mr. Benjamin
Franklin Shields.

Bowman, Mr. Benjamin married in Rutherford County on Tuesday evening
the 13th inst. to Miss Jane Brown.
National Banner & Nashville Whig (Mon., July 19, 1830)

Bowman, Miss Fanny married to Mr. Alexander Williams.

Bowman, Miss Jane married to Mr. Isaac Collier.

Bowman, Mr. John married in Rutherford county to Miss Mariah Woodruff.
National Banner & Nashville Whig (Sat., Oct. 7, 1826)

Bowman, Mr. John C. of Cincinnati married at the residence of Hugh
McGavock Esq. on Tuesday the 29th inst. by the Rev. J. B. Ferguson to
Miss Jane M. Hagan of Nashville.
Nashville True Whig & Weekly Commercial Register (Fri., Nov. 1, 1850)

Bowman, Dr. Joseph A. married on Thursday the 24th inst. at White Hall,
by the Rev. John W. Ogden, to Miss Lucy Caroline White, daughter of Gen.
William White, all of Davidson county.
Nashville Whig (Thurs., Aug. 31, 1843)

Bowman, Major William H. of Mississippi married on the 20th inst., by
the Rev. Dr. Edgar to Miss Elizabeth M. Maney daughter of Major William
Maney of Williamson County.
Nashville Whig (Sat., Sept. 23, 1843)

Bowmar, Miss Eliza Jane married to Col. William Barr.

Bowmar, Mr. Robert H. married in Frankfort, Ky., to Miss Martha H. Haggin.
National Banner & Nashville Whig (Sat., Aug. 30, 1828)

Bowshear, Miss Ann married to Mr. Robert M'Culloch.

Boyce, Mr. married in Henderson county to Mrs. Ott.
National Banner & Nashville Whig (Fri., Feb. 19, 1830)

Boyce, Miss Caroline married to Dr. William M. Shreve.

Boyce, Miss Sarah Jane married to Mr. Wm. Marquiss.

Boyd, Mr. Addison of Madison County married in Haywood County to Miss
Elizabeth Taylor
National Banner & Nashville Whig (Thurs., June 24, 1830)

Boyd, Miss Angelina married to Mr. Thomas F. Hicks.

Boyd, Mr. Benjamin S. married in Knox County to Miss Cynthia Brooks.
National Banner & Nashville Whig (Dec. 2, 1826)

Boyd, Miss Clemintine married to James T. Holman, Esq.

Boyd, Miss Elizabeth married to Mr. John N. Williams.

Boyd, Rev. Frederick W. of Vicksburg married on the 4th inst., at Oakland
near Natchez by the Rev. D. C. page to Miss Mary Eliza Railey, daughter
of Col. James Railey of Natxhez.
Nashville Whig (Thurs., Jan. 18, 1844)

Boyd, Miss Jane married to Capt. Daniel S. Hays.

Boyd, Major John married in this town last evening to Mrs. Lamira Ewing,
widow of the late Dr. John O. Ewing.
National Banner (Sat., June 13, 1829)

Boyd, Dr. John C. married in Clarksville, Tenn to Miss Mary Jane Chilton.
National Banner & Nashville Daily Advertiser (Sept..2, 1833)

(repeat of preceding)
Nashville Republican & State Gazette (Tues., Sept. 3, 1833)

Boyd, Mr. John W. of Grainger County married in Jefferson County to Miss
Leah Cox of Jefferson.
National Banner (Feb. 17, 1826)

Brack, Miss Laetitia married to Zachariah Coleman.

Boyd, Miss Leodocia J. married to Mr. Egbert A. Raworth.

Bradburn, Miss Henrietta N. married to Mr. George W. Doneghy.

Bradbury, Hezekiah, Esq. of Lexington, Tenn. married to Miss Mary D.
Shrewsbury in Hardin Co., Ky. on Thursday evening 13th inst.
National Banner & Nashville Advertiser (Thurs., Sept. 20, 1832)

Braden, Mr. Daniel P. married at Springfield, Robertson County by the
Rev. Mr. Gunn to Miss Emily L. T. Gorham.
National Banner & Nashville Whig (Fri., June 17, 1831)

Braden, Mr. James W. married in Maury Co., Tenn to Miss Mary P. Howard.
National Banner & Nashville Whig (Wed., Feb. 25, 1835)

Braden, Miss Margaret married to Mr. John Douglass.

Bradford, Mr. A. K. merchant of Dandridge, married in McMinn Co., to
Miss Jane Keith, daughter of Isham Keith, Esq.
National Banner & Nashville Whig (Fri., March 27, 1835)

Bradford, Major Alexander B., attorney at law of the Western District,
married in Knoxville on the 9th inst. to Miss Darthula O. Miller,
daughter of Pleasant M. Miller Esq.
Nashville Whig (Sept. 29, 1824)

Bradford, Benjamin M., Esq., Register of the Land Office, married near
Courtland, Ala., to Miss Martha Saunders, daughter of the Rev. Turner
Saunders.
National Banner & Nashville Whig (Mon., Jan. 3, 1831)

Bradford, Miss Cecilia married to Maj. William Carrol.

Bradford, Miss Eleanor, married to Mr. John J. Cowden.

Bradford, Mr. Eli M. married in Giles County to Miss Jane B. Burthall,
daughter of Matthew Burthall.
National Banner & Nashville Daily Advertiser (Tues., Nov. 19, 1833)

Bradford, Miss Eliza married at Lexington, Ky. to Mr. William R. Morton.

Bradford, Miss Evelina M. married to John Nichols, Esq.

Bradford, Frederick, Esq. married to Miss Elizabeth Virginia Demoss.

Bradford, Dr. H. C. of Huntsville married on Thursday evening the 18th inst. by the Rev. Mr. Hume to Miss Martha Turner, daughter of Mrs. M. Turner of this city.
The Nashville Whig (Sept. 15, 1817)

Bradford, Henry C. Esq married in M'Minn county to Miss Elizabeth Hard.
National Banner & Nashville Whig (Sat., Nov. 15, 1828)

Bradford, James F., Esq. married in Athens to Miss Nancy Kinder.
National Banner & Nashville Whig (Mon., April 11, 1831)

(repeat of preceding)
Nashville Republican & State Gazette (Tues., April 12, 1831)

Bradford, Joseph H. married at Pleasant Retreat near Winchester, on the 25th ult. to Miss Maria Catherine Spyker.
National Banner (Sat., Dec. 5, 1829)

Bradford, Miss Julia Matilda married to Dr. Samuel Hatch.

Bradford, Mr. Larkin of Huntsville married in Alabama to Miss Jane C. James.
National Banner & Nashville Whig (Fri., Feb. 6, 1835)

Bradford, Miss Louisa married to Mr. Alfred M. Hume.

Bradford, Miss Martha Elizabeth married to Capt. Robert C. Foster 3d.

Bradford, Miss Mary married to Mr. Benjamin W. Wilson.

Bradford, Miss Mary S. married to Mr. James Campbell.

Bradford, Mr. Miles H. married in Brownville to Miss Mary Cheatham, daughter of Mr. Peter Cheatham.
National Banner & Nashville Whig (Thurs., June 24, 1830)

Bradford, Mr. Robert married on the 30th by the Rev. Mr. Lapsley to Miss Eliza T. Hart, both of Nashville.
Nashville Republican (Sat., June 7, 1836)

Bradford, Sarah, married to John S. Fall, Esq.

Bradford, Thomas H. Esq. married in Woodford Co., Ky. to Miss S. C. Steele.
National Banner & Nashville Whig (Sat., Dec. 16, 1826)

Bradford, Mr. Thos. N. married in Aug. 1831 to Miss Mary Letta.
The Western Weekly Review (Franklin , Tenn, Fri., Sept. 2, 1831)

Bradford, Mr. Tipton of Bellefonte, Ala., married in Winchester on the 17th inst. to Miss Louisiana Taul.
National Banner (Sat. Nov. 21, 1829)

Bradley, Capt. Calvin married at Jersey Settlement to Miss Mary Nafe.
National Banner & Nashville Whig (Sat. Aug 4, 1827)

Bradley, Miss Elizabeth E. married to Mr. Zachariah T. Davis.

Bradley, Mr. H. D. married at Hopkinsville, Ky. to Miss J. S. Earl.
National Banner & Nashville Whig (Wed., June 8, 1831)

Bradley, Mr. Hugh H. married in Smith Co., Tenn to Miss Martha Dillon.
Nashville Republican & State Gazette (Tues., April 19, 1831)

Bradley, Rev. James married in Hawkins Co., Tenn to Miss Mary Magdalene
Kensinger.
National Banner & Nashville Whig (Fri., March 27, 1835)

Bradley, Jane married to James Huey, Esq.

Bradley, Miss Julia S. married to Mr. John K. Chester.

Bradley, Miss Mary married to Mr. Jackson Wallis.

Bradley, Miss Mary Jane married to Mr. James S. Conway.

Bradley, Mr. Robert Jr., married on Thursday the 1st inst. by the Rev.
R. B. C. Howell to Miss Margaret Perkins, both of Williamson County.
Nashville Whig (Thurs., Aug. 8, 1844)

Bradley, Miss Sarah married to Mr. Buxton Harris.

Bradley, Mr. Tompkin married in Logan Co., Ky. to Miss Mary Fugua.
National Banner & Nashville Whig (Sat., March 17, 1827)

Bradley, Mr. William married to Miss Mahala Kirkpatrick.
National Banner (March 10, 1826)

Bradley, Mr. William married on the 8th inst. in Smith County to Miss
Mary M'Alister.
National Banner & Nashville Whig (Mon. Nov. 29, 1830)

Bradshaw, Miss Elizabeth of Maury county married to Mr. George W. Gordon.

Bradshaw, Dr. John, of the Royal College of Surgeons of the City of
Dublin married on Thurs. 28th by Rev. J. Thos. Wheat to Mrs. Mary Jane
Hickey, at the residence of her mother Mrs. Jane Scott.
Daily Republican Banner (Fri., May 29, 1840)

(repeat of preceding)
Nashville Whig (Fri., May 20, 1840)

Bradshaw, Miss Margaret married to Mr. Elijah Brumat.
National Banner (April 14, 1826)

Bradshaw, Margaret married to Bernard Myers, Esq.

Bradshaw, Mr. Merryman married in Jessamine Co., Ky. to Miss Eliza Price.
National Banner (Sat.,July 18, 1829)

Brady, Mr. Benjamin married in Henry county, Tenn since the first of
Jan. to Miss Elizabeth Howell.
National Banner & Nashville Whig (Fri., Feb. 13, 1835)

Brady, Master Charles aged 18 married in Halifax (N. S.) to Mrs. Mary
Jackson aged 36.
National Banner & Nashville Whig (Fri., Nov. 11, 1831)

Brady, Miss Eliza married to Major Wallace Dixon.

Brady, Mr. Robert married in this town last evening to Miss Nancy Wright.
National Banner (Sat., Sept. 17, 1829)

Brady, Mrs. Rosanna married to Col. John Porter.

Brahan, Miss Jane married to Mr. Robert Patton.

Brahan, Miss Mary N. married to John D. Coffee, Esq.

Bramaker, Mrs. Bella Ann married to Smith Criddle, Esq.

Bramlett, Miss Adelaide married to A. H. Goff, Esq.

Branch, Miss Eliza M. married to Gen. Leigh Read

Branch, Miss Margaret married to Gen. Daniel S. Donelson.

Branch, Miss Mary W. married to Mr. Clay M. Ratcliff.

Branch, Miss Rebecca married to Col. R. W. Williams.

Branch, Miss Sarah married to Dr. James Hunter.

Brand, Miss Eliza married to Mr. Edward McAlister.

Brandon, Miss Caedonia R. married to Mr. John F. Mills.

Brandon, Miss Kesiah married to Mr. Joseph Cantre

Brandon, Miss L. C. married to Mr. William Jones.

Brandon, Miss Maria L. C. married to Mr. William Jones.

Brandon, Capt. Wm. M. married in Wilkinson County, Miss. to Miss Georgiana Ann C. Da
National Banner & Nashville Whig (Sept. 30, 1826)

Brannin, Miss Miriam married to Isaac H. Hilliard, Esq.

Bransford, Mr. Abraham married in Madison county, Ala to Miss Elizabeth
H. Ayers, daughter of the late Mr. Samuel Ayers.
National Banner & Nashville Daily Advertiser (Mon. July 23, 1832)

Bransford, Mr. Jacob H. married in Nashville to Miss Maria H. Hagey
on Thursday last.
Nashville Republican (Tues., March 17, 1835)

Bransford, Miss Mary C. married to Mr. William C. McLean.

Bransford, Miss Matilda S. married to Mr. Russell M. Kinnard, Merchant.

Bransford, Mr. Milton, Esq. late of the Clarksville Ark. bar, married
in Winchester, Tenn. on the 16th inst., by the Rev. A. J. Steele to
Miss Susan Frances Henderson, daughter of the Hon. Alfred Henderson.
The Politician & Weekly Nashville Whig (Fri., March 3, 1848)

Brantly, Mr. William married on Tuesday the 16th inst. to Miss Mary
Smith, daughter of Samuel Smith of Montgomery.
The Clarion & Tennessee Gazette (Jan. 30, 1821)

Brasfield, Mr. Isaiah married in Shelbyville to Miss Elizabeth C. Wade.
National Banner & Nashville Daily Advertiser (Fri., June 14, 1833)

Brashear, Miss Camilla L. married in Bolinggreen, Ky to W. P. Parker, Esq.

Brashear, Miss Pamela married to Rev. John P. Trotter.

Brashear, Miss Sarah F. married to Mr. J. C. Temple.

Brasheare, Mr. John married in Sullivan County to Miss Nancy Edgemond.
National Banner & Nashville Whig (Sat., July 29, 1826)

Brashears, Mr. Isaac W. married in Rutherford county to Miss Sarah Trott.
National Banner & Nashville Daily Advertiser (Sat., Feb 23, 1833)

Bratcher, Gen. F. H. Senator from Campbell married on Sunday 12th inst.
by Rev. Dr. Howell to Miss Nancy Ann Neugent of Nashville.
The Christian Record (Sat., Dec. 18, 1847)

(repeat of preceding)
The Politician & Weekly Nashville Whig (Fri., Dec. 24, 1847)

Bratton, Mrs. Catharine married to Mr. Thomas D. Jones

Brawdy, Miss Nancy married to Mr. Newton M'Conner.

Brazelton, Col. William amrried in Washington County to Miss Martha Gillespie.
National Banner & Nashville Whig (Sat., Feb. 7, 1829)

Brazil, Miss Polly married to Mr. James Rogers.

Breakinridge, Miss Mary C. married to Dr. Thomas P. Satterwhite.

Breast, Miss Sarah Jane married to Mr. J. A. Laird, Printer.

Breath, Rev. Jacob Jun. married in Fayette County to Mrs. Susan Bedford.
National Banner & Nashville Whig (Mon. Sept. 26, 1831)

Breathitt, Miss Eliza J. married to Col. William H. Carroll.

Breathitt, James Esq. of Hopkinsville, married at Frankfort, Ky. to Miss Gabriella Harvie, daughter of John Harvie, Esq.
National Banner & Nashville Whig (Fri., Feb. 19, 1830)

Breathitt, Miss Lucelia Jane married to James W. Ewing, Esq.

Breckenridge, Miss Eliza Ann married to Col. R. M. Williamson.

Breckenridge, Miss Elizabeth married to Mr. F. E. Dickey.

Breckenridge, Miss Frances A. married in Fayette county to Rev. John C. Young.

Breckenridge, Miss Jane married to Mr. Silas King.

Breckenridge, Rev. John, D. D., married at Stonington, Conn on the 2d Sept by Rev. John E. Edwards to Mary Ann Bobcock, daughter of the late Paul Babcock, Esq. Rev.Breckenridge of New Orleans.
Daily Republican Banner (Sat., Nov 14, 1840)

(repeat of preceding)
Nashville Whig (Fri. Nov. 13, 1840)

Breckenridge, Miss Martha married to Mr. Caleb Davis.

Breckenridge, Miss Mary C. married to Dr. Thomas P. Satterwhite.

Breecheen, Mr. Alanson married in Maury County to Miss Nancy Climer.
National Banner & Nashville Whig (Mon., Feb. 28, 1831)

Breechen, Mr. Josiah married near Athens, Ala to Miss Margaret D. Elliott.
National Banner & Nashville Daily Advertiser (Mon. Feb 18, 1833)

Breeden, Mr. Abel married in Cincinnati to Miss Martha B. Thompson.
National Banner & Nashville Whig (Mon. Aug. 30, 1830)

Breeden, Miss Sarah married in Jefferson county to Mr. Wm. Tillett.

Brelsford, Dr. John of Gallatin married in Nashville, by the Rev. Mr. Howell on Wed. the 7th inst to Miss Mary Ann Cook of Nashville.
National Banner & Nashville Whig (Fri., June 9, 1837)

(repeat of preceding)
Nashville Republican (Tues., June 13, 1837)

Bremaker, Mrs. Belle Ann married to Smith Criddle, Esq.

Brennan, Mr. John of Nashville married at Lexington, Ky on Thurs., 16th inst. to Miss Mary Morton, daughter of William R. Morton, Esq. of Lexington. National Banner & Nashville Daily Advertiser (July 25, 1833)

(repeat of preceding)
<u>Nashville Republican & State Gazette</u> (Fri., July 26, 1833)

Brent, Miss Elizabeth married to Henry Hart, Esq.

Brent, Mr. Hugh married in Fayette County to Miss Susan Lewis.
<u>National Banner</u> (Feb. 17, 1826)

Brevard, Miss Scyntha married to Mr. Goldman Donoho.

Brewer, Miss Elizabeth married to Mr. Thomas W. Shearon.

Brewer, Dr. James of Trenton married to Miss Ann Austin, in Nashville
on last evening.
<u>National Banner & Nashville Advertiser</u> (Thurs., Oct. 4, 1832)

Brewer, Miss Jane E. married to Sandy Holman, Esq.

Brewer, Miss Laetitia H. married to Mr. Thomas W. Shearon.

Brewer, Mr. Meredith married in Henry county to Miss Sina Steel.
<u>National Banner & Nashville Daily Advertiser</u> (Thurs., Sept. 6, 1832)

Brian, John C. married in Williamson county to Miss Seniza C. Holloway.
<u>The Western Weekly Review</u> (Franklin, Tenn, Dec. 14, 1832)

Briant, Miss Eleanor S. married to Mr. James W. Hilton.

Briant, Mr. James married in Maury county, Tenn to Miss Sarah Sprinkle.
<u>National Banner & Nashville Whig</u> (Wed., Feb. 25, 1835)

Briant, Mr. Samuel B. married in Murfreesborough, to Mrs. Tabitha A.
Thompson.
<u>National Banner & Nashville Whig</u> (Fri., June 10, 1831)

Briant, Mr. William T. married in Rutherford county to Miss Jane Kerr.
<u>National Banner</u> (Sat. Dec. 26, 1829)

Brickell, Henry B. Esq. married in Franklin to Miss Eliza P. Smith.
<u>Nashville Whig</u> (Mon. Jan 14, 1839)

Brickell, Col. James married in Limestone county to Miss Eliza Peel.
<u>National Banner & Nashville Whig</u> (Sat., March 31, 1827)

Bridges, Miss married in Haywood county to Mr. Joseph Bloodworth.
<u>National Banner & Nashville Advertiser</u> (Wed., Jan. 18, 1832)

Bridges, Miss Frances E. of Athens married to Mr. Thomas J. Campbell, Jr.

Bridges,Miss J. S. married to Mr. William M. Heren.

Bridges, Miss Martha Ann married to Mr. M. D. Carson.

Bridgeman, Miss Charlotte S. married to Mr. Richard D. Walker.

Bridgewater, Miss Mary E. married to Mr. Walter C. Allen.

Bridgman, Mr. Benjamin F. married in Pikeville to Miss Narcissa P. Massengill.
<u>National Banner & Nashville Whig</u> (Mon., Nov. 29, 1830)

Bridgman, Miss Eliza C. married to Mr. Samuel W. Robinson.

Bridgman, Miss Martha M. married to Mr. David Cleage.

Bridwell, Miss Mary J. married to Mr. George W. White.

Brien, John S., Esq. of Vicksburg, Miss married on Thurs. last at
Carthage, Smith county by the Rev. David Timberlake, to Miss Rosha M.
Howard, daughter of Samuel P. Howard, Esq.

Daily Republican Banner (Tues., Oct. 1, 1839)

Brigance, Mr. M. H. married in Sumner county to Miss Ann Dempsey.
National Banner & Nashville Whig (Mon., Feb. 21, 1831)

(repeat of preceding)
Nashville Republican & State Gazette (Feb. 22, 1831)

Brigg, Miss Sarah married in Henry county, Tenn. to Mr. James Johnson.

Briggs, Miss Julia E. married to Dr. Frederick A. M. Davis.

Briggs, Miss Rebecca married to Mr. John Polk.

Brigham, Miss Cornelia S. T. married to James Southgate, Esq.

Bright, Col. David married in Green county to Miss Lydia Collier.
National Banner & Nashville Daily Advertiser (Mon., June 17, 1833)

Bright, Miss Margaret married to Mr. Mathew Martin.

Bright, Martha R. married to Byrd Douglas.

Bright, Miss Mary A. married to Mr. James F. Drake.

Brinkley, R. C.Esq., attorney at law of Jackson, Tenn. married at the
residence of Mrs. Overtons in this vicinity on the 18th inst. by Philip
Lindsley, C. C. to Anna Overton, daughter of the late Judge Overton.
Nashville Whig (Wed., Oct. 20, 1841)

Brister, Miss Eliza married to Mr. James McClannahan.

Bristow, Miss Carolina married to Mr. Hiram W. Ashburn.

Britian, Miss Polly married to Mr. William Whalen.

Britt, Miss Martha married to Rev. F. E. Pitts.

Brittain, Capt. James, merchant of Shelbyville, married on Tues. evening
last by the Rev. Mr. Hume to Miss Maria Thompson, daughter of Col. Jason
Thompson, of Davidson county.
The Nashville Gazette (Sat., Feb. 17, 1821)

Brittan, Mr. James married in Franklin county to Miss Fanny Stovall.
National Banner & Nashville Whig (Sat., Feb. 23, 1828)

Brittan, William R., Esq. married in White county to Miss Matilda
Holland.
National Banner & Nashville Whig (Sat., June 9, 1827)

Brittle, Mr. George W. married on Thursday 26th inst., by the Rev. J.
R. Graves to Miss Melissa Dale, all of Nashville.
The Politician & Weekly Nashville Whig (Wed., Sept. 1, 1847)

Britton, Lieut. F., 7th U. S. Infantry, married at the Choctaw Agency
at the residence of Capt. William Armstrong, the 12th April by the Rev.
E. Dupy to Miss Rebecca Millard, late of Washington City.
The Union (Tues., May 24, 1836)

Britton, Miss Margaret married to Dr. D. G. Dismuke.

Broaddus, Mr. George W. married in Madison county, Ky. to Miss Elvira
Hooker.
National Banner & Nashville Whig (Sat., Jan. 10, 1829)

Broaddus, Miss Jane married to Mr. Christopher Rowland.

Broaddux, Miss Emily married to Mr. Silas Newland.

Broadnax, Mrs. married to Mr. Jesse Brown.

Broadway, Miss Sarah married to Mr. Phineas E. Hillis.

Brockway, Mr. R. Hyal of Nashville, Tenn. married in Philadelphia, on the 20th ult. by the Rev. G. S. Webb to Miss Elizabeth Ann Levering, daughter of Nathan Levering, Esq. of Philadelphia.
Nashville Whig (Thurs., Sept. 3, 1846)

Brondon, Capt. Wm. M. married in Wilkinson County, Miss to Miss Georgiana Ann C. Davis.
National Banner & Nashville Whig (Sat., Sept. 30, 1826)

Bronough, Miss Lucy married to Mr. William Tate.

Bronson, Miss Minerva married to Mr. Leonard Rogers.

Brook, Miss Lucy married to Dr. Daniel H. Johnson.

Brooks, Miss Abby married to Charles Francis Adams,Esq.

Brooks, Miss Barbary Jane married to Mr. Douglass R. Simms.

Brooks, Mr. Christopher of Nashville married in Sumner County on Thurs. last to Miss Betsey Bender, daughter of Mr. Daniel Bender.
National Banner & Nashville Whig (Tues., Feb. 23, 1830)

Brooks, Mr. Christopher married in Nashville on Wed. April 19, by Rev. Mr. Andrews to Mrs. Ann L. Kenley.
National Banner & Nashville Whig (Mon., April 24, 1837)

Brooks, Miss Cynthia married to Mr. Benjamin S. Boyd.

Brooks, Miss Cyprissa married to Mr. Elisha Q. Vance.

Brooks, Miss Elizabeth married to Mr. John L. Kamper.

Brooks, Miss Fanny married to Edward Macguire, Esq.

Brooks, Dr. Henry married in Smith County to Miss Burnethe Jones, on the 4th inst.
Nashville Republican (Tues., Nov. 10, 1835)

Brooks, Miss Jane married in Newport, E Tenn. to Mr. William Spillers.

Brooks, Mr. John married in Lexington, Tenn. to Miss Adeline Wilson.
Nashville Republican & State Gazette (Thurs., April 21, 1831)

Brooks, Miss Louisa married in Sumner county to Mr. John W. Crairy.
Nashville Whig (Tues., March 24, 1846)

Brooks, Miss Nancy married in Bedford county to Mr. Lee Lloyd.
National Banner & Nashville Whig (Sat., Jan. 10, 1829)

Brooks, Mr. M. D. F. H. of Davidson county married on the 18th by the Rev. Mr. McFerrin to Miss Melissa McGowen, eldest daughter of Mr. Robert McGowan of Maury county.
National Banner & Nashville Whig (Mon., Aug. 20, 1836)

Brooks, Miss Polly married to Capt. Micajah B. Belew.

Brooks, Miss Susan married to Mr. David Allen.

Brooks, Mr. William married in Lexington to Miss Violet Wilson.
National Banner & Nashville Whig (Fri., Feb. 26, 1830)

Brooks, Mr. William age 53 years of Weakley county, married in Henry County, Tenn. to Mrs. Susan P. C. Chandler age 27.
National Banner & Nashville Whig (Wed., Nov. 19, 1834)

(repeat of preceding)
National Banner & Nashville Whig (Nov. 26, 1834)

Brothers, Mr. Benjamin married in Rutherford County to Miss Jane Jetton.
National Banner (Feb. 10, 1826)

Broussard, Miss Emiline married to Calab Green Jr.

Browder, Frederick A. Esq., married in Wilkinson County, Miss. to Mrs.
Harriet Hook. National Banner & Nashville Whig. Sat. Sept.23,1826.
National Banner & Nashville Whig (Sat., Sept. 23, 1826)

Browder, Mr. Robert married in Christian Co., Ky to Miss Sarah Gilmer.
National Banner & Nashville Whig (Sat. Jan. 17, 1829)

Brown, Miss married to Mr. Theodore Staley.

Brown, Aaron V. Esq. of Paulaski married in Rutherford county to Miss
Sarah Burrus, of Rutherford.
National Banner (March 17, 1826)

Brown, Miss Amanda married to Mr. Joseph Reason.

Brown, Miss Ann married to Mr. Alexander Williamson, Esq.

Brown, Miss Ann E. married to Mr. Joshua B. Freirson.

Brown, B. C. Esq. married in Paris, Ten. to Miss L. N. Edmonds.
National Banner & Nashville Whig (Fri., June 10, 1836)

Brown, Benjamin C. Esq. married in Paris, Henry Co., to Miss Catherine
Lacy.
National Banner & Nashville Whig (Mon., June 21, 1830)

Brown, Mr. Benjamin Franklin, married on Tuesday the 5th inst., by the
Rev. Smith to Miss Ann James both of Nashville.
National Banner & Nashville Daily Advertiser (Thurs., Aug. 7, 1834)

Brown, Mr. Berry married in this town last evening to Miss Catharine
Marshall, by the Rev. Mr. Fall.
National Banner & Nashville Whig (Sat., Jan. 12, 1828)

Brown, Miss Caledonia married to the Hon. M. P. Gentry.

Brown, Miss Cynthia M. married to Mr. Francis N. Wisdom.

Brown, Dr. David F. married near Bolivar to Miss Jane Francis M'Neal.
National Banner (Sat., Nov. 7, 1829)

Brown, Miss Elizabeth married to Robert W. Scott, Esq.

Brown, Miss Elizabeth married to Mr. John Parker.

Brown, Miss Elizabeth married to Mr. John W. Koen.

Brown, Miss Elizabeth married to Henry M. Edwards.

Brown, Miss Elizabeth S. married to Vernon K. Stevenson,

Brown, Miss Francis married to Mr. Philip Willingham.

Brown, Mr. Franklin M. married in Bedford county on the 8th inst. to
Miss Polly Anthony.
National Banner (Jan. 27, 1826)

Brown, George B. Esq, Junior Publisher of the Nashville True Whig married
in Charlotte on the 27th inst. at the residence of W. James Esq. to Miss
Jane W. Williams, daughter of R. F. Williams, Esq. of Hardeman county,
Tenn.
Nashville True Whig & Weekly Commercial Register (Fri., Jan. 31, 1851)

Brown, Hartwell H. (Rev.) of Giles county married on Tuesday evening last to Miss Ann Herndon, daughter of Mr. Joseph Herndon of Maury Co.
Nashville Whig (Jan. 29, 1823)

Brown, Miss Henrietta of Frankfort, Ky. married to Hon. Wm. B. Reese

Brown, Mr. Henry L. of Huntsville, Ala married to Miss Laura P. Moseley of Mooresville, Ala daughter of Capt. W. H. Moseley in Fayetteville.
National Banner & Nashville Advertiser (Fri., July 6, 1832)

Brown, Hugh, Esq. married in Knox county to Miss Mary Ann Rice.
National Banner & Nashville Advertiser (Mon., April 23, 1832)

Brown, Mr. Isaac of Murfreesboro, married to Miss Jane Wade of Rutherford
Nashville Whig (Nov. 15, 1824)

Brown, Mr. J. G. married at Cincinnati, Ohio to Miss H. Kelly.
National Banner (Feb. 3, 1826)

Brown, Mr. James married in Hardeman County to Miss Mahala Juntor.
National Banner & Nashville Whig (Fri., July 15, 1831)

Brown, Mr. James married in Williamson county to Miss Charlotte McDaniel.
National Banner &Nashville Daily Advertiser (Mon., May 13, 1833)

Brown, Maj. James T. married in Madison County, Tenn to Miss Caroline D. Given.
National Banner & Nashville Whig (Fri., Dec. 12, 1834)

Brown, Miss Jane married to Mr. Benjamin Bowman.

Brown, Miss Jane married to Mr. John Turner.

Brown, Rev. Jefferson P. married in Louisville, Tenn. to Miss Hester Ann Cox, daughter of Mr. Nathaniel Cox.
National Banner & Nashville Whig (Fri., March 27, 1835)

Brown, Mr. Jesse married in Fayette County to Mrs. Broadnax.
Nashville Republican & State Gazette (Thurs., June 9, 1831)

Brown, General John married in Roane county to Miss Nancy Allison.
National Banner & Nashville Whig (Mon., Nov. 29, 1830)

Brown, Col. John of Sommerville married in Hardeman county to Miss Cinra W. Coleman, daughter of Col. William Coleman.
National Banner & Nashville Daily Advertiser (Mon., March 19, 1832)

Brown, John married in Williamson county to Miss Mary F. Montgomery.
The Western Weekly Review (Franklin, Tenn.) (Fri., May 11, 1832)

(repeat of preceding)
National Banner & Nashville Daily Advertiser (Wed., May 16, 1832)

Brown, John C. Esq. married on Tuesday evening 5th inst., by Rev. R. Caldwell, to Miss Mary E.Pointer all of Pulaski Tenn.
Nashville True Whig & Weekly Commercial Register (Fri., Nov. 15, 1850)

Brown, Mr. John G. married in Nashville on Thursday last 25th by the Rev. Philip Ball to Miss Martha E. Read, both of Nashville.
Nashville Whig (Mon., Nov. 29, 1841)

Brown, John J. married in Williamson county to Miss Elizabeth F. Carson.
The Western Weekly Review (Franklin, Tenn., Fri., March 8, 1833)

Brown, Mr. John L. married on Tuesday evening the 20th inst., by the Rev. Mr. Craighead to Miss Jane H. Weakley, daughter of Col. Robert Weakley of this county.
Nashville Whig (Feb. 2, 1824)

Brown, Mr. John M. of Mississippi married in Franklin, Williamson county on the 1st inst. by the Rev. Mr. Davis to Miss Eliza B. Harrison of Nashville.
National Banner & Nashville Daily Advertiser (Tues., March 5, 1833)

(repeat of preceding)
Nashville Republican & State Gazette (Wed., March 6, 1833)

Brown, John P. W. Esq, attorney at law, married last evening by the Rev. John T. Edagr, D. D. to Miss Jane Nichol, of Nashville, daughter of the late Josiah Nichol.
Daily Republican Banner (Fri., Nov. 17, 1837)

Brown, Mr. John S. of Roane county married at Selma, Ala to Miss Elizabeth H. Tarver.
National Banner & Nashville Whig (Sat., March 29, 1828)

Brown, Mr. John S. married at Frankfort, Ky. to Miss Mary Beckham.
National Banner & Nashville Whig (Mon., Aug. 23, 1830)

Brown, Mr. Jona married in Fayette county, Ky. to Miss Elizabeth Beauchamp.
National Banner (April 7, 1825)

Brown, Mr. Jordan married at Lebanon, on Wednesday evening last, to Miss Sarah Hill.
National Banner & Nashville Whig (Mon., Sept. 6, 1830)

Brown, Mr. Joseph married in Nashville on Thursday last, 20th inst. by the Rev. R. B. C. Howell to Miss Mary W. Staggs.
Nashville Whig (Fri., June 21, 1839)

Brown, Mr. Joseph P. Married in this town on Thursday evening 11th inst. to Miss Mary L. Brown.
National Banner & Nashville Whig (Sat., Sept. 13, 1828)

Brown, Mr. Joseph P. married in Randolph, Tenn to Miss Jane S. Frazier.
National Banner & Nashville Advertiser (Mon., April 9, 1832)

Brown, Mr. Josiah G. married on yesterday morning by the Rev. Mr. Howell to Miss Judith D. Scott, all of Nashville.
The Politician & Weekly Nashville Whig (Fri., Dec. 10, 1847)

Brown, Miss L. S. married in Wilson County to Dr. Watson of Williamson County.
National Banner & Nashville Whig (Wed., April 6, 1831)

Brown, Miss Laura L. married to Dr. F. J. Robertson.

Brown, Mr. Leonard married in Henry County to Miss Lydia Wright.
National Banner & Nashville Advertiser (Wed., Jan. 18, 1832)

Brown, Miss Louisa married to James Rucks, Esq.

Brown, Mrs. Louisa A. married to Dixon Allen, Esq.

Brown, Miss Lucinda married to Mr. James Bailey.

Brown, Miss Lucy married to Col. Richard Warner.

Brown, Miss Lucy H. married to Rev. Benjamin H. Sewell.

Brown, Miss Margaret married to Mr. Wm. B. Carnes, Esq.

Brown, Mr. Marquis L. married to Tuscumbia, Ala. to Miss Martha Franklin.
National Banner & Nashville Whig (Sat., Feb. 9, 1828)

Brown, Miss Martha L. married in Calhoun to Mr. Samuel J. Atkins.

Brown, Miss Mary married to Mr. Richard Figg.

Brown, Miss Mary married to Orlando Brown, Esq.

Brown, Mary married to Wright Perkins.

Brown, Miss Mary A. married to Capt. Thomas D. Martin.

Brown, Miss Mary C. married to Mr. E. G. Sevier.

Brown, Miss Mary E. married to Master Madison B. Gelusia.

Brown, Miss Mary L. married to Mr. James Graham.

Brown, Miss Mary L. married to Mr. Joseph P. Brown.

Brown, Miss Matilda married to A. H. White, Esq.

Brown, Mr Milton Esq. of Jackson married in Paris, Tenn to Miss Sarah Ann Toryann of Paris.
National Banner & Nashville Whig (Fri., Feb. 6, 1835)

Brown; Miss Minerva married to Dr. L. Conkey.

Brown, Morgan W. Esq. married last evening in this county to Miss Ann Maria Childress.
National Banner & Nashville Whig (Sat.,Nov. 11, 1826)

Brown, Miss Nancy married in Bedford county, Tenn to Mr. James Brown.
National Banner & Nashville Whig (Fri., June 10, 1836)

Brown, Neil S. Esq., attorney at Law of Pulaski, married on this morning by the Rev. Dr. Lindsley to Miss Mary Ann Trimble of Nashville, on the 26th.
Nashville Whig (Wed., Dec. 25, 1839)

Brown, Orlando, Esq. married in Frankfort, Ky. to Miss Mary Brown, daughter of the late Dr. Preston W. Brown.
National Banner & Nashville Whig (Aug. 9, 1830)

Brown, Percy J. of Mississippi married on Thursday evening by the Rev. J. T. Wheat to Miss Lisenka M. Campbell, daughter of the Hon. Geo. Washington Campbell, of Nashville.
Nashville Union (Fri., April 26, 1839)

Brown, Mr. Preston M. married to Miss Eliza Jane Geers in Lexington, Ky.
National Banner & Nashville Whig (Fri., Feb. 12, 1830)

Brown, Mr. Robert married in Madison County to Miss Susan Brown.
National Banner & Nashville Whig (Sat., April 12, 1828)

Brown, Mr. Samuel of Cooke County married in Grainger County to Miss Elizabeth S. Hightower.
National Banner & Nashville Whig (Mon., March 7, 1831)

Brown, Mr. Samuel married on Yesterday morning by the Rev. Dr. Howell to Miss Sarah E. Samuel, all of Nashville.
Nashville Whig (Thurs., Feb. 26, 1846)

Brown, Miss Sarah married to Mr. Bayles E. Bourland.

Brown, Miss Sarah married to Mr. John T. Harris.

Brown, Miss Sarah C. married to Mr. John W. Rush.

Brown, Miss Sarah E. married to Mr. Nath'l Ropes.

Brown, Miss Susan married to Mr. Robt Brown.

Brown, Miss Susan married to Mr. Isaac Wright.

Brown, Miss Susan married to William L. White, Esq.

Brown, Miss Susan Catherine married to Mr. Charles Ingersol.

Brown, Maj. Thomas A. married in Sullivan County to Miss Edna A. Trower.
National Banner & Nashville Whig (Mon., April 4, 1831)

(repeat of preceding)
Nashville Republican & State Gazette (Tues., April 5, 1831)

Brown, Mr. Thomas J. married in Shelbyville, Tenn. to Miss Elizabeth
Stoakes, daughter of Mr. Kinchin Stoaks.
National Banner & Nashville Whig (Wed., Dec. 3, 1834)

Brown, Mr. Thomas Jefferson married in Jessamine county, Ky. to Miss
Mary Jane Wallace.
National Banner (Sat., Aug. 8, 1829)

Brown, Miss Tyrana married to Mr. Robert J. Bell.

Brown, Unice T. married to Thomas Short.

Brown, Miss Virginia A. married to Mr. Alslon B. Estes.

Brown, Mr. W. M. married on the evening of the 8th inst., by the Rev.
Dr. Howell, to Miss Jane M. Morton, all of Nashville.
Nashville Whig (Tues., Sept. 10, 1844)

Brown, Mr. W. P. married Miss Polly Sans in Maury County.
National Banner & Nashville Whig (Fri., Feb. 12, 1830)

Brown, Mr. William of Williamson county aged 86 married on Friday 18th
inst. to Miss Mary Curry, age 56 of Wilson County.
The Western Weekly Review (Franklin, Tenn., Fri., Nov. 25, 1831)

(repeat of preceding)
National Banner & Nashville Whig (Sat., Nov. 26, 1831)

Brown, Mr. William married in Henry county to Miss Susan M'Cammon.
National Banner & Nashville Daily Advertiser (Fri., Jan. 27, 1832)

Brown, William L., Esq., married Miss Mary McNeill all of this city on
the morning of the 13th inst.,by the Rev. Dr. Edgar.
Republican Daily Banner & Nashville Whig (Mon., March 14, 1853)

Brown, Judge William T. married on Thursday the 14th inst., by the Rev.
Sam M. Williams to Mrs. Priscilla P. Boylan, of Fayette county.
Daily Republican Banner (Fri., March 29, 1839)

(repeat of preceding)
Nashville Whig (Fri., March 29, 1839)

Brownfield, Mr. William married Danville, Warren County on the 4th inst.
to Miss Cassy Chely.
National Banner & Nashville Whig (Sat., Dec. 27, 1828)

Browning, Miss Elenor married to Mr. Samuel Hudspeth.

Browning, Mr. Francis R. married at Russellville, Ky., to Mrs. Jane
Moore.
National Banner & Nashville Whig (April 14, 1827)

Browning, Mr. Henry R. married in Knox County to Miss Eliza Claiburn.
National Banner & Nashville Daily Advertiser (Nov. 5, 1832)

Browning, Mr. James married in Logan County, Ky., to Miss Margaret A.
Wallace.
National Banner & Nashville Whig (Mon., Dec. 29, 1834)

Browning, Miss Letitia married to Mr. David Jones.

Bruce, Mrs. Nancy G. married Mr. Walter Buster.

Brumat, Mr. Elijah married in Anderson County to Miss Margaret Bradshaw.
National Banner (April 14, 1826)

Brummitt, Mr. Wm. married in Maury County, on the 2d inst. to Miss
Elvira Pearce.
National Banner & Nashville Whig (Sept. 9,1830)

Brunner, Mrs. Frederica married to Mr. John Lindsey.

Brunson, Ashiel Esq., of Clarksville married yesterday afternoon by the
Rev. J. T. Edgar to Miss Emily Smiley of Nashville.
Nashville Whig (Fri., Feb. 8, 1839)

Brunson, Mr. J. E. married on Thursday the 6th inst., to Miss Levisa
Shelby, daughter of Col. John Shelby, of Montgomery County.
The Nashville Whig & Tenn. Advertiser (Nov. 17, 1817)

Brunson, Miss Mary Elizabeth married to Hugh S. Garland, Esq.

Brunson, Miss Penelope married to Mr. Willis Williams.

Bryan, Miss Araminta married to Mr. John W. Fitzhugh.

Bryan, Miss Caroline M. married to Joseph B. Crockett, Esq.

Bryan, Miss Elizabeth married to Mr. Richard Warmack.

Bryan, Mr. George married in Bourbon Co., Ky. to Mrs. J. Miller.
National Banner & Nashville Whig (Dec. 27, 1830)

Bryan, Miss Henrietta T. of Robertson Co., married Mr. Abraham B. Taylor.

Bryan, Mr. John G. married in Washington Co., Mo. to Miss Eveline
M'Llvaine.
National Banner & Nashville Whig (Sat., Jan. 12, 1828)

Bryan, Dr. John L. of Miss. married in Robertson County by the Rev.
A. L. P. Green to Miss Martha A.Woodson.
National Banner & Nashville Whig (Mon., Nov. 24, 1834)

Bryan, Rev. Lewis C. of Decatur, Ala., married on the 12th inst., by
the Rev. Philip P. Neeley to Miss Sarah A. D. King, daughter of Thos
S. King, Esq. of Davidson County.
Nashville Whig (Thurs., Oct. 19, 1843)

Bryan, Miss Lucinda R. married to Mr. Joseph P. Waddel.

Bryan, Miss Mary married to Mr. John Austin.

Bryan, Miss Roberta V. married to Mr. Henry Dickerson.

Bryan, Miss Sarah Y. married to Mr. James M. Beall.

Bryan, Miss Wealthy S. married to Maj. John E. Turner.

Bryan, Capt. William married to Miss Susan G. Innes, in Fayette Co., Ky.
National Banner & Nashville Whig (Sept. 20, 1830)

Bryan, Col. William married in Nashville on the evening of the 3rd inst.
by the Rev. A. L. P. Green to Miss Mary Macon Cannon, daughter fo the
late Gov. Cannon.
Nashville Whig (Oct. 8, 1844)

Bryan, Mr. William D. married Miss Polly Cannon.
The Western Weekly Review (Franklin, Tenn., Fri. Nov 11, 1831)

(repeat of preceding)
National Banner & Nashville Whig (Nov. 14, 1831)

Bryan, Mr. Willie B. of Nashville married on 23d inst. at Clarksville
by the Rev. A. S. P. Green to Miss Mary W. Bailey.
Daily Republican Banner (Tues., Nov. 28, 1837)

Bryant, Mr. Hardy married in Davidson County to Miss Margaret McGavock.
National Banner & Nashville Daily Advertiser (Tues., May 20, 1834)

Bryant, Miss Harriet married on the 16th inst. to Mr. Thomas J. Odell.

Bryant, Miss Sarah married to Mr. Alexander Allison.

Bryant, Miss Susan married to Mr. P. P. Collier.

Bryant, William married in Davidson county, on the 20th inst., by Rev.
Peter Fuqua to Mrs. Nancy Studervant, formerly the consort of the late
Josiah M. Studerbant.
National Banner & Nashville Daily Advertiser (Fri., Dec. 21, 1832)

Buchanan, Mrs. Argyle M. married to Miss Viena Lewis.
National Banner & Nashville Daily Advertiser (Wed., May 7, 1834)

Buchanan, Mr. Elbridge G. married in Fayetteville to Miss Catherine
Garner.
National Banner & Nashville Whig (Fri., Feb. 26, 1830)

Buchanan, Mrs. Elizabeth N. married to Mr. John Thompson.

Buchanan, Miss Frances T. married to Mr. John Crarren.

Buchanan, Mr. FrankS. of Lebanon, Merchant,married on the 17th December
by Rev. Mr. Lowery to Miss Ann E. Whorton, daughter of Mr. Joseph P.
Whorton of Wilson County.
Nashville True Whig & Weekly Commercial Register (Dec. 20, 1850)

Buchanan, Mr. George married to Miss Sarah M'Connell in Louisville, Ky.
National Banner & Nashville Whig (Fri., Feb 19, 1830)

Buchanan, Mr. Isaac married in Lincoln County to Miss Naomi Crawford.
National Banner & Nashville Whig (Oct. 6, 1827)

Buchanan, Miss Jane married to Mr. Reason Williams.

Buchanan, Mr. Richard married in Davidson County on the 26th June by
Rev. William Hume to Miss Martha Murphey.
National Banner & Nashville Daily Advertiser (Wed., June 27, 1832)

Buchanan, Mr. Robert married in this county to Miss Elizabeth Turley.
National Banner (March 3, 1826)

Buchanan, Mr. Robert married in this county on the 6th inst. to Barbara
Easter, daughter of Mr. Lahan Easters.
National Banner & Nashville Whig (Sat., July 15, 1826)

Buchanan, Miss Sarah married to Mr. B. A. Joyce.

Buck, Miss Ann W. married to Mr. Frederick E. Fisher.

Buck, Miss Martha A. married to Mr. Samuel D. Buck.

Buck, Mr. Samuel D. married in Montgomery County to Miss Martha A. Buck.
National Banner & Nashville Daily Advertiser (June 8, 1832)

Buck, Mr. Thos. M. married on the 31st ult by Rev. Sawrie to Miss
Martha Hanks.
Daily Republican Banner (Sat., Feb. 2, 1839)

Buckett, Miss Nancy married to Mr. Daniel Allen.

Buckley, Miss Eleanor married to Mr. James Nix.

Bucklin, James M. Esq. married in Huntsville, Ala. to Miss Mary Beckwith.
National Banner & Nashville Daily Advertiser (Mon., Aug. 19, 1833)

Bucknell, Miss Caroline Almira married to Mr..John B. Schenck.

Buckner, Miss Adeline married to Mr. Kennedy Foster.

Buckner, Miss Eliza A. C. married to David M. Porter, M. D.

Buckner, Miss Maria A. married to Mr. William Davidson.

Buckner, Miss Nancy married to Mr. William Pickett.

Budd, T. L. Esq. married by the Rev. Mr. Howell on the 9th inst. to
Miss Eliza Jane Moffitt, eldest daughter of Rev. John N. Moffitt, all
of Nashville.
Daily Republican Banner (Mon., Nov. 11, 1839)

(repeat of preceding)
Nashville Union (Mon., Nov. 11, 1839)

(repeat of preceding)
Nashville Whig (Mon., Nov. 11, 1839)

Buesley, Mr. Henry F. married in Warren county, Tenn to Miss Mary Ann
Walls.
National Banner & Nashville Daily Advertiser (Tues., Aug. 5, 1834)

Buffington, Mr. Anderson, Printer, married in Nashville, on the 1st
by the Rev. Mr. Robinson to Miss Parolee C. Cabler, both of Nashville.
National Banner & Nashville Whig (Fri., Oct. 3, 1834)

(repeat of preceding)
Nashville Republican & State Gazette (Sat., Oct. 4, 1834)

Buford, Charles Esq. married in Scott Co., Ky. to Miss Lucy Ann Duke.
National Banner & Nashville Whig (Wed., Feb. 25, 1835)

Buford, Miss Elizabeth married to Mr. Thomas Buford.

Buford, Miss Lucinda married to Mr. William L. Clark.

Buford, Martha married to Mr. Hardy.

Buford, Miss Sarah S. married to Mr. Thomas Hope.

Buford, Mr. Thomas of Giles County married in Williamson County, Tenn.
to Miss Elizabeth Buford of Williamson County.
National Banner & Nashville Whig (Wed., Nov. 26, 1834)

Bugg, Angelina married to Benj. R. Gant.

Bugg, Mr. Benjamin N. married in Williamson County, Tenn. to Miss Annis
Tucker.
National Banner & Nashville Whig (Mon., April 13, 1835)

Bugg, Mr. Samuel H. of Gallatin married by the Rev. Mr. Edgar to Miss
Catherine Smiley, of Nashville.
National Banner & Nashville Daily Advertiser (Tues., June 24, 1834)

Buice, Mr. John married on the 17th inst. to Miss Martha P. Hudson,
daughter of Mr. Isac Hudson, all of Davidson County.
Nashville Whig (July 28, 1823)

Buie, Miss Elizabeth married to Mr. John D. Goss.

Buie, Miss Flora married to Mr. Ephraim English.

Buie, Miss Malinda married to Mr. William M. Bowers.

Buie, Miss Martha Ann married to Mr. Hansel T. Wilkenson.

Bull, Mr. Corban, married in Shelby Co., Ky. to Mary Metcalfe.
National Banner & Nashville Whig (Sat., Feb. 7, 1829)

Bull, Miss Rebecca married in Sumner county to Mr. Benjamin Chapman.

Bull, Miss Sarah married in Louisville, Ky. to Mr. D. B. Leight.

Bull, Mr. William Izard married in Charleston, S. C. on the 26th Nov.
last to Miss Gracie C. Turnbull.
National Banner & Nashville Daily Advertiser (Sat., Jan. 18, 1834)

Bullard, Miss Ann E. married in Winchester last wekk to Mr. John C.
Pryor.

Bullard, Miss Octavia married to Mr. Jefferson I. Dodson.

Bullard, Miss Octavia married to Mr. Isaac J. Dotson.

Bullitt, Mr. Cuthbert of Louisville, Ky. married Miss Eliza White of
New Orleans, in Natchez, Miss.
National Banner & Nashville Advertiser (Mon., April 2, 1832)

Bullitt, Miss Mary Ann married to Gen. Henry Arkinson.

Bullock, Miss Mary Ann married in Fayette County, Ky. to Mr. Peter
Gordon Hunt.

Bullock, Miss Ophelia married to Mr. Samuel Beard.

Bullus, Miss Anne M. married to Daniel W. Adams, Esq.

Bullus, Miss Elizabeth M. married to Charles Scott, Esq.

Buman, Mr. Henry married to Miss Nancy F. Badgett in Knox County.
National Banner & Nashville Advertiser (Mon., Dec. 31, 1832)

Bunch, Mr. Thomas married in Henry County to Miss Nancy Hale.
National Banner & Nashville Whig (Wed., Dec. 28, 1831)

Bunker, Rev. J. B. married in Roan County to Mrs. Eliza Dover.
National Banner & Nashville Whig (Sat., Dec. 15, 1827)

Bunton, Miss Jane married to Mr. Daniel F. Carter.

Burch, Mr. Benjamin D. married in Bowling Green, Ky. to Miss Julie E.
Martin.
National Banner & Nashville Daily Advertiser (Sat.,April 28, 1832)

Burch, Miss Hannah married to Mr. Hamilton Archinson.

Burch, Mr. John married in Bullitt County, Ky. to Miss Mary Hardeman.
National Banner & Nashville Whig (Sat., July 8, 1826)

Burch, Miss Martha M. married in Rutherford County to George I Cain, Esq.

Burchitt, Mr. William married in Nashville on the 8th inst. to Miss
Fanny Elsberry, by Joseph Ferriss, Esq.
The Politician & Weekly Nashville Whig (Fri., July 16, 1847)

(repeat of preceding)
The Christian Record (Sat., July 17, 1847)

Burditt, Miss Epsabeth married to Mr. Sterling Goodrum.

Burditt, Miss Martha married to Mr. Andrew Davidson.

Burford, Mr. N. C. of Giles County married in Lincoln County to Miss Ann A Lesueur.
National Banner & Nashville Daily Advertiser (Fri., July 6, 1832)

Burge, Mrs. Eliza married in this county to Mr. Austin Gresham.

Burgess, Mr. Albert B. married on Tuesday evening last by Philip Lindsley to Miss Helen M. Stratton, both of Nashville.
National Banner & Nashville Whig (Fri., April 21, 1837)

(repeat of preceding)
Nashville Republican (Sat., April 22, 1837)

Burgess, Miss Esther married to Mr. Robert M. Pong.

Burgess, Miss Isabella M. married on 23d inst. to Mr. Thos C. Dabbs.

Burgess, Miss Mahala married to Mr. John B. Baker.

Burgess, Miss Mary married to Mr. J. Foster.

Burke, Miss Judith Ann married to Mr. John T. Dismukes.

Burke, Mr. Virgil of Columbus married in Noxubee Co., Mi. to Miss Lucy Ann Barnett.
National Banner & Nashville Daily Advertiser (Fri., July 18, 1834)

Burke, Mr. Walter Jun. married to Miss Roselee R. Egbert, in New Orleans on the 18th ult.
National Banner & Nashville Whig (Sat., June 14, 1828)

Burkhart, Miss Caroline Eliza Ann, married to Mr. Richard Kelley.

Burkley, Miss Isabel C. married to Mr. William F. Ready.

Burlington, Mr. John of Nashville married in Davidson County on Sunday last by the Rev. Mr. Whitsit to Miss Mary Ann Hollingsworth, of Davidson County.
Daily Republican Banner (Tues., Oct. 10, 1837)

Burnet, Miss Mary T. married to Mr. William Reasor.

Burnett, Mr. A. S. married at New Albaney, Ga. to Miss Eliza Gambill.
National Banner (Sat., May 2,1829)

Burnley, Abbot T., Esq. married at Frankford, Ky. to Miss Frances Ann Bibb.
National Banner & Nashville Whig (Sat., April 7, 1827)

Burnley, Mr. Hardin married to Miss Mary A. Wilkins.
National Banner & Nashville Daily Advertiser (Mon., Aug. 12, 1833)

(repeat of preceding)
National Banner & Nashville Daily Advertiser (Mon., Aug. 5, 1833)

Burns, Mr. Phenix married in Fayette Co., Ky. to Miss Ann Crocket.
National Banner & Nashville Whig (Sat., Nov. 18, 1826)

Burns, Miss Rachel S. married to Mr. WM. L. T. Edwards.

Burr, Col. Aaron married at Harlem Heights, N. Y. on the 1st inst. by the Rev. Dr. Bogart to Mrs. Eliza Jumel.
National Banner & Nashville Daily Advertiser (Mon., July 29, 1833)

Burr, Rev. Erastus married Worthington, Ohio, on the 7th Feb by the Rev. William Preston to Miss Harriet Griswold.
National Banner & Nashville Daily Advertiser (Thurs., Feb. 21, 1833)

Burrough, Mr. Gustavus J. married at New Orleans to Miss Alexandra Bauding.
National Banner & Nashville Whig (Sat., Jan. 6, 1827)

Burrow, Mr. John married in Bedford County to Miss Mary Snell.
National Banner & Nashville Daily Advertiser (Wed., March 28, 1832)

Burrow, Miss Mary married to Michael Fisher, Esq.

Burrow, Miss Miranda married to Mr. James G. Barby.

Burrow, Rev. Reuben married to Miss Elizabeth Bell in Franklin County.
National Banner & Nashville Whig (Sat., Feb. 23, 1828)

Burrow, Mr. Samuel G. married in Bedford county to Miss Jane Rozier.
National Banner & Nashville Daily Advertiser (Sat., July 28, 1832)

Burrows, Miss Ann Eliza married at Cincinnati to Mr. Saunders W. Hartsborne.

Burrus, Miss Sarah married to Aaron V. Brown, Esq.

Burrus, Miss Virginia B. amrried to Mr. Wesley Greenfield.

Burthall, Miss Jane married to Mr. Eli M. Bradford.

Burton, Miss Anne W. married to Mr. Thomas Rogers, of Bubuque, Iowa.

Burton, Major Charles F.,married to Miss Sophia King in Cumberland Co., Ky.
National Banner (March 10, 1826)

Burton, Miss Crissy H. married on the 20th to Mr. Henry B. Rogers.

Burton, Mr. Edmund married on the 5th inst. by the Rev. Mr. Bowman, to Miss Amanda Jones.
National Banner & Nashville Whig (Sat., July, 14, 1828)

Burton, Miss Eliba R. married to Thomas E. Morriss, Esq.

Burton, Miss Eliza married to Dr. George Crosthwait.

Burton, Miss Frances H. married to Col. Samuel Dickens.

Burton, Mr. Isaac married in Knox County to Miss Nancy Ingram.
National Banner & Nashville Whig (Sat., Dec. 15, 1827)

Burton, Mr. R. H. of Dickson County married Miss Mary Turner on the 9th Oct.
Nashville Republican (Tues., Jan. 19, 1836)

Burton, Mr. S. H. married on Oct. 26 to Miss Eliza Council, both of Dickson County.
Nashville Republican (Tues. Jan. 19, 1836)

Burtwell, Col. John T. married in Lauderdale County, Ala to Miss Cornelia M. Bedford.
National Banner & Nashville Daily Advertiser (Mon., Sept. 2, 1833)

(repeat of preceding)
Nashville Republican & State Gazette (Tues., Sept. 3, 1833)

Busby, Capt. John F. married in Woodford Co., Ky. to Miss Lucy Ann Thornton.
National Banner & Nashville Whig (Sat., Jan. 17, 1829)

Bush, Mr. John of Knoxville married in Grainger County to Miss Ellen Hommel.
National Banner & Nashville Daily Advertiser (Mon., June 17, 1833)

Buster, Miss Emily married to Mr. James Gorin.

Buster, Mr. Walter married Mrs. Nancy G. Bruce in Madison County, Ala. National Banner & Nashville Whig (Fri., Feb. 12, 1830)

Butler, Mr. A. W. married in this county on Thurs. evening 4th inst. to Miss Mary D. Hyde. National Banner (Sat., June 13, 1829)

Butler, Mr. Allen M. married in Madison County, Ky. to Miss Sally Stewart. National Banner (Feb. 3, 1826)

Butler, Edward S. of the firm of John W. Butler & Bro. Pittsburgh married at Cincinnati on the 17th Feb by the Rev. Mr. Wilson to Miss Margaret J. Smith, daughter of Joseph Smith, Esq. of Cincinnati. The Christian Record (Sat., March 13, 1847)

Butler, Miss Eliza married to Captain John Donelson Jr.

Butler, Miss Elizabeth married to Mr. William M'Cormack.

Butler, Mr. J. Williamson of Pittsburgh married in Nashville on the 16th by the Rev. J. Thomas Wheat to Miss Sarah G. Wilson, daughter of Col. G. Wilson. Nashville Whig (Tues., Jan. 18, 1842)

Butler, Mr. James H. married in Williamson County, Tenn. to Miss Eliza Stanley. National Banner & Nashville Whig (Fri., Feb. 13, 1835)

Butler, Miss Jane married to Mr. William Hawkins.

Butler, Miss Martha R. married to Mr. Smith Freeman.

Butler, Miss Mary married to Mr. Thos. G. Pate.

Butler, Miss Mary Ann married Mr. Benjamin R. Powell.

Butler, Mr. N. W. married to Miss Ann P. Marshall, on Wed. evening by the Rev. Doct. Edgar, both of Mississippi. National Banner & Nashville Whig (Fri., Aug 28, 1835)

Butler, Mrs. Nancy married to Joel Yowell, Esq.

Butler, Mrs. R. P. married to A. Hanson.

Butler, Mr. Robert of Davidson County married to Miss Rachel Hays of Davidson County on Sunday last. Impartial Review & Cumberland Repository (Thurs., Sept. 1, 1808)

Butler, Mr. Smith married in Henry County to Miss Sophia Biles. National Banner & Nashville Daily Advertiser (Thurs., March 22, 1832)

Butler, Maj. William O. married on the 17th inst. at Lexington, to Miss Eliza Todd. The Nashville Whig (April 30, 1817)

Butner, Mr. Martin married in Rutherford County to Miss Sarah Peake. National Banner & Nashville Whig (Fri., June 27, 1828)

Butt, Miss Harriet married in Maury County to Mr. Philip Meese.

Butt, Mr. Thomas P. married in Maury County to Miss Diana Donaldson. National Banner & Nashville Whig (Fri., Feb. 19, 1830)

Butterworht, Miss Permelia of Davidson married on Tuesday the 14th by the Rev. Mr. Gray to Mr. Thomas J. Talley of Sumner. Nashville Whig (Sat., Feb. 18, 1843)

Butterworth, Mr. R. married on Sunday the 21st inst by Rev. J. B. Ferguson to Miss Elizabeth Merritt, all of Nashville.
Nashville True Whig & Weekly Commercial Register (Fri., April 26, 1850)

Butts, Mr. Jacob married in Lincoln Co., Tenn to Miss Catherine Smith.
National Banner & Nashville Whig (Fri., Dec. 6, 1834)

Butts, Miss Mary G. married to Mr. Benjamin Blankenship.

Bynum, Chesley P., Esq. Editor of the Columbia Ten. Democrat, married on Friday Feb. 24th 1837 to Miss Mary Wingfield.
National Banner & Nashville Whig (Fri., March 10, 1837)

(repeat of preceding)
The Union (Sat., March 11, 1837)

Bynum, Miss Mary J. married to Mr. A. L. Cavender.

Byrd, Miss Eliza married to Mr. Henry Derroset.

Byrd, Mr. John married to Miss Martha Johnson in Madison Co., Ala.
National Banner & Nashville Whig (Sat., April 7, 1827)

Byrd, Mr. M. B. married in Smith Co., Tenn. to Miss Nancy Denny.
National Banner & Nashville Advertiser (Fri., March 23, 1832)

Byrd, Miss M. L. married to Mr. John W. Faulkner.

Byrn , Miss Fanny married to Mr. Bryant Piercy.

Byrn, Col. John W. married in Florence Ala. to Miss Mary Vigus.
Nashville Republican & State Gazette (Thurs., May 5, 1831)

Byrn, Miss Lucinda R. married to Mr. Joseph P. Waddel.

Byrn, Miss Sophia M. married to Maj. Thomas H. Bibb.

Byrns, Mr. James married in Fayette County, Ky. to Miss Nancy L. Crockett.
National Banner & Nashville Advertiser (Mon, March 12, 1832)

Cabble, Miss Mary married to Josiah Wilson.

Cabell, Mr. R. B. married at Henderson, Ky. to Miss Ann E. Hernden.
National Banner & Nashville Daily Advertiser (Mon., Feb. 18, 1833)

Cabill, Mr. Edwin married in Lexington, Ky. to Miss Margaret Adams.
National Banner & Nashville Whig (Fri., March 6, 1835)

Cabler, Mr. Edmund S. of Franklin married at Nashville on Thursday last
to Miss Leach of Nashville.
The Western Weekly Review (Franklin,Tenn. Fri., Dec. 16, 1831)

Cabler, Miss Parolee C. married in Nashville on the 1st by Rev. Mr.
Robinson to Mr. Anderson Buffington.

Caburit. Miss Catharine of Cincinnati married to Mr. Peter Billiard.

Cacey, Mr. Mathew C. married in Franklin to Miss Eliza A. Cameron.
National Banner & Nashville Advertiser (Tues., Sept. 25, 1832)

Cage, Miss Eveline A. B. married to Mr. Joel L. Abston.

Cage, Miss Harriet Caroline married to Thomas Fletcher, Esq.

Cage, Miss Solima married to Mr. D. E. Elliott.

Cage, Mr. Wilson of Sumner county married in Williamson County to Miss
Mary Crocket.
National Banner & Nashville Whig (Sat., Oct. 25, 1828)

Cage, Mr. Wilson J. married in Bedford county to Miss Mary B. Cardwell,
daughter of the Rev. Richard Cardwell.
National Banner (Sat., Aug. 29, 1829)

Cahal, Mr. John married in Henry County to Miss Elizabeth Wright.
National Banner & Nashville Advertiser (Fri., March 2, 1832)

Cahal, Hon. Terry H. of Maury County, Speaker of the Senate, married in
Sumner County on Thursday last by the Rev. James Smith to Miss Ann
Saunders, daughter of the late James Saunders of Sumner County.
Daily Republican Banner (Mon., Nov. 13, 1837)

Cahoon, Miss Ann married in Williamson County to John C. Neal.

Cain, Mr. of Paris married in Montgomery County to Mrs. Susan M'Clure.
National Banner & Nashville Daily Advertiser (Wed., Oct. 3, 1832)

(repeat of preceding)
Nashville Republican & State Gazette (Wed., Oct. 3, 1832)

Cain, Miss Caroline married to Mr. George Griffith.

Cain, Miss Caroline R. H. married to Mr. Samuel Spencer.

Cain, Miss Caroline R. R. married to Mr. Samuel Spencer.

Cain, George I., Esq. married to Miss Martha M. Burch, in Rutherford Co.
National Banner & Nashville Whig (June 27, 1828)

Cain, Miss Julia Ann married to Mr. George H. Graham.

Cain, Mr. Robert B. of McMinnville married in Nashville on Thursday the
29th inst. to Miss Mary Lawrence, daughter of Doct. Wm. P. Lawrence.
National Banner & Nashville Whig (Sept. 30, 1831)

Calcote, Mr. James L. of Mississippi married in the vicinty of Nashville,
on Tuesday last by the Rev. Dr. Edgar to Miss Elizabeth S. Overton,
daughter of Dr. James Overton.
Nashville Whig (March 19, 1846)

Caldwell, Mrs. married to Mr. Nelson Waters.

Caldwell, Mr. A. S. of Nashville married on Sat. the 23d inst. to Miss Matilda M. Shappard of Hardin County.
Daily Republican Banner (Feb. 27, 1839)

(repeat of preceding)
Nashville Union (Feb. 27, 1839)

(repeat of preceding)
Nashville Whig (Feb. 27, 1839)

Caldwell, Miss Ann married to M. B. Morton, Esq.

Caldwell, Mr. Benjamin H. married in Maury County Tenn. to Miss Maria M. Kirby.
National Banner & Nashville Whig (Feb. 25, 1835)

Caldwell, Dr. Daniel C. married in Russellville, Ky. to Miss Betsy King.
National Banner & Nashville Whig (Sat., Sept. 16, 1826)

Caldwell, David married to Miss Elizabeth Kelly, daughter of Col. Elexander Kelly, of Knox County.
Knoxville Gazette (Thurs., May 8, 1794)

Caldwell, Mr. David married in Blount County to Miss Sarah Yearout.
National Banner & Nashville Daily Advertiser (Wed., May 8, 1833)

Caldwell, Miss Elizabeth married to Mr. Albert G. Talbot.

Caldwell, Miss Harriet S. married to Mr. Steward Piokin.

Caldwell, John Esq., late of Nashville, married in Tuscumbia, Ala. to Miss Lucinda W. Haynie, daughter of the Rev. John Haynie.
National Banner & Nashville Whig (Sat., Dec. 15, 1827)

Caldwell, Mr. John, Editor of the evening Chronicle, married in Amesburg, Me. to Miss Mary Nason.
National Banner & Nashville Daily Advertiser (Thurs., Sept. 12, 1833)

Caldwell, Mr. Joseph married in Montgomery County, Tenn. to Miss Mary Nelson.
National Banner & Nashville Whig (Wed., Feb. 4, 1835)

(repeat of preceding)
Nashville Republican (Thurs., Feb. 5, 1835)

Caldwell, Miss Julia Ann married to Mr. Jonathan Keedy.

Caldwell, Mr. Leonard J. married in Smith county to Miss L. Robinson.
National Banner & Nashville Daily Advertiser (Fri., Feb. 10, 1832)

Caldwell, Miss Margaret married in this town on Thursday 15th inst. to Mr. James Erwin.
National Banner & Nashville Whig (Sat., Jan. 17, 1829)

Baldwell, Mrs. Mary Jane married to Dr. Nathaniel F. Daugherty.

Caldwell, Mr. Robert married in Giles County to Miss Roberta Elder.
Nashville Whig (Sat.,April 11, 1846)

Caldwell, Mr. St. Clair married in Maruy County to Miss Mary W. Pointer.
National Banner & Nashville Whig (Sat., Dec. 17, 1831)

Caldwell, Mr. Tho. J. married in Knoxville to Miss Lucinda Dardis, daughter of James Dardis, Esq.
National Banner & Nashville Whig (Sat., Dec. 9, 1826)

Calhoun, Mr. A. P., eldest son of the Hon J. C. Calhoun, married at
Columbia, S. C. to Miss Eugenia Chappell, eldest daughter of Col. J.
J. Chappell, on the 3d of January by the Rev. Mr. Henry.
National Banner & Nashville Daily Advertiser (Tues., Feb. 5, 1833)

Calhoun, Mr. James married at Columbia, to Miss Sarah Howard.
National Banner & Nashville Whig (Mon, July 12, 1830)

Calhoun, Miss Margaret married in Williamson County, Tenn. to Mr.
William Cathey.
National Banner & Nashville Whig (Mon., April 13, 1835)

Calhoun, Miss Martha married in Gallatin to Joseph M. Robb, Esq.
Nashville Whig (Wed., Oct. 7, 1840)

Calhoun, Meredith Esq. of Havre married at Natchez, Miss. to Mary Smyth
Taylor, daughter of the late Col. John Taylor, of South Carolina.
National Banner & Nashville Daily Advertiser (Thurs., June 19, 1834)

Call, Hon. Richard K. of Pensacola married on Wed. last by the Rev.
A. D. Campbell to Miss Mary L. Kirkman, of this place.
Nashville Whig (July 19, 1824)

Callahan, Mr. John K. married in Henry County to Miss Margaret Frwin,
daughter of Mr. Joseph Erwin.
National Banner & Nashville Whig (Mon., May 31, 1830)

Callaway, Miss Carolina married to Mr. Tho. B. Cox.

Callaway, Rev. Joseph R. married in Rhea City, Tenn. to Miss Mary Wilson,
daughter of James Wilson, Esq.
National Banner & Nashville Whig (Mon., Oct. 20, 1834)

Callaway, Miss Mary married to Dr. C. C. McReynolds.

Callaway, Miss Nancy married to Capt. George. M. Webb.

Callaway, Miss Rebecca C. married to Mr. Joseph Donohoo in Monroe County.
National Banner & Nashville Whig (Wed., July 27, 1831)

Callaway, William S. Esq. married in M'Minn County to Miss Sarah Ann
Hurst, daughter of Elijah Hurst, Esq.Wm.S. Callaway of Madisonville.
National Banner & Nashville Daily Advertiser (Tues., Nov. 27, 1832)

Callender, Mr. Thomas of Nashville married to Miss Mary Sangester.
National Banner & Nashville Whig (Mon., Feb. 28, 1831)

Callender, Mr. Thomas married on the 24th inst. to Miss Mary Sangster
of this county.
Nashville Republican and State Gazette (Feb. 26, 1831)

Callender, Mr. Thomas married on the 21st inst. by the Rev. Dr. Edgar
to Mrs. Catharine A. Dittmore, both of Nashville.
The Christian Record (Sat., Dec. 23, 1848)

Calliham, Miss Ann married to Mr. John Dunbar.

Callis, Miss Elizabeth O. married to Mr. William F. Latimer.

Callis, Miss Matilda married to Mr. Samuel Patton.

Calloway, Mr. J. F. Married in Monroe County to Miss Mary Cassander.
National Banner & Nashville Advertiser (Mon, Dec. 31, 1832)

Calloway, Miss Rebecca C. married to Mr. Joseph Donohoo.

Callum, Miss Eleanor married to Mr. Peter M'Nutt.

Calvert, Miss Rebecca married to Mr. Martin W. Cure.

Calvert, Mr. W. W. of Burlington, Ky. married on Sunday the 31st ult. by the Rev. J. B. Ferguson to Miss Samuella A. A. Holmes of Nashville. Nashville True Whig & Weekly Commercial Register (Fri., April 17, 1850)

Cameron, Mr. Donald, one of the editors of the Western Weekly Review, married on Wed. the 6th inst. by Rev. A. N. Cunningham to Miss Mary L. McClellan, daughter of Mr. George McClellan, all of Williamson Co. Nashville Whig (Thurs., May 14, 1846)

Cameron, Miss Eliza A. married in Franklin to Mr. Mathew C. Cacey. National Banner & Nashville Advertiser (Tues., Sept. 25, 1832)

Cameron, Mr. Ewen Jr. married near Bowling-green, Ky. on Thursday last by the Rev. Mr. Perry to Miss Clarissa Blakey. Daily Republican Banner (Tues., April 16, 1839)

Cameron, Mr. John married in Hawkins County to Miss Nancy Rodgers. National Banner & Nashville Whig (Sat., May 19, 1827)

Cameron, Mr. William of this place married in Warren county, Ky. on the 16th inst. to Miss Alzira H. Morehead. National Banner & Nashville Daily Advertiser (Mon., Aug. 20, 1832)

Cammack, Mr. George married in Christian Co., Ky. to Miss Joanna Thomas. National Banner & Nashville Daily Advertiser (Tues., Feb.5 , 1833)

Camon, Miss Sarah Jane married at Tuscumbia, Ala to Mr. John W. Mechan. National Banner (Sat., Aug 1, 1829)

Camp, Mr. Anthony S. married in Nashville on the 15th inst by the Rev. J. B. Ferugson to Miss Virginia Reynolds, daughter of the late Thomas L. Reynolds of Williamson County. The Politician & Weekly Nashville Whig (Fri., March 24, 1848)

Camp, Miss Elizabeth W. married to Mr. Silas Flournoy.

Camp, Mr. James married to Miss Sally Pearsall, on Tuesday the 27th ult., daughter of J. Pearsall, Esq. of Dickson County. Nashville Whig (July 4, 1815)

Camp, Col. James married in Maury County to Miss Mary J. Tate. National Banner & Nashville Whig (Mon., Sept. 26, 1831)

Camp, Capt. John of Davidson County married to Mrs. Martha Jones, of Davidson County, on Thursday last. Impartial Review & Cumberland Repository (Oct. 6, 1808)

Camp, Dr. John H. of Davidson County married to Miss Dolly Jones, of Davidson County on Monday last. Impartial Review & Cumerland Repository (June 23, 1808)

Camp, Miss Sarah P. married to Mr. Peter Perkins.

Campbe, Capt. James married in Grainger Co. to Miss Margery F. Blair. National Banner & Nashville Whig (Thurs., June 17, 1830)

Campbell, Rev. Alexander married at Wellsburg, Brooke Co., Va. to Miss Selina H. Bakewell. National Banner & Nashville Whig (Sat., Sept. 13, 1828)

Campbell, Col. Andrew married at Monroe County to Miss Mary Tedford. National Banner & Nashville Whig (Sat., Feb. 9, 1828)

Campbell, Mr. Andrew of Williamson County married in Winchester, Franklin Co., on the 14th inst., by the Rev. Copp to Miss Eliza Clarke. The Western Weekly Review (Franklin, Tenn., Fri., March 29, 1833)

Campbell, Andrew M. Esq. married in Henry County to Miss Sarah L. Hampton. National Banner (March 24, 1826)

Campbell, Miss Ann married to Mr. Wm. E. Owen.

Campbell, Miss Ann married to Mr. Cato Miller.

Campbell, Mis Caroline R. P. married to Mr. Richard Patterson.

Campbell, Mr. Charles married in Jefferson County to Miss Mary Stone, both of Grainger.
National Banner & Nashville Whig (Mon., Sept. 13, 1830)

Campbell, Miss Cynthia married in Fayetteville to Mr. Alexander R. Kerr.

Campbell, Miss Cynthia Ann married to Mr. George W. McGehee.

Campbell, Mr. Daniel of Henry County married on Wed. 13th inst. by the Rev. James W. Rea to Miss Elizabeth Cummins, daughter of Mr. Samuel Cummins, of Williamson County.
The Western Weekly Review (Fri., Feb. 22, 1833)

(repeat of preceding)
National Banner & Nashville Daily Advertiser (Mon., Feb. 25, 1833)

Campbell, Mr. Donald of Mooresville, Ala. married to Miss Elizabeth M'Kinley of Florence.
Nashville Republican & State Gazette (Sat., Sept. 21, 1833)

Campbell, Mr. Duncan married in Williamson County to Miss Nancy C. Anderson.
National Banner & Nashville Whig (Sat., Aug. 4, 1827)

Campbell, Miss Eliza A. married to Mr. Benjamin H. Ligon.

Campbell, Miss Elizabeth M. married to Mr. James A. Woods.

Campbell, Miss Emeline M. B. married to Mr. Nicholas H. Boyd.

Campbell Miss Emily, married in Maury County to Mr. Wm. W. Lane.

Campbell, Mr. Hardin married in this county to Miss Grace M'Cormack.
National Banner & Nashville Whig (Sat., Aug. 12, 1826)

Campbell, Miss Harriet Ann married to Mr. Wm. F. Birch.

Campbell, Miss Hariet married to Mr. William Rush.

Campbell, Col. J. P. of Columbia married on the 16th inst. at Planta Place, the residence of Mrs. Ann Minnick enar Nashville, by Judge Green, to Rebecca Warson Sims, daughter of Walter Sims, Esq. of Nashville.
Nashville Whig (Sat., Dec. 17, 1846)

(repeat of preceding)
The Christian Record (Sat., Dec. 26, 1846)

Campbell, Mr. James married at Chillicothe, O. to Miss Mary S. Bradford.
National Banner (Jan. 27, 1826)

Campbell, James Mason Esq. of Baltimore married in Washington City to Miss Ann Arnold Taney, daughter of the Hon. R. B. Taney, Secretary of the Treasury.
National Banner & Nashville Daily Advertiser (Thurs., June 19, 1834)

Campbell, James W. Esq. married in Knoxville to Miss Susan C. Morgan.
National Banner (Sat., June 6, 1829)

Campbell, Miss Jane married to Dr. Albert G. Ewing.

Campbell, Miss Jane L. married in Williamson County to Mr. Jacob T. Morris.

Campbell, Mr. Joel married in Logan Co., Y. to Miss Lydia Horn.
National Banner & Nashville Daily Adverliser (Tues. Nov. 13, 1832)

Campbell, Mr. John married in Knox County to Miss Elizabeth Armstrong, daughter of Mr. Moses Armstrong.
National Banner (Sat., July 18, 1829)

Campbell, John W. Esq. married in this town on Wed. evening last to Miss Jane Porter, daughter of Alexander Porter, Esq.
National Banner & Nashville Whig (Sat.,June 16, 1827)

Campbell, Mr. Jones married in Logan Co., Ky. to Miss Mary Ann Pert, daughter of Major James Pert.
National Banner & Nashville Whig (Mon., Dec. 29, 1834)

Campbell, Miss Lisenka M. married to J. Percy Brown.

Campbell, Miss Margaret married to Samuel W. Kilpatrick.

Campbell, Miss Margaret P. married to John Marshall, Esq.

Campbell, Miss Margaret W. married to Samuel W. Kilpatrick.

Campbell, Miss Martha C. married to Philo Beeman, Esq.

Campbell, Miss Martha Rebecca married to Dr. James W. Baxton.

Campbell, Miss Mary A. married to Mr. John M. Pilkinton.

Campbell, Miss Mary L. S. married to Mr. Thomas M. Patterson.

Campbell, Mr. Moses married in Logan Co., Ky. to Miss Surindia Parrish.
National Banner (March 10, 1826)

Campbell, Miss Nancy married to Maj. John Chase.

Campbell, Miss Nancy B. married to William D. V. Downing, Esq.

Campbell, Mrs. Polly L. married to Joseph Ficklin, Esq.

Campbell, Dr. R. M. of Dickson county married on 2d inst. to Miss Louisiana Park, of Davidson County.
Nashville Republican & State Gazette (Tues., Oct. 14, 1834)

Campbell, Miss Rebecca married to Mr. Thos D. Henley.

Campbell, Mr. Robt. of this vicinity, married to Miss Frances Ewell, in Smythe Co., Va.
Nashville Republican (Tues., Jan. 13, 1835)

(repeat of preceding)
National Banner & Nashville Whig (Wed., Jan. 21, 1835)

Campbell, Miss Sarah married in Grainger County to Mr. Michael H. Stone.
National Banner & Nashville Whig (Sat., April 7, 1826)

Campbell, Mr. Semple of Uniontown, married in Pittsburgh, Pa. to Miss Sarah A. Lowrie.
National Banner & Nashville Daily Advertiser (Mon., May 12, 1834)

Campbell, Miss Sophia married to Mr. Gedeon Riggs.

Campbell, Mr. Thomas J. Jr. of Georgia married in Athens, Tenn. to Miss Frances E.Bridges of Athens.
Nashville Whig (Thurs., June 25,1846)

Campbell, Mr. Urban married in Logan Co., Ky. to Miss Sarah C. Rush, daughter of the Rev. Grigsby Rush.
National Banner & Nashville Daily Advertiser (Sat., Oct. 13, 1832)

Campbell, W. R., Esq. married in Vicksburg, Miss to Miss Margaret P. H.
Tideman.
National Banner & Nashville Daily Advertiser (March 26, 1833)

Campbell, Mr. Washington married in Williamson County to Miss Mahala
Cartwright.
The Western Weekly Review (Franklin, Tenn., Friday Dec. 2, 1831)

(repeat of preceding)
National Banner & Nashville Whig (Wed., Dec. 7, 1831)

Campbell, Maj. William married in this town on Sat. last by the Rev.
Mr. Lindsey to Miss Frances Gill.
National Banner & Nashville Whig (Sat., Feb. 14, 1829)

Campbell, William G. M., Esq. of Davidson County married in Montgomery
County on the 26th inst. by the Rev. Mr. Williams to Miss Minerva Ann
Norfleet of Montgomery County.
Nashville Whig (Sat., April 29, 1843)

Campbell, Mr. Wm. M. married at Florence, Ala to Miss Mary Ann Glenn.
National Banner (March 3, 1826)

Campbell, Mr. Wm. P. married in this county on Thursday evening last to
Miss Lucy Wiggington.
National Banner & Nashville Whig (Sat., April 7, 1827)

Campton, Miss Elizabeth B. married to Mr. Hays Blackman.

Camron, Miss Catherine married to Capt. James Wortham.

Camron, Mr. John T. married in Rutherford county to Miss Sarah Ann
Harrison.
National Banner (Sat., July 25, 1829)

Canada, Miss Jane married to Mr. Samuel Evetts.

Cane, Miss A. A. married to Mr. Felix A. Harris.

Caneaster, Miss Martha married to Mr. Jarvis Williams.

Cannon, Mr. Alansin of Rutherford County married on the 21st inst. by
the Rev. Mr. Hall of Gallatin to Miss Elizabeth C. Sharp of Sumner County.
National Banner & Nashville Daily Advertiser (Tues., May 27, 1834)

Cannon, Miss Ann Matilda married to Benjamin W. McCulloch.

Cannon, Mr. Augusta married in Lincoln County to Miss Eliza Jane Holman.
National Banner & Nashville Whig (Sat., Sept. 8, 1827)

Cannon, Miss Elvira married to Mr. Hutchison Manley.

Cannon, Miss Evelina married to Lieut. Anderson K. Yookum.

Cannon, Miss Helen M. married in Shelbyville to Rev. George Newton.

Cannon, Mr. Henry married in Bedford County to Miss Sarah Tilmon.
National Banner & Nashville Daily Advertiser (Wed., Jan. 23, 1833)

Cannon, Miss Leah A. married to Thomas F. Perkins.

Cannon, Miss Mary Macon married to Col. William Bryan.

Cannon, Miss Polly married Mr. William D. Bryan.

Cannon, Thomas H. married to Miss Matilda C. Wynne in Madison County,
Tenn.
National Banner (Sat., July 10, 1829)

Cannon, Mr. William H., Merchant in Madisonville, married on the 2nd
ult. by Rev. A. A. Mathis to Miss Mary T. Heiskell, all of Monroe Co.,
East Tennessee.
The Christian Record (Sat., Jan. 22, 1848)

Cantreal, Mr. Steaphen of Davidson County married to Miss Juliet Windle,
of Davidson County, on Thursday evening last.
Impartial Review & Cumerland Repository (Jan. 17, 1807)

Cantrell, Miss Elizabeth married to Mr. Abraham Vanwyck.

Cantrell, Miss Elvina S. married to Mr. Edwin Ferguson.

Cantrell, Miss Emeline married to Mr. Alexander A. Caseday.

Cantrell, Mr. Joseph married in Giles county to Miss Kesiah Brandon.
Nashville Whig (Tues., July 14, 1846)

Cantrell, Miss Lucinda married in Lauderdale County, Ala., to Mr.
Canney Coburn.

Cantrell, Major Ota married lately in Rutherford county, Tenn. to Miss
Nelton Cummins.
The Nashville Whig & Tennessee Advertiser (Aug. 8, 1818)

Cantrell, Mr. William of Sumner county married in Williamson county on
Wed. evening last to Miss Sarah Gillespie.
National Banner & Nashville Whig (Sat., July 22, 1826)

Cantrill, Mr. Zebulon P. of this town married in Sumner county on Tues.
last to Miss Mary M. Sanderson by Rev. Mr. Hume.
National Banner (Sat., May 16, 1829)

Capen, Mr. Edward married in Stonington to Mrs. Mary Allen.
Nashville Republican & State Gazette (Tues., Sept. 20, 1831)

Caperton, Miss Sally G. married to Maj. Archibald Woods.

Capps, Miss Mary T. married to Mr. Lewis Castleman.

Car, Miss Marilda married to Mr. William G. Barnett.

Card, Miss Susan married to Col. Thomas Westgate.

Carden, Miss Mary Ann married to Dr. John Park.

Cardwell, Miss Dorothy J. married to Mr. Warner T. Rucks.

Cardwell, Miss Elizabeth Susan married to Rev. Jacob Nulty.

Cardwell, Mr. John B. married in Bedford county to Miss Elizabeth Taylor.
National Banner & Nashville Advertiser (Fri., March 9, 1832)

Cardwell, Miss Maria W. married to Mr. Robert Jouralman.

Cardwell, Miss Mary B. married to Mr. Wilson J. Cage

Carey, James K. Esq. married at Columbus, Ohio to Miss Maria Lawson.
National Banner (Feb. 3, 1826)

Cargill, Mr. Henry A. of New York married to Miss Mary Payson Hays last
evening.
Nashville Republican (Thurs., Aug. 6, 1835)

Cargill, Mr. Henry A. of New York married on the 5th inst. by the Rev.
Dr. Weller to Miss Mary Payson Hays, daughter of Andrew Hays, Esq.,
attorney General of the State.
National Banner & Nashville Whig (Fri., Aug. 7, 1835)

Cargill, Mary married to Royal C. Perry, D. D.

Carlile, Mr. W. of Baton Rouge, La married in Nashville on Oct. 2 by
W. H. Hunt to Miss Ann C. Huston of Nashville.
Daily Republican Banner (Wed., Oct. 3, 1838)

Carlisle, Mr. William M. married in Chillicothe to Miss Margaret H.
Steele.
National Banner & Nashville Whig (Sat.,July 22, 1826)

Carlock, Mr. Frederick married in Madison County, Ala. to Miss Milley
Ellett.
National Banner (April 14, 1826)

Carlton, Mr. John of Iresden married to Miss Susan Adams in Gibson Co.
National Banner & Nashville Whig (Sat., April 19, 1828)

Carmack, Samuel W. Esq. married in Lincoln County, Tenn. to Miss Margaret
Greer.
National Banner & Nashville Whig (Wed., Nov. 26, 1834)

Carman, Mr. Charles married in Louisville, Ky. to Miss Lucia Pickering.
National Banner & Nashville Daily Advertiser (Sat., June 2, 1832)

Carnage, Miss Rebecca married to Mr. Robert Griffith.

Carnes, Mr. John married in New Orleans to Miss Louise Emeline Bertus.
National Banner & Nashville Daily Advertiser (Thurs., June 28, 1832)

Carnes, Mr. WM. B. Esq. married in Knox county to Miss Margaret Brown.
National Banner & Nashville Whig (Sat., July 14, 1827)

Carney, Mr. Edward married in Todd county, Ky. on the 25th by Rev.
Stewart to Miss Elizabeth Garth.
National Banner (Sat., April 11, 1829)

Carney, Miss Evelina married to Mr. Henley Moses.

Carney, Mr. Legrand H. married in Rutherford County to Miss Catherine
Lytle daughter of Major John Lytle.
National Banner & Nashville Whig (Fri., Aug. 5, 1831)

Carns, Miss Mary married to Mr. Joel Ozier.

Carpender, Miss Margaret married to Mr. Jackson Gray.

Carpender, Miss Prudence married to Mr. Leroy Carpender.

Carpender, Mr. Leroy married in Knox County to Miss Prudence Carpender.
National Banner (Sat., Dec. 26, 1829)

Carpenter, Mr. Wm. married in Maury County on the 31st ult. to Miss
M'Duffy.
National Banner & Nashville Whig (Thurs., Sept. 9, 1830)

Carper, Mr. Sampson married in this town on Friday last to Miss Lavina
Austin.
National Banner & Nashville Whig (Sat., Jan. 10, 1829)

Carper, Miss Susan married to Mr. Bennet H. Beasley.

Carr, Miss Caroline E. married to Mr. John Woods.

Carr, Mr. David married in Russellville, Ky. to Miss Milly Dunn.
National Banner & Nashville Advertiser (Tues., June 26, 1832)

Carr, Miss Mary married to Mr. Miles G. Gilbert.

Carr, Miss Matilda married to Mr. William G. Barnett.

Carr, Mr. N. E. married in Logan County, Ky. to Miss Emily Davidson.
National Banner & Nashville Advertiser (Thurs., Aug. 23, 1832)

Carr, Miss Nancy married to Mr. Thomas O. Parran.

Carr, Mr. Robert D. married to Miss Elizabeth Ann Lowe on Thursday 22d
inst. in Robertson Co., Tenn.
Nashville Republican (Tues., Jan. 27, 1835)

Carr, Miss Samantha E. married to Mr. James M. Whiteside.

Carr, Miss Susan H. married to Mr. David V. Robinson.

Carrick, Mr. Moses married to Miss Susan Sawson.

Carrick, Samuel (Rev.) married on Monday last (Jan. 27, 1794) to Miss
Annis McClellen.
Knoxville Gazette (Thurs., Jan. 30, 1794)

Carriger, Miss Elizabeth married to Mr. James W. Nelson.

Carriger, Mr. Isaac married near Jonesborough, Tenn. to Miss Phoebe
Nave, daughter of Mr. Abraham Nave, all of Carter County.
National Banner & Nashville Whig (Mon., Nov. 10, 1834)

Carroll, Miss Catherine married to Mr. Caleb C. Norvell.

Carroll, Mr. George W. married at Tuscumbia, Ala to Miss Lucy H.
Lockhart.
National Banner & Nashville Whig (Sat., Jan. 12, 1828)

Carroll, Mrs. Milderd married in Alabama to Major William Acklen, Sen.

Carroll, Mr. M'William married on Sunday evening the 20th inst. by the
Right Rev'd Bishop Flashia to Miss Martha H. F. Meany, both of Nashville.
The Nashville Gazette (Sat., May 26, 1821)

Carroll, Thomas B. Esq. of Nashville married on the 2nd inst. by Rev.
Dr. Edgar to Miss Eliza B. Ham, daughter of Mr. Samuel Ham of Davidson
County.
Nashville Whig (Wed., June 3, 1840)

(repeat of preceding)
Daily Republican Banner (Sat., June 6, 1840)

Carroll, Maj. William married on Thursday to Miss Cecilia Bradford,
daughter of Maj. Henry Bradford.
The Clarion & Tennessee Gazette (Sept. 14, 1813)

Carroll, Col. William married in Nashville to Miss Eliza Jane Breathitt.
Daily Republican Banner (Tues., Nov. 6, 1838)

Carroll, Col. William H. married in Nashville on Monday evening last by
the Rev. J. T. Edgar, D. D., to Miss Eliza J. Breathitt, all of Nashville.
Nashville Whig (Fri., Nov. 9, 1838).Dau.of late Dr. E. Breathitt.

(repeat of preceding)
Nashville Union (Wed., Nov. 7, 1838)

Carson, Mr. David married in Maury County to Miss Septemma M'Daniel.
National Banner & Nashville Whig (Fri., Dec. 10, 1830)

Carson, Miss Eleanor D. married to Mr. Wilson L. Martin.

Carson, Miss Elizabeth H. married to John J. Brown.

Carson, Mr. Isaac N. married on the 3d inst. by the Rev. S. E. Gardner
to Miss Ann L. Jenkins, daughter of the late John Jenkins, Esq., all
of Wilson County.
Nashville True Whig & Weekly Commercial Register (Sept. 13, 1850)

Carson, Mr. James married in Butler County, Ky. to Miss Elizabeth M.
Stroud.
National Banner & Nashville Whig (Mon., Jan. 17, 1831)

Carson, Mr. John B. married on Thursday the 21st inst. by the Rev. Jas.
S. Shields to Miss Elizabeth C. Walker, all of this vicinity.
The Western Weekly Review (Fri., April 29, 1831)

Carson, Mr. John B. married in Williamson County to Miss Elizabeth C.
Walker.
National Banner & Nashville Whig (Mon., May 2, 1831)

(repeat of preceding)
Nashville Republican & State Gazette (Tues., May 3, 1831)

Carson, Miss Margaret married to Mr. Daniel Coggins.

Carson, Miss Mary married to Mr. George W. Drake.

Carson, Mr. N. D. of Nashville married in Williamson county on the 11th
inst. by the Rev. W. A. Scott to Miss Martha Ann Bridges, daughter of
Capt. H. Bridges.
Daily Republican Banner (Mon., April 15, 1839)

Carson, Miss Rebecca married to Mr. Isaac Ballard.

Carson, Hon. Samuel P. married in Rutherford County to Miss S. C. Wilson.
Nashville Republican & State Gazette (Thurs., June 9, 1831)

Carson, Mr. William married in Williamson County to Miss Almira Wilson.
National Banner & Nashville Whig (Sat., Feb. 3, 1827)

Carter, Miss Amanda N. married to Mr. James M. Miller.

Carter, Dr. Belfield of Charlotte married to Miss Sarah Ann Marable,
daughter of Dr. John H. Marable in Montgomery County.
National Banner & Nashville Whig (Fri., March 19, 1830)

Carter, Miss Charlotte married to Mr. John Warren.

Carter, Miss Charlotte, married to Mr. Charles Wade.

Carter, Mr. Daniel F. of Nashville married in Robinson County, Tenn.
on 23d inst. by the Rev. J. T. Edgar to Miss Mary Jane Bunton, daughter
of John Buntin, Esq.
National Banner & Nashville Whig (Fri., March 3, 1837)

Carter, Miss Elizabeth married to James C. Rhea.

Carter, Mr. Fountain B. married to Miss Mary A. Atkinson in Williamson
County.
Nashville Whig (July 7, 1823)

Carter, Miss Frances married to Mr. Thomas Montgomery.

Carter, Miss Harriet married to John Andrews, Esq.

Carter, Mrs. Harriet H. married to Capt. Jonas J. Bell.

Carter, Miss Jane married to Mr. William G. Loyd.

Carter, Lieut. Lawrence F. married in Miller County, A. T. to Miss
Lucinda Smith.
National Banner & Nashville Whig (Sat., March 10, 1827)

Carter, Mr. Levi married in Henry County, Tenn. to Miss Mila Kennedy.
National Banner & Nashville Daily Advertiser (Wed., April 4, 1832)

Carter, Miss Martha married to Larkin B. Orr.

Carter, Miss Mary R. married to Mr. Benj. R. Saunders.

Carter, Mr. Miller married on Sunday morning the 22d June last to Miss Pheby Phillips both of Wilson County.
The Nashville Whig (July 7, 1817)

Carter, Miss Pamelia married in Lincoln County, Ky. to Mr. James Crow.

Carter, Miss Peggy married to Mr. Jesse Stout.

Carter, Miss Sally married to Mr. William Currier.

Carter, Mr. Samuel J. married in Davidson county to Miss Ann C. Vaulx, eldest daughter of William Vaulx on the 29th ult by the Rev. Mr. Whitsett.
National Banner & Nashville Advertiser (Mon., Dec. 3, 1832)

Carter, Miss Sarah Elizabeth married to Mr. Robert Rodes.

Carter, Mr. William W. married to Miss Narcissa Holland in Maury County.
National Banner & Nashville Whig (Mon., Sept. 26, 1831)

Cartwright, Miss Elizabeth married in Sumner County on 12th to Mr. J. L. Warner.

Cartwright, Mr. Jefferson married in Nashville on the 24th inst. by Rev. Givin to Miss Margaret Payne.
National Banner & Nashville Whig (Monday, March 28, 1831)

(repeat of preceding)
Nashville Republican & State Gazette (Tues., March 29, 1831)

Cartwright, Mr. Jno. married in Davidson County to Miss Catherine Connell.
Nashville Republican & State Gazette (Sat., March 31, 1832)

Cartwright, Justinian Esq. aged 78 married on the 4th inst. by the Rev. Mr. Wilcox to Mrs. Mary Harris aged 75, both of Caldwell County, Ky.
National Banner & Nashville Whig (Wed., Nov. 24, 1830)

Cartwright, Miss Mahalia married to Mr. Washington Campbell.

Cartwright, Mr. Marcus L. married on the 13th inst. by the Rev. Mr. Schacht to Miss Sarah Ann Few, all of Nashville.
The Politician & Weekly Nashville Whig (Fri., Feb. 18, 1848)

Cartwright, Miss Pembroke married to Mr. Thomas Watkins.

Cartwrite, Miss Eliza married to Mr. Robert P. Estes.

Carty, Mr. Joseph R. married in Simpson Co., Ky. to Miss Martha See.
National Banner & Nashville Whig (Sat., July 14, 1827)

Carty, Mr. William married in Fayetteville, Tenn. to Miss Ann Russell.
National Banner & Nashville Daily Advertiser (Mon., May 12, 1834)

Caruthers, Miss Ara C. married to Mr. John C. Young.

Caruthers, Miss E. married to Mr. Richard G. Looney.

Caruthers, Miss Elizabeth married to Col. J. D. Love.

Caruthers, James Esq., Attorney at Law of the Western district, married on the 16th to Miss Frances M'Corry, daughter of Maj. Tho. M'Corry, of Anderson County.
Nashville Whig (Oct., 4, 1824)

Caruthers, John P. Esq. of Memphis, Tenn. married on the 24th at Hemphill, Christian Co., Ky. by the Rev. Samuel White to Miss Elizabeth R. McNeil, daughter of Mr. Malcom McNeil. Nashville Whig (Aug. 22, 1846)

Caruthers, Miss Nancy married to Mr. George K. Morton.

Caruthers, Robert L. Esq. married in Sumner County to Miss Sarah Saunders.
National Banner & Nashville Whig (Sat., Jan. 20, 1827)

Carven, Miss Martha H. married to Mr. Pleasent M. Lea.

Cary, Mr. Thomas married in Ross Co., Ohio, to Miss Mary Price.
National Banner & Nashville Whig (Sat., Dec. 30, 1826)

Cary, William Esq. married in Campbell County to Miss Melinda E. Wheeler, daughter of Thomas Wheeler, Esq.
National Banner & Nashville Advertiser (Tues., Dec. 18, 1832)

Case, Matilda married to Mr. Hardy Robinson.

Caseday, Mr. Alexander A. married in Nashville last evening by the Rev. Mr. Jennings to Miss Emeline Cantrell, daughter of Stephen Cantrell, Esq.
National Banner & Nashville Whig (Fri., Aug, 5, 1831)

Casey, Miss Delelah married to Mr. John Kimbrough.

Casey, Miss Rebecca married to Mr. James Jones.

Cash, Miss Harriet H. married to Mr. John R. H. Acklen.

Cash, Thomas W. Esq. of Nashville married at Franklin on the 29th ult.by the Rev. Mr. Otey to Miss Virginia Dudley, daughter of Col. Dudley of Franklin.
National Banner & Nashville Whig (Thurs., Sept. 2, 1830)

Cashburn, Mr. John A. married in Madison County to Miss Elizabeth W.Cole.
Nashville Whig (Tues., March 31, 1846)

Cassander, Miss Mary married to Mr. J. F. Callaway.

Cassedy, Miss Rebecca married to Mr. John Parkinson.

Cassel, Dr. John T. married in Fayette Co., Ky. to Mrs. Sarah Weagley.
National Banner & Nashville Whig (Mon., Dec. 27, 1830)

Cassilly, Mr. Philip of St. Louis married in Cincinnati to Miss Mary Ann M'Kenna.
National Banner & Nashville Whig (Fri., Dec. 3, 1830)

Cassitt, Maj. George married at Lagrange, Tenn. to Miss Lucy Mann, on the 12th inst.
Nashville Republican (Tues., May 19, 1835)

Casswell, Mr. Charles married at Little Rock to Miss Mary Bibb.
National Banner & Nashville Daily Advertiser (Fri., Aug. 16, 1833)

Castern, Miss Mary married to Mr. Tho. Palmer.

Castleman, David Esq. married in Fayette Co. to Miss Virginia Harrison.
Nashville Whig (Dec. 6, 1824)

Castleman, Mr. Lewis of Nashville married on the 23rd inst. by the Rev. J. S. Malone to Miss Mary T. Capps.
Nashville True Whig & Weekly Commercial Register (Fri., May 31, 1850)

Castons, Mr. E. married in Amite County, Mississippi to Miss Amanda Tolbert.
National Banner (Jan. 27, 1826)

Cate, Mr. John married in Jefferson County to Miss Martha Henry.
National Banner & Nashville Daily Advertiser (Mon, Jan. 14, 1833)

Cate, Miss Matilda married to Mr. Hardy Robinson.

Cates, Miss Susan J. married to Mr. Henry C. Bell.

Cathey, Miss Alice married to Dr. Eli Askew.

Cathey, Miss Mary married to Mr. George C. Armstrong.

Cathey, Mr. William married in Williamson County to Miss Margaret Calhoun.
National Banner & Nashville Whig (Mon., April 13, 1835)

Catron, John Esq., attorney at law of Nashville, married on Thursday evening last by the Rev. Mr. Campbell to Miss Matilda Childress, daughter of John Childress, deceased, of this vicinity.
Nashville Gazette (Jan. 27, 1821)

(repeat of preceding)
The Clarion & Tennessee Gazette (Jan. 30, 1821)

Caughran, Mr. Sam'l T. married in Maury County to Miss Rachael Watson.
National Banner & Nashville Whig (Fri., March 26, 1830)

Cauley, Miss America married in Garrard Co. Ky. to Mr. Reuben Price.

Cavender, Mr. A. L.married in Lewis County to Miss Mary J. Bynum.
Nashville Whig (Tues., May 5, 1846)

Cawley, Mr. James married in Nashville on Tuesday evening Oct. 1st by John Wright Esq. to Miss Nancy Maddin.
National Banner & Nashville Daily Advertiser (Thurs., Oct. 3,1833)

Cayce, Miss Caroline married to Mr. Henry Jeffreys.

Cayce, Mr. Joseph F. married in Nashville on 17th inst. by the Rev. Mr. Smith to Miss Isabella R. White.
National Banner & Nashville Daily Advertiser (Thurs., Oct. 18, 1832)

(repeat of preceding)
The Western Weekly Review (Fri., Oct. 19, 1832)

Cecil, Mr. James H. married on Thursday 21st inst. at the residence of Mr. Samuel Ingram, Maury county, by the Rev. Richard P. Miles, Bishop of Nashville to Miss Julia E. Ingram.
The Politician & Weekly Nashville Whig (Fri., Oct. 29, 1847)

Center, Miss Caroline married to Capt. Samuel B. Tate.

Center, Miss Eveline married to Mr. John Suddeth.

Cerre, Miss Catharine married to Mr. Pierre D. Papin.

Certain, Mrs. Dorcas married to Mr. James Givens.

Chadwell, Mr. Thomas merchant of Nashville married yesterday morning by the Rev. Dr. Howell to Miss Mary Ann Childress, eldest daughter of Edward Childress, Esq., of Davidson County.
Nashville Whig (Thurs., July 23, 1846)

Chaffin, Miss Pernetti married to Mr. Robert McMinn.

Chaffin, Mr. Prestley T. married in Maury Co., Tenn to Miss Eveline Coke.
National Banner & Nashville Whig (Fri., May 8, 1835)

Chaffin, Mr. T. married in Hardeman county to Miss Jennette Riddle, daughter of Benjamin Riddle, Esq.
National Banner & Nashville Daily Advertiser (Sat., Aug. 7, 1832)

Chairs, Mr. J. W. Merchant of Spring Hill married on Tuesday 1st day of

May by the Rev. Dr. Harlin to Miss Susan Pointer of Maury County.
Daily Republican Banner (Mon., May 7, 1838)

Chalmers, Miss Mary of Nashville married to Mr. James Hood.

Chamberlain, Miss Eleanor married to Mr. Nathan Mixer.

Chamberlain, Miss Elizabeth married to Mr. Joseph Taylor.

Chambers, Miss Blanche C. married to Mr. Thomas Shelton.

Chambers, David S. Esq. of Louisville married in Lexington, Ky. to
Miss Emily Postlethwait.
National Banner & Nashville Whig (Sat., June 9, 1827)

Chambers, John Esq. married to Mrs. Mary Tooley in Smith County.
National Banner (March 31, 1826)

Chambers, John R. married in Jefferson County, Tenn. to Miss Susan Ann
Huffar.
National Banner & Nashville Whig (Fri., Jan. 23, 1835)

Chambers, Miss R. S. married to Mr. Joe Shelby.

Chambers, Miss Sarah married to Mr. William G. Morris.

Chambliss, Miss Martha married to Mr. Augusta Cook.

Champ, Mr. Robert P. married in Nashville on Sunday morning last 26th
ult. to Miss Emily J. Singleton, all of Nashville.

The Christian Record (Sat., April 1, 1848)

Champion, Mr. Henry B. of Hartfort, Ct., married on Thursday 9th inst.
by the Rev. J. B. McFerrin to Miss Catherine C. Singleton, daughter of
Moses Singleton, Esq. of Nashville.
Nashville Whig (Sat., June 11, 1842)

Champion, Mr. Henry W. married in Princeton, Ky. to Miss Saran Ann
Wigginton on the 15th Jan.
Nashville Republican (Thurs., Feb. 5, 1835)

(repeat of preceding)
National Banner & Nashville Whig (Fri., Feb. 6, 1835)

Chancellor, Mr. William married in Macon County, Ky. to Miss Nancy Glenn.
National Banner & Nashville Whig (Sat., Dec. 16, 1826)

Chandler, Miss married to Mr. Preston Ayles.

Chandler, Miss Dorcas married to Mr. Edward George.

Chandler, James M. married in Williamson County to Miss Jane C. Price.
The Western Weekly Review (Fri., Dec. 14, 1832)

Chandler, Mrs. Susan P. C. married to Mr. William Brooks.

Chaney, Donora C., married to Granville P. Smith.

Chaney, Mr. Hampton J. married on the 4th inst. by the Rev. Mr. Pitts
to Miss Mary E. Smith, daughter of Mr. G. S. Smith.
National Banner & Nashville Daily Advertiser (Sat., Sept. 6, 1834)

Chaney, Mrs. Mary married to Col. A. W. Johnson.

Chaney, Miss Salley married to Mr. Samuel H. Dodson.

Chaple, Miss Parthena married to Mr. Charles Irvine.

Chapline, Miss Helen married to Mr. John B. Curd.

Chapman, Miss Acenith married to Mr. Henry D. Warnick.

Chapman, Mr. Benjamin married in Sumner County to Miss Rebecca Bull.
National Banner & Nashville Whig (Sat., Aug. 25, 1827)

Chapman, Miss Evelina married to Mr. John Purdy.

Chapman, Dr. John R. of Mississippi married on Tuesday the 10th inst.
by the Rev. J. T. Wheat to Miss Sarah Cheatham, daughter of Leonard P.
Cheatham, Esq. of Davidson County.
Nashville Whig (Thurs., Dec. 12, 1844)

Chapman, John S. Esq. of Frankford, Ky. married in Prince William Co.,
Va., to Miss Matilda L. A. Chapman
National Banner (April 7, 1826)

Chapman, Miss Mary R. married to Rev. S M. Williams.

Chapman, Miss Matilda L. A. married to Mr. John S. Chapman, Esq.

Chapman, Mr. Philip married in Sumner County to Miss Celia C. Hamilton.
National Banner & Nashville Daily Advertiser (Tues., March 11, 1834)

Chapman, Robert H. Esq. of Green County, Ala., married at Ashville, N.
C. to Miss Clarissa Evelina Chunn.
National Banner & Nashville Whig (Mon, Nov. 14, 1831)

Chapouil, Mr. Anthony married in Nashville to Miss Mary Humerickhouse.
Nashville Republican & State Gazette (Sat., March 10, 1832)

(repeat of preceding)
National Banner & Nashville Advertiser (Mon., March 12, 1832)

Chappell, Miss Eugenia married to Mr. A. P. Calhoun.

Chardovoyne, Mr. William V. married to Miss Martha Watkins, in Courtland,
Ala.
Nashville Republican & State Gazette (Mon., July 30, 1832)

Charles, Miss Ellen married to Mr. Diodate L. Arnold.

Charles, Miss Eliza married to Mr. John Kerr.

Charless, Mr. Joseph Jun. married in St. Louis to Miss Charlotte T.
Blow, daughter of Mr. Peter Blow.
National Banner & Nashville Whig (Mon., Nov. 28, 1831)

Charleston, Miss Agalae married to Dr. Thomas Hunt.

Charlton, Miss Ann married to Mr. Jacob Greenhalgh.

Chase, J. P. of Tennessee married in Greenville, S. C. on the 17th May
to Mary E. Bowen, daughter of Capt. George Bowen, of Waterloo, S. C.
National Banner & Nashville Whig (Fri., June 10, 1836)

Chase, Maj. John of Jefferson married in Knox County to Miss Nancy
Campbell.
National Banner & Nashville Whig (Sat., April 21, 1827)

Chatard, Frederick of the U. S. Navy married Miss Catherine Tierman in
Baltimore.
Nashville Republican & State Gazette (Sat., Oct. 29, 1831)

Chears, Miss Nancy R. married to Mr. Constantine B. Perkins.

Cheatham, Miss Amanda married to Robert J. Rivers, Esq.

Cheatham, Mr. D. S. of Virginia married in Logan Co., Ky. to Miss
Mary Simpson.
National Banner & Nashville Whig (Sat., Oct. 7, 1826)

Cheatham, Edward Esq. of Springfield married at Mansfield in this
vicinity last evening by the Rev. J. T. Wheat to Ellen Foster, daughter
of the Hon. Ephraim H. Foster.
Nashville Whig (Wed., Oct. 20, 1841)

Cheatham, Miss Elizabeth married in Robertson County to Mr. William K.
Turner.
National Banner & Nashville Whig (Sat., Aug. 12, 1826)

Cheatham, John A. Esq. married on Wed. evening last by the Rev. Mr.
Dobbs to Mrs. Ann Bass of this county.
Nashville Whig (May 24, 1824)

Cheatham, Leonard Esq., attorney at Law, married on the 11th inst. by
Mr. Hume to Miss Elizabeth Robertson, daughter of Jonathan Robertson,
deceased.
The Nashville Whig (Sept. 15, 1817)

Cheatham, Miss Martha Ann married in Florence to Dr. Niel Rowell.

Cheatham, Miss Martha married to Mr. John Keeble.

Cheatham, Miss Martha married to James Howard Esq.

Cheatham, Miss Martha Ann married to Mr. Cosby D. Johnson.

Cheatham, Miss Martha Washington married to John W. Walker, Esq.

Cheatham, Miss Mary married to Mr. Miles H. Bradford.

Cheatham, Miss Mary A. married to Doctor Edward Marshall.

Cheatham, Miss Medora married to Samuel J. Riggs, Esq.

Cheatham, Miss Sarah married to Dr. John R. Chapman.

Cheatham, Mr. Richard of Springfield married on Wednesday the 25th
inst. to Miss Susannah Saunders daughter of Major Edward Saunders, of
Maury County.
The Nashville Whig (Sept. 29, 1817)

Cheatham, Miss Olivia D. married to Maj. Granville A. Pillow.

Cheatham, Miss Susan L. married to William L. Foster, Esq.

Cheek, Mr. John married in Maury County to Miss Elizabeth Ryon.
National Banner & Nashville Whig (Mon., Oct. 4, 1830)

Cheek, Mr. S. R. married on Sunday the 13th by H. Towns, Esq. to Miss
Elizabeth Harris.
Daily Republican Banner (Thurs., April 19, 1838)

Cheeseman, Miss Charlotte married to Mr. John Latheret.

Chely, Miss Cassy married to Mr. William Brownfield.

Chenault, Miss Louisa W. married to Mr. James R. M'Gavock.

Cheney, Mr. Hampton J. married in Davidson County to Miss Mary E. Smith
on Thursday, 4th inst.
Nashville Republican & State Gazette (Sat., Sept. 6, 1834)

Cheney, Miss Leonora married to Dr. Granville P. Smith.

Chenoweth, Miss Ann Maria married to Mr. John Hickey.

Cherry, Miss Louama married to Mr. Hiram Partee.

Cherry, Mr. Pierce W. married on Tuesday the 20th inst. by the Rev. Peter
Fuqua to Miss Nancy A. Gleaves, all of Davidson County.
Nashville Whig (Thurs., Jan. 22, 1846)

Cherry, Col. Willes W. married in Lawrenceburg to Miss Frances Weir.
National Banner & Nashville Whig (Sat., Sept. 6, 1828)

Chester, Mr. John K. of Jackson married in Madison County to Miss Julia
S. Bradley.
National Banner (Sat., Aug. 8, 1829)

Chester, Mrs. Sophia married to Allen A. Hall.

Chester, Doctor Wm. P. of Carthage married on the 12th inst. to Miss
Sophia Hogg of Lebanon.
Nashville Whig (Feb., 23, 1824)

Chew, Mr. Henry M. of Prince George's County, Md., married in Georgetown
on the 15th inst. by the Rev. Mr. Brook to Elizabeth Ann Haw, youngest
daughter of John S. Haw, deceased.
National Banner & Nashville Daily Advertiser (Mon., Feb. 4, 1833)

Childress, Miss Ann Maria married to Morgan W. Brown, Esq.

Childress, Miss Ann P. married to Mr. Eramus Watker.

Childress, Mrs. Delina married to Mr. William H. Marshall.

Childress , Mr. Ed. H. married on Thursday 21st inst. by Dr. William H.
Wharton to Miss Elmira Read all of Davidson County.
the Politician & Weekly Nashville Whig (Fri., Oct. 29, 1847)

Childress, Edwin H. of Huntsville (AT.) married on Tuesday evening last
by the Rev. Mr. Hume to Miss Emily D. Hewett, daughter of Robert Hewett,
Esq., of this county.
the Nashville Whig & Tenn. Advertiser (Nov. 10, 1817)

Childress, Miss Elizabeth married to V. K. Stevenson.

Childress, Mr. George of Springfield married Miss Rebecca J. Murdaugh,
in Robertson County.
National Banner & Nashville Whig (Wed., Sept. 7, 1831)

Childress, Geo. C. Esq. married in this town Thursday evening 12th inst.
to Miss Margaret Vance.
National Banner & Nashville Whig (Sat., June 14, 1828)

Childress, Geo. C., Esq. married on the 12th inst. by the Rev. Mr. Edgar
to Miss Rebecca Jennings of Nashville.
Nashville Republican (Wed., Dec. 13, 1836)

(repeat of preceding)
National Banner & Nashville Whig (Dec., 14, 1836)

Childress, Mr. Gideon married in Logan Co., Ky. to Miss Martha M'Carlev
National Banner & Nashville Whig (Sat., March 31, 1827)

Childress, Mr. John aged 84 married in Warren County to Miss Catharine
T. Lewis aged 78.
National Banner & Nashville Whig (Sat., Jan. 27, 1827)

Childress, John Esq. married in Nashville to Miss Mary A. Goode by the
Rev. Mr. Hume.
National Banner & Nashville Advertiser (Thurs., Oct. 25, 1832)

Childress, Maj. John W. married in Rutherford County to Miss Sarah
Williams, daughter of Mr. Elisha Williams.
National Banner & Nashville Advertiser (Sat., Jan.7, 1832)

Childress, Miss Margaret married to Mr. John W. Martin.

Childress, Miss Margaret J. married to Mr. John W. Martin.

Childress, Miss Mary Ann married to Mr. Thomas Chadwell.

Childress, Miss Matilda married to John Catron, Esq.

Childress, Miss Paralee married to Mr. James J. Hanna.

Childress, Col. Robertson married in Little Rock to Miss Lorena Hall,
by the Rev. Moore.
Nashville Republican (Sat., July 25, 1835)

Childress, Col. Robertson married in Little Rock on the 14th July to
Miss Laurina Hall, daughter of S. S. Hall, Esq. of Arkansas Territory.
National Banner & Nashville Whig (Mon., Aug 3, 1835)

Childress, Samuel L. Esq., attorney at law married in Kingston, on the
7th inst., to Miss Ann Barry.
National Banner & Nashville Daily Advertiser (Wed., Jan. 30, 1833)

Childress, Miss Sarah of Murfreesborough married to Col. James K. Polk.

Childress, Dr. Stephen S. married in Madison County to Miss Drucilla
C. Dyer.
National Banner & Nashville Whig (Sat., March 10, 1827)

Childress, Miss Telid Ann married to Mr. Shadrack Kirkland.

Childress, Mr. Thomas J. married in Williamson County to Miss Lucindia
Walker by Rev. Mr. McConnico.
National Banner (Jan. 13, 1826)

Childress, W. married in Maury County to Miss Eliza Davis.
National Banner & Nashville Daily Advertiser (Thurs., April 5, 1832)

Childress, Mr. William married in Logan Co., Ky. to Miss Elizabeth
Miller.
National Banner & Nashville Whig (Sat., July 22, 1826)
Childs, Miss Mary married to Walter Lowrie, Esq.
Childs, Miss Maria O. married to Elijah Bigelow, Esq.

Chiles, Miss married in Clark Co., Ky. to Dr. James Taggart.

Chiles, Miss married in Anderson County to Mr. James Montgomery.

Chilton, Miss Emma M. married to Mr. Henry A. Fawlkes.

Chilton , Mr. James M. married on Sunday the 20th by Dr. W. H. Wharton,
to Miss Caroline M. Smith, all of Nashville.
Nashville Whig (Thurs., May 4, 1843)

Chilton, Miss Mary married to Dr. John C. Boyd.

Chilton, Miss Mary Jane married to Dr. John C. Boyd.

Chinn, Mr. Bolin married in Henry County, Tenn. since the first of Jan.
to Miss Miry Moore.
National Banner & Nashville Whig (Fri., Feb. 13, 1835)

Chinn, Mr. Morgan B. married in Franklin Co., Ky. to Miss Eliza Ann Macy.
National Banner (Sat., Aug. 29, 1829)

Chisolm, Miss Elizabeth married to Mr. John Sommerville.

Chisolm, Mr. Rufus K. married in Nashville on the 6th inst. by the Rev.
Mr. Pitts to Miss Emeline T. Nugent, daughter of Co. Nugent.
National Banner & Nashville Daily Advertiser (Tues., Feb. 11, 1834)

(repeat of preceding)
Nashville Republican & State Gazette (Tues., Feb. 11, 1834)

Choteau, Mr. Henry P. married at St. Louis to Miss Clemence Coursault.
National Banner & Nashville Whig (July 28, 1827)

Chowning, Miss Sarah J. married to Mr. William Roberts.

Chrisman, Martha married to William Stephens.

Christian, Miss Amanda married to Rev. William Potter.

Christian, Mr. Frederick married at Memphis to Miss Frances N. Robertson.
National Banner & Nashville Whig (Sat., Dec. 1, 1827)

Christian, Mr. George, son of George Christian, Esq. married at Hilham
to Miss Celina Fisk, eldest daughter of Moses Fisk, Esq.
National Banner (Sat. Aug. 15, 1829)

Christian, Miss Jane Maria married to George MacKenzie MacGregor.

Christian, Mr. John a blind alma seller aged 75 married to Miss Nelly
Palmer aged 64, at the Fayette poor-house near Lexington, KY.
National Banner & Nashville Whig (June 14, 1826)

Christman, Miss Elizabeth married lately in Woodford Co., Ky., to Mr.
James C. Lee.

Christmas, Mr. Richard married in Williamson County to Miss Emeline Smith.
National Banner & Nashville Daily Advertiser (Tues., Sept. 25, 1832)

Christopher, Mr. Andrew married in Lincoln Co., Ky. to Miss Sarah Robinson.
National Banner & Nashville Whig (Sat., Jan. 6, 1827)

Christopher, Mr. Thomas H. married in Madison Co., Ky. to Miss Mary Ann
Irvine.
National Banner (Feb. 10, 1826)

Christopher, Mr. William married in Maury Co., to Miss Margaret Smith.
National Banner & Nashville Daily Advertiser (Wed., March 6, 1833)

Christy, Mr. John H., Published of the Highland Messenger, married in
Ashville, N. C. by the Rev. McAnally to Miss A. Roberts, daughter of
Lawyer Roberts of Ashville.
Nashville Whig (Thurs., Sept. 8, 1842)

Christy, Mr. William T. of Murfreesborough married at Knoxville to. Miss
Ellen P. Morgan, daughter of Mr. Calvin Morgan.
National Banner & Nashville Daily Advertiser (Mon., July 23, 1832)

Chunn, Miss Clarissa Evelina married to Robert H. Chapman, Esq.

Church, Dr. Edward B. married in Lexington, Ky. to Miss Maria Innes
Bodley, daughter of Gen. Thomas Bodley.
National Banner & Nashville Daily Advertiser (Tues., March 19, 1833)

Church, Mr. J. M. married in Williamson County to Miss Sarah A. Sattef-
field.
Nashville Whig (Sat., July 11, 1846)

Church, Miss Mary E. married to Mr. John M. Younger.

Church, Mr. Robert married in Maury County to Miss Mary M. Smith.
National Banner & Nashville Whig (Mon., July 12, 1830)

Church, Mr. William married in Wilkinson Co., Miss., to Miss Jane Wilson.
National Banner (June 3, 1826)

Churchill, Warden P. Esq. married at Louisville, Ky. to Miss Mary J. Prather.
National Banner (Sat., May 2, 1829)

Churchman, Miss Sarah married to Mr. Vaden Perrin.

Cisna, Mr. William married in Nashville to Miss Mary Bennett.
National Banner & Nashville Daily Advertiser (Fri., Oct. 12, 1832)

Clack, Miss Matilda V. married to Maj. William S. McEwen.

Clack, Miss Parmelia married to Mr. John W. Goode.

Claiborne, Miss Charlotte Virginia married to J. B. Latrobe, Esq.

Claiborne, Ferdinand L. Esq. married at Natchez to Miss Courtney Ann Terrell.
National Banner & Nashville Whig (Sat., Aug. 9, 1828)

Claiborne, Mr. Henry L. of Nashville, Tenn. married in Christian Co., Ky. on the 11th inst. by Rev. W. D. Jones to Miss Lucy Ann Steele.
Nashville Whig (Thurs., Nov. 21, 1844)

Claiborne, Miss Martha married in Gibson County to Mr. Maxwell.
National Banner & Nashville Whig (Sat., Aug. 11, 1827)

Claiborne, Miss Mary married to Mr. Abraham P. Maury.

Claiborne. Mr. Thomas B. married in this county on the 5th inst. by the Rev. Mr. Hume to Miss Mary Maxwell.
National Banner & Nashville Whig (Sat., March 22, 1828)

Claiburn, Miss Eliza married to Henry R. Browning.

Clanton, Mr. Mathew married in Madison County to Miss Eliza Wilson.
National Banner & Nashville Whig (Sat., March 22, 1828)

Clardy, Mr. Peter married in Bedford County to Miss Eliza Moody.
Nashville Republican & State Gazette (Wed., Jan. 16, 1833)

(repeat of preceding)
National Banner & Nashville Daily Advertiser (Thurs., Jan. 17, 1833)

Clark, Alexr. R. married in Williamson County to Lucy Young.
National Banner & Nashville Daily Advertiser (Mon., Aug. 26, 1833)

Clark, Miss Alphia G. J. married in Christian Co., Ky. to William Ware.

Clark, Mrs. Ann S.married to Maj. Wm. Sebree.

Clark, Mr. Bantley M. married in Rutherford County to Miss Pamelia Anderson, daughter of Maj. Nelson Anderson.
National Banner (Jan. 27, 1826)

Clark, Mr. Benjamin P. merchant of the firm of Anderson & Clark, married on the 20th inst. by the Rev. Dr. Edgar to Miss Henrietta H. Morgan, second daughter of Samuel D. Morgan, Esq., all of Nashville.
Nashville Whig (Sat., May 23, 1846)

Clark, Miss Caroline married to Mr. Hickman Slayton.

Clark, Edwin T. Esq. married near Helena Ark. to Miss Harriet Stanford.
National Banner & Nashville Whig (Sat., May 12, 1827)

Clark, Miss Eliza married to Mr. John W. Locke.

Clark, Miss Elizabeth J. married to Mr. William Wood.

Clark, Miss Hester married to Mr. Thomas Moon.

Clark, Mr. Hezekiah aged 21 married in Burlingham, New York on the 3rd
inst. by the Rev. J. Langhead to Mrs. Ann Perkins, aged 42.
National Banner & Nashville Whig (Fri., March 6, 1835)

Clark, James P., attorney at Law, married on the 27th inst. at Knoxville,
by the Rev. Mr. Anderson to Miss Susan M'Corry, daughter of Thomas M'-
Corry Esq. of Knoxville.
The Clarion & Tennessee Gazette (July 18, 1820)

Clark, Miss Louisa married in Knox Co. to Col. John B. Rogers.

Clark, Miss Malinda D. married to Gen. William McQueston.

Clark, Miss Mary A. married to Mr. David W. Parish.

Clark, Miss Mary L. married to Mr. John W. Hill.

Clark, Miss Matilda married to Mr. Geo. Hickman.

Clark, Mr. Micajah married in Warren Co., Ky. to Miss Jane Hagerman.
National Banner & Nashville Whig (Fri., July 22, 1831)

Clark, Miss Polly married to Mr. John Keel, Jr.

Clark, Mr. Richard of Davidson County married to Miss Susan Clark of
Davidson County, on the 4th inst.
Nashville Republican (Tues., Jan. 19, 1836)

Clark, Miss Sally H. married to Mr. John C. Ward.

Clark, Miss Sally S. married to Dr. Archibald Rogers.

Clark, Miss Sarah M. married to Mr. Oliver J. Lindsev.

Clark, Miss Sophia married to Mr. Wm. Crosson.

Clark, Miss Susan married to Mr. William Wilson.

Clark, Miss Susan married to Mr. Richard Clark.

Clark, Miss Susan married to Mr. William W. Ellis.

Clark, Mr. Thomas married in Madison County, Ala. to Miss Hester Moon.
National Banner & Nashville Whig (Sat., March 17, 1827)

Clark, Mr. Thomas Jr. married in Christian Co., Ky. to Mrs. Frazier.
National Banner & Nashville Whig (Fri., Nov. 18, 1831)

Clark, Mr. Thomas C. of Crab Orchard married to Miss Elvira Moman of
Davidson County on Sunday 8, inst.
Impartial Review & Cumberland Repository (Sat., June 14, 1806)

Clark, Mr. Wm. married in Williamson County by the Rev. Thomas D. Porter
to Miss Ann B. Scales, daughter of Mr. Joseph Scales.
National Banner & Nashville Whig (Sat., May 19, 1827)

Clark, Mr. William of Louisville, Ky. married to Miss Priscilla Randolph.
National Banner & Nashville Advertiser (Wed., Jan. 4, 1832)

Clark, Mr. Wm. married in Cincinnati to Miss Lucy Ann Hicks.
National Banner & Nashville Advertiser (Thurs., Jan. 19, 1832)

Clark, Mr. William A. married in Logan Co., Ky. to Miss Mahala Roberts.
National Banner & Nashville Daily Advertiser (Mon., April 30, 1832)

Clark, Mr. William L. married in Giles County on Tuesdav the 27th ult.
to Miss Lucinda Buford.
National Banner & Nashville Whig (Mon., Nov. 8, 1830)

Clark, Mr. Sm. S. F. married in Sumner County to Miss Emma Douglass.
Nashville Republican & State Gazette (Thurs., April 2, 1831)

Clark, Mr. Wm. S. F. married in Sumner County to Miss Emma Douglass,
daughter of Mr. Reuben Douglass.
National Banner & Nashville Whig (Mon, April 4, 1831)

Clarke, Miss Eliza married in Winchester, Franklin Co., to Andrew Campbell.

Clarke, Mr. Lorenzo N. married at Little Rock, Ark. to Miss Arabella
Jane Bertrand.
National Banner (Sat., Nov. 21, 1829)

Clarke, Miss Nancy married to Mr. William Hamilton.

Clarkson, Mr. Robert B. married to Miss Maria J. Booker, in Tipton Co.
National Banner & Nashville Daily Advertiser (Mon., Sept. 9, 1833)

Clary, Mr. Urial A. married near Helena, Ark. to Miss Adelia Lattemore.
National Banner & Nashville Whig (Sat.,May 12, 1827)

Claxton, Miss Martha married to Mr. James Lively.

Claxton, Miss Martha married to Mr. James M. Williams.

Claxton, Miss Nancy married to Mr. Thomas Hefflin.

Clay, Miss Ann married to Mr. W. L. Earheart.

Clay, Mr. Cassius M. of Madison County married in Fayette Co., Ky. to
Miss Mary Jane Warfield, daughter of Dr. Elisha Warfield.
National Banner & Nashville Daily Advertiser (Thurs., Feb. 28, 1833)

Clay, Miss Frances married to Mr. John Stratton.

Clay, Henry Jr. married in Bourbon Co., Ky. to Miss Elizabeth Scott.
National Banner & Nashville Whig (Sat., Sept. 2, 1826)

Clay, Mr. Henry Jun. Esq., son of the Hon. Henry Clay, married at
Louisville, Ky. to Miss Mary Julia Prather, daughter of the late Thomas
Prather, Esq.
National Banner & Nashville Daily Advertiser (Tues., Oct. 16, 1832)

Clay, J. W. Esq. married in Davidson County to Miss Bethienia Walker,
on Thursday.
Nashville Republican (Sat., March 12, 1836)

Clay, Mr. Joseph W. of Virginia married in this county on Thursday evening last to Miss Elizabeth V. Harding.
National Banner & Nashville Whig (Sat., April 28, 1827)

Clay, Mr. Joseph W. married in Nashville yesterday to Miss Sarah Fletcher
daughter of Thomas B. Fletcher, Esq.
Daily Republican Banner (Wed., Jan. 1, 1840)

Clay, Miss Margaret married at Cincinnati, Ohio to Mr. Israel Bissell.

Clay, Miss Maria married to Mr. William Shealds.

Clay, Miss Martha married to Mr. Robert I. Moore.

Clay, Porter Esq. married in Franklin Co., Ky. to Mrs. Elizabeth Hardin,
relict of the late Gen. Martin D. Hardin.
National Banner & Nashville Whig (Tues., April 27, 1830)

Clay, Mrs. Sarah married to Mr. Jeptha Dudley.

Clay, Dr. William married in Tuscumbia, Ala., to Miss Alsy Johnston.
National Banner & Nashville Whig (Sat., Dec. 13, 1828)

Claybrooke, Mr. John S. married in Williamson County to Miss Mary A.
Perkins.
National Banner & Nashville Daily Advertiser (Thurs., May 1, 1834)

Clayter, Mr. Carter married in Rutherford County to Miss Elizabeth
Norman.
National Banner & Nashville Daily Advertiser (Sat., Feb., 23, 1833)

Clayton, Mr. David married in Knoxville to Miss Caroline Mason.
National Banner & Nashville Daily Advertiser (Mon., June 17, 1833)

Clayton, Miss Margaret married to Mr. Jeremiah Hughes.

Clayton, Mr. Robert married in Knox Co., Tenn. to Miss Elizabeth Hemmel.
National Banner & Nashville Daily Advertiser (Mon., Sept. 2, 1833)

Clayton, Mr. Solomon married in Knox Co. to Miss Minerva Jane Tipton.
National Banner & Nashville Advertiser (Mon., Nov. 12, 1832)

(repeat of preceding)
National Banner & Nashville Daily Advertiser (Nov. 23, 1832)

Cleage, Mr. David, Cashier of Branch, Planters Bank of Tennessee, at
Athens, married in Bledsoe County, to Miss Martha M. Bridgman.
Nashville Whig (Tues., July 14, 1846)

Clear, Miss Lucinda married to Mr. Henry Pyle.

Cleaveland, Mr. H. B., formerly of South Carolina, married in Maury
Co., Tenn. to Miss Sarah E. Stone.
National Banner & Nashville Daily Advertiser (Wed., Sept. 25, 1833)

Clegg, Miss Jane married to Joseph L. Woods.

Cleland, Mr. Horatio, merchant of this town, married to Miss Sally Irvine
of Mercer Co., Ky.
Nashville Whig (Wed., Dec. 20, 1814)

Clem, Miss Sarah married to Mr. James McLin.

Clement, Miss Martha M. married to Mr. John M. Barnett.

Clements, Mr. Aaron married in Henry County to Miss Nancy Yarborough.
National Banner & Nashville Advertiser (Tues., July 3, 1832)

Clements, Miss Martha M. married in Madison County, Tenn. to Mr. John M.
Barnet.
National Banner & Nashville Whig (Fri., Oct. 17, 1834)

Clemer, Miss Nancy married to Mr. Alanson Breecheen.

Clemmons, Miss Winey married to Mr. John A. Shannon.

Clendenin, Lieut. J. M.(U. S. Army, married at Fort Brady, M. T. to
Miss Henrietta King, late of Rochester, N. Y.
National Banner & Nashville Daily Advertiser (Tues., Dec. 17, 1833)

Cleveland, Miss Carline married in Montgomery, Ala. to Ebenezer Pond,
Esq.

Cleveland, Charles, professor of Language, married to Miss Alison Nisbet
M'Corskry, in Carlisle, Pa.
Nashville Republican & State Gazette (Sat., April 23, 1831)

Clevinger, Mr. Thomas married in Jefferson Co., Tenn. to Miss Patsy Neal.
National Banner & Nashville Whig (Mon., May 11, 1835)

Cliff, Miss Elizabeth married to Capt. Lee Smith.

Clifton, Mr. Casswell R. Esq. of Huntsville married in Alabama to Miss Eliza M. Dancy, daughter of Col. David Dancey, of Limestone county.
National Banner & Nashville Whig (Fri., Feb. 6, 1835)

Clifton, Miss Maria Louisa married in Huntsville, Ala. to Mr. Albert J. Watkins.
National Banner & Nashville Daily Advertiser (Wed., Aug. 21, 1833)

Clifton, Miss Sarah married to Mr. Frederick A. Muller.

Climer, Mr. John married to Miss Lucy C. Poyner, in Williamson County.
The Western Weekly Review (Fri., Dec. 23, 1831)

Climer, Miss Nancy married to Mr. Alanson Breecheen.

Clinard, Miss Caroline Malissa married to Mr. Northflet E. Webb.

Clinard, Miss Evelina married to Mr. George S. Gross.

Cline, Miss Elizabeth married to Mr. George Notham.

Clopper, Miss Ellenore Adeline married to Eliakim Lilly, Esq.

Clopton, Miss Elizabeth H. married to Mr. William Harding.

Clopton, Mr. Monroe married in Madison Co., Ala. to Miss Caroline E. Hunter.
National Banner & Nashville Advertiser (Thurs., Aug. 23, 1832)

Cloud, Miss Bartheny married to Rev. Josiah R. Smith.

Cloud, Mr. Eldridge married in Williamson County to Miss Nancy McGavock.
The Western Weekly Review (Fri., Dec. 2, 1831)

(repeat of preceding)
National Banner & Nashville Whig (Wed., Dec. 7, 1831)

Cloud, Mr. John married in Logan Co., Ky. to Miss Elizabeth Rutherford.
National Banner (Feb. 10, 1826)

Cloud, Dr. Joseph married in Shelby County to Miss Jane M. Vaughan.
National Banner & Nashville Advertiser (Wed., Feb. 8, 1832)

Clowney, Miss Esther A. married to Maj. Henry S. Purris.

Clowney, Miss Martha married to Dr. Jas. P. Montgomery.

Cloys, Miss Mary married in Henry County to Mr. John E. Oliver.

Coady, Miss Lucinda married to Mr. Samuel Hays.

Coapland, Miss Elizabeth married to Mr. George W. Roads.

Coates, Mr. William L. married to Miss Elizabeth L. Runkle, in this town.
National Banner (March 24, 1826)

Cobb, Mr. of Georgia married in Madison County,Tenn. to Miss Frances Meriwether, daughter of Maj. James Meriwether.
National Banner & Nashville Whig (Wed., Dec. 17, 1834)

Cobb, Miss Elizabeth married to Mr. Wm. Watson.

Cobb, Mr. James H. married on the 23d inst. at the residence of Capt. G. S. Smith near Nashville by Rev. Dr. Edgar to Mrs. Margaret J. Boyce,both of Sumner County.
Nashville Whig (Wed., May 26, 1841)

Cobb, Miss Martha married to Mr. James R. Smart.

Cobb, Miss Sarah married to Mr. Charles B. Hodges.

Cobbler, Mr. Edward of Franklin, married in Nashville on Thursday evening last by the Rev. Mr. Greene to Miss Rebecca M. Leech.
National Banner & Nashville Whig (Sat., Dec. 17, 1831)

Coburn, Mr. Canney married in Lauderdale Co., Ala. to Miss Lucindia Cantrell.
National Banner & Nashville Whig (July 1, 1826)

Cockran, Mr. James married at Murfreesborough, Tenn. to Miss Nancy McDowell.
National Banner & Nashville Daily Advertiser (Wed.,March 26, 1834)

Cochran, Miss Mary married to Mr. Maleca Sovy.

Cockran, Miss Mary A. E. H. married to Dr. Martin Guest.

Cockran, Mr. Samuel married in Maysville, Ky. to Miss Mary Bland.
National Banner & Nashville Whig (Sat., Dec.16, 1826)

Cock, Mr. Singleton, Married in Gibson County to Miss Margaret Dickson.
National Banner & Nashville Whig (Sat., July 28, 1827)

Cock, Mr. William married in Wilson County to Miss Minerva Bloodworth.
National Banner & Nashville Whig (Mon., Nov. 14. 1831)

Cockburn, Miss Tabitha married in Bolivar to Mr. William Reynolds.

Cocke, Miss Eleanora married to Maj. Thomas J. Dye.

Cocke, Dr. James R. of Rutledge married to Miss Alice G. Hagan in Hawkins County.
National Banner (Sat., Nov. 28, 1829)

Cocke, Mr. John married at Knoxville to Miss Lavinia King.
Nashville Union (Mon., Dec. 2, 1839)

Cocke, Miss Martha A. W. married to Mr. Edmond Winston.

Cocke, Miss Sarah Frances married to Mr. William M. Cocke.

Cocke, Mr. William M. married in Grainger Co., Tenn. to Miss Sarah Frances Cocke, daughter of Dr. William E. Cocke.
National Banner & Nashville Whig (Feb., 4, 1835)

Cockrel, Miss A. E. married to Mr. Arthur F. McCain.

Cockrill, Mr. W. S. of Memphis married on Wed. last at the home of J. L. Webb by the Rev. Mr. Coons to Miss M. E. Bosley, of Shelby County.
Memphis Appeal
Nashville True Whig & Weekly Commercial Register (Fri., Aug 9, 1850)

Cockrum, Mr. D. W. married in Henry County to Miss Sabina Page.
National Banner & Nashville Daily Advertiser (Thurs., March 20, 1834)

Cody, Miss Elizbeth Jane married to Mr. Isaac C. Black.

Cody, Mr. George W. married on the 24th to Miss Malinda Jenkins.
The Christian Record (Sat., Oct. 28, 1848)

Coe, Mr. Leven of Bolivar married Miss Maria J. Lindsey, in Maury County.
Nashville Republican & State Gazette (Thurs., June 23, 1831)

Coffee, John D. Esq. married in Florence, Ala. on Feb. 4th to Miss Mary N. Brahan, daughter of the late Gen. Brahan.
Nashville Republican (Tues., Feb. 16, 1836)

Coffee, Miss Mary married to Mr. Andrew J. Hutchins.

Coffee, Miss Rebecca married to Mr. Alfred Tribble.

Coffin, Miss Eliza H. married to Langdon Bowie, Esq. of Abbeville, S. C.

Coffin, Mr. J. A., clerk of the Chancery Court, at Madisonville, married in Jefferson County, Tenn. to Miss Margaret Martin.
National Banner & Nashville Daily Advertiser (Sat., Sept. 13, 1834)

Coffman, Miss Eliza married to Mr. Lafayette Booker.

Coffman, Mr. John N. married in Russellville, Ala. to Miss Nancy Wood.
National Banner & Nashville Whig (Sept. 9, 1826)

Coffman, Mr. Ralph, merchant of Madisonville, Mi., married in Salem, Ten. on the 18th inst. by Rev. H. Larkin to Miss Eliza S. McWhorter, daughter of the late James S. McWhorter
National Banner & Nashville Whig (Fri., Oct. 3, 1834)

Coggins, Mr. Daniel married in Williamson County to Miss Margaret Carson.
The Western Weekly Review (Fri., Dec. 2, 1831)

(repeat of preceding)
National Banner & Nashville Whig (Wed.,Dec 7, 1831

Cogswell, Miss Eunice married to Mr. Benj. M'Carty.

Coke, Miss Eveline married to Mr. Prestley T. Chaffin.

Cokner, Miss Sarah H. married to Mr. Wm. W. Potter.

Colby, Mrs. Rebecca married to Capt. John Hamilton.

Caldwell, Mr. St. Clair F.married in Maury County to Miss Mary W. Pointer.
National Banner & Nashville Whig (Sat., Dec.17, 1831)

Cole, Mr. David A. married on the 18th inst. by the Rev. Dr. Edgar to Miss Sarah J. Penticost, both of Nashville.
Nashville Whig (Sat., Dec. 21, 1844)

Cole, Mr. E. married in Maury County to Polly Hodge.
National Banner & Nashville Advertiser (Thurs., April 5, 1832)

Cole, Miss Elizabeth married at Tuscaloosa, Ala. to Mr. John W. Andrews.
National Banner & Nashville Whig (Sat., Nov. 17, 1827)

Cole, Miss Elizabeth W. married to Mr. John A. Cashburn.

Cole, Miss Fanny married to Mr. Henry Moore.

Cole, Mr. John L. married in Madison County to Miss Lucy Waddel.
National Banner & Nashville Whig (Sat., Feb. 14, 1829)

Cole, Dr. P. H. of Clarksville married on the 13st ultimo, to Miss Nancy Pathia of Montgomery.
The Nashville Whig & Tenn. Advertiser (Jan. 10, 1818)

Cole, Miss Rebecca C. married to Mr. Hugh M'Kenzie.

Cole, Mr. S. married at St. Louis, Mo. to Madame Theresa Reed.
National Banner & Nashville Daily Advertiser (Wed., July 10, 1834)

Cole, Miss Sarah married in Woodford Co. to Mr. Henry B. Lewis.

Coleman, Miss married to Mr. Thomas Johnson.

Coleman, Miss Abigail married to Mr. George Haynes.

Coleman, Mr. Basil W. married in Mercer Co., Ky. to Miss Mary F. Dedman, daughter of Philip D. Dedman.
National Banner & Nashville Daily Advertiser (Tues., Dec.18, 1832)

Coleman, Miss Catherine E. married to Robert Frazer, Jun., Esq.

Coleman, Chapman, Esq. married in Frankfort Ky. to Miss Ann Mary B. Crittenden, daughter of John J. Crittenden, Esq.
National Banner & Nashville Whig (Mon., Nov. 29, 1830)

Coleman, Charlotte married to William Denton.

Coleman, Miss Christiana W. married to Mr. John Cottart.

Coleman, Miss Cinra W. married to Col. John Brown.

Coleman, Miss Eliza W. married to Mr. Thomas Figures.

Coleman, Miss Helen married to A. G. Slauter, Esq.

Coleman, Mr. J. B. of Green Co., Ala. married in Bibb Co., Ala to Miss Mary Anne Crawford, daughter of the Hon. T. Crawford.
National Banner & Nashville Daily Advertiser (Mon., March 31, 1834)

Coleman, Mr. J. P. married on the 20th inst. by the Rev. Dr. Howell, to Miss Emily H. Taylor, both of Nashville.
Nashville Whig (Sat., Nov. 23, 1844)

Coleman, Mr. James of Todd Co., Ky. married in Logan Co., Ky. to Mrs. Susan H. Batts.
National Banner & Nashville Whig (Mon., Dec. 29, 1834)

Coleman, Jas. A. married in Williamson County to Sarah A. Denton.
The Western Weekly Review (Fri., Feb. 10, 1832)

Coleman, Mr. John married near Bardstown, Ky. to Miss Rossella G. Thompson.
National Banner & Nashville Daily Advertiser (Mon., July 21, 1834)

Coleman, John B. Esq. married in Lexington, Ky. to Miss Catherine M. Ellis, daughter of the late Armstrong Ellis, of Miss.
National Banner & Nashville Whig (Wed., Sept. 21, 1831)

Coleman, Mr. Jonathan married in Adams Co., Miss. to Miss Caroline L. Mann.
National Banner & Nashville Whig (Sat., Feb. 23, 1828)

Coleman, Miss Julia M. married to Doctor W. Taff.

Coleman, Mr. Leroy C. married on Monday morning Dec. 30 by the Rev. Dr. Edgar to Mrs. Caroline Smith, all of Nashville.
Nashville True Whig & Weekly Commercial Register (Fri., Jan. 3, 1851)

Coleman, Miss Mary Ann married to Mr. Nelson Prewitt.

Coleman, Miss Mary Ann married to Mr. John J. Hudgins.

Coleman, Miss Nancy S. married to Mr. John E. Edmondson.

Coleman, Nichols D. Esq. married in Macon Co., Ky. to Miss Lucy A. Marshall.
National Banner & Nashville Whig (Sat., Nov. 18, 1826)

Coleman, Miss Sarah Elizbaeth married to Mr. John E. Thomas.

Coleman, Mr. Thomas married at Louisville to Miss Mary Ann Taylor.
National Banner (Sat., April 25, 1829)

Coleman, Mr. Thomas married in Maury Co. to Miss Charlotte Magors.
National Banner & Nashville Whig (Sat., Dec. 17, 1831)

Coleman, Mr. Thomas B. married in Lincoln Co., Tenn. to Miss Maria
E. Harper.
National Banner & Nashville Whig (Fri., Jan. 23, 1835)

Coleman, Mr. Turner married in Williamson County to Miss Eliza J. Jones.
National Banner & Nashville Whig (Mon., Oct. 20, 1834)

Coleman, Mr. William M. of Maury County married in Williamson County to
Miss Mary G. Johnson.
National Banner & Nashville Daily Advertiser (Sat., July 28, 1832)

Coleman, Col. William W. married on the 10th Nov. by the Rev. Duncan
Brown, to Miss Jeannette M. Frierson, daughter of Thomas J. Frierson,
all of Maury County.
National Banner & Nashville Whig (Mon., Nov. 16, 1835)

Coleman, Zachariah married in Williamson County to Miss Laetitia Brock.
The Western Weekly Review (Fri., March 23, 1832)

Coleman, Zachariah married in Williamson County to Miss Letitia Black.
National Banner & Nashville Daily Advertiser (Mon., March 26, 1832)

Collart, Mr. John married in Williamson County to Miss Christiana Bostick,
on 28th ult.
Nashville Republican & State Gazette (Thurs., Dec. 5, 1833)

Callender, Mr. Thomas of Nashville married in Davidson County on the 24th
Feb. by the Rev. Mr. Hume to Miss Mary Sangster.
National Banner & Nashville Whig (Mon., Feb.28, 1831)

Coller, Miss Rachel married in Campbell County to Mr. Wyatt Kincaid.
National Banner & Nashville Daily Advertiser (Fri., March 1, 1833)

Collier, Miss Anna A. married at Jackson to Mr. Erasmus D. Tenner.

Collier, Chas. married in Williamson County to Mary J. Meadows.
The Western Weekly Review (Fri. Feb. 10, 1832)

Collier, Miss Charlotte R. married to Mr. Reuben M. Cother.

Collier, Gen. George married at St. Charles, Missouri to Miss Euphrasia
Morrison.
National Banner (Jan. 27, 1826)

Collier, Henry W. Esq. married at Tuscaloosa, Ala to Mary Ann Battle.
National Banner (May 13, 1826)

Collier, Mr. Isaac married near Cairo to Miss Jane Bowman.
National Banner & Nashville Whig (Sat., Jan. 6, 1827)

Collier, Miss Lydia married to Col. David Bright.

Collier, Mr. P. P. of Covington, Tenn. married in Rutherford County, to
Miss Susan Bryant, daughter of Mr. Needham Bryant.
National Banner & Nashville Whig (Mon., July 26, 1830)

Collier, Mr. William E. married at Triana, Ala. to Miss Jane O. Slaughter.
National Banner (Sat., Dec. 26, 1829)

Collier, Mr. Wyatt of Ala. married in This town on Thurs. evening to
Miss Janet Walker.
National Banner & Nashville Whig (Sat., April 5, 1828)

Collin, Mr. Harry married in Henry County, Tenn. since the first of Jan.
to Miss Elizabeth Hartsfield.
National Banner & Nashville Whig (Fri., Feb. 13, 1835)

Collingman, Miss Susan married to Mr. John P. Erness.

Collins, Miss Amelia Ann married to Mr. Thomas S. Griges.

Collins, Miss Cary D. married to Howell W. Runnels, Esq.

Collins, Miss Emily married to Mr. Wm. S. Pratt.

Collins, Mr. George of Clarksville married in Logan Co., Ky. to Miss
Elizabeth Frazier
National Banner (May 20, 1826)

Collins, Mr. John G. married on Thursday evening, the 11th inst. by the
Rev. Mr. Campbell to Miss Sirrenne Donoho, both of this place.
The Clarion & Tennessee Gazette (Jan. 23, 1821)

Collins, Mr. John L. of Nashville, Tenn. married on the 2nd inst. at
Hopkinsville, Ky. by the Rev. L. B. Davidson, to Miss Elizabeth A. Mc-
Cool, daughter of Mrs. McCool of Hopkinsville, Ky.
Nashville Whig (Thurs., April 9, 1846)

Collins, Mr. William married in Madison County, Illinois to Miss Elizabeth
Hertzog.
National Banner (March 17, 1826)

Collins, Mr. William of Miss. married in Montgomery County to Miss Mary
Powell.
National Banner & Nashville Whig (Sat., Dec. 27, 1828)

Collins, Mr. William B. married in Montgomery County, Tenn. to Miss
Frances Williams, daughter of Mr. Henry Williams.
National Banner & Nashville Whig (Fri., April 17, 1835)

Colnesil, Mr. John D. maried in Jefferson Co., Ky. to Miss Courtney
Ann Taylor.
National Banner & Nashville Whig (Sat., Dec. 16, 1826)

Colshire, Mr. John married at Louisville, Ky. to Miss Tena Ann Kice.
National Banner & Nashville Whig (Sat., April 26, 1828)

Colvin, Mr. Thomas married in Cincinnati to Mrs. Hannah Conn.
National Banner & Nashville Whig (Sat., July 22, 1826)

Colwell, Capt. Wm. A., late of Huntsville, Ala., married in Franklin
Co., Tenn. on the 3d inst. by Rev. John Dougan, to Miss Ellenor Foster.
National Banner & Nashville Daily Advertiser (Mon., April 7, 1834)

Combs, Dr. married in Logan Co., Ky. to Mrs. Piper.
National Banner (Sat., Aug. 29, 1829)

Combs, Miss Harriet H. married to Col. Wm. Quarles.

Combs, Mr. William married in Jefferson County to Miss Jincey Peerman.
National Banner (Sat., Dec. 19, 1829)

Comfort, Joseph W. married in Nashville to Miss Nancy A. Williams.
Nashville Republican & State Gazette (Sat., March 31, 1832)

Compton, Miss Mary Ann married to Mr. Richard Abbay.

Compton, Miss Rebecca married to Mr. Thos. Alderson.

Compton, Miss Rebecca married to Mr. James D. Hill.

Compton, Miss Susan L. married to Mr. Anthony S. Abbey.

Compton, Mr. Thomas of Shelby County married in Nashville on Tuesday
last by the Rev. Dr. Howell to Miss Susan Murphy of Nashville.
Nashville Whig (Thurs., April 2, 1846)

Connally, Mr. John of Ala. married in Lincoln Co., Tenn. to Miss Frances Jones.
National Banner & Nashville Whig (Fri., June 10, 1836)

Condlay, Mr. Abraham D. married in Knox County to Miss Sarah Hoskins.
National Banner & Nashville Whig (Mon., Sept. 13, 1830)

Condon, Miss Julia, married to Mr. Samuel M'Minnis.

Condon, Mr. Robert V. mzrried in Williamson County by the Rev. Mr. Whitsett to Miss Eleanor White.
National Banner (Sat., May 30, 1829)

Conger, Mr. Charles H. married on the 29th by Rev. J. B. McFerrin to Mrs. Mary A. Williams, all of Nashville.
The Politician & Weekly Nashville Whig (Fri., May 7, 1847)

Conk, Mr. Greenberry married in Knox Co., Tenn. to Miss Phebe Olinger.
National Banner & Nashville Whig (Mon., April 13, 1835)

Conkey, Dr. L. married in Maury County to Miss Minerva Brown, daughter of Col. Joseph Brown.
National Banner & Nashville Whig (Sat., Jan. 3, 1829)

Conlan, James W. Esq. married on the 27th inst. by Rev. Dr. Edgar at the residence of Capt. Miller, of Nashville to Miss Catherine A. West.
Nashville Whig (Wed., Aug. 28, 1839)

Conn, Mrs. Hannah married to Mr. Thomas Colvin.

Conn, Mr. Jesse formerly of Penn. married by the Rev. Mr. Salter on Thursday 23rd inst. to Miss Eliza E. Reynolds of Nashville.
The Politician & Weekly Nashville Whig (Wed., Sept. 29, 1847)

Conn, Mr. Robert of Knox County married in Blount Co., Tenn. to Miss Abigail Hood, daughter of Nathaniel Hood.
National Banner & Nashville Whig (Mon., Nov. 10, 1834)

Connell, Miss Catherine married to Mr. Jno. Cartwright.

Connel, Miss Jane married to Mr. Jacob Swisher.

Connell, Miss Sarah Jane married to Mr. Robert Baxter.

Conner, Mr. Cornelius married in this town last evening by the Rev. Mr. Hume to Miss Menerva A. Eakin.
National Banner & Nashville Whig (July 13, 1832)

Conner, Mr. Wm. married in Knoxville to Miss Martha Gammon.
National Banner & Nashville Advertiser (Mon., April 9, 1832)

Conner, Mr. William R. married in Knox County to Miss Martha Gammon, daughter of Lewis Gammon.
National Banner & Nashville Advertiser (Mon., March 12, 1832)

Conover, James F. Esq. married in Cincinnati to Miss Julia A. E. Sellman, daughter of the late Dr. Sellman of Cincinnati.
National Banner & Nashville Daily Advertiser (Mon., Feb. 6, 1832)

Conrad, Miss Minerva A. married to Dr. Joel M. Jones.

Conway, Mr. James S. married at Long Prarie, A. T. to Miss Mary Jane Bradley, daughter of Maj. John Bradley, of Wilson County.
National Banner & Nashville Whig (Sat., March 10, 1827)

Cook, Miss married to Mr. Buckner Miller.

Cook, Mr. Augusta married in Jefferson County, Miss. to Miss Martha Chambliss.
National Banner & Nashville Whig (Sat., Dec. 9, 1826)

Cook, Miss Eliza A. married to Mr. Philip Allenworth.

Cook, Miss Eliza Ann married to Mr. Edward Powell.

Cook, Miss Elizabeth married to Mr. Bryant Wilcox.

Cook, Mr. Ezekiel of the Steamvessel Talleyround married on the 27th
at the residence of Capt. Johnson by the Rev. Dr. Edgar to Miss Lucy
Jones of Nashville.
Nashville Whig (Thurs., Nov. 30, 1843)

Cook, Mr. George married in Richmond, Ky. to Miss Mary Porter.
National Banner & Nashville Whig (Sat., Aug. 19, 1826)

Cook, Mr. George W. of Lebanon married on Yesterday morning to Miss
Callie Douglass of Sumner.
Nashville True Whig & Weekly Commercial Register (Fri., Feb. 21, 1851)

Cook, Mr. Greenville of Nashville married on Thursday last to Miss
Eleanor P. Long.
Nashville Republican (Sat., Sept. 5, 1835)

(repeat of preceding)
Nation1 Banner & Nashville Whig (Mon., Sept. 8, 1835)

Cook, Mr. Henry married in Williamson County to Miss Martha Sheppard.
Nashville Whig (Aug. 11, 1823)

Cook, Mr. James M. married in Warren Co., Ky. to Miss Sally Turner.
National Banner & Nashville Whig (Sat., March 10, 1827)

Cook, John B. Esq. married at Claiborne, Ala. to Miss Mary Slina Simpson.
National Banner & Nashville Whig (Sat., Nov. 18, 1826)

Cook, Mr. John B. married in Ross Co., Ohio, to Miss Hetty Halloway.
National Banner & Nashville Whig (Sat., Dec. 30, 1826)

Cook, Mr. John F. of Mississippi married by the Rev. A. L. P. Green on
the 14th inst. to Miss Carolina A. Duval, daughter of A. D. Duval, Esq.
of Davidson County.
Nashville Whig (Wed., Oct. 20, 1841)

Cook, Mr. John H. married at Tuscumbia, Ala., to Miss Susan M. N. Lightfoot.
National Banner & Nashville Whig (Mon., Oct. 31, 1831)

Cook, Miss Mary married at Shawneetown to Mr. Frederick Oldenberg.

Cook, Miss Mary married to Seth Wheatley Esq.

Cook, Miss Mary Ann married to Dr. John Brelsford.

Cook, Miss Sarah W. married to Mr. A. W. Hicks.

Cook, Miss Susan married to Mr. Samuel Parkes.

Cook, Miss Susan married in Logan Co., Ky. to Mr. William Beaumont.

Cook, Mr. William A. of Cookville, White County, married in Smith County
to Miss Amanda Strother, daughter of Judd Strother, Esq.
National Banner & Nashville Daily Advertiser (Wed., June 5, 1833)

Cook, Mr. William B. of Maury County married on Thursday the 20th inst.to
Miss Mary Ann A. Watson, daughter of Lewis Watson of Hickman County.
National Banner & Nashville Daily Advertiser (Thurs., Feb. 27, 1834)

Cook, Mr. William B. of Maury County married in Hickman County to Miss
Mary Ann Watson.
Nashville Republican & State Gazette (Thurs., March 13, 1834)

Cook, Mr. William C. married in Williamson County to Miss Elizabeth
Putnam.
The Western Weekly Review (Fri., Dec. 2, 1831)

(repeat of preceding)
National Banner & Nashville Whig (Wed., Dec. 7, 1831)

Cooke, Miss Catherine married to Dr. Henry Hopson.

Cooke, Dr. M. B. of Lexington married to Miss Lucy Ann Jones, daughter
of the Rev. Edmund Jones, in Madison Co., Tenn.

National Banner & Nashville Whig (Sat., Feb. 9, 1828)

Cooke, Miss Margaret R. married to Mr. Reuben Daughty.

Cooke, Lieutenant Philip St. George, U. S. A., married at Cantonment,
Leavenworth, Mo. to Rachel W. Hertzog.
National Banner & Nashville Whig (Fri., Nov. 26, 1830)

Cooke, Mr. Stephens married at Frankford, Ky. to Miss Ann Baxter.
National Banner (March 31, 1826)

Cooke, Col. Watson M., merchant of the firm of Hart & Cooke, married at
the residence of Thomas L. Bransford, Esq., Gainsboro, Tenn., on the 2nd
inst. by Rev. Gideon H. Bransford, to Miss Mary Ann Shores, daughter of
Mr. Wilson Shores, of Flovanna Co., Va.
Nashville Whig (Fri., Nov. 12, 1841)

Cooke, Mr. William, merchant, married on 23d Feb. at Bowling Green, Ky.
to Miss Mary Jane Vanmeter, daughter of Mr. Jacob Vanmeter, all of
Bowling Green, Ky.
National Banner & Nashville Whig (Fri., March 3, 1837)

Coolidge, Miss Ann Maria married to Mr. William S. Sampson.

Cooms, Miss Nancy married to Mr. William Pittman.

Coons, Miss Barthena married to Mr. Andrew Turner.

Cooper, Miss Ann L. B. married to Dr. Fielding Deadrick.

Cooper, Miss Ann Letitia married to Dr. Fielding Deadrick.

Cooper, Miss Catharine Ann married to Major J. T. Dent.

Cooper, Charles, clark of the Bank of the State of Tennessee, married on
Sunday evening last, to Miss Ann Marie Eastland, daughter of Mr. Thomas
Eastland, all of this town.
The Clarion & Tennessee Gazette (November 21, 1820)

Cooper, Miss Jane married to Col. Hannibal Harris.

Cooper, Dr. John married in Knoxville to Miss Susan W. Veal, daughter of
Mr. John C. Veal.
National Banner & Nashville Whig (Monday, May 2, 1831)

Cooper, Mr. John married in Smith County to Miss Rebecca Gillam.
National Banner & Nashville Advertiser (Fir., May 4, 1832)

Cooper, Capt. John B. of Bedford County, married in Madison County,
Ala. to Miss Eliza Sivley.
National Banner & Nashville Advertiser (Wed., June 20, 1832)

Cooper, Dr. Langston, married in Giles County to Miss Nancy Wilkinson.
Nashville Republican & State Gazette (Sat., April 23, 1831)

(repeat of preceding)
National Banner & Nashville Whig (Wed., Apirl 27, 1831)

Cooper, Miss Margaret married to Mr. Anderson Beadles.

Cooper, Miss Margaret Ann married to Frederick B. Pennybaker.

Cooper, Maria married to L. B. Knott.

Cooper, Miss Mary married to Mr. Charles Hamilton.

Cooper, Mr. Matthew D. married in Davidson County to Miss Elizabeth Jane Frierson on the 9th inst.
Nashville Republican (Tuesday, July 14, 1835)

Cooper, Miss Sarah married to Mr. Hugh C. Haskins.

Cooper, Mr. Washington B. Portrait Painter. Married in Nashville on Thursday last, by the Rev. A. L. P. Green. To Ann Letton daughter of Joseph Litton Esq.
Nashville Whig (Mon., Jan. 21, 1839)

Cooper, Mr. William. Married in Jackson, Mi. to Miss Clara A. Wardell.
National Banner & Nashville Whig. (Wed., Jan. 21, 1835)

Cooxey, Mr. John. Married in Henry County to Miss Rebecca Rose.
National Banner & Nashville Daily Advertiser. (Fri., Feb. 15, 1833)

Copeland, Miss Elizabeth married to George W. Roads.

Copeland, Mr. Hugh S. married in Knox County to Miss Frances Bibbs.
National Banner & Nashville Daily Advertiser. (Mon., April 9, 1832)

Copper, Mr. Thomas A. Formerly of Phila. Married on Thursday the 9th by the Rev. Mr. J. F. Wheat to Miss Martha Hall of Nashville, Tenn.
Daily Republican Banner (Wed., Nov. 15, 1837)

Corbett, Mr. Willy. Married in Nashville on the 1st inst. to Miss Elizabeth Moore all of Nashville.
National Banner & Nashville Daily Advertiser (Fri., May 2, 1834)

Corbitt, Miss Mahala married to Mr. J. Stewart.

Corbitt, Mr. Wylly B. married in Nashville to Mrs. Elizabeth Moore on 1st inst.
Nashville Republican & State Gazette (Sat., May 3, 1834)

Cornelius, Miss Rebecca married to Mr. William A. Owen.
National Banner & Nashville Daily Advertiser (Mon., Aug. 12, 1833)

Cornell, Miss Sarah Ann married to Mr. Cooper Settle.

Corzine, Mr. Eli M. married in Williamson County to Miss Elizabeth W. Johnson.
National Banner & Nashville Whig. (Fri., Jan. 9, 1835)

Cossitt, Miss Ann C. married to Col. James H. Fisher.

Cother, Mr. Reuben M. married in Sumner County to Miss Charlotte R. Collier.
National Banner & Nashville Daily Advertiser. (Wed., March 7, 1832)

Cottart, Mr. John married in Williamson County on the 28th ult. to Miss Christiana W. Coleman.
National Banner & Nashville Daily Advertiser. (Fri., Dec. 6, 1833)

Cotton, Mr. Charles married in Davidson County to Miss Francis S. Pilant on 4th inst.
Nashville Republican (Tues., June 9, 1835)

Cotton, Miss Tabitha married to Mr. E. J. B. Gosey.

Couch, Mr. Andrew married near Florence, Ala. to Miss Pauline G. Baker.
National Banner & Nashville Daily Advertiser (Tues., Aug. 19, 1834)

Couch, Mr. James married in Claiborne County, Miss. to Miss Polly Edes.
National Banner (May 10, 1826)

Couch, Miss Martha Jane married to Mr. Thos. H. Fite.

Couch, Miss Martha Jane married to Mr. Thomas H. Fite.

Coughanour, David married in Williamson County, Ten. to Malinda Irvin.
National Banner & Nashville Whig. (Wed., Dec. 17, 1834)

Coulson, Mr. William married in Knoxville to Miss Margaret Slatery.
National Banner & Nashville Daily Advertiser. (Mon., Jan. 9, 1832)

Coulter, Mr. Moses S. of Virginia. Married at Hanover, Indiana on the 1st inst. by the Rev. J. F. Crawe D.D. to Miss Caroline E. Crawe of Hanover, Indiana.
The Christian Record (Sat., Jan. 20, 1849)

Council, Miss Eliza married to Mr. S. H. Burton.

Council, Miss Lovy married to Mr. Travice Staden.

Courier, Miss Elizabeth married to Mr. James H. Johnson.

Coursault, Miss Clememce married to Mr. Henry P. Choteau.

Coursey, Charles married in Williamson County to Miss Matilda Manire.
The Western Weekly Review (Friday, Dec. 14, 1832) Franklin, Tenn.

Coursey, James R. Married in Williamson County to Miss Malinda Manier.
The Western Weekly Review - Franklin, Tenn. (Fri., Feb. 1,1833)

Courtney, N. married in Williamson County to Miss Judith B. Womack.
The Western Weekly Review - Franklin, Tenn. (Fri., Dec. 14, 1832)

Courtney, Mr. W. of Louisiana married by the Rev. Mr. Lapsley to Miss Agnes Adine Woods daughter of the late Mr. Andrew Woods of Missouri.
National Banner & Nashville Whig (Wed., Oct. 14, 1835)

Courtney, Mr. W. of La. married to Miss Agness Adine Woods of Missouri.
Nashville Republican (Thurs., Oct. 15, 1835)

Courts, Miss Emily married to Mr. Thomas Pollard.

Coussens, Mr. John H. married on Thursday the 24th inst. by the Rev. Mr. Fanning to Miss Mary E. P. Royister both of Nashville.
Nashville Whig (Mon., Dec. 28, 1840)

Covey, Miss Jane D. married to Mr. Joshua Jones.

Covey, Miss Jane D. married to Mr. Joshua Jones.

Covington, Miss Cornelia married to Sydney L. Johnson Esq.

Covington, Miss Cornelia F. married to Sidney L. Johnson Esq.

Covington, Miss Eliza W. married to Hon. Robert W. Wells.

Covington, Miss Julia Ann to Mr. John A. Fraker.

Covington, Miss Mary married to William H. Betty.

Cowan, Miss Ann E. married to Dr. Alexander H. Smiley.

Cowan, Mr. Henry L. married in Lincoln County, Ky to Miss Chloe Ely.
National Banner & Nashville Whig (Sat., Sept. 1, 1827)

Cowan, Mr. James H. Married in Knoxville to Miss Lucinda Dickinson.
National Banner & Nashville Whig. (Mon., Dec. 6, 1830)

Cowan, Mr. James H. married in Blount County to Miss Margaret Berry.
National Banner & Nashville Advertiser. (Mon., Oct. 1, 1832)

Cowan, John married in Williamson County to Miss America Johnson.
The Western Weekly Review - Franklin, Tenn. (Fri., Dec. 14, 1832)

Cowden, Mr. John J. of Rodney, Mi. Married on Thursday evening last
by Mr. T. Fanning to Miss Eleanor Bradford eldest daughter of Capt.
Simon Bradford of Nashville.
Daily Republican Banner. (Fri., Aug. 14, 1840)

Cowan, Mr. John W. married in Shelbyville, Ten. to Miss Jane Eakin.
National Banner & Nashville Daily Advertiser (Sat., Aug. 24, 1833)

Cowan, Miss Letitia married in Blount county to Mr. George Graham.
National Banner & Nashville Whig. (Sat., Oct. 11, 1828)

Cowan, Miss Mary P. married to Dr. Samuel C. M'Whirter.

Cowan, Miss Menerva married to Mr. Alfred Kincaid.

Cowan, Mr. P. William married in Wilson County to Miss Mary M.
Mosely daughter of Capt. Peter Moseley.
National Banner & Nashville Whig. (Sat., Dec. 2, 1826)

Cowan, Samuel married at Jonesborough, Mr. Samuel Cowan, merchant of
this town, to Miss Jane Montgomery, of Salisbury, North Carolina.
Knoxville Gazette (Thurs., May 8, 1794)

Cowan, Mr. William married in Wilson County on the 28th of Sept.
to Miss Mary M. Moseley daughter of Capt. Peter Moseley.
National Banner & Nashville Whig. (Sat., Nov. 4, 1826)

Cowan, Mr. William of Memphis. Married in Murfreesborough to Miss
Mary Elizabeth Johns.
National Banner & Nashville Daily Advertiser. (Mon., April 29, 1833)

Cowen, Miss Eleanor married in Williamson County to William Baxter.
The Western Weekly Review - Franklin, Tenn. (Fri., Dec. 14, 1832)

Cowen, Mrs. Mary M. married to Everett Owen, Esq.

Cowgill, Mrs. Mary M. married to Mr. B. A. Knighton.

Cox, Mr. Benjamin married in Davidson County on Thursday the 9th
inst. by William E. Watkins to Miss Irean Watkins daughter of Capt.
Isaac Watkins.
National Banner & Nashville Daily Advertiser (Mon., Feb. 13, 1832)

Cox, Miss Frances married to Mr. Thomas Booth.

Cox, Mr. George jun. married in Huntsville, Ala. to Miss Elizabeth
Patterson.
National Banner & Nashville Daily Advertiser. (Mon., Dec. 31, 1832)

Cox, Miss Hester Ann daughter of Mr. Nathaniel Cox married in
Louisville, Tenn. to Jefferson P. Brown.
National Banner & Nashville Whig (Fri., March 27, 1835)

Cox, Mr. Isaac M. married on Thursday 5th inst. by Josiah Ferguson
Esq. to Mrs. Mary Ann Cunningham all of Nashville.
Nashville Whig. (Sat., March 7, 1846)

Cox, Mr. John. married at Cincinnati to Nancy Hanna.
National Banner & Nashville Whig (Sat., Jan. 3, 1828)

Cox, Miss Leah of Jefferson married in Jefferson County to Mr.
John W. Boyd of Granger County.
National Banner (Feb. 17, 1826)

Cox, Miss Martha married to Mr. Jonathan Tipton.

Cox, Miss Martha Ann married to Mr. William George.

Cox, Miss Mary married to Capt. Thomas Yardy.

Cox, Mr. Robert married in Madison County, Ky to Miss Elly Ballard.
National Banner (March 3, 1826)

Cox, Miss Sarah married to John A. Nevand.

Cox, Mr. Stephens married in Madison County, Ky. to Miss Sally
Hieatt.
National Banner (March 3, 1826)

Cox, Thomas Esq. Married on the 16th inst. by Rev. Dr. Edgar to
Miss Adda Gowdey daughter of Thomas Gowdey Esq. all of Nashville.
The Christian Record (Sat., Nov. 25, 1848)

Cox, Mr. Tho. B. married in Knox County to Miss Caroline Callaway.
National Banner. (Sat., May 9, 1829)

Cox, Mr. William of St. Louis married at Pittsburgh to Miss Elizabeth
Beltzhoover.
National Banner & Nashville Whig. (Thurs., Sept. 23, 1830)

Cozart, Miss Elizabeth R. married to Mr. Benj. A. West.

Cozzen, Brown Esq. married at Natchez to Miss Eliza Martin.
National Banner & Nashville Whig (Sat., May 17, 1828)

Crabb, Miss Eleanor married to Dr. W. Estill.

Crabb, Henry Esq. Attorney at law. Married at the residence of
Willie Barrow Esq. in the vicinity of this place on Thursday evening
28th by the Rev. Mr. Hume. Henry Crabb of this place. To Miss Jane
A. Barrow daughter of the first named Gentleman.
The Nashville Whig (Sept. 1, 1817)

Crabb, Mrs. Jane married to Harry L. Douglass, Esq.

Crabb, Col. Ralph of Winchester married in the vicinity of Nashville
on the 17th inst. to Mrs. Miriam Lewis relict of Col. Joel Lewis.
The Nashville Whig & Tenn. Advertiser (March 21, 1818)

Crabb, Mr. William married at New Orleans to Miss Mary Spider.
National Banner & Nashville Whig. (Sat., June 2, 1827)

Crabtree, Mrs. Frances E. married to Mr. S. L. Graham.

Craddock, Miss Caroline married to James B. Wallace Esq.

Craddock, Miss Harriet married to Mr. Nichols P. Perkins.

Craddock, Miss Margaret married to Mr. John Harris.

Craddock, Mr. R. S. married on Thursday last by Rev. Judd to Miss Eliza Beard all of Nashville.
Nashville Union (Sat., March 17, 1838)

Craddock, Mr. R. S. married on Thursday last by the Rev. Judd to Miss Eliza Beard all of Nashville.
Daily Republican Banner. (Wed., March 21, 1838)

Craddock, Mr. R. S. married on Thursday evening by the Rev. Mr. Judd to Miss Eliza Beard all of Nashville.
Nashville Whig. (Wed., March 21,1838)

Craddock, Richard L. married in Maury County to Miss Noamy Due.
National Banner & Nashville Daily Advertiser. (Thurs., April 5, 1832)

Craff, Miss Susan married to Rev. David Adams.

Craig, Miss Araminta married to Mr. Asa N. Vaughn.

Craig, Mrs. Clarissa married to David Hooks.

Craig, Mr. Elijah T. married on Thursday last by the Rev. Mr. Howell to Miss Sarah Dew both of Nashville.
Nashville Whig. (Sat., June 29, 1844)

Craig, Miss Elizabeth married to Lieut. Edmond B. Alexander.

Craig, Miss Elizabeth married to Mr. Z. Herndon.

Craig, Miss Elizabeth married to Mr. Thomas S. Proctor.

Craig, Miss Elizabeth married to Clairborne Watkins.

Craig, Miss Ellen married to Dr. R. T. Maury.

Craig, Harriet E. married to Abner M. Vaughn.

Craig, James T. Esq. Proprietor of the Lebanon Mirrow. Married on Tuesday evening 18th inst. by the Rev. Mr. Green to Miss Mary E. Robertson of Nashville.
National Banner & Nashville Whig. (Wed., Jan. 20, 1836)

Craig, James Thomas. Proprietor of the Labanon Morror. Married on Tuesday the 19th instant by Rev. Mr. Green to Miss Mary E. Robertson of Nashville.
The Union. (Thurs., Jan. 21, 1836)

Craig, Mr. John. Married in Scott County, Ky. to Miss Harriet Johnson.
National Banner & Nashville Whig. (Sat., Dec. 2, 1826)

Craig, Mr. John. Married in Maury County, Ten. to Miss Mary Gordon.
National Banner & Nashville Whig. (Wed., Feb. 25, 1835)

Craig, Miss Martha married to Mr. John Benford.

Craig, Miss Malissa married to Mr. William Vaughn.

Craig, Mr. Robert. Married in Knox County to Miss Elizabeth Jones.
National Banner & Nashville Whig (Sat., Aug. 30, 1828)

Craig, Dr. William married in Lincoln County, Ky to Miss Martha Green.
National Banner & Nashville Whig. (Sat., Aug. 4, 1827)

Craig, Mr. Wm. P. Married in Franklin County, Ten. on the 22nd
of Aug. to Miss Martha V. Alexander.
National Banner & Nashville Daily Advertiser. (Fri., Aug. 30, 1833)

Craig, Mr. Wm. P. Married in Franklin County, Tennessee to Miss
Martha V. Alexander of the 22 of Aug.
Nashville Republican & State Gazette (Sat., Aug. 31, 1833)

Craighead, Miss Eliza H. Married to James M. N. White Esq.

Craighead, Mr. J. E. Married in Fayette County on the 30th ult.
to Miss Phereby Whyte daughter of the Hon. R. Whyte of Nashville.
National Banner & Nashville Daily Advertiser. (Wed., Aug. 14, 1833)

Craighead, Mr. J. E. married in Fayette County, Ten. to Miss Phereby
Whyte of Nashville.
Nashville Republican & State Gazette (Thurs., Aug. 15, 1833)

Craighead, Maj. John. Married in Knox County to Miss Tinsey Gibbs.
National Banner & Nashville Whig. (Sat., Oct. 28, 1826)

Craighead, Mr. John B. Married on Thursday evening last. To Mrs.
Lavina Beck, relict of John E. Beck Esq.
Nashville Whig. (Nov. 17. 1823)

Craighead, Miss Malinda married to Mr. Samuel Thatcher.

Craighead, Rev. T. B. of Louisiana married in Williamson County to
Miss Tennessee Virginia Johnson of Williamson.
Nashville Whig. (Tues., July 7, 1846)

Craighead, Mrs. Tinsey married to Samuel Frazier, Esq.

Craine, Mr. John married in Smith County to Miss Mary Barkley.
National Banner & Nashville Daily Advertiser (Fri., May 18, 1832)

Crairy, Mr. John W. Married in Sumner County to Miss Louisa Brooks.
Nashville Whig (Tues., March 24, 1846)

Crampton, Mr. Henry R. Married in Cincinnati to Miss Mary Andrews.
National Banner & Nashville Whig. (Sat., Aug. 5, 1826)

Crane, Rev. Simeon N. Married in Lexington, Ky. to Miss Amanda Taylor.
National Banner & Nashville Whig. (Sat., Dec. 2, 1826)

Crank, Mr. Jesse married in Knox County to Miss Eliza George.
National Banner & Nashville Whig. (Sat., Feb. 21, 1829)

Crarren, Mr. John. Married in Giles County to Miss Frances T.
Buchanan.
National Banner & Nashville Daily Advertiser. (Thurs., Jan. 17, 1833)

Craven, Mr. Ernsley married in Howard County, Missouri to Miss
Sarah Kivett.
National Banner & Nashville Whig. (Sat., Jan. 6, 1827)

Craven, Martha H. married to Mr. Pleasant M. Lea.

Cravens, Miss Abigail married to Mr. Squire Stites.

Craw, Mr. Isaac of Athens married in Roane County to Miss Catherine
Senter.
National Banner & Nashville Whig (Sat., Jan. 17, 1829)

Craw, Mr. James married in Lincoln County, Ky. to Miss Pamelia Carter.
National Banner (Feb. 3, 1826)

Craw, Miss Mary married to Mr. J. H. Durrett.

Crawe, Miss Caroline E. married to Moses S. Coulter.

Crawford, Mr. A. C. married on Tuesday last by Phillip Lindsley D.D. to Miss Martha A. Lytle.
Nashville Republican (Sat., April 22, 1837)

Crawford, Mr. Andrew C. married at Shawneetown to Miss Sarah Hamilton.
National Banner (Feb. 24, 1826)

Crawford, Miss Ann married to Mr. C. K. Isbell.

Crawford, Miss Cynthia married to Capt. James English.

Crawford, Mr. D. B. married in Bedford County to Miss Algeline Shockley.
National Banner & Nashville Whig. (Fri., Nov. 18, 1831)

Crawford, Mr. David married at Laurel Furnace, Dickson County on the 21st. ult. to Miss Elizabeth D. Fulcher.
National Banner (Sat., July 18, 1829)

Crawford, Miss Elizabeth A. married to George M. Porter.

Crawford, Rev. J. Y. married at Rogersville to Miss Mary White.
National Banner & Nashville Whig (Sat., Oct. 6, 1827)

Crawford, Mr. James married at Shipping port, Ky. to Miss Elizabeth Shaw.
National Banner (May 4, 1826)

Crawford, Miss Jane married in Henry County to Mr. Franklin T. Frazier on 10th inst.
Nashville Republican & State Gazette (Sat., Sept. 14, 1833)

Crawford, Mr. Wm. married in Lincoln County to Miss Nancy Gardner.
National Banner & Nashville Whig (Sat., March 17, 1827)

Crawford, Mr. William B. married in Lincoln County, Ten. to Miss Martha B. Moore.
National Banner & Nashville Whig (Mon., Jan. 5, 1835)

Creath, Rev. Jacob jun. married in Fayette County, Ky. to Mrs. Susan Bedford.
National Banner & Nashville Whig (Mon., Sept. 26, 1831)

Creath, Miss Margaret M married to Mr. Ambros Gibson.

Creek, Miss Elizabeth married to Geo. Hopkins.

Creek, Newton C. married in Williamson County to Miss Cynthia Pope.
The Western Weekly Review - Franklin Tenn. (Fri., Dec. 14, 1832)

Creighton, Charles Esq. married in Louisville, Ky. to Miss Margaret G. Martin daughter of George W. Martin Esq. of New Orleans.
National Banner & Nashville Whig. (Mon., Aug. 16, 1830)

Crendshaw, Mr. Chester married in Williamson County to Miss Sarah Crenshaw.
National Banner & Nashville Whig (Mon., Nov. 14, 1831)

Crenshaw, Mr. Chester married to Miss Sarah Crenshaw.
The Western Weekly Review - Franklin, Tenn. (Fri., Nov. 11, 1831)

Crenshaw, Maj. James W. married at Athens, Ala to Miss Narcissa Beaty.
National Banner & Nashville Whig. (Fri., Feb. 18, 1831)

Crenshaw, John T. Esq. married in Oseola St. Clair County, Mo. by
Rev. Dr. Browning to Miss Sarah Nash all of Oseola.
The Politician & Weekly Nashville Whig (Wed., Sept. 1st. 1847)

Crenshaw, Miss Louisa married near Montgomery, Ala. to Mr. Saml.
R. Davenport.
National Banner & Nashville Whig (Sat., April 14, 1827)

Crenshaw, Miss Martha married to Mr. F. Martin.

Crenshaw, Miss Sarah married to Mr. Chester Crenshaw.

Crenshaw, Miss Susannah S. V. married to Jabez R. Townsend, Esq.

Crenshaw, Mr. William married to Miss Elizabeth R. B. Davis.

Crenshaw, Mr. Wm. married in Williamson County to Miss Elizabeth
R. B. Davis.
National Banner & Nashville Whig. (Wed., Dec. 7, 1831)

Creswell, Mr. James married in Pittsburgh to Miss Mary Ann Dickens.
National Banner & Nashville Daily Advertiser (Mon., July 21, 1834)

Creswell, Mr. Samuel M. married in Blount county to Miss Catherine
S. Williams.
National Banner & Nashville Daily Advertiser (Wed., May 8, 1833)

Crew, Capt. Pleasant married in McMinn County, Tenn. to Mrs.
Frances Riddle.
National Banner & Nashville Daily Advertiser (Mon., June 18, 1832)

Crews, Mr. John married in Florence, Ala. to Miss Jane Terry.
National Banner & Nashville Daily Advertiser (Mon., May 28, 1832)

Crews, Mr. Milton married in Madison County, Ky to Miss Mary Fox.
National Banner & Nashville Whig (Sat., Feb. 23, 1828)

Creyon, Miss Catharine M. married to Mr. John Duncan, jun.

Crickner, Mr. James M. married in Williamson county to Miss Minerva
Francis.
The Western Weekly Review - Franklin, Tenn. (Fri., June 29, 1832)

Crickner, Mr. James M. of Williamson county married to Miss Minerva
Francis.
National Banner & Nashville Advertiser (Tues., July 3, 1832)

Criddle, Miss Adeline married to Mr. Wm. M. Hinton.

Criddle, Miss Amanda E. married to Mr. C. J. Fox Wharton.

Criddle, Miss Amanda E. married to Mr. C. J. Fox Wharton.

Criddle, Miss Harriet S. of Davidson County married in Nashville on
the 3d inst. by the Rev. Mr. Hume to Benjamin D. Smith, Esq. of
Williamson.
National Banner & Nashville Daily Advertiser (Fri., May 4, 1832)

Criddle, Mr. Smith of Davidson married on Thursday last to Miss
Lucinda Whitfield daughter of H. Whitfield Esq. of Williamson County.
The Western Weekly Review - Franklin, Tenn. (Fri., Sept. 7, 1832)

Criddle, Mr. Smith of Davidson County married in Williamson County
to Miss Lucinda Whitfield.
National Banner & Nashville Daily Advertiser (Mon., Sept. 10, 1832)

Criddle, Smith Esq. married on the 16th by the Rev. R. B. C. Howell
to Mrs. Belle Ann Bremaker.
Daily Republican Banner (Fri., Oct. 18, 1839)

Criddle, Smith Esq. married on the 16th inst at the residence of
Mr. George Graham by the Rev. R. B. C. Howell to Mrs. Belle Ann
Bremaker all of Nashville.
Nashville Union (Fri., Oct. 18, 1839)

Criddle, Smith Esq. married on Wednesday the 16th inst. by the Rev.
R. B. C. Howell to Mrs Belle Ann Bramaker all of Nashville.
Nashville Whig (Fri., Oct. 18, 1839)

Criswell, Miss Hannah married in Williamson County to Mr. J. T. Martin.
Nashville Whig (Sat., July 11, 1846)

Crittenden, Miss Ann Mary B. daughter of John B. Crittendon Esq.
married at Frankfort, Ky. to Chapman Coleman Esq.
National Banner & Nashville Whig. (Mon., Nov. 29, 1830)

Crittenden, Mr. James married in Franklin, Ten. to Miss Stagg.
Nashville Republican & State Gazette (Thurs., April 14, 1831)

Crittenden, Mr. James G. married on Thursday evening last by the Rev.
Robert Davis to Miss Narcissa Staggs daughter of Mr. Thomas Staggs
of Williamson county.
The Western Weekly Review - Franklin, Tenn. (Thurs., April 14, 1831)

Crittenden, John J. Esq. married in Frankford, Ky. to Mrs. Maria K.
Todd widow of John H. Todd Esq.
National Banner & Nashville Whig (Sat., Dec. 2, 1826)

Crittenden, Mr. John P. married in Salem, Franklin county on the 11th
inst. to Miss Martha R. Tripplin.
National Banner & Nashville Whig (Wed., Sept. 21, 1831)

Crittenden, Mr. Robert H. married in Frankfort, Ky. on the 17th
inst. by the Rev. C. B. Parsons to Miss Adeline Theobald.
Nashville Whig (Tues., Oct. 29, 1844)

Crocker, Miss Gerusha married to Mr. William Hooper.
National Banner & Nashville Whig (June 24, 1826)

Crocket, Miss Ann married to Mr. Phenix Burns.

Crockett, Miss America S. married to Mr. W. G. W. Beaty.

Crockett, Miss Elizabeth S. married to Mr. James Wood Jr.

Crockett, Miss Elizabeth S. married to Mr. James Woods

Crockett, Joseph B. Esq. married at Hopkinsville, Ky. married Miss.
Caroline M. Bryan daughter of Mr. John Bryan.
National Banner & Nashville Advertiser (Fri., Nov. 22, 1832)

Crockett, Miss Mary married to Mr. Wilson Cage.

Crockett, Miss Martha married to James Knox.

Crockett, Miss Nancy married to Col.A. M. M. Upshaw.

Crockett, Miss Nancy L. married to Mr. James Byrns.

Crofford, Mr. Charles D. married in Maury County to Miss Susan
Wantland.
National Banner & Nashville Whig (Fri., March 26, 1830)

Croft, Miss Martha married to Maclin Cross Esq.

Croghan, Wm. Esq. of Louisville married Miss O'Hare at Pittsburgh.
Nashville Whig (Feb. 26, 1823)

Cromwell, Mr. Alexander H. Merchant of Clarksville married in
Robinson County on the 4th inst. to Miss Margaret E. Williamson
daughter of Thos. Williamson Esq.
National Banner & Nashville Whig (Fri., Oct. 14, 1836)

Cromwell, Miss Ann married to Mr. David Armour.

Cromwell, Mr. George of Jackson married Miss Elizabeth Moale late
of Baltimore.
National Banner & Nashville Whig (Fri., March 6, 1835)

Crook, Mr. John married in Henderson county, Ten. to Miss Martha J.
Still only daughter of Maj. W. Still.
National Banner & Nashville Whig (Wed., Jan. 21, 1835)

Crookshank, Miss Eliza married in Washington Co. Ten. to Maj.
Washington Willett.
National Banner & Nashville Daily Advertiser (Tues., Aug. 19, 1834)

Crosby, Mr. Samuel married at Columbus, Ohio to Miss Margaret M'Lene.
National Banner & Nashville Whig (Sat., Dec. 23, 1826)

Cross, Mr. married in Bedford County to Miss Reeves.
National Banner & Nashville Daily Advertiser. (Fri., Jan. 27, 1832)

Cross, Maclin Esq. married in M'Nairy county to Miss Martha Croft.
National Banner & Nashville Whig (Sat., April 21, 1827)

Cross, Mr. Nathaniel married in Nashville on the 3d inst. by the
Rev. Doctor Lindsley to Miss Ann Caroline Bonny.
National Banner & Nashville Whig (Tues., April 6, 1830)

Cross, Miss Rebecca O. married to Mr. Lemuel Philips.

Crosson, Mr. Wm. married at Cincinnati to Miss Sophia Clark.
National Banner & Nashville Whig (Sat., May 12, 1827)

Crossway, Mr. James married in Sumner County to Miss Winnay Joyner.
National Banner & Nashville Whig (Mon., Oct. 4, 1830)

Crosthwait, Dr. George married in Rutherford County, near Murfrees-
borough by the Rev. Mr. Eagleton to Miss Eliza Burton daughter of
Col. F. N. W. Burton.
The Union (Tues., Dec. 13, 1836)

Crouch, Miss Susan married to Mr. Armistead Morehead.
National Banner & Nashville Daily Advertiser (Wed., June 13, 1832)

Crouch, Mr. William H. of Franklin married on Wednesday last by the
Rev. Joel Anderson to Miss Eliza Stone daughter of Capt. Stone of
Williamson County.
The Western Weekly Review - Franklin, Tenn. (Fri., Dec. 7, 1832)

Crouch, Mr. William H. married in Williamson county to Miss Eliza
Stone.
National Banner & Nashville Daily Advertiser (Mon., Dec. 10, 1832)

Crouse, Miss Mary Ann married to Gen. Thomas J. Porter.

Crowder, Mr. R. D. married in Henry County, Ten. to Miss Virginia S.
Kay.
National Banner & Nashville Whig (Wed., April 8, 1835)

Crowdus, Miss Harriet E. married to John A. Nooe Esq.

Crowdus, Dr. John A. married in Logan county, Ky. to Miss Juliet
Stevenson.
National Banner & Nashville Whig (Sat., Sept. 20, 1828)

Crozier, Mr. Arthur of Knoxville, Ten. married in Wythe Cty, Va. to Miss Nancy Henderson.
National Banner & Nashville Whig (Mon., Oct. 20, 1834)

Crozier, Miss Betsey Jane married to Mr. David A. Deaderick.

Crozier, Mr. Carrick W. late a merchant of Knoxville, Ten. married in Clay County, Ky. to Miss Elizabeth Baker daughter of Abner Baker Esq.
National Banner & Nashville Whig (Fri., Jan. 23, 1835)

Crozier, Mr. Clark G. married in Anderson county to Miss Abiah Roberts daughter of Mr. Collin Roberts.
National Banner & Nashville Daily Advertiser (Fri., Nov. 23, 1832)

Crozier, Miss Eliza married to Judge Wilkerson.

Crozier, Mr. R. G. married in Tuscumbia, Ala. to Miss Susan H. Harding.
National Banner & Nashville Whig (Sat., Feb. 16, 1828)

Crudeson, Mr. George married in Logan County, Ky. to Miss Polly Ann Edgar.
National Banner & Nashville Whig (Sat., March 10, 1827)

Crumbaugh, Mr. Eli married in Logan County, Ky. to Miss Elizabeth Townsent.
National Banner & Nashville Daily Advertiser (Tues., Feb. 14, 1832)

Crunk, N. S. married in Williamson County to Miss Lavinia S. Pratt.
The Western Weekly Review - Franklin, Tenn. (Fri., Feb. 1, 1833)

Crutcher, Miss Esther married to Mr. James S. Fall.

Crutcher, Miss Esther O. married to Mr. James S. Fall.

Crutcher, Miss Frances married to Mr. Solomon George.

Crutcher, Col. James A. married on Thursday evening last by Rev. Dr. Howell to Miss Pheriba C. McCullough all of Davidson county.
The Christian Record (Sat., April 3, 1847)

Crutcher, Miss Martha married to Mr. A. M. Osborne.

Crutcher, Miss Nancey married to Mr. Preston Blackwell.

Crutcher, Mr. W. N. married in Franklin County, Ky. to Miss Elizabeth Rupe.
National Banner & Nashville Whig (Sat., Jan. 12, 1828)

Crutcher, Mr. William of Pittsburgh married to Miss Emma C. Pike of Nashville on July 20.
Nashville Republican (Thurs., Aug. 6, 1835)

Crutcher, Mr. William merchant of Pittsburgh married on Thursday July 20th by the Rev. Dr. Weller to Miss Emma C. Pike second daughter of the late John M. Pike of this city.
National Banner & Nashville Whig (Fri., Aug. 7, 1835)

Crutchfield, Mr. James S. married in Jefferson County, Ky. to Miss Frances T. G. Taylor.
National Banner & Nashville Whig (Fri., Oct. 20, 1826)

Crutchfield, Mr. John L. married in Madison County, Ky. to Miss Sarah Jerman.
National Banner & Nashville Whig (Sat., Sept. 9, 1826)

Crutchfield, Miss Rosanna married to Mr. Jesse M. Henson.

Crutchlow, H. S. married in Williamson County to Martha A. Williamson.
The Western Weekly Review - Franklin, Tenn. (Fri., Feb. 10, 1832)

Cryer, Rev. Hardy M. of Sumner County, Ten. married in Logan County,
Ky. to Miss Susan Ann Duvall.
Nashville Republican & State Gazette (Sat., Oct. 26, 1833)

Culler, Mr. Eason married in Lincoln County to Miss Jane Cuningham.
National Banner & Nashville Whig (Sat., Sept. 9, 1826)

Cullum, Miss Polly married to Col. Pleasant M. Armstrong.

Cully, Mr. Robert married on Sunday the 29th inst. by C. W. Nance
Esq. to Miss Emily Work all of Davidson County.
Nashville Whig (Thurs., Nov. 2, 1843)

Cummings, Miss Emily married to Mr. Lewis Holt.

Cummings, Mr. Robt. S. married in Blount County to Miss Frances Smith.
National Banner (Sat., June 13, 1829)

Cummins, Miss Elizabeth married to Mr. Daniel Campbell.

Cummins, Miss Elizabeth married to Mr. David Campbell.

Cummins, Miss Elizabeth L. married to Mr. Robert N. Herbert.

Cummins, Mr. John O. of Tuscaloosa, Alabama married on Thursday
the 19th inst. to Miss Martha M'Cawley daughter of James M'Cawley
of Smithville, Kentucky.
Nashville Whig. (Oct. 25, 1824)

Cummins, Miss Mary married to Mr. John Edmonson.

Cummins, Miss Nelton married to Major Ota Cantrell.

Cummins, Uriah S. Esq. married in Rutherford County to Miss Martha L.
Tilford.
National Banner & Nashville Daily Advertiser (Fri., May 11, 1832)

Cummins, Mr. Walter married in Williamson County to Miss Martha Hunter.
National Banner & Nashville Whig (Fri., Feb. 13, 1835)

Cuney, Dr. Richard R. married in Lexington, Ky. to Miss Millisent
F. Cayle.
National Banner (April 28, 1826)

Cunningham, Rev. Alexander of Montgomery, Ala. married in Jonesborough,
Ten. to Miss Margaret Ann Eason.
National Banner & Nashville Daily Advertiser (Tues., Aug. 19, 1834)

Cunningham, Charles M. Esq. married in Harrodsburg, Ky. to Miss
H. M. Magoffin.
National Banner & Nashville Whig (Thurs., Oct. 7, 1830)

Cunningham, Mr. Edward A. of Arkansas married in Davidson County on
Tuesday evening 15th inst. by Rev. Mr. Hall to Miss Susan T. Dismukes
daughter of Paul Dismukes Esq.
National Banner & Nashville Daily Advertiser (Thurs., Jan. 17, 1833)

Cunningham, Miss Eliz. married in Clarke County, Ky. to Mr. D. J.
Flournoy.
National Banner (April 28, 1826)

Cunningham, Miss Elizabeth married to Mr. Burgess Gray.

Cunningham, Miss Elizabeth married to Hon. James Gallagher.

Cuningham, Mr. Gideon B. married in Lincoln County, Ten. to Miss Mary R. Davis.
National Banner & Nashville Whig (Fri., Dec. 6, 1834)

Cunningham, Mr. James married in Lincoln County to Miss Nancy Groce.
National Banner (May 27, 1826)

Cuningham, Mr. James D. of Huntsville married in Lincoln Cty, Ten. to Miss Sarah Turner of Lincoln County.
National Banner & Nashville Whig. (Mon., Oct. 20, 1834)

Cunningham, Miss Jane married to Mr. Eason Culler.

Cunningham, Miss Jane married to Daniel M'Neil, Esq.

Cunningham, John Jr. of M'Minville married to Miss Mary Ann Mabry of Vicksburg, Miss. on Thursday May 21st.
Nashville Republican (Tues., June 9, 1835)

Cunningham, Miss Maria married to Mr. Matthew Hume.

Cuningham, Mrs. Mary Ann married to Mr. Isaac M. Cox.

Cunningham, Mr. Pleasant T. married in M'Minn County to Miss Evelina Smith.
National Banner (Sat., June 13, 1829)

Cuningham, Mr. Samuel married in Lincoln County to Miss Mary Ellis.
Nashville Whig (Tues., May 5, 1846)

Cunningham, Miss Sarah married to Mr. Lewis Harris.

Cuningham, Mr. Valentine E. married in Sumner County to Miss Mary P. Steele.
National Banner (Sat., May 2, 1829)

Cuningham, Mr. William B. married in Jefferson County to Miss Eliza S. Peck.
National Banner & Nashville Whig (Mon., Dec. 27, 1830)

Cuny, Dr. Richard R. of La. married at Cincinnati to Miss Clara Miller.
National Banner (Sat., April 25, 1829)

Curd, Miss Elizabeth married to Mr. Nimrod Long.

Curd, Miss Fanny married to Mr. Samuel Matthes.

Curd, Mr. John B. married in Mercer county, Ky. to Miss Helen Chapline.
National Banner & Nashville Whig (Sat., March 31, 1827)

Curd, Miss Mary Ann C. married to Mr. Wm. H. Hawkins.

Curd, Miss Patsy married to Mr. John Small.

Curd, Mr. William married in Logan county, Ky. to Miss Mariah Ely.
National Banner & Nashville Whig (Mon., Jan. 17, 1831)

Curd, Mr. William P. married to Miss Mary A. Megowan in Lexington, Ky.
National Banner & Nashville Whig (Fri., Jan. 29, 1830)

Cure, Mr. Martin W. Married at Lexington, Ky. to Miss Rebecca Calvert.
National Banner & Nashville Whig (Sat., Dec. 6, 1828)

Curington, Mr. Robert married in Jefferson county, Ten. to Miss Dolly Weaver.
National Banner & Nashville Daily Advertiser. (Mon., May 28, 1832)

Curl, Miss Susan married to Robert Walker.

Curle, Mr. Jefferson married in Madison county, Ky. to Miss Mary Ann Estill.
National Banner (March 31, 1826)

Currey, Mr. G. W. J. Esq. of Nashville married at Clifton on Thursday the 10th inst. by the Rev. Dr. Lapsley to Miss Emily Donelson Martin daughter of Maj. James Glasgow Martin of Davidson county.
Nashville Whig (Sat., Sept. 12, 1846)

Currey, Robert B., Jr. married at Clifton on the 7th inst. by the Rev. Dr. Lapsley to Miss Mary D. Martin daughter of Maj. James G. Martin.
The Politician & Weekly Nashville Whig (Wed., Sept. 15, 1847)

Currey, Miss Susannah E. married to De. James M. Perkins.

Currier, Mr. William married in Madisonville, Monroe county to Miss Sally Carter.
National Banner & Nashville Whig (Wed., Nov. 2, 1831)

Currin, Miss Cassandra C. married to Horace P. Keeble.

Curry, Miss Elizabeth married to Mr. Shackleford Glass.

Curry, Mr. James W. married in Williamson county to Miss Eliza Hungerfond.
National Banner & Nashville Whig. (Sat., Dec. 30, 1826)

Curry, Miss Mary married to Mr. Rob. G. Johnson.

Curry, Miss Mary married to Mr. William Brown.

Curry, Dr. Richard O. married on Thursday the 26th inst. at the residence of Stockley Donelson, Esq. to Miss Rachel J. Easton all of Davidson county.
Nashville Whig (Tues., May 31, 1842)

Curry, Robert B. Jr. married at Clifton on Tuesday the 7th inst. by the Rev. Dr. Lapsley to Miss Mary D. Martin daughter of Maj. James G. Martin.
The Christian Record (Sat., Sept. 11, 1847)

Curry, Miss Sarah married to Mr. Robert Hamilton.

Curry, Miss Susanna E. married to Dr. James Madison Perkins.

Curtis, Miss Caroline E. married to Mr. James F. Blount.

Curvin, Miss Cassandra C. married to Horace P. Keeble.

Cusick, Mr. David of Sevier married in Blount county to Miss Ellen Williams.
National Banner & Nashville Daily Advertiser (Mon., March 18, 1833)

Custer, Miss Celina married to Mr. Nelson Bennett.

Custis, Miss Caroline E. married to Mr. James F. Blount.

Cutter, Hon. George W. member of the House of Representative of Indiana married in Indianpolis to Mrs. A. Drake the well known actress.
Daily Republican Banner (Thurs., Feb. 6, 1840)

Dabbs, Mr. Edwin of Limestone married in Madison County, Ala. to Miss Elizabeth J. Lewis, daughter of Mr. Corbin Lewis.
National Banner and Nashville Whig (Wed., Sept. 28, 1831)

Dabbs, Mr. John R. married in Davidson County on the 31st ult. by the Rev. Mr. Whitsett to Miss Eliza Menees.
National Banner and Nashville Whig (Mon., April 4, 1831)

Dabbs, Miss Mary married to Mr. Tazewell J. Dabbs.

Dabbs, Doctor Samuel A. R. married on the 8th inst. by the Rev. Mr. Clayed to Miss Elizabeth M. Martin all of Wilson County.
National Banner and Nashville Daily Advertiser (Tues., Jan. 14, 1834)

Dabbs, Mr. Tazewell J. married in this County on the 17th inst. to Miss Mary Dabbs.
National Banner and Nashville Whig (Fri., July 25, 1828)

Dabbs, Mr. Thos. C. of Davidson County married to Miss Isabella M. Burgess on 23rd inst.
Nashville Republican (Thurs., July 30, 1835)

Dabney, Miss Frances married to Mr. William R. Rainer.

Dabney, Miss Lucy A. married to James H. F. Atkins.

Dabney, Miss Margaret married to Mr. Sidney P. Smith.

Dabney, Miss Mildred married to Mr. John Rivers.

Dabney, Dr. Samuel H. married in Montgomery County to Miss Cordelia Minor.
National Banner (Sat., Dec. 19, 1829)

Dabney, Miss Sarah Elizabeth married to Mr. John S. Langhorne.

Dabney, Mr. Walter D. married in Shelby County on the 19th ult. by L. Henderson Esq. to Miss Lucy H. Sappington formerly of Nashville.
National Banner (Sat., Dec. 5, 1829)

Dabney, Esq. William H. in Montgomery County married Miss Fredonia Marable daughter of Dr. John H. Marable.
National Banner and Nashville Whig. (Fri., April 23, 1830)

Daily, Mrs. Ellen married in New Orleans, La. to Dr. Samuel McKay.
National Banner and Nashville Whig (Wed., Nov. 12, 1834)

Dains, Mr. Samuel A. merchant of Maysville married on the 18th inst. by Howard W. Turner Esq. to Miss Sarah Garrett of Dickson County.
Nashville Republican (Tues., May 30, 1837)

Dair, Mr. John married at Cincinnati to Miss Julia Ann Martin daughter of Mr. John Martin.
National Banner and Nashville Daily Advertiser (Fri., Aug. 17, 1832)

Dale, Edward W. Esq. married at Columbia to Mrs. Baird of this town.
National Banner (Sat., Oct. 3, 1829)

Dale, Mr. John A. married at Louisville, Ky. to Miss Elizabeth Patton
National Banner and Nashville Whig (Sat., April 14, 1827)

Dale, Miss Martha married to Mr. John Davison .

Dale, Mr. Isaac A. married on Thursday the 8th inst. by the Rev. R. Graves to Miss Nancy F. Long all of Nashville.
Nashville Whig (Tues., Oct. 13, 1846)

Dale, Mr. William married in Columbia, Tenn. to Miss Mary E. O'Riley.
National Banner and Nashville Whig (Wed., Dec. 3, 1834)

Dale, Miss Melissa married to Mr. George W. Brittle.

Dallahite, Miss Mahala married to Mr. John J. Daniel.

Dana, Mr. Charles D. married in Cincinnati, Ohio to Miss Sarah P. Lyman.
National Banner and Nashville Daily Advertiser. (Fri., June 22, 1832)

Dance, Miss Christiana G. married to Dr. Geo. W. Jones.

Dance, Maj. Russell of Rutherford County married to Miss Mary Martin
in Davidson County.
Nashville Republican and State Gazette (Tues., Jan. 28, 1834)

Dance, Maj. Russell, merchant of Murfreesborough married in Davidson
County on Thursday 23rd ult. to Miss Mary Martin, daughter of Thomas
Martin Esq. of Davidson County
National Banner and Nashville Daily Advertiser (Mon., Feb. 3, 1834)

Dancy, Miss Eliza M. married to Mr. Casswell R. Clifton Esq.

Dancy, Doctor Francis of Ala. married in Jackson, Tenn. to Miss
Rebecca Mason.
National Banner & Nashville Daily Advertiser (Fri., Aug. 15, 1834)

Dancy, Lieut. H. L. U. S. Army married in Florida to Miss Florida
Forsyth Reid daughter of Hon. R. R. Reid.
National Banner & Nashville Daily Advertiser (Fri., Nov. 15, 1833)

Dancy, Miss Sarah Margaret F. married to Daniel Fisher, Esq.

Danforth, Mr. J. B. married at Louisville, Ky. to Miss Ann R. Talbot.
National Banner & Nashville Daily Advertiser (Mon., July 21, 1834)

Daniel, Mr. John J. married in Henry County to Miss Mahala Dollahite.
National Banner & Nashville Advertiser (Thurs., Sept. 27, 1832)

Daniel, Miss Lucretia married to Mr. Ephraim Baker.

Daniel, Margaret married to Mr. J. J. Lenn.

Daniel, Mr. Oswy at Frankfort, Ky. married to Miss Eliza D. Vaughan.
National Banner and Nashville Whig. (Fri., Feb. 19, 1830)

Danks, Dr. John W. married in Simpson County, Ky. to Miss E. F. Jones.
National Banner and Nashville Whig. (Mon., Nov. 1, 1830)

Dannaby, Mr. Edward married in Bedford County, Tenn. to Mrs. Eleanor
Thornton.
National Banner & Nashville Whig (Fri., March 6, 1835)

Danner, Mr. Jacob married in Louisville, Ky. to Miss Paulina Long.
National Banner & Nashville Whig (Fri., March 13, 1835)

Darden, Miss Harriet married to Mr. Horatio Nelson.

Darden, Mr. John C. married in Nashville on Wednesday 2d inst. by the
Rev. Dr. Howell to Miss Virginia Demoville daughter of Peter Demoville
Esq., deceased.
The Politician & Weekly Nashville Whig (Fri., June 4, 1847)

Dardis, Miss Lucinda married to Mr. Tho. J. Caldwell.

Dardis, Miss Margaret married to Mr. Demarcus G. Stacks.

Darnell, Miss Minerva married to Mr. Pinckney Erwin.

Dashiell, Miss Sophia R. married to Maj. William F. Lytle.

Daughtery, Miss Catherine married to Mr. M. A. Parrish

Daughty, Mr. Reuben married in Knox County to Miss Margaret R. Cooke.
National Banner & Nashville Advertiser (Mon., Dec. 31, 1832)

Daughty, Dr. Simpson married in Monroe County to Miss Rachel Goodman.
National Banner & Nashville Whig (Sat., Feb. 7, 1829)

Davenport, Mr. David married in Claiborne county to Miss Hetty Miller.
National Banner & Nashville Whig (Sat., March 31, 1827)

Davenport, Mr. Sam'l R. married near Montgomery, Ala. to Miss Louisa
Crenshaw.
National Banner & Nashville Whig (Sat., April 14, 1827)

Davenport, Mr. William S. married in Giles county to Miss Willamina
Reynolds.
National Banner & Nashville Daily Advertiser (Thurs., Sept. 6, 1832)

David, Dr. Amos of Fayette County married on the 14th in Fayette
county, Ten. by the Rev. J. H. Cobb to Miss Minerva Ellen W. Garland
late of Amherst County, Va.
Daily Republican Banner (Tues., Oct. 3, 1837)

Davidge, Miss Julia H. married to Wm. Fry, Esq.

Davidge, Miss Juliana married to Robert H. Adams, Esq.

Davidson, Mr. Abraham S. married in Rutherford County to Miss L. M.
Stoddard.
National Banner (Jan. 6, 1826)

Davidson, Mr. Andrew married in Bedford county to Miss Martha Burditt
daughter of Jesse Burditt, Esq.
National Banner & Nashville Daily Advertiser (Mon., May 6, 1833)

Davidson, Miss Emily married to Mr. N. E. Carr.
National Banner and Nashville Daily Advertiser (Thurs., Aug. 23, 1832)

Davidson, Mrs. Harriet married in Bedford County to Rev. Case
Ferguson.
National Banner and Nashville Whig (Fri., Oct. 20, 1826)

Davidson, Mr. James late of Romelton, Ireland married in Fayetteville
on 13th inst. by William Nield Esq. to Miss Mary Margant Fulton eldest
daughter of Col. James Fulton of Fayetteville.
Nashville Whig (Tues., Sept. 20, 1842)

Davidson, Miss Margaret married to Mr. Guinn.

Davidson, Rev. Robert in Lexington, Ky. married to Miss Adeline
Therese Doren.
Nashville Republican and State Gazette (Sat., Aug. 24, 1833)

Davidson, Rev. Samuel C. married in Jefferson County, Tenn. to Miss
Isabella McClanahan.
National Banner and Nashville Daily Advertiser (Mon., May 28, 1832)

Davidson, Rev. Samuel R. married in Haywood County, Tenn. to Mrs.
Mary H. Gray.
National Banner and Nashville Whig (Wed., Nov. 12, 1834)

Davidson, Rev. Thomas P. married in Haywood County to Miss Elizabeth
Terry.
National Banner and Nashville Whig (Thurs., July 29, 1830)

Davidson, Thomas W. married in Williamson county to Bethenia B. Blackburn.
National Banner & Nashville Whig (Wed., Sept. 24, 1834)

Davidson, Mr. William married at Louisville, Ky. to Miss Maria A. Buckner.
National Banner & Nashville Advertiser (Fri., Sept. 7, 1832)

Davis, Miss Amanda married in Williamson county to Mr. Eli S. Ray.
The Western Weekly Review - Franklin, Tenn. (Fri., Dec. 2, 1831)

Davis, Miss Amanda married to Mr. Eli S. Ray.

Davis, Miss Ann A. married to Rev. Stephen Foster.

Davis, Miss Ann V. married to Mr. James W. Ivens.

Davis, Anthony H. Esq. married in Tuscumbia, Ala. to Miss Emily Aldridge.
National Banner & Nashville Whig (Sat., Sept. 1, 1827)

Davis, Anthony H., Esq. married at Florence, Ala. to Miss Emily Aldridge.
National Banner & Nashville Whig (Sept. 8, 1827)

Davis, Miss Aurelia Davis married to Gen. E. W. Ripley.

Davis, Mr. Caleb married at Franklinton, O. to Miss Martha Breckinridge.
National Banner & Nashville Whig. (Sat., April 21, 1827)

Davis, Miss Carolina married to Mr. Felding Park.

Davis, Miss Caroline married to Capt. B. Figures.

Davis, Miss Caroline C. married to Mr. W. G. West.

Davis, Miss Eliza married to Mr. Newton Forsyth.

Davis, Eliza married to Mr. W. Childress.

Davis, Miss Eliza married to Everitt Davis.

Davis, Miss Elizabeth married to Mr. Hiram Dillingham.

Davis, Miss Elizabeth Jane married to Mr. Asa Jackson, Jr.

Davis, Miss Elizabeth R. B. married to Mr. William Crenshaw.

Davis, Miss Emily O. married to Mr. Drury Robertson.

Davis, Everett married in Williamson County to Miss Eliza R. Davis.
The Western Weekly Review - Franklin, Tenn. (Fri., Dec. 14, 1832)

Davis, Miss Frances married to Mr. Allen Phillips.

Davis, Dr. Frederick A. M. of Augusta married at Lexington, Ky. to Miss Julia E. Briggs.
National Banner (Feb. 10, 1826)

Davis, Garret, Esq. married in Bourbon County, Ky. to Miss Rebecca Trimble.
National Banner & Nashville Whig. (Sat., Oct. 28, 1826)

Davis, Miss Georgiana Ann C. married to Capt. Wm. M. Brandon.

Davis, Hilliard married in Williamson County to Miss Malinda Perry.
The Western Weekly Review - Franklin, Tenn. (Fri., Dec. 14, 1832)

Davis, Mr. Jackson C. married in this county to Miss Elizabeth
Patterson.
National Banner & Nashville Whig (Sat., Jan. 17, 1829)

Davis, Mr. James B. Married in Rutherford County to Miss Martha
Sheerman.
National Banner & Nashville Whig (Mon., Nov. 29, 1830)

Davis, Capt. James L. married in Knox County to Miss Evelina J.
McMillan daughter of John McMillan, Esq.
National Banner & Nashville Daily Advertiser (Tues., Nov. 27, 1832)

Davis, Mr. James L. married in Maury County, Ten. to Miss Jane Beard.
National Banner & Nashville Whig (Fri., May 8, 1835)

Davis, Mr. James M. married in Ross county, Ohio to Miss Elizabeth
Hampton.
National Banner (May 10, 1826)

Davis, Mr. James O. married in Giles county to Sarah A. Gooding, Miss.
Nashville Whig (Tues., April 21, 1846)

Davis, Miss Jane daughter of Col. Robt. Davis married in Butler County,
Ky. on the 8th ult. to Mr. Edmund Hyde of this county.
Mational Banner (Jan. 6, 1826)

Davis, Mr. John married in Maury County to Miss Mary Wright.
National Banner & Nashville Whig. (Fri., Dec. 10, 1830)

Davis, Mr. Johnson married in Maury county to Miss Eliza Johnson.
National Banner & Nashville Whig (Fri., Dec. 10, 1830)

Davis, Mr. Jonathan of Spencer county, Ky. married at Louisville, Ky.
to Miss Susan Thronberry.
National Banner & Nashville Whig (Mon., June 27, 1831)

Davis, Miss Julia married to Mr. W. Smith.

Davis, Julia Ann married to Mr. Richard Fox Sullivan.

Davis, Miss Julia G. married to Mr. Edmund Powell.

Davis, Miss Julian married to Mr. R. F. Sullivan.

Davis, Lavinia married to Geo. G. Mays.

Davis, Miss Lydia married to Aaron White, Esq.

Davis, Miss Madeline married to Mr. Doak M'Millen.

Davis, Miss Margaret married to Mr. Joseph Haines.

Davis, Miss Martha married to Mr. George Simpson.

Davis, Miss Martha married to George W. Lane, Esq.

Davis, Miss Mary married to Mr. John North.

Davis, Miss Mary married to Mr. N. M. Price.

Davis, Miss Mary E. married to Mr. Frederick R. Jackson.

Davis, Miss Mary Jane married to Mr. John M. Speckernagle.

Davis, Miss Mary R. married to Mr. Gideon B. Cuningham.

Davis, Miss Nancy married to Mr. Wm. Moulden.

Davis, Mr. Nathaniel A. married in Warren County, Ky. to Miss
Catharine C. Atchison.
National Banner and Nashville Daily Advertiser (Fri., March 9, 1832)

Davis, Peggie Miss married to Robert Houston, Esquire.

Davis, Dr. Preston W. married in this county by the Rev. Mr. Hume to
Miss Amanda Sumner.
National Banner & Nashville Whig. (Sat., May 3, 1828)

Davis, Mr. Robert married in Williamson County to Miss Eliza Hudgins.
The Western Weekly Review - Franklin, Tenn. (Fri., March 29, 1833)

Davis, Mr. Robert married in Williamson County to Miss Eliza H.
Hudgins.
National Banner & Nashville Daily Advertiser (Mon., April 1, 1833)

Davis, Miss Ruth married in Lincoln County to Col. Davis Smith.
National Banner and Nashville Whig (Sat., Feb. 23, 1828)

Davis, Mr. Sandy married in Madison County to Miss Lucy Haines.
National Banner & Nashville Whig (Wed., June 29, 1831)

Davis, Miss Sarah married to Jeptha Mathis.

Davis, Miss Sarah A. married to Mr. John Miller.

Davis, Sarah Ann Miss married to Dr. Barksdale.

Davis, Mr. Sterling married in Williamson County to Miss Martha
Applewhite.
The Western Weekly Review - Franklin, Tenn. (Fri., Dec. 23, 1831)

Davis, Miss Susan P. married to Mr. Samuel S. Rayburn.

Davis, Miss Susannah married to Mr. William Baggett.

Davis, Thomas Esq. Postmaster married at Shelbyville to Miss Eliza
Stevenson.
National Banner & Nashville Whig (Sat., Nov. 29, 1828)

Davis, Mr. Thomas C. married in Limestone county to Miss Nancy Harris.
National Banner. (Jan. 27, 1826)

Davis, Rev. Thomas E. of North Carolina married in Greene county to
Miss Harriett L. Dobson of Greene County.
Nashville Whig (Tues., March 31, 1846)

Davis, Capt. Valentine married in Blount county to Miss Rebecca Tipton.
National Banner & Nashville Daily Advertiser (Wed., May 8, 1833)

Davis, William Esq. married in Sommerville to Miss Malvina Henderson
daughter of Bennet H. Henderson Esq.
National Banner (Sat., July 11, 1829)

Davis, Maj. William M. Married at Frankfort, Ky. to Miss Arabella
Scott.
National Banner & Nashville Daily Advertiser (Mon., Jan. 9, 1832)

Davis, Mr. Zachariah T. married in Logan county, Ky. to Miss Elizabeth
E. Bradley.
National Banner & Nashville Whig. (Sat., March 31, 1827)

Davison, Mr. John of Sumner married in Rutherford County to Miss
Martha Dale.
National Banner (Sat., Aug. 8, 1829)

Davolt, Mr. Peter married in Washington county to Miss Mary Ann Hoss.
National Banner & Nashville Whig (Friday, Nov. 11, 1831)

Dazey, Nathan A. married in Williamson county to Eliza S. Adams.
National Banner & Nashville Daily Advertiser (Mon., Aug. 26, 1833)

Deaderick, Mr. David A. married in Knox county to Miss Betsey Jane Crozier daughter of Capt. John Crozier.
National Banner & Nashville Whig. (Wed., Aug. 1 (or 17?), 1831)

Deaderick, Dr. Fielding married on the 24th inst. by the Rev. John T. Edgar to Miss Ann L. B. Cooper all of this place.
National Banner & Nashville Daily Advertiser (Fri., April 25, 1834)

Deaderick, Dr. Fielding married in Nashville to Miss Ann Letitia Cooper on Thursday last.
Nashville Republican & State Gazette (Sat., April 26, 1834)

Deaderick, Mr. John T. of Jonesborough married in Greenville, Ten. to Miss Rebecca L. Williams daughter of Jos. Williams, Esq. of North Carolina.
National Banner & Nashville Whig (Mon., Sept. 26, 1831)

Deaderick, Mr. Joseph married at Jonesborough to Miss Emeline Anderson daughter of James V. Anderson Esq.
National Banner & Nashville Whig (Mon., Jan. 31, 1831)

Deadrick, David married January 1, 1795. Mr. David Deadrick, merchant of Jonesborough to Miss Anderson of Washington County.
Knoxville Gazette (Fri., January 9, 1795)

Deadrick, Mr. David A. married in Knox county to Miss Betsey Jane Crozier.
National Banner & Nashville Whig (Mon., Aug. 1, 1831)

Deadrick, Mr. Walter of Jonesborough married to Miss Anderson of Washington County on the first inst.
Knoxville Gazette (Fri., Jan. 9, 1795)

Deagned, Miss Joyce married to Rev. Wm. Warfield.

Dean, Elijah married in Williamson County to Jane B. McCarroll.
The Western Weekly Review - Franklin, Tenn. (Fri., Dec. 14, 1832)

Dean, Francis A. L. of Rutherford County married to Miss Jane Alley of Nashville on the 17th inst.
Nashville Republican and State Gazette (Tues., Oct. 21, 1834)

Dean, Francis A. L. of Rutherford County married in Nashville on the 17th by Mr. John Wright Esq. to Miss Jane Alley of Nashville.
National Banner Nashville Whig (Wed., Oct. 22, 1834)

Dean, Mr. John married in Bedford County to Miss Mary Ann Price.
National Banner and Nashville Whig (Fri., March 27, 1835)

Dean, Miss Mary married on Thursday evening the 9th inst. by the Rev. Joshua White to Mr. Thomas Gleaves Jur. both of this County.
The Nashville Whig and Tenn. Advertiser (Oct. 13, 1817)

Dean, Dr. R. of West Tenn. married in Bedford County to Miss Eliza R. McKissick, daughter of Col. James McKissick.
National Banner and Nashville Daily Advertiser (Fri., March 28, 1834)

Dean, Mr. Robert married in Madison County to Miss Elizabeth Stewart.
National Banner and Nashville Daily Advertiser (Thurs., Sept. 27, 1832)

Dearing, Mr. J. W. married in Tuscaloosa, Alabama to Miss Eliza Noon.
National Banner Nashville Daily Advertiser (Mon., July 21, 1834)

Dearing, James H. Capt. merchant of St. Stephen, Alabama Territory
married to Miss Julia Ann Searcy, daughter of Thomas Searcy, Esq. at
Mount Pleasant North Carolina on the 10th instant by Rev. Benj. Fewel.
The Clarion and Tennessee Gazette (June 29, 1819)

Dearmond, Miss Elizabeth married in Knox County to Mr. Duke Hawe.
National Banner (March 24, 1826)

Deavers, Mr. Neal C. married in Giles County to Miss Matilda Birdwell
daughter of Mr. John Birdwell.
National Banner and Nashville Daily Advertiser (Wed., Jan. 30, 1833)

Deberry, Miss Eliza Jane eldest daughter of Mathine Deberry Esq.
married in Madison City, Tenn. to Mr. David Meriwether.
National Banner and Nashville Whig (Fri., Dec. 12, 1834)

Decamp, Mr. Gideon of Green County, Ky. married on the 11th June by
the Rev. William Fugua to Miss Elizabeth Dougal, of Davidson County.
Nashville Whig (Thurs., July 18, 1844)

Decherd, Mr. David married at Salem, T. on the evening of the 5th
inst. by the Rev. Aaron Alexander to Miss Elizabeth Calloway Patrick
daughter of the late John Patrick Esq.
National Banner (Sat., May 16, 1829)

Deckard, Mr. Peter S. married in Franklin County 6th inst. to Miss
Francis S. Holder.
National Banner and Nashville Whig (Sat., Nov. 17, 1827)

Deckinson, Miss Sophia married to Mr. Joel Johns.

De Clausell, Miss Martha S. married to Mr. John R. Howard.

De Clauselle, Miss Martha S. married to Mr. John R. Howard.

Dedman, Miss Mary F. married to Mr. Basil W. Coleman.

Deer, Mr. Ephraim married to Miss Nancy Henderson.

Dempsey, Miss Ann married to Mr. M. H. Brigance.

Dempsey, Miss Ann married to Mr. M. N. Briganel.

Dempsey, Mr. Hugh married in Williamson County to Miss Nancy Allen.
National Banner and Nashville Daily Advertiser (Mon., Sept. 9, 1833)

Denham, Mr. George W. married in Henry County, Tenn. to Miss Lydia
Bennett.
National Banner and Nashville Whig (Mon., Feb. 23, 1835)

Deniston, Mr. John W. married in Jefferson County, Missouri to Miss
Ann Maria Vansant.
National Banner (Feb. 17, 1826)

Dennis, Mrs. Catherine married to Mr. Robert Mullins.

Dennis, Miss Elizabeth married to Mr. Richard B. Elam.

Dent, Major J. T. of the United States Army married at Charleston,
S. C. to Miss Catharine Ann Cooper of New York.
The Nashville Whig (April 2, 1817)

Dent, Miss Caroline married to Mr. Philip May.

Dent, Doctor H. of Triana married in Limestone, Ala. to Miss Anna
R. Longstreet.
National Banner and Nashville Daily Advertiser (Mon., Feb. 18, 1833)

Dennison, Miss Delany married to Mr. Alexander Willis.

Denny, Miss Nancy married to Mr. M. B. Byrd.

Denton, Sarah A. married to Jas A. Coleman.

Denton, William married in Williamson County to Charlotte Coleman.
The Western Weekly Review - Franklin, Tenn. (Fri., Feb. 10, 1832)

Denty, Mr. Thomas J. married in Giles County to Miss Elizabeth
Abernathy.
National Banner and Nashville Daily Advertiser. (Mon., March 25, 1833)

Depriest, Miss Harriet Calista married to Sidney C. Possy, Esq.

Dereussaux, Miss Matilda married to Mr. Etienne Vaugine.
National Banner and Nashville Whig (Sat., Feb. 24, 1827)

Derickson, Miss Julia married to Maj. Ebenezer Stone.

Derosset, Mr. Henry married to Miss Eliza Byrd in Blount County.
National Banner (March 17, 1826)

Derryberry, Mr. David L. married in Williamson County to Miss Evelina
Andrews.
The Western Weekly Review - Franklin, Tenn. (Fri., Dec. 23, 1831)

Derybery, Miss S. married to E. Hardison.

Deshazo, Mr. Benjamin H. married in Louisville, Ky to Miss Elizabeth
S. Lewis.
National Banner and Nashville Daily Advertiser. (Thurs., Aug. 15, 1833)

Deugued, Miss Joyce married in Todd County, Ky to Rev. Wm. Warfield.
National Banner and Nashville Whig (Mon., April 18, 1831)

Devier, Miss Mary Ann married at Louisville, Ky to Mr. Samuel
Pennington.
National Banner and Nashville Daily Advertiser (Tues., July 10, 1832)

De Villemon, Miss Matilda married to Mr. Francis Vaugine Jr.

Devinny, Mr. Charles B. married in Nashville on Thursday by the
Rev. Dr. Howell to Miss Esther Rose.
Nashville Whig (Sat., Aug. 8, 1846)

Devor, Miss Martha married to Mr. Joseph Loveitt.

Devore, Mr. Samuel P. married in Fayette County, Ky. to Miss Mary E.
Johnson.
National Banner and Nashville Whig (Fri., June 20, 1828)

Dew, Mr. Joseph J. married in Bolivar to Miss Martha Greenleaf.
National Banner and Nashville Whig (Wed., Aug. 3, 1831)

Dew, Miss Sarah married to Mr. Elijah T. Craig.

Dewitt, Mr. G. V. H. married in Cincinnati to Miss Julia Kilgour.
National Banner and Nashville Daily Advertiser (Thurs., Jan. 19, 1832)

Dewly, Dr. Joseph married in Clarksville to Miss Lucy Gayle.
National Banner and Nashville Whig (Fri., July 15, 1831)

Dial, Miss Esther married to Mr. Samuel W. Fleming.

Dibble, Miss Mary Jane married to Mr. Sumner R. Mason.

Dibrell, Miss Elizabeth married to Mr. John B. Pease.

Dibrell, Elizabeth Watson married to John B. Pease.

Dibrell, Doctor M. W. married in Athens, Mississippi on the 29th
by the Rev. Henry W. Pasley to Miss Martha Louisa Hill, daughter
of Col. William Hill.
National Banner and Nashville Whig (Wed., Aug. 2, 1837)

Dibrell, Mary J. married to Mr. J. Wesley Woodson.

Dickens, Miss Ann P. married to James L. Talbot Esq.

Dickens, Miss Mary married to Mr. Jesse H. Hicks.

Dickens, Miss Mary Ann married to Mr. James Creswell.

Dickens, Col. Samuel of Madison County, Tenn. married in Williams-
borough, Granville County, N. C. to Miss Frances H. Burton.
National Banner and Nashville Whig (Mon., Sept. 5, 1831)

Dickerson, Mr. Henry of Nashville married on the 8th at the resi-
dence of William K. Turner, Esq. of Montgomery County to Miss
Robert A. V. Bryan, daughter of Col. Henry H. Bryan of Montgomery
County.
Daily Republican Banner (Sat., Dec. 12, 1840)

Dickerson, Miss Mary Eliza married to Mr. John Roling.

Dickerson, Mr. Wm. R. married in Rutherford County to Miss Rhoda T.
Johns.
National Banner and Nashville Whig (Sat., April 7, 1827)

Dickey, Mr. F. E. married in Georgetown, Ky. to Miss Elizabeth
Breckinridge.
National Banner and Nashville Whig (Sat., Feb. 17, 1827)

Dickey, Miss Harriet Jane married to Mr. W. O. Ferguson.

Dickey, Mr. John married in Simpson County to Miss Bethia Duncan.
National Banner and Nashville Whig (Sat., Feb. 10, 1827)

Dickey, Mr. Robert married in Florence, Ala. to Miss Elizabeth
Anderson.
National Banner and Nashville Daily Advertiser (Mon., July 23, 1832)

Dickey, Mr. Samuel married in Louisville, Ky. to Miss Elizabeth
Barrett.
National Banner and Nashville Daily Advertiser (Wed., Aug. 22, 1832)

Dickins, Miss Ann P. married to Mr. James L. Talbot.

Dickins, Miss Elizabeth F. married to Mr. William H. Hunt.

Dickinson, Miss Belinda married to Mr. William H. Polk.

Dickinson, Mr. Chs. H. married in this town on the 17th to Miss
Maria W. Turner.
National Banner and Nashville Whig (Sat., April 19, 1828)

Dickinson, Col. David W. of Rutherford County married at Maj. William
Maney's near Franklin by the Rev. Dr. Lindsley to Miss Sally B.
Murfree of Williamson County on the 7th inst.
Nashville Whig (Fri., Oct. 8, 1841)

Dickinson, Miss E. Llewellyn married to Doct. Robert Martin.

Dickinson, Miss E. Llewellyn married to Doct. Robert Martin.

Dickinson, Miss Fanny Priscilla married to William L. Murfree, Esq.

Dickinson, John Esq. of Nashville, Tenn. married to Miss Jean Lytle of Rutherford County.
Impartial Review and Cumberland Repository published at Nashville. (Thurs., May 12, 1808)

Dickinson, Miss Lucinda married to Mr. James H. Cowan.

Dickinson, Miss Martha married to Louis G. Galloway.

Dickinson, Miss Mary married to Mr. James Bell.

Dickinson, Mr. William married in Fayette County, Ky. to Miss Eleanor Murdock.
National Banner and Nashville Whig (Sat., Dec. 23, 1826)

Dickson, David Esq. of Dickson County married to Miss Eliza McNairy of Dickson County Thursday the 16th inst.
Impartial Review and Cumberland Repository, published at Nashville. (Thurs., June 30, 1808)

Dickson, Mr. Henry married in Hardem County to Miss Francis Micham.
National Banner and Nashville Whig (Sat., July 28, 1827)

Dickson, Miss Isabella M. married to Mr. William McLean.

Dickson, Mr. J. W. of Sommerville married in Fayette County, Tenn. to Miss Ann Jane Wormac formerly of Hillsborough, N. C.
National Banner and Nashville Whig. (Fri., March 6, 1835)

Dickson, Mr. James W. married in Bedford County to Miss Martha Harsby.
National Banner and Nashville Whig (Sat., Jan. 3, 1829)

Dickson, Mr. Joseph H. married in Jackson to Miss Eliza Vannoy.
National Banner and Nashville Daily Advertiser. (Thurs., July 12, 1832)

Dickson, Mr. Lewis married at Tuscumbia, Ala. to Mrs. Ann Moore.
National Banner and Nashville Whig (Sat., Feb. 9, 1828)

Dickson, Mr. Malton of Charlotte married to Miss Martha Strong of Dickson County on Tuesday, 3rd inst.
Impartial Review and Cumberland Repository - published at Nashville. (Saturday, Feb. 14, 1807)

Dickson, Miss Margaret married to Mr. Singleton Cock.

Dickson, Miss Martha Jane married to Mr. Richard B. Hatter.

Dickson, Miss Mary Florida married to Henry Baldwin jun.

Dickson, Nancy married to Mr. John C. Smith.

Dickson, Miss Sarah married to Capt. William Harpole.

Dickson, Mr. William married in Bedford County to Miss Wortham, daughter of John Wortham Esq.
National Banner and Nashville Whig (Sat., Dec. 23, 1826)

Dickson, Mr. Wm. married at Clinton, Tenn. to Miss Elizabeth Barton.
National Banner (Sat., May 16, 1829)

Diel, Ester, Miss married to Mr. Samuel W. Fleming.

Diggons, Miss Susannah married to Dr. George M'Daniel.

Diggs, Mr. Benjamin married in Henry County to Mrs. Mary McCorkle.
National Banner and Nashville Daily Advertiser (Tues., Aug. 7, 1832)

Dill, Miss Lavinia married to Mr. Dennis P. Posey.

Dill, Mr. M. M. married in Rutherford County to Miss Mary Ann Sanders.
National Banner and Nashville Whig. (Fri., May 27, 1831)

Dillahunty, Miss Harriet T. married in Lauderdale County, Ala. to
Mr. Lassiter, of Laurince County, Ala.
National Banner and Nashville Daily Advertiser (Tues., March 19, 1833)

Dillahunty, Maj. John B. in Florence married to Miss Sarah N. Savage
National Banner and Nashville Advertiser (May 8, 1832)

Dillard, Dr. of Tuscumbia married in Franklin County, Ala to Miss
Nancy Winston.
National Banner and Nashville Whig (July 8, 1826)

Dillard, Miss Peggy married to Mr. Henry L. Traywich.
National Banner and Nashville Daily Advertiser (Fri., May 4, 1832)

Dillingham, Mr. Hiram in Maury County married to Miss Elizabeth Davis.
Nashville Republican and State Gazette (Thurs., June 9, 1831)

Dillingham, Mr. Hiram married in Maury County on the 11th of May to
Miss Elizabeth Davis.
National Banner and Nashville Whig (Fri., June 10, 1831)

Dillon, Mr. John married in Logan County, Ky. to Miss Jane Edes.
National Banner and Nashville Daily Advertiser (Mon., April 30, 1832)

Dillon, Miss Mary Ann married to Mr. Littlebury Bachelar.
National Banner and Nashville Whig (Mon., Dec. 13, 1830)

Dirickson, Mr. David S. of Davidson County married on the 28th inst.
by Rev. Mr. Roswell to Miss Mary S. Wilson daughter of Samuel Wilson
of Rutherford County.
The Union (Tues., Feb. 2, 1836)

Dirickson, Mr. David S. of Davidson County married on 28th Jan. by
the Rev. Mr. Roswell to Miss Mary Wilson, daughter of Samuel Wilson,
daughter of Samuel Wilson of Rutherford County.
Nashville Republican (Thurs., Feb. 4, 1836)

Dishon, Henry married in Williamson County to Miss Icy Roberts.
The Western Weekly Review - Franklin, Tenn (Fri., March 23, 1832)

Dishon, Henry married in Williamson County to Miss Icy Roberts.
National Banner and Nashville Advertiser (Mon., March 26, 1832)

Dismuke, Dr. D. G. of Macon, Miss. married on the 10th inst. by Rev.
D. Lawsy to Miss Margaret Britton of Lebanon, Tenn.
Nashville True Whig and Weekly Commercial (Wed., Dec. 25, 1850)

Dismukes, Mrs. Fanny married to Mr. Frank Parrish.

Dismukes, Mr. George of Sumner County married on Tuesday evening
22nd inst. to Miss Harriet Williamson, daughter of Jno. Williamson
dec'd of Davidson County.
National Banner and Nashville Daily Advertiser (Thurs., July 24, 1834)

Dismukes, Mr. John T. married on Thursday evening last to Miss Royster
all of Davidson County.
The Nashville Gazette (Sat., Jan. 29, 1820)

Dismukes, Mr. John T. of Tennessee (Russellville, Ky. June 8) married on the 7th inst. by the Rev. R. T. Anderson to Miss Judith Ann Burke of Kentucky.
National Banner and Nashville Whig (Wed., June 22, 1836)

Dismukes, Miss Susan T. married to Mr. Edward A. Cuningham.

Dittmore, Mrs. Catharine A. married to Mr. Thomas Callender.

Dixon, Mr. Henry O. of Abingdon, Va. married on the 16th inst. by the Rev. John W. Hanner to Miss Ann M. Patterson of Davidson County.
Nashville Whig (Fri., Nov. 19, 1841)

Dixon, Miss Lucy P. married to Mr. Jeremiah H. Morgan.

Dixon, Miss Nancy married to John C. Smith.

Dixon, Miss Nancy B. married to Mr. Robert E. Hardin.

Dixon, Major Wallace of Russellville, Ky married on Wednesday evening last by the Rev. John T. Hamilton to Miss Eliza Brady of this place (Nashville).
Nashville Whig (Oct. 6, 1823)

Doak, Miss Charlotte married to Mr. Thomas B. Flintum.

Doan, Mr. Ira married in McMinn County to Miss Nancy Triplett.
National Banner & Nashville Advertiser (Mon., June 18, 1832)

Dobbins, Mr. R. married in Sumner County to Miss Nancy M'Lin.
National Banner & Nashville Daily Advertiser (Thurs., March 20, 1834)

Dobbins, Miss Sarah married to Mr. David Anderson.

Dolbee, Miss Mary married to Mr. Nicholas Wintersteen.

Dollahite, Miss Mahala married to Mr. John J. Daniel.

Dollahite, Mr. Nathaniel married in Henry County to Miss Martha Fawler.
National Banner and Nashville Whig (Sat., March 17, 1827)

Donald, John T. Esq. of Mobile married on the 23rd inst. near Nashville at the residence of Henry Norwell, Esq. by the Rev. Dr. Edgar to Miss Eliza M. Sevier, daughter of Col. George W. Sevier.
The Politician and Weekley Nashville Whig (Wed., Sept. 1st 1847)

Donald, Mr. William W. married at the residence of Miss Harris in Wilson County on the 17 inst. by Rev. B. D. Moore to Miss Frances H. Harris all of Wilson County.
Nashville Whig (Tues., Dec. 22,1846)

Donald, Mr. William W. married at the residence of Mrs. Harris in Wilson County on Thursday, 17th inst. by the Rev. B. D. Moore to Miss Frances H. Harris all of Wilson County.
The Christian Record (Sat., Dec. 26, 1846)

Donaldson, Miss Diana married to Mr. Thomas P. Butt.

Donaldson, Mrs. E. married to John Anderson, Esq.

Donaldson, Mr. James T. merchant of Bowling-Green married in Logan County, Ky to Miss Mary Murrell daughter of Col. William Murrell of Clarksville, Ten.
National Banner & Nashville Whig (Mon., Dec. 29, 1831)

Donaldson, Miss Mariah married to Mr. W. M. Barton.

Donegan, Miss Ellen M. married to Mr. James H. Weakley.

Doneghy, Mr. George W. married at Danville, Ky. to Miss Henrietta
N. Bradburn.
National Banner (March 31, 1826)

Doneghy, Mr. Georgw W. married at Danville, Ky. to Miss Henrietta
Bradburn.
National Banner (April 21, 1826)

Doneghy, Miss Harriet married to Mr. John Allen.

Donelson, Maj. A. J. married on the 10th inst. by Rev. Mr. Lapsley
to Mrs. Elizabeth A. Randolph all of Davidson County.
Nashville Whig (Fri., Nov. 12, 1841)

Donelson, Gen. Daniel S. of Tennessee married at Washington and the
18th ult. to Miss Margaret Branch, daughter of the Hon. John Branch
Secretary of the Navy.
National Banner and Nashville Whig (Mon., Nov. 8, 1830)

Donelson, Emily Miss married to Andrew Jackson Donelson.

Donelson, Mr. John jun. married in Nashville on Thursday 24th inst. by
the Rev. Mr. Edgar to Miss Laura M. Lawrence daughter of Dr. William
P. Lawrence.
National Banner & Nashville Daily Advertiser (Fri., Oct. 25, 1833)

Donelson, Captain John Jr. of Alabama to Miss Eliza Butler married
on Thursday evening last at the seat of Judge McNairys.
Nashville Whig (Nov. 10, 1823)

Donelson, Mr. John Jr. in Nashville married to Miss Laura M. Lawrence
Nashville Republican and State Gazette (Oct. 29, 1833)

Donelson, Lucinda R. Miss married in Davidson County on the 13th ult.
Maj. George W. Martin of Courtland.
National Banner & Nashville Whig (Mon., Oct. 4, 1830)

Donelson, Miss Mary married to Dr. Hamblin.

Donelson, Miss Phereby E. R. married to B. Harper Sheppard.

Donelson, Stockly Esq. married in this town on Thursday evening 19th
inst. by Rev. Hume to Miss Philian Lawrence.
National Banner & Nashville Whig (Fri., June 27, 1828)

Donelson, Mr. Thomas in Davidson County married to Miss Emma Y.
Farqhar at the Hermitage seat of the President Jackson last evening
by the Rev. Mr. Weller.
National Banner and Nashville Advertiser (Sept. 18, 1832)

Donelson, Mr. Thomas J. married last evening by the Rev. Mr. Weller
at the Hermitage the seat of President Jackson in Davidson County to
Miss Emma Y. Farguhar.
National Banner & Nashville Daily Advertiser (Tues., Sept. 18, 1832)

Donelson, Mr. William married in this county on the 14th ult. to Miss
Elizabeth Anderson.
National Banner & Nashville Whig (Sat., July 14, 1827)

Donnahoo, Mr. John M. married in Lincoln county to Miss Mary Giverly.
National Banner & Nashville Whig (Fri., Jan. 23, 1835)

Donnel, Mr. Robert in Sumner County married to Miss Mary Jane Wallace.
Nashville Republican and State Gazette (Oct. 17, 1833)

Donnell, Robert Rev. married in Lawrence County, Ala. to Miss Clarissa
W. Lindley late principal of Oakville Female Academy.
National Banner and Nashville Daily Advertiser (Sat., July 28, 1832)

Donoho, Mr. A. G. married in Sumner County on the 29th ult. by Rev.
Joyner to Miss Cynthia Wynn.
National Banner (Sat., Nov. 14, 1829)

Donoho, Mr. Goldman of Damascus, Sumner County married on Tuesday
last to Miss Scyntha Brevard daughter of John Brevard Esq. of Smith
County.
The Nashville Gazette (Sat., Aug. 28, 1819)

Donoho, Sirrenne married to Mr. John G. Collins.

Donohoo, John Esq. married in Lauderdale County, Ala. to Miss Betsy
Fuguea.
National Banner & Nashville Whig (Sat., Dec. 2, 1826)

Donohoo, Mr. Joseph married in Monroe County to Miss Rebecca C.
Callaway daughter of Joseph Calloway Esq.
National Banner and Nashville Whig (Wed., July 27, 1831)

Donohoo, Miss Sarah married to Col. John J. Hurphreys.

Dooley, Miss Surrilda L. married to Mr. Jas. Mathews.

Dooly, Miss Cynthia married to Mr. James Kimes.

Dooly, Mr. Lyttleton J. of Mary County married in this county to
Miss Mary E. Bell.
National Banner & Nashville Whig (Sat., Oct. 7, 1826)

Doom, Miss Alison E. married to Mr. Robert A. Sanders.

Doores, Mr. French married in Mercer County, Ky to Miss Sarah Taylor.
National Banner and Nashville Whig (Sat., Feb. 21, 1829)

Doran, Miss Minerva married in Rutherford County on the 4th inst. by
the Rev. Jesse Alexander to Mr. Samuel Armstrong.
National Banner and Nashville Whig (Fri., Jan. 14, 1831)

Dorch, Miss Marinda married to Mr. Henry Toney.

Doren, Miss Adeline Therese married to Rev. Robert Davidson.

Doris, Miss Ann married to Mr. Kinchen Bass.

Dorman, Mr. Solomon V. married in Ross County, Ohio to Miss Jane M'Dill.
National Banner & Nashville Whig (Sat., Feb. 3, 1827)

Dorris, Miss Frances married to Mr. Joseph West.

Dorris, Mr. H. P. married in Jackson to Miss Sarah Shropshire.
National Banner & Nashville Daily Advertiser (Wed., July 3, 1833)

Dorsey, Dr. married in Flemingsburg, Ky. to Miss Jane Whittington.
National Banner (May 27, 1826)

Dorsey, Miss Sarah married near Manchester on Thursday last to O. D.
Gibbs Esq. Attorney at law both of Manchester.
Daily Republican Banner (Tues., Dec. 4, 1838)

Dortch, Mr. David married in Maury County to Miss Nancy Dodson.
National Banner & Nashville Whig (Wed., June 1, 1831)

Dortch, Capt. Jesse L. married in this town last evening by the Rev.
Mr. Paine to Miss Nancy Adams all of this city.
National Banner & Nashville Whig (Sat., Jan. 5, 1828)

Dorton, Miss Rebecca married to Mr. Ainsworth Harrison.

Dotson, Miss Elizabeth married to Mr. John Pennington.

Dotson, Mr. Isaac J. married in Lebanon to Miss Octavia Bullard.
Nashville Republican & State Gazette (Tues., May 6, 1834)

Dotson, Mr. James E. married in Davidson County to Miss Rebecca Hope.
Nashville Republican (Tues., Jan. 27, 1835)

Dotson, James M. married in Williamson County to Miss Susan Hardeman.
The Western Weekly Review - Franklin, Tenn. (Fri., Dec. 14, 1832)

Dotson, Miss Nancy T. C. married to Joseph Waller.

Dotson, Mr. Presley married in Williamson County to Miss Ann Harper.
National Banner & Nashville Whig (Wed., Dec. 7, 1831)

Dotson, Mr. Rawliegh married in Maury County to Miss Parthena Witherspoon.
National Banner & Nashville Whig (Mon., Sept. 26, 1831)

Dougal, Miss Elizabeth married to Mr. Gideon Decamp.

Dougherty, Miss Harriett married to Mr. Shadrack S. Hosea.

Dougherty, Dr. Nathaniel E. of Tennessee married in Lexington, Ky.
to Mrs. Mary Jane Caldwell.
National Banner & Nashville Daily Advertiser (Wed., July 9, 1834)

Doughty, Mr. Bushrod T. married on Thursday 12th inst. by the Rev.
Dr. Howell to Miss Martha Jane Tindal all of Nashville.
The Politician & Weekly Nashville Whig (Wed., Aug. 18, 1847)

Doughty, Miss Lyda Jane married to Mr. James Wilkinson.

Douglas, Addison H., Esq. of Sommerville married at Boliver on the
2d inst. at the residence of Gen. J. C. N. Robertson by the Rev
John T. Boscoville to Miss Martha A. Robertson, daughter of Gen.
J. C. N. Robertson.
Nashville Whig (Feb. 19, 1842)

Douglas, Alfred H. Esq. Clerk of Sumner County married on Thursday
evening last to Miss Rebecca Louisa, youngest daughter of David
Fulton, Esq. all of Sumner County.
Nashville Whig. (Feb. 19, 1823)

Douglas, Byrd of the firm of H. & B. Douglas married on the 23d
October by the Rev. M. M. Marshall to Martha R. Bright third daughter
of James Bright, Esq. all of Lincoln County, Tenn.
Nashville Whig (Fri., Nov. 2, 1838)

Douglas, Miss Emma married to Mr. Wm. S. F. Clark.

Douglas, Miss Mary married to Mr. Jared C. Martin.

Douglass, Miss Callie married to Mr. George W. Cook.

Douglass, Miss Caroline married to Mr. S. H. Shaw.

Douglass, Mr. Cullen E. of Sumner County married on the morning of the
4th inst. by the Rev. J. R. Bain to Miss Harriett Newell Bain daughter
of Rev. J. B. Bain of Davidson County.
The Christian Record (Sat., April 8, 1848)

Douglass, Miss Elizabeth S. married to Prof. Andrew Henry Edgar.

Douglass, Harry L. Esq. of Lebanon married in this town on Tuesday
evening last to Mrs. Jane Crabb widow of the late Henry Crabb.
National Banner (Sat., Dec. 19, 1829)

Douglass, Mr. John married in Madison County to Miss Margaret Braden.
National Banner & Nashville Whig (Sat., March 31, 1827)

Douglass, Capt. Kelsey H. married in Tipton County to Miss Minerva
Hulme.
National Banner & Nashville Whig (Sat., Jan. 17, 1829)

Douglass, Miss Lamira L. married to Doctor John D. Erwin.

Douglass, Miss Mary Ann married to Mr. Merry C. Abstin.

Douglass, Miss Mary Ann married to Mr. M. C. Aleston.

Douglass, Miss Mary Catharine married to Mr. John F. Sanderson.

Douglass, Miss Peggy Ann married to Mr. Barkley V. Walker.

Douglass, Miss Priscilla married to Dr. Robert Martin.

Douglass, Mr. Robert married in Smith County to Miss Pamelia Hodges.
National Banner & Nashville Whig (Fri., Dec. 30, 1831)

Douglass, Mr. Robert G. married in Sumner County to Miss Elizabeth
Blythe.
National Banner & Nashville Whig (Mon., June 7, 1830)

Dougle, Miss Mary married to Mr. Kindle Webb.

Douthitt, Mr. Robert H. married in Pittsburgh, Pa. to Miss Adelaide
C. Gleim.
National Banner & Nashville Daily Advertiser (Mon., Sept. 9, 1833)

Dover, Mrs. Eliza married to Rev. J. B. Bunker.

Dowdy, Frances married in Williamson County, Ten. to J. W. Wilson.
National Banner & Nashville Daily Advertiser (Mon., Aug. 26, 1833)

Downing, William D. V. Esq. of Port Gibson, Miss married on the 13th
by the Rev. Dr. Edgar to Miss Nancy B. Campbell daughter of James
Campbell, Esq. of Nashville.
Nashville Whig (Sat., Oct. 15, 1842)

Doyle, Dr. Henry George married in Jefferson County, Miss. to Mrs.
Ann M. Dunbar daughter of Rev. Jacob Creathsen of Kentucky.
National Banner & Nashville Advertiser (Mon., Feb. 6, 1832)

Dozier, Miss Edna H. married to H. T. Wilkinson Esq.

Drake, Mrs. A. married to Hon. George W. Cutter.

Drake, Miss Amanda V. married to Dr. Joseph N. M'Dowell.

Drake, Mrs. Anne married to Mr. Richard Ambrose Turner.

Drake, Mr. Blount married in Davidson county by the Rev. Mr. Pitts
to Miss Mary Hyde.
National Banner & Nashville Whig (Wed., Jan. 21, 1835)

Drake, Charles D. Esq. formerly of Cincinnati married at St. Louis,
Mo. on Tuesday 8th inst. to Miss Martha Ella Taylor of Florence, Ala.
Nashville Republican (Tues., Sept. 26, 1835)

Drake, Mrs. Charlotte married to Mr. John M. Wilkinson.

Drake, Mr. Elijah H. of Lexington married in Fayette County, Ky. to
Miss Emerine Thomson daughter of Clifton Thomson Esq.
National Banner (Sat., Nov. 7, 1829)

Drake, Miss Eliza married to Mr. C. W. Nelson.

Drake, Miss Eveline married to Mr. L. L. Stone.

Drake, Mr. George W. married in Jefferson County to Miss Mary Carson.
National Banner & Nashville Whig (Mon., Oct. 31, 1831)

Drake, Mr. James married in Madison County, Ala. to Miss Honora G.
Rootes.
National Banner & Nashville Whig (Sat., April 7, 1827)

Drake, Mr. James F. of Madison County, Ala. married in Huntsville,
Ala. by the Rev. Mr. McEwen to Miss Mary A. Bright daughter of
James Bright Esq. of Fayetteville.
Daily Republican Banner. (Fri., Oct. 27, 1837)

Drake, Miss Julia married to Mr. Thomas H. Fosdick.

Drake, Miss Mary married to Mr. John D. Stovall.

Drake, Mr. Nathan S. married in Lexington, Ky. to Miss Adelia Thompson.
National Banner & Nashville Advertiser (Fri., Feb. 24, 1832)

Drake, Mrs. Olivia E. married to Mr. D. E. A. Strong.

Drake, Mr. Sevier of this county married in Giles County on the 3d
inst. to Miss Mary P. Mitchell of Giles.
National Banner & Nashville Whig (Sat., Aug. 12, 1826)

Drake, Miss Temperence married to Mr. Exum P. Sumner.

Drane, Lieut A. married in Louisville, Ky. to Miss Elizabeth Rebecca
Ferguson.
National Banner & Nashville Whig (Sat., Dec. 13, 1828)

Drane, Miss Rachel married to Mr. Willer Holland.

Draper, Mr. Ariel married at Louisville, Ky. to Miss Martha Maria
Spencer.
National Banner & Nashville Whig (Fri., Sept. 9, 1831)

Draper, Mr. D. married in Lincoln Co., Ky. to Miss Mary Orr.
National Banner & Nashville Daily Advertiser (Mon., June 30, 1834)

Draper, Mr. Thomas M. recently of Jackson County, Tennessee married
in Monroe County, Arkansas to Miss Eveline Wright.
National Banner & Nashville Whig (Mon., Aug. 15, 1836)

Drennen, Miss Ann married to Maj. John C. Hampton.

Drennan, Miss Anne married to Maj. John C. Hampton.

Dresback, Miss Mary married to Mr. Christopher Ross.

Drew, Miss Ariana married to Mr. William Berry Hurt.

Drew, Miss Juliet married to Mr. Tazewell M. Mart.

Drew, Miss Mary Ann married to Mr. E. S. Vick.

Drew, Thomas Stephenson Esq. formerly of Wilson County, Tenn. married
in Greenville, Mo. to Miss Cinderella Bettis.
National Banner & Nashville Whig (Sat., March 17, 1827)

Drish, Miss Catherine L. married to Pleasant N. Wilson, Esq.

Driver, Mr. Burrell married in Nashville, Monday 18th Feb. to Miss.
Rebecca McDuffy.
National Banner & Nashville Daily Advertiser (Tues., Feb. 19, 1833)

Driver, Mr. Eli M. married in Madison County, Ala. to Miss Julia Sophia Scruggs.
National Banner & Nashville Daily Advertiser (Mon., May 20, 1833)

Driver, Mr. Henry married in Nashville on last evening by the Rev. Mr. Givin to Miss Elizabeth C. Maclin.
National Banner & Nashville Whig (Wed., April 15, 1835)

Driver, Mr. Henry married in Nashville to Miss Elizabeth C. Maclin on Tuesday last.
Nashville Republican (Thurs., April 16, 1835)

Driver, Capt. Wm. of Salem, Mass. married on Sunday the 14th inst. in Christ Church by the Rector, Rev. Mr. Wheat to Miss Sarah Jane Park of Cornersville.
Daily Republican Banner - Nashville (January 19, 1838)

Drummond, Mr. Charles married at Tuscaloosa, Ala. to Miss Elizabeth Taliaferro.
National Banner (April 21, 1826)

Dse-go-eh married at the Valley Towns by the Rev. E. Jones 12th April 1830 to On-dsa-lu-de.
National Banner & Nashville Whig (Mon., July 26, 1830)

Dso-sdo-suh- married at the Valley Towns by the Rev. E. Jones 12th April 1830 to Du-na-ye.
National Banner & Nashville Whig (Mon., July 26, 1830)

Dsu-do-dsa-la married at the Valley Towns by Rev. E. Jones 12th April, 1830 to Ga-lu-sda-ye.
National Banner & Nashville Whig (Mon., July 26, 1830)

Duchouquette, Mr. J. B. married at St. Louis to Miss Amelia Roy.
National Banner & Nashville Daily Advertiser (Sat., July 28, 1832)

Dudgeon, Miss Margaret married to Dr. D. P. Wilson.

Dudley, Mr. A. H. of Christian married in Todd County, Ky. to Miss Susan Anderson.
National Banner & Nashville Whig (Wed., Nov. 24, 1830)

Dudley, Mr. Edward A. married to Miss Margaret Talbot.

Dudley, Miss Elizabeth H. married to Mr. George F. Barnes.

Dudley, Miss Elizabeth Jane married to Mr. William Steel.

Dudley, Mr. Francis N. B. married in Knox County to Miss Nancy Myers.
National Banner (Sat., Nov. 28, 1829)

Dudley, Dr. Japptha married in Clarksville to Miss Lucy Gayle.
Nashville Republican & State Gazette. (Tues., July 12, 1831)

Dudley, Mr. Jeptha of Frankfort married in Madison County, Ky. to Mrs. Sarah Clay widow of the late Gen. Green Clay.
National Banner & Nashville Whig (Mon., April 25, 1831)

Dudley, Miss Julia A. M. married to Mr. James Bosworth.

Dudley, Miss Matilda married to Mr. John Weatherford.

Dudley, Miss Sarah married to Mr. James Lumpkins.

Dudley, Miss Virginia married to Thomas W. Cash, Esq.

Due, Miss Noamy married to Richard L. Craddock.

Duff, Miss Jane N. married to Mr. James W. Hope.

Duff, Miss Sally married to Mr. Gideon Kirk.

Dugger, Mr. Alexander married in Maury County to Miss Catherine Reynolds
National Banner & Nashville Whig (Mon., July 12, 1830)

Dugger, Miss Jane married to Mr. Britian Willieford.

Dugger, Mr. Jones married in Maury County to Miss Sarah S. Jones.
National Banner & Nashville Whig (Fri., Dec. 10, 1830)

Dugger, Miss Lydia married to Mr. Benjamin Hasty.

Duglass, Miss Emma married to Mr. Wm. S. F. Clark.

Duke, H. C. married in Williamson County to Martha Pewit.
The Western Weekly Review - Franklin, Tenn. (Fri., Feb. 10, 1832)

Duke, Dr. J. B. married in Frankford, Ky. to Miss Caroline A. Thomas
National Banner & Nashville Whig (Sat., Oct. 25, 1828)

Duke, Mr. John of Clarksville married in Robinson County on the 9th
inst. to Miss Bobo daughter of Mr. Chaney Bobo.
National Banner & Nashville Whig (Sat., Dec. 27, 1828)

Duke, Miss Julian married to Mr. Ephraim Reinhardt.

Duke, Miss Lucy Ann married to Charles Buford, Esq.

Duke, Mr. Thomas married at Lexington, Ky. to Miss Nancy Ashby.
National Banner (Feb. 24, 1826)

Duke, Mr. Thomas married to Miss Nancy Ashby at Lexington, Ky.
National Banner (Feb. 24, 1826)

Dulancy, Mr. Frank C. married in Warren County, Ky. to Miss Sarah S.
Duncan daughter of Mr. Edmund Duncan.
National Banner & Nashville Whig (Mon., Nov. 22, 1830)

Dulany, Mr. Wm. married in Logan County, Ky. to Miss Nancy W. Morton.
National Banner & Nashville Whig (Sat., Nov. 18, 1826)

Dun, Mr. Samuel married in Danville, Ky. to Miss Susan Sprawl.
National Banner & Nashville Whig (Sat., July 29, 1826)

Dunaway, Lawson H. married in Williamson county to Miss Rebecca Long.
The Western Weekly Review - Franklin, Tenn. (Fri., Dec. 14, 1832)

Du - Na - Ye married at the Valley Towns by the Rev. E. Jones 12th
April 1830 to Dse - sdo - suh.
National Banner and Nashville Whig (Mon., July 26, 1830)

Dunbar, Mrs. Ann M. married to Dr. Henry George Doyle.

Dunbar, Mr. Elza married to Miss Nancy Stokes.

Dunbar, Mr. John married in Wilkinson County, Miss. to Miss Ann
Calliham.
National Banner & Nashville Whig (Sat., Feb. 24, 1827)

Dunbar, Miss Rhoda Ann married to Mr. Taply M. Maddox.

Dunbar, Mr. Robert married in Louisville, Ky. to Mrs. Mineda Rall.
National Banner & Nashville Daily Advertiser (Mon., April 7, 1834)

Duncan, Mr. Albert G. married in Hardeman County to Mrs. Mary D.
Jarmon widow of Maj. William Jarmon.
National Banner & Nashville Whig (Fri., Aug. 26, 1831)

Duncan, Miss Ann E. married to Mr. James S. Irwin.

Duncan, Miss Bethia married to Mr. John Dickey.

Duncan, Miss Caroline married to Mr. William McWhorter.

Duncan, Mrs. Catherine married to Mr. Nehemiah Anderson.

Duncan, Miss Celia married to Capt. Charles Taws.

Duncan, Mr. Coleman of Louisville, Ky married at Lexington, Ky.
to Miss Mary Postlethwait daughter of John Postlethwait, Esq.
National Banner & Nashville Whig (Wed., April 27, 1831)

Duncan, Mr. Garnett of Louisville married at Lexington, Ky. Sat.,
July 15, 1826 to Miss Patsey W. Martin daughter of John L. Martin,
Esq.
National Banner & Nashville Whig (Sat., July 15, 1826)

Duncan, Mr. Jesse S. married at Cincinnati to Miss Elizabeth Patterson.
National Banner & Nashville Advertiser (Wed., Feb. 8, 1832)

Duncan, Mr. John jun. of Mobile married in Autauga County, Ala. to
Miss Catharine M. Creyon.
National Banner (April 7, 1826)

Duncan, Mr. John married in Jonesborough, T. to Miss Rachel G. Duncan.
National Banner & Nashville Whig (Sat., Sept. 2, 1826)

Duncan, Hon. Joseph of Illinois married in Washington city to Miss
Elizabeth Caldwell Smith.
National Banner & Nashville Whig (Sat., May 31, 1828)

Duncan, Mr. Joseph married in Maryville to Miss Susannah Norwood.
National Banner & Nashville Whig (Sat., Nov. 1, 1828)

Duncan, Mr. Lemuel H. married in Muary County on the 3d inst. by the
Rev. Mr. Porter to Miss Emily L. Webster.
National Banner & Nashville Whig (Fri., July 18,1828)

Duncan, Miss Mary D. married in Smith County to Mr. Leonard Saunderson.

Duncan, Miss Mary I. married to Mr. William Moore.

Duncan, Mr. Oliver married in Logan County, Ky. to Miss Roham Priest.
National Banner & Nashville Whig (Mon., Oct. 4, 1830)

Duncan, Miss Rachel G. married to Mr. John Duncan.

Duncan, Miss Sarah married to Mr. Jos. Waters.

Duncan, Miss Sarah S. married to Mr. Frank C. Dulancy.

Duncan, Mr. William M. married in Blount County to Miss Eliza A.
Edmonson.
National Banner & Nashville Advertiser (Mon., Oct. 1, 1832)

Dunham, Mr. Hiram married on the evening of the 1st. of May by the
Rev. W. G. Canders to Mrs. Caroline Smith all of Mt. Pleasant, Maury
County, Tenn.
The Christian Record (Sat., June 10, 1848)

Dunham, Mr. James married in Cincinnati to Miss Rhoda Wooley.
National Banner & Nashville Whig (Sat., Feb. 16, 1828)

Dunham, Miss Sarah married to Mr. Edward M. Temple.

Dunigan, Elizabeth married to Mr. Richard V. Tear.

Dunken, Mr. George married in Blount County to Miss Nancy Jones.
National Banner & Nashville Whig (Sat., Oct. 11, 1828)

Dunkin, Miss Mary E. married to Mr. B. M. Runyan.

Dunlap, Miss Charlotte Eliza married to Maj. Alexnader Hamilton.

Dunlap, Hugh married on Thursday, the 12th of June, 1794. Mr. Hugh
Dunlap, of this town, a merchant to Miss Susannah Ellish Gilliam,
daughter of Captain Gilliam of Knox County.
Knoxville Gazette (Thurs., June 19, 1794)

Dunlap, Hugh W. Esq. of Paris, Ten. married Miss Susannah M'Kiernan
daughter of B. M'Kiernan Esq. in Franklin County, Ala. on the 9th
inst.
National Banner & Nashville Whig (Fri., Feb. 12, 1830)

Dunlap, Miss Martha Jane married to Capt. David S. Greer.

Dunlap, Miss Martha Jane married to Capt. David B. Greer.

Dunlap, Miss Melinda married to John A. Hodges.

Dunlap, Mrs. Nancy of Maury County, Ten. married Rev. Isaac Jones
of Williamson County on the 8th inst.
Nashville Republican & State Gazette (Fri., May 17, 1833)

Dunlap, Gen. Richard G. late Minister from Texas married in Washington
City to Miss Mary Louise Winn.
Daily Republican Banner (Fri., June 5, 1840)

Dunlap, Mr. Samuel married in Williamson County to Miss Mary P.
Henley.
The Western Weekly Review - Franklin, Tenn. (Fri., Dec. 23, 1831)

Dunn, Miss Ann married at Knoxville to Mr. James Hubbard.

Dunn, Ann E. married to John R. Blocker, Esq.

Dunn, Maj. D. married to Mrs. S. B. Hawkins.

Dunn, Maj. D. married to Mrs. S. B. Hawkins.

Dunn, Dr. Dudley married in Memphis to Miss P. Perkins.
National Banner & Nashville Daily Advertiser (Wed., July 17, 1833)

Dunn, Dr. Dudley of Big Creek married Mrs. P. Perkins of Memphis on
Wednesday the 3d inst.
Nashville Republican & State Gazette (Wed., July 17, 1833)

Dunn, Miss Eliza married to Mr. Alpheus Lyon.

Dunn, Miss Elizabeth married to Mr. E. D. Farnsworth.

Dunn, Mr. George J. G. married in Knox County, Ten. to Miss Edy Stow.
National Banner & Nashville Whig (Wed., Dec. 17, 1834)

Dunn, Miss Margaret married to Mr. Lee Shute.

Dunn, Miss Margaret married to Mr. Lee Shute.

Dunn, Miss Martha A. married to Mr. William Mankins.

Dunn, Miss Martha Ann married to Mr. H. Rollings.

Dunn, Miss Mary married to Mr. E. Parkham.

Dunn, Miss Milly married to Mr. David Carr.

Dunn, Miss Penia married to Benj. M. M'Farland, Esq.

Dunn, Miss Penina married to Mr. B. M. M'Farland.

Dunn, Miss Penina C. married to Mr. B. McFarland.

Dunn, Miss Susan married to Mr. Stephen Haynes.

Dunn, Miss Susan Ann married to Mr. Lafayette Jones.

Dunn, Mr. Thomas T. married in Louisville, Ky. to Miss Mary Ann Ridge.
National Banner and Nashville Whig (Fri., March 13, 1835)

Dunn, Col. William D. of Mobile married January 20, 1848 by Rev. Dr. Lapsley to Miss Louisa Horton daughter of the late Joseph W. Horton of the vicinity of Nashville.
The Christian Record (Sat., Jan. 22, 1848)

Dunn, Col. William D. of Mobile married Jan. 20, 1848 by the Rev. Dr. Lapsley to Miss Louise Horton daughter of the late Joseph W. Horton of the Nashville vicinity.
The Politician and Weekly Nashville Whig (Fri., Jan. 28, 1848)

Dunn, Mr. Wilson of Ky. married on the 31st ult. by the Rev. Dr. Edgar to Miss Martha M. Pentecost daughter of Mr. John Pentecost of Nashville.
Nashville Whig (Sat., Sept. 2, 1843)

Dunseth, Miss Julia married at Cincinnati to Capt. J. Strodes.
National Banner & Nashville Whig (Sat., June 2, 1827)

Duralde, Miss Clarice married to Wm. C. C. Claiborne.

Durden, Mr. Anthony married on the 18th inst. Miss Helen Hooper by the Rev. Mr. Hume.
The Nashville Whig & Tenn. Advertiser (Dec. 29, 1817)

Durham, Mr. James married in Maury County, Ten. to Miss Prudence Perdew.
National Banner & Nashville Whig (Wed., Feb. 25, 1835)

Durham, Mr. Joseph H. married in Smith County to Miss Matilda Nichols.
National Banner & Nashville Daily Advertiser (Fri., May 18, 1832)

Durham, Miss Louisa married to Mr. David Taylor.

Durham, Miss Nancy married to Mr. Samuel H. Baughn.

Durham, Mr. Thomas A. of Warren County married in Smith County to Miss Maria Nicholas daughter of Capt. Matthews Nichols.
National Banner & Nashville Daily Advertiser (Wed., April 24, 1833)

Durrett, Mr. J. H. married in Christian County, Ky. to Miss Mary Crow.
National Banner & Nashville Whig (Sat., Jan. 3, 1829)

Durring, Miss Mariah married to Mr. E. Anderson Jr.

Dustin, Miss Elizabeth H. married to Col. John Lane.

Duty, Mr. Solomon married in Madison County to Miss Margaret M'Donald.
National Banner & Nashville Whig (Sat., March 31, 1827)

Duty, Mr. William B. married on Thursday evening 9th inst. to Miss Sarah Wilkins daughter of James Wilkins Esq.
The Western Weekly Review - Franklin, Tenn. (Fri., Feb. 10, 1832)

Duval, Miss Caroline A. married to Mr. John F. Cook.

Duval, Miss Elizabeth C. married to Mr. Laurence Finn.

Duval, Miss Elizabeth P. married to William H. McNairy.

Duvall, Miss Ann married to Mr. Thomas Richards.

Duvall, Miss Susan Ann married to Rev. Hardy M. Cryer.

Dwiggins, Miss Mary A. married to Mr. Enoch Russhing.

Dwyer, Miss Catharine married to Mr. Joseph Dwyer.

Dwyer, Miss Elizabeth married to Col. Wm. Phillips.

Dwyer, Miss Jane married to Mr. David M. Saunders, Esq.

Dwyer, Mr. John of this town married in New York to Miss Mary C. Tierney.
National Banner (Sat., Aug. 8, 1829)

Dwyer, Mr. Joseph of Franklin married in this town on the 29th by Wm. William Esq. to Miss Catharine Dwyer of Nashville.
National Banner & Nashville Whig (Sat., March 8, 1828)

Dwyer, Miss Sally married to Mr. Andrew Far.

Dwyer, Miss Sarah Maria married to Richard W. Otis, Esq.

Dyas, Mr. Alexander J. of Nashville married at Columbia on the 21st inst. by the Rev. Mr. Sherman to Miss Sarah B. Jackson of Columbia.
Nashville Whig (Fri., Oct. 29, 1841)

Dyche, Mr. John married in Green County to Miss Nancy Williams daughter of Mr. Enos Williams.
National Banner & Nashville Daily Advertiser (Fri., March 29, 1833)

Dye, Mr. Stephen W. married in Louisville, Ky. to Miss Eliza Plew.
National Banner & Nashville Advertiser (Tues., June 26, 1832)

Dye, Maj. Thomas J. of Lincoln County married in Maury County to Miss Eleanor Cocke.
National Banner & Nashville Whig (Mon., Aug. 8, 1831)

Dyer, Mr. Abner S. married in Maury County on the 2d inst. to Miss Martha Hall.
National Banner & Nashville Whig (Thurs., Sept. 9, 1830)

Dyer, Mr. Abraham married at Louisville, Ky. to Miss Maria King.
National Banner & Nashville Advertiser (Mon., July 30, 1832)

Dyer, Miss Drucilla C. married to Dr. Stephen S. Childress.

Dyer, Frances Miss married to Mr. Thomas Mitchell.

Dyer, Miss Francis E. married to Mr. E. F. Parker.

Dyer, Joel H. Esq. married in Jackson to Miss Sarah L. Miller daughter of Pleasant M. Miller, Esq.
National Banner & Nashville Whig (Sat., Feb. 17, 1827)

Dyer, Mary married in Williamson County, Ten. to Jacob Scott, Jr.
National Banner & Nashville Daily Advertiser (Mon., Aug. 26, 1833)

Dyer, Miss Sarah E. married to James L. Totten, Esq.

Dyer, Miss Sophia married to William R. Hess, Esq.

Eagan, Mr. Samuel R. married in Wilson county on Sunday 2d inst. to Miss Myra Harris.
National Banner & Nashville Whig (Fri., Aug. 7, 1835)

Eakin, Mr. A. P. married on Tuesday 15th inst. by the Dr. Edgar, at the residence of John M. Hill Esq. to Miss Louise P. Wright all of Nashville.
The Christian Record (Sat., Dec. 26, 1846)

Eakin, Miss Eleanor V. married on the same evening (Thursday last) to Mr. Benjamin W. Wilson both of this town.
Nashville Whig (Nov. 10, 1823)

Eakin, Miss Jane married in Shelbyville, Ten. to Mr. John W. Cowan.

Eakin, Miss Eleanor V. married to Mr. Benjamin W. Wilson.

Eakin, Miss Jane married to Mr. John W. Cowan.

Easkin, John R. Esq. of Nashville married in Huntsville, Ala. on Monday last, by the Rev. Mr. Wright to Miss Bettie Erwin daughter of Andrew Erwin Esq.
The Christian Record (Sat., Aug. 5, 1848)

Easkin, Miss Minerva A. married in Nashville last evening, by the Rev. William Hume to Mr. Cornelius Conner.
National Banner & Nashville Daily Advertiser (Fri., July 13, 1832)

Eakin, Miss Myra P. married to Capt. T. P. Minor.

Easkin, Thomas of Nashville married in Philadelphia on the 19th inst. by the Rev. Dr. Bethune to Sarah Ewing eldest daughter of the late Henry Ewing, Esq. of Philadelphia.
Nashville Whig (Tues., Sept. 29, 1846)

Eakin, William Esq. merchant of the house of W. & T. Eakin & Co. married in Nashville on 5th inst. by the Rev. Dr. Edgar to Felicia Ann Grundy youngest daughter of Hon. Felix Grundy, deceased.
Nashville Whig (Thurs., July 7, 1842)

Eales, Miss Louisa married in Bourbon county, Ky. to Mr. Joseph F. Taylor.

Eames, Miss Elizabeth B. married to Rolla P. Raines Esq.

Earhart, Mr. Adam married in Davidson County to Miss Mary Sturdivant.

Earheart, Mr. W. L. married on the 2d inst. by the Rev. J. B. McFerrin to Miss Ann Clay.
Daily Republican Banner (Sat., April 4, 1840)

Earie, Mr. Jacob W. married at Louisville, Ky. to Miss Maryann Bell.
National Banner & Nashville Whig (Sat., April 7, 1827)

Earl, Miss J. S. married to Mr. H. D. Bradley.

Earley, Miss Jane married to Mr. Andrew Gould.

Earnest, Mr. Frederick B. married at Louisville, Ky to Miss Eleanor Garrard.
National Banner & Nashville Whig (Sat., Jan. 10, 1829)

Earthman, Miss Mary married to Dr. Peter Smith.

Earwood, Miss Jane married to Mr. Robert B. Thompson.

Easley, Mr. Hugh married in Madison county, Ala. to Miss Murrell.
National Banner & Nashville Daily Advertiser (Aug. 23, 1832)

Easley, Mr. Hugh married at Huntsville, Ala. to Miss Margaret Murrell.
National Banner & Nashville Daily Advertiser (Wed., Aug. 29, 1832)

Eason, Mr. Howel D. married in Madison County, Ala. to Mrs. Mary Hays.
National Banner (Sat., Oct. 17, 1829)

Eason, Maj. James K. married in Statesville, Ten. to Miss Jane Fisher on the 8, inst. daughter of Mr. John Fisher.
National Banner & Nashville Whig (Mon., Sept. 12, 1831)

Eason, Miss Margaret Ann married to Rev. Alexander Cuningham.

Eason, Mr. Randolph married at Athens to Mrs. Margaret L. Fyffe widow of Isaac W. Fyffe Esq. deceased.
National Banner & Nashville Whig (Fri., June 10, 1831)

Eason, Mr. William H. of Wilson County married on the 29th ult. by the Rev. T. W. Haynes to Miss Nancy A. Whittemore of Davidson.
Nashville Whig (Tues., March 5, 1844)

East, Mrs. Elizabeth married to Mr. Seymour Powell.

East, Miss Elizabeth married to Mr. Seymour Powell.

East, Capt. Thomas of Giles County married to Miss Sarah J. Alderson.
National Banner (Sat., Oct. 17, 1829)

East, Dr. William A. married in Nashville on Tuesday evening 5th inst. by the Rev. C. D. Elliott to Miss Elizabeth H. Searcy daughter of W. W. Searcy Esq. of Jackson.
Nashville Whig (Thurs., May 7, 1846)

Easters, Miss Barbara married to Mr. Robert Buchanan.

Eastin, Miss Mary A. married to Lucius J. Polk Esq.

Eastin, Miss Sarah married to Mr. Samuel Sparkman.

Eastland, Miss Ann Marie married to M. Charles Cooper.

Eastland, Capt. Thomas merchant of this town married on Thursday evening last, by the Rev. Mr. Craighead to Miss Polly Swann of Davidson County.
The Nashville Whig (July 7, 1817)

Eastland, Mr. Thomas B. married at Murfreesborough on the 21st. inst. to Miss Josephine M. Green.
National Banner (Sat., April 11, 1829)

Eastland, Mr. Wm. married in Limestone County, Ala. to Miss Ann P. Borrough.
National Banner & Nashville Whig (Sat., April 7, 1827)

Easton, Mr. E. married in Cincinnati to Miss Mary D. Kemper.
National Banner & Nashville Whig (Fri., Nov. 11, 1831)

Easton, Miss Rachel J. married to Dr. Richard O. Curry.

Eaton, Miss Hannah married to Mr. James M. Prescott.

Eaton, Hezekiah H. Esq. assistant professor of Chemestry at Transylvania University, married at Lexington, Ky. to Miss Mary R. Harper daughter of the late James Harper, Esq.
National Banner & Nashville Whig (Sat., Dec. 17, 1831)

Eaton, Hon. John H. of the U. S. Senate married on Thursday 1st. Jan. 1829 in Washington City to Mrs. Margaret Timberlake.
National Banner & Nashville Whig (Sat., Jan. 24, 1829)

Eaton, Miss Mary married to Mr. William L. Lindslay.

Eaton, Miss Temperance married to Lunsford L. Alsobrook Esq.

Eaton, Mr. Wm. a soldier of the revolution, aged 64 to Miss Lovey
Worthy Woods aged 29 daughter of Phillip W. Woods.
National Banner (Sat., June 6, 1829)

blen, Miss Lucinda married to Mr. Wm. M'Elwee.

Echols, Miss Eliza married to Mr. Larkin F. Wood.

Echols, Miss Sarah W. married to Capt. John R. Kent.

Eddings, Miss Arraminta married to Mr. Spencer W. Scruggs.

Eddings, Miss Elizabeth C. married to Mr. John R. M'Carroll.

Eddings, Miss Louisa married to Mr. Byrel Hill.

Eddins, Miss Elvira married to Mr. William D. Jones.

Eddins, Mr. Lewis T. married in Madison County, Ten. to Miss
Elizabeth Lacy.
National Banner & Nashville Daily Advertiser (Wed., April 4, 1832)

Edes, Miss Jane married to Mr. John Dillon.

Edes, Miss Polly married to Mr. James Couch.

Edgar, Andrew H. of Nashville married at Gallatin on the 16th by
the Rev. John W. Hall to Miss Iva Ann Henderson of Gallatin.
Nashville Whig (Fri., April 20, 1840)

Edgar, Andrew H. Esq. of Nashville married at Gallatin on the 16th
by the Rev. John W. Hall to Miss Iva Ann Henderson daughter of the
late Charles Henderson of Gallatin.
Daily Republican Banner (Tues., April 21, 1840)

Edgar, Prof. Andrew Henry married at Gallatin on the 27th inst. by
the Rev. Dr. Edgar to Miss Elizabeth S. Douglass daughter of the
late Alfred H. Douglass, Esq.
The Politician & Weekly Nashville Whig (Fri., Feb. 4, 1848)

Edgar, Prof. Andrew Henry married at Gallatin, Tenn. on the 27th
by the Rev. Dr. Edgar to Miss Elizabeth S. Douglass daughter of the
late Alfred H. Douglass, Esq.
The Christian Record (Sat., Feb. 5, 1848)

Edgar, Mr. John Todd of Nashville married at Canonsburg, Pa. on the
15th inst. by the Rev. Dr. R. J. Breckenridge to Miss Fanny Smith
daughter of the Rev. William Smith D. D. of Jefferson College.
The Politician & Weekly Nashville Whig (Fri., June 25, 1847)

Edgar, Mr. John Todd of Nashville married at Canonsburg, Pa. on the
15th inst. by the Rev. Dr. R. J. Breckenridge to Miss Fanny Smith
daughter of the Rev. William Smith, D. D. of Jefferson College.
The Christian Record (Sat., June 26, 1847)

Edgar, Miss Margaret Anne married to Mr. Charles A. R. Thompson.

Edgar, Miss Margaret Ann married to Mr. Charles A. R. Thompson.

Edgar, Miss Mary married to Thomas J. Wharton.

Edgar, Miss Polly Ann married to Mr. George Crudeson.

Edgemond, Miss Nancy married to Mr. John Brasheare.

Edgerton, Miss Diana married to Mr. James Mitchell.

Edington, Mr. Nicholas married in Knox County, Ten. to Miss Patience Wright.
National Banner & Nashville Whig (Mon., April 13, 1835)

Edmiston, Miss Eliza Ann married to Mr. Wm. M. Old.

Edmiston, Miss Mary married to Mr. William B. M'Cutchen.

Edmonds, Miss F. C. married to Maj. A. M. Hamptramck.

Edmonds, Miss L. N. married to B. C. Brown Esq.

Edmondson, Mr. Andrew married in Williamson County on Feb. 17th by the Rev. William A. Whitsette to Miss Sarah J. Holland.
The Politician & Weekly Nashville Whig (Fri., Feb. 25, 1848)

Edmondson, Miss Eliza A. married to Mr. William M. Duncan.

Edmondson, Miss Esther S. married to Mr. David Glass.

Edmondson, Miss Eveline married to Mr. William Edmondson.

Edmonson, Mr. John married in Williamson County to Miss Mary Cummings.
National Banner & Nashville Whig (Sat., Oct. 6, 1827)

Edmondson, Mr. John C. married in Williamson County, Ten. to Miss Nancy S. Coleman.
National Banner & Nashville Whig (Mon., April 13, 1835)

Edmondson, Miss Mary J. married to Mr. John B. Miles.

Edmondson, Miss Sarah Ann married to Mr. Greenbury Fleece.

Edmondson, Mr. William married in Williamson County, Ten. to Miss Eveline Edmondson.
National Banner & Nashville Whig (April 13, 1835)

Edmundson, Mr. John K. married in Nashville on Thursday evening last by Rev. Geo. Weller to Miss Matilda G. Wilson daughter of Col. George Wilson all of Nashville.
Nashville Republican (Sat., April 29, 1837)

Edmundson, Mr. Ross B. of Tennessee married in Logan County, Ky to Miss Vesta L. Wilson daughter of Samuel Wilson Esq.
National Banner & Nashville Daily Advertiser (Mon., Jan. 9, 1832)

Edney, Miss Nancy married to Mr. Orion S. Perry.

Edson, Miss Lucy married to Mr. Regen Jones.

Edwards, Mr. Amos A. married on Sunday 4th inst. by William B. Cook, Esq. to Miss Malinda Anderson daughter of Capt. John G. Anderson all of Hickman County.
Nashville Republican (Wed., Sept. 8, 1836)

Edwards, Mr. Amos A. married on Sunday the 4th inst. by William B. Cook, Esq. to Miss Melinda Anderson daughter of Capt. John G. Anderson all of Hickman County.
National Banner & Nashville Whig (Fri., Sept. 9, 1836)

Edwards, Mr. Augustus married in Madison County to Miss Mary Van.
National Banner & Nashville Advertiser (Wed., March 28,1832)

Edwards, Miss Chancy married to Mr. James Van Pelt.

Edwards, Mr. Henry M. married in Henry County to Elizabeth Brown
National Banner & Nashville Advertiser (Monday, April 23, 1832)

Edwards, Mr. Joseph, merchant, married on the evening of the 24th
at the residence of John W. Walker Esq. by Rev. Dr. Edgar to Miss
Sarah E. Keenan all of Nashville.
The Christian Record (Sat., Feb. 19, 1848)

Edwards, Joseph Esq. of the house of J. W. Walker & Edwards of Nash-
ville. Married on Tuesday last 24th inst. by the Rev. Dr. Edgar to
Miss Sarah Elizabeth Keenan of Florence, Ala.
The Politician & Weekly Nashville Whig (Fri., March 3, 1848)

Edwards, Miss Judith married to Mr. Thomas Nelson.

Edwards, Miss Lucy married to Mr. Joseph Martin.

Edwards, Miss M. J. married to John L. Lancaster Esq.

Edwards, Miss Marillas married to Mr. Leaman Haile.

Edwards, Miss Mary married to Mr. John B. Slaughter.

Edwards, Mrs. Mary W. married to A. W. Putnam Esq.

Edwards, N. W. Esq. married in Lexington, Ky. to Miss Elizabeth Todd
daughter of Robert S. Todd Esq.
National Banner & Nashville Advertiser (Fri., March 9, 1832)

Edwards, Miss Nancy married to Mr. Andrew Beard.

Edwards, Mr. Silas married in Williamson County to Miss Mary Bagby.
The Western Weekly Review - Franklin, Tenn. (Fri., Dec. 2, 1831)

Edwards, Mr. Silas married in Williamson County to Miss Mary Bagby.
National Banner & Nashville Whig (Wed., Dec. 7, 1831)

Edwards, Mr. Wm. married in Logan County to Miss Adeline Amos.
National Banner (Sat., May 2, 1829)

Edwards, Mr. William married at Bowling Green to Miss Ann Virginia
West.
National Banner (Sat., Sept. 26, 1829)

Edwards, Mr. Wm. L. T. married in Wayne County on the 4th inst. by the
Rev. Mr. Barnett to Miss Rachel S. Burns.
National Banner & Nashville Whig (Fri., July 18, 1828)

Edwards, Mr. Young married in Christian County, Ky to Miss Elizabeth
Williams.
National Banner & Nashville Advertiser (Thurs., Oct. 18, 1832)

Eelbeck, Henry married in Williamson County to Miss Sarah Williamson.
Nashville Whig (Aug. 11, 1823)

Egbert, Miss Roselie R. married to Mr. Walter Burke, Jun.

Eggleson, Mr. Edward C. married in August 1831 to Miss Matilda Seay.
The Western Weekly Review - Franklin, Tenn. (Fri., Sept. 2, 1831)

Elam, Miss America R. married to Mr. William Bass.

Elam, Miss Elizabeth W. married to Mr. Francis Vannerson.

Elam, Mr. Richard B. married at Little Rock, Ark. to Miss Elizabeth
Dennis.
National Banner & Nashville Whig (Sat., Sept. 8, 1827)

Elam, Maj. S. Muel married on the 22nd day of November last at
Petersburg, Va. to Mrs. Elizabeth Stokes of Petersburg, Va.
The Nashville Gazette (Sat., Dec. 30, 1820)

Elam, Mr. William married to Miss Jamina Strange in Rutherford County
on Thursday evening last.
National Banner & Nashville Whig (Tues., Feb. 9, 1830)

Elben, Miss Ann married to Mr. Sylvester Freeman.

Elder, Mrs. married to Mr. James B. Reynolds, Esq.

Elder, Mr. Benjamin married in Rutherford County to Miss Eliza A.
Wade.
National Banner & Nashville Whig (Sat., Feb. 24, 1827)

Elder, Miss Frances married in Rutherford County to Mr. David Baxter.
National Banner & Nashville Daily Advertiser (Sat., April 14, 1832)

Elder, Miss Lucretia E. married to Mr. Wm. Oldham.

Elder, Miss Roberta married to Robert Caldwell.

Elder, Miss Sarah W., Jr. [sic] married to Mr. Edward Tanner.

Elder, Mr. William married in Louisville, Ky. to Miss Cynthia Ann
Fultrell.
National Banner & Nashville Whig (Fri., March 13, 1835)

Elderberry, Miss C. married to Mr. N. Blackberry.

Eldridge, Miss Elizabeth married to Archibald Wright, Esq.

Eldridge, Miss Julia married to Rev. William L. Lacy.

Eldridge, Miss Julia married to Rev. Wm. L. Lacy.

Eli, Miss Polly W. married to Samuel Hutchins Esq.

Elizer, Mr. James of Williamson married in Sumner County to Miss
Mary Garnett.
National Banner (Sat., Sept. 19, 1829)

Elkins, Mr. Abel G. married in Madison County, Ky. to Miss Elizabeth
Hogan.
National Banner & Nashville Whig (Sat., Oct. 28, 1826)

Ellet, Miss Elizabeth married to Mr. James A. Johnson.

Ellett, Miss Milley married to Mr. Frederick Carlook.

Elliot, Mr. D. of Lebanon married in Sumner County to Miss Solima
Cage.
National Banner & Nashville Whig (Mon., Jan. 10, 1831)

Elliot, Hugh Esq. of the House of Grigg & Elliot, Booksellers. Married
in Philadelphia, on the 20th by the Rev. Epra Stiles Ely to Mary
Stuart Robinson daughter of J. J. Robinson Esq. of Montgomery County,
Ten.
Nashville Whig (Sat., July 1st 1843)

Elliot, James Mr. married in Williamson County on Thursday evening
27th inst. to Miss Mary Bobbitt.
National Banner & Nashville Whig (Mon., Jan. 31, 1831)

Elliot, Miss Kitturah married to Mr. Dawson H. Robinson.

Elliott, Miss Eliza Ann married to Mr. Joseph Henderson.

Elliott, Miss Elizabeth married to George A. Wyllie, Esq.

Elliott, Miss Margaret D. married to Mr. Josiah Breechen.

Ellis, Miss Catherine M. married to John B. Coleman.

Ellis, Harvey W. Esq. married in Tuscaloosa County, Ala. to Miss
Catherine Parish.
National Banner & Nashville Daily Advertiser (Sat., July 7, 1832)

Ellis, Mr. Isaac married in Wilson County to Miss Nancy Jennings.
National Banner & Nashville Whig (Sat., Nov. 17, 1827)

Ellis, Mary Miss married in Lincoln County to Mr. Samuel Cuningham.

Ellis, Hon. Powhatan Senator from Mississippi married to Miss Eliza
Winn in Washington City.
Nashville Republican & State Gazette (Sat., March 19, 1831)

Ellis, Hon. Powhatan Senator in Congress from Miss. married at
Washington City to Miss Eliza Winn daughter of Timothy Winn Esq.
National Banner & Nashville Whig (Mon., March 21, 1831)

Ellis, Richard W. Esq. of Smithville, Arkansas married in McMinnville
on the 8th inst. by the Rev. A. M. Stone to Eliza Jane Ford eldest
daughter of John W. Ford Esq.
Nashville Whig (Sat., Dec. 19, 1846)

Ellis, Richard W. Esq. of Smithville, Arkansas married in McMinnville
on the 8th inst. by Rev. A. M. Stone to Miss Eliza Jane Ford eldest
daughter of John W. Ford, Esq.
The Christian Record (Sat., Dec. 26, 1846)

Ellis, Mr. Robert married in Montgomery County to Miss Ann Williamson.
National Banner (March 17, 1826)

Ellis, Mr. Rowland married at Cincinnati to Miss Mary C. Rogers.
National Banner & Nashville Whig (Sat., Jan. 3, 1829)

Ellis, W. M. Esq. married in Dickson County on 12th inst. to Miss
George Ann West of Dickson County
Nashville Whig (Tues., April 19, 1842)

Ellis, Mr. William W. of the Tennessee Iron Works, Caldwell Co., Ky.
married yesterday morning by the Rev. Dr. Howell to Mrs. Susan Clark
of Nashville.
The Politician & Weekly Nashville Whig (Wed., Aug. 18, 1847)

Ellison, Miss Eliza married to Mr. Leonard Launtz.

Elliston, Miss Mary A. E. married to Rev. A. L. P. Greene.
Nashville Republican & State Gazette (Sat., Oct. 22, 1831)

Elliston, William R. Esq. of this vicinity married on the 12th inst. by
the Rev. A. L. P. Green to Miss Elizabeth B. Boddie eldest daughter of
Elijah Boddie Esq. of Sumner County.
Daily Republican Banner (Wed., May 13, 1840)

Elsberry, Miss Fanny married to Mr. William Burchitt.

Elsberry, Miss Fanny married to Mr. William Burchitt.

Ely, Miss Chloe married to Mr. Henry L. Cowan.

Ely, Mr. Jesse married in Montgomery County to Miss Charlotte Jamison.
National Banner & Nashville Whig (Mon., Jan. 10, 1831)

Ely, Miss Lucy married to Mr. Ridley Morgan.

Ely, Miss Mariah married to Mr. William Curd.

Ely, Miss Nancy married to Mr. Thomas Dodson.

Ely, Mr. Nelson of Overton County married in Monroe County, Ten. to Miss Margaret Tate of Monroe.
National Banner & Nashville Whig (Wed., Feb. 4, 1835)

Elzy, Miss Elizabeth married to Mr. Solomon Rutter.

Emack, Miss Harriet Hargrove married to Mr. Thomas R. Kennedy.

Embree, Miss Eliza married to Mr. Jefferson Wilson.

Embry, Mr. Bowling married in Mountsterling, Ky. to Miss Louisa Howard.
National Banner (March 17, 1826)

Embry, Miss Patsy married to Dr. George Tribble.

Embry, Mr. Squire married in Henry County to Miss Christa Snider.
National Banner & Nashville Daily Advertiser (Thurs., March 22, 1832)

Emerson, Mr. Henry married in Cincinnati to Miss Eveline Benbride.
National Banner & Nashville Whig (Sat., Jan. 19, 1827)

Emmerson, Thomas, Esq. married in Jonesborough to Miss Catherine Jacobs.
National Banner & Nashville Daily Advertiser (March 18, 1833)

Emmerson, Hon. Thomas formerly one of the judges of the Supreme Court of this state married in Jonesborough on the 7th ult. to Miss Catherine Jacobs.
National Banner & Nashville Daily Advertiser (Wed., April 3, 1833)

Emmerson, Mr. Thomas B. married in Jonesborough, Ten. to Miss Eliza. Green.
National Banner & Nashville Daily Advertiser (Fri., Sept. 6, 1833)

Emmit, Miss M. L. married to Mr. F. S. Allison.

Enders, Mr. Robert of Shawneetown married in Union County, Ky. to Miss Amanda Barbee.
National Banner (Feb. 24, 1826)

England, Miss Frances married to Mr. Geo. Stamer.

English, Dr. Charles G. of Tallahassee, Florida married in Nashville on the 24th of Sept. by the Rev. Mr. Elliott to Miss Martha E. Southall of North Carolina.
Nashville Whig (Tues., Oct. 31,1843)

English, Mr. Ephraim married in Henry County to Miss Flora Buie.
National Banner & Nashville Advertiser (Wed., Feb. 8, 1832)

English, Miss Hetty married to Mr. Henry Wayland, Jr.

English, Capt. James married at Tuscumbia to Miss Cynthia Crawford.
National Banner & Nashville Whig (Sat., Dec. 23, 1826)

English, Jane B. married to John J. Akin.

English, Mr. Thomas married at Pittsburgh to Miss Mary O'Donnell.
National Banner & Nashville Advertiser (Tues., July 10, 1832)

Ensley, Miss Mary Paralee married to Robert N. Williams Esq.

Enoch, Mr. Alfred married in this County on the 3d inst. to Miss E. S. Famborough.
National Banner & Nashville Whig (Sat., April 12, 1828)

Enness, Mr. John B. married at Cincinnati to Mrs. Eliza Biddle.
National Banner & Nashville Daily Advertiser (Wed., Aug. 15, 1832)

Eppes, Miss Polly married to Mr. Nicholas Gibbs.

Epps, Miss Martha C. married to Mr. James H. W. Stanback.

Epps, Miss Martha C. married to Mr. James W. Stainback.

Erich, Miss Elizabeth married to Mr. Thomas B. Hooper.

Erness, Mr. John P. married in Cincinnati to Miss Susan Collingman.
National Banner & Nashville Whig (Sat., Oct. 28, 1826)

Erwin, Miss Amelia married to Mr. William T. Yeatman.

Erwin, Miss Amelia married to Mr. William T. Yeatman.

Erwin, Mr. Andrew Jr. married on the 12th inst. at the house of John P.
Erwin, Esq. to Miss Elvira J. Searcy, daughter of Maj. Robert Searcey,
dec'd.
The Nashville Gazette (Sat., Oct. 14, 1820)

Erwin, Miss Bettie married to John R. Eakin, Esq.

Erwin, Miss Catherine married to Mr. Joseph H. B. Wilson.

Erwin, Mr. Hugh of Nashville married on 23d inst. by the Rev. Mr.
Lapsley to Miss Margaret Bosley of this vicinity.
Nashville Republican (Thurs., Feb. 25, 1836)

Erwin, Mr. James married in this town on Thursday 15th inst. to Miss.
Margaret Caldwell.
National Banner & Nashville Whig (Sat., Jan. 17, 1829)

Erwin, Rev. James of Centerville, Hickman County married in Davidson
County on the 24th inst. by the Rev. Martin Clark to Miss Francis A.
Jefferson of Davidson County.
National Banner & Nashville Daily Advertiser (Fri., Jan. 27, 1832)

Erwin, Miss Jane married to Mr. Thomas Yeatman.

Erwin, Mr. John married to Miss Peggy Rivers of Davidson County on
Oct. 5, 1808.
Impartial Review & Cumberland Repository - Published at Nashville
(Thurs., Oct. 6, 1808)

Erwin, Doctor John D. of this town married on the 7th inst. to Miss
Lamira L. Douglass of Louisville, Ky.
Nashville Whig (Nov. 24, 1823)

Erwin, John E. married in Williamson County to Miss Elizabeth H.
McFadden.
The Western Weekly Review - Franklin, Tenn. (Fri., Dec. 14, 1832)

Erwin, Miss Nancy married to Col. Andrew Hynes.

Erwin, Miss Laura married to Mr. William J. Ledyard.

Erwin, Miss Laura married to Mr. William J. Ledyard.

Erwin, Miss Leodocia married to Mr. Wm. B. Robertson.

Erwin, Miss Margaret G. married to Mr. John K. Callahan.

Erwin, Miss Olivia married to Mr. Jeremiah Swing.

Erwin, Mr. Pinckney married in Maury County to Miss Minerva Darnell.
National Banner & Nashville Whig (March 8, 1828)

Erwin, Miss Rebecca J. married to Major Andrew F. Goff.

Erwin, Miss Sarah married to Rev. Albert G. Gibson.

Espy, Miss Maria married to Mr. William D. Turner.

Esselman, Miss Ann C. married to Mr. Samuel H. London.

Estell, Mr. Philemon of M'Minn County, married in Rhea County to Miss
Emeline Day.
National Banner & Nashville Whig (Sat., Feb. 2, 1828)

Estes, Mr. Alston B. married in Pulaski to Miss Virginia A. Brown.
Nashville Republican & State Gazette (Mon., Feb. 4, 1833)

Estes, Mr. Henderson married in Columbia to Miss Martha White.
National Banner & Nashville Daily Advertiser (Thurs., Dec. 27, 1832)

Estes, Mr. L. H. married at Tuscaloosa, Ala. to Miss Ann Neal.
National Banner & Nashville Daily Advertiser (Mon., March 31, 1834)

Estes, Miss Martha married to Mr. Thomas Fuzzell.

Estes, Mr. Robert P. of Nashville married to Miss Eliza Cartwright of
Davidson County.
Nashville Republican & State Gazette (Thurs., June 23, 1831)

Estes, Miss Virginia T. married to Dr. Paca Wilson.

Estill, Miss Jane W. married to Mr. James R. Hobbs.

Estill, Miss Mary Ann married to Mr. Jefferson Curle.

Estill, Miss Rebecca married to Mr. James R. Slatter.

Estill, Dr. W. married in Winchester on the 8th inst. to Miss Eleanor
Crabb daughter of Col. R. Crabb.
The Nashville Whig & Tenn. Advertiser (Jan. 24, 1818)

Estlin, Miss Rebecca married to Mr. John Starr.

Ethridge, Mr. David married in Henry County to Miss Lucinda Ray.
National Banner & Nashville Daily Advertiser (Fri., April 12, 1833)

Eubanks, Mr. Richardson married in Logan County, Ky to Elizabeth
Richardson.
National Banner & Nashville Whig (Sat., Sept. 6, 1828)

Evans, Miss Eleanor married to Mr. Isaac Finlay.

Evans, Miss Malvina married to Col. Wm. C. Garrison.

Evans, Mrs. Mary married to Mr. Samuel B. Wright.

Evans, Miss Mary married to Mr. Edmund Odum.

Evans, Miss Mary B. married to Mr. William Galbreath.

Evans, Mr. Nathaniel of Somerville, Ala. married near Whitesburg, Ala.
on the 3d ult. by the Rev. James H. Lorance to Miss Sarah Jane
Richardson of Whitesburg.
The Christian Record (Sat., Dec. 4th, 1847)

Evans, Mr. William T. married in Logan County, Ky to Miss Amelia
Williams of Robertson County, Ten.
National Banner & Nashville Whig (Mon., Dec. 29, 1834)

Everett, Miss Louisa married to Mr. John Roe, Jr.

Everett, Miss Louisa married to Mr. John Roe, Jr.

Everett, Miss Sarah A. B. married to Mr. Hanse H. Ridley.

Everheart, Mr. Martin married in Washington County, Ky to Miss Eliza. McLlroy.
National Banner & Nashville Whig (Sat., Jan. 27, 1826)

Eversoll, Miss Ann married to Mr. William Tabler.

Eves, Mr. Bartlet married in Henry County to Miss Levina Walker.
National Banner & Nashville Daily Advertiser (Wed., Feb. 8, 1832)

Evetts, Mr. Samuel married in Smith County to Miss Jane Canada.
National Banner & Nashville Whig (Fri., Nov. 18, 1831)

Ewalt, Mr. Samuel married in Lexington, Ky. to Miss Eliza P. Smith.
National Banner & Nashville Daily Advertiser (Thurs., June 19, 1834)

Ewell, Miss Frances married to Mr. Robert Campbell.

Ewen, Capt. John M. married in Kingston to Miss Nancy Patton.
National Banner & Nashville Daily Advertiser (Wed., Jan. 9, 1833)

Ewing, Mr. Andrew married on Thursday, Feb. 4th by the Rev. Dr. Lindsley. to Miss Margaret Haynes, eldest daughter of Col. Andrew Haynes all of Nashville.
Nashville Republican (Sat., Feb. 6, 1836)

Ewing, Mr. B. W. married in Oldham County, Ky. to Miss Ann Eliza Barbour.
National Banner and Nashville Daily Advertiser (Mon., July 20, 1834)

Ewing, Edwin H. Esq. of Davidson County married in Davidson County on the 20th inst. by the Rev. Mr. Hume to Miss Rebecca P. Williams of Davidson County.
National Banner & Nashville Daily Advertiser (Mon., Dec. 24, 1832)

Ewing, Miss Eliza C. married in Logan County Ky. to Mr. Andrew Jackson M'Lean.
National Banner and Nashville Whig (Sat., Jan. 19, 1828)

Ewing, George W. Esq. of Russellville, Ky married on the 18th at the Cross plains, Robertson County, Tenn. to Miss Susan C. Moss.
National Banner & Nashville Whig (Mon., Feb. 1, 1836)

Ewing, Henry of this town married on the 23rd ult. to Miss Susan C. Grundy daughter of George Grundy of Washington County, Ky.
Nashville Whig (Oct. 4, 1824)

Ewing, James W. Esq. of Hopkinsville married in Russellville, Ky. to Miss Lucelia Jane Breathitt.
National Banner and Nashville Whig (Sat., Jan. 31, 1829)

Ewing, John H. married yesterday morning by the Rev. Mr. Fanning to Susan H. Goodwin.
Daily Republican Banner (Fri., Nov. 9, 1838)

Ewing, Mr. Joseph L. married on Thursday evening last to Miss Sally M'Gavock, daughter of David M'Gavock Esq. all of this County.
Nashville Whig (Nov. 15, 1824)

Ewing, Mrs. Lamira married to Major John Boyd.

Ewing, Miss Martha married to Capt. Lamb.

Ewing, Miss Mary married to Frances Shannon.

Ewing, Mary Ann Elizabeth married to John H. Miller

Ewing, Miss Mary Jane married to Mr. Pleasant Smith.

Ewing, Miss Mary Y. married to Mr. John B. Garner.

Ewing, Orville Esq. of Nashville, Tenn. on 28 inst. married to
Miss Melbrey H. Williams, daughter of John F. Williams by the Rev.
Mr. Hume.
National Banner and Nashville Daily Advertiser (Mon., Jan. 30, 1832)

Ewing, Sarah married to Thomas Eakin.

Ezell, Miss Sarah married to Joseph P. Hood.

Fackler, Mr. John A. married at Huntsville, Ala. to Miss Elizabeth
A. Turner.
National Banner (Jan. 27, 1826)

Fagundus, Mr. Theadore of Nashville married in Davidson County on the
4th May to Miss Levenia Saunders daughter of William Saunders.
National Banner & Nashville Whig (Fri., May 6, 1836)

Fain, Miss Eliza R. married to Dr. A. C. White.

Fain, Dr. G. S. of Nashville married on Tuesday evening the 17th inst.
by the Rev. C. Foster Williams to Margaret E. Witson of Maury County.
Nashville Daily Gazette (Dec. 22, 1857)

Fain, Mr. Samuel married in this town on Tuesday evening last to Miss
Susan S. Wharton.
National Banner & Nashville Whig (Sat., June 7, 1828)

Faircloth, Miss Mary Ann married to Mr. Joseph T. Wilson.

Fairfax, Miss Matilda F. married to Mr. Robert Lusk.

Fairly, Miss Elizabeth married to Mr. Elihu J. Marshall.

Falconer, Miss Martha married to Dr. Hugh W. Henry.

Falger, Mr. John of Cincinnati married in Vicksburgh, Mi. to Mrs.
Martha Habbell of Philadelphia.
National Banner & Nashville Daily Advertiser (Sat., Aug. 17, 1833)

Falkenberry, Miss Ruth married to Mr. Melton Fowler.

Fall, Alexander Esq. married at Hazlewood in this vicinity by the
Rev. Mr. Howell to Miss Elizabeth Horton third daughter of Joseph W.
Horton Esq.
Nashville Whig (Tues., Oct. 25, 1842)

Fall, Miss Charlotte married to Rev. T. Fanning.

Fall, Mr. James S. junior editor of the Mississippian married in
Jackson, Miss. to Miss Esther O. Crutcher daughter of the late George
R. Crutcher.
National Banner & Nashville Whig (Wed., Jan. 20, 1836)

Fall, Mr. James S. Junior editor of the Mississippian. Married in
Jackson, Miss. on the 31st inst. by the Rev. L. B. Hollaway to Miss
Esther O. Crutcher daughter of the late Geo. B. Crutcher.
Nashville Republican (Thurs., Jan. 21, 1836)

Fall, Mr. James A. Junior editor of the Mississippian married in
Jackson, Mississippi to Miss Esther O. Crutcher daughter of the late
George B. Crutcher, deceased.
The Union (Thurs., Jan. 21, 1836)

Fall, John S. Esq. one of the Publishers of the Agriculturist married
in Nashville last evening by the Rev. T. Fanning to Sarah Bradford
daughter of Simon Bradford Esq.
Nashville Whig (Wed., Sept. 29, 1841)

Fall, Miss Marianna married in Nashville on Wednesday evening 28th
inst. by the Rev. Mr. Hume to Mr. Orin A. Kinne.
National Banner & Nashville Whig (Thurs., July 29, 1830)

Falls, Miss Fanny M. married to S. B. Lanier Esq.

Falls, Mr. James of Murfreesborough married in this county to Miss
Frances Love.
National Banner & Nashville Whig (Sat., March 10, 1827)

Famborough, Miss E. S. married to Mr. Alfred Enoch.

Fanning, Rev. T. of Nashville, Tenn. married in Nicholasville, Ky. on the 5th inst. by Rev. Dr. B. F. Hall to Miss Sarah Ann Shreve daughter of Judge W. Shreve.
National Banner & Nashville Whig (Fri., Nov. 13, 1835)

Fanning, Rev. T. married on Thursday 22nd Dec. by the Rev. Philip Lindsey D. D. to Miss Charlotte Fall all of Nash.
National Banner & Nashville Whig (Fri., Dec. 23, 1836)

Fanning, Rev. T. of Nashville, Tenn. married Miss Charlotte Fall on 22nd of Dec.
Nashville Republican (Sat., Dec. 24, 1836)

Fannyline, Miss married to Dr. F. J. Jones.

Far, Mr. Andrew merchant of this town married on Wednesday evening last to Miss Sally Dwyer of Franklin.
Nashville Whig (April 30, 1823)

Faris,. Miss Eliza F. married to Gregory D. Stone Esq.

Faris, Mr. Eneas married in Smith County to Miss Hannah Symmes.
National Banner & Nashville Whig (Sat., Feb. 24, 1827)

Faris, Mr. Hezekiah married in Amhurst County, Va. to Miss Sarah Young.
National Banner (March 17, 1826)

Faris, Mr. Joseph Belt married in Fleming County, Ky to Miss Betsy Ann Finley.
National Banner & Nashville Whig (Sat., Jan. 20, 1826)

Faris, Miss Sally married to Richard Anderson Esq.

Farley, Major John F. married in Limestone County, Ala. to Miss Mary Allen.
National Banner (April 21, 1826)

Farley, Miss Martha married to Mr. Farney.

Farley, Miss Martha J. married to Capt. Thomas L. Stevens.

Farmer, Baily W. married in Murfreesborough to Miss Susan M. Fletcher.
National Banner & Nashville Whig (Fri., Sept. 16, 1831)

Farmer, Mr. Collins married in Rutherford County to Miss Elizabeth Kelton.
National Banner & Nashville Advertiser (Sat., July 14, 1832)

Farmer, Miss Judith Ann married to Mr. Thomas M. Aiken.

Farmer, Mr. Moses E. married in August 1831 to Miss Jane Williams.
The Western Weekly Review - Franklin, Tenn. (Fri., Sept. 2, 1831)

Farmer, Miss Sarah D. married to Mr. William Work.

Farney, Mr. married in Shelbyville to Miss Martha Farley.
National Banner & Nashville Whig (Oct. 7, 1826)

Farnham, Miss Adeline married to Augustus D. Berry Esq.

Farnsworth, Mr. E. D. of Nashville married in New Orleans on the 21st inst. by the Rev. Mr. Wheedon to Miss Elizabeth Dunn of New Orleans.
Nashville Whig (Sat., April 30, 1842)

Farnsworth, Miss Mary Ann married to Dr. Joseph E. Bell.

Farguhar, Miss Emma married to Mr. Thomas J. Donelson.

Farquharson, Miss Nancy married to Mr. Hiram F. Delancy.

Farr, Mr. Perran married in Courtland, Ala. to Miss Rebecca S. Freeman.
National Banner & Nashville Whig (Fri., Dec. 10, 1830)

Farran, Mr. W. E. married in Maury County to Miss Rachel Reynolds.
National Banner & Nashville Whig (Sat., Oct. 7, 1826)

Farrar, Mr. John married in Bedford County to Miss Mariam Blair.
National Banner & Nashville Daily Advertiser (Sat., Oct. 6, 1832)

Farrell, Dr. of New Orleans married in Nashville on Monday evening by the Rev. Phillip Lindsley, D. D. to Miss Jane Kirkman daughter of the late Thomas Kirkman of Nashville.
Nashville Whig (Fri., Oct. 19, 1838)

Farrell, Doctor of New Orleans married in Nashville on Monday by the Rev. Philip Lindsley, D. D. to Miss Jane Kirkman daughter of the late Thomas Kirkman of Nashville.
Nashville Union (Fri., Oct. 19, 1838)

Farrell, Mr. Andrew married at Louisville, Ky. to Miss Sarah Mathena.
National Banner (Sat., June 27, 1829)

Farrell, Doctor John of New Orleans married on Monday last by the Rev. Philip Lindsley to Miss Jane Kirkman of Nashville.
Daily Republican Banner (Fri., Oct. 19, 1838)

Farrer, Mrs. Martha W. of Dickson County married on the 6th inst. to Mr. James Gould of Nashville.
Nashville Whig (Fri., Oct. 11, 1839)

Farrer, Preston W. Esq. Attorney at Law married at Oak Grove the residence of Gov. Scott to Miss Eliza Scott only daughter of the Governor.
National Banner & Nashville Daily Advertiser (Thurs., April 11, 1833)

Farrer, Mr. Samuel married at Cincinnati to Miss Sarah H. Howard.
National Banner (Feb. 24, 1826)

Farrington, Miss Priscilla P. married to Mr. James H. Gaines.
National Banner & Nashville Whig (Wed., May 25, 1831)

Farrington, Miss Priscilla P. married to Mr. James H. Gains.

Farris, Carey A. Esq. married in Williamson County on the 14th inst. by Rev. Otey to Miss Martha F. Maury.
National Banner & Nashville Whig (Sat., Jan. 24, 1829)

Farwater, Mr. David married in Knox County, Ten. to Miss Emelia Summers.
National Banner & Nashville Whig (Mon., Jan. 5, 1835)

Fauleoner, Mr. Absalom married in Fayette County, Ky to Miss Clarissa Perkins.
National Banner & Nashville Whig (Mon., Sept. 13, 1830)

Faulk, Dr. Wilson married in Jefferson County, Miss. to Mrs. Martha Valentine.
National Banner & Nashville Whig (Sat., Oct. 28, 1826)

Faulkner, James T. of Nashville married on the 4th inst. by the Rev. Dr. Howell to Miss Margaret M. Howerton of Davidson County.
The Politician & Weekly Nashville Whig (Fri., Jan. 7, 1848)

Faulkner, Mr. John W. married near Montgomery, Ala. to Miss M. L.
Byrd.
National Banner & Nashville Whig (Sat., Sept. 27, 1828)

Faulkner, Mr. Robert P. married on the 16th inst. by Rev. A. Goodlet
to Miss Mary A. Hunter.
Nashville Whig. (Tues., July 21, 1846)

Fauntleroy, Mrs. Emily married to Mr. George Webb.

Fausett, Miss Rebecca married to Mr. George Turner.

Fearn, Dr. Richard L. married in Madison County, Ala. to Miss Maria
Jane Walker.
National Banner & Nashville Whig (Sat., Feb. 7, 1829)

Fearn, Miss Sophronia L. married to Mr. John M. Putnam.

Feltus, Mr. Edward married at Woodville, Miss. to Miss Sarah W.
Marshall.
National Banner (April 28, 1826 and April 21, 1826)

Feltz, Miss Eliza married to Mr. Thomas H. Harris.

Fenn, Miss Caroline J. married to Major John E. Fenn.

Fenn, Major John E. of this town married at Petersburg, Va. to Miss
Caroline J. Fenn.
National Banner & Nashville Whig (April 14, 1827)

Fennell, Mr. Hubbard H. married in Madison County, Ala. to Miss Mary
Smith.
National Banner & Nashville Whig (Sat., March 29, 1828)

Fenner, Miss Eliza married to Mr. James Vaulx.

Fenner, Mr. Erasmus D. married at Jackson to Miss Ann A. Collier.
National Banner & Nashville Advertiser (Wed., Feb. 8, 1832)

Fentress, David Esq. of Bolivar married in Murfreesborough to Miss
Matilda M'Iver.
National Banner & Nashville Daily Advertiser (Sat., Jan. 26, 1833)

Fentress, David, Esq. of Bolivar married to Mrs. Matilda M'Iver.
Nashville Republican & State Gazette. (Fri., January 30, 1833)

Fentress, Miss Rebecca married to Mr. W. R. Hicks.

Ferebee, Geo. W. Esq. married to Miss Hannah Montgomery.

Ferguson, Adam Esq. married in Carthage on Wednesday 24th of June to
Miss Hester Ann Hazard.
National Banner (Sat., July 11, 1829)

Ferguson, Rev. Case married in Bedford County to Mrs. Harriet Davidson.
National Banner & Nashville Whig. (Fri., Oct. 20, 1826)

Ferguson, Mr. D. of St. Louis married in Herculaneum, Misso. to Miss
Jane Lewis.
National Banner & Nashville Whig (Sat., Dec. 13, 1828)

Ferguson, Mr. Edwin of New Orleans married at A. A. Cassedays by the
Rev. Dr. Edgar to Miss Elvina S. Cantrell all of Nashville.
Nashville Whig (Thurs., Jan. 15, 1846)

Ferguson, Miss Eleanor E. married to Mr. George Starkley.

Ferguson, Miss Eliza J. married to Mr. William B. Shepheard.

Ferguson, Miss Elizabeth Rebecca married to Lieut A. Drane.

Ferguson, James Esq. married in Natchez, Mi. to Miss Josephine Quiggles.
National Banner & Nashville Daily Advertiser (Wed., Aug. 14, 1833)

Ferguson, Mr. James B., Jr. married in Nashville on Monday 25th inst. by the Rev. Jesse B. Ferguson to Miss Elizabeth M. Robinson daughter of John McNairy Robinson of Baton Rouge, La.
The Christian Record (Sat., Sept. 30, 1848)

Ferguson, Miss Jane married to Maj. John B. Nash.

Ferguson, Mr. John married to Miss Margaret A. Gillespie.
The Western Weekly Review - Franklin, Tenn. (Fri., Nov. 11, 1831)

Ferguson, Mr. John married in Williamson County to Miss Margaret A. Gillespie.
National Banner & Nashville Whig (Mon., Nov. 14, 1831)

Ferguson, Mrs. Nancy married to Mr. Lewis Talbert.

Ferguson, Miss Philadelphia married to Mr. Francis Niblett.

Ferguson, Mr. Samuel married in Blount County to Miss Elizabeth Patrick.
National Banner & Nashville Daily Advertiser (Mon., April 29, 1833)

Ferguson, Mr. W. O. married in Maury County to Miss Harriet Jane Dickey.
National Banner & Nashville Daily Advertiser (Thurs., March 20, 1834)

Ferguson, Wm. D. Esq. married in Sumner County to Mrs. Margaret D. Neely widow of the late Capt. A. B. Neely.
National Banner (Sat., Oct. 17, 1829)

Fernandez, Mr. Francis married at New Orleans on the 26th by the Rev. Theo Clapp to Mrs. Eleonore Pienovi civorcee of Mr. F. C. Bamcier.
National Banner & Nashville Daily Advertiser (Sat., July 12, 1834)

Fernival, Mr. Henry Lewis of Baltimore married to Miss Polly Perry of Davidson County on Sunday evening last.
Impartial Review & Cumberland Repository - Published at Nashville (Sat., July 26, 1806)

Ferree, Miss Ellen R. married to Mr. Isaac C. Ashton.

Ferrel, Mr. Binonn formerly of Sumner County, aged 44 married in Hickman County, Ky. on Sunday 17th Oct. by the Rev. Mr. Samuel Gibson to Mrs. Elender Ray aged 52.
National Banner & Nashville Whig (Mon., Nov. 22, 1830)

Ferris, Mr. Douglass married in Rutherford County to Miss Mary Ward.
National Banner & Nashville Daily Advertiser (Sat., Jan. 26, 1833)

Ferry, Monsier G. married in Louisville, Ky. to Mademoiselle Mary Murray.
National Banner & Nashville Daily Advertiser (Tues., March 11, 1834)

Few, Miss Sarah Ann married to Mr. Marcus L. Cartwright.

Ficklin, Joseph Esq. editor of the Kentucky Gazette married in Christian County, Ky. to Mrs. Polly L. Campbell.
Nashville Whig (Jan. 22, 1823)

Ficklin, Mrs. Maria married to Arch'd Yell.

Field, Eli married in Williamson County to Sarah Hodge.
The Western Weekly Review - Franklin, Tenn. (Fri., Feb. 10, 1831)

Field, Miss Haniel married to Mr. John Hutt.

Field, Miss Margaret Y. married to Col. Joseph C. Rhea.

Field, Dr. Edward R. married in Pulaski on the 16th inst. to Miss
Julia Ann Flournoy.
National Banner & Nashville Whig (Sat., Jan. 26, 1828)

Fields, Mr. Eli married in Williamson County to Miss Sarah Hodge on
Thursday the 9th inst.
National Banner & Nashville Advertiser (Mon., Feb. 13, 1832)

Fields, Miss Nancy C. married to Mr. Greenville Hanks.

Fields, Miss Sarah J. married to Mr. James Harberson.

Fields, Mr. Silas married in Louisville, Ky. to Miss Eliza Miller
daughter of Major Anderson Miller
National Banner (Jan. 20, 1826)

Fields, Mr. William of Knoxville, Ten. married to Miss Minerva H.
Mayes of Davidson County.
Nashville Republican & State Gazette (Sat., Nov. 1, 1834)

Fields, Mr. William Jr. printer of Knoxville married on Thursday
evening last by the Rev. Wm. White to Miss Minerva H. Mayes daughter
of Mr. Gardner Mayes of this county.
National Banner & Nashville Whig (Mon., Nov. 3, 1834)

Figg, Mr. Richard married in Mercer County, Ky to Miss Mary Brown.
National Banner & Nashville Whig (Sat., March 31, 1827)

Figuers, Miss Caroline married in Wilson County, on the 9th ult. to
Capt. William Dudley Smith.

Figures, Capt. B. married in Wilson C., Ten. to Miss Caroline Davis.
National Banner & Nashville Daily Advertiser (Thurs., June 19, 1834)

Figures, Miss Martha of Wilson County married on Thursday evening last,
by the Rev. Mr. Malone to Mr. James W. Lewis Esq. of Franklin County.
The Nashville Whig (Sept. 17, 1816)

Figuers, Miss Mary married to Mr. Robert B. Porterfield.

Figuers, Mr. Thomas of Springfield married to Miss Eliza W. Coleman of
Robertson County, on Wednesday 4, inst.
Impartial Review & Cumberland Repository. - Published at Nashville
(Sat., Feb. 14, 1807)

Files, Miss Maria T. married to Mr. James Rice.

Finch, Mr. Wm. of Davidson County married in Nashville on the 22d of
May to Miss Mary Stephen of Nashville.
National Banner & Nashville Daily Advertiser (Mon., May 26, 1834)

Finch, Mr. William of Hayesboro married to Miss Mary Stephens of
Nashville on 22 inst.
Nashville Republican & State Gazette (Tues., May 27, 1834)

Fine, Miss Margaret E. married to Mr. John Monoham.

Finlay, Mr. Isaac married in Sparta, White Co. to Miss Eleanor Evans.
National Banner (Sat., Aug. 15, 1829)

Finlay, Mr. John C. married in Madison County, Ala. to Miss Cynthia Hamblet.
National Banner (April 7, 1826)

Finley, Alvah Esq. married in Madison County, Ala. to Miss Sarah T. F. Hall.
National Banner & Nashville Whig (Wed., July 6, 1831)

Finley, Mr. Andrew married in Shelby County, Ky. to Miss Icephena Younger.
National Banner (March 17, 1826)

Finley, Miss Betsy Ann married to Mr. Joseph Belt Faris.

Finley, Major J. J. Attorney at law of Grenada, Miss. married at Memphis, Tennessee to Miss Eliza H. Lamb of Memphis.
Nashville Whig (Fri., Jan. 11, 1839)

Finn, Mr. Laurence of Franklin, Ky. married in Robertson County on the 4th inst. to Miss Elizabeth C. Duval.
National Banner & Nashville Daily Advertiser (Mon., Sept. 10, 1832)

Finnell, Miss Lucy C. married to Mr. John T. Timmerman.

Fiser, Mr. John B. of Springfield married in Robertson County, Ten. to Miss Angeline Binkley.
National Banner & Nashville Whig (Mon., Sept. 19, 1831)

Fisher, Miss Adeline married to Mr. Elias H. Simpson.

Fisher, Miss Clara married to Mr. James Gaspard Meader.

Fisher, Daniel Esq. of Murfreesborough married at Decatur, Ala. to Miss Sarah Margaret F. Dancy daughter of Col. Francis Dancy.

Fisher, Colonel Daniel of La. married yesterday at 5 p.m. in Christ Church by Rev. Thomas Wheat to Mrs. Penelope Williams of Nashville.
Nashville Whig (Wed., Sept. 15, 1841)

Fisher, Miss Elizabeth married to Capt. Jacob Gingery.

Fisher, Miss Frances G. married to Mr. James Wise.

Fisher, Miss Frances G. married to Mr. James Wise.

Fisher, Mr. Fred married in Williamson County, Ten. to Miss Rebecca S. McCurdy.
National Banner & Nashville Whig (Fri., Jan. 9, 1835)

Fisher, Mr. Frederick E. married in this town on Tuesday the 1st inst. by the Rev. Mr. Hume to Miss Ann W. Buck.
National Banner & Nashville Whig (Sat., April 12, 1828)

Fisher, Mr. George married in Bedford County to Miss Rebecca Shearon.
National Banner & Nashville Whig (Wed., Dec. 14, 1831)

Fisher, Col. James H. married in Lebanon on the 29th inst. by the Rev. C. G. Macpherson to Miss Ann C. Cossitt daughter of the Rev. Dr. F. R. Cossitt.
Nashville Whig (Sat., Sept. 2, 1843)

Fisher, Miss Jane daughter of Mr. John Fisher married to Maj. James K. Eason.

Fisher, Mr. John married in Maury County to Miss Sarah D. Hurt.
National Banner & Nashville Whig (Thurs., Nov. 18, 1830)

Fisher, Mr. John B. of Springfield married to Miss Angelina Binkley in Robertson County.
National Banner & Nashville Whig (Mon., Sept. 19, 1831)

Fisher, Michael Esq. married in Bedford County to Miss Mary Burrow.
National Banner & Nashville Advertiser (Thurs., July 12, 1832)

Fisk, Miss Caroline married to Sam Turney, Esq.

Fisk, Miss Caroline married to Samuel Turney, Esq.

Fisk, Miss Celina married to Mr. George Christian.

Fisk, Mr. Isaac to Miss Elizabeth Johnson. Married on Thursday last Feb. to the 1806 Mr. Isaac Fisk of Jackson County to Miss Elizabeth Johnson of this place (Nashville)
Impartial Review (Feb. 8th, 1806)

Fisk, Rev. Nathaniel married in Hilham to Miss Martha Goodpasture.
National Banner and Nashville Daily Advertiser (Fri., Feb. 10, 1832)

Fisk, Miss Onela married to Daniel Ames, Esq.

Fisk, Miss Perilla married to Mr. S. L. Leonard.

Fisk, Miss Sarah P. married to Mr. Sidney H. Little of Ohio.

Fite, Mr. L. B. merchant of Nashville married on the 1st inst. by the Rev. Mr. Bowen to Miss Amanda F. Reynolds of Smith County.
Nashville Whig (Mon., Jan. 13, 1840)

Fite, Mr. Thomas H. married on the 6th day of Sept. 1840 by Edder S. Lindsley to Miss Martha Jane Couch both of Nashville.
Nashville Whig (Wed., Sept. 9, 1840)

Fite, Mr. Thomas J. of Trenton married in Dyer County to Miss J. C. Henderson.
Nashville Whig (Tues., April 21, 1846)

Fitz, Abraham a soldier of the revolution, aged 72 years. Married in Abemarle County, Va. to Mrs. Lucy Dawson aged 56 years.
National Banner & Nashville Whig (Wed., Jan. 21, 1835)

Fitz, Minerva Ann married to James Poteete.
National Banner & Nashville Daily Advertiser (Mon., Aug. 26, 1833)

Fitzgerald, Miss Nancy married to Mr. Geo. Bealer.

Fitzgerald, Miss Nancy married to Mr. John Bowden.

Fitzgerald, Nancy married to Mr. Geo. W. Shelton.

Fitzhugh, Mr. John W. of Davidson married in Madison County to Miss Araminta Bryan.
National Banner & Nashville Whig (Sat., Feb. 14, 1829)

Fitzhugh, Miss Lucy Ann married to Henry S. Coxe, Esq.

Fitzhugh, Mr. Samuel married in Madison County, Ala to Miss Mary Bibb.
National Banner & Nashville Whig (Sat., Dec. 30, 1826)

Fleece, Mr. Greenbury married in Washington County, Ky. to Miss Sarah Ann Edmondson.
National Banner & Nashville Whig (Sat., Jan. 27, 1827)

Fleming, Mr. Hugh married in Lexington, Ky. to Miss Mary Grooms.
National Banner (May 20, 1826)

Fleming, Major John D. married in Maury County to Miss Margaret Williams.
National Banner & Nashville Daily Advertiser (Wed., Oct. 3, 1832)

Fleming, Mr. Samuel W. married in Henry County to Miss Esther Dial.
National Banner & Nashville Advertiser (Tues., July 17, 1832)

Fleming, Miss Susan B. married to Mr. John C. Atkinson.

Flemming, Mr. Ferguson of the firm of Flemming & Co. married in Nashville on the 25th inst. by the Rev. A. L. P. Green to Miss Frances J. McCombs daughter of James McCombs Esq.
Nashville Whig (Thurs., Jan. 27, 1842)

Flemming, Mr. John married in Madison County, Ten. to Miss Margaret Knight.
National Banner & Nashville Daily Advertiser (Tues., Sept. 16, 1834)

Fleshart, Miss Jane married to Mr. Ephram Noel.
National Banner & Nashville Whig (Mon., April 11, 1831)

Fletch, Mr. Peyton married to Mrs. Sarah W. Graves in Davidson County on the 26th.
National Banner & Nashville Whig (Tues., Feb. 2, 1830)

Fletcher, Col. Elliott married at Fayetteville to Miss Frances Hickman on Thursday the 6th inst.
Nashville Republican & State Gazette (Sat., Jan., 22, 1831)

Fletcher, Col. Elliot married at Fayetteville to Miss Frances Hickman.
National Banner & Nashville Whig (Mon., Jan. 24, 1831)

Fletcher, Mr. J. M. married on the 8th inst. near Nashville by the Rev. R. B. C. Howell to Miss Maria Ann Hooper.
Nashville Whig (Tues., Jan. 11, 1842)

Fletcher, Miss Mary M. married to Mr. Josiah Ligon.

Fletcher, Miss Mary M. married to Mr. Rufus Jetton.

Fletcher, Mr. Russell married in Henry County to Miss Elizabeth Lee.
National Banner & Nashville Daily Advertiser (Fri., Feb. 22, 1833)

Fletcher, Mr. Russell married in Henry County to Miss Elizabeth Lee.
Nashville Republican & State Gazette (Fri., Feb. 22, 1833)

Fletcher, Miss Ruth Talbot married to Gen. William H. Loving.

Fletcher, Miss Ruth Talbot married to Gen. William H. Loving.

Fletcher, Sarah married to Joseph W. Clay.

Fletcher, Miss Susan M. married to Mr. Baily W. Farmer.

Fletcher, Thomas Esq. of the Natchez Bar married on the 5th inst. by the Rev. Dr. Edgar to Miss Harriet Caroline Cage daughter of Jesse Cage Esq. of Sumner County.
Nashville Whig (Fri., Oct. 8, 1841)

Flint, Miss Elizabeth married to Mr. James Bankhead.

Flint, Mrs. Eunice married to Doctor John Waters.

Flint, James T. Esq. married on the 12th ult. at Alexandria, La. by the Rev. George R. Waters to Miss Susan T. Martin daughter of the late Thomas Martin of Davidson County.
Nashville Whig (Tues., Jan. 2, 1844)

Flint, Thos. G. married in Bedford County to Mary A. Newton.
National Banner & Nashville Daily Advertiser (Tues., Dec. 17, 1833)

Flintum, Mr. Thomas B. married in Bedford County to Miss Charlotte
Doak daughter of Capt. David Doak.
National Banner & Nashville Daily Advertiser (Fri., Feb. 22, 1833)

Flintum, Mr. Thomas B. married to Miss Charlotte Doak in Bedford
County.
Nashville Republican & State Gazette. (Fri., Feb. 22, 1833)

Flournoy, Mr. D. J. married in Clarke County, Ky to Miss Eliz.
Cunningham.
National Banner (April 28, 1826)

Flournoy, Miss Julia Ann married to De. Edward R. Field.

Flournoy, Maj. Notley M. married in Lexington, Ky to Margaret G. Keen.
National Banner & Nashville Whig (Sat., Sept. 30, 1826)

Flournoy, Mr. Silas married near Pulaski, Ten. to Miss Elizabeth W.
Camp.
National Banner & Nashville Daily Advertiser (Mon., March 3, 1834)

Flournoy, Victor M. Esq. married in Scott County, Ky. to Miss Elizabeth
J. Johnson daughter of John T. Johnson Esq.
National Banner (Sat., Oct. 10, 1829)

Flournoy, Mr. William of Shrevesport, La. married on Tuesday morning
by the Rev. C. D. Elliott to Miss Elizabeth M. Armstrong daughter
of Gen. Robert Armstrong.
Nashville Whig (Thurs., Nov. 12, 1846)

Flournoy, Mr. William of Shrevesport, La. married on Tuesday morning
by the Rev. C. D. Elliot to Miss Elizabeth M. Aronstrong of Nashville.
The Christian Record (Sat., Nov. 14, 1846)

Floyd, Mr. Drury married in Williamson County to Miss Ann Rowlett.
Nashville Whig (Sat., July 11, 1846)

Floyd, Miss Elizabeth N. married to Runwick A. Gault.

Floyd, Miss Letetia married to Col. William L. Lewis.

Floyd, Mr. William W. married in Limestone County, Ala. to Miss
Margaret Ann Trier.
National Banner & Nashville Daily (Mon., Oct. 1, 1832)

Flawes, Mr. Andrew married in Todd County, Ky to Miss Mary Isbille.
National Banner & Nashville Daily Advertiser (Wed., June 13, 1832)

Fly, John Esq. married in Madison County to Miss Eliza Ann Tyson.
National Banner & Nashville Whig (Fri., May 7, 1830)

Fly, Miss Sarah married to Mr. Zachariah H. Roberts.

Fly, Mr. William D. married on Sunday morning 18th inst. by the Rev.
F. E. Pitts to Miss Cornelia A. Mullun both of Nashville.
The Politician & Weekly Nashville Whig (Fri., March 24, 1848)

Fogg, Francis H. Esq. Attorney at law married on Wednesday even. 15th
inst. by the Rev. Mr. Campbell to Miss Mary daughter of Maj. Henry M.
Rutledge all of this place.
Nashville Whig (Oct. 20, 1823)

Fogg, Godfrey M. Esq. of the firm of Foster & Fogg married last evening
by the Rev. Robert A. Lapsley to Miss Ellen Stevenson of Nashville.
Nashville Whig (Wed., Dec. 18, 1839)

Fogg, Godfrey M. of the firm of Foster & Fogg Attornies. Married on
Tuesday last by the Rev. Robt. A. Lapsley to Miss Ellen Stevenson of
Nashville.
Daily Republican Banner (Thurs., Dec. 19, 1839)

Fogg, Godfrey M. Esq. married in Nashville by the Rev. Robert A.
Lapsley to Miss Ellen Stevenson.
Nashville Union (Fri., Dec. 20, 1839)

Fogg, Capt. Joseph married in Madison County to Miss Eliza Mading.
National Banner (Sat., June 27, 1829)

Fagg, Mr. Julius married in Maryville to Miss Elizabeth Smith.
National Banner (Sat., Sept. 26, 1829)

Folsom, Miss Nancy married to Mr. Skidmore Barker.

Folwell, Miss Arabella married to Mr. Jesse W. Page.

Folwell, Miss Eliza A. married to Capt. Robert Graham.

Foote, Henry S. Esq. married in Tuscumbia, Ala. to Miss Elizabeth
Winter.
National Banner & Nashville Whig (Sat., March 31, 1827)

Foote, Miss Mary E. married to LeRoy Pope Jr., Esq.

Fooy, Miss Charlotte married to Mr. Archibald Hubbird.

Forbes, Mr. Moses married in Henry County to Miss Priscilla Harrison.
National Banner & Nashville Whig (Fri., Nov. 18, 1831)

Forbes, Dr. Robert married in Giles County to Miss Elzira Long.
National Banner & Nashville Daily Advertiser (Fri., Dec. 21, 1832)

Ford, Miss Ann married to Mr. John C. Weaver.

Ford, Miss Elizabeth married to Mr. Wm. London.

Ford, Mr. Frederick married in Knox County to Miss Rhoda Maxey.
National Banner & Nashville Whig (Wed., March 16, 1831)

Ford, Eliza Jane married to Richard W. Ellis Esq.

Ford, Mr. James C. of Mississippi married in Paris, Ky. to Miss Mary
Trimble daughter of the late Judge Trimble.
National Banner & Nashville Whig (Mon., June 21, 1830)

Ford, Dr. John P. of Florence, Ala. married in Davidson County to
Miss Ann S. Jefferson.
National Banner & Nashville Daily Advertiser (Sat., March 10, 1832)

Ford, Dr. John R., of Florence, Ala. married in Davidson County to
Miss Ann S. Jefferson.
National Banner & Nashville Daily Advertiser (March 9, 1832)

Ford, Mr. Newton married in Huntsville, Ala. to Miss Applis Frazier.
National Banner & Nashville Daily Advertiser (Fri., Aug. 1, 1834)

Formwalt, Mr. John married in Fayetteville to Miss Matilda Moyers.
National Banner & Nashville Whig (Sat., July 8, 1826)

Forrest, Edwin Esq. married on the 23d June in London to Catherine
Sinclair daughter of John Sinclar, Es. of the Theatre Royal, Drury Lane.
National Banner & Nashville Whig (Fri., Aug. 4, 1837)

Forrest, Edwin Esq. married in London, on the 23d June to Catherine
Sinclair daughter of John Sinclair Esq.
Nashville Republican (Thurs., Aug. 11, 1837)

Forrester, John B. Esq. of McMinnville married in Lebanon on the 17th
inst. by Rev. Calhoun to Miss Elizabeth Emma Hall eldest daughter of
John Hall, Esq.
National Banner & Nashville Whig (Mon., June 21, 1830)

Forsyth, Mr. Henry of the house R. & H. Forsyth, Louisville, Ky.
married at Pittsburgh to Miss Eleanor Riddle daughter of the Hon.
James Riddle.
National Banner & Nashville Whig (Fri., Dec. 3, 1830)

Forsyth, Miss Maria Jane married at Natchez to Mr. Dempsey P. Jackson.
National Banner & Nashville Whig (Sat., Feb. 23, 1828)

Forsyth, Mr. Newton married in Ross County, Ohio to Miss Eliza Davis.
National Banner (May 10, 1826)

Fort, Miss Frances E. of Hardeman County married at Bolivar on the
17th inst. by the Rev. H. C. Chisholm to Col. William Wallace Wear
of Davidson County.
Nashville Whig (Mon., Feb. 22, 1841)

Fort, Miss Martha married in Robertson County to Mr. Thomas J. Fort.
National Banner & Nashville Daily Advertiser (Sat., March 3, 1832)

Fort, Miss Martha W. married to William N. Bilbo, Esq.

Fort, Mr. Thomas J. married in Robertson County to Miss Martha Fort.
National Banner & Nashville Advertiser (Sat., March 3, 1832)

Fort, Mr. Whitnell of Robertson County married to Miss Dorothy Wimberly
Robertson County on Thursday 13 inst.
Impartial Review & Cumberland Repository - published at Nashville
(Thursday, October 27, 1808)

Fosdick, Mr. Thomas H. of Cincinnati married on the first inst. at
Louisville to Miss Julia Drake late of the Nashville Theatre.
Nashville Whig (March 12, 1823)

Fossee, Miss Mary P. married to Mr. Bennett Maxey.

Foster, Miss Angelina married to Mr. Walter C. Smith.

Foster, Col. B. F. of Davidson County married last evening by the Rev.
Mr. Fanning to Miss Agnes E. Temple of Nashville.
National Banner & Nashville Whig (Wed., July 22, 1835)

Foster, Col. B. F. of Davidson County married to Miss Agness E. Temple
of Nashville.
Nashville Republican (Thurs., July 23, 1835)

Foster, Miss Elizabeth of Pittsburgh married to Capt. Andrew Morrison.

Foster, Ellen married to Edward Cheatham, Esq.

Foster, Miss Ellenor married to Capt. Wm. A. Colwell.

Foster, Ephraim H., Jr. of Clarksville, Tennessee married near Courtland,
Ala. on the 7th inst. by the Rev. Dr. Wardsworth to Miss Susan A.
Watkins daughter of T. J. Watkins Esq. of Lawrence County, Ala.
The Politician & Weekly Nashville Whig (Fri., July 16, 1847)

Foster, Ephraim H., Jr. of Clarksville, Tenn. married near Courtland,
Ala. on the 7th inst. by the Rev. Dr. Wardsworth to Miss Susan A.
Watkins daughter of T. J. Watkins, Esq. of Lawrence County, Ala.
The Christian Record (Sat., July 17, 1847)

Foster, Miss Frances married to Mr. Malcomb J. Gilchrist.

Foster, Miss Hannah S. married to Mr. John H. Hicks.

Foster, Mr. J. married in Christian County to Miss Mary Burgess.
National Banner & Nashville Whig (Sat., March 31, 1827)

Foster, Mr. James W. of Wilson Co. married on Tuesday the 22nd inst.
by Rev. Mr. Baker, Pastor of the 1st Baptist Church to Miss Locisa E.
McIntosh daughter of John McIntosh of Nashville.
Nashville True Whig & Weekly Commercial Register (Fri., Oct. 25, 1850)

Foster, Mr. John married in Bedford County, Ten. to Miss Eliza Harmon.
National Banner & Nashville Whig (Fri., Jan. 23, 1835)

Foster, Miss Julia Ann married to John M. Hood, Esq.

Foster, Mr. Kennedy married in Louisville, Ky. to Miss Adeline
Buckner.
National Banner & Nashville Whig (Sat., March 7, 1829)

Foster, Miss Martha Jane married to Mr. Samuel J. Watkins.

Foster, Miss Mary married to Mr. George W. Tucker.

Foster, Rob. C. of Ky. married in Montgomery County to Miss Jane H.
Sims.
National Banner & Nashville Whig (Sat., Jan. 17, 1829)

Foster, Capt. Robert C. 3d married in Nashville on the 6th inst. at
the residence of Mr. John Nicholas by the Rev. Dr. Edgar to Miss
Martha Elizabeth Bradford daughter of the late Armistead Bradford,
Esq. of Jefferson County, Mississippi.
The Christian Record (Sat., April 15, 1848)

Foster, Rev. Stephen Professor of language in East Tenn. College
married in Knox County to Miss Ann A. Davis.
National Banner & Nashville Whig (Fri., July 15, 1831)

Foster, Thomas Esq. married in Logan County, Ky to Miss Patsey Smith.
National Banner & Nashville Whig (Sat., May 19, 1827)

Foster, Thomas J. Esq. of this place married near Courtland, Ala. on
30th ult. to Miss Virginia Watkins.
Nashville Republican & State Gazette (Sat., Nov. 30th, 1833)

Foster, Thomas J. of this vicinity married near Florence, Alabama
to Miss Jane Hood daughter of the late James Hood of Lauderdale County,
Ala.
Nashville Whig (Wed., March 17, 1841)

Foster, Turner Esq. of Memphis married on Wednesday the 18th ult. by
the Rev. Robert Payne to Ann Eliza Wilson daughter of Col. John S.
Wilson of Florence, Ala.
Nashville Whig (Thurs., March 3, 1846)

Foster, Miss Virginia married to Mr. John Wetherill.

Foster, Mr. Washington of Franklin, Ten. married near Tuscumbia, Ala.
to Miss Sarah Watkins.
National Banner (Sat., Oct. 31, 1829)

Foster, William L. Esq. Attorney at law of Nashville married in Spring-
field on the 28th inst. by the Rev. D. R. Harris to Miss Susan L.
Cheatham daughter of Gen. Richard Cheatham of Springfield.
Nashville Whig (Mon., Nov. 1, 1841)

Foster, Miss Wilmonth married to Mr. J. B. Grisham.

Fothergill, Mr. William married in Lexington, Ky. to Miss Catherine Robinson.
National Banner & Nashville Whig (Feb. 25, 1835)

Fothergill, Mr. William married in Lexington, Ky. to Miss Catherine Robinson.
National Banner & Nashville Whig (Fri., March 6, 1835)

Fowler, Miss Charlotte married to Mr. John Saylor.

Fowler, Mr. Joseph T. married in Denmark, Ten. to Miss Eliza Hewlitt daughter of Mr. Thomas Hewlitt.
National Banner & Nashville Daily Advertiser (Fri., Aug. 15, 1834)

Fowler, Miss Martha married to Mr. Nathaniel Dallahite.

Fowler, Miss Mary Ann married to Mr. Willis Hall.

Fowler, Mr. Milton married in Rutherford County to Miss Ruth Falkenberry.
National Banner & Nashville Whig (Sat., Nov. 18, 1826)

Fowler, Miss Miriam E. married to Lt. Thomas Jefferson Ayre.

Fowler, Mr. Richard married in Madison County, Ky. to Miss Malinda Bentley.
National Banner & Nashville Whig (Sat., March 31, 1827)

Fowler, Mr. Thos. married in Madison County, Ky. to Miss Emily Tevis.
National Banner & Nashville Whig (Sat., March 31, 1827)

Fowlkes, Mr. Henry A. of Gainesville, Ala. married on Sunday the 22nd. inst. by the Rev. Doct. Mullen to Miss Emma M. Chelton daughter of Joseph Chelton of Clarksville, Tenn.
Nashville Whig, (Fri., Sept. 27, 1839)

Fowlkes, Dr. J. of Memphis married on Sat., the 24th inst. by the Rev. J. T. Wheat, D.D. to Miss Maria J. Ward of Davidson County.
Nashville Whig (Thurs., Jan. 29, 1846)

Fox, Miss Mary married in Madison County, Ky to Mr. Milton Crews.
National Banner & Nashville Whig (Sat., Feb. 23, 1828)

Foxwell, Miss Elizabeth married in St. Clair County, Ill. to Mr. Edward West.

Fraker, Mr. John A. married in Bowling Green, Ky. to Miss Julia Ann Covington.
National Banner & Nashville Daily Advertiser (Sat., April 28, 1832)

Francis, Mr. Joseph married in Nashville on Thursday evening last by the Rev. Mr. Green. to Miss Eliza Speece.
National Banner & Nashville Daily Advertiser (Fri., Jan. 11, 1833)

Francis, Miss Malinda J. married to Mr. Edward L. Woodward.

Francis, Miss Margaret A. married to Maj. Edward L. Givins.

Francis, Miss Mary married to Mr. James L. Back.

Francis, Miss Minerva married to James M. Crickner.

Francis, Miss Theresa married to Hopkins L. Turney Esq.

Franklin, Mr. Albert C. married in Sumner County to Miss Henrietta E. Watkins.
Nashville Republican (Thurs., April 7, 1836)

Franklin, Miss Elizabeth married to Mr. Isaac Perry.

Franklin, Isaac Esq. of Sumner County married on the 2nd inst. by the
Rev. Dr. Edgar to Miss Adelicia Hayes daughter of Rev. O. B. Hayes
of this vicinity.
Nashville Whig (Fri., July 5, 1839)

Franklin, Col. Isaac of Sumner County married on Tuesday 2d inst. by
the Rev. J. T. Edgar to Miss Adeletia Hays daughter of O. B. Hays of
this vicinity.
Nashville Union (Mon., July 8, 1839)

Franklin, Mr. John married at Cincinnati to Miss Julia DeForest.
National Banner (April 21, 1826)

Franklin, Lavinia married in Williamson County to Anthony Job.
National Banner & Nashville Whig (Wed., Sept. 24, 1834)

Franklin, Capt. Lawson D. married in Cocke County to Miss Elizabeth
Rodgers.
National Banner & Nashville Whig (Sat., April 21, 1827)

Franklin, Miss Martha married to Mr. Marquis L. Brown.

Franklin, Miss Mary M. married to Mr. Robert Sanderson.

Franklin, Miss Pocahontas married to Mr. Albert J. Saddler.

Franklin, Mr. Robert married in Gibson County to Miss Elizabeth Page.
National Banner & Nashville Whig (Sat., Aug. 30, 1828)

Frazer, Mr. Alexander married in Warren County, Ky. to Miss Zurrah N.
Atchison.
National Banner & Nashville Whig (Sat., May 12, 1827)

Frazer, Miss Lucy married to Mr. Thomas H. Bartlett.

Frazer, Miss Martha Jane married to Jordon Stokes, Esq.

Frazer, Robert Jun. Esq. married in Louisville, Ky. to Miss Catherine
E. Coleman.
National Banner & Nashville Whig (Mon., May 2, 1831)

Frazer, Mr. William in Logan County, Ky. married to Miss Mary Ann
Perkins.
National Banner & Nashville Whig (Fri., Feb. 26, 1830)

Frazier, Miss married to Mr. Haner.

Frazier, Mrs. married to Mr. Thomas Clark, Jr.

Frazier, Miss Applis married to Newton Ford.

Frazier, Miss Carolina Georgiana married to Prince Lucien Murat.

Frazier, Miss Cynthia married to Mr. William Ricketts.

Frazier, Miss Elizabeth married to Mr. George Collins.

Frazier, Mr. Franklin T. married to Miss Jane Crawford in Henry County
on the 10th inst.
Nashville Republican & State Gazette (Sat., Sept. 14, 1833)

Frazier, Miss Harriet married to Mr. Wm. Pendleton.

Frazier, Mr. James of Ala. married in Montgomery County to Miss Sarah
Jamison.
National Banner & Nashville Whig (Sat., Oct. 7, 1826)

Frazier, Miss Jane S. married to Mr. Joseph P. Brown.

Frazier, Mr. Levi married in Logan County, Ky. to Miss Mary Orear.
National Banner & Nashville Whig (Sat., March 10, 1827)

Frazier, Miss Phetney M. married to Mr. Wm. E. Looney.

Frazier, Samuel Esq. married in Knox County to Mrs. Tinsey Craighead daughter of Mr. Jacob Gibbs.
National Banner & Nashville Daily Advertiser (Mon., Feb. 20, 1832)

Frazier, Dr. Samuel W. married in Knox County, Tenn. to Miss Lydia Julian daughter of Stephen Julian.
National Banner & Nashville Whig (Mon., April 13, 1835)

Frazier, Wm. Esq. married at Lexington, Ky. to Miss Ann Overton.
National Banner & Nashville Whig (July 1, 1826)

Frazor, Miss Rebecca Ann married to Rev. William Smith.

Freburger, Miss Rebecca married to Mr. Isaac Needy.

Freeburger, Mr. Samuel married to Miss Elizabeth Ann Boots.

Freeling, Miss Elizabeth married to Mr. John V. Anderson.

Freeman, Miss Rebecca S. married to Mr. Perran Farr.

Freeman, Mr. Smith of Nashville married in the Baptist Church of Nashville by the Rev. R. B. C. Howell to Miss Martha R. Butler of Davidson County.
Nashville Whig (Thurs., Dec. 28, 1843)

Freeman, Mr. Sylvester married in Roane County to Miss Ann Eblen.
National Banner & Nashville Whig (Sat., Jan. 10, 1829)

French, Miss Lucy Ann married to Mr. Edward H. Hudson.

French, William B. Esq. of Knoxville married on the 2nd inst. at the residence of Mrs. Overtons. by the Rev. Dr. Edgar to Miss Isabella White daughter of the late Hon. Hugh L. White.
Nashville Whig (Sat., Feb. 4, 1843)

Friend, Mr. Daniel B. married in Madison County, Ala. to Miss Maria B. Bentley.
National Banner & Nashville Whig (Sat., Sept. 30, 1826)

Frier, Miss Margaret Ann married to Mr. William W. Floyd.

Frierson, Miss Elizabeth Jane married to Mr. Mathew D. Cooper.

Frierson, Mr. Gardner married in Maury County to Miss Levina Williams.
National Banner & Nashville Whig (Sat., Oct. 6, 1827)

Frierson, Miss Jennette M. married to Col. William W. Coleman.

Frierson, Mr. Joshua B. married in Maury County to Miss Ann E. Brown daughter of the Rev. Duncan Brown, D. D.
National Banner & Nashville Daily Advertiser (Thurs., Feb. 23, 1832)

Frierson, Miss Martha W. married to Mr. Samuel D. Frierson.

Frierson, Mr. Robert M. married in Maury County to Miss Jane E. Stephenson.
National Banner & Nashville Whig (Sat., Aug. 12, 1826)

Frierson, Mr. Samuel D. married in Maury County to Miss Mary Mays.
National Banner & Nashville Whig (Fri., Oct. 20, 1826)

Frierson, Mr. Samuel D. married in Maury County to Miss Martha W. Frierson.
National Banner & Nashville Whig (Mon., Aug. 8, 1831)

Frierson, Miss Selina J. married to John A. McEwen.

Frindell, Miss Catherine married to Mr. James Paton.

Frith, Mr. Henry married on the 27th inst. by the Rev. J. S. Molone to Miss Harriet Harman all of Nashville.
Nashville True Whig & Weekly Commercial Register (Fri., Aug. 30, 1850)

Firzell, Mr. Joseph married in Russellville, Ky to Miss Sally Frizell.
National Banner & Nashville Whig (Sat., Oct. 6, 1827)

Frizell, Mr. William married in Simpson County, Ky. to Miss Barbara Graham.
National Banner & Nashville Daily Advertiser (Mon., Sept. 17, 1832)

Frohock, Miss Mary M. married to Mr. William C. Hazen.

Frost, Miss married to Mr. Lewis Nolen.

Frost, Miss Louisa married to Mr. Thomas H. Perkins.

Frost, Miss Louisa married to Mr. Thomas H. Perkins.

Frozell, Mr. Benj. B. married in Logan County, Ky. to Miss Eliza Wilson.
National Banner & Nashville Advertiser (Sat., Aug. 4, 1832)

Fruit, Mr. Thompson married in Christian County, Ky to Miss Elizabeth Underwood.
National Banner & Nashville Daily Advertiser (Fri., Nov. 23, 1832)

Fry, George W. Esq. married in Carroll County to Miss Elizabeth T. Bledsoe.
National Banner & Nashville Whig (Wed., June 29, 1831)

Fry, Miss Nancy married to Mr. Thomas Barbee.

Fry, Mr. Nicholas married to Miss Moore. in Knox County.
National Banner (March 24, 1826)

Fry, Wm. Esq. married at Hopkinsville, Ky. to Miss Julia H. Davidge.
National Banner & Nashville Whig. (Sat., Nov. 29, 1828)

Frye, Mr. Jas. C. married in Columbus, O. to Miss Eliza Sterling Wright.
National Banner & Nashville Daily Advertiser (Thurs., Sept. 12, 1833)

Fulbright, Mr. John married in Henry County, Ten. since the first of Jan. to Miss Mary Atkins.
National Banner & Nashville Whig (Fri., Feb. 13, 1835)

Fulcher, Miss Elizabeth D. married to Mr. David Crawford.

Fulcher, Miss Lucy A. married to Mr. F. O. Hurt.

Fulcher, Miss Margaret married to Mr. Phineas Garrett.

Fulgham, Maj. W. W. married on Wednesday 23d inst. by B. M. Barnes Esq. to Miss Martha A. M. McQuary both of Davidson County.
Daily Republican Banner (Mon., Sept. 28, 1840)

Fullilove, Mr. J. S. married near Bardstown, Ky. to Miss Margaret Eliza Gore daughter of Henry Gore Esq.
National Banner & Nashville Whig (Wed., Nov. 18, 1834)

Fullmer, Mr. John S. merchant of Nashville married this morning by

Rev. Mr. Howell to Miss Mary Ann Price daughter of John Price, Esq.
National Banner & Nashville Whig (Wed., May 24, 1837)

Fullmer, Mr. John S. merchant of Nashville married yesterday morning
by the Rev. Mr. Howell to Miss Mary Ann Price daughter of John Price,
Esq.
Nashville Republican (Thurs., May 25, 1837)

Fullmer, John S. married on Wednesday 24th inst. by the Rev. R. B. C.
Howell to Miss Mary Ann Price daughter of John Price, Esq. all of
Nashville.
The Union (Sat., May 27, 1837)

Fulsom, Mr. David married at Indianapolis to Miss Polly Lamaster.
National Banner (April 14, 1826)

Fulton, Mr. J. W. married in Jeffersonville, Ia. to Miss Ann D. Lee.
National Banner & Nashville Whig (Sat., Sept. 9, 1826)

Fulton, Mr. James married in Henry County to Miss Elizabeth Nunley.
National Banner & Nashville Advertiser (Thurs., Aug. 16, 1832)

Fulton, Miss Mary Margaret eldest daughter of Col. James Fulton of
Fayetteville married to Mr. James Davidson.

Fulton, Miss Rebecca Louisa married to Alfred H. Douglas Esq.

Fultrell, Miss Cynthia Ann married to Mr. William Elder.

Fuqua, Miss Betsey married in Lauderdale County, Ala. to John Donohoo,
Esq.
National Banner & Nashville Whig (Sat., Dec. 2, 1826)

Fuqua, Miss Mary married in Logan County, Ky. to Mr. Tompkins Bradley.

Fuqua, Mr. Stephens Jr. married in Logan County, Ky. to Miss Sophia
W. Ross.
National Banner (March 31, 1826)

Fuqnea, Miss Betsy married to John Donohoo, Esq.

Fursman, Miss B. married to Mr. Monroe Bell.

Fursman, Miss E. married to Mr. Monroe Bell.

Fussell, Miss Catherine V. married to Mr. Willie B. Blakemore.

Fussell, Mr. John O. married in Maury County to Miss Docia Ragsdale.
National Banner & Nashville Whig (Fri., March 26, 1830)

Fuzzell, Mr. Thomas married in Henry County, Ten. since the first of
Jan. to Miss Martha Estes.
National Banner & Nashville Whig (Fri., Feb. 13, 1835)

Fyffe, Mrs. Elizabeth Jane married to Mr. Hugh Smith.

Fyffe, Miss Margaret L. married to Mr. Randolph Eason.

Gadsey, Mr. John E. married on the evening of the 12th by the Rev.
T. L. Douglass to Mrs. Sarah Hamilton daughter of Mr. Andrew Johnson
all of Franklin, Tenn.
The Western Weekly Review - Franklin, Tenn. (Fri., May 13, 1831)

Gailbreath, Mr. Benjamin A. married on Thursday Oct. 8th by the Rev.
Dr. Powell to Miss Jane Gailbreath all of Nashville.
Nashville Whig (Sat., Oct. 10, 1846)

Gailbreath, Miss Jane married to Mr. Benjamin A. Gailbreath.

Gaines, Mr. Henry P. married in Robertson County to Miss Frances T.
Norman.
National Banner & Nashville Daily Advertiser (Wed., Jan. 4, 1832)

Gaines, Mr. James H. married in Sparta to Miss Priscilla P. Farrington.
National Banner & Nashville Whig (Wed., May 25, 1831)

Gaines, Miss Martha Susan married to Mr. George W. Petway.

Gaines, R. M. Esq. of Natchez married in Adams County, Miss. to Miss
Eliza B. Hutchins.
National Banner & Nashville Whig (Mon, June 7, 1830)

Gaines, Mr. Samuel D. married in Sullivan County to Miss Sarah Gaines.
National Banner & Nashville Whig. (Mon., Sept. 19, 1831)

Gaines, Miss Sarah married in Sullivan County to Mr. Samuel D. Gaines.

Gains, Mr. Armstrong married in Knox County to Miss Polly Swaggerty.
National Banner & Nashville Whig (Wed., March 16, 1831)

Gains, Mrs. Fanny married to Mr. Ernst Benoit.

Gains, Mr. Henry P. of Robertson County married to Miss Frances T.
Norman Robertson County.
National Banner & Nashville Advertiser (Wed., Jan. 4, 1832)

Gains, Mr. James H. married in Sparta, Tenn. to Miss Priscilla P.
Farrington.
Nashville Republican & State Gazette. (Tues., May 24, 1831)

Gains, Mr. James H. married in Sparta to Miss Priscilla P. Farrington.
National Banner & Nashville Whig (Wed., May 25, 1831)

Gains, Miss Sarah married to Mr. Wm. Scarborough.

Gaitwood, Mr. Thomas married in Henderson County to Miss Elizabeth
Trice.
National Banner (Sat., Aug. 15, 1829)

Galbreath, Miss Mary Ann married to Mr. Rolla Harrison.

Galbreath, Mr. William married at Shelbyville to Miss Mary B. Evans
daughter of Jesse Evans Esq.
National Banner (Feb. 24, 1826)

Gale, Miss Emeline married to Mr. J. Hart.

Gallagher, Hon. James of Moulton married in Lauderdale County, Ala.
on the 11th by the Rev. Mr. Sloss to Miss Elizabeth Cunningham of
Lauderdale.
Daily Republican Banner (Thurs., Aug. 1, 1839)

Gallagher, Miss Sarah married to Mr. Weisey Knight.

Gallaher, Mr. George married in Knox County to Miss Lucinda King.
National Banner & Nashville Whig (Mon., Sept. 19, 1831)

Gallegher, Mr. John married in Lincoln County to Miss Fanny Blackemore.
National Banner & Nashville Whig (Sat., March 17, 1827)

Galloway, Louis G. Esq. of New Orleans married on Thursday the 10th
inst. at Murfreesboro, by the Rev. Joseph H. Eaton. to Miss Martha
Dickinson daughter of David Dickinson Esq. of Murfreesboro.
Nashville Whig (Sat., Sept. 12, 1846)

Galloway, Miss Mary A. J. married to Mr. Caswell Martin.

Ga-lo-Nus-gee married at the Valley Towns by the Rev. E. Jones April
12, 1830 to A-ga-lu-ga.
National Banner & Nashville Whig (Mon., July 26, 1830)

Ga-lu-sda-ye married at the Valley Towns by the Rev. E. Jones, 12th
April, 1830 to Dsu-do-dsa-la.
National Banner & Nashville Whig (Mon., July 26, 1830)

Gambell, William N. C. married in Maury County Miss Jane E. Tate.
Nashville Whig (Tues., July 14, 1846)

Gambill, Miss Eliza married at New Albany Ia to Mr. A. S. Burnett.

Gamble, Mr. A. H. married in Athens, E. Tenn. to Miss Martha Kinder.
National Banner & Nashville Daily Advertiser (Wed., July 16,1834)

Gamble, Mrs. Polly married to Col. John A. Hooke.

Gamble, Mr. W. T. married in Limestone Co., Ala. to Miss Caroline T.
Harris.
National Banner & Nashville Daily Advertiser (Mon., June 30, 1834)

Gammon, A. L. of Jonesborough married in Rogersville, Ten. to Miss
Nancy Anderson.
National Banner & Nashville Daily Advertiser (Mon., June 30, 1834)

Gammon, Miss Jane G. married to Mr. S. E. Stuart.

Gammon, Miss Martha married to Mr. William R. Conner.

Gammon, Miss Martha married to Mr. Wm. Connor.

Gann, Mr. Enoch married in Smith County to Miss Elizabeth Moore,
National Banner & Nashville Whig (Fri., Nov. 25, 1831)

Gannaway, Mr. R. A. of Murfreesboro married in Nashville at the resi-
dence of Mr. Woolford on 23rd inst. by the Rev. Dr. Lapsley to Miss
Frances Westervelt of Pittsburgh, Pa.
The Politician & Weekly Nashville Whig (Fri., July 2, 1847)

Gant, Benj. R. married in Williamson County to Angelina Bugg.
National Banner & Nashville Daily Advertiser (Mon., Aug. 26, 1833)

Gant, Miss Lucy married in Maury County to Mr. Jonathan Webster.

Garbra, Mr. James S. married in Nashville on Thursday Dec. 6th to
Miss Mary Shepherd.
National Banner & Nashville Daily Advertiser (Sat., Dec. 8, 1832)

Gardener, Miss Elizabeth H. married to Jeptha Gardner Esq.

Gardener, John of this place married on the same (Wednesday) eveing
to Miss Eliza Ham daughter of Mr. Samuel Ham of this County.
The Nashville Whig (Sept. 1st, 1817)

Gardiner, Mary married to Walter Gardener.

Gardiner, Walter married in Williamson County to Mary Gardiner.
Western Weekly Review - Franklin, Tenn. (Feb. 10, 1832)

Gardner, Maj. Alfred married in Weakley County to Miss Mary Ann
Stovall.
National Banner & Nashville Advertiser (Tues., Nov. 13, 1832)

Gardner, Jeptha, Esq. of Dresden, Ten. married to Miss Elizabeth H.
Gardener.
Nashville Republican and State Gazette (Feb. 22, 1833)

Gardner, Miss Lalvina married to Mr. David Safferans.

Gardner, Miss Nancy married to Mr. Wm. Crawford.

Gardner, Robert H. merchant of Nashville married in Knoxville, on
Thursday 9th inst. by the Rev. Mr. Mack to Miss Margaret McClung
eldest daughter of Col. Matthew McClung of Knox County.
Nashville Whig (Tues., June 21, 1842)

Gardner, Mr. Uriah married in Rutherford County to Miss Elizabeth C.
Featherston.
National Banner & Nashville Whig (Sat., Oct. 7, 1826)

Garland, Hugh S. Esq. of Nashville married in Clarksville the 12th
inst. by A. A. Muller D. D. to Miss Mary Elizabeth Brunson daughter
of the late Dr. Ashbel Brunson of Montgomery County.
Daily Republican Banner (Tues., Nov. 19, 1839)

Garland, Miss Minerva Ellen W. married to Dr. Amos David.

Garland, Rice Esq. married at Opelousas, La. to Miss Celeste
Lastropes.
National Banner (April 21, 1826)

Garner, Miss Catherine married to Mr. Elbridge G. Buckhanan.

Garner, Miss Elizabeth married to Mr. A. B. Sluder.

Garner, Mr. Jesse married in Willaimson County to Miss Clarissa
Rutherford.
The Western Weekly Review - Franklin, Tenn. (Fri., Dec. 2, 1831)

Garner, Mr. Jesse married in Williamson County to Miss Clarissa
Rutherford.
National Banner & Nashville Whig (Wed., Dec. 7, 1831)

Garner, Mr. John B. of Arkansas married in Logan County, Ky to Miss.
Mary Y. Ewing.
National Banner & Nashville Whig (Sat., Sept. 15, 1827)

Garner, John E. Printer of Nashville married in Springfield on the
18th. by the Rev. George McNelly to Miss Elizabeth Thomas daughter
of Dr. A. Thomas of Springfield.
Nashville Whig (Mon., Jan. 20, 1840)

Garner, John E. Printer of Nashville married in Springfield on the
18th by the Rev. George McNelly to Miss Elizabeth Thomas daughter
of Dr. A. Thomas of Springfield, Ten.
Daily Republican Banner (Tuesday, Jan. 21, 1840)

Garner, Mr. John J. married in Florence, Ala. to Miss Mary A. Williams.
National Banner & Nashville Advertiser (Mon., April 30, 1832)

Garner, Miss Lamira D. married to Mr. Leonard D. Baker.

Garner, Mr. Lewis married in Rutherford County to Miss Lucy W. Rucker.
National Banner & Nashville Whig (Sat., April 12, 1828)

Garner, Mr. N. B. of Selma, Ala. married in Fayetteville to Miss
Ann L. M'Connell daughter of the late Mr. John P. M'Connell.
National Banner & Nashville Whig (Wed., Sept. 28, 1831)

Garner, Mr. William married on the same evening (Thursday) by the
Rev. Mr. Whitsitt to Miss Lucinda Hill both of this place.
The Nashville Whig & Tenn. Advertiser (Oct. 27, 1817)

Garnet, Miss Elizabeth married to Mr. Philander Barclay.

Garnett, Miss Mary married to Mr. James Elizer.

Garnett, Miss Mary married to Mr. Samuel Parrish.

Garrard, Miss Elenear married to Mr. Frederick B. Earnest.

Garrett, Miss married to Mr. Samuel Parrish.

Garrett, Mr. Ashton married at Lexington, Ky to Miss Mary M. Spangler.
National Banner & Nashville Whig (Sat., Dec. 6, 1828)

Garrett, Miss Elizabeth married in Clarksville to Mr. James Allison.

Garrett, Miss Elizabeth M. married to Mr. Thomas Wells.

Garrett, Mr. James married in Warren County, Ky. to Miss Cassondra
Penic.
National Banner & Nashville Whig (Sat., Dec. 16, 1826)

Garrett, Miss Juliet married to Rev. Josiah Rhoton.

Garrett, Lewis A. Esq. attorney at law of Tazewell married on the
25th at Rocky Springs, Grainger County by Rev. Mr. Rhoton to Miss
Harriet Jack daughter of the late Judge Jack of Grainger.
Nashville Whig (Wed., March 18, 1840)

Garrett, Miss Louisa married to Mr. James Croach.

Garrett, Mr. Pheneas married on the 31st ult. by the Rev. E. P. Neely
to Miss Margaret Fulcher both of Nashville.
Nashville Whig (Sat., Aug. 3, 1844)

Garrett, Mrs. S. married to Mr. Hiram Green.

Garrett, Miss Sarah married to Mr. Samuel A. Dams.

Garrett, Thomas M. married in Giles County to Miss Margaret M. Reed.
National Banner & Nashville Daily Advertiser (Tues., Dec. 17, 1833)

Garrett, Mrs. Winny married to Mr. Braddock Richmond.

Garrick, Mr. James married to Miss Finnetta Lowry in White County.
National Banner & Nashville Whig (Fri., Jan. 29, 1830)

Garrison, Col. Wm. C. married in Liberty to Miss Malvina Evans on
the 7th inst.
Nashville Republican & State Gazette (Thurs., Aug. 15, 1833)

Garth, Miss Elizabeth married to Mr. Edward Carney.

Garth, Mr. William A. married to Miss Elizabeth Saffarans.

Gash, Mr. Barnard P. married in Lewis County, Ky. to Miss Abbey Barr.
National Banner (May 10, 1826)

Gash, Mr. Bernard P. married in Lewis County, Ky to Miss Ibby Barr.
National Banner (April 7, 1826)

Gaston, Mr. William married in Madison County to Miss Epsey B. Avent. National Banner & Nashville Daily Advertiser (Tues., Sept. 4, 1832)

Gately, Mr. Thomas married in Henry County, Tenn. to Miss Zerilda Hind. National Banner & Nashville Daily Advertiser (Mon., May 28, 1832)

Gatewood, Miss Ann Eliza married to Dr. Francis A. Williamson.

Gatewood, Mr. James married near Haydensville, Todd County, Ky on Tuesday 14th by the Rev. Mr. Wats. to Miss Ann A. Miller. Nashville Union (Thurs., Nov. 23, 1837)

Gatlin, Miss Sarah married to Isaac Shaw.

Gaugh, Mr. Percival married in Lexington, Ky. to Miss Julia C. Megowan. National Banner & Nashville Daily Advertiser (Tues., June 26, 1832)

Gault, Isaiah C. married in Williamson County, Ten. to Mary Ramey. National Banner & Nashville Whig (Wed., Dec. 17, 1834)

Gault, Mr. James M. married on Tuesday last in Franklin by the Rev. Mr. Porter to Miss Mary Jane Coehms. The Western Weekly Review - Franklin, Tenn. (Fri., Oct. 28, 1831)

Gault, Mr. James M. married in Franklin to Miss Mary Jane Rhems. Nashville Republican & State Gazette (Tues., Nov. 1, 1831)

Gault, Mr. John married in Blount County to Miss Susan Culton. National Banner & Nashville Daily Advertiser (Mon., April 29, 1833)

Gault, Runwick A. married in Williamson County to Miss Elizabeth N. Floyd. The Western Weekly Review (Franklin, Tenn.) (Fri., March 8, 1833)

Gault, Miss Susan married to Mr. John Gault.

Gautier, Miss Fanny married to Mr. James Perkins.

Gay, Edward J. Esq. of St. Louis married last evening by the Rev. Dr. Edgar to Miss Lavinia Hynes daughter of Col. Andrew Hynes of Nashville. Nashville Whig (Fri., Oct. 23, 1840)

Gay, Mr. Lemuel of McNairy County married to Miss Eliza Wilkinson of Hardeman County on the 2d inst. by Elder Reddick. Nashville Republican & State Gazette (Thurs., Jan. 23, 1834)

Gayle, Miss Lucy married to Dr. Japptha Dudley.

Gayle, Miss Lucy married in Clarksville to Dr. Joseph Dewly.

Gee, Mr. James H. of Carroll County, Tenn. married in Lauderdale County, Ala. to Miss Ann Hawkins. National Banner & Nashville Whig (Sat., Nov. 18, 1826)

Gee, John H. married in Williamson County to Miss Julia A. Turner. The Western Weekly Review - Franklin, Tenn. (Fri., Dec. 14, 1832)

Geers, Miss Eliza Jane married to Mr. Preston M. Brown.

Gelusia, Mr. Madison B., aged 16 married in Providence, R. I. to Miss Mary E. Brown, aged 14 all of Lynn, Mass. National Banner & Nashville Whig (Wed., Aug. 17, 1831)

Genett, Cha. Jr. married in New York to Miss Elizabeth E. Adrian. National Banner & Nashville Daily Advertiser (Thurs., Sept. 19, 1833)

Gentry, Miss Elizabeth married to Mr. George F. Reynolds.

Gentry, Mr. James O. married in Knox County to Miss Charlotte Reynolds.
National Banner (Feb. 17, 1826)

Gentry, Mr. Joseph married in Franklin County to Mrs. Roache.
National Banner & Nashville Whig (Sat., Sept. 9, 1826)

Gentry, Hon. M. P. married on the 19th inst. in the vicinity of
Franklin, at the residence of Hon. A. P. Maury to Miss Caledonia
Brown.
Nashville Whig (Sat., Sept. 21, 1846)

Gentry, Miss M. married to Mr. Robert Stone.

Gentry, Col. Meredith P. of Williamson County married in Sumner County
on Thursday last by the Rev. James Smith to Miss Emily Saunders
daughter of the late James Saunders of Sumner.
Nashville Whig (Mon., Feb. 20, 1838)

George, Mr. Barnett married in Louisville, Ky. to Mrs. Elizabeth
Banister.
National Banner & Nashville Daily Advertiser (Sat., June 1, 1832)

George, Mr. Edward married in Blount County, Tenn. to Miss Dorcas
Chandler.
National Banner & Nashville Advertiser (Tues., May 22, 1832)

George, Miss Eliza married to Mr. Jesse Crank.

George, Miss Eliza J. married to Mr. Greenbury Swope.

George, Mr. Leonard Jun married in Jefferson County, Ky. to Miss.
Esther M. Hughes.
National Banner (Sat., Oct. 10, 1829)

George, Miss Martha Ann married to Capt. Lewis Landram.

George, Mr. Presly of Mississippi married in Franklin County, Ten.
on Thursday 25th ult. by the Rev. Mr. Spyker to Miss Sarah Moore.
The Western Weekly Review (Fri., Nov. 9, 1832)

George, Mr. Presly married in Franklin County to Miss Sarah Moore.
National Banner & Nashville Daily Advertiser (Tues., Nov. 13, 1832)

George, Mr. Solomon married in Limestone County, Ala. to Miss Frances
Crutcher.
National Banner & Nashville Whig (Sat., June 2, 1827)

George, Mr. W. B. B. married in Knox County to Miss Hannah Aldridge.
National Banner & Nashville Daily Advertiser (Wed., Aug. 29, 1832)

George, Mr. William late from Baltimore married on the 14th inst. by
the Rev. Edmund Lanier to Miss Martha Ann Cox daughter of Mr. John
Cox of Nashville.
The Nashville Gazette (Sat., Dec. 18, 1819)

George, Mr. Wyly married in Maury County to Miss Mary Meeks.
National Banner & Nashville Advertiser (Fri., Jan. 27, 1832)

Gerale, Mr. E. married at New Harmony, Ia. to Miss Mary Wheatcraft.
National Banner (Feb. 24, 1826)

German, Mr. Daniel married in Williamson County to Miss Elizabeth
Raunsavall.
National Banner & Nashville Whig (Sat., Feb. 23, 1828)

Gholson, Miss Melinda married to Mr. Thomas W. Ament.

Cholson, Thomas Esq. of Columbus, Miss. married on Thursday last at Villa de-Rose to Miss Catherine D. McLemore daughter of Col. J. C. McLemore of Fort Pickering.
Nashville Whig (Fri., Sept. 24, 1841)

Fholson, Mr. Wm. T. married in Shelby County to Miss Sarah Hart.
National Banner & Nashville Whig (Mon., April 18, 1831)

Gibbes, Miss Julia G. married to Mr. Samuel L. Hill.

Gibbons, Mr. Thomas married in Jefferson County to Miss Kitchens.
National Banner & Nashville Whig (Fri., 14th Jan. 1831)

Gibbs, Mr. Joseph married at Louisville, Ky. to Miss Henrietta Arcambal.
National Banner & Nashville Whig (Sat., April 14, 1827)

Gibbs, Miss M. W. married to Rev. William C. Paine.

Gibbs, Miss Martha Catharine married to David D. Bill, Esq.

Gibbs, Mr. Nicholas married in Knox County to Miss Polly Eppes.
National Banner (Jan. 13, 1826)

Gibbs, O. D. Esq. Attorney at law married near Manchester on Thursday last to Miss Sarah Dorsey both of Manchester.
Daily Republican Banner (Tues., Dec. 4, 1838)

Gibbs, Miss Tinsey married to Maj. John Craighead.

Gibson, Rev. Albert G. of Lincoln married in Hazlegreen, Ala. to Miss Sarah Erwin.
National Banner & Nashville Whig (Sat., Dec. 13, 1828)

Gibson, Mr. Ambros married at Port Gibson, Miss. to Miss Margaret M. Creath.
National Banner (March 31, 1826)

Gibson, Mr. William married in Monroe County to Miss Lumima Axley.
National Banner & Nashville Whig (Fri., Sept. 9, 1831)

Gibson, Miss Ann married to Mr. Joseph Mason.

Gibson, Col. D. C. formerly of Georgia married on Thursday evening 23d April by the Rev. Robert Dougan to Miss Jane Griffin of Winchester, Ten.
National Banner & Nashville Whig (Wed., May 6, 1835)

Gibson, Miss Derinda married to Mr. John M. Slealey.

Gibson, Miss Elizabeth married to Mr. Asa Messer.

Gibson, Mr. Joseph married in Nashville to Miss Sophia W. Hall on last Tuesday.
Nashville Republican & State Gazette (Wed., July 17, 1833)

Gibson, Mr. Joseph F. married in Nashville, Tuesday evening 16th inst. by the Rev. P. B. Robinson to Miss Sophia W. Hall.
National Banner & Nashville Daily Advertiser (Thurs., July 18, 1833)

Gibson, Josiah Esq. married in Warren County, Miss. to Miss Mary Hamer.
National Banner & Nashville Whig (Sat., Dec. 30, 1826)

Gibson, Miss Mary married to Mr. Willy Whitfield.

Gibson, Mr. Robert merchant, married on Tuesday evening last. to Miss Jane Adams both of this town.
Nashville Whig (Nov. 24, 1823)

Gibson, Mr. Stephen aged 59 married in Manchester, Ky. to Miss Amelia Strong aged 16.
National Banner & Nashville Whig (Wed., March 23, 1831)

Gibson, Mr. Thomas married in Jefferson county to Miss Kitchens.
National Banner & Nashville Whig (Fri., Jan. 14, 1831)

Gibson, Mr. Robias of Mississippi married to Miss Louisiana B. Hart.
National Banner & Nashville Whig (July 28, 1827)

Gibson, Mr. Wm. married on Tuesday evening last by the Revd. Mr. Campbell to Miss Rebecca Adams both of this city.
The Clarion & Tennessee Gazette (November 21, 1820)

Gideon, Miss Mary W. married to David T. Moss.

Gifford, Miss Ann married to Mr. William Louallen.

Gift, Mr. Robt. married in Shelby County, Ten. to Mrs. Williams.
National Banner & Nashville Daily Advertiser (Mon., Aug. 26, 1833)

Gilbert, Mr. Ambrose B. married in Lincoln County to Miss Sarah Wright.
National Banner & Nashville Whig (Sat., Aug. 12, 1826)

Gilbert, Miss Catherine married to Mr. George Green.

Gilbert, Mr. James married in Logan County, Ky. to Miss Jane Rush.
National Banner & Nashville Whig (Sat., July 29, 1826)

Gilbert, Mr. John C. married in Bedford County to Miss Rachel Roberts.
National Banner & Nashville Daily Advertiser (Thurs., June 20, 1833)

Gilbert, Miss Lucy Ann married to Mr. John M'Gonegil.

Gilbert, Miss Mary married to Mr. George L. Lenard.

Gilbert, Mr. Miles G. married in Logan County, Ky. to Miss Mary Carr.
National Banner & Nashville Whig (Sat., Dec. 30, 1826)

Gilchrist, Miss Catherine married to Mr. George Green.

Gilchrist, Mr. Malcomb J. of Lawrence County, Ala. married on Wednesday the 17th inst. at Farmers Joy by the Rev. C. D. Elliott to Miss Frances A. Foster daughter of James H. Foster of Davidson County.
The Christian Record (Sat., Nov. 27, 1847)

Gilchrist, Mr. Philip P. of Ala. married by the Rev. Dr. Lapsley on the 23rd inst. to Miss Sarah E. Moore eldest daughter of Rebert I. Moore, Esq. of Nashville.
The Politician & Weekly Nashville Whig (Wed., Sept. 29, 1847)

Gilchrist, William Esq. Attorney at law of Shelbyville married in Bedford County to Miss Martha A. Jones eldest daughter of the late Col. Fanning Jones.
National Banner & Nashville Daily Advertiser (Thurs., Oct. 18, 1832)

Giles, Miss married to Mr. James Shaffer.

Giles, Miss Lucy W. married to Mr. Wm. O. Smithson.

Giles, Mr. Milton married near Cairo to Miss Sarah Hamilton.
National Banner & Nashville Whig (Sat., Jan. 6, 1827)

Giles, Mr. Wm. married in Williamson County, Ten. to Miss Mary Young.
National Banner & Nashville Whig (Fri., Jan. 9, 1835)

Gilhouley, Miss Mary married to Mr. Hugh O'Neil, Jr. Esq.

Gilis, Mr. James H. married in Maury County to Miss M. S. Robinson.
National Banner & Nashville Advertiser (Thurs., April 5, 1832)

Gilkey, Mr. Chs. married in Fayette County to Miss Agnes Barnett.
National Banner (Mar. 17, 1826)

Gill, Miss Frances married to Maj. William Campbell.

Gill, Miss Harriet married to Charles Atkin.

Gill, Dr. Joseph married in Fayette County, Ky. to Miss Maria Lamb.
National Banner & Nashville Whig (Sat., Jan. 17, 1829)

Gill, Mr. Joseph J. S. married in Lincoln County, Ten. to Miss Angelina
Moore.
National Banner & Nashville Whig (Wed., Dec. 17, 1834)

Gill, Miss Martha married to Mr. Chesley Jarnagan.

Gillam, Miss Fanny married to Mr. James McFarland, Jr.

Gillam, Mr. Finney B. married in Logan County, Ky. to Miss Martha C.
Martin.
National Banner (Sat., May 16, 1829)

Gillam, Mr. Levi S. married in Wilson County on Thursday 18th ult. by
the Rev. R. W. Morris to Miss Eliza C. Hodges.
National Banner & Nashville Whig (Tues., March 2, 1830)

Gillam, Miss Rebecca married in Smith County, Tenn. to Mr. John
Cooper.
National Banner & Nashville Daily Advertiser (Fri., May 4, 1832)

Gillee, Mr. Pearce married in Jefferson County, Ky. to Miss Catherine
Johnson.
National Banner & Nashville Daily Advertiser (Fri., Feb. 15, 1833)

Gilleland, Miss Mary married in Spencer County, Ky. to Mr. Allen Taylor.

Gillespie, Ch. K. Esq. of Washington, Rhea County married Miss Evelina
E. C. Taylor on 22d ult.
Nashville Republican (Thurs., Oct. 8, 1835)

Gillespie, Col. David of Lebanon married in Sumner County on the 19th
inst. by the Rev. John W. Hall to Miss Mary L. Tyree.
National Banner & Nashville Daily Advertiser (Fri., Feb. 22, 1833)

Gillespie, Col. David of Lebanon married to Miss Mary L. Tyree.
Nashville Republican & State Gazette (Fri., Feb. 22, 1833)

Gillespie, Geo. M. married in Williamson County to Francis L. Morton.
The Western Weekly Review - Franklin, Tenn. (Fri., Feb. 10, 1832)

Gillespie, Mr. James married in Blount County to Miss Hesther Ann
Talbott.
National Banner (April 14, 1826)

Gillespie, Miss Jane B. married in Maury County to Mr. Addison S. Hall.

Gillespie, Mr. John L. married in Williamson County to Miss Tabitha
Gray.
National Banner & Nashville Whig (Fri., Jan. 9, 1835)

Gillespie, Miss Margaret A. married to Mr. John Ferguson.

Gillespie, Miss Margaret A. married to Mr. John Ferguson.

Gillespie, Miss Martha married to Col. William Brazelton.

Gillespie, Miss Mary married to Mr. George W. Stone.

Gillespie, Miss Nancy Ann married to E. B. M'Coy Esq.

Gillespie, Miss Nancy M. married to Mr. William H. Moffatt.

Gillespie, Mr. Robert of Washington, Rhea County married Miss Hannah
Leuty in M'Minn County.
National Banner & Nashville Whig (Thurs., May 27, 1830)

Gillespie, Robert married in Williamson County, Ten. to Marietta
Gleaves.
National Banner & Nashville Daily Advertiser (Mon., Aug. 26, 1833)

Gillespie, Miss Sarah married to Mr. William Cantrell.

Gillespy, Col. Berry of Paris married at Purdy to Miss Emily B. Lane.
National Banner & Nashville Daily Advertiser (Wed., Jan. 4, 1832)

Gilliam, Col. James married in Rutherford County to Miss Margaret
Lorance daughter of Mr. Alexander Lorance.
National Banner & Nashville Advertiser (Fri., Jan. 13, 1832)

Gilliam, James of the County of York married in James City, Va. to
Mrs. Mary A. Piggott relict of F. Piggott, deceased.
National Banner & Nashville Daily Advertiser (Thurs., June 19, 1834)

Gilliam, Miss Susannah Ellis of Knox County married to Mr. Hugh Dunlap.

Gillian, Miss Rachel married to Mr. Willis Mitchell.

Gillingwater, Mr. Elijah married in M'Minn County to Miss Polly
Weaver.
National Banner (Sat., Dec. 26, 1829)

Gillispie, Sophia Miss married to Thomas M. Laughlin.

Gillium, Mr. John married in Logan County, Ky. to Miss Brunetta
Baker.
National Banner & Nashville Whig (Mon., Dec. 29, 1834)

Gillmore, Dr. Frederick H. married in Logan County, Ky. to Miss Sarah
Jane Loving.
National Banner & Nashville Whig (Thurs., June 17, 1830)

Gills, Thomas married in Williamson County to Miss Prudence Ranea.
The Western Weekly Review - Franklin, Tenn. (Fri., Feb. 1, 1833)

Gilman, Miss Jane married to Mr. W. E. Howlet.

Gilman, Miss Jane A. M. married to Mr. William E. Hewlett.

Gilmer, Mr. J. married in Maury County to Miss Nancy F. Patterson.
National Banner & Nashville Daily Advertiser (Thurs., May 17, 1832)

Gilmer, Miss Sarah married in Christian County, Ky to Mr. Robert Browder.

Gilston, Mr. Samuel married near Carmi, Ill. to Miss Elizabeth M'Henry.
National Banner & Nashville Whig (Sat., Oct. 28, 1826)

Gingery, Capt. Jacob of Shelbyville married in Rutherford County to
Miss Elizabeth Fisher.
National Banner & Nashville Whig (Sat., Oct. 7, 1826)

Ginn, Mr. Edmund married in Wilkinson County, Miss to Mrs. Eliza Ann
Harris.
National Banner & Nashville Whig (Sat., Aug. 12, 1826)

Girard, Mr. William married on the 16th inst. by the Rev. Mr. Wheat to Miss Sarah B. Smith both of Nashville.
Nashville Whig (Mon., Sept. 20, 1841)

Gist, Mrs. Julia A. M. of Baltimore County married to L. C. Levin Esq.

Gist, Dr. Robert P. married in Jefferson County, Ky. to Miss Eliza Love, Esq. daughter of Matthew Love, Esq.
National Banner & Nashville Whig (Sat., Aug. 9, 1828)

Gist, Lieut, Spencer C. of the Navy married in Sevier County to Miss Angelina F. Porter daughter of George W. Porter Esq.
National Banner & Nashville Daily Advertiser (Wed., April 3, 1833)

Gist, Mrs. Thermusthus married to Mr. John Hogan.

Gist, Miss Thermusthus married to Mr. John Hogan.

Given, D. A. Esq. of New Orleans married in Princeton, Ky. to Miss Clarisse H. Goodall of Tompkinsville, Ky.
Nashville Whig (Sat., Jan. 27, 1838)

Givens, Miss Caroline D. married in Madison Cty, Ten. to Maj. James T. Brown.

Givens, Mr. James married in Knox County to Mrs. Dorcas Certain.
National Banner & Nashville Whig (Mon., May 9, 1831)

Givins, Maj. Edward L. of Alexandria, Ala. married in Nashville on the 24th May by the Rev. William Garrett to Miss Margaret A. Francis daughter of Col. Miller Francis Treasurer of the State of Tennessee.
Daily Republican Banner (Fri., May 25, 1838)

Givins, Mr. R. H. married in Madison County, Ten. to Miss Lucinda Hill.
National Banner & Nashville Whig (Wed., Aug. 17, 1831)

Glascock, Edwin R. married on Thursday 24th inst. by the Rev. Dr. Davis to Miss Olivia F. Andrews all of Nashville.
The Union (Sat., May 27, 1837)

Glascock, Dr. Hiram of Madison County, Ala. married in Maury County to Miss Ann H. Sanford daughter of the late Col. James T. Sanford.
National Banner & Nashville Whig (Mon., July 11, 1831)

Glascock, Mrs. Margaret married to Mr. Elias P. Smith.

Glasgow, Mr. James of Nashville married on Tuesday the 6th inst. at Kingston, Ten. to Miss Lydia White of Knoxville.
The Nashville Whig (Feb. 26, 1817)

Glasgow, Miss Susan daughter of Col. James Glasgow of this County married to Thomas Haywood Esq.

Glasgow, Miss Maria A. married to Mr. Henry Jordan.

Glasier, Dr. Charles married in Nashville on the 3rd inst. by the Rev. J. B. McFerrin to Miss Margaret Weakley daughter of Mrs. E. Weakley.
Nashville Whig (Tues., March 7, 1843)

Glass, Miss Catherine S. married to Mr. Samuel E. Shaw.

Glass, Mr. David married in Knox County to Miss Esther S. Edmondson.
National Banner & Nashville Whig (Thurs., July 29, 1830)

Glass, Mr. Shackleford married in Maury County to Miss Elizabeth Curry.
National Banner & Nashville Whig (Mon., Feb. 23, 1835)

Glasscock, Mr. Edwin R., printer married on Thursday 25th inst. by the Rev. Dr. Davis to Mrs. Olivia Andrews all of Nashville.
National Banner & Nashville Whig (May 26, 1837)

Glasscock, Dr. Hiram of Madison County, Ala. married to Miss Ann H. Sandford in Maury County.
Nashville Republican & State Gazette (Thursday, July 7, 1831)

Glassock, Miss Eliza married to Mr. Eli Lunn.

Gleaves, Miss Caroline married to Mr. Kirkpatrick.

Gleaves, Miss Caroline married to Mr. Kirkpatrick.

Gleaves, Emeline married to Mr. James Wright.

Gleaves, John Ewing Attorney at law of Nashville married on April 5th by the Rev. Mr. Huntington to Manilla L. Massey daughter of William G. Massey.
The Christian Record (Sat., April 10, 1847)

Gleaves, Marrietta married to Robert Gillespie.

Gleaves, Miss Missouri married to Mr. Henry F. Smith.

Gleaves, Miss Nancy A. married to Mr. Pierce W. Cherry.

Gleaves, Mr. Thomas Jun. married on Thursday evening the 9th inst. by the Rev. Joshua White to Miss Mary Dean both of this county.
The Nashville Whig & Tenn. Advertiser (Oct. 13, 1817)

Gleim, Miss Adelaide C. married to Mr. Robert H. Douthitt.

Glenn, Miss Ann married to Dr. Wm. H. Jenkins.

Glenn, Mr. John of Williamson County married in Robertson County on the 2d inst. to Mrs. Elizabeth Bottitt late of Williamson County.
National Banner & Nashville Daily Advertiser (Wed., June 6, 1832)

Glenn, Mrs. Mary married to Mr. John Stephens.

Glenn, Miss Mary Ann married to Mr. Wm. M. Campbell.

Glenn, Miss Mary C. married to Mr. James G. Reno.

Glenn, Miss Nancy married to Mr. William Chancellor.

Glenn, Mr. William married in Williamson County to Miss Zilpah Magness.
The Western Weekly Review - Franklin, Tenn. (Fri., Dec. 2, 1831)

Glenn, Mr. William married in Williamson County to Miss Eilpah Magness.
National Banner & Nashville Whig (Wed., Dec. 7, 1831)

Glisson, Mr. B. B. married in Henry County to Miss Polly Williams.
National Banner & Nashville Whig (Fri., Nov. 25, 1831)

Glover, Dr. George A. of Giles County married in Columbia to Miss Maria S. Bell.
National Banner & Nashville Daily Advertiser (Wed., July 10, 1833)

Glover, Miss Rhoda married to Mr. Charles Phifer.

Glover, Mr. William married in Giles County to Miss Nancy Phifer.
National Banner & Nashville Daily Advertiser (Mon., March 25, 1833)

Glymph, Miss Sally married to Jeremiah Jenkins.

Goadon, Mr. William H. merchant of Nashville married on Thursday
last, by the Rev. Mr. Tomes to Miss Susan Litton daughter of Mr.
Benjamin Litton of this vincinity of Nashville.
Nashville True Whig & Weekly Commercial Register (Wed., Dec. 25, 1850)

Goddard, Miss Catherine married to Geo. Manus.

Goddard, Francis E. Esq. of Louisville, Ky. married in Charlestown,
Mass. to Miss Martha Bartlett.
National Banner (Sat., Oct. 31, 1829)

Godwin, Mr. Riddeck married in Williamson County to Miss Mary A.
Beasly.
The Western Weekly Review - Franklin, Tenn. (Fri., Dec. 2, 1831)

Godwin, Mr. Riddeck married in Williamson County to Miss Mary A.
Beasley.
National Banner & Nashville Whig (Wed., Dec. 7, 1831)

Goff, A. F. Esq. married in Pulaski to Miss Adelaide Bramlitt.
Nashville Republican & State Gazette (Tues., July 29, 1834)

Goff, A. H. Esq. married in Giles County, Ten. to Miss Adelaide
Barmlett daughter of Judge Bramlett.
National Banner & Nashville Daily Advertiser (Tues., Aug. 5, 1834)

Goff, Major Andrew F. Attorney at law of Winchester, Ten. married on
the 3d inst at White Cottage by Rev. Dr. Edgar to Miss Rebecca J.
Erwin daughter of John P. Erwin, Esq.
Nashville Whig (Tues., July 4, 1843)

Goff, Miss Jane married in Williamson County to Mr. Joseph F. McMahon.

Goff, Miss Jane L. married to Mr. Joseph F. McMahon.

Goff, Nancy M. married to Lewis D. Inman.

Goff, Mr. Thomas J. married in Columbia to Miss Eliza P. White.
National Banner & Nashville Whig (Sat., Feb. 10, 1827)

Goforth, Miss Sarah married to Mr. John H. Peck.

Goin, Mr. Alfred married on Monday the 18th inst. by Felix G.
Earthman, Esq. to Miss Rhoda Dorcus Thompson all of Davidson County.
The Christian Record (Sat., Oct. 30, 1847)

Goldsborough, Lewis M. of the U. S. Navy married at Baltimore to Miss
Elizabeth Gamble Wirt daughter of the Hon. William Wirt.
National Banner & Nashville Whig (Friday, Nov. 18, 1831)

Gooch, Mr. Allen T. married in Rutherford County to Miss Elizabeth
Morton.
National Banner & Nashville Whig (Sat., Sept. 16, 1826)

Gooch, Miss Catherine E. married to Volney N. Howard Esq.

Gooch, Miss Lucinda married to Geo. King.

Gooch, Miss Lucinda married to George King.

Goodall, Miss Clarisse H. married to D. A. Given Esq.

Goodall, Miss Eleanor married to Col. Arthur T. Isom.

Goodall, Miss Eliza married to Mr. Robert Robinson.

Goode, Mr. John W. married in Giles County to Miss Parmelia W. Clack.
Nashville Republican & State Gazette (Tues., May 13, 1834)

Goode, Miss Juliana married to William J. Bledsoe.

Goode, Miss Mary A. married to John Childress, Esq.

Goode, Mr. W. married in Wilkinson County, Miss to Miss Francis
T. Slocumb.
National Banner & Nashville Daily Advertiser (Mon., Feb. 17, 1834)

Gooding, Miss Sarah A. married to Mr. James O. Davis.

Goodlet, Mr. Robert married on Thursday 25th April by the Rev. Mr.
Ogden to Miss Louisa McMurry all of Davidson County.
Nashville Whig (Mon., May 6, 1839)

Goodlett, M. C. Attorney at law of Nashville married on the 17th inst.
in Christian County, Ky. by the Rev. Charles Day to Mrs. Mary Ann
Woodward daughter of Mr. James Miller.
The Politician & Weekly Nashville Whig (Fri., June 25, 1847)

Goodlett, Mr. William C. married on Tuesday the 14th inst. by the
Rev. Dr. Wharton to Miss Martha Washington.
The Christian Record (Sat., Dec. 18, 1847)

Goodlett, Mr. William C. married on Tuesday the 14th inst. by the
Rev. Dr. Wharton to Miss Martha Ann Washington.
The Politician & Weekly Nashville Whig (Fri., Dec. 24, 1847)

Goodlin, Dr. Cyrus M. Jefferson County married to Miss Priscilla
S. H. Talbot.
National Banner & Nashville Whig (Mon., July 18, 1831 & Aug. 3, 1831)

Goodloe, Miss Attelia Alice married to Mr. Richard C. Williams.

Goodloe, Miss Cynthia married to Mr. James D. Orr.

Goodloe, Mr. S. D. Jr. married at Tuscumbia, Ala. to Miss Ann J. Winter.
National Banner & Nashville Daily Advertiser (Thurs., March 29, 1832)

Goodloe, Miss Eliza Martha married to Dr. Benj. F. Robertson.

Goodloe, Miss Rebecca married to Mr. Lewis Jetton.

Goodman, Miss Rachel married to Dr. Simpson Doughty.

Goodner, Mr. Jacob married in Smith County to Miss Charlotte Kemp.
National Banner & Nashville Advertiser (Fri., Jan. 13, 1832)

Goodner, Miss Louisa D. married to Mr. Robert Dowell.

Goodnough, Mr. Josiah married in this place on Thursday evening to
Miss Sarah Smith.
The Nashville Whig & Tenn. Advertiser (March 21, 1818)

Goodpasture, Miss Martha married to Rev. Nathaniel Fisk.

Goodrich, Col. A. W. married in Washington City on the 6th inst. to
Miss Eliza Jane Thaw.
National Banner & Nashville Whig (Mon., Sept. 19, 1831)

Goodrich, Miss Ann Courtney W. married to Mr. Thomas D. Mosely.

Goodrich, Edmund W. formerly of Va. married to Miss Lucy A. B. Goodrich
of this vicinity.
Nashville Republican & State Gazette (Sat., Dec. 18, 1830)

Goodrich, Mr. Edmund W., Jr. formerly of Davidson County, Ten. married

near Claysville, Ala. on the 24th inst. to Miss Mary Wilburn daughter of Major Wilburn.
National Banner & Nashville Daily Advertiser (Fri., Feb. 1, 1833)

Goodrich, Mr. Edmund W. Jun. married in Claysville, Ala. to Miss Mary Wilburn on the 24th ult.
Nashville Republican & State Gazette (Fri., Feb. 1, 1833)

Goodrich, Miss Eliza S. married to Col. John L. Harris.

Goodrich, Mr. James M. married in this County on the 27th ult. to Miss Susan P. Wells.
National Banner & Nashville Whig (Sat., Feb. 7, 1828)

Goodrich, Mr. John married in August 1831 to Miss Milly Short.
The Western Weekly Review - Franklin, Tenn. (Fri., Sept. 2, 1831)

Goodrich, Miss Lucy A. B. of this vicinity married to Mr. Edmund W. Goodrich.

Goodrich, Mr. Silas C. married in Madison County to Miss Mary Stewart daughter of Col. B. G. Stewart.
National Banner & Nashville Whig (Wed., Sept. 7, 1831)

Goodrum, Mr. John married in Warren County, Ten. to Miss Elizabeth Bond.
National Banner & Nashville Daily Advertiser (Tues., Aug. 5, 1834)

Goodrum, Mr. Sterling married in Shelbyville, Ten. to Miss Epsabeth Burditt.
National Banner & Nashville Daily Advertiser (Sat., Aug. 24, 1833)

Goodsen, Mr. R. aged 85 married in Maury County to Mrs. Hood aged 75.
National Banner & Nashville Whig (Sat., Dec. 1, 1827)

Goodwin, Mrs. Elizabeth married to Dr. Jos. K. Sparks.

Goodwin, Harriet married to Jas. Stephens.

Goodwin, Miss Martha married to Mr. Chauncy Richardson.

Goodwin, Susan H. married to John H. Ewing.

Gorby, Mr. Lewis H. formerly of Philadelphia married last evening 15th inst. by the Rev. Dr. Howell to Miss Mary E. Horn daughter of Capt. W. H. Horn all of Nashville.
The Politician & Weekly Nashville Whig (Wed., Sept. 22, 1847)

Gordley, Mr. William married to Miss Sidney Ann Stevenson in Fayette County.
National Banner & Nashville Whig (Fri., Jan. 22, 1830)

Gordon, Miss Ann Harrison married to Mr. Hugh White Jr.

Gordon, Ann Jannette married to C. C. Norvell.

Gordon, Major Bolling of Tennessee married in Buckingham County, Va. to Miss Mary Elizabeth Watkins daughter of Joel Watkins Esq.
National Banner & Nashville Whig (Mon., May 9, 1831)

Gordon, Maj. Bolling of Tennessee married to Miss Mary E. Watkins. in Buckingham County, Va.
Nashville Republican & State Gazette (Tues., May 10, 1831)

Gordon, Miss Caledonia married to Mr. John H. Petway.

Gordon, Miss Dorothy married to Charles W. Weber Esq.

Gordon, Mr. Francis H. President of Clinton College married in Smith

County, Ten. to Miss Rhoda M. Moores.
National Banner & Nashville Daily Advertiser (Tues., Aug. 19, 1834)

Gordon, Col. George H. married in Wilkinson County, Mi. to Miss
Leonora N. Nelson
Nashville Banner & Nashville Daily Advertiser (Thurs., May 17, 1832)

Gordon, Mr. George W. Esq. married in Maury County to Miss Elizabeth
Bradshaw of Maury County.
National Banner & Nashville Daily Advertiser (Fri., Jan. 17, 1833)

Gordon, Mr. Jefferson married in Madison County, Ky. to Miss Eliza
Harris.
National Banner & Nashville Whig (Sat., Feb. 10, 1827)

Gordon, Mr. John married in Louisville, Ky. to Miss Louise Baxter.
National Banner & Nashville Whig (Sat., March 22, 1828)

Gordon, Miss Judith A. married to Mr. Samuel M'Alexander.

Gordon, Miss Margaret A. married to Mr. Jonathan Rothrock.

Gordon, Miss Margaret A. married to Mr. Jonathan Rothrock.

Gordon, Miss Mary married to Mr. John Craig.

Gordon, Miss Nancy married to Dr. Wm. B. Moores.

Gordon, Rev. Neal M. of Nicholasville, Ky. married in Shelbyville,
Ky. on the 1st day Jan. by the Rev. James Smith to Catharine M. Smith
daughter of Dr. Smith.
The Christian Record (Sat., Jan. 20, 1849)

Gordon, Major W. B. of Texas married in Rutherford County on the
31st Oct. by the Rev. J. M. Watson to Miss Virginia A. Russworm
daughter of Gen. Russworm.
Nashville Whig (Fri., Nov. 16, 1838)

Gordon, Maj. Wiley of Texas married in Rutherford County on the 31st
inst. to Miss Virginia Russworm daughter of Gen. Russworm.
Nashville Union (Mon., Nov. 5, 1838)

Gore, Miss Margaret Eliza married to Mr. J. S. Fullilove.

Gowen, Matilda A. married to Mr. William S. Anthony.

Gowin, Mr. Wilford B. married in this County yesterday to Miss Ursula
Rains.
National Banner & Nashville Whig (Sat., July 29, 1826)

Gorham, Miss Emily L. T. married to Mr. Daniel P. Braden.

Gorham, Mr. John W. married in Springfield, Tenn. on Friday the
20th inst. by the Rev. R. Harris to Miss Laroah A. Johnson both of
Nashville
Nashville Union (Thurs., April 26, 1838)

Gorham, Mr. Simpson married in Lexington, Ky. to Miss Letitia Boyd.
National Banner (Sat., Nov. 28, 1829)

Gorin, Franklin Esq. of the Kentucky Bar married on Friday 30th inst.
by Rev. J. Thomas Wheat to Mrs. Frances C. Boardman of England.
Nashville Whig (Mon., Aug. 2, 1841)

Gordin, Mr. Gladin married in Madison County, Ten. to Miss Jane B.
Wormley daughter of Hugh W. Wormley Esq.
National Banner & Nashville Whig (Fri., Dec. 12, 1834)

Gorin, Mr. James married in Bowling Green, Ky. to Miss Emily Buster.
National Banner & Nashville Daily Advertiser (Mon., Aug. 26, 1833)

Gorman, Mr. James O. married Miss Mary Ann Hewlett daughter of Mr.
William Hewlett in Nashville by Wilkins Tannehill Esq. married Jan.
20, 1830
National Banner & Nashville Whig (Fri., Jan. 22, 1830)

Gosey, Mr. E. J. B. of Williamson County married on the 8th of Jan.
by the Rev. Mr. Hobdy to Miss Talitha Cotton daughter of Mr. Monoah
Cotton of Sumner County.
Nashville Whig (Sat., Jan. 17, 1846)

Goss, Mr. John D. married in Davidson County on Tuesday last by the
Rev. Mr. M'Dowell to Miss Elizabeth Buie.
National Banner & Nashville Whig (Mon., Dec. 20, 1830)

Gossett, Mr. Andrew married in Hardeman County to Miss Rhoda W.
Mulder.
National Banner & Nashville Daily Advertiser (Sat., Jan. 7, 1832)

Gott, Mr. John of Tennessee married on Feb. 19th by the Rev. Mr. Parsons
to Miss Margaret Bean.
National Banner & Nashville Whig (Mon., March 20, 1837)

Gough, Mr. Percival married in Lexington, Ky. to Miss Julia C. Megowan.
National Banner & Nashville Advertiser (Tues., June 26, 1832)

Gould, Mr. Andrew married in Blount County, Ten. to Miss Jane Earley
daughter of Mr. Andrew Earley.
National Banner & Nashville Whig (Mon., Nov. 10, 1834)

Gould, Mr. James of Nashville married on the 6th inst. to Mrs. Martha
W. Farrar of Dickson County.
Nashville Whig (Fri., Oct. 11, 1839)

Govin, Mr. H. H. married in Henry County to Miss Elvira Atkins.
National Banner & Nashville Daily Advertiser (Tues., Aug. 7, 1832)

Gowdey, Miss Adda married to Thomas Cox Esq.

Gowdy, Miss Anna married to Hon. Thomas C. McCampbell.

Gowen, Mr. John J. married on the 8th inst. to Miss Tabitha Hays
daughter of Mr. Charles Hays all of this County.
Nashville Whig (May 14, 1823)

Gowen, Miss Matilda A. married in Williamson Co. to Mr. Wm. S. Anthony.

Grace, Miss Mary married to Mr. John Lawrence.

Grace, Miss Nancy married to Mr. James Cuningham.

Grady, Miss Caroline A. married to Mr. Silas N. Macey.

Grady, Miss Eley married to Mr. Elisha Jenkins.

Graham, Dr. Albert B. married in Greenburg, Ky. to Miss Lavenia I.
Herdman.
National Banner & Nashville Advertiser (Sat., April 14, 1832)

Graham, Mr. Alexander married in Sumner County to Miss Violet Tucker.
Nashville Whig (Tues., March 24, 1846)

Graham, Miss Barbara married to Mr. William Frizell.

Graham, Miss Catherine married to Mr. George W. Gwinn.

Graham, Daniel Esq. Secretary of State, married on Thursday evening to Miss Maria M'Iver daughter of Col. John M'Iver of Murfreesborough. Nashville Whig (May 14, 1823)

Graham, Mr. Dudley married in Rutherford County to Miss Mary Jetton. National Banner & Nashville Whig (Fri., Nov. 11, 1831)

Graham, Mr. George married in Blount County to Miss Letitia Cowan. National Banner & Nashville Whig (Sat., Oct. 11, 1828)

Graham, Mr. George H. married in Huntsville, Ala. to Miss Julia Ann Cain. National Banner & Nashville Daily Advertiser (Mon., Feb. 18, 1833)

Graham, Mr. James of Florence, Ala. married in New York to Miss Mary L. Brown of Cincinnati. National Banner & Nashville Whig (June 24, 1826)

Graham, Mr. James M. married in Maury County to Miss Cynthia Ann Lusk. National Banner & Nashville Daily Advertiser (Tues., Dec. 17, 1833)

Graham, Miss Jane married to Mr. Thomas H. Newell.

Graham, Miss Margaret married to James W. Robertson, Esq.

Graham, Miss Milly R. married to Mr. Samuel B. Lusk.

Graham, Miss Rachel married to Mr. William Hansard.

Graham, Mr. Richard married in Sumner County on the 2nd inst. to Miss Martha Blythe. National Banner (Sat., May 30, 1829)

Graham, Capt. Robert married on Thursday 18th inst. by the Rev. Dr. Edgar to Miss Eliza A. Folwell all of Nashville. Nashville Union (Fri., Oct. 26, 1838)

Graham, Mr. S. L. of Franklin married in Columbia to Mrs. Frances E. Crabtree. Nashville Whig (Tuesday, March 24, 1846)

Graham, Mr. Samuel married in Williamson County to Miss Jane Thompson. National Banner & Nashville Daily Advertiser (Mon., May 13, 1833)

Graham, Miss Sarah married to Capt. Ira A. Stout.

Graham, Miss Sarah Ann married to D. Alexander Esq.

Grant, Mr. James A. married on the 27th ult. by Rev. J. G. Ward to Miss Frances E. Roberts both of Montgomery County, Tenn. Nashville True Whig & Weekly Commercial Register (Fri., July 19, 1850)

Grant, Rev. John married in Roan County to Miss Dolly Winton daughter of the Rev. John Winton. National Banner & Nashville Whig (Mon., Oct. 11,1830)

Grant, Miss Lucy married in to Mr. William R. Pope.

Grant, Miss Nancy L. married to Mr. Lewis Mountany.

Grant, Mr. Smith married at Louisville, Ky. to Miss Jane Smith. National Banner & Nashville Whig (June 14, 1826)

Grant, Miss Susan married to Mr. Timothy Sanderson.

Grat, Miss Sarah married to Mr. John A. Holland.

Graven, Miss Julia Ann married to Mr. George F. Razor.

Graves, Miss Martha married to Dr. Thomas B. Jefferson.

Graves, Miss Sarah W. married to Mr. Peyton Fletch.

Graves, Mr. William married in Blount County to Miss Mary Holloway
National Banner & Nashville Daily Advertiser (Wed., May 8, 1833)

Gray, Capt. Angerean. Married in Louisville, Ky. to Miss Myrah
M'Connell.
National Banner & Nashville Whig (Sat., Aug. 30, 1828)

Gray, Dr. Benjamin married in Fayette County, Ky. to Miss Mary Young.
National Banner (May 4, 1826)

Gray, Mr. Burgess married in Lincoln County, Ten. to Miss Elizabeth
Cuningham.
National Banner & Nashville Whig (Fri., Jan. 23, 1835)

Gray, Capt. C. H. married in Sumner County to Miss Catherine S.
Hassell.
National Banner & Nashville Advertiser (Mon., Dec. 31, 1832)

Gray, Mrs. Catharine Dangerfield married to Achille Murat, Esq.

Gray, Mr. Harvey married in Williamson County to Miss Malinda Wood.
The Western Weekly Review - Franklin, Tenn. (Fri., Dec. 2, 1831)

Gray, Mr. Harvey married in Williamson County to Miss Malinda Wood.
National Banner & Nashville Whig (Wed., Dec. 7, 1831)

Gray, Mr. Jackson of the Theatre married on Wednesday last in this
town by the Rev. Mr. Lanier to Miss Margaret Carpender
National Banner & Nashville Whig (Sat., Sept. 8, 1827)

Gray, Miss Margaret married to Mr. Kendall.

Gray, Miss Mary E. married to Mr. James E. Marshall.

Gray, Mrs. Mary H. married to Rev. Samuel R. Davidson.

Gray, Miss Susan married to Peter R. Booker.

Gray, Miss Sarah A. married to John W. Walker.

Gray, Miss Susan married to Mr. John A. McLung.

Gray, Miss Susan married to Mr. John A. M'Clung.

Gray, Miss Tibitha married to Mr. John L. Gillespie.

Gray, Wm. Esq. married in Warren County, Ten. to Mrs. Sarah Hays.
Nashville Republican & State Gazette (Tues., Sept. 20, 1831)

Gray, Mr. William married in Sumner County to Miss Margaret Houdyshelt.
National Banner & Nashville Advertiser (Mon., Oct. 29, 1832)

Gray, Mr. Wm. H. married in Muary County to Miss Emeline Hackney.
National Banner & Nashville Whig (Sat., Dec. 17, 1831)

Graysen, Mr. John married at Florence, Ala. to Miss Delia Hooks.
National Banner & Nashville Whig (Sat., Feb. 23, 1828)

Grayson, Mr. Daniel married in LaGrange, Ala. to Miss Martin.
National Banner & Nashville Daily Advertiser (Mon., Jan. 16, 1832)

Calab, Green Jr. Esq. of Saratoga, New York married in Attakapas,
Parish, La. to Miss Emiline Braussard.
National Banner & Nashville Daily Advertiser (Fri., May 16, 1834)

Green, Miss Catharine M. married to Mr. James R. White.

Green, Mr. David D. married to Miss Jane Inglish.

Green, Edward H. Esq. married in Hopkinsville, Ky. to Miss Arietta
J. Ward daughter of Mr. George Ward.
National Banner & Nashville Daily Advertiser (Mon., July 2, 1832)

Green, Miss Eliza married to Mr. Thomas Emmerson.

Green, Miss Elizabeth married to Mr. Joel Simons.

Green, Mr. George married in Maury County to Miss Catharine Gilchrist.
National Banner & Nashville Whig (Mon., Aug. 8, 1831)

Green, Mr. George W. of Natchez Miss. married yesterday at the
Episcopal Church in Nashville by the Rev. J. T. Wheat to Miss Amanda
M. Austin of Concordia, La.
Daily Republican Banner (Wed., Sept. 18, 1839)

Green, Mr. George W. of Natchez, Miss married in Nashville by the
Rev. J. T. Wheat to Mrs. Amanda Austin of Concordia, La.
Nashville Union (Fri., Sept. 20, 1839)

Green, Mr. Hiram married in Nashville last evening by the Rev. Mr.
Hume to Mrs. S. Garrett.
National Banner & Nashville Daily Advertiser (Fri., June 1, 1832)

Green, J. married in Maury County to Miss E. Hinson.
National Banner & Nashville Daily Advertiser (Thurs., April 5, 1832)

Green, Mr. James of Nolensville, Williamson County married in Davidson
County on the 15th inst by the Rev. Mr. Porter to Miss Elizabeth H.
Hyde daughter of the late Henry Hyde of this County.
National Banner & Nashville Whig (Fri., Dec. 10, 1835)

Green, Miss Josephine M. married to Mr. Thomas B. Eastland.

Green, Mr. M. J. of Williamson County married on the 20th ult. by the
Rev. R. W. January to Miss Martha M. Willis of Wilson County.
Nashville Whig (Tues., March 5, 1844)

Green, Miss Martha married to Dr. William Craig.

Green, Miss Martha married to Ozwell Newby.

Green, Martha married to Mr. Ozewell Newby.

Green, Miss Mary married to Mr. Joshua Scott.

Green, Miss Nancy married to Capt. Robt. Moore.

Green, Miss Nancy W. married to Rev. Samuel K. Sneed.

Green, Hon. Nathan of the Supreme Bench of Tennessee married on the
8th inst. by the Rev. James Arkin Presiding Elder of the Knoxville
District to Mrs. E. A. Purris of Roane County.
Nashville True Whig & Weekly Commercial Register (Fri., Aug. 16, 1850)

Green, Mr. Orville married in Smith County to Miss Levisa Moore
daughter of Capt. Armstead Moore.
National Banner & Nashville Daily Advertiser (Tues., June 11, 1833)

Green, Mr. Samuel married on Thursday the 18th inst. by the Rev. Dr. Lapsley to Miss Susan Greenhalch all of Nashville.
The Christian Record. (Sat., May 27, 1848)

Green, Miss Sarah married to Mr. Oliver H. Wilson.

Green, Miss Sarah married to Mr. Oliver H. Wilson.

Green, Maj. Thomas J. of Tallahasee, Fla. married to Miss Sarah Wharton daughter of Jessee Wharton, Esq.
National Banner & Nashville Whig (Fri., Jan. 15, 1830)

Greene, Rev. A. L. P. married in Nashville to Miss Mary A. E. Elliston.
Nashville Republican & State Gazette (Sat., Oct. 22, 1831)

Greene, Mr. James H. married in Davidson County on the 30th ult. to Miss Mary D. Menifee.
National Banner & Nashville Whig (Wed., Sept. 7, 1831)

Green, Dr. Lewis married in Lauderdale County to Miss Lucinda W. M'Donald.
National Banner & Nashville Daily Advertiser (Mon., Oct. 29, 1832)

Greene, Miss Susan Jane married to Mr. Albert G. Payne.

Greenfield, Miss Minerva married to Mr. Henry Roberts.

Greenfield, Mr. Thomas married to Miss Lucy Hanna.

Greenfield, Mr. Wesley married in Todd County to Miss Virginia B. Burrus.
National Banner & Nashville Whig (Sat., Feb. 3, 1827)

Greenfield, William Esq. married in Robinson County to Miss Piety H. Yancey.
National Banner & Nashville Whig (Sat., Nov. 15, 1828)

Greenhalch, Miss Susan married to Mr. Samuel Green.

Greenhalgh, Mr. Jacob married to Miss Ann Charlton.

Greenleaf, Miss Martha married to Mr. Joseph J. Dew.

Greenstead, Miss Harriet married to Mr. A. C. Hurt.

Greenwell, Miss Julian married to Mr. Stephen T. Twyman.

Greenwood, Mrs. Ann L. married to Rev. James O. Andrew.

Greenwood, Mr. Robert H. of Nashville, Tenn. formerly of Greensboro, Ga. married in St. Louis on the 19th inst. by the Rev. Nathaniel Childs Jr. to Miss Mary A. Jamison daughter of Mr. David S. Jamison of St. Louis.
Nashville Whig (Tues., March 3, 1846)

Greer, Miss Amy married to Mr. Archibald M'Niell.

Greer, Miss Ann married to Mr. Francis Hargrove.

Greer, Capt. David B. married in Henry County, Ten. to Miss Martha Jane Dunlap.
National Banner & Nashville Whig (Fri., March 6, 1835)

Greer, Capt. David S. married in Henry County to Miss Martha Jane Dunlap.
Nashville Republican (Thurs., March 5, 1835)

Greer, Miss Emily married to Mr. John Spencer.

Greer, Miss Eliza married to Mr. Benajah Bosworth.

Greer, Miss Elizabeth married to Mr. Preston A. Hughes.

Greer, Miss Emily married to Mr. John Spencer.

Greer, Mr. Greenbury married in Davidson County to Miss Lucinda Robertson.
National Banner & Nashville Whig (Tues., Dec. 20, 1831)

Greer, Miss Hetty E. K. married to Wm. D. Thompson Esq.

Greer, Joseph married Miss Polly Mitchell on Thursday the 16th June, 1814 inst. Mr. Joseph Greer to Miss Polly Mitchell of this County.
Clarion (June 21, 1814)

Greer, Miss Margaret married to Samuel W. Carmack Esq.

Greer, Miss Ruth T. married to George McNeill Esq.

Gregg, Mr. Will M. married in Lawrence County, Ala. to Miss Francis Townes.
Nashville Republican & State Gazette (Sat., Sept. 24, 1831)

Gregory, Miss Susannah married to Mr. Henry Parks.

Grengrey, Miss Catherine married to Mr. John E. Barrow.

Gresham, Mr. Archibald married in Christian County, Ky. to Miss Susan Boyd.
National Banner & Nashville Daily Advertiser (Tues., Oct. 30, 1832)

Gresham, Mr. Austin of this town married in this County last evening to Mrs. Eliza Burge.
National Banner (Sat., July 25, 1829)

Grider, Mr. Wm. married near La Grange to Miss Sarah Taylor.
National Banner & Nashville Whig (Thurs., July 22, 1830)

Grierson, Miss Margaret married to Mr. Thomas C. Phillips.

Griffin, Mrs. Ann W. married to Mr. Francis T. Moody.

Griffin, Miss Jane married to Col. D. C. Gibson.

Griffin, Mr. Jefferson married in Knox County to Miss Mary Simpson.
National Banner & Nashville Daily Advertiser (Mon., Feb. 6, 1832)

Griffin, Miss Martha married to Mr. John D. Lankford.

Griffis, Mr. Wm. A. married in Lincoln County, Ten. to Miss Mahala Johnson.
National Banner & Nashville Whig (Fri., Dec. 5, 1834)

Griges, Mr. Thomas S. married on Thursday 3d inst. by Joseph L. Jarrell Esq. to Miss Amelia Ann Collins all of Davidson County.
Nashville True Whig & Weekly Commercial Register (Fri., Oct. 11, 1850)

Grigg, Mr. Lewis M. married in Williamson County to Miss Sarah M. Yearger.
The Western Weekly Review - Franklin, Tenn. (Fri., Dec. 2, 1831)

Grigg, Mr. Lewis M. married in Williamson County to Miss Sarah M. Yearger.
National Banner & Nashville Whig (Wed., Dec. 7, 1831)

Griggs, Miss Mary married to Mr. Hosea Stanfield.

Griggs, Miss Sophia married to Mr. Oscar Staley.

Griggsby, Miss married to Mr. William M. McBridge.

Grigsby, Dr. J. B. of Greene County married in Granger County to Miss Caroline A. Jarnagin daughter of J. Jarnagin Esq.
National Banner & Nashville Daily Adv. (Mon., Jan. 21, 1833)

Grigsby, Dr. J. B. of Green County married to Miss Caroline A. Jarnagin of Granger County on the 10 inst.
Nashville Republican & State Gazette (Mon., Jan. 21, 1833)

Grills, Miss Mary C. married to Mr. Isam P. Alley.

Grimes, Miss Jane married in Madison County, Ky. to Mr. James T. Smith.

Grimes, Miss Mary Ann R. married to Dr. H. H. Sugg.

Grimes, Mr. William C. married in Wayne County to Miss Sally Shull.
National Banner & Nashville Daily Advertiser (Fri., Sept. 20, 1833)

Grisham, Mr. George W. married in Lauderdale County, Ala. to Miss Mary Ann Thornton.
National Banner & Nashville Whig (Mon., Nov. 28, 1831)

Grisham, Mr. J. B. married in Maury County to Miss Wilmouth Foster.
National Banner & Nashville Whig (Mon., Aug. 8, 1831)

Grisham, Mr. Wm. married in Smith County to Miss Nancy Haley.
National Banner & Nashville Advertiser (Fri., Jan. 27, 1832)

Grissum, Miss Susan married to Mr. George Patton.

Griswold, Miss Harriet married to Rev. Erastus Burr.

Grizzard, Miss Ann Eliza married to Mr. Richard C. Bandy.

Grizzard, Mr. Edmund of Huntingdon, Tenn. married in Monroe County, Miss. on the 25th Dec. by the Rev. Mr. Cook to Miss Lydia Boggan.
National Banner & Nashville Daily Advertiser (Mon., Jan. 14, 1833)

Grizzard, Miss Frances married to Mr. Ortho H. Moores.

Grizzard, Mr. J. W., merchant of Huntington, Tenn. married in Brownsville on Tuesday 4th inst. by the J. Fannington Esq. to Miss C. C. Towns daughter of Col. James Towns formerly of Nashville.
National Banner & Nashville Whig (Mon., July 17, 1837)

Grizzard, Mr. J. W., merchant of Huntington, Tenn. married in Brownsville on Friday the 4th inst. by the Mr. J. Farrington, Esq. to Miss C. C. Towns daughter of Col. James Towns.
Nashville Republican (Tues., July 18, 1837)

Grizzard, Miss Louisa Ann married to Henry E. A. Mason Esq.

Grizzard, Miss Nancy J. married to Mr. Joel R. Smith.

Grizzard, Miss Sarah E. married to Mr. J. D. Aydelott.

Grooms, Miss Mary married to Mr. Hugh Fleming.

Cross, Mr. George S. married in this town to Miss Evelina Clinard.
National Banner & Nashville Whig (Sat., Jan. 17, 1829)

Gross, Mr. John of Ky. married in Cincinnati, Ohio to Miss Ann Haven Woodward.
National Banner & Nashville Daily Advertiser (Thurs., June 19, 1834)

Grosvenor, Miss Laura C. married to Mr. George Washington Sutton.

Grove, Mr. married in Christian County, Ky. to Miss Barnett.
National Banner & Nashville Whig (Wed., Oct. 19, 1831)

Grove, Miss Elizabeth M. married to Mr. Samuel A. Holmes.

Grove, Mr. William B. married in Hardeman to Miss Emeline C. Rives.
National Banner & Nashville Daily Advertiser (Wed., Jan. 18, 1832)

Groves, Mr. Alexander married in Maury County, Ten. to Miss Francis White.
National Banner & Nashville Whig (Wed., March 4, 1835)

Groves, Mr. Alexander married in Maury County to Miss Frances White.
Nashville Republican (Thurs., March 5, 1835)

Groves, Miss Sarah S. married to Mr. Thomas M. Rives.

Grundy, Miss Eliza married to Mr. Ramsey Mason.

Grundy, Felicia Ann married to William Eakin Esq.

Grundy, James P. H. Esq. married in Trenton to Miss Eliza Hogg daughter of Maj. John B. Hogg.
National Banner & Nashville Whig (Sat., May 24, 1828)

Grundy, Miss Malvina married to Mr. John M. Bass.

Grundy, Maria G. married to William W. Materson Esq.

Grundy, Miss Maria G. married to Mr. William W. Masterson.

Grundy, Miss Martha A. F. married to V. P. Winder.

Grundy, Miss Mary E. married to Mr. Walter Scott.

Grundy, Miss Mary E. married to Mr. Walter Scott.

Grundy, Rev. R. C., D.D. Pastor of the Presbyterian Church in Maysville married in Cincinnati, Ohio on May 30th by the Rev. S. Ramsay Wilson to Miss Ellen Suzett Kemper eldest daughter of James Kemper Esq. of Cincinnati.
The Christian Record (Sat., June 17, 1848)

Grundy, Miss Susan C. married to Henry Ewing.

Gub-na-ne-da married at Valley Towns by the Rev. E. Jones, 12th April, 1830 to Yo-gwe-se.
National Banner & Nashville Whig (Mon., July 26, 1830)

Guest, Miss Elizabeth married to Mr. Benj. B. Reynolds.

Guest, Dr. Martin of Fayette County, Tenn. married on 7th Dec. to Miss Mary A. E. H. Cochran daughter of John Cockran, Esq. of Fayette County, Ala.
National Banner & Nashville Whig (Fri., Dec. 30, 1831)

Guidry, Miss Felonist married to Mr. T. De Valcourt.

Guild, J. C. Esq. married at Gallatin to Miss Catharine Blackmore.
National Banner & Nashville Whig (Sat., Dec. 30, 1826)

Guinn, Mr. of Warren County married in Bedford County to Miss Margaret Davidson daughter of Hugh Davidson Esq.
National Banner & Nashville Daily Advertiser (Tues., Nov. 13, 1832)

Guinn, Mr. Christopher married to Miss Martha B. Robinson.
National Banner & Nashville Whig (Fri., March 6, 1835)

Guion, Miss Isabella married to Mr. Francis Labeau.

Guion, John J. Esq. married in Claiborne County, Mo. to Miss Lucinda Jane McCaleb.
National Banner & Nashville Daily Advertiser (Tues., May 20, 1834)

Gun, Mr. William G. married in Petersburg, Va. by the Rev. Mr. Cannon to Miss Emily Maria Pistol.
Nashville Whig (July 7, 1823)

Gunn, Mr. Ed. H. married at Russellville, Ky. to Miss Catherine Orndorff.
National Banner & Nashville Advertiser (Tues., May 8, 1832)

Gunn, Mr. Lyman T. married on Wednesday the 22d inst. by the Rev. A. L. P. Green to Miss Caroline M. Morehead all of Nashville.
Daily Republican Banner (Fri., Jan. 24, 1840)

Gunter, Miss Eleanor married to Mr. Gideon Ward.

Gunter, Miss Eliza married to Mr. Rewben P. Hayes.

Guthrie, Mr. E. A. married in Williamson County to Miss Lucy Bomar.
The Western Weekly Review - Franklin, Tenn. (Fri., Dec. 2, 1831)

Guthrie, Mr. E. A. married in Williamson County to Miss Lucy Bomar.
National Banner & Nashville Whig (Wed., Dec. 7, 1831)

Guthrie, Mr. Jacob E. married in Williamson to Miss Nancy Orton.
National Banner & Nashville Whig (Sat., Dec. 30, 1826)

Guthrie, Mr. James of Green County married at Rogersville, Ten. to Miss Mary Ann Simpson daughter of William Simpson Esq. of Rogersville.
National Banner & Nashville Daily Advertiser (Mon., Feb. 4, 1833)

Guthrie, Mr. Jno. W. married in Jackson to Miss Dolly Prewitt.
Nashville Republican & State Gazette (Wed., Jan. 16, 1833)

Guthrie, Mr. John W. married in Jackson to Miss Dolly Prewett.
National Banner & Nashville Daily Advertiser (Thurs., Jan. 17, 1833)

Guy, Miss Mary Elizabeth of Davidson County married on Feb.8th 1848 by the Rev. F. E. Pitts to Mr. George W. McCown of Nashville.

Gwathney, Miss Mary Eliza married to Mr. Frances B. Tillay.

Gwin, Dr. Daniel M. married in Hardeman County to Miss Olivia Ricks.
National Banner & Nashville Daily Advertiser (Thurs., Sept. 27, 1832)

Gwin, Miss Elizabeth P. married to Mr. James C. Mosby.

Gwin, Dr. William M. U. S. Marshall for Mississippi married on the 23d of March at the residence of Dr. Bill, near Francisville, La. by the Hon. Judge Dawson to Mrs. Mary E. Logan of Texas.
The Union (Thurs., April 13, 1837)

Gwinn, Dr. Daniel M. married in Hardeman County to Miss Oliva Ricks.
National Banner & Nashville Advertiser (Thurs., Sept. 27, 1832)

Gwinn, Mr. George W. married in Frankfort, Ky. to Miss Catherine Graham.
National Banner (Sat., Oct. 3, 1829)

Haaen, Mr. Gilbert married in Nashville on the 24th May by the Rev.
Mr. Wheat to Miss Caroline Sittler daughter of the late Isaac Sittler
Esq.
Daily Republican Banner (Fri., May 25, 1838)

Habbell, Mrs. Martha married to Mr. John Talger.

Hackett, Mr. William P. married in Arkansas County A. T. to Mrs.
Polly Taylor.
National Banner & Nashville Whig (Sat., March 10, 1827)

Hackney, Miss Emeline married to Mr. Wm. H. Gray.

Hackney, Mr. Geo. W. married in Maury County to Miss Mary W. Johnson.
National Banner & Nashville Whig (Sat., Feb. 14, 1829)

Hackney, Miss Jemimah married to Mr. Edward Warmack.

Hackney, Mr. John R. married in Campbell County to Miss Rachel Arwine.
National Banner & Nashville Daily Advertiser (Fri., May 10,1833)

Haddox, Miss Mary married to Mr. William L. Banks.

Haden, Miss Emily married to Mr. Joseph Rogers.

Haden, Mr. James married at Maryville to Miss Nancy Hood.
National Banner & Nashville Whig (Sat., April 14, 1827)

Haden, Mr. Resin P. married in the vicinity of Russellville, Ky. to
Miss Eleanor Ann Blakey.
National Banner & Nashville Daily Advertiser (Sat., Feb. 2, 1833)

Haden, Mr. Richard married in Clarksville, Tenn. to Mrs. Elizabeth
E. Porter.
National Banner & Nashville Advertiser (Sat., June 2, 1832)

Hadley, Miss Amelia married to Dr. John L. Hadley.

Hadley, Miss Eveline married to Dr. James A. Blackmore.

Hadley, James H., Esq. married in Sumner County to Emeline M. Blackmore.
National Banner (Aug. 8, 1829)

Dr. John L. Hadley of this town (Nashville) married to Miss Amelia
Hadley of Sumner County.
Nashville Whig (Wed., December 20, 1815)

Hadley, Dr. John L. Jun. of Williamson County married in Sumner County
on Tuesday 11th inst. to Miss Elizabeth Bledsoe daughter of Mr.
Isaac Bledsoe of Sumner County.
National Banner & Nashville Whig (Thurs., May 20, 1830)

Haffy, Mr. Hugh married in Nashville to Miss Emeline Thweat of Franklin
County.
Nashville Republican (Tues., Nov. 10, 1835)

Hagan, Miss Alice G. married to Dr. James R. Cocke.

Hagan, Miss Jane M. married to Mr. John C. Bowman.

Hagan, Letitia C. married to Andrew J. McCreary.

Hageman, John F. Councellor at Law married at Princeton, New Jersey on
Wednesday 26th by the Rev. Dr. Miller to Sarah Sergeant Miller daughter
of Rev. Dr. Miller.
The Christian Record (Sat., June 18, 1847)

Hageman, John F. Councellor at Law married in Princeton, New Jersey on the 26th ult. by the Rev. Dr. Miller to Sarah Sergeant Miller daughter of Rev. Dr. Miller.
The Politician & Weekly Nashville Whig (Fri., June 25, 1847)

Hagen, Mary W. married to Hugh W. McGavock, Esq.

Hager, Mr. Jonathan B. married in Lexington, Ky. to Miss Sarah Springle.
National Banner & Nashville Whig (Thurs., July 1st. 1830)

Hagerman, Miss Jane married to Mr. Micajah Clark.

Hagey, Miss Maria H. married to Mr. Jacob H. Bransford.

Haggan, Miss Ann married to P. S. Laughborough Esq.

Haggard, Mr. J. married in Christian County, Ky. to Miss Mary J. Thompson.
National Banner & Nashville Daily Advertiser (Tues., Feb. 5, 1833)

Haggard, Miss Sarrah married to Mr. John Shields.

Haggatt, Mrs. Amanda married to Mr. Wharton.

Haggin, Miss Martha H. married to Mr. Robert H. Bowmar.

Hagle, Mr. John married in Madison County, Ala. to Miss Elizabeth Scruggs.
National Banner & Nashville Whig (Sat., March 17, 1827)

Hail, Miss Eliza Ann married to Mr. William McCall.

Hail, Miss Louisa Walker married to Rev. Herbert C. Thomson.

Haile, Mr. Leaman married in Rutherford County to Miss Marillas Edwards.
National Banner & Nashville Daily Advertiser (Fri., Jan.27, 1832)

Haile, Mr. Pumfrey married in Bedford County to Miss Susan Hively Bedford County.
National Banner & Nashville Advertiser (Wed., Jan. 4, 1832)

Haile, Mr. Thomas I. married in Nashville to Miss Evelinia Ambress on Tuesday evening 2d inst. by the Rev. James Gwinn.
National Banner & Nashville Whig (Wed., Aug. 3, 1831)

Hailey, Mr. Anderson married in Bedford Co., Ten. to Mrs. Ruth McFarland.
National Banner & Nashville Daily Advertiser (Tues., Aug. 19, 1834)

Haines, Mr. Joseph married in Madison County to Miss Margaret Davis.
National Banner & Nashville Whig (Wed., June 29, 1831)

Haines, Miss Lucy married to Mr. Sandy Davis.

Haines, Mr. Thomas married in Fayette County, Ky. to Miss Mary Merrill.
National Banner & Nashville Whig (Sat., March 17, 1827)

Hair, Mr. James married in Knox County to Miss Betsey McCampbell.
National Banner & Nashville Whig (Sat., Jan. 26, 1828)

Haiston, Mr. Robert married in Bedford County to Miss Isabella M'Clain.
National Banner & Nashville Daily Advertiser (Sat., Oct. 6, 1832)

Hakill, Mr. Oliver married at Maysville, Ky. to Miss Hetty Bell.
National Banner & Nashville Whig (Sat., Dec. 23, 1826)

Halbrook, Mr. John married Miss Mecca F. Moore.
The Western Weekly Review - Franklin, Tenn. (Fri., Nov. 11, 1831)

Halbrook, Mr. John married in Williamson County to Miss Mecca F. Moore.
National Banner & Nashville Whig (Mon., Nov. 14, 1831)

Halcum, Mr. Charles married in Warren County, Ten. to Miss Charlotte
Allen daughter of Thos. Allen Esq.
National Banner & Nashville Whig (Wed., Feb. 4, 1835)

Hale, Mr. Albert G. married in Marion County, Ten. to Miss Nancy Oats
daughter of Col. David Oats.
National Banner & Nashville Whig (Mon., Jan. 5, 1835)

Hale, Miss Catharine married to Mr. James King.

Hale, E. C. W. of Sumner County married in Gibson County, Tenn. at
the residence of Burton Jordan to Mrs. Martha Jordan.
Daily Republican Banner (Sat., Dec. 7, 1839)

Hale, Miss Martha married to Mr. Andrew Harris.

Hale, Miss Nancy married to Mr. Thomas Bunch.

Hale, Mr. Samuel married at Shippingport, Ky. to Mrs. Rebecca Wells.
National Banner & Nashville Whig (Thurs., Sept. 2, 1830)

Haley, Mr. Benj. married in Madison County to Miss Martha F. M'Clelan.
National Banner & Nashville Whig (Sat., May 12, 1827)

Haley, Mr. James married in Madison County to Miss Martha Weaver.
National Banner & Nashville Whig (Sat., Jan. 6. 1827)

Haley, Miss Nancy married to Mr. Wm. Grisham.

Haley, Miss Nancy married to Robert Wilson.

Haley, Miss Nancy married to Mr. James Roberts.

Haley, Miss Paulina T. married to Mr. Willis D. Bennett.

Halfacre, Mr. Andrew married in Williamson County to Miss Mary Barnes.
National Banner & Nashville Whig (Wed., Sept. 24, 1834)

Halfacre, Jacob married in Williamson County to Miss Elizabeth
Rucks.
The Western Weekly Review - Franklin, Tenn. (Fri., March 8, 1833)

Miss A. Hall married to Mr. Sampson Lane.

Mr. Addisson S. Hall married in Maury County to Miss Jane B. Gillespie.
National Banner & Nashville Whig (Fri., Dec. 10, 1830)

Hall, Dr. Alexander married in Christian County, Ky. to Miss Selina
Wilson aged 12 years and 9 months.
National Banner (Jan. 20, 1826)

Hall, Allen A. Esq. Nashville, Tenn. married Mrs. Sophia Chester
daughter of Dr. John Hogg Thursday evening 1st. inst. by the Rev. Mr.
Hume.
National Banner & Nashville Advertiser (Fri., March 2, 1832)

Miss Ann Hall married to Mr. Abiel Smith.

Hall, Mr. Augustus in Fayette County, Ky. to Miss Sarah Henderson.
National Banner & Nashville Whig (Jan. 19, 1831)

Hall, Miss Caroline Matilda married to Mr. William C. Blake.

Hall, Cornelia Miss married to Edward D. Hicks, Esq.

Hall, Miss E. T. B. married to Mr. Miles Kirby.

Hall, Mr. E. S. married to Miss Sophai Talbot.

Eliha S. Hall, Esq. married in this town last evening to Mrs.
Rhoda Boyd.
National Banner & Nashville Whig (Sat., Oct. 20, 1826)

Hall, Miss Elizabeth married to Mr. Joseph Herron.

Hall, Miss Elizabeth married to Joseph M. Lapsley.

Hall, Miss Elizabeth married to Joseph H. Lapsley, Esq.

Hall, Miss Elizabeth Emma married to John B. Forrester, Esq.

Hall, Miss Emily married to James Alderson.

Hall, Miss Isabell married to Rev. Thomas W. Tory.

Hall, Mr. J. H. M. of Nashville married on the 25th ult. at Lagrange,
Tenn. to Miss Ann R. Rhodes formerly of Warren County, N. C.
Daily Republican Banner (Thurs., May 3, 1838)

Hall, Mr. James H. M. of the firm of Hall & Washington of Nashville
married on the 25th ult. at Lagrange, Tenn. to Miss Ann R. Rhodes of
Nashville.
Nashville Union (Fri., May 4, 1838)

Hall, Mr. James H. M. of the firm of Hall & Washington of Nashville
married on the 25th ult. at Lagrone in Tennessee to Miss Ann R.
Rhodes of Lagrong, Tenn.
Nashville Whig (Fri., May 4, 1838)

Hall, Hon. Judge married in Alachua, E. Florida to Miss Dorothy
Deering, late of Portsmouth, N. H.
National Banner & Nashville Daily Advertiser (Sat., Aug. 10, 1833)

Hall, Miss Laurena daughter of S. S. Hall Esq. of Arkansas Territory
married in Little Rock on the 14th July to Col. Robertson Childress.
National Banner & Nashville Whig (Mon., Aug. 3, 1835)

Hall, Mr. Lawrence H. married in Todd County, Ky to Miss Mary M.
Terry daughter of Col. Nathaniel Terry.
National Banner & Nashville Daily Advertiser (Mon., July 2, 1832)

Hall, Miss Lorena married to Col. Robertson Childress.

Hall, Miss Martha married to Mr. Abner S. Dyer.

Hall, Miss Martha married to Mr. Thomas A. Copper.

Hall, Miss Mary Ann married to Mr. Porter J. Stoner.

Hall, Mr. Robert B. in Nashville to Miss Mary P. Musgrove both of
Glasgow, Ky.
National Banner and Nashville Whig (Sept. 2, 1831)

Hall, Miss S. J. at Carthage married to Mr. William A. Lack.

Hall, Mr. Samuel S. married on the 6th inst. by Rev. Mr. Hayes to
Miss Hadassah Neely, daughter of William Neely Esq. all of Davidson
County.
National Banner & Nashville Whig (June 10, 1836)

Hall, Miss Sarah married to Mr. Geo. D. Harle.

Hall, Miss Sarah T. F. married to Alvah Finley Esq.

Hall, Miss Sophia W. married to Mr. Joseph Gibson.

Hall, Miss Sophis W. married to Mr. Joseph F. Gibson.

Hall, Mr. T. A. married to Miss Elizabeth T. Nowlin by Rev. Mr. Newton daughter of Jabus Nowlin Esq. of Bedford County.
Nashville Union (Tues., Nov. 14, 1837)

Hall, Mr. Thomas Douglass married in Knox County, Ten. to Miss Telitha Emeline Weir.
National Banner & Nashville Daily Advertiser (Tues., Aug. 19, 1834)

Hall, Mr. William B. Hall formerly of S. C. married in Madison County, Ten to Miss Susan M. Senter.
National Banner & Nashville Daily Advertiser (Tues., Sept. 20, 1833)

Hall, Mr. Willis married in Franklin County to Miss Mary Ann Fowler.
National Banner & Nashville Whig (Sat., Sept. 9, 1826)

Hall, Mr. Wm. B. S. in Madison County married to Miss Susanna M. Senter.
Nashville Republican and State Gazette (Sept. 21, 1833)

Halley, Mr. Washington G. married at Cincinnati to Miss Rachel P. Westcoat.
National Banner & Nashville Whig (Sat., Feb. 10, 1827)

Halloway, Miss Hetty married to Mr. John B. Cook.

Halloway, Mr. Wm. married in Williamson County, Ten. to Lucinda Lumpkins.
National Banner & Nashville Daily Advertiser (Mon., Aug. 26, 1833)

Hallu, Miss Emily married to Mr. James H. Hodges.

Hallum, James R. Esq. Editor of the Pulaski Whig Carrier married at Fayetteville, Lincoln County on the 21st inst. by the Rev. M. M. Marshall to Miss Clarena M. Baily of Fredericksburg, Va.
Nashville Whig (Mon., Jan. 25, 1841)

Hallum, Mr. John married in Smith County to Miss Eliza H. Patterson daughter of Capt. Wm. Patterson.
National Banner & Nashville Daily Advertiser (Wed., June 19, 1833)

Ham, Miss Eliza married to Mr. John Gardener.

Ham, Miss Eliza B. married to Thomas B. Carroll Esq.

Hambaugh, Mr. D. C. married in Louisville, Ky. to Eliza Mann.
National Banner & Nashville Whig (Sat., Nov. 15, 1828)

Hamblen, Dr. married in Davidson on the 24th inst. to Mary Donelson daughter of Col. Wm. Donelson.
The Nashville Whig & Tenn. Advertiser (Feb. 28, 1818)

Hamblet, Miss Cynthia married to Mr. John C. Finlay.

Hamblin, Mr. Arthur married in Bedford County to Miss Sarah Nelson.
National Banner & Nashville Advertiser (Thurs., Aug. 16, 1832)

Hamblin, Miss Eliza J. married to Capt. Benjamin W. Williams.

Hamer, Miss Mary married to Josiah Gibson Esq.

Hamer, Mr. Milton J. married in September 1831 to Miss Emily M. Roberts.
The Western Weekly Review - Franklin, Tenn. (Fri., Sept. 23, 1831)

Hamilton, Maj. Alexander married in Pair to Miss Charlotte Eliza Dunlap.
National Banner & Nashville Whig (Sat., Oct. 7, 1826)

Hamilton, Mr. Andrew McNairy married at the residence of W. McIntosh, Esq. on the 18th inst. by the Rev. Dr. Edgar to Miss Nancy Ellen Hoobury all of the vicinity of Nashville.
The Politician & Weekly Nashville Whig (Fri., July 23, 1847)

Hamilton, Mr. Andrew McNairy married at the residence of W. McIntosh on the 18th inst. by the Rev. Dr. Edgar to Mrs. Nancy Ellen Hoobury all of Nashville vicinity.
The Christian Record (Sat., July 24, 1847)

Hamilton, Miss Celia C. married to Mr. Philip Chapman.

Hamilton, Mr. Charles married near Port Gibson, Miss to Miss Mary Cooper.
National Banner (March 17, 1826)

Hamilton, Miss Eliza married to Mr. Patrick Lewis.

Hamilton, Miss Eliza E. married to Mr. James D. Smith.

Hamilton, Mr. James M. of Nashville married at Elmwood on the 26th inst. by the Rev. Dr. Edgar to Miss Mary Louise Berry daughter of Dr. David Berry.
Nashville Whig (Sat., Oct. 28, 1843)

Hamilton, Miss Jane married to Maj. Joseph Lynn.

Hamilton, Capt. John married in Wiscassett to Mrs. Rebecca Colby.
Nashville Republican & State Gazette (Sat., Jan. 8, 1831)

Hamilton, Mr. Joseph of Trenton married in Gibson County to Miss Margaret M'Cleary daughter of Mr. Andrew M'Cleary.
National Banner & Nashville Whig (Thurs., Aug. 12, 1830)

Hamilton, Miss Lucinda married to Mr. Greenberg.

Hamilton, Miss M. L. married to Mr. David Trotter.

Hamilton, Miss Mary A. married to Mr. W. W. Woodruff.

Hamilton, Miss Mary A. married to Mr. E. J. Kreider.

Hamilton, Mr. Mortimore married on Thursday the 3d inst. by the Rev. E. D. F. Sawrie to Miss Emaline Hill all of Nashville.
Nashville Union (Fri., Sept. 6, 1839)

Hamilton, Mr. Mortimer formerly of Russellville, Ky. married on the 5th inst. by the Rev. W. D. F. Sawrie to Miss Emeline Hill daughter of the late Thomas Hill of Nashville.
Daily Republican Banner (Sat., Sept. 7, 1839)

Hamilton, Mr. Robert married in Scott County, Ky. to Miss Sarah Curry.
National Banner & Nashville Whig (Sat., Dec. 23, 1826)

Hamilton, Miss Sarah married to Mr. Andrew C. Crawford.

Hamilton, Miss Sarah married to Mr. Milton Giles.

Hamilton, Mrs. Sarah married to Mr. John E. Gadsey.

Hamilton, Mr. William married on the 6th inst. by the Rev. Dr. Edgar to Miss Nancy Clarke all of Nashville.
Nashville Whig (Sat., July 8, 1843)

Hamilton, Mr. Wm. S. married in Williamson County to Miss Sarah
Johnston.
National Banner & Nashville Whig (Sept. 2, 1826)

Hamlet, Miss Nancy married to Mr. Bennett Siris.

Hamlet, Miss Nancy married to Mr. Bennett Siris.

Hammon, Mr. Thomas married in Maury County to Miss Sarah Osborne.
National Banner & Nashville Whig (Fri., April 16, 1830)

Hammond, C. Esq. of Cincinnatti married at Zaneville, Ohio Jan. 2
by the Rev. Mr. Smallwood to Miss Elizabeth B. Morehead of Zaneville.
Nashville Republican (Thurs., Jan. 14, 1836)

Hammonds, Mr. William married in Williamson County to Miss Mary Ingram.
National Banner & Nashville Whig (Fri., Feb. 13, 1835)

Hamner, Dr. Austin M. of Columbia married at the Columbia Female
Institute on Thursday Aug. 26th by the Rev. F. G. Smith to Miss Ann
Eliza Anthony daughter of Samuel Anthony Esq. of Pattonburg, Va.
The Politician & Weekly Nashville Whig (Wed., Sept. 15, 1847)

Jamner, Mr. Herekiah F. formerly of Scottsville, Va. married in
Shelby County, Ten. to Miss Caledonia M. Scales.
National Banner & Nashville Whig (Fri., Jan. 9, 1835)

Hamner, Miss Lucy married to Mr. Thomas Potts.

Hannah, Miss Mary married to Mr. Henry Smith.

Hampton, Miss Eliza married to Mr. James R. Tate.

Hampton, Miss Elizabeth married to Mr. James M. Davis.

Hampton, Maj. John C. formerly of Surry County, N. C. married in
Franklin on the 24th to Miss Anne Drennan daughter of James Drennan
of Wilson Co.
National Banner & Nashville Daily Advertiser (Wed., March 26, 1834)

Hampton, Maj. John C. formerly of Surry County, N. C. married in
Franklin to Miss Ann Drennen.
Nashville Republican & State Gazette (Thurs., March 27, 1834)

Hampton, Mr. John R. married at Tuscaloosa, Ala. to Miss Frances Webb.
National Banner & Nashville Daily Advertiser (Feb. 25, 1832)

Hampton, Mr. Phineas D. married in Warren County, Ky. to Miss Caroline
Hines.
National Banner & Nashville Whig (Fri., July 22, 1831)

Hampton, Miss Sarah married to Andrew M. Campbell, Esq.

Hampton, Miss Sarah L. married to Andrew M'Campbell, Esq.

Hamptramck, Maj. A. M. married in Paris, Tenn. to Miss F. C. Edmonds.
National Banner & Nashville Whig (Fri., June 10, 1836)

Hamptramck, Miss Rebecca married to Capt. T. J. Harrison.

Hancock, Ann married to Jannathan Jenkins.

Hancock, Mr. B. C. married in Rutherford County to Miss F. L. O. A.
Bennett.
National Banner & Nashville Daily Advertiser (Tues., Dec. 24, 1833)

Hancock, Miss Emily married to Mr. Thomas C. Jones.

Hancock, Miss Lucinda M. married to Mr. Tate Morton.

Hancock, Miss Nancy married to Mr. Tate Morton.

Hancock, Mr. Stephen married on Thursday the 28th inst. to Miss Emeline Lane both of Maury County.
The Western Weekly Review - Franklin, Ten. (Fri., July 6, 1832)

Handy, Edward Smith, Esq. married at West Wood in this vicinity last evening to Theora Jane Woods second daughter of Robert Wood Esq.
Nashville Whig (Sat., Jan. 22, 1842)

Handy, Mr. Edward Smith merchant of Philadelphia married on Thursday last by Rev. Mr. Lapsley to Miss Margaret F. Woods eldest daughter of James Woods Esq. of Nashville.
Nashville Whig (Sat., Dec. 9, 1843)

Handy, Mr. Thomas K. married in Franklin, Ten. to Miss Maria Henderson.
Nashville Republican & State Gazette (Tues., Sept. 23, 1834)

Handy, Thomas K. married in Williamson County to Miss Maria Henderson.
National Banner & Nashville Whig (Wed., Sept. 24, 1834)

Haner, Mr. married in Warren County, Ky. to Miss Frazier.
National Banner & Nashville Whig (Sat., Dec. 16, 1826)

Hanes, Mr. Stephen J. of Madison County married in Lauderdale County, Ala. to Miss Elizabeth Pritchard.
National Banner & Nashville Whig (Fri., March 6, 1835)

Hanks, Mr. Greenville married in Maury County to Miss Nancy C. Fields daughter of Major William Fields.
National Banner & Nashville Whig (Mon., July 4, 1831)

Hanks, Miss Martha married to Mr. Thomas M. Buck.

Hanks, Dr. Robert T. of North Carolina married at Citico to Miss Margaret A. W. Morgan daughter of Col. Gideon Morgan.
National Banner & Nashville Daily Advertiser (Wed., May 15, 1833)

Hanks, Dr. Robert T. married in Monroe County to Miss Margaret Morgan.
National Banner & Nashville Daily Advertiser (May 18, 1833)

Hanna, Mr. James J. married on the 6th inst. to Miss Paralee Childress all of Lauderdale County, Al.
Nashville Whig (Feb. 19, 1823)

Hanna, Miss Latitia married to Mr. Edward Odgen.'

Hanna, Miss Lucy married to Mr. Thomas G. Greenfield.

Hanna, Miss Nancy married to Mr. John Cox.

Hanna, Miss Sarah married to Edward York Esq.

Hannah, Miss Lucinda married to Rev. Lewis W. Woodson.

Hannah, Miss Mary married to Mr. Thos. Docker.

Hanner, Rev. J. W. married in Williamson Co., Tenn. to Miss Elizabeth R. Park.
National Banner & Nashville Daily Advertiser (Mon., June 9, 1834)

Hanner, Mrs. Susan married to Maj. Ambrose Bates.

Hanniss, Miss Lucinda married to Mr. James Wilkison.

Hansaid, Mr. Robert of Knox County married in Tazewell, Claiborne
County to Miss Louisa Ann Catherine Hodges.
National Banner & Nashville Whig (Tues., April 27, 1830)

Hansard, Mr. Samuel H. married in Knox County to Miss Arminia Weir.
National Banner & Nashville Daily Advertiser (Tues., Dec. 18, 1832)

Hansard, Mr. Samuel H. of Anderson County married in Knox County to
Miss Arminia Weir.
National Banner & Nashville Advertiser (Dec. 27, 1832)

Hansard, Mr. William married in Knox County to Miss Rachel Graham.
National Banner (Sat., July 4, 1829)

Hanson, A. Esq. of N. O. Married in New Orleans to Mrs. R. P. Butler
of Cincinnati, Ohio.
National Banner & Nashville Daily Advertiser (Fri., Aug. 15, 1834)

Haralson, Miss Mary H. married to Mr. James A. Steel.

Haralson, Col. Joseph T. married in Denmark, Te. to Miss Frances Watts.
National Banner & Nashville Whig (Fri., June 20, 1828)

Harberson, Mr. James married in Maury County to Miss Sarah J. Fields.
National Banner & Nashville Whig (Mon., Sept. 26, 1831)

Hard, Miss Elizabeth married to Henry C. Bradford, Esq.

Hardaway, Miss Elizabeth M. married to Capt. James G. Hicks.

Hardcastle, Mr. B. F. married on Tuesday the 26th March by the Rev.
A. L. P. Green to Miss Minerva H. White all of Nashville.
Nashville Whig (Wed., April 3, 1839)

Hardeman, Miss Anna G. married to Mr. J. P. Sessions.

Hardeman, Mr. John married in Hardeman County on the 15th inst. to Miss
Mary Hardeman.
National Banner & Nashville Whig (Sat., May 31, 1828)

Hardeman, Miss Mary married in Bullitt County to Mr. John Burch.
National Banner & Nashville Whig (Sat., July 8, 1826)

Hardeman, Miss Mary married to Mr. John Hardeman.

Hardeman, Miss Mary married to William P. Scales, Esq.

Hardeman, Miss Matilda J. married to Mr. W. H. January.

Hardeman, Miss Polly married to Mr. Thomas H. Perkins.

Hardeman, Miss Sarah E. married to Benjamin D. Hynds.

Hardeman, Miss Susan married in Williamson Co. to James M. Dotson.

Hardeman, Thomas Esq. married in Williamson County to Miss Berthunia
H. Perkins.
National Banner & Nashville Whig (Mon., Aug. 30, 1830)

Hardeman, Mr. Thomas married in Williamson County to Miss Hannah
McCrory.
National Banner & Nashville Whig (Wed., Sept. 24, 1834)

Harden, Miss Frances married to Mr. Thomas Parrent.

Harden, James of Va. married on Sunday last to Miss Sussannah Shute
of Davidson County
Impartial Review & Cumberland Repository. (Aug. 9, 1806)

Harden, Mr. William Giels married in this town last evening by the
Rev. Mr. Hume to Miss Mary Selina McNairy daughter of Nath. A.
M'Nairy.
National Banner (Sat., Nov. 21, 1829)

Hardgraves, Miss N. M. married to Samuel Harkreader.

Hardgrove, Miss Elizabeth married to Mr. John Beale.

Hardin, Alexander M. Esq. of Maury County to Miss Elizabeth Jane
Robinson of Hardin County on Thursday evening 16th inst.
Nashville Republican (Thurs., April 23, 1835)

Hardin, Mr. Alexander M. Esq. of Maury County married in Savannah, Ten.
to Miss Elizabeth Jane Robinson daughter of David Robinson Esq.
National Banner & Nashville Whig (Wed., April 29, 1835)

Hardin, Miss Ann married to Mr. David B. Phillips.

Hardin, Mrs. Elizabeth married to Porter Clay Esq.

Hardin, Miss Emily Esq. married to Dr. Robert C. Palmer.

Hardin, Mr. H. H. married in Franklin County, Ky to Miss Eliza Milam
daughter of Mr. John Milam.
National Banner & Nashville Whig (Jan. 23, 1835)

Hardin, Miss Lucinda B. married to John L. Helm Esq.

Hardin, Mrs. M. married to Dr. William McNeil.

Hardin, Miss Matilda married to Benjamin Rush Montgomery Esq.

Hardin, Miss Nancy Jane married to Mr. James Saunders.

Hardin, Mr. Robert E. married in Wayne County to Miss Nancy B. Dixon.
National Banner & Nashville Daily Advertiser (Fri., Sept. 20, 1833)

Hardin, Miss Sally married to Mr. John M. Holderby.

Hardin, Miss Sarah R. married to Mr. Jas. Aston.

Hardin, Miss Sarah R. married to Mr. James Aston.

Hardin, Mr. William married in Knoxville, Tenn. to Miss Mary Bell
daughter of Mr. Joseph Bell.
National Banner & Nashville Whig (Fri., Jan. 9, 1835)

Harding, Mr. married on Thursday evening last to Miss Elizabeth Bosley
daughter of Mr. John Bosley.
The Nashville Gazette (Sat., Jan. 29, 1820)

Harding, Mr. David married in Greensborough, Ala. to Miss Mary S.
Alston.
National Banner & Nashville Whig (Sat., Jan. 19, 1828)

Harding, Mr. Edward aged 83 Married in Lincoln County Mrs. Nancy
Whitington aged 70.
Nashville Whig (Sat., July 11, 1846)

Harding, Miss Elizabeth V. married to Mr. Joseph W. Clay.

Harding, Jacob Esq. married at Knoxville to Miss Love Nelson.
National Banner & Nashville Whig (Sat., July 14, 1827)

Harding, Miss Margery married to Mr. Thompson Harden.

Harding, Miss Rachel N. married to Mr. John Overton.

Harding, Miss Susan H. married to Mr. R. G. Crozier.

Harding, Mr. William married in Davidson County on Wednesday last by the Rev. Mr. Hume to Miss Elizabeth H. Clopton.
National Banner & Nashville Whig (Fri., May 14, 1830)

Harding, Mr. William G. married on the 26th ult. at Belle Meade, the residence of W. G. Harding by the Rev. Dr. Wharton to Miss Marion C. Roberts.
Nashville Whig (Tues., Dec. 8, 1846)

Harding, Miss Willie E. married to Mr. David R. McGacock.

Hardison, Mr. E. married in Maury County to S. Derybery.
National Banner & Nashville Advertiser (Thurs., April 5, 1832)

Hardwick, Mr. Christopher married in Franklin County, Ky to Miss Catharine Pemberton.
National Banner (March 31, 1826)

Hardwick, Mr. Dillard of Charlotte, Tenn. married in Chactaw County, Miss. on the 21st July last to Miss Mary C. Boykin of Miss.
Nashville Republican (Tues., Aug. 15, 1837)

Hardwick, Mr. Dillard of Charlotte, Ten. married in Chocktaw County, Mississippi 21st July last. to Miss Mary E. Boykin of Miss.
National Banner & Nashville Whig (Wed., Aug. 16,1837)

Hardy, Mr. married in Giles County to Martha Buford.
National Banner & Nashville Daily Advertiser (Tues., Dec. 17, 1833)

Hardy, Miss Elizabeth married to Mr. Robert S. Williamson.

Hargrave, Mr. William M. married on Thursday 7th inst. by the A. S. Tiggs to Miss Elizabeth D. Mitchell all of Nashville.
Nashville Whig (Sat., Nov. 11, 1843)

Hargraves, Mr. R. married in Florence, Ala. to Miss Angeline Heslep.
National Banner & Nashville Daily Advertiser (Tues., March 11, 1834)

Hargrove, Miss Elizabeth married to Mr. John Beal.

Hargrove, Mr. Francis married in Madison County to Miss Ann Greer.
National Banner & Nashville Whig (Thurs., June 17, 1830)

Harker, Mr. E. J. married in Cincinnati to Miss Maria Louisa Birdsall.
National Banner & Nashville Daily Advertiser (Thurs., July 10, 1834)

Harkreader, Samuel married in Williamson County to Miss N. M. Hardgraves.
The Western Weekly Review - Franklin, Tenn. (Fri., Feb. 1, 1833)

Harlan, Miss Mary married in Lincoln County to Joseph Wallace.

Harle, Mr. Geo. D. married in Blunt County to Miss Sarah Hall.
Nashville Republican & State Gazette (Thurs., Oct. 17, 1833)

Harman, Mr. Charles R. of Warren married in Girard Mahoning County, O. on March 2nd by the Rev. Mr. Boardman of Youngstown to Miss Mary Hezlep.
The Politician & Weekly Nashville Whig (Fri., March 31, 1848)

Harman, Miss Harriet married to Mr. Henry Frith.

Harman, Miss Julia married to Capt. Henry Wolf.

Harman, Mr. Richard married in Nashville to Miss Sarah Hughes on Thursday 13 inst.
National Banner & Nashville Advertiser (Sat., Sept. 15, 1832)

Harmon, Dr. D. Peyton married at Vicksburgh, Mi. to Miss Mary L. Whiting.
National Banner & Nashville Daily Advertiser (Fri., Sept. 20, 1833)

Harmon, Miss Eleanor married to Mr. Robert J. Allen.

Harmon, Miss Eliza married to Mr. John Foster.

Harmon, Mr. William married near Florence, Ala. to Miss Lucinda P. Murphy.
National Banner & Nashville Daily Advertiser (Wed., March 26, 1833)

Harney, Maj. Robt. B. married at Elkton, Giles County to Miss Mary E. Miller on Monday 7th inst.
Nashville Republican & State Gazette (Sat., Feb. 12, 1831)

Harney, Maj. Rob. B. married in Giles County at Elkton to Miss Mary E. Miller.
National Banner & Nashville Whig (Mon., Feb. 14, 1831)

Harney, Miss Susan married to Mr. John Reynolds.

Harp, Miss Elizabeth married to Mr. Courtney Talbot.

Harper, Miss Ann married to Mr. Presley Dodson.

Harper, Miss Ann married to Mr. Presly Dotson.

Harper, Miss Averella married to Hon. James H. Thomas.

Harper, Mr. McLin married in Sumner County to Miss Sarah Malone.
National Banner & Nashville Daily Advertiser (Fri., Aug. 16, 1833)

Harper, Miss Maria E. married in Lincoln County, Ten. to Mr. Thomas B. Coleman.

Harper, Miss Martha S. married to Charles McAlister, Esq.

Harper, Miss Mary married to Captain Miles Phillips.

Harper, Miss Mary married to Mr. Alexander M'Donald.

Harper, Miss Mary R. married to Hezekiah H. Eaton Esq.

Harper, Mr. Robert married in Smith County to Miss Hannah Johnson.
National Banner & Nashville Daily Advertiser (Thurs., Jan. 5, 1832)

Harpole, Capt. William married in Weakley County on the 5th inst. to Miss Sarah Dickson.
National Banner (Sat., Nov. 21, 1829)

Harreld, Maj. Alfred married in Logan County to Miss Amanda L. Wilson.
National Banner & Nashville Whig (Mon., April 25, 1831)

Harrell, Mr. Thomas M. married in Sumner County to Miss Frances A. Willis.
National Banner & Nashville Daily Advertiser (Mon., July 14, 1834)

Harrell, Mr. William of Gallatin married in Huntingdon on the 13th ult. to Miss Malinda M'Cracken daughter of Mr. Robert MCracken.
National Banner & Nashville Whig (Mon., Nov. 8, 1830)

Harrington, Doctor W. H. married in Lagrange, Ala. to Miss Riley.
National Banner & Nashville Daily Advertiser (Mon., May 28, 1832)

Harris, Mrs. married to Capt. Joh Beck.

Harris, Dr. Alfred W. of Nashville married in Bellmont, Tenn. on the
3rd inst. to Miss Mary Louisa Sale daughter of Rev. Henry W. Sale.
Nashville Whig (Sat., March 21, 1846)

Harris, Mr. Alfred W. R. married in Louisville to Miss Mary Jane D.
Johnson.
National Banner & Nashville Whig (Sat., Sept. 9, 1826)

Harris, Lieut. A. 7th U. S. Infantry married at the Choctow Agency
at the residence of Capt. William Armstrong on the 12th April by the
Rev. C. Washburn to Miss Susan Armstrong daughter of Col. Robert
Armstrong.
The Union (Tues., May 24, 1836)

Harris, Mr. Andrew married in Smith County to Miss Martha Hale.
National Banner & Nashville Whig (Tues., Dec. 13, 1831)

Harris, Mr. Arthur married in Montgomery County to Miss Elizabeth
Ramey.
National Banner (Sat., Oct. 3, 1829)

Harris, Mr. Buxton of Nashville married on the 4th inst in Smith
County to Miss Sarah Bradley daughter of the late Capt. James Bradley.
National Banner & Nashville Whig (Mon., Nov. 29, 1830)

Harris, Miss Caroline T. married to Mr. W. T. Gamble.

Harris, Dr. Crampton S. married in Jefferson County to Miss Maria J.
M'Farland daughter of Col. John M'Farland.
National Banner & Nashville Daily Advertiser (Mon., July 15, 1833)

Harris, Rev. Eleazar of Calloway County, Ky. married in Obion County
to Miss Martha Hutchinson daughter of Mr. William Hutchinson.
National Banner & Nashville Daily Advertiser (Mon., May 13, 1833)

Harris, Mr. Elisha W. of Hardeman County, Ten. married in Tuscumbia,
Ala. to Miss Clestia A. Whittaker.
National Banner & Nashville Whig (Wed., Sept. 28, 1831)

Harris, Miss Eliza married to Mr. Jefferson Gordon.

Harris, Mrs. Eliza Ann married to Mr. Edmund Ginn.

Harris, Miss Elizabeth married to Mr. Benjamin Williamson.

Harris, Miss Elizabeth married to Mr. David E. Putney.

Harris, Miss Elizabeth married to Mr. S. R. Cheek.

Harris, Mrs. Elizabeth married to Mr. Birdwell.

Harris, Mr. Felix A. of Arkansas, formerly of Nashville married on the
8th inst. by the Rev. C. D. Elliott to Miss A. A. Cane of Nashville.
Nashville Whig (Sat., April 22, 1843)

Harris, Rev. Finis married in Madison County, Ala. to Miss Barbara
Monroe.
National Banner & Nashville Whig (Wed., Oct. 19, 1831)

Harris, Miss Frances H. married to Mr. William W. Donald.

Harris, Miss Frances H. married to Mr. William W. Donald.

Harris, Geo. Esq. of Tellico married in Jefferson County to Miss
Matilda Roper.
National Banner & Nashville Whig (Sat., March 10, 1827)

Harris, Mr. George W. married in Batavia, N. Y. by the Hon. Simion Cummings to Mrs. Lucinda Morgan widow of the late Capt. William Morgan.
National Banner & Nashville Whig (Wed., Dec. 22, 1830)

Harris, Mr. Gideon married in Maury County to Miss Lucy Ledbetter.
National Banner & Nashville Whig (Sat., Dec. 17, 1831)

Harris, Col. Hannibal of Paris married in Henry County on the 18th of Jan. by Rev. Samuel McGowen to Miss Jane Cooper daughter of Blunt Cooper Esq. of that County.
National Banner & Nashville Whig (Mon., Feb. 7, 1831)

Harris, Miss Harriet married to Mr. James H. Moran.

Harris, Miss Harriett B. married to Mr. Henry McCarlin.

Harris, Miss Harriett P. married to Mr. Hillery Moseley.

Harris, Col. J. George Editor of the Union married in Williamson County on the 5th inst. by Rev. Dr. Edgar to Miss Lucinda McGavock daughter of the late James McGavock Esq. of Davidson County.
Nashville Whig (Sat., May 7, 1842)

Harris, Mr. John married in Madison County, Ala. to Miss Margaret Craddock.
National Banner & Nashville Whig (Sat., Sept. 27, 1828)

Harris, Mr. John B. married on Sunday the 20th inst. by the Rev. Thomas Wheat to Miss Sarah B. Humphreys.
Nashville Whig (Tues., Nov. 22, 1842)

Harris, Capt. John H. married on the 22nd inst. by Rev. Mr. Lapsley to Miss Mary E. Sledge daughter of John P. Sledge Esq. of this vicinity.
Nashville Whig (Thurs., Feb. 24, 1842)

Harris, Col. John L. married in this county on the 28th ult. by the Rev. William White to Miss Eliza S. Goodrich of this County.
National Banner & Nashville Whig (Sat., Sept. 9, 1826)

Harris, Mr. John T. married to Miss Sarah Brown.
The Western Weekly Review - Franklin, Tenn. (Fri., Nov. 11,1831)

Harris, Mr. John T. married in Williamson County to Miss Sarah Brown.
National Banner & Nashville Whig (Mon., Nov. 14, 1831)

Harris, Mr. Joseph married in Louisville, Ky. to Miss Martha Ann Lawless.
National Banner & Nashville Whig (Sat., Sept. 27, 1828)

Harris, Miss Judith married to Major Samuel Meredith.

Harris, Mr. Lewis married to Miss Sarah Cunningham.

Harris, Miss Margaret married to Mr. William Waind.

Harris, Miss Martha W. married to Mr. Jerome B. Pillow.

Harris, Mrs. Mary married to Justinian Cartwright Esq.

Harris, Miss Mary A. married to Rev. Isaac Sullivan.

Harris, Miss Mary B. married to Rev. Isaac Sullivan.

Harris, Miss Myra married to Mr. Samuel R. Eagan.

Harris, Miss Nancy married to Mr. Thomas C. Davis.

Harris, Miss Olivia married to Mr. John Allen Read.

Harris, Miss Olivia married to Mr. John A. Reed.

Harris, Mr. Richard N. married in Courtland, Ala. to Miss Amanda
Banks.
Nashville Republican & State Gazette (Thurs., April 28, 1831)

Harris, Mr. Richard N. married in Courtland, Ala. to Miss Amanda
Banks.
National Banner & Nashville Whig (Fri., April 29, 1831)

Harris, Miss Rosini C. married to Mr. James H. Thompson.

Harris, Temple O. Esq. of Nashville married at Lebanon on the 13th
inst. by the Rev. D. Lowery to Miss Martha M. McGregor eldest daughter
of John M. McGregor.
Nashville Whig (Sat., Jan. 17, 1846)

Harris, Thankful Miss married to Mr. Olivar Wallace.

Harris, Mr. Thomas H. married on the evening of the 30th of Sept.
by J. L. Jarrell Esq. to Miss Eliza Felts all of Davidson County.
Nashville True Whig & Weekly Commercial Register (Fri., Oct. 4, 1850)

Harris, Thomas Jefferson Esq. merchant of Pittsburgh, Pa. married on
last evening by the Rev. J. T. Edgar D.D. to Miss Eliza Leak of
Memphis.
Nashville Whig (Wed., March 21, 1838)

Harris, Dr. Thomas W. married in Jackson, Madison County on the 24th
ult. by Rev. John Finlay to Miss Mary E. Turley daughter of Hon.
William B. Turley Judge of Supreme Court of Tennessee.
Nashville Whig (Sat., April 16, 1842)

Harris, Mr. W. O. married in Nashville on last evening by the Rev.
A. L. P. Green to Miss Frances A. Bartee.
Daily Republican Banner (Fri., July 27, 1838)

Harris, Mr. W. O. married in Nashville last evening by the Rev.
A. L. P. Green to Miss Frances A. Bartee.
Nashville Whig (Fri., July 27, 1838)

Harris, Mr. W. S. married in Obion County to Miss Angelletta Meadow.
National Banner & Nashville Whig (Fri., July 22, 1831)

Harris, Mr. William married in Lincoln County, Ten. to Miss Eliza
Old.
National Banner & Nashville Whig (Wed., Dec. 17, 1834)

Harris, Mr. Wm. married in Lincoln County to Miss Eliza Old.
National Banner & Nashville Whig (Mon., Jan. 5, 1835)

Harris, Mr. William F. married in Wilson County to Miss Margaret B.
M'Neely.
National Banner & Nashville Daily Advertiser (Wed., June 13, 1832)

Harris, Dr. Zeno T. of Elkton married near Tuscumbia, Ala. to Miss
Harriet M. Hawkins.
National Banner (Feb. 3, 1826)

Harrison, Mr. Ainsworth married in Wilson County, Tenn. to Miss
Rebecca Dorton.
National Banner & Nashville Whig (Mon., May 4, 1835)

Harrison, Miss Eliza B. married to Mr. John M. Brown.

Harrison, Miss Eliza M. married to Mr. H. M. Jones.

Harrison, Mr. George married in Henry County to Miss Rachel Rhoads
National Banner & Nashville Daily Advertiser (Thurs., March 20, 1834)

Harrison, Mrs. H. H. married to Miss Rebecca Pearson.

Harrison, Mrs. Isabelle married to Mr. Thomas Lewis.

Harrison, Miss Kitty married to Mr. Hamilton Atchison, Sr.

Harrison, Miss Louisa married to Robert Hill Esq.

Harrison, M. V. Esq. married in Montgomery County, Ky. to Miss Dulcina
M. Bledsoe.
National Banner & Nashville Whig (Sat., Sept. 8, 1827)

Harrison, Mrs. Margaret married to Willis L. Reeves, Esq.

Harrison, Miss Margaret C. married to Noah C. Summers.

Harrison, Miss Martha L. married to Dr. Daniel Moore.

Harrison, Miss Mary E. married to Mr. James McGrath.

Harrison, Miss Nancy married to Mr. John Williams.

Harrison, Miss Priscilla married to Mr. Moses Forbes.

Harrison, Mr. Rolla in Davidson County married to Miss Mary Ann
Galbreath on the 14th inst.
Nashville Republican (Tues., May 19, 1835)

Harrison, Miss Sarah Ann married to Mr. John T. Camron.

Harrison, Miss Sarah E. married to Dr. Llewellyn Powell

Harrison, Steth Esq. married in Wilson County on the 4th inst. to
Miss Harriet Wood.
National Banner & Nashville Whig (Sat., Sept. 13, 1828)

Harrison, Capt. T. J. married in St. Louis to Miss Rebecca Hamstramck.
National Banner & Nashville Whig (Sat., May 19, 1827)

Harrison, Miss Virginia married to David Castleman Esq.

Hart, Miss Eliza B. married to Dr. Solon Barland.

Hart, Miss Eliza T. married to Mr. Robert Bradford.

Hart, Miss Ellen R. married to Mr. William A. Johnson.

Hart, Henry Esq. of Lexington married in Paris, Ky. to Miss Elizabeth
Brent youngest daughter of Hugh Brent, Esq.
National Banner & Nashville Whig (Fri., Jan. 23, 1835)

Hart, Mr. J. of Maury County married to Miss Emeline Gale of Miss.
on Nov. 27th.
Nashville Republican (Tues., Dec. 1, 1835)

Hart, Miss Jane D. married to Mr. Thomas J. Allen.

Hart, Mr. John H. married on 19th inst. by the Rev. Dr. Davis to
Miss Mary Ann Bosworth both of Nashville.
Daily Republican Banner (Tues., Oct. 24, 1837)

Hart, Mr. John S. of the House of Hart & Kennedy married at Clarks-
ville on the 27th ult. by the Rev. John W. Hanner to Mrs. Martha A.
Miller all of Clarksville.
Nashville Whig (Thurs., Aug. 3, 1843)

Hart, Miss Leodocia R. married to Mr. James B. Nichol.

Hart, Miss Louisiana B. married to Mr. Robias Gibson.

Hart, Miss Mary married to Col. W. C. Loftin.

Hart, Mr. R. W. of Nashville married Miss Martha Thompson Richland
Creek on Thursday last.
Impartial Review & Cumberland Repository - Published at Nashville
(Thurs., Sept. 29, 1808)

Hart, Miss Sarah married to Mr. Wm. T. Gholson.

Hart, Miss Sarah W. married in Muary County, Ten. to Mr. Enus Robinson.

Hart, Miss Sinia A. married to William B. M'Laughlin Esq.

Hart, Mr. Tho. P. married at Lexington, Ky to Miss Sally Postlethwait.

Hart, Mr. Winslow. married in Lebanon by the Rev. Mr. Claiborn to
Miss Agnes Smith.
National Banner & Nashville Whig (Mon., July 12, 1830)

Hartley, Miss Amanda S. married to Mr. James M. Hughes.

Hartley, Miss Eliza Ann married to Mr. John N. Spain.

Hartley, Miss Sarah married to Doct. James C. O'Reiley.

Hartsborne, Mr. Saunders W. married at Cincinnati to Miss Ann Eliza
Burrows.
National Banner & Nashville Whig (Fri., Feb. 18, 1831)

Hartsfield, Miss Elizabeth married to Mr. Harry Collin.

Hartshorn, Mr. Saunders W. married to Miss Ann Eliza Burrows at
Cincinnati.
National Banner & Nashville Whig (Fri., Feb. 18, 1831)

Harvey, Mr. Garrett married at Louisville, Ky. to Miss Sally Longust.
National Banner & Nashville Whig (June 14, 1826)

Harvey, Miss Narcissa married to Mr. Granville H. Hogan.

Harvey, Mr. William, Printer, Athens, Ten. married in Knoxville, Ten.
to Miss A. H. Bell daughter of Mr. Joseph Bell of Knox County.
National Banner & Nashville Whig (Wed., Jan. 21, 1835)

Harvie, Miss Gabriella married to James Breathitt Esq.

Harvy, Mr. Wm. married in Knoxville to Miss Mary A. H. Bell on the
27th ult.
Nashville Republican (Tues., Jan. 27, 1835)

Harwell, Mr. Featherston married to Miss Eliz Owen.
National Banner & Nashville Whig (Fri., March 6, 1835)

Harwell, Miss Hannah married to Mr. James Harwell.

Harwell, Mr. James married in Maury County to Miss Hannah Harwell.
National Banner & Nashville Whig (Mon., Feb. 23, 1835)

Harwell, Mrs Susan married to Mr. B. B. Trousdale.

Harwichalte, Miss Marinda married to Mr. R. C. McAlpin Esq.

Harwood, Miss Martha married to Mr. Jones.

Haskell, Mr. James G. married in Madison County, Ten. to Miss Susan Alexander.
Nashville Whig (Jan. 22, 1823)

Haskell, Miss Mary Ann married to William N. Porter, Esq.

Haskin, Mr. John G. married in Knox County to Miss Barsheba Lorew.
National Banner & Nashville Whig (Mon., June 13, 1831)

Haskins, Miss Sarah married to Mr. Abraham D. Condlay.

Haslett, Miss Eliza married to Mr. James Balch.

Haslope, Mr. George married in Louisville, Ky. to Miss Dorinda W. Austin.
National Banner & Nashville Whig (Mon., Aug. 16, 1830)

Hassell, Miss Catherine S. married to Capt. C. H. Gray.

Hassell, Zebulon married in Williamson County to Miss Unity Shields.
The Western Weekly Review - Franklin, Tenn. (Fri., March 23, 1832)

Hassell, Zebulon married in Williamson County to Miss Unity Shields.
National Banner & Nashville Daily Advertiser (Mon., March 26, 1832)

Hastings, Miss Jane married to Mr. James Andrews.

Hasty, Mr. Benjamin married in Wayne County to Miss Lydia Dugger.
National Banner & Nashville Whig (Fri., Sept. 20, 1833)

Hatch, Mr. married to Miss Polly Ann Bisor daughter of Mr. John W. Bisor married in Davidson County on the 26th.
National Banner & Nashville Whig (Tues., Feb. 2, 1830)

Hatch, Miss Caroline married in Fayette County to Mr. Henry Smith.

Hatch, Miss Elizabeth married to Mr. George M. Smith.

Hatch, Dr. Samuel of Georgetown, Ky. married at Lexington, Ky to Miss Julia Matilda Bradford daughter of Daniel Bradford Esq.
National Banner & Nashville Whig (Fri., Feb. 11, 1831)

Hatchen, Mr. Edward married in Henry County to Miss Betsy Green.
National Banner & Nashville Advertiser (Tues., Aug. 7,1832)

Hatcher, Miss Mary married to Mr. William Williams.

Hatchett, Miss Nancy married to Mr. Granville Arnett.

Hathaway, Miss Ann married to Mr. William Hathaway.

Hathaway, Mr. William of Nashville married on Wednesday evening last by the Rev. Mr. Johnson to Miss Ann Hathaway of Davidson County.
The Nashville Gazette (Sat., May 6, 1820)

Hatter, Miss Elizabeth married to Mr. Elizah Rush.

Hatter, Mr. Richard B. married in Greenborough, Ala. to Miss Martha Jane Dickson.
National Banner & Nashville Daily Advertiser (Wed., Aug. 22, 1832)

Hatton, Miss Mary married to Joseph H. Peyton, Esq.

Haughton, Miss Emelia D. married to Mr. Thomas Rawlins.

Haughton, Miss Jane married to Mr. Charles Morrison.

Havely, Miss Eliza Catharine married to Mr. John Mill McKee.

Haw, Miss Elizabeth Ann married to Mr. Henry M. Chew.

Hawkin, Mr. John married in Columbus, Ohio to Miss Eliza Johnson.
National Banner & Nashville Whig (Sat., Sept. 8, 1827)

Hawkins, Miss Ann married in Lauderdale County, Ala. to Mr. James H.
Gee.

Hawkins, Mrs. Caroline M. married to Col. Thomas T. Patton.

Hawkins, Miss Catherine married to Mr. Robert L. Sims.

Hawkins, Miss Evaline married to Mr. Thomas Kennedy.

Hawkins, Miss Aabriella Augusta married to Mr. Geo. Washington.

Hawkins, Miss Harriet M. married to Dr. Zeno T. Harris.

Hawkins, Henry B. Esq. married in Madison County, Ky. to Miss Margaret
Baxter.
National Banner & Nashville Whig (Sat., Sept. 20, 1828)

Hawkins, Mr. Henry T. married in Jefferson County to Miss Francis Pate
daughter of Mr. Bird Pate.
National Banner & Nashville Daily Advertiser (Mon., Jan. 14, 1833)

Hawkins, Mr. James M. merchant married on Thursday 14th inst. by Rev.
C. D. Elliott to Miss Elizabeth S. Seigler daughter of Mr. John
Seigler all of Nashville.
Nashville Whig (Sat., May 16, 1846)

Hawkinds, Mr. Joseph J. married in Brownsville to Mrs. Sarah Minor.
Nashville Republican & State Gazette (Thurs., March 10, 1831)

Hawkins, Mrs. Julia married to Mr. John Willis.

Hawkins, Miss Louisa married to Mr. B. S. Parsons.

Hawkins, Miss Lucy Jane married to Mr. Wm. Shamon.

Hawkins, Miss Rebecca married to Mr. Edmund A. Bacon.

Hawkins, Mr. Robert married in this County on Thursday 8th inst. to
Miss Rosetta Inyard.
National Banner & Nashville Whig (Sat., Jan. 10, 1829)

Hawkins, Mrs. S. B. married to Maj. D. Dunn.

Hawkins, Mrs. S. B. married to Maj. D. Dunn.

Hawkins, Dr. Thomas P. of Weakly County married in Gallatin on the
15th inst. by the Rev. J. W. Hume to Miss Frances Rhea of Nashville.
The Christian Record (Sat., Nov. 25, 1848)

Hawkins, Mr. W. N. married in Nashville on the evening of the 11th
inst. by the Rev. J. T. Edgar to Miss Elizabeth Saunders.
National Banner & Nashville Daily Advertiser (Wed., March 12, 1834)

Hawkins, Mr. W. N. married in Nashville to Miss Elizabeth Saunders
on 11th inst.
Nashville Republican & State Gazette (Thurs., March 13, 1834)

Hawkins, Mr. William married at Port William, Ky. to Miss Jane Butler.
National Banner & Nashville Whig (Sat., Dec. 19, 1826)

Hawkins, Mr. Wm. H. married in Logan County, Ky. to Miss Mary Ann C.
Curd.
National Banner (Sat., April 11, 1829)

Hawlett, Miss Mary Ann married in Williamson County to Mr. William A. Williams.

Haws, Miss Masey married to Mr. Amazon King.

Hay, Miss Adelaida married to Wm. H. Savage Esq.

Hay, Miss Amanthis P. married to Mr. John P. McCall.

Hay, Richard married in Williamson County to Miss Susan Walker.
The Western Weekly Review - Franklin, Tenn. (Fri., Dec. 14, 1832)

Hayden, Miss Eliza married to Mr. John Poland.

Haydon, Mrs. Margaret married to Mr. William Walden.

Hayes, Miss Adelicia married to Isaac Franklin Esq.

Hayes, Miss Martha married to Mr. Thompson.

Hayes, Mr. Reuben P. married in Franklin to Miss Eliza Gunter.
National Banner & Nashville Whig (Sat., Jan. 26, 1828)

Hayes, Roswell P., M. D. of Cincinnati, O. married in Philadelphia, Ohio to Miss Cornelia C. Snowden.
National Banner & Nashville Daily Advertiser (Thurs., July 10, 1834)

Hayley, Miss Sarah G. married to Mr. A. M. Neal.

Haynes, Mr. Aaron of Perry County married in Nashville to Miss Sarah G. M. Barry of Nashville.
National Banner & Nashville Whig (Mon., Jan. 10, 1831)

Haynes, Abram married in Williamson County to Miss Sarah Haynes.
The Western Weekly Review - Franklin, Tenn. (Fri., Dec. 14, 1832)

Haynes, Miss Almyra married to Mr. Randall M'Gavock.

Haynes, Miss Elizabeth married to Mr. John W. Smith.

Haynes, Miss Elizabeth J. married to Mr. R. H. Barry.

Haynes, Mr. George married in Ross County, Ohio to Miss Abigail Coleman.
National Banner & Nashville Whig (Sat., Dec. 23, 1826)

Haynes, Mr. John married to Miss Virginia Kennedy.'
National Banner & Nashville Whig (Fri., March 6, 1835)

Haynes, Capt. Jonathan married in Sumner County to Miss Woods.
National Banner & Nashville Whig (Sat., Sept. 20, 1828)

Haynes, Miss Julia A. married to Mr. James C. Karr.

Haynes, Miss Margaret married to Mr. Andrew Ewing.

Haynes, Mr. Preston G. married to Miss Minerva Hays, married in Henry County.
National Banner & Nashville Daily Advertiser (Fri., Feb. 22, 1833)

Haynes, Mr. Preston G. married in Henry County to Miss Minerva Hays.
Nashville Republican & State Gazette (Fri., Feb. 22, 1833)

Haynes, Mr. R. R. married in Williamson County to Miss Sarah Meritt.
The Western Weekly Review - Franklin, Tenn. (Fri., Dec. 2, 1831)

Haynes, Mr. R. R. married in Williamson County to Miss Sarah Meritt.
National Banner & Nashville Whig (Wed., Dec. 7, 1831)

Haynes, Mr. Stephen married at Knxoville to Miss Susan Dunn daughter
of Mr. Jonathan Dunn.
National Banner & Nashville Daily Advertiser (Mon., Feb. 20, 1832)

Haynie, Miss Lucinda W. married in Tuscumbia, Ala. to Mr. John Caldwell,
Esq.

Haynie, Mr. S. G. married to Miss Julia M. Lucas married at Tuscumbia,
Ala.
National Banner & Nashville Advertiser (Thurs., March 29, 1832)

Hays, Miss Adelitia married to Col. Isaac Franklin.

Hays, Miss Ann married to Mr. Lewis Charles Levine.

Hays, Miss Ann married to Mr. Lewis Charles Levin.

Hays, Col. Blackburn of Davidson Co., Tenn. married by Rev. James
Whitsett on Monday Jan. 1st. 1844 to Miss Nancy b. Blackman daughter
of James Blackman of Ala.
Nashville Whig (Tues., Jan. 2, 1844)

Hays, Mr. Charles M. of Davidson County married on Thursday 20th
July by the Rev. Dr. Edgar to Miss Louisa Jane Smiley daughter of
the late Robert Smiley.
Nashville Whig (Sat., July 22, 1843)

Hays, Capt. Daniel S. married at Hopkinsville, Ky. to Miss Jane Boyd.
National Banner (Feb. 3, 1826)

Hays, Capt. George of Green County married in Cocke County to Miss
Sarah W. Rodgers daughter of Mr. Robert Rodgers.
National Banner & Nashville Daily Advertiser (Wed., May 22, 1833)

Hays, Miss Jane married to Samuel T. M'Kenney Esq.

Hays, Dr. John B. married in Columbia to Miss Ophelia Polk.
National Banner (Sat., Oct. 3, 1829)

Hays, Mrs. Mary married to Mr. Howel E. Eason.

Hays, Miss Mary Payson married to Mr. Henry A. Cargill.

Hays, Miss Mary Payson married to Mr. Henry A. Cargill.

Hays, Miss Matilda married to Mr. Micajah P. Hedgepeth.

Hays, Miss Minerva married to Mr. Preston G. Haynes.

Hays, Miss Minerva married to Mr. Preston G. Haynes.

Hays, Miss Nancy married to Mr. George S. Koontz.

Hays, Miss Rachel married to Mr. Robert Butler.

Hays, Mr. Samuel married in Henry County to Miss Lucinda Coady.
National Banner & Nashville Whig (Wed., Dec. 28, 1831)

Hays, Samuel G. of Lincoln County, Ky. married on Tuesday 17th inst.
near Shelbyville, Tenn. by the Rev. S. S. Moody of Alabama to Miss
Frances Jane Doke daughter of Samuel Doke Esq. of Bedford County,
Tenn.
Nashville Whig (Sat., Nov. 21, 1846)

Hays, Mrs. Sarah married to Wm. Gray Esq.

Hays, Miss Sarah Jane married to Mr. John H. Rawlings.

Hays, Miss Tabitha married to Mr. John J. Gowen.

Hayward, Dr. Joshua H. of Boston married at Cincinnati to Miss Sarah A. McLean daughter of the Hon. John McLean Judge of the Supreme Court of the United States.
National Banner & Nashville Whig (Mon., Aug. 2, 1830)

Haywood, Egber Esq. married in Hardeman County to Miss Sally Johnson.
National Banner & Nashville Whig (Sat., May 24, 1828)

Haywood, Miss Eliza married to Mr. William Morgan.

Haywood, Miss Eliza married to Mr. Wm. Morgan.

Haywood, Thomas Esq. married on Tuesday evening last by the Rev. Mr. Craighead to Miss Susan Glasgow daughter of Col. James Glasgow of this County.
The Nashville Whig & Tenn. Advertiser (Oct. 20, 1817)

Hazard, Mr. Evan M. married in Huntsville, Ala. on the 26th ult. to Miss Jane Hume.
National Banner & Nashville Whig (Wed., Feb. 3, 1836)

Hazard, Miss Hester Ann married to Adam Ferguson Esq.

Hazard, Miss Louisa married to Mr. W. E. Jones.

Hazen, Mr. Gideon M. married in Knoxville, Ten. to Miss Mary Strong.
National Banner & Nashville Whig (Fri., April 10, 1835)

Hazen, Mr. William C. married in Tipton County to Miss Mary M. Frohock.
National Banner (Sat., Nov. 7, 1829)
                    Nov. 21, 1829

Head, Miss Penelope married to Maj. William A. Lauderdale.

Headache, Charles Esq. married in Philadelphia to Mary Workman daughter of Maurice Workman.
National Banner & Nashville Whig (Wed., Sept. 24, 1834)

Headrick, Miss Susannah married to Mr. Robert Patterson.

Heard, Miss Minerva Ann married to Pryor Lea, Esq.

Heaton, Miss Mary married to Mr. Hillary Lyles.

Hebert, Miss Mary married to Mr. William Baker.

Heddinburg, Mr. Charles of Texas married in Davidson County Thursday 1st inst. by Rev. A. L. P. Green to Mrs. Mary Higginbotham of this vicinity.
Nashville Whig (Fri., July 16, 1841)

Hedgepath, Mr. Micajah P. married in Lincoln County, Ten. to Miss Matilda Hays.
National Banner & Nashville Whig (Fri., Jan. 23, 1835)

Hedspeth, Mr. James married in Henry County to Miss Cary M'Lin.
National Banner & Nashville Daily Advertiser (Fri., Feb. 15, 1833)

Hefflin, Mr. Thomas married in Bedford County to Miss Nancy Claxton.
Nashville Republican & State Gazette (Wed., Dec. 12, 1832)

Hegan, Mr. John of St. Louis married on Wednesday last by Bishop Miles to Miss Mary H. Barry daughter of W. L. Barry Esq. of Nashville.
The Christian Record (Sat., Oct. 30, 1847)

Heiskell, Miss Mary T. married to Mr. William H. Cannon.

Helfenstein, Miss Matilda married to Benjamin Patton Jr.

Helm, John L. Esq. married in Bardstown, Ky. to Miss Lucinda B.
Hardin daughter of Benjamin Hardin Esq.
National Banner & Nashville Whig (Mon., Aug. 23, 1830)

Hemingway, Mr. Thomas married at Lexington to Miss Jane Hilton.
National Banner (Sat., April 25, 1829)

Hemmel, Miss Elizabeth married to Mr. Robert Clayton.

Henby, Miss Elizabeth married to Mr. Michael T. Weldie.

Henderson, Miss Ann married to Mr. Samuel M. Sharp.

Henderson, Miss Elizabeth married to Mr. William B. Vincent.

Henderson, Rev. Greenville T. married in Murfreesborough to Miss
Matilda Keyser.
National Banner & Nashville Daily Advertiser (Fri., March 29, 1833)

Henderson, Miss Isabella married to Mr. Ransford M'Gregor.

Henderson, Miss Iva Ann married to Andrew H. Edgar Esq.

Henderson, Miss J. C. married to Mr. Thomas J. Fite.

Henderson, Mr. James of Rutherford County married at Columbia to
Miss Amanda Voorhies.
National Banner & Nashville Daily Advertiser (Thurs., Dec. 27, 1832)

Henderson, Miss Jane E. married to Mr. William S. Moore.

Henderson, Mr. John L. married in Madison County to Miss Letitia
Reynolds.
National Banner & Nashville Whig (Sat., Jan. 6, 1827)

Henderson, Mr. Joseph married at Little Rock, Ark. to Miss Eliza Ann
Elliott.
National Banner & Nashville Whig (Sat., July 8, 1826)

Henderson, Miss Malvina married to William Davis Esq.

Henderson, Miss Maria married to Mr. Thomas K. Handy.

Henderson, Miss Martha L. married to Mr. George W. Becton.

Henderson, Miss Martha married to George W. Winters.

Henderson, Miss Matilda married to Mr. John N. M'Nairy.

Henderson, Miss Melinda married to Mr. Alexder Blair.

Henderson, Miss Nancy married to Mr. Arthur Crozier.

Henderson, Miss Nancy married to Mr. Ephraim Deer.

Henderson, Mr. Ramsay married in August 1831 to Miss Elizabeth Ott.
The Western Weekly Review - Franklin, Tenn. (Fri., Sept. 2, 1831)

Henderson, Miss Sarah married to Mr. Augustus Hall.

Henderson, Mr. O. P. of Ky. married in Jonesborough to Miss Keziah
Vance.
Nashville Whig (Thurs., March 19, 1846)

Henderson, Miss Susan Frances married to Mr. Milton Bransford Esq.

Henderson, Miss Violet C. married to Mr. Wm. T. Lytle.

Hendley, Miss Mary E. B. married to Mr. Arbraham Smith.

Hendon, Miss Keren Happuch married to Mr. William B. Taliaferro.

Hendon, Miss Louisa A. married to Mr. John H. Seawell.

Hendrick, Miss Elizabeth F. married to Mr. James Banks.

Hendrex, Mr. William married in Williamson County to Miss Nancy Wood.
National Banner & Nashville Whig (Wed., Dec. 7, 1831)

Hendricks, Mr. William married in September 1831 to Miss Nancy Wood.
The Western Weekly Review - Franklin, Tenn. (Fri., Sept. 23, 1831)

Hendrix, Mr. John M. married in Monroe County to Miss Jane V. Blair.
National Banner & Nashville Daily Advertiser (Mon., April 9, 1832)

Hendrixson, Miss Elizabeth married to Mr. Christian Baker.
National Banner & Nashville Whig (Thurs., May 20, 1830)

Henkle, Miss Mary Ann married to Mr. David Lockran.

Henley, Miss Mary P. married to Mr. Samuel Dunlap.

Henley, Mr. Osborne married in Fayette County, Ky. to Miss Sarah
Vaughn.
National Whig (Feb. 10, 1826)

Henley, Mr. Thos. D. married in Williamson County, Ten. to Miss
Rebecca M. Campbell.
National Banner & Nashville Whig (Fri., Feb. 13, 1835)

Henley, Mr. Turner B. of this city married on Thursday evening last
to Miss Susan D. House of Rutherford County.
The Clarion & Tennessee Gazette (Dec. 26, 1820)

Hennen, Mr. Duncan N. of New Orleans married on Tuesday the 20th by
the Rev. Dr. Lindsley to Miss Eleanor R. Robertson daughter of
Dr. Felix Robertson of Nashville.
National Banner & Nashville Whig (Mon., Sept. 26, 1836)

Hennenger, Mr. H. aged 104 married in Marion, Fla. to Mrs. E. A. Peak
aged 83.
National Banner & Nashville Whig (Wed., Nov. 11, 1835)

Henning, Mr. Joseph, merchant, married on Sunday April 1st, by the
Rev. Mr. Winburn to Miss Eliza Litton both of Nashville.
Nashville Whig (Fri., April 6, 1838)

Henning, Miss Susan W. married to Mr. Edward D. Hobbs.

Henrie, Major John M. married Miss Priscilla A. Nixon daughter of
George A. Nixon, Esq. of Texas married at the residence of Dr. Martin
of this City on Tuesday evening the 16th inst.
Nashville Daily Republican Banner (January 18, 1838)

Henry, Miss Elizabeth married to Mr. William Woodward.

Henry, Gustavus S. Esq. married in Montgomery County to Miss Marian
M'Clure.
National Banner & Nashville Daily Advertiser (Mon., Feb. 25, 1833)

Henry, Dr. Hugh W. married at Montgomery, Ala. to Miss Martha Falconer.
National Banner & Nashville Whig (Sat., March 1, 1828)

Henry, Mr. Isaac N. one of the Editors of the St. Louis Enquirer
married Miss P. C. Bennett.
The Clarion & Tennessee Whig (October 3, 1820)

Henry, Dr. John F. married in Lexington, Ky. to Miss Lucy E. F. Ridgley.
National Banner & Nashville Whig (Sat., Jan. 12, 1828)

Henry, Miss Lucy married to Warren L. Underwood Esq.

Henry, Miss Martha married to Mr. John Cate.

Henry, Mrs. Nancy married to Mr. Edward Bacon.

Henslett, Col. James A. married in Hardeman County to Miss Emily
Philpot.
National Banner & Nashville Whig (Sat., May19, 1827)

Hensley, Miss Ellen married to Mr. Burgess Phelps.

Hensley, Miss Fanny married to Mr. James Robinson.

Hensley, Mr. John B. married in McMinnville to Miss Mary Wilson.
National Banner & Nashville Daily Advertiser (Tues., May 27, 1834)

Hensley, Mr. Joseph C. married at Florence, Ala. to Miss Charlotte
Stephens.
National Banner & Nashville Whig (Sat., June 14, 1828)

Henson, Mr. Jesse M. married in Henry County to Miss Rosanna Crutchfield.
National Banner & Nashville Daily Advertiser (Wed., Jan. 18, 1832)

Herbert, Miss Rebecca married to Mr. D. Matthews.

Herbert, Mr. Robert N. married Miss Elizabeth L. Cummins.
The Western Weekly Review - Franklin, Tenn. (Fri., Nov. 11, 1831)

Herbert, Mr. Thomas S. married in Wilkinson County, Miss to Miss
Susan F. Hughes.
National Banner & Nashville Whig (Sat., Sept. 16, 1826)

Herdman, Miss Lavenia I. married to Dr. Albert B. Graham.

Heren, Mr. William M. married in M'Minn County to Miss J. S. Bridges
daughter of Jas. S. Bridges Esq.
National Banner & Nashville Daily Advertiser (Mon., March 11, 1833)

Herndon, Miss Ann married to Rev. Hartwell H. Brown.

Hernden, Miss Ann E. married to Mr. R. B. Cabell.

Herndon, Miss Ann Hall married to Matthew F. Maury, Esq.

Herndon, Mr. Augustus G. married in Bourbon County, Ky. to Miss Eliza
G. Herndon.
National Banner & Nashville Whig (Sat., Nov. 17, 1827)

Herndon, Miss Martha T. married to Wm. Berry Esq.

Herndon, Miss Rebecca G. married to Mr. James B. Houston.

Herndon, Mr. Z. married in Scott County, Ky. to Miss Elizabeth
Craig.
National Banner & Nashville Whig (Sat., Dec. 2, 1826)

Herne, Milbry F. Esq. married on the 25th Jan. by the Rev. John F.
Hughs to Miss Elizabeth Jane Johnson daughter of Robertson Johnson
Esq. all of Wilson County.
Nashville Whig (Mon., Feb. 18, 1839)

Heron, William R. Esq. formerly of Philadelphia married last night
in Christs Church by the Rev. J. Thomas Wheat to Miss Ellen Diggons
daughter of James Diggons Esq. of Nashville.
Nashville Whig (Wed., Sept. 2, 1840)

Herpin, Miss Nathalie married to Dominibue Salle.

Herr, Mr. Alfred Married in Jefferson City, Ky. to Miss Mary Ann
Shirley.
Nashville Republican & State Gazette. (Thurs., Dec. 16, 1830)

Herren, Rev. Andrew Jr. married in August 1831 to Miss Lydia W. Warren
daughter of Edward Warren all of Williamson County.
The Western Weekly Review - Franklin, Tenn. (Fri., Sept. 2, 1831)

Herring, Miss Catherine married to Mr. Hiram Sharp.

Herring, Mr. William B. married near Franklin on the 27th inst. by
the Rev. A. L. P. Green to Miss Jane Foster Lytle daughter of
Archibald Lytle Esq. of Williamson County.
Nashville Whig (Sat., Jan. 29, 1842)

Herrison, James C. Esq. married in Lexington, Ky. to Miss Margaret
Ross.
National Banner & Nashville Whig (Mon., Aug. 2, 1830)

Herron, Mr. Joseph married last evening to Miss Elizabeth Hall both
of this town.
Nashville Whig (Feb. 5, 1823)

Herron, Miss Sarah married to Mr. Joel Winn.

Herron, Mr. Thomas B. married in Jackson to Miss Mary Wynne.
National Banner & Nashville Advertiser (Thurs., July 12, 1832)

Hertzog, Miss Elizabeth married to Mr. William Collins.

Hertzog, Rachel W. married to Lieutenant Philip St. George Cooke.

Heslep, Miss Angeline married to Mr. R. Hargoaves.

Hess, William R. Esq. Attorney at law of Shelbyville married Miss
Sophia W. Dyer daughter of Major Joel Dyer of Murfreesboro.
The Nashville Whig (June 10, 1817)

Hester, Mr. David married in Nashville to Miss Mary Booen both of New
Albany, Ind. on last evening.
National Banner & Nashville Whig (Fri., Aug. 26, 1831)

Hetherington, Miss Julia married to Mr. Christian Weller.

Hewes, Miss Ann married to Hon. George Poindexter.

Hewes, Mr. Daniel married in Louisville, Ky. to Miss Mary A. Spence.
National Banner & Nashville Daily Advertiser (Sat., July 7, 1832)

Hewett, Miss Emily D. married to Edwin H. Childress.

Hewett, Mr. H. married on Thursday evening last to Miss Newsome both
of this County.
The Clarion & Tennessee Gazette (Dec. 26, 1820)

Hewett, John M. Esq. married in Wolcox County, Ala. to Martha Perkins.
National Banner (Feb. 10, 1826)

Hewett, Miss Matilda married to Mr. William E. Watkins.

Hewgley, Col. John W. of Wilson married on the 22nd inst. by the
Rev. R. B. C. Howell to Miss Jane C. Whitsitt of Davidson, daughter
of William D. Whitsitt, dec'd.
Daily Republican Banner (Tues., Aug. 27, 1839)

Hewitt, Miss Evelina married to Mr. John H. Summerville.

Hewlett, Mrs. married to Mr. Scruggs.

Hewlett, Miss Marie A. married to J. B. Robinson.

Hewlett, Mr. William B. of Davidson County married on the 19th inst.
by the Rev. Dr. Edgar to Miss Mary Ann Woodford daughter of John
Woodford Esq. of Nashville.
Nashville Whig (Sat., July 22, 1843)

Hewlett, Mr. William E. of Nashville married on Thursday evening 25th
June by the Rev. Mr. Hanner to Miss Jane A. M. Gilman daughter of
Major Timothy Gilman of Davidson County.
National Banner & Nashville Whig (Wed., July 1, 1835)

Hewlitt, Miss Eliza married to Mr. Joseph T. Fowler.

Hew, Mr. Daniel in Louisville, Ky. married to Miss Mary A. Spence.
National Banner & Nashville Advertiser (Sat., July 7, 1832)

Hezlep, Miss Mary married to Mr. Charles R. Harman.

Hickerson, Miss Eliza M. married to Mr. Samuel Thompson.

Hickey, Mr. Calvin M. married in Nashville last evening by the
Rev. Mr. Weller to Miss Mary Jane Scott.
National Banner & Nashville Daily Advertiser (Fri., Sept. 21, 1832)

Hickey, Mr. John married in Knox County to Miss Ann Maria Chenoweth.
National Banner & Nashville Daily Advertiser (Tues., Oct. 30, 1832)

Hickey, Miss Martha married to Mr. Simon W. Walsh.

Hickey, Miss Mary Jane married to Dr. John Bradshaw.

Hickey, Miss Sally married to Mr. Isaac Baker.

Hickle, Mr. John married in Knoxville to Miss Parthena Moore.
National Banner & Nashville Daily Advertiser (Mon., April 16, 1832)

Hickman, Miss Catharine C. married to Mr. James K. Marshall.

Hickman, Miss Elizabeth married to Mr. John Murphy.

Hickman, Miss Frances married to Col. Elliot Fletcher.

Hickman, Mr. Geo. married in Logan County to Miss Matilda Clark.
National Banner (Sat., May 16, 1829)

Hickman, Maj. John P. married on Tuesday the 19th inst. by the Rev.
T. B. Craighead to the amiable and lovely Miss Narcissa A. Weakly
daughter of Colonel Robert Weakley of this County.
The Nashville Whig (Dec. 28, 1815)

Hickman, Mr. Thomas married in Lexington, Ky. to Miss Elizabeth
Shryock.
National Banner & Nashville Whig (Sat., Dec. 2, 1826)

Hicks, Mr. Alfred M. married on Tuesday evening 2nd inst. by the Rev.
R. B. C. Howell to Miss Mary Winston Demoville all of Nashville.
Nashville Whig (Fri., March 5, 1841)

Hicks, Miss Amanda married to Mr. Robert Travis.

Hicks, Mr. A. W. of La Grang, Furnace, Tenn. married at Paris, Tenn. on the 5th inst. to Miss Sarah W. Cook daughter of the Hon. J. W. Cook.
Nashville Republican (Tues., Oct. 11, 1836)

Hicks, Edward D. Esq. of the House of Hicks, Ewing & Co. of Nashville. Married in Lebanon on May 4th by the Rev. Mr. Donald to Miss Cornelia Hall daughter of John Hall, Esq. of Lebanon.
National Banner & Nashville Whig (Wed., May 11, 1836)

Hicks, Miss Elizabeth S. married to Mr. Baldwin Hudnell.

Hicks, Capt. James G. married on Wednesday last to Miss Elizabeth M. Hardaway.

Hicks, Mr. Jesse H. married in Madison County, Ky. to Miss Mary Dickens.
National Banner & Nashville Whig (Sat., Aug. 11, 1827)

Hicks, Mr. John H. married in Russellville, Ky. to Miss Hannah S. Foster.
National Banner & Nashville Daily Advertiser (Sat., Feb. 16, 1833)

Hicks, Miss Lucy Ann married to Mr. William Clark.

Hicks, Miss Polly married to Mr. Henry Ash.

Hicks, Mr. Reuben married in Maury County to Miss Maria Jones.
National Banner & Nashville Whig (Fri., March 26, 1830)

Hicks, Mr. Thomas F. married in Kingston to Miss Angelina Boyd.
National Banner & Nashville Daily Advertiser (Tues., Dec.18, 1832)

Hicks, Mr. W. R. merchant of Charlotte married in Montgomery County on the 11th ult. to Miss Rebecca Fentress daughter of James Fentress Esq.
National Banner & Nashville Whig (Mon., Nov. 15, 1830)

Hieatt, Miss Sally married to Mr. Stephens Cox.

Higgenbothem, John R. of Texas married on the 13th by the Rev. J. B. McFerrin to Miss Mary E. Barnes of Tenn.
Daily Republican Banner (Sat., Nov. 16, 1839)

Higginbotham, Mrs. Mary married to Mr. Charles Heddinburg.

Higgins, Miss America married to Major Alexander G. Morgan.

Higgins, Miss Carolina V. married to Thomas H. Waters, Esq.

Higgins, Mr. Joseph R. married in Mason County, Ky. to Miss Narcissa Owen.
National Banner (March 24, 1826)

Higgins, Miss Margaret married to Mr. Isaac Worthington.

Higgins, Mr. Peter married Monday evening last by the Rev. Lewis Garrett to Mrs. Ann Rogers all of Nashville.
Nashville Union (Wed., Oct. 2, 1839)

Higgins, R. Esq. of Lexington, Ky. married in Jessamine County, Ky. to Miss Nancy Young relict of Hon. Richard Young.
National Banner & Nashville Daily Advertiser (Mon., May 12, 1834)

Higgins, Mr. Richard Jun. married in Fayette County, Ky. to Miss Sarah M. Shelby daughter of Major Thomas H. Shelby.
National Banner & Nashville Daily Advertiser (Fri., Jan. 27, 1832)

Higgins, Miss Winifred married to Mr. N. Batterson.

Higgs, Miss Nancy married to Mr. George L. Thompson.

Highland, Miss Cedonia married to Mr. Charles M. Smith.

Hightower, Miss Elizabeth S. married to Mr. Samuel Brown.

Hikes, Miss Elizabeth married to Mr. Robert Ayars.

Hilderbrand, Mr. Benjamin married in Shelby County to Miss Susan Robinson.
National Banner & Nashville Daily Advertiser (Mon., April 8, 1833)

Hildreth, Paul Esq. married to Miss Eliza Otey married in Madison County, Ala.
National Banner & Nashville Whig (Tues., Feb. 2, 1830)

Hill, Mrs. married to Mr. Charles C. Locke.

Hill, Miss married to Mr. Richard Hunning.

Hill, Mr. Anderson married in Knoxville to Miss Nancy Seay daughter of the late Mr. William Seay.
National Banner & Nashville Whig (Mon., Nov. 29, 1830)

Hill, Mr. Benjamin F. married on Thursday 21st inst. at the residence of Mr. Samuel Ingram Maury County to Miss Susan Ingram.
The Politician & Weekly Nashville Whig (Fri., Oct. 29, 1847)

Hill, Miss Betsy married to Mr. Tiller Blancett.

Hill, Mr. Byrel married in Madison County to Miss Louisa Eddings.
National Banner & Nashville Whig (Thurs., June 24, 1830)

Hill, Mr. Daniel B. married in Nashville, last evening by the Rev. Mr. Hume to Miss Margaret J. Stout.
National Banner & Nashville Daily Advertiser (Fri., Feb. 24, 1832)

Hill, Miss Elizabeth married to Mr. Richard Alman.

Hill, Miss Elizabeth P. married to Dr. H. W. K. Myrick.

Hill, Miss Elizabeth married to Mr. Loyd Rutherford.

Hill, Miss Emaline married to Mr. Mortimore Hamilton.

Hill, Miss Emeline married to Mr. Mortimer Hamilton.

Hill, Miss Evalina E. married to Mr. Lorenzo D. Turner.

Hill, Mr. Henry R. W. married in Franklin to Miss Margaretta E. M'Alister.
National Banner & Nashville Whig (Sat., Aug. 18, 1827)

Hill, Mr. James B. married on Thursday May 19th by Rev. James W. Rea to Miss Narcissa Hughes all of Williamson County.
The Western Weekly Review - Franklin, Tenn. (Fri., June 10, 1831)

Hill, Mr. James D., printer, married at Tuskaloosa, Ala. on the 25th ult. to Miss Rebecca Compton of Tuskaloosa.
The Politician Weekley Nashville Whig (Fri., June 18, 1847)

Hill, James F. married in Williamson County to Miss Elizabeth W. Payne.
The Western Weekly Review - Franklin, Tenn. (Fri., Dec. 14, 1832)

Hill, John D. married in Williamson County to Annis L. Hodges.
National Banner & Nashville Whig (Wed., Sept. 24, 1834)

Hill, Mr. John T. married in this town on Wednesday evening by Rev.
Mr. Hume to Miss Georgianna Beck.
National Banner & Nashville Whig(Sat., Jan. 26, 1828)

Hill, Mr. John W. married in Columbus, Miss on the 7th June by the
Rev. Mr. North to Miss Mary L. Clark daughter of Mr. Alexander Clark.
of Williamson County, Ten.
National Banner & Nashville Whig (Fri., July 1, 1836)

Hill, Mr. Joshua D. married in Murfreesborough on the 5th inst. to
Miss Elizabeth M'Cutchen.
National Banner & Nashville Whig (Sat., Feb. 14, 1829)

Hill, Miss Lucinda married to Mr. William Garner.

Hill, Miss Lucinda married to Mr. R. H. Givins.

Hill, Miss Lyda married to Mr. Butwell Kannon.

Hill, Miss Martha A. married to Mr. Hugh B. Bozeman.

Hill, Miss Martha J. married to Mr. John Crook.

Hill, Miss Martha Louisa married to Doctor M. W. Dibrell.

Hill, Miss Martha M. married to Mr. John G. C. Wilson.

Hill, Miss Mary married to Mr. Zacheus Little.

Hill, Robert Esq. married in Davidson County to Miss Louisa Harrison
on Thursday last.
Nashville Republican & State Gazette (Sat., May 17, 1834)

Hill, Mr. Robert of this County married on Thursday evening last to
Mrs. Eliza Perkins of Williamson County.
Nashville Whig (Jan. 29, 1823)

Hill, Mr. Robert T. married on the 21st by the Rev. Dr. Edgar to
Miss Catherine Stout daughter of S. V. D. Stout Esq. both of Nashville.
Nashville Whig (Sat., Sept. 23, 1843)

Hill, Mr. Samuel L. of the house of S. L. Hill & Co. married in New
Orleans by the Rev. Dr. Scott on the 9th inst. to Miss Julia G.
Gibbes late of Charleston, S. C.
The Christian Record (Sat., Nov. 25, 1848)

Hill, Miss Sarah married to Mr. Jordan Brown.

Hill, Miss Sarah E. married to Mr. Daniel Williams.

Hill, Mr. Turner G. married to Miss Harriet W. Arms.
The Western Weekly Review - Franklin, Tenn. (Fri., Nov. 11, 1831)

Hill, Mr. Turner G. married in Williamson County to Miss Harriet W.
Arms.
National Banner & Nashville Whig (Mon., Nov. 14, 1831)

Hill, Mr. William married in Knox County to Miss Margaret Low.
National Banner (Sat., Nov. 28, 1829)

Hilliard, Isaac H. Esq. of Arkn's. married on the 28th ult. by the
Rev. William Leacock to Miss Miriam Brannin daughter of Daniel Brannin
Esq. of New Castle, Ky.
The Politician & Weekly Nashville Whig (Wed., Aug. 4, 1847)

Hilliard, Miss Nancy married to Mr. Solomon Hunt.

Hilliard, Miss Sally married to George W. Polk Esq.

Hillis, Mr. Phineas E. married in Henry County to Miss Sarah Broadway.
National Banner & Nashville Whig (Fri., Dec. 9, 1831)

Hillman, Mr. Charles E. married in Nashville on the 19th inst. by the
Rev. Mr. Neeley to Miss Elizabeth M. Jones daughter of the late
Amzi Jones both of Nashville.
Nashville Whig (Sat., July 22, 1843)

Hills, Mr. H. W. of New Orleans married on Aug. 22d at Craigfont by
the Rev. Jno. W. Hull to Miss Susan W. Robeson daughter of the late
Gen. W. L. Robeson.
Daily Republican Banner (Thurs., Aug. 31, 1837)

Hills, Mr. H. H. of New Orleans married on Tuesday Aug. 22d at Craigfont, by the Rev. John W. Hall to Miss Susan W. Robeson daughter of
the late W. L. Robeson.
The Union (Sat., Sept. 2, 1837)

Hillsman, Miss Mary married to Mr. Gordon Mayatt.
Nashville Republican & State Gazette. (Mon., April 29, 1833)

Hilton, Mr. James W. of Bowling Green to Miss Eleanor S. Briant.
National Banner (Sat., Sept. 26, 1829)

Hilton, Miss Jane married to Mr. Thomas Hemingway.

Hind, Miss Zerilda married to Mr. Thomas Gately.

Hindman, Mr. Silas married in Lincoln County, Ten. to Miss Synthia J.
Smith.
National Banner & Nashville Whig (Fri., Dec. 5, 1834)

Hinds, Miss Mary married to Col. Charles Prentice.

Hines, Miss Caroline married to Mr. Phineas D. Hampton.

Hines, Miss Mary married to Mr. Joseph Walker.

Hines, Capt. Thomas of South Carolina married in Lincoln County to
Miss Mary R. Moores.
National Banner & Nashville Whig (Sat., Aug. 12, 1826)

Hines, Mr. W. H. married in Elyton, Ala. to Miss Sarah N. Barker
both of Tuscaloosa.
National Banner & Nashville Daily Advertiser (Wed., March 26, 1833)

Hinkle, Miss Mary W. married to Mr. W. D. Lacky.

Hinson, Miss E. married to Mr. J. Green.

Hinson, Miss Margaret married to Mr. James Younger.

Hillsman, Miss Mary married to Mr. Gordan Mynatt.

Hinson, Miss Margaret married to Mr. James Younger.

Hinton, Mr. C. H. married on Thursday 3d inst. by Rev. J. B. McFerrin
to Miss Mary Jane Watkins all of Davidson County.
Nashville True Whig & Weekly Commercial Register (Fri., Oct. 11, 1850)

Hinton, Miss Elizabeth married to Mr. John M'Gavock.

Hinton, Miss Frances married to William Yates.

Hinton, Mr. Harrison Boyd married in Davidson County to Miss Isabella
Turner.
Nashville Republican & State Gazette (Sat., July 23, 1831)

Hinton, Mr. Jesse married in Maury County, Ten. to Miss Katherine Agent.
National Banner & Nashville Whig (Mon., March 30, 1835)

Hinton, Mr. Wm. M. married on Tuesday 4th inst. by the Rev. Parson
Lanier to Miss Adeline Criddle both of this County.
The Clarion & Tennessee Gazette (July 25, 1820)

Hise, Elijah, Esq. of Russellville, Ky. married in Davidson County to
Miss Alvira Stewart on Tuesday evening last.
National Banner & Nashville Advertiser (Tues., Oct. 16, 1832)

Hitchcock, Charles L. Esq. married at Louisville, Ky. married Miss
Janette Racine.
National Banner & Nashville Whig (Tues., March 2, 1830)

Hite, Mr. Abraham of Louisville, Ky. married at Salem, Ind. to Miss
Sarah Parke daughter of Judge Parke.
National Banner (April 21, 1826)

Hite, Mr. Ormsby married at Louisville, Ky. to Miss Amelia P. Matthews.
National Banner (Sat., June 27. 1829)

Hite, Mr. Thos. H. married on Sabbath evening the 6th inst. by
Elder S. Lindsley to Miss Martha Jane Couch both of Nashville.
Daily Republican Banner (Tues., Sept. 8, 1840)

Hiter, Miss Eliza R. married to Mr. Yancy Simmons.

Hively, Miss Susan married to Mr. Pumfrey Haile.

Hix, Miss Rebecca married to Mr. Charles T. Philpot.

Hoard, Thomas Esq. Attorney at law married in Rutherford County, Tenn.
to Miss Mary E. M'Cullock.
National Banner & Nashville Daily Advertiser (Mon., April 7, 1834)

Hobbs, Miss Catharine married to Mr. H. Vaughn.

Hobbs, Miss Catharine C. married to Mr. Hiram Vaughan.

Hobbs, Mr. Edward D. married in Jefferson County, Ky. to Miss Susan
W. Henning.
National Banner & Nashville Advertiser (Mon., Dec. 17, 1832)

Hobbs, Mr. James R. formerly of Huntsville, Ala. married in Winchester,
Tenn. on the 16th Dec. by the Rev. Robert Dongan to Miss Jane W.
Estill, daughter of James Estill, Esq.
National Banner & Nashville Whig (Mon., Jan. 5, 1835)

Hobbs, Miss Julia Ann married to Mr. Powhaten W. Maxey.

Hobbs, Miss Mary C. married to William Atkinson.

Hobson, Miss Catherine married to Mr. N. A. McNairy.

Hobson, Miss Martha married to Mr. William Petway.

Hobson, Miss Mary C. married to Mr. James Knox.

Hobson, Miss Susan married to Mr. Charles Shepperd.

Hobson, Miss Susan married to Mr. Joseph Vaulx.

Hobson, Mr. Thomas married on Thursday 6th inst. by Rev. J. B. McFerrin
to Miss Sarah Ann Tally daughter of Mr. Reuben Tally all of Nashville.
Nashville Whig (Sat., July 8, 1843)

Hocker, Miss Elvira married to Mr. George W. Broaddus.

Hockersmith, Mr. Judiah married at Lawrenchburgh, Ky. to Miss Maria Story.
National Banner (April 14, 1826)

Hodge, Mr. Francis L. married in Williamson County to Miss Mary Polk.
National Banner & Nashville Whig (Fri., Jan. 9, 1835)

Hodge, James married in Williamson County to Miss Nancy B. Atkinson.
The Western Weekly Review - Franklin, Tenn. (Fri., Dec. 14, 1832)

Hodge, Miss Jane married to W. Woodall.

Hodge, Miss Polly married to Mr. E. Cole.

Hodge, Mr. Samuel of Sumner married in Rutherford to Miss Sarah Mitchell.
Nashville Whig (April 9, 1823)

Hodge, Sarah married to Eli Field.

Hodge, Miss Sarah married to Mr. Eli Fields.

Hodge, Mr. Wm. of Flemingsburgh, Ky. to Miss

Hodge, William F. Esq. married in Fayette County to Miss Sophia B. M'Clellan.
National Banner & Nashville Whig (Wed., July 6, 1831)

Hodge, William R. married in Williamson County to Francis L. Atkinson.
National Banner & Nashville Whig (Wed., Sept. 24, 1834)

Hodges, Mr. Albert G. publisher of the Lexington Whig married at Frankford, Ky. to Miss Elizabeth S. Todd.
National Banner (Feb. 17, 1826)

Hodges, Annis L. married to John D. Hill.

Hodges, Mr. Charles B. of Jefferson County married in Knox County to Miss Sarah Cobb.
National Banner & Nashville Advertiser (Tues., July 17, 1832)

Hodges, Miss Eliza C. married to Mr. Levi S. Gillam.

Hodges, Miss Euseba married to Mr. John Thompson.

Hodges, Miss Frances married to Mr. Joseph D. Hodges.

Hodges, Mr. James H. married in Smith County to Miss Emily Hallum daughter of Mr. Andrew Hallum.
National Banner & Nashville Daily Advertiser (Wed., July 17, 1833)

Hodges, Mr. John A. married at Tuscaloosa to Miss Melinda Dunlap.
National Banner (Sat., July 18, 1829)

Hodges, Mr. Joseph D. married in Jefferson County to Miss Frances Hodges.
National Banner & Nashville Advertiser (Mon., Feb. 27, 1832)

Hodges, Miss Louisa Ann Catherine married to Mr. Robert Hansaid.

Hodges, Miss Mary Jane married to Mr. George B. Holloway.

Hodges, Miss Pamelia married to Mr. Robert Douglass.

Hodges, William F. Esq. married in Fayette County to Miss Sophia B. M'Clellan.
National Banner & Nashville Whig (Wed., July 6, 1831)

Hodslew, Mr. Robert H. married in Blount County to Miss Elizabeth Hook. duaghter of Mr. Robert Hook.
National Banner & Nashville Daily Advertiser (Tues., Oct. 9, 1832)

Hoffar, Mr. Walker A. married in Knox County to Miss Mary R. Walker.
National Banner & Nashville Whig (Sat., Feb. 21, 1829)

Hoffer, Mr. A. M. married in Philadelphia to Miss Abigal E. Swift on Wednesday 30 ult.
National Banner & Nashville Whig (Sat., Dec. 17, 1831)

Hofstetter, Mr. Christian of Fountain of Health married on the 27th ult. by the Rev. Dr. Edgar to Miss Cahtarine Scheider of Nashville.
The Christian Record (Sat., July 1st. 1848)

Hogan, Miss A. C. married to Mr. H. W. Prout, Esq.

Hogan, Miss Elizabeth married to Mr. Abel G. Elkins.

Hogan, Miss Fanny married to Mr. Robert Rankin.

Hogan, Mr. Granville H. married in Franklin County to Miss Narcissa Harvey.
National Banner & Nashville Whig (Sat., Sept. 9, 1826)

Hogan, Mr. Jacob R. of Davidson County married on the 15th by the Rev. Mr. Green to Miss Harriett D. Taliaferro of Williamson County.
National Banner & Nashville Whig (Mon., Oct. 26, 1835)

Hogan, Mr. John married in Franklin County, Ala. to Miss Thermusthus Gist.
Nashville Republican & State Gazette (Sat., Nov. 23, 1833)

Hogan, Miss Louisa B. married to Col. Samuel Meredith.

Hoge, Mr. Moses married in Giles County to Miss E. M. Young.
National Banner & Nashville Whig (Sat., Jan. 10, 1829)

Hogg, Miss Eliza married to James P. H. Grundy Esq.

Hogg, Miss Rebecca R. married to James Young, M. D.

Hogg, Dr. Samuel of Wilson County married to Miss Polly Talbot of Davidson County on Tuesday last.
Impartial Review & Cumberland Repository - Published at Nashville (Sat., April 5, 1806)

Hogg, Miss Sophia married to Doctor Wm. P. Chester.

Hoggatt, Mr. Abraham S. married in Prince Edward County, Va. to Miss Amanda F. Walker of Buckingham.
Nashville Whig (Jan. 12, 1824)

Hoggatt, Miss Anges W. married to Richard S. Williams Esq.

Hoggatt, Dr. James W. Davidson County married Miss Mary Ann Saunders in Sumner County on last eveing by the Rev. Mr. Hume daughter of James Saunders Esq.
National Banner & Nashville Whig (Wed., Oct. 19, 1831)

Hogsett, Mr. Charles T. married in Jackson to Miss Jemima C. Sharp.
Nashville Whig (Tues., March 24, 1846)

Hogshead, Miss Nancy married to Mr. William McAdoo.

Hogue, Mr. James married near Florence, Ala. to Miss Maty Ann Parker.
National Banner & Nashville Daily Advertiser (Mon., May 12, 1834)

Hogue, Mrs. Patsey married to Mr. Jacob Young.

Hohe, Mr. Marcus L. merchant of Lincolnton married in Ashville, N. C.
to Miss Harriet E. Smith daughter of Col. J. M. Smith.
National Banner & Nashville Daily Advertiser (Wed., July 9, 1834)

Halbert, J. Bentley Esq. of Columbus, Miss. married in the vicinity
of Nashville on the 9th inst. by the Rev. C. D. Elliott to Miss
Catherine W. Bostick daughter of Hardin P. Bostick Esq. of Nashville.
The Politician & Weekly Nashville Whig (Wed., Sept. 22, 1847)

Holcomb, Mr. Alfred married in Maury County to Miss Sebina Porter.
National Banner & Nashville Whig (Mon., Feb. 28, 1831)

Holcomb, Mr. Caleb B. married in Cincinnati to Miss Temperance Mooney.
National Banner & Nashville Whig (Sat., Feb. 24, 1827)

Holden, Miss Joanna married to Mr. Albert G. Underwood.

Holder, Miss Ann married in Maury County to Mr. Claiborn Pigg.

Holder, Miss Francis H. married to Mr. Peter S. Deckard.

Holder, Miss Sophia married to Mr. James A. Sowden.

Holder, Miss Sophia married to Mr. James A. Snowden.

Holderby, Mr. John M. married in Frankfort, Ky. to Miss Sally Hardin.
National Banner (Sat., Oct. 3, 1829)

Holdin, Miss Catharine married to Mr. Gideon Riggs.

Holeman, Mr. John P. age 17 married in Wilson County on Friday 19th
inst. by the George H. Bullard, Esq. to Miss Lavina Randolph age 45.
National Banner & Nashville Whig (Sat., Sept. 20, 1828)

Holiday, Mr. Allen J. married in Madison County to Miss Nancy D. Blair.
National Banner & Nashville Daily Advertiser (Wed., May 1, 1833)

Holland, Mr. Benj. married in Bedford County to Miss Maria Yates.
National Banner & Nashville Whig (Sat., Nov. 15, 1828)

Holland, Mr. Benjamin married in Hardeman County to Miss Mary T. Allen.
National Banner & Nashville Whig (Wed., Dec. 14, 1831)

Holland, Mr. H. H. of Nashville married on Tuesday the 12th inst.by
the Rev. Mr. Howell to Miss Amanda M. F. Webb of this vicinity.
Nashville Whig (Thurs., March 14, 1844)

Holland, Mr. John A. married in Williamson County to Miss Sarah Grat.
Nashville Whig (Aug. 11, 1823)

Holland, Miss Mary Ann married to Mr. Robert M. Tarlton.

Holland, Miss Matilda married to William R. Brittan, Esq.

Holland, Miss Narcissa married to Mr. William W. Carter.

Holland, Miss Sarah J. married to Mr. Andrew Edmondson.

Holland, Miss Sarah M. married to Rev. Frederick A. Thompson.

Holloway, Miss Mary married to Mr. William Graves.

Hollowell, Mr. Joseph married in Rutherford County to Miss Louisa
Beasley.
National Banner & Nashville Advertiser (Sat., Feb. 25, 1832)

Holman, Miss Eliza Jane married to Mr. Augusta Cannon.

Holman, James T. Esq. Member of the Senate from White County married
in Davidson County on Thursday evening, Oct. 11 by the Rev. Mr. Hume.
To Miss Clemintine H. Boyd.
National Banner & Nashville Advertiser (Fri., Oct. 12, 1832)

Holman, Sandy Esq. married in Franklin County, Ky. to Miss Jane H.
Brewer.
National Banner & Nashville Whig (June 24, 1826)

Holmes, Mr. James of Murfreesborough married in Rutherford County to
Miss Mary daughter of Charles Ready Sr. Esq.
National Banner (Sat., May 2, 1829)

Holmes, Miss Jane married to Mr. George Nulands.

Holmes, Mr. Phineas in Nashville married by the Rev. Mr. Hume on the
13th inst. to Miss Eliza J. Read.
National Banner & Nashville Whig (Thurs., May 20, 1830)

Holmes, Mr. Samuel A. merchant of Covington, Tipton County. Married
in Haywood County Oct. 3 by the Rev. Mr. Rogers to Miss Elizabeth
M. Grove of Haywood daughter of the late Hon. William B. Grove formerly
of Fayetteville, N. C.
National Banner & Nashville Daily Advertiser (Sat., Oct. 20, 1832)

Holmes, Miss Samuella A. A. married to Mr. W. W. Calvert.

Holmes, Miss Susan married to Mr. Mitchum Webb.

Holmes, Vivian B. Esq. married in this County on Thursday evening last
to Miss Susan B. Wiggington.
National Banner & Nashville Whig (Sat., April 7, 1827)

Holmes, Mr. Wm. N. near Pulaski, Ten. married Miss Eliza Ann Yarbrough
of Hillsborough, N. C. on the 15th of October.
Nashville Republican (Thurs., November 19, 1835)

Holsapple, Miss Catherine married to Mr. Andrew Stichies.

Holstead, Miss Malinda married to Abner C. Potts.

Holston, Mr. Henry of Grainger County married in Jefferson County to
Miss Maria C. Peck.
National Banner & Nashville Whig (Mon., Dec. 27, 1830)

Holt, Mrs. married in Florence, Ala. to Mr. Isaac Hooks.

Holt, Mr. Calvin M. married in Maury County to Miss Maria Patton.
National Banner & Nashville Whig (Wed., April 27, 1831)

Holt, Dr. David married in Little Rock, Ark to Mrs. J. J. Shall
daughter of David Fulton, Esq.
Nashville Republican (Tues., Aug. 9, 1836)

Holt, Miss Emily B. married to Mr. Ira Ingram.

Holt, Mr. F. married in Smith County to Miss Diana Hughes.
National Banner & Nashville Daily Advertiser (Fri., Feb. 24, 1832)

Holt, Miss Harriet H. married to Major Joseph W. E. Wallace.

Holt, Mr. Lewis married in Williamson County, Ten. to Miss Emily
Cummings.
National Banner & Nashville Whig (Mon., Nov. 10, 1834)

Holt, Miss Mary married to Mr. John Reeves.

Holt, Miss Nancy married to Mr. Philip Vacaro.

Holt, Nicholas P. married in Williamson County, Ten. to Tobitha C. Hughes.
National Banner & Nashville Daily Advertiser. (Mon., Aug. 26, 1833)

Holt, Mr. Robert S. of McMinn County married in Monroe County to Miss Elizabeth Ragan daughter of Peter Ragan, Esq.
National Banner & Nashville Daily Advertiser (Mon., July 2, 1832)

Holt, Mr. Thomas married at St. Louis to Miss Sarah Slater.
National Banner & Nashville Whig (Sat., Feb. 21, 1829)

Holt, Mr. William married in Williamson County to Miss Polly White.
National Banner & Nashville Whig (Fri., Jan. 9, 1835)

Holtzclaw, Mr. B. W. of Sumner County married in Wilson County on the 5th inst. to Miss Martha Leech.
National Banner & Nashville Whig (Wed., Oct. 12, 1831)

Hommedieu, Mr. Samuel L. married at Cincinnati to Miss Eliza Swift.
National Banner & Nashville Whig (Sat., July 8, 1826)

Hommel, Miss Ellen married to Mr. John Bush.

Hooberry, Miss Martha married to Mr. James A. White.

Hoobury, Mrs. Nancy Ellen married to Mr. Andrew McNairy Hamilton.

Hood, Mrs. married to Mr. R. Good. sen.

Hood, Miss Abagail married to Mr. Robert Conn.

Hood, Mr. James of Alabama married on Thursday evening last to Miss Mary Chalmers of Nashville.
The Nashville Gazette (Sat., Nov. 20, 1819)

Hood, Miss Jane married to Thomas J. Foster, Esq.

Hood, John M. Esq. of Florence, Ala. married at Mansfield on Tuesday moring 26th inst. by the Rev. Dr. Edgar to Miss Julia Ann Foster daughter of the Hon. Ephraim H. Foster.
The Christian Record (Sat., Sept. 30, 1848)

Hood, Mr. Joseph P. married at Dr. La Ezells June 26th by Joseph Jarrell Esq. to Miss Sarah Ezell all of the Valley of Mill Creek.
Nashville True Whig & Weekly Commercial Register (Fri., July 5, 1850)

Hood, Miss Nancy married to Mr. James Haden.

Hook, Miss Elizabeth married to Mr. Robert H. Hodslew.

Hook, Mrs. Harriet married to Frederick A. Browder, Esq.

Hooke, Miss Adelaide Louisa married to Mr. John K. Whiteside.

Hooke, Col. John A. married in Kingston to Mrs. Polly Gamble.
National Banner & Nashville Whig (Mon., Dec. 27, 1830)

Hooks, Mr. David married in Giles County to Mrs. Clarissa Craig.
National Banner & Nashville Whig (Sat., Aug. 16, 1828)

Hooks, Miss Delia married to Mr. John Graysen.

Hooks, Mr. Isaac married in Florence, Ala. to Mrs. Holt.
National Banner & Nashville Whig (Sat., July 8, 1826)

Hooks, Miss Mary A. married to Col. Thomas M'Callie.

Hooper, Miss Helen married to Mr. Anthony Durden.

Hooper, Miss Indiana J. married to Mr. David Wilkins.

Hooper, Miss Maria Ann married to Mr. J. M. Fletcher.

Hooper, Mr. Thomas B. of Newburgh, Ind. married at Louisville, Ky. to Miss Elizabeth Erich daughter of Mr. A. D. Erich.
National Banner & Nashville Daily Advertiser (Fri., Aug. 10, 1832)

Hooper, Mr. William married in Vandalia, Ill. to Miss Gerusha Crocker.
National Banner & Nashville Whig (June 24, 1826)

Hooser, Miss Eliza C. married to Mr. William Young.

Hooser, Mr. John H. married on Tuesday the 25th of Feb. to Miss Martha King both of Todd County, Kentucky.
National Banner & Nashville Daily Advertiser (Fri., March 14, 1834)

Hoover, J. Esq. of Murfreesborough married in Davidson County on the 4th inst. by the Rev. Mr. Edgar Andrew to Miss Martha Shute of this neighborhood.
National Banner & Nashville Daily Advertiser (Mon., Sept. 9. 1833)

Hoover, Maj. John married in Bedford County to Miss T. Murphee.
National Banner & Nashville Advertiser (Wed., March 28, 1832)

Hoover, Miss Martha married to Dr. Patrick D. Neilson.

Hoover, Mr. Philip of this town married in this County on Thursday evening by the Rev. Mr. Fall to Miss Sarah Ann Priestley.
National Banner & Nashville Whig (Sat. Oct. 6, 1827)

Hoover, Mr. William married in Bedford County to Miss Sarah Ann L. Lingo.
National Banner & Nashville Daily Advertiser (Thurs., Sept. 6, 1832)

Hope, Mr. David L. married Miss Mary E. Welch in Knoxville.
National Banner & Nashville Whig (Tues., Feb. 2, 1830)

Hope, Mr. James W. married on Thursday 31st ult. by the Rev. J. B. McFerrin to Miss Jane N. Duff both of Nashville.
Nashville Whig (Mon., Jan. 6, 1841)

Hope, Miss Julia married to Mr. Charles Shaffer.

Hope, Miss Nancy married to Capt. Mathew P. Walker.

Hope, Miss Rebecca married to Mr. James E. Dobson.

Hope, Miss Rebecca married to Mr. James E. Dotson.

Hope, Miss Sarah married to Mr. Jacob Bentlinger.

Hope, Mr. Thomas married in Shelby County, Ky. to Miss Sarah S. Buford.
National Banner (Sat., Aug. 22, 1829)

Hopkins, Mr. Benj. H. married at Hopkinsville, Ky. to Miss Salina M. Wheatley.
National Banner & Nashville Daily Advertiser (Mon., Aug. 5, 1833)

Hopkins, Miss Elizabeth married to Mr. Caleb E. Witt.

Hopkins, Geo. married in Williamson County to Miss Elizabeth Creek.
The Western Weekly Review - Franklin, Tenn. (Fri., Dec. 14, 1832)

Hopkins, Miss Luzena married to Mr. Finis Reed.

Hopp, Miss Virginia married to Mr. James S. Shaw.

Hopson, Dr. Henry of Clarksville married in Lexington, Ky. to Miss
Catherine Cooke daughter of Professor John E. Cooke.
National Banner & Nashville Whig (Mon., Nov. 29, 1830)

Hopson, Mr. Morgan married in Christian County, Ky. to Miss Ann Wills.
National Banner & Nashville Whig (Fri., June 20, 1828)

Horatio, Mr. merchant of this town married on the 10th to Miss Sally
Irwin of Mercer County, Kentucky.
The Nash. Whig & Tenn. Advertiser (Dec. 20, 1815)

Horn, Miss Lydia married to Mr. Joel Campbell.
National Banner & Nashville Advertiser (Tues., Nov. 13, 1832)

Horn, Miss Mary E. married to Mr. Lewis H. Gorby.

Horne, Mr. Anderson married in Jackson to Miss Sarah Horne.
Nashville Whig (Tues., March 24, 1846)

Horne, Rev. George married in Knox County to Miss Amanda M. Luttrell.
National Banner & Nashville Whig (Sat., Oct. 28, 1826)

Horne, Miss Sarah married to Mr. Anderson Horne.

Horne, William P. Esq. Editor of the Florence Gazette married in
Lawrence County to Miss Mary M. Stribling.
Nashville Whig (Thurs., March 19, 1846)

Horner, Miss Eliza married to Mr. J. J. Marshall.

Hornsby, Miss Martha married to Mr. James W. Dickson.

Horseford, Miss Nancy married to Joseph White.

Horton, Ann Weston married to Francis M. Mayson Esq.

Horton, Miss Elizabeth married to Alexander Fall, Esq.

Horton, Miss Ellen married to Col. William W. Woodford.

Horton, Mr. Joseph W. married on Thursday evening the 19th inst.
January 19, 1815 to Miss Sophia Western Davis both of this County,
Davidson.
Nashville Whig (Tues., Jan. 24, 1815)

Horton, Miss Louisa married to Col. William D. Dunn.

Horton, Miss Louise married to Col. William D. Dunn.

Horton, Mr. William D. married on Tuesday evening last of this County
to Miss Rhoda B. Love of this town.
Nashville Whig (July 19, 1824)

Hosea, Mr. Shadrack S. married in Louisville, Ky. to Miss Harriet
Dougherty.
National Banner & Nashville Advertiser (Tuesday, June 26, 1832)

Hosea, Mr. Shadrack S. married in Louisville, Ky. to Miss Harriet
Dougherty.
National Banner & Nashville Daily Advertiser (Tues., June 26, 1832)

Hoskins, Mr. Hugh C. of Tenn. married to Miss Sarah Cooper near
Courtland, Ala.
National Banner & Nashville Advertiser (Sat., July 28, 1832)

Hoss, Miss Mary Ann married to Mr. Peter Davolt.

Hoss, Miss Salina married to Mr. Cornelius Yerger.

Hoster, Mr. Franklin married in Henry County, Ten. to Miss Winnie Jackson.
National Banner & Nashville Whig (Fri., May 1, 1835)

Houdyshelt, Miss Margaret married to Mr. William Gray.

Hough, Mr. Thomas J. married on the 8th inst. by the Rev. F. E. Pitts to Miss Margaret F. Wilson all of Nashville.
Nashville Whig (Sat., Oct. 10, 1846)

House, Miss Adaline married to Mr. Hubbard S. Wilkinson.

House, Mr. Ambrose of Rutherford County married in Davidson County to Margaret Weatherald of Davidson County.
National Banner & Nashville Daily Advertiser (Sat., Sept. 14, 1833)

House, Miss Martha M. married to Mr. Alexander C. McLaren.

Houser, Mr. Philip P. married in Knoxville to Miss Jane Morrow.
National Banner (May 13, 1826)

House, Miss Susan D. of Rutherford County married to Mr. Turner B. Henley

Houston, Eliza married to Volney H. Steel.

Houston, Mr. James B. of Nashville, Tenn. married on Thursday evening last by the Rev. Mr. Kilpatrick to Miss Rebecca G. Herndon daughter of Joseph Herndon Esq. of Maury County.
The Nashville Gazette (Sat., Aug. 28, 1819)

Houston, Dr. Joel B. of North Carolina married in Maury County to Miss Elizabeth L. M'Corcle daughter of Mr. Alexander M'Corcle of Bedford County.
National Banner & Nashville Whig (Sat., Oct. 7, 1826)

Houston, Dr. John B. married in Williamson County to Miss Charlotte Kinnard.
National Banner & Nashville Whig (Sat., July 15, 1826)

Houston, Robert Esq. of Knox County married to Miss Peggie Davis on Thursday last (Mar. 20.)
Knoxville Gazette (Thurs., March 27, 1794)

Houston, Miss Rutilia married to Mr. James Isbell.

Houston, Hon. Samuel married in Sumner County on Thursday evening, 22d inst. to Miss Eliza Allen.
National Banner & Nashville Whig (Tues., Jan. 27, 1829)

Houston, Genl. Samuel of Texas married on the 8th inst. in Marion, Ala. to Miss Margaret Lea.
Daily Republican Banner (Tues., May 19, 1840)

Houston, Mr. William of Brownville married in Sommerville, Fayette County to Miss Mary Bell daughter of Maj. John Bell.
National Banner & Nashville Daily Advertiser (Mon., April 15, 1833)

Houston, Marj. William of Brownville married at Somerville on the 4th ult. Miss Mary E. Ball.
National Banner & Nashville Daily Advertiser (May 6, 1833)

Hover, Andrew J. Esq. of Murfreesborough married in Davidson County to Miss Martha Shute.
Nashville Republican & State Gazette (Tues., Sept. 10, 1833)

Howard, Miss Agnes married to Mr. Richard C. Blain.

Howard, Miss Aminta married to Mr. Charles E. Beynroth.

Howard, Mr. Benjamin R. married in Sumner County to Miss Mary Baker daughter of Isaac Baker Esq.
National Banner & Nashville Daily Advertiser (Tues., June 24, 1834)

Howard, Miss Berrilla married to Mr. George James Poor.

Howard, James Esq. of Sumner County married to Martha Cheatham of this County.
Nashville Republican & State Gazette (Sat., Dec. 25, 1830)

Howard, James Esq. of Sumner County married in Davidson County on the 21st inst. by the Rev. Mr. Hume to Miss Martha Cheatham.
National Banner & Nashville Whig (Mon., Dec. 27, 1830)

Howard, Mr. John married in M'Minn County to Miss Elizabeth Steed.
National Banner & Nashville Daily Advertiser (Mon., Jan. 14, 1833)

Howard, Mr. John P. of Oak Grove on the 23d November married to Miss Martha S. DeClausell of Paris.
Nashville Republican (Sat., Dec. 5, 1835)

Howard, Mr. John R. of Oak Grove married in Paris, Henry County on the 23d Nov. to Miss Martha S. De. Clauselle of Paris.
National Banner & Nashville Whig (Wed., Dec. 9, 1835)

Howard, Miss Louisa married to Mr. Bowling Embry.

Howard, Miss Mary P. married to Mr. James W. Braden.

Howard, Memucan H. Esq. of the Western District married in Nashville on the 11th inst. by the Rev. Mr. Hume to Miss Rebecca Porter.
National Banner & Nashville Daily Advertiser (Mon. Nov. 12, 1832)

Howard, Miss Rosha M. married to John S. Brien, Esq.

Howard, Miss Sarah married to Mr. James Calhoun.

Howard, Miss Sarah H. married to Mr. Samuel Farrer.

Howard, Volney N. Esq. Editor of the Mississippian of Jackson, Mi. married in Baltimore on the 6th March to Miss Catherine E. Gooch of Washington.
National Banner & Nashville Whig (Mon., March 27, 1837)

Howard, Mr. Wardlow merchant married in Hardeman County, Ten. to Miss Mary Polk daughter of Willie Polk Esq.
National Banner & Nashville Whig (Fri., Jan. 23, 1835)

Howard, Mr. William H. of Nashville married in Paris, Henry County to Miss Eliza B. Yarnell of Louisville, Ky.
National Banner & Nashville Daily Advertiser (Tues., Dec. 17, 1833)

Howell, Mr. Duke married in Knox County to Miss Mary Yoast.
National Banner & Nashville Whig (Sat., Nov. 1, 1828)

Howe, Mr. Duke married in Knox County to Miss Elizabeth Deramond.
National Banner (March 24, 1826)

Howell, Mrs. Catharine married to Mr. Thomas Loftin.

Howell, Mr. D. married in Maury County to Miss H. Howell.
National Banner & Nashville Advertiser (Thurs., May 17, 1832)

Howell, Miss E. married to Charles McKinney Esq.

Howell, Miss Elizabeth married to Mr. Benjamin Brady.

Howell, Miss H. married to Mr. D. Howell.

Howell, Mr. James married in Sparta to Miss Nancy Williams.
National Banner & Nashville Whig (Sat., July 22, 1826

Howell, Mr. James married in Rutherford County to Miss Martha Pope.
National Banner & Nashville Daily Advertiser (Sat., Aug. 10, 1833)

Howell, Mr. Seth married in Logan County, Ky. to Miss Selitia Willis.
National Banner & Nashville Whig (Mon., May 23, 1831)

Howerton, Miss Margaret married to Mr. James T. Faulkner.

Howett, Miss Caroline C. married to Mr. Joseph P. Wharton, sen.

Howlett, W. E. Mr. of Nashville married to Miss Jane Gilman of
Davidson County on June 25.
Nashville Republican (Sat., July 4, 1835)

Howlett, Miss Florida married to Mr. William Sandy.

Howlett, Miss Mary Ann married to Mr. James O. Gorman.

Howser, Miss Joanna Wilhelmena married to Mr. Philip Winn.

Hoy, Miss Martha C. married to Mr. Washington C. McCutcheon.

Hubbard, Mr. James married at Knoxville to Miss Ann Dunn.
National Banner (Sat., Nov. 14, 1829)

Hubbard, Mr. James married at Knoxville to Miss Ann Dunn.
National Banner (Sat., Nov. 21, 1829)

Hubbard, Miss Mary M. married to Mr. Reddick P. Moore.

Hubbard, Mr. Obadiah R. married in Smith County to Miss Prudence B.
Rucks daughter of the Rev. Josiah Rucks.
National Banner & Nashville Daily Advertiser (Thurs., Jan. 5, 1832)

Hubbard, Dr. R. D. married in Statesville, Ten. on the 2d inst. by
the Rev. Mr. Picket to Miss Frances Pemberton of that vicinity.
Daily Republican Banner (Tues., Nov. 21, 1837)

Hubbell, Capt. Julius married in Mobile to Miss Mary Ingelson both
of New Orleans.
National Banner & Nashville Whig (Sat., Sept. 9, 1826)

Hubbird, Mr. Archibald B. married in Critteden County, Ark. Ter. to
Miss Charlotte Fooy.
National Banner (Sat., Sept. 5, 1829)

Hubble, Miss Lucretia married to Mr. Mason Pilcher.

Hubble, Parish married in Giles County to Margaret Blain.
National Banner & Nashville Daily Advertiser (Tues., Dec. 17, 1833)

Hudgens, Mr. James A. married in Williamson County to Miss Nancy
Vaughn.
The Western Review - Franklin, Tenn. (Fri., Dec. 23, 1831)

Hudgins, Miss Eliza married to Mr. Robert Davis.

Hudgens, Miss Eliza H. married to Mr. Robert Davis.
National Banner & Nashville Daily Advertiser (Mon., April 1, 1833)

Hudgins, John J. married in Williamson County to Miss Mary Ann Coleman.
The Western Weekly Review - Franklin, Tenn. (Fri., March 8, 1833)

Hudnell, Mr. Baldwin married in Madison County, Miss. on April 19th
by the Rev. Mr. Crawford to Miss Elizabeth S. Hicks.
Daily Republican Banner (Thurs., May 10, 1838)

Hudnell, Miss Elizabeth married to Mr. Leroy P. Walker.

Hudnell, Miss Nancy married to Capt. John Simmons.

Hudson, Mr. Edward married at Moscow, Hickman County, Ky. Oct. 14th.
to Miss Lucy Ann French both of that place.
National Banner & Nashville Whig (Wed., Nov. 4, 1835)

Hudson, Miss Jane married to Rev. Edmund Jones.

Hudson, Mr. John H. married in Henry County to Miss Nancy Wright.
National Banner & Nashville Daily Advertiser (Fri., Jan. 27, 1832)

Hudson, Mr. John Washington married on Sunday the 1st inst. at
Smyrna Meeting House by Thomas Palmer Esq. to Miss Mary Tilly daughter
of George Tilly all of Dickson County.
Daily Republican Banner (Dec. 6, 1839)

Hudspeth, Miss Nancy married to Mr. William Ransome.

Hudspeth, Mr. Samuel married in Franklin County, Tenn. on the 17th inst
by the Rev. William Woods to the beautiful Miss Elenor Browning
daughter of Capt. Robt. S. Browning.
National Banner & Nashville Daily Advertiser (Wed., Sept. 25, 1833)

Huffar, Miss Susan Ann married to Mr. John R. Chambers.

Hugher, Mr. Jeremiah married in Henry County, Ten. since the first of
Jan. to Miss Margaret Clayton.
National Banner & Nashville Whig (Fri., Feb. 13, 1835)

Hughes, Miss Charlotte married to Mr. Benjamin Waxler.

Hughes, Mr. Daniel of Logan County, Ky. married in Lincoln County, Tenn.
to Miss Nancy King daughter of Mr. Turner King of Lincoln Co.
National Banner & Nashville Whig (Wed., Nov. 12, 1834)

Hughes, Miss Diana married to Mr. F. Holt.

Hughes, Miss Elizabeth married to Matthew Jenkins, Esq.

Hughes, Miss Elizabeth married to Mr. Ananias B. Smith.

Hughes, Miss Esther M. married to Mr. Leonard George jun.

Hughes, Mr. Jas. married in Jackson to Miss Martha Parrum.
Nashville Republican & State Gazette (Wed., Jan. 16, 1833)

Hughes, Mr. James M. married on the 21st inst. by the Rev. Mr. R. B. C.
Howell to Miss Amanda S. Hartley all of Nashville.
Nashville Whig (Fri., May 22, 1840)

Hughes, Miss Jane married to Mr. Wm. Neill.

Hughes, Miss Martha J. married to Dr. Henry Y. Webb.

Hughes, Miss Narcissa married to Mr. James B. Hill.

Hughes, Mr. Oliver of Nashville married on Thursday last to Miss Sarah
Ann Morton.
Nashville Republican (Sat., March 7, 1835)

Hughes, Mr. Preston _. married near Port Gibson, Miss. to Miss Elizabeth
Greer.
National Banner & Nashville Whig (Sat., Oct. 28, 1826)

Hughes, Mr. Samuel C. married in August 1831 to Miss Nancy W. Anderson.
The Western Weekly Review - Franklin, Tenn. (Fri., Sept. 2, 1831)

Hughes, Miss Sarah married to Mr. Richard Harman.

Hughes, Miss Sarah Ann married to Mr. Jeremiah L. Smith.

Hughes, Miss Sarah married to Mr. John Tucker.

Hughes, Miss Susan F. married to Mr. Thomas S. Herbert.

Hughes, Miss Susan T. married to Mr. Llewellen A. Temple.

Hughey, James Esq. married in Maury County to Miss Jane Bradley.
National Banner & Nashville Daily Advertiser (Thurs., April 5, 1832)

Hughlett, Miss Elizabeth married to Capt. Samuel Wilson.

Hughlett, Miss Mary married to Mr. Thomas R. Sumner.

Hughlett, Mr. P. M. married in Madison County, Ten. to Miss Unice W. White.
National Banner & Nashville Whig (Fri., Dec. 12, 1834)

Hughs, Miss Christiana T. married to David R. Owen.

Hughs, John F. married in Williamson County to Miss Jane B. Baldridge.
The Western Weekly Review - Franklin, Tenn. (Fri., Dec. 14, 1832)

Hughs, Miss Nancy P. married to Mr. W. B. Dawson.

Hughs, Miss Susan T. married to Mr. Llewellen A. Temple.

Hughs, Tabitha C. married to Nicholas P. Holt.

Hukill, Mr. Joseph married at Louisville, Ky. to Miss Sarah Sinclair.
National Banner & Nashville Whig (Sat., April 26, 1828)

Hulett, Miss Sally married to Mr. James Watts.

Hulin, Mr. James W. married in Williamson County to Miss Mary Murry.
The Western Weekly Review - Franklin, Tenn. - (Fri., Dec. 2, 1831)

Hull, Mr. John married at Steubenville, Ohio to Miss Mary Wampler.
National Banner (June 10, 1826)

Hull, Mr. John M. married last evening by the Rev. Dr. Wharton to Miss Susan G. Lanier all of Nashville.
Nashville Whig (Sat., July 11, 1846)

Hulme, Miss Mary married in Williamson County to Maury Jones.
The Western Weekly Review - Franklin, Tenn. (Fri., March 23, 1832)

Hulme, Miss Menirva married to Capt. Kelsey H. Douglass.

Hulme, William B. married in Williamson County to Miss Mary Leigh.
The Western Weekly Review - Franklin, Tenn. (Fri., March 8, 1833)

Huly, James, Esq. in Maury County married to Jane Bradley.
National Banner & Nashville Advertiser (Thurs., April 5, 1832)

Hume, Mr. Alfred M. married in Davidson County to Miss Louisa Bradford on 12th inst.
Nashville Republican & State Gazette (Thurs., Aug. 14, 1834)

Hume, Ebenezer J. of Nashville married at Washington City on the 26th ult. to Miss Barbara Ellen Berry of Washington.
National Banner & Nashville Daily Advertiser (Wed., March 13, 1833)

Hume, Miss Eliza M. married to Mr. Caleb H. Jones.

Hume, Mr. Fountain married in this town on the 21st ult. to Miss
Alcenia A. Austin.
National Banner (Sat., Nov. 14, 1829)

Hume, Miss Jane married to Mr. Samuel B. Snowden.

Hume, Miss Jane married to Mr. Evan M. Hazard.

Hume, Miss Mary married to Mr. J. M. Turman.

Hume, Mr. Matthew married in Clark County, Ky. to Miss Maria Cunningham.
National Banner & Nashville Whig (Sat., Nov. 22, 1828)

Hume, Mr. Thomas W. married in Knox County, Ten. to Miss Cornelia
Williams daughter of Etheldred Williams Esq.
National Banner & Nashville Whig (Wed., Dec. 17, 1834)

Hume, Mr. William P. of Nashville married on Tuesday the 14th in
Rutherford County, by the Rev. John Henderson to Miss Sarah Ann Manley.
Nashville Whig (Fri., Oct. 16, 1840)

Humerickhouse, Miss Mary married to Mr. Anthony Chapouil.
National Banner & Nashville Daily Advertiser (Mon., March 12, 1832)

Humes, Miss Martha married to Mr. David Speak.

Humes, Miss Mary married to Mr. John White Esq.

Humes, Mr. Thos. W. in Knoxville, Tenn. married to Miss Cornelia
Williams.
Nashville Republican & State Gazette (Tues., Dec. 16, 1834)

Humphress, Mr. Alexander of Blount County married in Knox County to
Miss Isabella Johnson.
National Banner & Nashville Daily Advertiser (Wed., Jan. 30, 1833)

Humphreys, Charles Esq. married at Lexington, Ky. to Elizabeth Rigg.
National Banner & Nashville Whig (Sat., Nov. 4, 1826)

Humphreys, Dr. Charles married in Sommerville, Ala. to Miss Ann Roby.
National Banner & Nashville Whig (Sat., March 31, 1827)

Humphreys, Miss Elizabeth married to Robert S. Todd Esq.

Humphreys, Miss Elizabeth married to Robert S. Todd Esq.

Humphreys, Mrs. Elizabeth married to Daniel Mays Esq.

Humphreys, Miss Elizabeth A. married to Mr. Thomas B. McIlwee.

Humphreys, Miss Elizabeth T. married to Mr. Caleb Bates.

Humphreys, Mr. G. W. married on Oct. 29th to Miss Laurel Sutton both
of Dickson County.
Nashville Republican (Tues., Jan. 19, 1836)

Humphreys, Mr. Hilton married at Athens, Tenn. to Miss Lucinda Toncry.
National Banner & Nashville Daily Advertiser (Mon., Jan. 14, 1833)

Humphreys, Mr. James married in Blount County to Miss Nancy M'Clung.
National Banner & Nashville Whig (Sat., Feb. 23, 1828)

Humphreys, Col. John J. married in Monroe County to Miss Sarah Donohoo.
National Banner & Nashville Whig (Wed., July 27, 1831)

Humphreys, Mr. Julius married on Wednesday 29th June by Rev. Dr. Edgar
to Miss A. E. Lathrop all of Nashville.
National Banner & Nashville Whig (Fri., July 1, 1836)

Humphreys, Miss Mary married to Isham G. Trotter Esq.

Humphreys, Miss Mary Angeline married to Mr. Elijah Morton.

Humphreys, Miss Mary Angeline married to Mr. Elijah Morton.

Humphreys, Mr. Samuel married in Nashville by the Rev. A. L. P. Green to Miss Dorcas Price.
Nashville Republican (Sat., April 16, 1836)

Humphreys, Miss Sarah B. married to Mr. John B. Harris.

Humphreys, Miss Sarah Elizabeth married to Mr. Robert Thompson.

Humphreys, Miss Sarah L. married to Mr. John A. Barnes.

Humphreys, Dr. W. W. married in Madison County, Ala. to Miss Margaret S. Walton.
National Banner & Nashville Daily Advertiser (Thurs., Feb. 21, 1833)

Humphreys, West H. Esq. Attorney at law of Sommerville married in Nashville last evening at the residence of John W. Saunders Esq. by the Rev. J. T. Edgar D.D. to Miss Amanda Pillow of Nashville.
Nashville Union (Wed., Jan. 2, 1839)

Humphreys, West H. Esq. Attorney at Law of Sommerville married in Nashville last evening at the residence of John W. Saunders Esq. by the Rev. J. T. Edgar D.D. to Miss Amanda Pillow of Nashville.
Nashville Whig (Wed., Jan. 2, 1839)

Humphreys, West H. Esq. Attorney at law of Sommerville married in Nashville by the Rev. J. T. Edgar D.D. to Miss Amanda Pillow of Nashville.
Daily Republican Banner (Thurs., Jan. 3, 1839)

Hungerford, Miss Eliza married to Mr. James W. Curry.

Hunning, Mr. Richard married in Madison County, Ten. to Miss Hill.
National Banner & Nashville Whig (Wed., Oct. 19, 1831)

Hunt, A. D. Esq. married in Lauderdale County, Ala. to Miss Ellen Jackson daughter of James Jackson Esq.
National Banner & Nashville Whig (Mon., July 5, 1830)

Hunt, Mr. Charles W. married on the 3d inst. at Valmont to Miss Lucy Ann Ruffin daughter of Maj. James Ruffin all of Hardeman County.
National Banner & Nashville Daily Advertiser (Sat., Sept. 13, 1834)

Hunt, Mr. Douglass R. married in La Grange, Tenn. to Miss Mary Polk.
Nashville Whig (Tues., May 5, 1846)

Hunt, Miss Harriet L. married to Lieut E. Sproat Sibley.

Hunt, Miss Henrietta married to Col. Calvin G. Morgan.

Hunt, Miss Martha married to Mr. Absalem G. Wynne.

Hunt, Miss Minerva married to Mr. Thomas G. McGehee.

Hunt, Mr. Peter Gordon married in Fayette County, Ky to Miss Mary Ann Bullock daughter of Walter Bullock Esq.
National Banner & Nashville Whig (Mon., July 19, 1830)

Hunt, Mr. Ralph P. married in Cincinnati to Miss Adareen Vanderpool.
National Banner (April 7, 1826)

Hunt, Mr. Solomon married in Montgomery County to Miss Nancy Hilliard.
National Banner & Nashville Whig (Fri., May 20, 1831)

Hunt, Dr. Thomas formerly of Charleston, S. C. married at New Orleans to Miss Aglae Charleston of that city.
National Banner & Nashville Daily Advertiser (Tues., May 6, 1834)

Hunt, Mr. William H. of Fayette County married in Madison County to Miss Elizabeth F. Dickins daughter of Capt. Wm. Dickens.
National Banner & Nashville Whig (Mon., Aug. 30, 1830)

Hunter, Miss Amanda married to Mr. Thomas H. Albright.

Hunter, Mrs. Ann D. married to T. Batte Jr. A.P.M.

Hunter, Mrs. Ann O. married to Thomas Batte A.P.M.

Hunter, Miss Caroline E. married to Mr. Monroe Clopton.

Hunter, Miss Eliza Cecil married to Hon. John Macpherson Berrien.

Hunter, Miss Eliza H. married to Mr. Reddick Kitrell.

Hunter, Miss Eliza Sophia married to Mr. Henry Wilkeson.

Hunter, Capt. Jacob married on the 4th inst. by John Wright Esq. to Miss Mary Bolton of Smithland, Ky.
National Banner & Nashville Whig (Mon., June 8, 1835)

Hunter, Dr. James married in Enfield, N. C. to Miss Sarah Branch daughter of the Hon. John Branch.
National Banner & Nashville Daily Advertiser (Fri., Aug. 16, 1833)

Hunter, Dr. James married at Enfield, Halifax County, N. C. to Miss Sarah Branch.
Nashville Republican & State Gazette (Sat., Aug. 17, 1833)

Hunter, Mr. James A. of Wilson married in Smith County to Miss Mary Ann Thompson.
National Banner & Nashville Daily (Mon., Dec. 10, 1832)

Hunter, Mr. Joseph married in Jefferson County to Miss Sarah Kimbrough.
National Banner & Nashville Whig (Fri., Sept. 9, 1831)

Hunter, Leyton Esq. married in Sumner County on Monday 29th ult. to Miss Elizabeth Robertson.
National Banner & Nashville Whig (Sat., Oct. 11, 1828)

Hunter, Miss Margaret J. married to Rev. James Marshall.

Hunter, Miss Martha married to Mr. Walter Cummins.

Hunter, Miss Mary A. married to Mr. Robert P. Faulkner.

Hunter, Mr. Thomas married in Smith County on the 18th inst. to Miss Masey Beasley.
National Banner & Nashville Daily Advertiser (Fri., Jan. 27, 1832)

Huntley, Mr. Luther married in Windham, Conn. to Miss Eunice Lincoln. both parties above seventy years old.
National Banner & Nashville Daily Advertiser (Sat., Nov. 23, 1833)

Huntsman, Adam Esq. married in Madison County to Miss Elizabeth Todd.
National Banner (Sat., June 17, 1829)

Huntsman, Mr. William married in Shelby County to Miss Eliza Banks.
National Banner & Nashville Whig (Sat., Feb. 14, 1829)

Hurts, Mr. Frederick a dwarf, 40 inches in Height married in All Saints Poplar England to Miss Caroline Appleby a lady nearly six feet high.
National Banner & Nashville Whig (Wed., June 7, 1837)

Hurst, Miss Sarah Ann married to William S. Callaway Esq.

Hurst, William Henry Esq. married in Lexington, Ky. to Miss Ann J. Bodley daughter of Gen. Thomas Bodley.
National Banner & Nashville Whig (Fri., April 16, 1830)

Hurt, Mr. A. C. married in Lexington, Ky. to Miss Harriet Grenstead.
National Banner & Nashville Whig (Sat., Feb. 3, 1827)

Hurt, Mr. F. O. married on Thursday the 23d inst. by the Rev. P. P. Neeley to Miss Lucy A. Fulcher daughter of the late J. J. Fulcher all of Nashville
Nashville Whig (Sat., May 25, 1844)

Hurt, Mr. George of Sumner County married in Smith County to Miss Matilda Baker.
National Banner & Nashville Whig (Wed., Jan. 21, 1835)

Hurt, Miss Sarah D. married to Mr. John Fisher.

Hurt, Mr. William late of Va. married in this County on the 10th ult. by the Rev. Mr. White to Miss Elizabeth Bowers.
National Banner & Nashville Whig (Sat., Feb. 21, 1829)

Hurt, Mr. William Berry married in Russellville, Ky. to Miss Ariana Drew.
National Banner & Nashville Daily Advertiser (Sat., March 30, 1833)

Husbands, Mills. married in Williamson County to Miss Sophia W. Nicholson.
The Western Weekly Review - Franklin, Tenn. (Fri., Feb. 1, 1833)

Hussey, Miss Jane married to Ephraim Robins Esq.

Hussey, Miss Margaret married to Mr. William Valiant.

Hussey, Miss Margaret married to Mr. William Valient.

Huston, Miss Ann C. married to Mr. W. Carlile.

Hutcheson, Mr. William C. married in Madison County to Miss Elizabeth May.
National Banner & Nashville Whig. (Thurs., June 3, 1830)

Hutchings, Mr. Andrew J. married in this vicinity on the 14th inst. to Miss Mary Coffee eldest daughter of the late Genl. John Coffee, deceased (Florence Gazette).
The Nashville Republican & State Gazette (Nov. 23, 1833)

Hutchings, Mrs. Elizabeth married to Mr. Phares T. Posey.

Hutchings, Miss Rachel married to Mr. James S. Rollings.

Hutchins, Mr. Andrew J. married near Florence, Ala. to Miss Mary Coffee eldest daughter of the late Gen. Coffee.
National Banner & Nashville Daily Advertiser (Tues., Nov. 19, 1833)

Hutchins, Mr. Andrew J. married in this vicinity to Miss Mary Coffee on the 14th inst.
Nashville Republican & State Gazette (Sat., Nov. 23, 1833)

Hutchins, Miss Eliza married to Mr. W. Williford.

Hutchins, Miss Eliza married to James Robinson Esq.

Hutchins, Miss Eliza B. married to R. M. Gaines Esq.

Hutchins, Miss Elizabeth married to Maj. Jason H. Wilson.

Hutchins, Miss Mary A. married to George W. White, Esq.

Hutchinson, Miss Ann married to Mr. J. T. Adams.

Hutchinson, Mr. John married in Fayette County, Ky. to Miss Alley Parker.
National Banner (Sat., Sept. 5, 1829)

Hutchinson, Miss Martha daughter of Mr. William Hutchinson married to Rev. Eleazar Harris.

Hutchinson, Miss Mary Ann married to Mr. David Laudensan.

Hutchinson, Samuel Esq. married in Russellville, Ky. to Miss Polly W. Eli daughter of Mr. Lawrence Eli.
National Banner & Nashville Whig (Wed., Nov. 26, 1834)

Hutson, Mr. W. G. married on the 31st Dec. by the Rev. J. B. M'Farren to Miss Mary A. Allen both of Davidson County.
The Union (Sat., Jan. 2, 1836)

Hutt, Mr. John married in Shelby County to Miss Haniel Field Shelby County.
National Banner & Nashville Advertiser (Wed., Jan. 4, 1832)

Hutton, Miss Harriet married to Mr. Elias Kane.

Hutton, Miss Sarah married to Mr. William Moore.

Hyde, Mr. Edmund of this County married in Butler County, Ky. on the 8th ult. to Miss Jane Davis daughter of Col. Robert Davis.
National Banner (Jan. 6, 1826)

Hyde, Mr. Edmund married in this County on Thursday 8th inst. to Miss Christiana Rain.
National Banner & Nashville Whig (Sat., Jan. 10, 1829)

Hyde, Miss Elizabeth H. married to Mr. James Green.

Hyde, Miss Mary married to Mr. Blount Drake.

Hyde, Miss Mary D. married to Mr. A. W. Butler.

Hyde, Miss Sarah G. married to Mr. Lawrence S. Mason.

Hyder, Mr. Joseph of Carter County married in Washington County, Tenn. to Miss Ann Elizabeth Nelson daughter of Mr. Jesse Nelson of Jonesboro.
National Banner & Nashville Whig (Fri., Jan. 9, 1835)

Hydes, Miss Ann Eliza married on the 1st inst. by the Rev. P. P. Neely to Mr. Robert A. Barnes all of Davidson County.
Nashville Whig (Sat., May 9, 1844)

Hynds, Benjamin D. married on 28th ult. by Rev. J. Allison to Miss Sarah E. Hardeman daughter of Constant Hardeman, Esq.
Daily Republican Banner (Tues., Oct. 3, 1837)

Hynes, Col. Andrew of this place married at the residence of Captain Joseph Erwin on Sunday evening the 2nd inst. by the Rev. Mr. Blackburn to Miss Nancy Erwin daughter of the first named Gentleman Joseph Erwin.
The Nashville Whig (March 5, 1817)

Hynes, Miss Finetta married to Mr. Eli Moores.

Hynes, Miss Lavinia married to Edward J. Gay Esq.

Hynes, Miss Margaret married to Mr. Andrew Ewing.

Hynes, Miss Mary Jane married to Mr. Phocion R. McCreery.

Hynes, Miss Rachel married to Mr. Seth Stowell.

Hynson, Miss Harriet Overton married to Rev. Alexander Van Court.

Inge, Miss Agnes married to Mr. James C. Jones.

Inge, Mr. Robert of Tenn. married at Tuscaloosa to Miss Agatha S. Marr.
National Banner & Nashville Advertiser (Fri., Dec. 21, 1832)

Ingelson, Miss Mary married to Capt. Julius Hubbell.

Ingersol, Mr. Charles married in Philadelphia to Miss Susan Catherine Brown daughter of the late Dr. Samuel Brown.
National Banner & Nashville Whig (Wed., Dec. 14, 1831)

Inglis, Miss Frances Erskine married to Chavalier A. Calderon DeLa Barca.

Inglish, Miss Jane married to Mr. David D. Green.

Ingram, Miss Charlate married to James Adams.

Ingram, Miss Charlotte married to James Adams.

Ingram, Mr. Henry of Nashville married to Miss Susan Nichols on Sunday last.
Impartial Review & Cumerland Repository - published at Nashville. (Thurs., Aug. 11, 1808)

Ingram, Mr. Ira married on the 13th inst. at New Orleans to Miss Emily B. Holt recently of this town.
Nashville Whig (April 2, 1823)

Ingram, Mr. J. C. merchant of Dover married in Christian County, Ky. to Miss Margaret Kay daughter of Mr. James Kay.
National Banner & Nashville Daily Advertiser (Sat., Sept. 1, 1832)

Ingram, Miss Julie E. married to Mr. James H. Cecil.

Ingram, Miss Mary married to Mr. William Hammonds.

Ingram, Miss Nancy married to Mr. Isaac Burton.

Ingram, Miss Susan married to Mr. Benjamin F. Hill.

Ingram, Mr. Thomas C. married at Hopkinsville to Miss Martha Myers.
National Banner & Nashville Advertiser (Mon., Setp. 17, 1832)

Inis, Mr. Henry married in Franklin County, Ky. to Miss Penelope Sullinger.
National Banner & Nashville Whig (Sat., May 19, 1827)

Inman, Lewis D. married in Williamson County, Ten. to Nancy M. Goff.
National Banner & Nashville Daily Advertiser (Mon., Aug. 26, 1833)

Inman, Miss Margaret H. married to Maj. Jonathan Wood.

Inman, Mr. Wilson married in Jefferson County to Miss Ann Lea.

Innes, Miss Susan G. married to Capt. William Bryan.

Instone, Miss Jane Isibell married to Mr. William Botts.

Inyard, Miss Rosetta married to Mr. Robert Hawkins.

Iradale, Miss Elizabeth married to Capt. Daniel T. Sanders.

Irby, Dr. Edmund married in Huntsville to Miss Mary G. Mastin.
Nashville Republican & State Gazette (Wed., Jan. 30, 1833)

Irby, Mr. Francis W. married at Abingdon, Va. to Miss Jane Preston.
Nashville Whig (Feb. 26, 1823)

Iredale, Miss Sally married to Mr. Joseph Keen.

Irion, Dr. Robert A. of this State married in Vicksburg, Miss. to Miss Ann A. Vick.
National Banner & Nashville Whig (Sat., Aug. 12, 1826)

Irvin, Mr. Abraham married in Lincoln County, Ky. to Miss Pamelia Moss.
National Banner (Feb. 3, 1826)

Irvin, Matilda married in Williamson County, Ten. to David Coughanour.

Irvine, Mr. Charles married in Maury County to Miss Parthena Chaple.
National Banner & Nashville Whig (Mon., Sept. 26, 1831)

Irvine, Miss Sally Ann married to Mr. Madison C. Johnson.

Irwin, Mr. Allen H. married in Madison County, Ala. to Miss Eliza Waddell.
National Banner & Nashville Whig (Mon., May 23, 1831)

Irwin, Miss E. married to Thomas J. Long.
National Banner & Nashville Daily Advertiser (Mon., June 30, 1834)

Irwin, James Esq. of Florence, Ala. married at Pittsburgh to Miss Emily Boggs.
National Banner & Nashville Whig (Sat., Aug. 4, 1827)

Irwin, Mr. James of Murfreesborough married in Harden County to Miss Ann Sevier of Green County.
National Banner & Nashville Whig (Sat., Jan. 17, 1829)

Irwin, Mr. James S. of Pittsburg married in Louisville, Ky. to Miss. Ann E. Duncan.
National Banner & Nashville Whig (Fri., May 20, 1831)

Irwin, Mr. Joseph C. married in Louisville, Ky. on the 9th inst. by the Rev. G. W. Ashbridge to Miss Ann O. Showard.
National Banner & Nashville Daily Advertiser (Sat., July 13, 1833)

Irwin, Miss Margaret married to Mr. Edward Alford.

Irwin, Miss Mary Ann married to Mr. James H. Christopher.

Irwin, Miss Nancy married to Captain William Armstrong.

Irwin, Miss Nancy married to Mr. John Alford.

Irwin, Miss Sally married to Mr. Horatio.

Irwin, William M. Esq. of Nashville married on the 27th inst by the Rev. Dr. Edgar to Miss Elizabeth McKeage daughter of Mr. John McKeage of Clarksville, Tenn.
Nashville Whig (Mon., Aug. 31, 1840)

Irwine, Mr. Charles married in Maury County to Miss Parthena Chapel.
National Banner & Nashville Whig (Mon., Sept. 26, 1831)

Isaacs, Miss Coerella married to Mr. O. D. Williams.

Isaacks, Mr. Smith married in Campbell County to Miss Polly Ballard.
National Banner & Nashville Whig (June 14, 1826)

Isbell, Mr. C. K. married in Athens, Ala. to Miss Ann Crawford.
National Banner & Nashville Daily Advertiser (Wed., July 10, 1834)

Isbell, Mr. James of Ala. married in Knox County to Miss Rutilia Houston daughter of Robert Houston, Esq.
National Banner & Nashville Daily Advertiser (Wed., April 3, 1833)

Isbille, Miss Mary married to Mr. Andrew Flowes.

Isham, Miss Mary married to Rev'd. Silas Totten.

Isom, Col. Arthur T. of Maury County married to Miss Eleanora D.
Goodall in Rutherford County on Wednesday 5 inst.
National Banner & Nashville Whig (Fri., Oct. 7, 1831)

Israel, Miss Nancy married to Dr. Williams.

Ivens, Mr. James W. of Gallatin married on Wednesday the 27th ult.
by Rev. J. B. Ferguson to Miss Ann V. Davis of Nashville.
Nashville True Whig & Weekly Commercial Register (Fri., April 5, 1850)

Ivey, Capt. Charles married in Rutherford County, Tenn. to Miss
Judy Wood.
National Banner & Nashville Whig (Wed., Sept. 24, 1834)

Ivy, Mr. Isaac married in Williamson County to Miss Nancy Spence.
The Western Weekly Review - Franklin, Tenn. (Fri., Dec. 23, 1831)

Ivy, Miss Joannah married to Mr. J. W. Pritchard.

Jabine, Mr. Charles married in Louisville, Ky. to Miss Hudley Ann Eliza Reel.
National Banner & Nashville Whig (Sat., July 29, 1826)

Jack, Miss Harriet married to Lewis A. Garrett Esq.

Jack, Mr. Turner F. married in Giles County on Tuesday evening last to Miss Caroline L. Perry daughter of James Perry Esq.
National Banner (Sat., Nov. 14, 1829)

Jackson, Andrew Jun, Esq. adopted son of the President of the United States married in Philadelphia by the Rev. Mr. Barnes on the 15th ult. to Miss Sarah Yorke daughter of the late Peter York Esq.
National Banner & Nashville Whig (Mon., Dec. 12, 1831)

Jackson, Mr. Asa Jr. married on the 14th inst. by the Rev. John Kelley to Miss Elizabeth Jane Davis daughter of Isham C. Davis all of Wilson County.
Nashville Whig (Tues., Nov. 14, 1844)

Jackson, Mr. Dempsey P. married at Natchez to Miss Maria Jane Forsyth.
National Banner & Nashville Whig (Sat., Feb. 23, 1828)

Jackson, Miss Ellen married to A. D. Hunt, Esq.

Jackson, Mr. Frederick R. married in Tipton County to Miss Mary E. Davis.
National Banner & Nashville Whig (Sat., Dec. 16, 1826)

Jackson, Mr. James married in Amite County, Mississippi to Miss Ann Berryhill.
National Banner (Jan. 27, 1826)

Jackson, Mr. John R. married in Gallatin, Ten. to Miss Julia B. Watwood.
National Banner & Nashville Daily Advertiser (Wed., March 21, 1833)

Jackson, Mrs. Mary married to Master Charles Brady.

Jackson, Miss Mary T. married to Mr. Hawkins Simmons.

Jackson, Miss Mary T. married to Mr. Hawkins Simmons.

Jackson, Rachel Miss married to Dr. John W. Lawrence.

Jackson, Miss Sarah B. married to Mr. Alexander J. Dyas.

Jackson, Mr. Thomas married last evening by the Rev. Dr. Edgar to Miss Mary Keys both of Nashville.
Nashville Whig (Fri., July 5, 1839)

Jackson, Mr. Thomas married on Thursday last by the Rev. Dr. Edgar to Miss Mary Keyes all of Nashville.
Nashville Union (Mon., July 8, 1839)

Jackson, Mr. William married in Maury County to Miss Mary Kitnell.
National Banner & Nashville Daily Advertiser (Wed., March 6, 1833)

Jackson, Mr. William late of New York married on the 4th inst. by the Rev. G. A. Goodlett to Miss Emily Jointer of Sumner County,Tenn.
The Christian Record (Sat., March 13, 1847)

Jackson, Miss Winnie married to Mr. Franklin Hoster.
National Banner & Nashville Whig (Fri., May 1, 1835)

Jacobs, Miss Catherine married to Hon. Thomas Emmerson.

Jacobs, Miss Catherine married to Mr. Joseph Toca.

Jacobs, Miss Elizabeth married to Mr. Jeremiah Baxter.

Jagges, Mr. Thos. J. married in Williamson County to Miss Frances A. Bateman.
National Banner & Nashville Whig (Fri., Feb. 13, 1835)

James, Miss Ann married to Mr. Jacob Shall.

James, Miss Ann married to Mr. Benjamin Franklin Brown.

James, Mrs. Catherine married to Maj. William E. Owen.

James, Miss Jane C. married to Mr. Larkin Bradford.

James, Mr. John J. married at Cincinnati to Miss Margaret Keating.
National Banner & Nashville Whig (Sat., July 15, 1826)

James, Mr. Thos. A. married in August 1831 to Miss Elizabeth A. Baily.
The Western Weekly Review - Franklin, Tenn. (Fri., Sept. 2, 1831)

Jamison, Miss Charlotte married to Mr. Jesse Ely.

Jamison, Miss Mary A. married to Mr. Robert H. Greenwood.

Jamison, Miss Sarah married to Mr. James Frazier.

January, Mr. W. H. married in Rutherford County to Miss Matilda J. Hardeman.
Nashville Whig (Tues., April 21, 1846)

Jarman, Miss Sally married to Mr. Thomas Price.

Jarmon, Mrs. Mary D. married to Mr. Albert G. Duncan.

Jarnagan, Mr. Chesley married in Granger County to Miss Martha Gill.
National Banner (Feb. 10, 1826)

Jarnagin, Miss Caroline A. married to Dr. J. B. Grisby.

Jarnagin, Miss Caroline A. married to Dr. J. B. Grigsby.

Jarnagin, Miss Lavinia L. married to Dr. Wm. J. J. Morrow.

Jarnegin, Mr. Thomas P. married in Henry County to Miss E. K. Randle.
Nashville Whig (Tues., May 5, 1846)

Jarred, Mr. Samuel married in Smith County to Miss Mary Scruggs.
National Banner & Nashville Daily Advertiser (Sat., March 3, 1832)

Jarrett, Mr. Jacob married in Rutherford County to Miss Mary Morris.
National Banner & Nashville Whig (Sat., Feb. 3, 1827)

Jarrett, Miss Mary Ann married to Mr. Robert Bensford.

Jarrett, Miss Purlener N. married to Mr. Wm. E. North.

Jauralman, Mr. Robert married in Knox County, Tenn. to Miss Maria W. Cardwell daughter of the Rev. P. Cardwell.
National Banner & Nashville Whig (Wed., March 11, 1835)

Jefferson, Miss Ann S. married to Dr. John R. Ford.

Jefferson, Miss Frances A. married to Rev. James Erwin.

Jefferson, Miss Melissa married to Mr. John B. Ashe.

Jefferson, Dr. Thomas B. of Summer County married in this county on Thursday evening last to Miss Martha Graves.
National Banner & Nashville Whig (Sat., April 28, 1827)

Jeffords, Mrs. Sarah married to Mr. William K. Lawson.

Jeffreys, Miss Helen Love married to Mr. Augustus Williams.

Jeffreys, Mr. Henry married on Thursday evening 26th inst. to Miss Caroline Caycè all of Nashville.
National Banner & Nashville Daily Advertiser (Fri., Dec. 27, 1833)

Jeffreys, Miss Lucy P. married to Mr. Alexander Thompson.

Jeffreys, Miss Sarah T. married to Mr. William T. Williamson.

Jemison, Miss Nancy E. married to Mr. John Scott.

Jenckes, Edwin of Smithfield, Rhode Island married in this city (Prividence, R. I.) Tuesday 14th inst. by the Rev. Mr. Boyden to Mary Adaline Johnson daughter of the late Joseph H. Johnson of Nashville, Tenn.
Nashville True Whig & Weekly Commercial Register (Fri., May 31, 1850)

Jenkins, Miss Ann L. married to Mr. Isaac N. Carson.

Jenkins, Mr. Benjamin F. married in Franklin County, Tenn. to Miss Eliza Johnson daughter of John O. Johnson, Esq.
National Banner & Nashville Whig (Wed., May 13, 1835)

Jenkins, Catharine married to Mr. Benjamin B. Smith.

Jenkins, Mr. Ebenezer married at Maysville, Ky. to Miss Sarah Wood.
National Banner & Nashville Daily Advertiser (Mon., July 30, 1832)

Jenkins, Mr. Elisha married Miss Eley Grady in Lexington, Ky.
National Banner & Nashville Whig (Fri., Feb. 12, 1830)

Jenkins, Jeremiah married in Williamson County to Miss Sally Glymph.
The Western Weekly Review - Franklin, Tenn. (Fri., Dec. 14, 1832)

Jenkins, Jonnathan aged 74 married in Garrard County to Ann Hancock aged 73.
National Banner & Nashville Whig (Sat., Sept. 2, 1826)

Jenkins, Miss Malinda married to Mr. George W. Cody.

Jenkins, Matthew Esq. married in St. Augustine, Florida to Miss Elizabeth Hughes late of Lexington, Ky.
National Banner & Nashville Whig (Sat., Sept. 2, 1826)

Jenkins, Mr. Philip H. of Maury married in Williamson County to Miss Sarah Parham.
National Banner & Nashville Whig (Sat., Aug. 11, 1827)

Jenkins, Miss Sarah E. married to Mr. James F. Roberts.

Jenkins, Mr. Valentine Hardeman County married to Frances Thompson daughter of the Rev. Henry Thompson.
National Banner & Nashville Whig (Fri., May 27, 1831)

Jenkins, Rev. William married in Bedford County to Miss Mary Uliss.
National Banner & Nashville Whig (Sat., Feb. 7, 1829)

Jenkins, Dr. William H. of Ala. married in Dresden, Tenn. to Miss Ann Glenn.
Nashville Republican (Tues., Jan. 5, 1836)

Jennings, Miss married to Col. Young Ewing in Christian County, Ky.
National Banner & Nashville Whig (Sat., Nov. 4, 1826)

Jennings, Miss Ann E. married to Henry A. Wise Esq.

Jennings, Miss Mary S. married to F. H. Morgan.

Jennings, Miss Nancy married to Mr. Isaac Ellis.

Jennings, Miss Rebecca married to Geo. C. Childress, Esq.

Jent, Miss Christiana married to Mr. Joseph Seay.

Jerman, Miss Sarah married to Mr. John L. Crutchfield.

Jeter, Miss Elizabeth married to William W. Jeter.

Jeter, William W. married in Williamson County to Miss Elizabeth Jeter.
The Western Weekly Review - Franklin, Tenn. (Fri., May 11, 1832)

Jeter, Mr. Wm. W. married in Williamson County to Miss Elizabeth Jeter.
National Banner & Nashville Advertiser (Wed., May 16, 1832)

Jetton, Miss Jane married to Mr. Benjamin Brothers.

Jetton, Mr. Lewis married in Rutherford County to Miss Rebecca Goodloe.
National Banner & Nashville Whig (Sat., Feb. 21, 1829)

Jetton, Miss Mary married to Mr. Dudley Graham.

Jetton, Mr. Rufus married at Murfreesboro to Miss Mary M. Fletcher daughter of Mr. Jeremiah W. Fletcher.
National Banner (Sat., Nov. 14, 1829)

Jetton, Miss Susan married to Francis Norman.

Jewett, Thomas L. Esq. of New York City married in Smithland, Ky. by the Rev. Mr. Willis to Miss Jane G. Balknap of Smithland, Ky.
National Banner & Nashville Whig (Fri., April 21, 1837)

Jewett, Thos. L. of the city of New York married in Smithland, Ky. by the Rev. Mr. illis to Miss Jane G. Belknap of Smithland, Ky.
Nashville Republican (Sat., April 22, 1837)

Job, Anthony married in Williamson County to Lavinia Franklin.
National Banner & Nashville Whig (Wed., Sept. 24, 1834)

Jackers, Mr. C. J. married on the 15th by Rev. Dr. Lapsley to Mrs. S. A. Whalon.
Nashville True Whig & Weekly Commercial Register (Fri., Oct. 18, 1850)

Jogan, Miss Caroline E. married to Mr. James Longenatti.

Johns, Miss Martha married to Dr. William Thompson.

Johns, Miss Martha married to Dr. William L. Thompson.

Johns, Miss Mary Elizabeth married to Mr. William Cowan.

Johns, Miss Rhoda T. married to Mr. Wm. R. Dickerson.

Johns, Miss Sarah Ann married to Mr. William J. Biles.

Johns, Miss Sarah H. married to Mr. John Postlhwait Jr. of Covington.
Nashville Republican & State Gazette (Fri., Feb. 1, 1833)

Johns, Miss Sarah H. married to Mr. John Postlethwait Jr.

Johnson, Mr. A. J. married on Sunday last by Rev. John L. Smith to Mrs. Sophia McBride all of Nashville.
Nashville True Whig & Weekley Commercial Register (Fri., Oct. 25, 1850)

Johnson, Col. A. W. of the House of Johnson, Rayburn & Co. married
recently in Nashville by the Rev. McFerrin to Mrs. Mary Chaney
daughter of Capt. George S. Smith of this vicinity.
Nashville Whig (Wed., Aug. 9, 1838)

Johnson, Lieut. Albert married in Louisville, Ky. to Miss Henrietta
Preston.
National Banner & Nashville Whig (Sat., Feb. 7, 1829)

Johnson, Miss America married to John Cowan.

Johnson, Miss Ann married to Mr. Philip Bailey.

Johnson, Mr. Ben married in Williamson County, Ten. to Miss Adelia
C. Nolen daughter of Lee Nolen Esq.
National Banner & Nashville Whig (Fri., March 6, 1835)

Johnson, Mr. Benjamin married in Williamson County to Miss Adelia C.
Nolen, daughter of Mr. Lee Nolen, Esq.
National Banner & Nashville Whig (Feb. 13, 1835)

Johnson, Miss Brittania married in Williamson Co. to Richard C. Jones.

Johnson, Miss Catharine married to Mr. Stephen White.

Johnson, Miss Catharine married to Mr. S. White.

Johnson, Miss Catherine married to Mr. Pearce Gillee.

Johnson, Mr. Cosby D. married in Davidson County to Miss Martha Ann
Cheatham.
Nashville Republican (Tues., July 14, 1835)

Johnson, Miss Cynthia married to Dr. James Q. Anthony.
Johnson, Dr. Daniel H. of Bedford County married in Weakly County, Ten.
by John H. Moor Esq. to Miss Lucy Brook daughter of William Brook.
National Banner & Nashville Daily Advertiser (Sat., June 16, 1832)

Johnson, Miss Eliza married to Mr. Edward Oliver.

Johnson, Miss Eliza married to Mr. John Hawkin.

Johnson, Miss Eliza married to Mr. Johnson Davis.

Johnson, MIss Eliza married to Mr. Marshall P. Pinckard.

Johnson, Miss Eliza married to Mr. Marshall P. Pinkard.

Johnson, Miss Eliza married to Mr. Benjamin F. Jenkins.

Johnson, Miss Elizabeth married to Mr. Isaac Fisk.

Johnson, Miss Elizabeth married to Mr. Josiah Purdy.

Johnson, Miss Elizabeth J. married to Victor M. Flournoy, Esq.

Johnson, Miss Elizabeth Jane married to Milbry F. Herne Esq.

Johnson, Elizabeth W. married to Eli M. Corzine.

Johnson, Miss Esther D. married to Mr. Alexander D. Ayres.

Johnson, Mr. Freeman married in Williamson County to Miss Sarah McGuire.
National Banner & Nashville Whig (Fri., Feb. 13, 1835)

Johnson, Mr. George J. married in Nashville on Thursday evening last
by the Rev. Mr. Robertson to Miss Martha Ann Spain.
National Banner & Nashville Daily Advertiser (Fri., Jan. 11, 1833)

Johnson, Miss Hannah married to Mr. Robert Harper.

Johnson, Miss Harriet married to Mr. John Craig.

Johnson, Mr. Henry Clerk & Post Master married at Red River Forge Montgomery County on the 14th ult. to Miss Sarah Northington.
National Banner & Nashville Whig (Sat., Dec. 9, 1826)

Johnson, Hon. Henry late Governor of La. married at Georgetown, D.C. to Miss Elizabeth Key daughter of the late Philip Barton Key.
National Banner (Sat., Oct. 31, 1829)

Johnson, Isaac married in Williamson County, Ten. to Lucy Williams.
National Banner & Nashville Whig (Wed., Dec. 17, 1834)

Johnson, Miss Isabella married to Mr. Alexander Humphress.

Johnson, Mr. J. married in Williamson County, Ten. to Miss Minerva Jordan.
National Banner & Nashville Whig (Fri., Feb. 13, 1835)

Johnson, Mr. James married in Louisville, Ky. to Miss Sarah Smetson.
National Banner & Nashville Whig (Sat., Nov. 15, 1828)

Johnson, Mr. James married in Bedford County to Miss Jane Rolling.
National Banner & Nashville Daily Advertiser (Wed., June 27, 1832)

Johnson, Mr. James married in Williamson County, Tenn. to Miss Narcissa Merritt.
National Banner & Nashville Whig (Mon., Nov. 10, 1834)

Johnson, Mr. James married in Henry County, Ten. to Miss Sarah Brigg.
National Banner & Nashville Whig (Fri., May 1, 1835)

Johnson, Mr. James A. married in Madison County, Ala. to Miss Elizabeth Ellett daughter of Mr. Richard Ellett.
National Banner & Nashville Whig (Wed., Mar. 16, 1831)

Johnson, Mr. James H. married in Knox County to Miss Elizabeth Courier.
National Banner (Sat., Dec. 19, 1829)

Johnson, Miss Jane married to Mr. James Alston.

Johnson, Mr. John married in Chillicothe, Ohio to Miss H. A. Rogers.
National Banner & Nashville Whig (Sat., Dec. 9, 1826)

Johnson, Mr. John married in Madison County, Ten. to Miss Temperance S. Alston.
National Banner & Nashville Whig (Wed., Aug. 17, 1831)

Johnson, Mr. John B. married in Columbia to Miss Eliza Ann Baird on the 8th inst.
Nashville Republican (Tues., Oct. 20, 1835)

Johnson, Mr. Joseph H. married in this town on Thursday evening 8th inst. to Miss Harriet Richmond.
National Banner & Nashville Whig (Sat., Jan. 10, 1829)

Johnson, Miss Laroah A. married to Mr. John W. Gorham.

Johnson, Mr. Levi married in Bedford County, Ten. to Miss Elizabeth Nash daughter of Mr. Travis C. Nash.
National Banner & Nashville Whig (Wed., Feb. 25, 1835)

Johnson, Miss Lucinda married to Mr. John A. Wheeler.

Johnson, Mr. Madison C. married in Madison County, Ky. to Miss Sally Ann Irvine.
National Banner & Nashville Whig (Sat., Jan. 10, 1829)

Johnson, Miss Mahala married to Mr. Wm. A. Griffis.

Johnson, Miss Martha married to Mr. John Byrd.

Johnson, Miss Mary married to Mr. Joseph B. Knowles.

Johnson, Miss Mary married to Mr. Samuel S. Perkins.

Johnson, Mary Adaline married to Edwin Jenckes.

Johnson, Miss Mary D. married to Mr. Dempsey Weaver.

Johnson, Miss Mary D. married to Dempsey Weaver, Esq.

Johnson, Miss Mary E. married to Mr. Samuel P. Devore.

Johnson, Miss Mary G. married to Mr. William M. Coleman.

Johnson, Miss Mary H. married to Rev. John B. M'Kinney.

Johnson, Miss Mary Jane D. married to Mr. Alfred W. R. Harris.

Johnson, Miss Mary S. married to Mr. Thompson P. Anderson.

Johnson, Miss Mary S. married to Mr. Thomas P. Anderson

Johnson, Miss Mary W. married to Mr. Geo. W. Hackney.

Johnson, Miss Milly married to Mr. Hosen Ward.

Johnson, Miss Nancy L. married to Mr. Isaac N. McGinnis.

Johnson, Miss Polly married to Mr. Wiley Beasley.

Johnson, Mr. R. B. of Lebanon married in Gallatin, Ten. to Miss E. T.
Winchester of Sumner County.
National Banner & Nashville Daily Advertiser (Fri., Sept. 19, 1834)

Johnson, Mr. Reuben married at Carthage on the 27th ult. to Miss
Matilda Wilkinson both of Lebanon.
National Banner & Nashville Whig (Wed., Nov. 2, 1831)

Johnson, Mr. Rob. G. married in Perry County, Ala. to Miss Mary Curry.
National Banner (Feb. 17, 1826)

Johnson, Mr. Robert married in Madison County, Ky. to Miss Hannah
M'Queen.
National Banner (Sat., May 16, 1829)

Johnson, Miss Sally married to Edger Haywood Esq.

Johnson, Sidney L. Esq. Attorney at Law, N. Orleans married on Sunday
20th inst. by the Rev. Dr. Edgar to Miss Cornelia F. Covington daughter of Gen. Covington, of Bowling Green, Ky.
Daily Republican Banner (Tues., Oct. 22, 1839)

Johnson, Mr. Simeon W. married in Louisville, Ky. to Miss Eliza M.
Suel.
National Banner & Nashville Daily Advertiser (Thurs., June 19, 1834)

Johnson, Simon married in Maury County to Miss Nicy Swim.
National Banner & Nashville Daily Advertiser (Thurs., April 5, 1832)

Johnson, Miss Susan H. married to Mr. Andrew A. F. Allen.

Johnson, Miss Susanna L. married to Rev. Wm. F. Spann.

Johnson, Sydney L. Esq. of New Orleans married on the 20th inst. by
Rev. Dr. Edgar at the residence of Mr. John P. Erwin to Miss Cornelia

daughter of Gen. Covington.
Nashville Whig (Wed., Oct. 23, 1839)

Johnson, Miss Tennessee Virginia married to Rev. T. B. Craighead.

Johnson, Mr. Thomas married in Maury County to Miss Coleman daughter
of Col. Thomas Coleman.
National Banner (Feb. 10, 1826)

Johnson, Mr. Thomas B. married in Fayette County, Ky. to Miss Harriet
Patterson.
National Banner & Nashville Whig (Sat., March 1, 1828)

Johnson, Mr. Thomas H. married in Nashville to Miss Ellen Ann Weaver.
Nashville Union (Mon., Dec. 2, 1839)

Johnson, Mr. W. of Livingston County married in Frankfort, Ky. to Miss.
Catherine Scott.
National Banner & Nashville Daily Advertiser (Thurs., June 19, 1834)

Johnson, Mr. William A. married on Tuesday evening 31st inst. by the
Rev. Dr. Wharton to Miss Ellen R. Hart all of Nashville.
Nashville Whig (Thurs., Nov. 9,1843)

Johnson, Mr. William H. married on Thursday the 10th inst. by the
Rev. J. B. McFerrin to Miss Mongiana Napier daughter of the late
James Napier all of Nashville.
Nashville Whig (Sat., Sept. 12, 1846)

Johnson, Mr. William S. married at Frankford, Ky. to Miss Rebecca C.
Miller.
National Banner & Nashville Whig (Sat., Aug. 9, 1828)

Johnston, Miss Alsy married to Dr. William Clay.

Johnston, Mr. Daniel A. of Springfield married on Thursday 26th inst.
by the Rev. Mr. West to Miss Arabella Williams daughter of Harris
Williams of Nashville.
The Politician & Weekly Nashville Whig (Wed., Sept. 1st, 1847)

Johnston, George W. Esq. married in Columbia to Mrs. Nancy W. Andrews.
Nashville Whig (Tues., May 5, 1846)

Johnston, Miss Maria married to Capt. J. V. Troup.

Johnston, Miss Sarah married to Mr. Wm. S. Hamilton.

Joiner, Miss Emily married to Mr. William Jackson.

Joiner, Miss Martha married to Mr. Frederick Leaticker.

Jokes, Mr. Thomas married at Pittsburgh to Mrs. Ann Smith.
National Banner & Nashville Whig (Sat., Feb. 23, 1828)

Joman, Nancy A. married to John Yates.

Jones, Miss married to Mr. John L. Terrell.

Jones, Mr. married in Bedford Co., Tenn. to Miss Virginia Webster
daughter of Col. J. Webster.
National Banner & Nashville Daily Advertiser (Tues., Aug. 19, 1834)

Jones, Mr. married in Giles County to Miss Martha Harwood.
National Banner & Nashville Daily Advertiser (Tues., Sept. 9, 1834)

Jones, Mr. Abner married in Maury County to Miss Maria Bobbitt.
National Banner & Nashville Whig (Fri., Feb. 19, 1830)

Jones, Miss Aly married to Mr. Hugh D. Neilson.

Jones, Miss Amanda married to Mr. Edmund Burton.

Jones, Miss Amelia A. married to Mr. John M. Hannah.

Jones, Miss Ann Eliza married to Mr. John K. Yerger.

Jones, Miss Ann Eliza married to Nathan Ross Jr. Esq.

Jones, Mr. Barnett married in Williamson County to Miss Mary Martin.
The Western Weekly Review - Franklin, Tenn. (Fri., Dec. 2, 1831)

Jones, Mr. Barnett married in Williamson County to Miss Mary Martin.
National Banner & Nashville Whig (Wed., Dec. 7, 1831)

Jones, Mr. Berthier of Memphis, Tenn. married in Emelia County, Va.
on the 25th ult. to Miss Martha Ward Baker.
National Banner & Nashville Advertiser (Thurs., Aug. 23, 1832)

Jones, Mr. Bird S. married in Madison County to Miss Abigail M. Arnold.
National Banner & Nashville Whig (Fri., Nov. 18, 1831)

Jones, Miss Burnethe married to Dr. Henry Brooks.

Jones, Mr. Caleb H. of Winchester married on the 24th inst. by the
Rev. Dr. Weller to Miss Eliza M. Hume daughter of the late Rev. Wm.
Hume.
National Banner & Nashville Whig (Mon., May 25, 1835)

Jones, Calvin Esq. of Pulaski, Ten. married in Person County, N. C. on
the 15th Oct. to Miss Mildred Williamson daughter of the late James
Williamson.
National Banner & Nashville Whig (Wed., Nov. 11, 1835)

Jones, Miss Catherine married to Wm. Hart.

Jones, Mr. Daniel D. married in Bardstown, Ky. to Miss Mary M. Simpson.
National Banner & Nashville Whig (Sat., Feb. 7, 1829)

Jones, Mr. David married in Knox County to Miss Letetia Browning.
National Banner & Nashville Whig (Sat., Dec. 30, 1826)

Jones, Miss Dolly married to Dr. John H. Camp.

Jones, Miss E. F. married to Dr. John W. Danks.

Jones, Rev. Edmund married in Madison County to Miss Jane Hudson.
National Banner (Sat., April 11, 1829)

Jones, Edward H. married in Giles County to Emeline Keeling.
National Banner & Nashville Daily Advertiser (Tues., Dec. 17, 1833)

Jones, Mr. Elisha married in Maury County, Ten. to Miss Charlotte
Shelton.
National Banner & Nashville Whig(Wed., Feb. 25, 1835)

Jones, Miss Eliza J. married to Mr. Turner Coleman.

Jones, Miss Elizabeth married to Mr. Wm. Pulley.

Jones, Miss Elizabeth married to Mr. Robert Craig.

Jones, Miss Elizabeth Ann married to Mr. Jesse Bell.

Jones, Miss Elizabeth M. married to Mr. Martin W. Oakley.

Jones, Miss Elizabeth M. married to Mr. Charles E. Hillman.

Jones, Miss Ellen married to Mr. John Work.

Jones, Miss Elvira married to Mr. Thomas J. Winston.

Jones, Dr. F. J. of Trenton married in Logan County, Ky. to Miss Fannyline.
National Banner & Nashville Whig (Sat., June 16, 1827)

Jones, Miss Frances married to Mr. John Conally.

Jones, G. W. Esq. Attorney at Law married in Fincastle, Va. to Miss Mary T. Anderson daughter of Col. Wm. Anderson.
National Banner & Nashville Daily Advertiser (Wed., July 16, 1834)

Jones, Rev. Gilford married in Carthage, Tenn. to Miss Mary Lee.
National Banner & Nashville Whig (Wed., Nov. 26, 1834)

Jones, Dr. Geo. W. of Dinwiddie County, Va. married on Wednesday the 10th inst. to Miss Christina G. Dance of Wilson County, Tennessee.
The Nashville Whig & Tenn. Advertiser (Dec. 29, 1817)

Jones, Mr. H. M. married to Miss Eliza M. Harrison
National Banner & Nashville Whig (Fri., March 6, 1835)

Jones; Miss Harriet married to Mr. William Willis.
National Banner & Nashville Whig (Mon., Aug. 8, 1831)

Jones, Rev. Isaac of Williamson County married to Mrs. Nancy Dunlap of Maury County,Ten. on 8th inst.
Nashville Republican & State Gazette (Fri., May 17, 1833)

Jones, Mr. Isaac M. merchant of Nashville married on Tuesday the 13th by the Rev. C. D. Elliott to Miss Sarah A. Demoss daughter of A. Demoss all of Davidson Co.
The Politician & Weekly Nashville Whig (Fri., April 16, 1847)

Jones, Mr. Isaac M. merchant of Nash. married on Tuesday evening last the 13th by the Rev. C. D. Elliott to Miss Sarah A. Demoss daughter of A. Demoss all of Davidson Co.
The Christian Record (Sat., April 17, 1847)

Jones, Mr. James married at Hunters Hill in this County on the 27th inst. to Miss Sarah Munford of Mercer County, Ky.
National Banner (Sat., Aug. 29, 1829)

Jones, Mr. James of Bath County, Ky. married in Carter County, Ten. to Miss Pualina Renfro.
National Banner & Nashville Whig (Mon., April 13, 1835)

Jones, Mr. James married in Hardeman County, Ten. to Miss Rebecca Casey.
National Banner & Nashville Whig (Wed., April 29, 1835)

Jones, Mr. James C. married in Smith County to Miss Agnes Inge.
National Banner & Nashville Daily Advertiser (Thurs., Jan. 5, 1832)

Jones, Mr. Jas. G. married in Williamson County to Miss Minerva Jordan.
The Western Weekly Review - Franklin, Ten. (Fri., Dec. 2, 1831)

Jones, Mr. James G. married in Williamson County to Miss Minerva Jordan.
National Banner & Nashville Whig (Wed., Dec. 7, 1831)

Jones, Mr. James H. Esq. merchant of Nashville married on Thursday 23d inst. by the Rev. Mr. Howlett at the residence of her father on Mill Creek to Miss Tabitha Barnes of Davidson County.
Nashville Whig (Sat., June 25, 1842)

Jones, Col. Joel L. of Fayette County married to Mrs. Minerva Turner in Nashville on Sunday.
Nashville Republican & State Gazette (Tues., Nov. 18, 1834)

Jones, Joel married to Miss Sophia Dickinson in Davidson County.
National Banner & Nashville Whig (Fri., Jan. 1st 1830)

Jones, Dr. Joel M. married in Springfield, Tenn. on the 23d of February
by the Rev. J. J. Ellis to Miss Minerva A. Conrad.
The Christian Record (Sat., March 13, 1847)

Jones, Mr. John T. Attorney at law, Washington, Ark. married on Tuesday
the 13th Aug. by the Rev. Dr. Lapsley to Miss Sarah Caroline McEwen
daughter of Col. R. H. McEwen.
Daily Republican Banner (Fri., Aug. 16, 1839)

Jones, Mr. John T. Attorney at law, of Washington, Ark. married on
Tuesday 13th Aug. in Nashville by the Rev. Dr. Lapsley to Miss Sarah
Caroline M'Ewen daughter of Col. R. H. M'Ewen.
Nashville Whig (Fri., Aug. 16, 1839)

Jones, Mr. Joseph married in August 1831 to Miss Betsy Taylor
The Western Weekly Review - Franklin, Tenn. (Fri., Sept. 2, 1831)

Jones, Mr. Joseph married in Smith County to Miss Betsy Lynch.
National Banner & Nashville Whig (Fri., Nov. 25, 1831)

Jones, Mr. Joshua married in Maury County to Miss Jane D. Covey.
National Banner & Nashville Whig (Mon., Jan. 26, 1835)

Jones, Mr. Joshua married in Davidson County to Miss Jane D. Covey.
Nashville Republican (Tues., Jan. 27, 1835)

Jones, Mr. Lafayette married in Shelby County to Miss Susan Ann Dunn.
National Banner & Nashville Daily Advertiser (Mon., April 9, 1832)

Jones, Miss Levina married to Mr. Henry A. Rard.

Jones, Miss Lucindia married to Mr. Garret Dehaven.

Jones, Miss Lucy married to Mr. Ezekiel Cook.

Jones, Miss Lucy Ann married to Dr. M. B. Cook.

Jones, Miss Maria married to Mr. Reuben Hicks.

Jones, Miss Maria married to Mr. William Strother.

Jones, Mrs. Martha married to Capt. John Camp.

Jones, Miss Martha married to Mr. James Newbern.

Jones, Miss Martha married to William Gilchrist, Esq.

Jones, Miss Martha Ann married to Mr. Arthur H. W. Uphaw.

Jones, Martin S. married in Giles County to Mary J. Mennifee.
National Banner & Nashville Daily Advertiser (Tues., Dec. 17, 1833)

Jonston, Miss Mary married to Mr. Samuel S. Perkins.

Jones, Miss Mary Ann H. married to Mr. Thos. Armstrong.

Jones, Miss Mary Ann H. married to Mr. Thomas T. Armstrong.

Jones, Miss Mary B. married to Mr. Calvin H. Nicholson.

Jones, Miss Mary B. married to Mr. George B. McCombs.

Jones, Miss Mary E. E. married to Mr. Samuel T. King.

Jones, Miss Mary Frances married to Mr. James H. Lander.

Jones, Maury married in Williamson County to Miss Mary Hulme.
The Western Weekly Review - Franklin, Tenn. (Fri., March 23, 1832)

Jones, Mr. Maury married in Williamson County to Miss Mary Hulme.
National Banner & Nashville Advertiser (Mon., March 26, 1832)

Jones, Miss Millberry Ann married in Lincoln County, Ten. to Mr. John
Weigart.
National Banner & Nashville Whig (Fri., June 10, 1836)

Jones, Miss Nancy married in Blount County to Mr. George Dunken.
National Banner & Nashville Whig (Sat., Oct. 11, 1828)

Jones, Miss Nancy married to Mr. William Outon.

Jones, Miss Polly married to Rev. Harmon Barrott.

Jones, Mr. Rezen married in Jefferson County, Ky. to Miss Lucy Edson.
National Banner (April 21, 1826)

Jones, Lieut Richard A. of the Navy married to Miss Emily Pinckney
Baltimore.
Nashville Republican & State Gazette (Thurs., April 21, 1831)

Jones, Richard C. married in Williamson County to Miss Brittania
Johnson.
The Western Weekly Review - Franklin, Tenn. (Fri., Dec. 14, 1832)

Jones, Mr. Robert H., merchant, married on Sunday evening 18th inst. by
the Rev. A. L. P. Green to Miss J. J. Price all of Nashville.
Nashville Union (Tues., March 20, 1838)

Jones, Robert H. Esq. merchant married on Sunday evening last by the
Rev. Mr. Green to Miss J. J. Price daughter of John Price Esq. all of
Nashville.
Nashville Whig (Wed., March 21, 1838)

Jones, Mr. S. A. married on the evening of the 22nd inst. by the
Rev. J. B. Ferguson to Miss Lucinda Boon.
Nashville True Whig & Weekly Commercial Register (Fri., May 31, 1850)

Jones, Miss Sally married to Mr. John P. Bonham.

Jones, Miss Sarah married to Mr. Henry Ault.

Jones, Miss Sarah Jane married to Col. Samuel Mitchell.

Jones, Miss Sarah S. married to Mr. Jones Dugger.

Jones, Miss Sophronia Macon married to Mr. Samuel Stevens.

Jones, Thomas married in Williamson County, Ten. to Susan Riddle.
National Banner & Nashville Daily Advertiser (Mon., Aug. 26, 1833)

Jones, Mr. Thomas C. married near Little Rock, Ark. to Miss Emily
Hancock daughter of Mr. Joseph Hancock.
National Banner & Nashville Whig (Wed., Nov. 26, 1834)

Jones, Mr. Thomas D. married at Clarksville to Mrs. Catharine Bratton.
National Banner (April 21, 1826)

Jones, Mr. W. E. of Nashville married on the 30th ult. to Miss Louisa
Hazard daughter of Lot Hazard Esq. of Carthage, Tenn.
National Banner & Nashville Whig (Fri., May 15, 1835)

Jones, Mr. Wesley W. married in Henry County to Miss Charity Rowe.
National Banner & Nashville Daily Advertiser (Wed., Jan. 11, 1832)

Jones, Mr. Westley W. married in Henry County to Miss Charity Rowe.
National Banner & Nashville Advertiser (Wed., Jan. 11, 1832)

Jones, Mr. Wm. married in Tuscaloosa, Ala. to Miss Priscilla Hall.
National Banner & Nashville Whig (Sat., Aug. 5, 1826)

Jones, Mr. William married in Madison County, Ala. to Miss L. C.
Brandon daughter of Col. William Brandon.
National Banner & Nashville Whig (Wed., Sept. 7, 1831)

Jones, Mr. Wm. married in Bairdstown, Ky. to Miss Louisa Ann Lucas.
National Banner & Nashville Daily Advertiser (Thurs., June 19, 1834)

Jones, William Carey of New Orleans married in Washington City, on
Thursday 18th inst. by the Rev. Mr. French to Miss Eliza Preston
Carrington Benton daughter of the Hon. Thomas H. Benton of Missouri.
The Christian Record (Sat., April 3, 1847)

Jones, Mr. William D. married in Tuscaloosa, Ala. to Miss Elvira Eddins.
National Banner & Nashville Whig (Sat., July 29, 1826)

Jones, Mr. William J. married in Madison County to Miss Angelina Bond.
National Banner & Nashville Whig (Sat., Jan. 3, 1829)

Jones, Mr. Wilie married on the 1st inst. to Miss Nancy Nolen daughter
of Wm. Nolen Esq. all of Williamson County.
The Clarion & Tennessee Gazette (Aug. 15, 1820)

Jones, Mr. Willis of Gibson County married in Maury County to Miss
Susan C. Tindall.
National Banner & Nashville Daily Advertiser. (Thurs., Dec. 27, 1832)

Jonte, Miss Harriet A. of Nashville married to Mr. N. Y. Stanley.

Jopland, Mr. William married in Wilson County to Miss Mary Stone.
National Banner & Nashville Whig (Mon., Aug. 1, 1831)

Jordan, Dr. Flemming married in Madison County, Ala. to Miss Lucy
Jane M. Moore daughter of Wm. H. Moore Esq.
National Banner (Sat., July 11, 1829)

Jordan, Mr. Henry married in Huntsville, Ala. to Miss Maria A.
Glasglow.
National Banner & Nashville Whig (Dec. 14, 1831)

Jordan, Mr. James E. married in Lexington to Miss Jane Wilson.
National Banner & Nashville Whig (Fri., Feb. 26, 1830)

Jordan, Mr. John married in Williamson County to Miss Grizell Taylor.
The Western Weekly Review (Franklin, Tenn. Fri., Dec. 23, 1831)

Jordan, Miss Lucy married in Davidson Co. to Mr. John Nash.

Jordan, Mrs. Martha married to E. C. W. Hale.

Jordan, Mary A. married to Isaac B. Wilson.

Jordan, Miss Minerva married to Mr. Jas. G. Jones.

Jordan, Miss Minerva married to Mr. James G. Jones.

Jordan, Miss Minerva married to Mr. J. Johnson.

Jordan, Miss Phoebe E. married to Abner D. Porter.

Jordan, Mr. Warren married on the 10th inst. by the J. C. Lovel Esq.
to Miss Sarah A. Allison daughter of the late Richard Allison Esq. all
of Davidson County.
Nashville Whig (Tues., Dec. 12, 1843)

Jordan, Miss Winefred married to Mr. James Westbrook.

Joseph, Mr. Isaac married on Thursday evening last by Rev. Mr. Judd
to Miss Elizabeth Smith all of Nashville.
Nashville Whig (Tues., Oct. 31, 1843)

Joseph, Mr. J. G., merchant, married on Wednesday afternoon 25th inst.
by the Rev. Judal L. Levetus High Priest from Jerusalam to Miss
Rebecca Symonds daughter of Mr. L. Symonds all of Nashville.
National Banner & Nashville D. Advertiser (Sat., Jan. 4, 1834)

Joslin, John married on Thursday the 21st by Riddick Dishongh Esq. to
Miss Jincy W. Thomas both of Hardeman County.
National Banner & Nashville Daily Advertiser (Fri., Nov. 29, 1833)

Jouett, Miss Catherine married to Mr. James Mansfield.

Jouett, Mr. John married in Montgomery County, Ky. to Miss Phebe
M'Donnold.
National Banner (June 3, 1826)

Jouitt, Miss Sarah B. married to Richard H. Menefee, Esq.

Journey, Miss Ann D. married to Mr. John W. Read.

Journey, Miss Lucretia married to Mr. Nathan Vaught.

Joyce, Mr. B. A. married on Monday 5th inst. by the Rev. R. B. C.
Howell to Miss Sarah A. Buchanan all of Davidson County.
Daily Republican Banner (Tues., Oct. 13, 1840)

Joyce, Miss Susan C. married to Mr. Jo. A. Aldrich.

Joyce, Miss Susannah married to Mr. James Kirby.

Joyes, John Esq. to Miss Harriet Martin.

Joyner, Capt. Jesse married on the 8th inst by the Rev. J. B. McFerrin
to Miss Julia Nutt all of Nashville.
Nashville Whig (Sat., March 11, 1843)

Joyner, Miss Winnay married to Mr. James Crossway.

Judkins, Mr. John W. merchant of Cross Plains, Robinson County, Ten.
married in Logan County, Ky. to Miss Eliza Ann Townsend.
National Banner & Nashville Daily Advertiser (Mon, June 3, 1833)

Judkins, Mr. John W. of Cross Plains, Robertson County, Ten. married in
Logan County to Miss Eliza Ann Townsend.
Nashville Republican & State Gazette (Wed., June 5, 1833)

Judson, Mr. Zephaniah H. married at St. Louis to Miss Lydia Boss.
National Banner & Nashville Whig (Mon., Sept. 6, 1830)

Judy, Miss Nancy married to Mr. Moses Whiteside.

Judy, Mr. Thomas married in Madison County, Ill. to Miss Louisa Snider
National Banner (April 21, 1826)

Julian, Miss Lydia married to Dr. Samuel W. Frazier.

Juman, Miss Nancy A. married to John Yates.

Jumel, Mrs. Eliza married to Col. Aaron Burr.

Juntor, Miss Mahala married to Mr. James Brown.

Kamper, Mr. John L. married in Madison County, Ala. to Miss Elizabeth Brooks.
National Banner & Nashville Whig (Thurs., Oct. 14, 1830)

Kane, Mr. Elias married in Louisville, Ky. to Miss Harriet Hutton.
National Banner & Nashville Daily Advertiser (Tues., May 20, 1834)

Kannon, Mr. Butwell married Miss Lyda Hill in Maury County on the 26th inst.
National Banner & Nashville Whig (Fri., Jan. 29, 1830)

Karcher, Mr. Jacob married in Jefferson County, Ky. to Miss Sarah B___en.
National Banner & Nashville Whig (March 22, 1828)

Karnes, Miss Catharine married to Mr. Miles C. Vernon.

Karr, Mr. James C. married on Thursday last by the Rev. James Porter to Miss Julia A. Haynes both of this vicinity.
The Western Weekly Review - Franklin, Tenn. (Fri., July 13, 1832)

Karr, Mr. James C. married in Williamson County to Miss Julia A. Haynes.
National Banner & Nashville Daily Advertiser (Tues., July 17, 1832)

Kavanaugh, Miss Ann C. married to Mr. David Whitaker.

Kay, James Esq. married at Dover, Tenn. to Miss Mary Ann Eliza Bailey on 3d inst.
Nashville Republican (Sat., March 12, 1836)

Kay, Mr. Joseph L. married in Maury County, Ten. to Miss Margaret Overton.
National Banner & Nashville Whig (Mon., Jan. 26, 1835)

Kay, Miss Margaret married to Mr. J. C. Ingram.

Kay, Nimrod E. Esq. late merchant of this city, now of Pine Bluff, Ark. married near Haydensville, Todd Co., Ky. Dec. 31st by the Rev. Mr. Carry to Elizabeth M. Allensworth daughter of the late Philip Allensworth of Ky.
Nashville Whig (Mon., Jan. 6, 1840)

Kay, Mr. Reuben L. of the firm of Kay & Thomas merchants married in Nashville on the 25th Aug. by the Rev. Mr. Lapsley to Miss Elspa M. Walker.
National Banner & Nashville Whig (Fri., Aug. 26, 1836)

Kay, Miss Rosey Ann married to Mr. Richard Allen.

Kay, Miss Susan L. married to William Green Kirby.

Kay, Miss Susan L. married to Mr. William Green Kirby.

Kay, Miss Thyrsa married to Mr. James C. Bernard.

Kay, Miss Virginia S. married to Mr. R. D. Crowder.

Kaykendall, Miss R. married to Mr. John Lane.

Keane, Miss Eleanor E. S. married to Dr. Wm. L. Richards.

Kearney, Mr. Phillip J. married in Hardeman County to Miss Sarah Ramsey.
National Banner & Nashville Whig (Sat., Feb. 7, 1829)

Keas, Miss Mary C. married to Dr. Robert C. Price.

Keating, Mr. John married at Cincinnati to Miss Mary R. Wheelwright.
National Banner (May 13, 1826)

Keating, Miss Margaret married to Mr. John J. James.

Keeble, Edwin A. Esq. married in Murfreesborough by Rev. William
Eagleton to Miss Mary W. Maney daughter of Doctor James Maney.
Nashville Republican (Sat., Dec. 10, 1836)

Keeble, Edwin A. Esq. Attorney at Law married in Murfreesborough by
the Rev. Mr. Eagleton to Miss Mary W. Maney daughter of Dr. J. Maney.
The Union (Tues., Dec. 13, 1836)

Keeble, Miss Eliza married to Dr. George Thompson.
National Banner & Nashville Whig (Sat., Nov. 18, 1826)

Keeble, Horace P. Attorney at law married at Murfreesboro on the 22nd
inst. by the Rev. Dr. Edgar to Miss Cassandra C. Currin daughter of
the late Jonathan Currin Esq.
The Politician & Weekly Nashville Whig (Fri., June 25, 1847)

Keeble, Horace P. Attorney at law married at Murfreesboro on the 22nd
inst. by the Rev. Dr. Edgar to Miss Cassandra C. Currin daughter of
the late Jonathan Currin Esq.
The Christian Record (Sat., June 26, 1847)

Keeble, Mr. John G. married Miss Martha Cheatham.
National Banner & Nashville Whig (Mon., Jan. 26, 1835)

Keeble, Mr. John G. of Nashville married in Davidson County to Miss
Martha Cheatham.
Nashville Republican (Jan. 27, 1835)

Keedy, Mr. Jonathan married at Russellville, Ky. to Miss Julia Ann
Caldwell daughter of Gen. Samuel Caldwell.
National Banner & Nashville Whig (Mon., Aug. 2, 1830)

Keel, Mr. John jun. married in Warren County to Miss Polly Clark.
National Banner & Nashville Whig (Mon., Aug. 1, 1831)

Keele, Miss Nancy married to Mr. Silas Reynolds.

Keen, Mr. Joseph married Miss Sally Iredale on Thursday evening.
Daughter of Mr. John Iredale.
The Nashville Whig & Tenn. Advertiser (May 9, 1818)

Keen, Margaret G. married to Maj. Notley M. Flournoy.

Keenan, Miss Sarah E. married to Mr. Joseph Edwards.

Keenan, Miss Sarah Elizabeth married to Joseph Edwards, Esq.

Keepers, William R. of the U. S. Army married at Baton Rougue, La.
to Miss Juliam Maria Saunders.
National Banner & Nashville Daily Advertiser (Fri., May 16, 1834)

Keiser, Miss Eliza married to Mr. James Markham.

Keith, Rev. William J. married in Athens, Ten. to Miss Margaret J.
Shumate.
National Banner & Nashville Whig (Fri., March 20, 1835)

Keller, Miss Paulina married to Mr. Lewis Shirley.

Kelley, Mr. Richard of M'Minn County married in Knox County to Miss
Caroline Eliza Ann Burkhart daughter of Mr. Peter Burkhart.
National Banner & Nashville Daily Advertiser (Tues., Oct. 9, 1832)

Kelly, Mr. A. M. married in Williamson County to Miss Sarah B. Womack.
The Western Weekly Review - Franklin, Tenn. (Fri., Dec. 2, 1831)

Kelly, Capt. Edwin married in Christian County, Ky. to Mrs. Redd.
National Banner & Nashville Whig (Fri., Nov. 18, 1831)

Kelly, Elizabeth Miss married to Mr. David Caldwell.

Kelly, Mr. George of Montgomery married on Thursday evening last by
the Rev. P. Lee to Miss Ellen Ostrander of Shawangunt.
National Banner & Nashville Whig (Fri., March 6, 1835)

Kelly, Miss H. married to Mr. J. G. Brown.

Kelly, Miss Letitia married to Mr. Peter Marrison.

Kelly, Miss Martha married to Mr. Abel M. Willis.

Kelly, Mr. Samuel married in Monroe County to Miss Eliza Upton.
National Banner & Nashville Whig (Sat., Jan. 5, 1828)

Kelly, Miss Susan married to Mr. Sidney Rose.

Kelso, Miss Terrissa M. married to Mr. Isaac W. Price.

Kelton, Miss Elizabeth married to Mr. Collins Farmer

Kelvey, Mr. Henry G. married at Sinking Springs, O. to Miss Susanna
Miles.
National Banner & Nashville Whig (July 1, 1826)

Kemp, Miss B. married to Mr. C. Richards.

Kemp, Miss Charlotte married to Mr. Jacob Goodner.

Kemp, Capt. Joseph of Cincinnati married Miss Louisiana Barton at
Louisville, Ky.
National Banner & Nashville Advertiser (Wed., Aug. 22, 1832)

Kemper, Miss Ellen Suzett married to Rev. R. C. Greendy D.D.

Kemper, Mr. John married in Mercer County, Ky. to Miss Frances Ann
Doggett.
National Banner & Nashville Whig (Mon., Aug. 30, 1830)

Kemper, Miss Mary D. married to Mr. E. Easton.

Kendall, Mr. merchant of Elkton, Ky. married in Elkton, Todd County, Ky.
to Miss Margaret Gray daughter of Maj. John Gray.
National Banner & Nashville Daily Advertiser (Tues., Aug. 20, 1833)

Kendall, Mr. Amos Editor of the Frankford Argus to Miss Jane Kyle.
National Banner (Jan. 20, 1826)

Kendall, Miss Feriby married to Mr. Miles Wood.

Kendall, Richmond G. married in Henry County to Martha Atkins.
National Banner & Nashville Daily Advertiser (Mon., April 23, 1832)

Kendrick, Mr. James H. of Jackson, La. married in Nashville on the
16th inst. by the Rev. J. B. McFerrin to Miss Sarah H. Bateman of
Nashville.
Nashville Whig (Wed., March 18, 1840)

Kendrick, Mr. William married at Louisville, Ky. to Miss Maria S.
Schwing.
National Banner & Nashville Daily Advertiser (Fri., Jan. 27, 1832)

Kenley, Mrs. Ann L. married to Mr. Christopher Brooks.

Kenley, Miss Susan Catherine married to Dr. Pascal W. Saunders.

Kennard, Mr. Lewis M. at Huntsville, Ala. married to Miss Catherine
Spence.
National Banner & Nashville Whig (Mon., Oct. 31, 1831)

Kennard, Mr. Lewis M. married at Huntsville, Ala. to Miss Catharine
Spence.
National Banner & Nashville Whig (Mon., Oct. 31, 1831)

Kennedy, Mr. Jas. married in August 1831 to Miss Elizabeth P. Bennett
daughter of Dr. Geo. Bennett, dec'd.
The Western Weekly Review - Franklin, Tenn. (Fri., Sept. 2, 1831)

Kennedy, James married in Williamson County to Miss Lavinia Long.
The Western Weekly Review - Franklin, Tenn. (Fri., Feb. 1, 1833)

Kennedy, James married in Williamson County to Miss Lavinia Long.
The Western Weekly Review - Franklin, Tenn. (Fri., March 8, 1833)

Kennedy, Miss Martha married to Capt. John P. McConnel.

Kennedy, Miss Mila married to Mr. Levi Carter.

Kennedy, Mr. Thomas married in Madison County, Ky. to Miss Evelina
Hawkins.
National Banner & Nashville Whig (Sat., Aug. 11, 1827)

Kennedy, Dr. Thomas J. married in Giles County, Ten. to Miss Almina
K. Lindsey.
National Banner & Nashville Daily Advertiser (Thurs., March 29, 1832)

Kennedy, Mr. Thomas R. of Jonesborough, Tennessee married in Washington
City, D. C. to Miss Harriet Hargrove Emack of Washington.
National Banner & Nashville Daily Advertiser (Fri., Aug. 1, 1834)

Kennedy, Miss Virginia married to Mr. John Haynes.

Kennedy, Capt. George H. of St. Louis married Miss Abzeere Menard.
National Banner (Jan. 27, 1826)

Kenney, Dr. Daniel of Jonesborough married to Mrs. Minerva Nelson
daughter of James Sevier Esq. in Washington County.
National Banner & Nashville Whig (Mon., Aug. 1, 1831)

Kensinger, Miss Mary Magdalene married to Rev. James Bradley.

Kent, Capt. John R. married in Shelby County to Miss Sarah W. Echols.
National Banner (Sat., Dec. 19, 1829)

Kent, Mr. Joseph K. married in Sumner County to Miss Jane Trigg.
National Banner & Nashville Whig (Thurs., Oct. 21, 1830)

Keplinger, Mr. John married again on Wednesday the 7th inst. by the
Rev. Mr. Morris to his former wife Mrs. Mary Keplinger both of Baltimore.
National Banner & Nashville Daily Advertiser (Tues., April 17, 1832)

Keplinger, Mrs. Mary married to Mr. John Keplinger.

Kerly, William Green of the Texan Army married in Nashville on the 12th
inst. by the Rev. Mr. Howell to Miss Susan I. Kay.
Republican Banner (Nov. 13, 1839)

Kerley, Miss Lydia married to Mr. Wm. Wooten.

Kerley, Mr. William married in Smith County to Miss Matilda Scott.
National Banner & Nashville Daily Advertiser (Thurs., Jan. 5, 1832)

Kerley, Mr. William Green of the Texan Army married in Nashville on the
12th inst by the Rev. Mr. Howell to Miss Susan L. Kay.
Nashville Whig (Nov. 13, 1839)

Kern, Mr. Wm. P. married in Madison County to Miss Ann M. Robinson.
National Banner (Sat., May 16, 1829)

Kernahan, Mrs. Martha married to Mr. Robert Kernahan.

Kernahan, Mr. Robert married at Florence, Ala. to Mrs. Martha Kernahan.
National Banner & Nashville Daily Advertiser (Mon., June 9, 1834)

Kerr, Rev. A. H. married in Shelby County, Tenn. on the 3d inst. at
the residence of Mrs. Sarah Ward by the Rev. John R. Gray to Miss
M. J. C. Ward of Davidson County.
Nashville Whig (Tues., March 31st 1846)

Kerr, Mr. Alexander R. merchant married in Fayetteville to Miss
Cynthia Campbell both of that town.
Nashville Whig (March 26, 1823)

Kerr, Fanny J. married in Giles County to William D. Orr.
National Banner & Nashville Daily Advertiser (Tues., Dec. 17, 1833)

Kerr, Mr. H. married in M'Minn County, Ten. to Miss Mary Ann Robison
both of Va.
National Banner & Nashville Daily Advertiser (Mon., Sept. 2, 1833)

Kerr, Miss Jane married to Mr. William T. Briant.

Kerr, Mr. John married at St. Louis to Miss Eliza Charless.
National Banner & Nashville Whig (Sat., Sept. 15, 1827)

Kerron, Mr. Alvin of Ky. married in Weakley County to Miss Nancy
Pursell daughter of A. Pursell, Esq.
National Banner (Sat., Nov. 21, 1829)

Kersey, Miss Biddy married to Mr. Henry Patterson.

Ketchum, Mr. Levi married in Maury County to Miss Barcenia Black
daughter of James Black Esq.
National Banner (Jan. 13, 1826)

Key, Miss Elizabeth married to Hon. Henry Johnson.

Key, Miss Mary T. married to Mr. John Ware.

Keys, Miss Mary married to Mr. Thomas Jackson.

Keyes, Miss Mary married to Mr. Thomas Jackson.

Keys, Miss Polly Z. married to Capt. Calvin H. M'Knight.

Keyser, Miss Mary married to Rev. Jarman Baker.

Keyser, Miss Matilda married to Rev. Greenville T. Henderson.

Kezer, Mr. Horace P. merchant married in Nashville, Tenn. on the 1st.
April, by the Rev. Mr. Edgar to Miss Emeline Maynard.
National Banner & Nashville Whig (Fri., April 3, 1835)

Mr. T. Kezer married in Nashville on Tuesday the 11th inst. by the
Rev. Dr. Edgar to Miss Ellen Temple eldest daughter of Mr. S. H.
Laughlin.
National Banner & Nashville Daily Advertiser (Thurs., Feb. 13, 1834)

Kezer, Mr. T. married in Nashville on Tuesday last to Miss Ellen
Tempe Laughlin.
Nashville Republican & State Gazette (Thurs., Feb. 13, 1834)

Kice, Miss Tena Ann married to Mr. John Colshire.

Kid, Miss Margaret married to Mr. John Anderson.

Kidd, Mr. Hudson H. of Welumpka, Alabama married in Nashville on
Tuesday last at the residence of Gen. Zollicoffer by the Rev C. D.
Elliott to Miss Martha A. Williams of Nashville.
Nashville Whig (Sat., Feb. 4, 1843)

Kidd, Miss Mahana married to Mr. Matthew Thompson.
National Banner & Nashville Daily Advertiser (Sept. 10, 1832)

Kidrell, Mr. James F. married in Giles County to Miss Jane Morris.
Nashville Whig (Sat., April 11, 1846)

Kieth, Mr. D. printer of the St. Louis Observer married in St. Louis,
Mo. to Miss Esther Woods.
National Banner & Nashville Daily Advertiser (Tues., March 25, 1834)

Kieth, Miss Jane married to Mr. A. K. Bradford.

Kilcrease, Miss Katherine married to Mr. Nathaniel Nicholson.

Kilcrease, Miss Kathrine married to Mr. Nathaniel Nicholson.

Kilgore, Miss Nancy married to Mr. John Masoner.

Kilgour, Miss Julia married to Mr. G. V. H. Dewitt.

Killough, Mr. Isaac married in Rutherford County to Miss Mary D. M'Kean.
National Banner & Nashville Whig (Sat., March 10, 1827)

Killough, Mr. John H. married in Rutherford County to Miss Nancy
Lawrence daughter of Mr. John Lawrence.
National Banner & Nashville Whig (Mon., Jan. 31, 1831)

Kilpatrick, Mr. Enos J. married in Maury County to Miss Martha M'Corpen.
National Banner & Nashville Whig (Fri., Feb. 19, 1830)

Kilpatrick, Samuel W. married in Williamson County to Miss Margaret W.
Campbell.
The Western Weekly Review - Franklin, Tenn. (Fri., May 11, 1832)

Kilpatrick, Samuel W. married in Williamson County to Margaret W.
Campbell.
National Banner & Nashville Advertiser (Wed., May 16, 1832)

Kilpatrick Dr. T. J. of Maury County married at the City Hotel on the
5th inst. by the Rev. Mr. Green to Miss Mary Smithers of Boonville
Missouri.
The Politician & Weekly Nashville Whig (Fri., June 11, 1847)

Kilpatrick, Dr. T. J. of Maury Co. married at the Cty. Hotel on the
5th inst. by the Rev. Mr. Green to Miss Mary Smithers of Boonville,
Missouri.
The Christian Record (Sat., June 12, 1847)

Kimbell, Mrs. Polly married to Dr. Isaac J. Thomas.

Kimbro, Mr. Benj. married in Bedford County to Miss Ann Payne.

Kimbro, Mr. Levi married in Bedford County to Miss Margaret Anthony.
National Banner & Nashville Advertiser (Fri., March 9, 1832)

Kimbrough, Amanda N. J. married to John Mitchell.
National Banner & Nashville Daily Advertiser (Tues., Dec. 17, 1833)

Kimbrough, Mr. John married in Cynthiana, Ky. to Miss Delelah Casey.
National Banner & Nashville Whig (Sat., Sept. 16, 1826)

Kimbrough, Miss Sarah married to Mr. Joseph Hunter.

Kimbrough, Mr. Wiley of Fayette County married to Miss Isabella Titus Fayette County.
National Banner & Nashville Advertiser (Wed., Jan. 4, 1832)

Kimes, Mr. James married in Maury County to Miss Cynthia Dooly.
National Banner (Jan. 13, 1826)

Kimmer, Miss Rebecca married to Mr. Hamden S. Scott.
National Banner & Nashville Whig (Fri., Jan. 23, 1835)

Kincade, Miss Jane married to Mr. Samuel Younce.

Kincaid, Mr. Alfred married in Campbell County to Miss Minerva Cowan daughter of the Rev. Samuel Cowan.
National Banner & Nashville Advertiser (Mon., March 12, 1832)

Kincaid, Mr. Anderson married in Henry County to Miss Martha Miller.
National Banner & Nashville Advertiser (Wed., Jan. 18, 1832)

Kincaid, Doctor Joseph married in Shelbyville, Ten. to Miss Arey Eliza McGimpsey.
National Banner & Nashville Whig (Wed., Dec. 3, 1834)

Kincaid, Mr. Wyatt married in Campbell County to Rachel Coller.
National Banner & Nashville Daily Advertiser (Fri., March 1, 1833)

Kincannon, Mr. L. A. of M'Minnville married in Rutherford County, Tenn. to Miss Serena G. Robertson.
National Banner & Nashville Daily Advertiser (Sat., Sept. 6, 1834)

Kindall, Mr. Richmond G. married in Henry County to Miss Martha Atkins.
National Banner & Nashville Advertiser (Mon., April 23, 1832)

Kinder, Miss Martha married to Mr. A. H. Gamble.

Kinder, Miss Nancy married to James F. Bradford, Esq.

Kinder, Miss Nancy married to James F. Bradford, Esq.

King, Mr. Amazon in Franklin County married to Miss Masey Haws.
National Banner & Nashville Whig (Fri., March 26, 1830)

King, Maj. Austin A. married in Gibson County to Miss Nancy Roberts.
National Banner & Nashville Whig (Sat., May 24, 1828)

King, Miss Betsy married to Dr. Daniel C. Caldwell.

King, Miss Catherine Ann married to Mr. Joseph L. King.

King, Mr. Charles L. formerly of Nashville married on 2d inst. to Miss Sarah M. Patrick of Decatur, Ala.
National Banner & Nashville Whig (Mon., March 21, 1836)

King, Mr. Edward of Nashville married in Nashville on the 11th inst. by Rev. Mr. Elliott to Miss Emilie L. Snider of Philadelphia.
The Christian Record (Sat., Jan. 15, 1848)

King, Miss Elizabeth married to Mr. Henry R. Swishar.

King, Miss Elizabeth married to Rev. Dr. Stephen B. Balch.

King, Miss Elizabeth Ray married to Henry Van Rensselaer.

King, Miss Frances L. married to Dempsey Weaver.

King, Geo. married in Williamson County to Lucinda Gooch.
The Western Weekly Review - Franklin, Tenn. (Fri., March 23, 1832)

King, Mr. George married in Williamson County to Lucinda Gooch.
National Banner & Nashville Advertiser (Mon., March 26, 1832)

King, Miss Harriet married to Mr. Burrell Griffith.

King, Miss Henrietta married to Lieut J. M. Clendenin.

King, Mr. James married in Louisville, Ky. to Miss Catharine Hale.
National Banner & Nashville Whig (Sat., Oct. 6, 1827)

King, Mr. James B. married in Sumner County to Miss Elizabeth Blythe.
National Banner & Nashville Whig (Thurs., Aug. 12, 1830)

King, John married in Williamson County to Sarah Taylor.
National Banner & Nashville Whig (Wed., Sept. 24, 1834)

King, Mr. Joseph L. merchant of Knoxville, Ten. married in Montgomery
Co., Va. to Miss Catherine Ann King.
National Banner & Nashville Daily Advertiser (Mon., June 30, 1834)

King, Miss Lavinia married to Mr. John Cocke.

King, Miss Lucinda married to Mr. Elkanah Pepper.

King, Miss Lucinda married in Knox County to Mr. George Gallaher.

King, Miss Maria married to Mr. Abraham Dyer.

King, Miss Martha married to Mr. John H. Hooser.

King, Miss Mary A. married to Mr. Robert Nelson.

King, Miss Nancy married to Mr. Daniel Hughes.

King, Mr. Samuel T. married in Wilkinson County, Missis. to Miss Mary
E. E. Jones.
National Banner & Nashville Whig (June 24, 1826)

King, Mrs. Sarah married to Mr. Joseph C. Smith.

King, Miss Sarah A. D. married to Rev. Lewis C. Bryan.

King, Mr. Silas married in Frankfort, Ky. to Miss Jane Breckenridge.
National Banner (Sat., Oct. 3, 1829)

King, Miss Sophia married to Major Charles F. Burton.

King, Walter married on the 1st January, 1795 Mr, Walter King to Miss
Nancy Sevier, daughter of General Sevier.
Knoxville Gazette (Fri., Jan. 9, 1795)

King, Mr. William married in Williamson County, Ten. to Miss Rebecca
Marine.
National Banner & Nashville Whig (Fri., Jan. 9, 1835)

King, Rev. Wm. A. of Middletown, Ky. married at Louisville, Ky. to
Miss Jane M. Blackburn.
National Banner & Nashville Whig (June 14, 1826)

King, Mr. William G. of Jackson, Tennessee married at Louisville, Ky.
by Rev. Mr. Fagg to Miss Rose A. Oliver of Louisville.
National Whig (Thurs., Feb. 9,1843)

Kingston, Mr. William married in Davidson County to Miss Matilda Roach.
National Banner & Nashville Whig (Wed., Nov. 12, 1834)

Kinhead, Mr. Guy married in Christian County, Ky. to Miss Allen.
National Banner & Nashville Whig (Thurs., Nov. 11, 1830)

Kinnannon, Miss Elizabeth married to Mr. John D. Berry.

Kinnard, Miss Charlotte married to Dr. John B. Houston.

Kinnard, Hon. G. L. of Indiana died at Cincinnati from being scalded while on his way to Washington.
Teh Union (Sat., Dec. 10, 1836)

Kinnard, Mr. Russell M., merchant, married in Gainsborough, Tenn. on Tuesday the 21st inst. by the Rev. William Burr, of the M. E. Church to Miss Matilda S. Bransford daughter of Mr. Thomas L. Bransford.
The Politician & Weekly Nashville Whig (Fri., March 31, 1848)

Kirby, Mr. Benjamin of Springfield married at Port Royal, Montgomery County on Tuesday evening 21st inst. to Miss Mary Sample.
National Banner & Nashville Whig (Mon., Dec. 27, 1830)

Kirby, Mr. James married in Maury County to Miss Susannah Joyce.
National Banner & Nashville Whig (Mon., Sept. 26, 1831)

Kirby, Mr. Jesse married in Madison County to Miss Bennett.
Nashville Whig (Thurs., March 19, 1846)

Kirby, Mr. John M. married in Nashville to Miss Margaret H. M. White on Tuesday last.
Nashville Republican & State Gazette (Thurs., Feb. 13, 1834)

Kirby, Mr. John M. married in Nashville on Tuesday the 11th inst. by The Rev. Mr. Green to Miss Margaret H. M. White.
National Banner & Nashville Daily Advertiser (Fri., Feb. 14, 1834)

Kirby, Miss Maria M. married to Mr. Benjamin H. Caldwell.

Kirby, Mr. Miles married at Springfield on the 3d by the Rev. Thomas Gunn to Miss E. T. B. Hall.
National Banner & Nashville Daily Advertiser (Thurs., May 10, 1832)

Kirk, Miss Eleanor married to Mr. Pinckney Baird.

Kirk, Mr. Gideon married in Mason County, Kentucky to Miss Sally Duff.
National Banner (March 3, 1826)

Kirk, Mr. John of Columbia married in Murfreesborough on Tuesday 21st inst. to Miss Mary S. Spence of the former place.
National Banner & Nashville Whig (Wed., June 29, 1831)

Kirk, Mr. John married on Thursday 6th inst. by the Rev. F. E. Pitts. to Miss Eliza Ann Blake daughter of Mr. N. O. Blake all of Nashville.
The Christian Record (Sat., Jan. 8, 1848)

Kirk, Miss Nancy G. married to Major Jas. Beaver.

Kirkland, Mr. Shadrack married in Henry County, Ten. to Miss Telid Anne Childress.
National Banner & Nashville Whig (Wed., April 6, 1835)

Kirkman, Hugh Esq. of the House of H. & J. Kirkman & Co. married on Tuesday evening last to Miss Eleanora Vanleer daughter of A. W. Vanleer Esq.
Daily Republican Banner (Thurs., Jan. 24, 1839)

Kirkman, Mr. Thomas married in Lauderdale County, Ala. to Miss Elizabeth McCulloch.
National Banner & Nashville Whig (Sat., Nov. 18, 1826)

Kirkman, Miss Jane of Nashville married to Doctor John Farrell.

Kirkman, Miss Jane married to Doctor Farrell.

Kirkman, Miss Mary L. married to Hon. Richard K. Call.

Kirkpatrick, Mr. of Sumner County married in Wilson County to Miss Caroline Gleaves.
National Banner & Nashville Daily Advertiser (Mon., Dec. 17, 1832)

Kirkpatrick, Mr. married in Wilson County to Miss Caroline Gleaves.
Nashville Republican & State Gazette (Mon., Dec. 17, 1832)

Kirkpatrick, Miss Mahala married to Mr. William Bradley.

Kirkpatrick, Mr. Thos. married in Bourbon County, Ky. to Miss Elizabeth Miller.
National Banner & Nashville Whig (Sat., Oct. 6, 1827)

Kise, Mr. Wm. married in Fayette County, Ky. to Mrs. Harriet Stout.
National Banner & Nashville Whig (Sat., Feb. 17, 1827)

Kitchens, Miss married to Mr. Thomas Gibson.

Kitnell, Miss Mary married to Mr. William Jackson.

Kitrell, Mr. Reddick married in Maury County to Miss Eliza H. Hunter.
National Banner & Nashville Whig (June 24, 1826)

Kivett, Miss Sarah married to Mr. Ernsley Craven.

Kizer, Miss M. married to Mr. D. Lefler.

Knight, Mr. J. D. of Nashville married in Russellville, Ky. on Tuesday the 29th inst. by the Rev. W. McAllen to Miss Louisa A. Wilson of Russellville, Ky.
Nashville Whig (Fri., Oct. 2, 1840)

Knight, Mr. J. D. of Nashville married in Russellville, Ky. on Tuesday evening the 29th inst. by the Rev. W. McAllen to Miss Louisa A. Wilson of Russellville.
Daily Republican Banner (Fri., Oct. 3, 1840)

Knight, Mr. John married on Thursday evening last by the Rev. Mr. Hume to Miss Mary Scott both of this city.
The Clarion & Tennessee Gazette (Jan. 30, 1821)

Knight, Miss Margaret married to Mr. John Flemming.

Knight, Miss Martha married to Mr. Obadiah Knight.

Knight, Miss Mary married to Mr. John M. Little.

Knight, Mr. Obadiah married in Bedford County to Miss Martha Knight daughter of Allen Knight Esq.
National Banner & Nashville Daily Advertiser (Wed., Jan. 23, 1833)

Knight, Mr. Weisey of Pickaway County, Ohio married in Fleming County, Ky. to Miss Sarah Gallagher.
National Banner & Nashville Whig (Sat., Jan. 20, 1827)

Knighton, Mr. B. A. married in Little Rock, Ark. to Mrs. Mary M. Cowgill.
National Banner & Nashville Whig (Fri., March 13, 1835)

Knoepple, Mr. F. married on the 21st inst. by Rev. Dr. Lapsley to Miss Eve Snider.
Nashville True Whig & Weekly Commercial Register (Fri., Oct. 25, 1850)

Knott, Mr. Andrew married in Knox County to Miss Sarah Lonas daughter of Mr. Henry Lonas.
National Banner & Nashville Whig (Tues., Feb. 2, 1830)

Knott, L. B. married in Bedford County to Maria Cooper.
National Banner & Nashville Daily Advertiser (Tues., Dec. 17, 1833)

Knowles, Mr. Joseph B. married on Thursday evneing last by the Rev.
Wm. Hume to Miss Mary Johnson.
The Nashville Clarion (April 18, 1821)

Knowles, Capt. Leander married in Nashville to Miss Frances Stout of
Louisville, Ky.
Nashville Republican & State Gazette (Tues., June 24, 1834)

Knowles, Capt. Leander of the steamboat Eclipse married in Nashville
by the Rev. Mr. Adams to Miss Frances Stout of Louisville, Ky.
National Banner & Nashville Daily Advertiser (Tues., June 24, 1834)

Knox, Mr. James merchant married on Thursday evening last to Miss
Mary C. Hobson both of this town.
Nashville Whig (Oct. 4, 1824)

Knox, James of Philadelphia, Pa. married in Nashville yesterday morning
by the Rev. J. T. Edgar to Miss Martha Crockett daughter of George
Crockett Esq. all of Nashville.
Nashville Whig (Fri., Nov. 9, 1838)

Knox, Miss Jone E. married to Mr. S. D. McAlister.

Knox, Miss Mary Ann married to Mr. Richard Richardson.

Knox, Mr. Wm. married in Franklin County on the 7th inst to Miss Ann Lewis
National Banner & Nashville Whig (Sat., Nov. 17, 1827)

Koance, Miss Sarah married to Mr. James G. Shaw.

Koen, Mr. John W. married in Stewart Co. to Miss Elizabeth Brown.
National Banner & Nashville Advertiser (Sat., April 7, 1832)

Koontz, Mr. George S. married in Murfreesborough to Miss Nancy Hays.
National Banner & Nashville Daily Advertiser (Tues., May 27, 1834)

Kreider, Mr. E. J. of Nashville married on Sunday the 1st inst. by the
Rev. C. D. Elliott to Miss Mary A. Hamilton of La.
Daily Republican Banner (Tues., Nov. 3, 1840)

Kuykendall, Mr. J. married in Henry County to Miss Ann Ridgway.
National Banner & Nashville Whig (Fri., Nov. 18, 1831)

Kyle, Miss Jane married to Mr. Amos Kendall.

Kyle, Mr. William P. married to Miss Rachel M'Carty in Hawkins County.
National Banner & Nashville Advertiser (Tues., Oct. 9, 1832)

Labeau, Mr. Francis married at St. Louis to Miss Isabella Guion.
National Banner & Nashville Whig (Wed., June 8, 1831)

Labouisse, Miss Maria Adele married to Mr. Paul Negrin.

Lack, Miss Martha married to Dr. William Robinson.

Lack, Mr. William A. married at Carthage to Miss S. J. Hall.
National Banner & Nashville Advertiser (Thurs., Aug. 23, 1832)

Lacky, Mr. W. D., merchant married at Fayetteville, Tenn. on the 13th
by the Rev. Hirschell S. Porter to Miss Mary W. Hinkle daughter of
Joseph Hinkle Esq. all of Fayetteville.
Nashville Whig (Feb. 19, 1840)

Lacy, Rev. Beverly T. Pastor of the Presbyterian Church of Winchester,
Va. married at Clifton near Lexington, Va. on the 29th April by Rev.
J. Skinner, D.D. to Miss Agnes R. Alexander daughter of Maj. J. Alex-
ander of Clifton.
The Christian Record (Sat., June 26, 1847)

Lacy, Miss Catherine married to Benjamine C. Brown Esq.

Lacy, Mr. D. R. married in Hickman County on the 20th ult. to Miss
Jane Bailey daughter of Col. J. Bailey.
National Banner & Nashville Whig (Sat., Dec. 13, 1828)

Lacy, Miss Elizabeth married in Madison County, Tenn. to Mr. Lewis T.
Eddins.

Lacy, Mr. Hugh R. married in Madison County to Miss Smith.
National Banner & Nashville Advertiser (Wed., May 9, 1832)

Lacy, Mr. Jesse married in Madison County to Miss Powell daughter
of Mr. John Powell.
National Banner & Nashville Daily Advertiser (Fri., July 6, 1832)

Lacy, Miss Mary Jane married to Dr. Daniel O. Williams.

Lacy, Mr. Robert J. married in Maury County, Ten. to Miss Mary J.
Bobbitt.
National Banner & Nashville Whig (Mon., Jan. 26, 1835)

Lacy, Mr. Theophilus of Huntsville married in Huntsville, Ala. to Miss
Francis Binford of Limestone County, Ala.
Nashville Whig (Wed., Dec. 26, 1838)

Lacy, Rev. William L. married in Pulaski, Tenn. to Miss Julia Eldridge.
National Banner & Nashville Daily Advertiser (Mon., Sept. 9, 1833)

Lafever, Mr. Samuel married in Louisville, Ky. to Miss Louisa Luster.
National Banner & Nashville Whig (Mon., July 4, 1831)

La Grasse, Mrs. Louisa married to Mr. John S. Perkins.
National Banner & Nashville Whig (Mon., Nov. 21, 1831)

Laird, Miss Ann married to Mr. Franklin T. McLaurine.

Laird, Mr. J. A. printer married on Thursday the 25th inst. by the
Rev. Dr. Lapsley to Miss Sarah Jane Breast daughter of C. A. Breast
all of Nashville.
The Christian Record (Sat., May 27, 1848)

Laird, Miss Louisa married to Mr. Terrell.

Lake, Col. Robert H. married in Madison County to Miss Mary M. Sanders.
National Banner & Nashville Whig (Sat., Sept. 13, 1828)

Lamar, Gen. Mirabeau B. married in New Orleans on Wednesday 29th
Jan. at Christ Church, by Rev. Mr. Nevell to Miss Henrietta Moffitt
daughter of the late J. Newland Moffitt both of Texas.
Nashville True Whig & Weekly Commercial Register (Fri., March 7, 1851)

Lamaster, Miss Polly married to Mr. David Fulsom

Lamb, Capt. married in Russellville, Ky. to Miss Martha Ewing.
National Banner & Nashville Advertiser (Wed., June 13, 1832)

Lamb, Mr. A. L. married on Wednesday the 6th inst. by the Rev. Dr.
Wharton to Miss Catharine Thompson all of Nashville.
The Politician & Weekly Nashville Whig (Fri., Oct. 15, 1847)

Lamb, Miss Eliza H. married to Major J. J. Finley.

Lamb, Miss Maria married to Dr. Joseph Gill.

Lamb, Miss Paulina married to Edwards Stevens Jr.

Lamb, Miss Paulina married to Edward Stevens Jr.

Lamb, Mr. William married in Louisville, Ky. to Miss Elizabeth F.
Williams.
National Banner (Sat., June 27, 1829)

Lambe, Mr. Augustus L. married in Davidson County at the residence of
Mrs. William Harris by the Rev. Dr. Wharton to Miss Catharine J.
Thompson.
The Politician & Weekly Nashville Whig (Fri., Oct. 8, 1847)

Lambs, Miss Hannah married to Thomas Martin Esq.

Lampton, Miss Mary married to Mr. Jesse M. Reily.

Lamsden, Miss Dorinda marred to Rev. Cyrus Smith.

Lancaster, John L. Esq. of Jackson, Tenn. married in Christian County,
Ky. on the 11th of Oct. by the Rev. Mr. White to Miss M. J. Edwards
daughter of Mr. N. Edwards.
The Christian Record (Sat., Dec. 26, 1846)

Lancaster, Miss Judith married to Dr. William D. Lester.

Land, Miss Eliza married to Mr. James Scott.

Lander, Mr. James H. married in Christian County, Ky. to Miss Mary
Frances Jones.
National Banner & Nashville Daily Advertiser (Mon., Aug. 5, 1833)

Landers, Miss Phoebe married to Mr. Jacob Anthony.

Landman, Mr. Robert married at Louisville, Ky. to Miss Narcissa
Warbriden.
National Banner (April 21, 1826)

Landram, Capt. Lewis married in Mercer County, Ky. to Miss Martha Ann
George.
National Banner & Nashville Whig(Sat., March 31, 1827)

Landrum, Mr. John W. married in M'Minn County to Miss Charity Newman.
National Banner & Nashville Whig (Thurs., July 22, 1830)

Landrum, Miss Martha S. married to Mr. Wm. D. Allen.

Lands, Miss Susan married to Mr. James Swan.

Lane, Miss Emeline married to Mr. Stephen Hancock.

Lane, Miss Emily B. married to Col. Berry Gillespy.

Lane, George W. Esq. married at Athens, Ala. to Miss Martha Davis.
National Banner & Nashville Whig (Mon., Nov. 10, 1834)

Lane, Mr. James married in Henry County to Miss Elizabeth Turpin.
National Banner & Nashville Advertiser (Sat., Oct. 13, 1832)

Lane, Mr. John married in Conway County, Ark. to Miss R. Kaykendall.
National Banner & Nashville Whig (Sat., Aug. 26, 1826)

Lane, Col. John married near Shawneetown, Ill. to Miss Elizabeth H.
Dustin.
National Banner & Nashville Whig(Sat., Jan. 6, 1827)

Lane, Miss Mary married to Col. Richard G. Waterhouse.

Lane, Mr. Sampson married in Sumner County to Miss A. Hall.
National Banner & Nashville Whig (Mon., Jan. 10, 1831)

Lane, Mr. Samuel married in Roane County to Miss Frances Robinson
daughter of Mr. Thomas Robinson.
National Banner & Nashville Daily Advertiser (Mon., Feb. 6, 1832)

Lane, Mr. Turner jun. married in White County to Miss Mary Scoggins.
National Banner & Nashville Whig (Fri., Jan. 22, 1830)

Lane, Mr. Wm. W. married in Maury County to Miss Emily Campbell.
National Banner & Nashville Whig (Sat., Feb. 17, 1827)

Langford, Miss Martha married to Mr. John Reddich.

Langford, Miss Martha married to Mr. J. Reddich.

Langfort, Miss Sophia married to Mr. Jacob Millison.

Langley, Miss Martha married to Mr. Hamlet Bates.

Langsdon, Miss Mary married to Mr. John P. Smith.

Langston, Miss Mary married to Mr. John P. Smith.

Lanier, Miss Angelina M. married to Mr. Edward F. Musgrove.

Lanier, Miss Henrietta W. married to Hon. C. S. Spann.

Lanier, Miss Louisa A. married to Thomas J. Sumner, Esq.

Lanier, S. B. Esq. of Mississippi Co. Arkansas married on the 8th
inst. by the Rev. Dr. Wharton to Miss Fanny M. Falls daughter of
Mrs. Frances Falls of Nashville.
Nashville Whig (Sat., Feb. 10, 1844)

Lanier, Miss Susan G. married to Mr. John M. Hull.

Lankford, Mr. John D. married in Madison County, Ala. to Miss Martha
Griffin.
National Banner (Feb. 3, 1826)

Lankford, Miss Nancy married to Mr. Manoah M. Priest.

Lanning, Miss Mary Ann married to Mr. Charles Morrison.

Lanphear, Miss Adelaide A. married to Mr. Samuel M'Cormick.

Lans, Miss Sarah J. married to Mr. William Ragland.

Lape, Miss Christina married to Mr. John Armstrong.

Lapsley, Miss Adeline married to Dr. Joseph Barclay.

Lapsley, Joseph M. of Carrolton, Miss. married on Tuesday last to
Miss Elizabeth Hall daughter of Capt. John Hall of Nashville.
Daily Republican Banner (Fri., Sept. 15, 1837)

Lapsley, Joseph H. Esq. of Carrollton, Mississippi married on Tuesday
morning by the Rev. R. A. Lapsley to Miss Elizabeth Hall of Nashville.
The Union (Sat., Sept. 16, 1837)

Lapsley, Rev. Robert A. D.D. Pastor of the second Presbyterian Church
of Nashville married at Carthage on the 28th ult. by Rev. A. H. Kerr.
to Mrs. Alethia Allen relict of the late Hon. Robert Allen of Smith
County.
The Christian Record (Sat., Dec. 2, 1848)

Lapsley, Mrs. Sarah W. married to Thomas Witherspoon Esq.

Larew, Miss Barsheba married to Mr. John G. Haskins.

Larew, Miss Phoebia married to Mr. Willie O'Neal.

Large, Miss Mary Ann married to Mr. Wm. Price.

Larimore, Mr. David R. married on the 6th inst. by the Rev. Dr. Edgar
to Miss Keziah Patterson.
Nashville Whig (Sat., Jan. 8, 1842)

Lassiter, Mr. of Lawrence County, Ala. married in Lauderdale County,
Ala. to Miss Harriet T. Dillahunty.
National Banner & Nashville Daily Advertiser (Tues., March 19, 1833)

Lastropes, Miss Celeste married to Rice Garland, Esq.

Latapie, Mr. Anthony married in this town on the 15th inst. to Miss
Sophia Ann Josephine Martin.
National Banner (Fri., Dec. 23, 1825)

Latheret, Mr. John married in West Union, O. to Miss Charlotte Cheeseman.
National Banner & Nashville Whig (Sat., Aug. 5, 1826)

Lathrop, Miss A. E. married to Mr. Julius Humphries.

Latimer, Mr. William F. married in Sumner County on Wednesday the 20th
inst. by Samuel Kirkpatrick, Esq. to Miss Elizabeth O. Callis all of
Sumner County.
Nashville Whig (Sat., May 30, 1846)

Latrobe, J. B. of Baltimore married near Natchez to Miss Charlotte
Virginia Claiborne daughter of the late Gen. F. L. Claiborne.
National Banner & Nashville Daily Advertiser (Tues., Dec. 18, 1832)

Latta, Mr. Anderson A. married in Fayette County to Miss Sarah W.
Reaves.
National Banner & Nashville Daily Advertiser (Fri., Nov. 29, 1833)

Lattemore, Miss Adelea married to Mr. Urial A. Clary.

Laudeman, Mr. David married in Lexington, Ky. to Miss Mary Ann Hutchinson
National Banner & Nashville Daily Advertiser (Wed., July 31, 1833)

Lauderdale, Maj. William A. married in Sumner County to Miss Penelope
Head.
National Banner & Nashville Daily Advertiser (Mon., Nov. 19, 1832)

Laughborough, P. S. Esq. married at Franford, Ky. to Miss Ann Haggan.
National Banner & Nashville Whig (Sat., Oct. 6, 1827)

Laughlin, Miss Ellen Tempe married to Mr. T. Kezer.

Laughlin, John R., Esq. of Murfreesborough married on Thursday evening last to Miss Nancy K. Ledbetter of Rutherford County.
Nashville Whig (Oct. 6, 1823)

Laughlin, Mr. Thomas M. married at the same place (Winchester) to Miss Sophia Gillispie.
The Nashville Whig & Tenn. Advertiser (Jan. 24, 1818)

Laughlin, Capt. William H. M. married on the 25th inst. by the Rev. J. Moore to Miss Catherine Peeples all of Davidson County.
The Nashville Whig & Tenn. Advertiser (Dec. 29, 1817)

Launtz, Mr. Leonard married in West Union, Ohio to Miss Eliza Ellison.
National Banner & Nashville Whig (Sat., Aug. 19, 1826)

Laurison, Mr. J. T. married in Robertson County to Miss Susan F. Lowe on the 3d inst.
Nashville Republican (Tues., March 8, 1836)

Lavender, Miss Elizabeth P. married to Rev. Acton Young.

Lavender, Nelson married in Williamson County to Miss Pamelia White.
The Western Weekly Review - Franklin, Tenn. (Fri., March 23, 1832)

Lavender, Nelson married in Williamson County to Miss Pamelia White.
National Banner & Nashville Daily Advertiser (Mon., March 26, 1832)

Laverty, Mr. Edward married in Knoxville to Miss Minerva T. Veal daughter of Mr. John C. Veal.
National Banner & Nashville Daily Advertiser (Tues., June 11, 1833)

Lavisson, Miss Patronille Mary married to Mr. C. F. Shultz.

Lawrence, Miss Caroline M. married to Rev. A. Stephens.

Lawrence, Miss Cynthia married to Mr. Joseph Witt.

Lawrence, Miss Frances married to Mr. John S. Williams.

Lawrence, Miss Jane H. married to Mr. Thomas Porter.

Lawrence, Mr. John of Nashville married in Philadelphia to Miss Mary Grace of Philadelphia.
National Banner & Nashville Whig (Sat., March 17, 1827)

Lawrence, John W. Dr. married Miss Rachel daughter of Andrew Jackson, Esq. on Tuesday evening the 25th inst. at the Hermitage.
Republican Daily Banner and Nashville Whig - Nashville, Tennessee, (Thurs., Jan. 27, 1853)

Lawrence, Dr. John M. of Nashville married to Miss Rachel Jackson on Tuesday 25 inst.
Republican Banner & Nashville Whig (Thurs., Jan. 27, 1853)

Lawrence, Miss Laura M. married to Mr. John Donelson jun.

Lawrence, Miss Laura M. married to Mr. John Donelson jr.

Lawless, Miss Martha Ann married to Mr. Joseph Harris.

Lawrence, Miss Mary married to Mr. Robert B. Cain.

Lawrence, Miss Minerva married to Mr. A. Stephens.

Lawrence, Miss Nancy married to Mr. John H. Killough.

Lawrence, Miss Philian married in this town on Thursday evening 19th inst. by Rev. Mr. Hume to Mr. Stockly Donelson, Esq.
National Banner & Nashville Whig (Fri., June 27, 1828)

Lawrence, Miss Sarah P. married to Mr. Anthony North.

Lawrence, Miss Virginia married to Mr. Howard Matthews.

Lawrence, Mr. William of Illinois married in Russellville, Ky. to Miss Rebecca Dawes.
National Banner & Nashville Whig (Sat., Nov. 15, 1828)

Lawrie, Miss Sarah A. married to Mr. Semple Campbell.

Lawrisen, Mr. J. T. married in Robertson County on the 3rd inst. by the Rev. John B. M'Ferrin to Miss Susan Lowe.
Nashville Republican (Tues., March 8, 1836)

Lawrison, Miss Sidney married to Mr. John R. Pidgeon.

Lawson, Mr. David of Natchez married at Lexington, Ky. on Tuesday Aug. 3d. to Miss Catharine May.
National Banner & Nashville Whig (Mon., Sept. 6, 1830)

Lawson, Mr. Horace married in Sumner County on the 29th ult. to Miss. Tabitha Alexander.
National Banner (Sat., Nov. 14, 1829)

Lawson, Miss Maria married to James K. Cary Esq.

Lawson, Mr. William K. married at Columbus, Ohio to Mrs. Sarah Jeffords.
National Banner (Feb. 3, 1826)

Lawton, Mr. Charles married in Warren County, Ky. to Miss Lucy Ann Perkins.
National Banner & Nashville Whig (Wed., Sept. 21, 1831)

Layborne, Miss Emily married to Mr. James Willis.

Lazenbury, Frances married to Smith Manning.

Lea, Miss Ann married to Mr. Wilson Inman.

Lea, Miss Caroline married to Mr. John Phelps.

Lea, Mr. Caswell married in Sevier County to Miss Ann Sharp.
National Banner & Nashville Daily Advertiser (Mon., April 29, 1833)

Lea, Dr. James W. married in Blount County to Miss Malvina Weir.
National Banner & Nashville Whig (Wed., July 27, 1832)

Lea, Miss Margaret married to Genl. Samuel Houston.

Lea, Mr. Pleasent M. married in Roane County to Miss Martha H. Craven.
National Banner & Nashville Advertiser (Mon., Feb. 27, 1832)

Lea, Pryor Esq. of Knoxville married in M'Minn County to Miss Minerva Ann Heard.
National Banner (Sat., June 6, 1829)

Leach, Miss married to Mr. Edmund S. Cabler.

Leach, Mr. John C. married in Louisville, Ky. to Miss Margaret Darkies.
National Banner & Nashville Whig (Sat., July 8, 1826)

Leak, Miss Eliza married to Thomas Jefferson Harris, Esq.

Leath, Mr. James T. married in Sumner County to Miss Martha Anderson daughter of Thomas Anderson Esq.
National Banner & Nashville Whig (Mon., March 21, 1831)

Leatherman, Mr. C. of Giles County married in Rutherford County, Ten. to Miss Eliza Alexander daughter of D. Alexander Esq.
National Banner & Nashville Daily Advertiser (Wed., July 9, 1834)

Leathers, Miss Delia Jane married to Col. William A. Booth.

Leaticker, Mr. Frederick married in Henry County to Miss Martha Joiner.
National Banner & Nashville Daily Advertiser (Fri., Feb. 15, 1833)

Leaton, Miss Rachel married to Franklin Alexander.

Leaver, Mr. Lewis married at Mobile to Miss Mary Motley.
National Banner & Nashville Whig (July 1, 1826)

Leavy, Miss Amanda married to Charles S. Morehead, Esq.

Leavy, Miss Margaret married to Charles S. Morehead, Esq.

Leavy, William A. Esq. married at Lexington, Ky. to Miss Mary Ann Trotter.
National Banner (Sat., July 18, 1829)

Lebeaum, Mr. Augustus married at St. Louis to Miss Elizabeth McPherson.
National Banner & Nashville Whig (Sat., Jan. 27, 1827)

Ledbetter, Miss Lucy married to Mr. Gideon Harris.

Ledbetter, Miss Mary married to Mr. William Mitchell.

Ledbetter, Miss Nancy K. married to John R. Laughlin.

Ledbetter, Maj. William married in Williamson County to Miss Eliza Adeline Wellborne.
National Banner & Nashville Whig (Sat., May 17, 1828)

Ledyard, Mr. William J. merchant of Mobile married in Nashville on Monday 14th inst. by the Rev. Mr. Edgar to Miss Laura Erwin daughter of John P. Erwin, Esq.
National Banner & Nashville Daily Advertiser (Tues., April 15, 1834)

Ledyard, Mr. William J. of Mobile married to Miss Laura Erwin on Monday 14th inst.
Nashville Republican & State Gazette (Tues., April 15, 1834)

Lee, Miss Ann D. married in Jeffersonville, Ia. to Mr. J. W. Fulton.

Lee, Miss Elizabeth married to Mr. Russell Fletcher.

Lee, Miss Hester C. married to Mr. William Taylor.

Lee, Mr. James C. of this place. Married lately in Woodford Co., Kentucky to Miss Elizabeth Christman daughter of Jonas Christman, dec'd.
The Nashville Whig & Tenn. Advertiser (June 13, 1818.

Lee, Mr. John married in Madison County to Miss Mary Lilly.
National Banner (Jan. 27, 1826)

Lee, Mr. Joseph of Nashville married in Davidson County on Wednesday 1st by the Rev. Mr. M'Donnell to Mrs. Catherine Parrish.
National Banner & Nashville Whig (Mon., Dec. 6, 1830)

Lee, Miss Mary married to Rev. Gilford Jones.

Lee, Miss Nelly married to Mr. Joseph Wimberly.

Lee, Mr. Sampson married in Henry County to Miss Lucinda B. Woodside.
National Banner & Nashville Advertiser (Thurs., Sept. 27, 1832)

Lee, Samuel B. Esq. married on Thursday the second inst. near Charlotte,
Dickson County to Miss Susan Amanda Napier daughter of John W. Napier,
Esq.
Nashville Union (Tues., Nov. 14, 1837)

Lee, Mr. Seth married in Knox County to Miss Maria Bearden.
National Banner & Nashville Whig (Mon., April 11, 1831)

Leech, Miss Martha married to Mr. B. W. Holtzclaw.

Leech, Miss Rebecca M. married to Mr. Edward Cobbler.

Leek, Miss Eliza married to Mr. William Northern.

Leetch, Miss Margaret married to Mr. Payne.

Leetch, Miss Margaret married to Mr. Payne.

Leeper, Miss Nancy married to Mr. Jefferson Alexander.

Leeper, Miss Narcissa married to Mr. Bedford Miles.

Lefler, Mr. D. married at Cincinnati, Ohio to Miss M. Kizer.
National Banner (Feb. 3, 1826)

Leftwich, Miss Polly R. married to Mr. Joel Reece.
National Banner & Nashville Whig (Fri., Jan. 29, 1830)

Leggitt, Mr. John T. married at Port Gibson, Mississippi to Miss Phebe
Rundell.
National Banner (March 10, 1826)

Le Grand, Miss Elizabeth F. married to Dr. N. B. Atwood.

Leigh, Miss Eliza H. married to John P. Perkins, Esq.

Leigh, Miss Mary married to William B. Hulme.

Leight, Mr. D. B. married in Louisville, Ky. to Miss Sarah Bull.
National Banner & Nashville Daily Advertiser (Mon., Dec. 10, 1832)

Lemons, Miss Elizabeth married to Mr. Philip W. Baugh.

Lenard, Mr. George L. married in Lincoln County to Miss Mary Gilbert.
National Banner & Nashville Whig (Sat., Aug. 12, 1826)

Lenderman, Mr. Dickenson married in Louisville, Ky. to Miss Eliza
Vance of Louisville, Ky.
National Banner & Nashville Advertiser (Wed., Jan. 4, 1832)

Lenn, Mr. J. J. married at New Orleans to Margaret Daniel.
National Banner & Nashville Daily Advertiser (Fri., May 16, 1834)

Lenner, Miss Mary married to Mr. George Tuirer.
National Banner & Nashville Whig (Sat., Oct. 28, 1826)

Leonard, Mr. S. L. married at Hilham to Miss Perilla Fisk daughter
of Moses Fisk Esq.
National Banner & Nashville Daily Advertiser (Mon., Jan. 21, 1833)

Leonard, Mr. William W. married in Bolivar to Miss Lucy N. Polk.
National Banner & Nashville Whig (Sat., May 12, 1827)

Leroy, Miss Carolina married to Hon. Daniel Webster.

Lester, E. W. married on the 28th Jan. by the Rev. J. Lester to Miss Amercia Warson all of Wilson County.
Nashville Republican (Sat., Feb. 6, 1836)

Lester, Mr. Fountain of Logan County, Ky. married to Miss Sally Fox Napier Dixson County Thursday 3 inst.
Impartial Review & Cumberland Repository - Published at Nashville (Thurs., March 10, 1808)

Lester, Mr. Fountain of Pulaski married in Columbia by the Rev. Thomas Maddin to Miss Caroline Sutton daughter of Jasper R. Sutton of Maury County.
National Banner & Nashville Daily Advertiser (Tues., April 29, 1834)

Lester, Mr. Fountain C. married in Maury County to Miss Caroline Sutton.
Nashville Republican & State Gazette (Thurs., May 1, 1834)

Lester, Mr. German Clerk of the County Court of Giles County married in this County (Davidson) on Thursday evening 19th inst. by the Rev. Mr. Hume to Miss Elizabeth Lewis sister of William B. Lewis, Esq.
National Banner & Nashville Whig (July 28, 1827)

Lester, Miss Maria Louisa married to Col. Samuel S. Stockard.

Lester, Miss Maria Louisa married to Col. Samuel S. Stockard.

Lester, Mr. S. H. of Pulaski married in Maury County to Miss Rebecca Todd.
National Banner & Nashville Daily Advertiser (Wed., March 6, 1833)

Lester, Mr. Sterling H. of Elkton, Giles County married to Miss Martha A. Wharton daughter of the late William Wharton of this County.
Nashville Whig (June 21, 1824)

Lester, Miss Tralucca H. married to Mr. Phillip O'Riely.

Lester, W. P. married in Williamson County to Miss Rebecca Pinkston.
The Western Weekly Review - Franklin, Tenn. (Fri., Dec. 14, 1832)

Lester, Dr. William D. married to Miss Judith Lancaster.
National Banner & Nashville Whig (Nov. 11, 1831)

Lesueur, Miss Ann A. married to Mr. N. C. Burford.

Letta, Miss Mary married to Mr. Thos. N. Bradford.

Leuty, Miss Hannah married to Mr. Robert Gillespie.

Levering, Miss Elizabeh Ann married to Mr. R. Hyal Brockway.

Levin, L. C. Esq. of Tenn. married on Wednesday to Mrs. Julia A. M. Gist of Baltimore County.
Nashville Republican & State Gazette (Sat., Dec. 27, 1834)

Levin, Mr. Lewis Charles of Mississippi married in Nashville to Miss Ann Hays on Jan. 2d.
Nashville Republican & State Gazette (Fri., Jan. 4, 1833)

Levine, Mr. Lewis Charles of Mississippi married in Nashville on Wednesday evening Jan. 2d by the Rev. Mr. Weller to Miss Ann Hays daughter of Andrew Hays Esq.
Nashville Banner & Nashville Daily Advertiser (Thurs., Jan. 3, 1833)

Levition, Miss Providence, married to Nelson T. Raymond.

Lewin, Miss Susan S. married to Mr. Blackstone Waterhouse.

Lewis, Capt. A. S. of the U. S. Army married in Newport, Ky. to Miss Mary A. Mayo daughter of Daniel Mayo, Esq.
National Banner (Sat., Nov. 7, 1829)

Lewis, Miss Ann married to Mr. Wm. Knox.
National Banner & Nashville Whig (Sat., Nov. 17, 1827)

Lewis, Lt. C. N. of the Rifle Corps married on the 12th inst. (January 12, 1815) to Miss Figures of Wilson County.
Nashville Whig (Tues., Jan. 24, 1815)

Lewis, Miss Elizabeth married to Mr. German Lester.

Lewis, Miss Elizabeth married to Mr. William Lynn.

Lewis, Miss Elizabeth J. married to Mr. Edwin Dabbs.

Lewis, Miss Elizabeth S. married to Mr. Benjamin H. Deshazo.

Lewis, Elum married in Williamson County to Elizabeth Wood.
The Western Weekly Review - Franklin, Tenn. (Fri., Feb. 10, 1832)

Lewis, Miss Gabrilla married to Mr. William Mathews.

Lewis, Dr. H. F. of Hardensburgh married at Lexington to Miss Letitia Downing.
National Banner (May 10, 1826)

Lewis, Mr. Henry B. married in Woodford County, Ky. to Miss Sarah Cole.
National Banner (Sat., Oct. 17, 1829)

Lewis, Mr. Hickman of Huntsville married to Miss Virginia Lindslay daughter of Col. Wm. Lindsay of U. S. Army in Limestone County.
National Banner & Nashville Whig (Sat., Aug. 14, 1835)

Lewis, Mr. Hickman of Huntsville married in Limestone County to Miss Virginia Lindslay.
Nashville Republican (Aug. 15, 1835)

Lewis, James W. Esq. of Franklin County married on Thursday evening last by the Rev. Mr. Malone to Miss Martha Figuers of Wilson County.
The Nashville Whig (Sept. 17, 1816)

Lewis, Miss Jane married to Mr. D. Ferguson.

Lewis, Mr. John married at Russellville, Ky. to Miss Mary Morton daughter of William I. Morton Esq.
National Banner & Nashville Whig (Wed., Sept. 7, 1831)

Lewis, Mr. John C. married in Hickman County by the Rev. Samuel H. Peak to Miss Agness Powell all of this State.
National Banner & Nashville Daily Advertiser (Tues., April 29, 1834)

Lewis, Mr. John H. married in Cincinnati to Miss Phebe L. Vanhouton.
National Banner & Nashville Whig (Fri., Nov. 11, 1831)

Lewis, Mrs. Louisa married to Mr. A. C. Sublett.

Lewis, Miss Mary Ann married to Alphonso Pageat Esq.

Lewis, Mrs. Miriam married to Col. Ralph Crabb.

Lewis, Mr. Patrick of Memphis married in Sommerville, Fayette County to Miss Eliza Hamilton.
National Banner & Nashville Daily Advertiser (Mon., April 15, 1833)

Lewis, Dr. R. H. of La Grange married in Fayette County, Ten. to Miss. Sarah Ann Minter daughter of Mr. Wm. Minter of Columbia.
National Banner & Nashville Whig (Wed., May 6, 1835)

Lewis, Miss Sally married to Wm. D. Boyer, Esq.

Lewis, Mr. Samuel M. married in Mercer County, Ky. to Miss Susan Taylor.
National Banner & Nashville Whig (Mon., Oct. 4, 1830)

Lewis, Miss Sarah W. married to Mr. Thomas J. Trice.

Lewis, Shedrick married in Henry County to Miss Mary McDaniel.
National Banner & Nashville Daily Advertiser (Mon., April 23, 1832)

Lewis, Miss Susan married to Mr. Hugh Brent.

Lewis, Miss Susan married to Mr. Abram Shelton.

Lewis Mr. Thomas married in Hardin County, Ky. to Mrs. Isabelle Harrison.
National Banner & Nashville Whig (Sat., Oct. 28, 1826)

Lewis, Miss Viena married to Mr. Argyle M. Bauchanan.

Lewis, Mr. Waller married in Logan County, Ky. to Miss Emily Washington
National Banner & Nashville Whig (Wed., March 23, 1831)

Lewis, Col. William L. of S. C. married in New Orleans on the 13th ult. to Miss Letetis Floyd the eldest daughter of Gen. John Floyd late Governor of Virginia.
The Union(Thurs., Apirl 13, 1837)

Lewis, Col. Wm. T. married in Woodville, Missis. to Miss Virginia E. Marshall.
National Banner & Nashville Whig (Sat., March 17, 1827)

Lidey, Mr. Samuel married in Chillicothe to Miss Miranda Noble.
National Banner & Nashville Whig (Sat., Aug. 12, 1826)

Lientz, Miss Elizabeth married to George Tompkins.

Lightfoot, Miss Susan M. M. married to Mr. John H. Cook.

Ligon, Mr. Benjamin H. married in Haywood County to Miss Eliza A. Campbell daughter of Dr. Alexander A. Campbell.
National Banner & Nashville Daily Advertiser (Sat., Jan. 7, 1832)

Ligon, Mr. Josiah married in Wilson County to Miss Mary M. Fletcher.
National Banner & Nashville Whig (Sat., July 22, 1826)

Likins, Miss Lucinda D. married to Rev. Joseph Wilson.

Likins, Miss Martha A. married to Mr. John Spencer.

Lile, Rev. Daniel married in Jefferson County to Miss Lucinda Mathews.
National Banner & Nashville Whig (Wed., Oct. 12, 1831)

Lillard, Mr. William B. married in Rutherford County to Miss Mary Smith.
National Banner & Nashville Whig (Fri., Sept. 16, 1831)

Lillard, Mr. William B. married in Rutherford County to Miss Mary Smith
Nashville Republican & State Gazette (Tues., Sept. 20, 1831)

Lilly, Eliakim Esq. married at Pittsburgh on the 23th ult. by the Rev. Mr. Hopkins to Miss Ellenore Adeline Clopper formerly of Philadelphia.
National Banner & Nashville Whig (Fri., March 19, 1830)

Lilly, Miss Mary married to Mr. John Lee.

Limbert, Mr. Wm. H. married at N. Orleans to Miss Judith Suares.
National Banner (April 7, 1826)

Linch, Mr. Aden married in Rutherford County to Miss Susan Linch.
National Banner & Nashville Whig (Wed., Dec. 17, 1834)

Linch, Miss Elizabeth married to Mr. John G. Phillips.

Linch, Miss Susan married to Mr. Aden Linch.

Lincoln, Miss Eunice married to Mr. Luther Huntley.

Lindell, Mr. Jesse G. married in St. Louis to Miss Jemima Smith.
National Banner (Jan. 6, 1826)

Lindley, Miss Clarissa W. married to Rev. Robert Donnell.

Lindley, Miss Rebecca married to Mr. Elijah O'Neal.

Lindsay, Mr. Edward married in Henry County to Miss Louisa Rumbly.
National Banner & Nashville Daily Advertiser (Wed., Jan. 18, 1832)

Lindsay, Miss Rebecca married to Mr. Elisha F. Omall.

Lindsey, Almina K. married to Dr. Thomas J. Kennedy.

Lindsey, Mr. Dudley married in Rutherford County to Miss Charlotte
Puckett.
National Banner (Sat., Nov. 28, 1829)

Lindsey, Mr. John married in Lincoln County, Ky. to Miss Catharine
Miller.
National Banner & Nashville Whig (Sat., Aug. 4, 1827)

Lindsey, Mr. John married in Louisville, Ky. to Mrs. Frederica Brunner.
National Banner & Nashville Daily Advertiser (Mon., Jan. 30, 1832)

Lindsey, Miss Margaret married to Mr. Alpha Walter.

Lindsey, Miss Maria J. married to Mr. Leven Coe.

Lindsey, Mr. Oliver J. married in Franklin, County to Miss Sarah M.
Clark.
National Banner & Nashville Whig (Sat., April 7, 1827)

Lindsey, Mr. Phinchas C. married on Wednesday the 1st inst. at the
residence of Mrs. Maria Rice by the Rev. Isaac Cochran to Miss Ann
Maria Rice youngest daughter of the late Thomas Rice all of Prince
Edward County, Va.
Nashville True Whig & Weekly Commercial Register (Fri., Jan. 24, 1851)

Lindsey, Thos. S. Esq. Attorney at law of Princeton married in Frankfort,
Ky. to Miss Isabella Weisiger.
National Banner & Nashville Daily Advertiser (Sat., Sept. 6, 1834)

Lindsey, Miss Virginia married to Mr. Hickman Lewis.

Lindslay, Miss Virginia married to Mr. Hickman Lewis.

Lindslay, Mr. William L. married at Maysville, Ky. to Miss Mary Eaton.
National Banner & Nashville Whig (Fri., July 18, 1828)

Lindsley, A. V. S. Esq. Attorney at law married last evening by the
Rev. Philip Lindsley, D.D. to Miss Eliza M. Trimble all of Nashville.
Nashville Whig (Fri., April 13, 1838)

Lindsley, A. V. S. Esq. Attorney at law married in Nashville on Wednesday last by the Rev. Dr. Lindsley to Miss Eliza M. Trimble.
Daily Republican Banner (Sat., April 14, 1838)

Lindsley, Maj. N. Lawrence of Greenwood Cottage, Wilson County married
Miss Julia M. Stevens daughter of the late Moses Stevens Esq. of this
vicinity by the Rev. Dr. Lindsley, on Monday Oct. 18th.
Nashville Whig (Wed., Oct. 20, 1841)

Lindsley, Rev. Philip P. D. D. President of the University married
Mrs. Mary Ann Ayres of New Albany, Indiana on Thursday evening April
19, (1849) by the Rev. Dr. Wood.
Knoxville Register (Tues. morning May 8, 1849)

Linebaugh, Miss Margaret Catharine married to Robt. B. Mitchell.

Lingo, Miss Sarah Ann L. married to Mr. Williams Hoover.

Lipscomb, Mr. Dabney M. married in Franklin County, Tenn. to Miss
Lucy Ann Woods daughter of Capt. Andrew Wood.
National Banner & Nashville Daily Advertiser (Sat., Feb. 22,1834)

Lipscomb, Dr. E. P. married in E. T. in Calhoun to Miss N. M. S.
Williams daughter of Colonel J. G. Williams.
National Banner & Nashville Daily Advertiser (Wed., July 17, 1833)

Lipscomb, Miss Keren C. married to Prof. N. B. Smith.

Lipscomb, Doctor Thomas married in Shelbyville, Tenn. on Tuesday 22nd
May by the Rev. George Newton to Miss Rebecca Stevenson.
National Banner & Nashville Daily Advertiser (Thurs., May 31, 1832)

Lischer, Mr. George married in Nashville on Thursday last by the Rev.
Mr. Judd to Miss Sophia Stimball.
Nashville Whig (Mon., Aug. 2, 1841)

Lishy, L. C. merchant married on Tuesday the 8th inst. by the Rev.
Mr. McFerrin to Mrs. Mary Ann Sledge daughter of John T. Smith Esq.
all of Nashville.
Daily Republican Banner (Sat., Dec. 12, 1840)

Lister, Miss Nancy married to Mr. Samuel Bailies.

Little, Mr. Alfred L. married in Williamson County to Miss Martha Pope.
National Banner & Nashville Whig (Fri., Feb. 13, 1835)

Little, Miss Eliza married to Mr. Martin Stanley.

Little, Miss Elizabeth married to Mr. William Willhite.

Little, Miss Jane married to Mr. Jonathan Peach.

Little, Mr. John M. married in Williamson County, Ten. to Miss Mary
Knight.
National Banner & Nashville Whig (Fri., Feb. 13, 1835)

Little, Mr. Martin S. married in Williamson County to Miss Mary Dobson.
National Banner (Sat., Oct. 3, 1829)

Little, Mr. Robert A. of Nashville married in Philadelphia on the 10th
Nov. by the Rev. Mr. Wood to Elizabeth Catharine Solms of Philadelphia.
Nashville Whig (Thurs., Dec. 8, 1842)

Little, Mr. Sidney H. of Ohio married at Hilham to Miss Sarah P. Fisk
daughter of Moses Fisk Esq.
National Banner & Nashville Whig (Fri., Aug. 19, 1831)

Little, Mr. Thomas married in Overton County to Miss Frances Quarles.
National Banner & Nashville Whig (July 22, 1826)

Little, Mr. Zacheus married in Williamson County to Miss Mary Hill.
The Western Weekly Review - Franklin, Ten. -(Fri., Dec. 2, 1831)

Little, Mr. Zacheus married in Williamson County married to Miss Mary
Hill.
National Banner & Nashville Whig (Wed., Dec. 7, 1831)

Littleford, Miss Mary married to Andrew M'Millan.

Litton, Miss Ann married to Mr. Washington B. Cooper.

Litton, Miss Eliza married to Mr. Joseph Henning.

Litton, Miss Elizabeth married to Jesse Thomas.

Litton, Miss Elizabeth married to Mr. Jesse Thomas.

Litton, Miss Susan married to Mr. James C. Robinson.

Litton, Miss Susan married to Mr. William H. Goadon.

Lively, Mr. George married in Warren County, Ky. to Miss Lucinda R.
Alcock.
National Banner & Nashville Whig (Mon., Oct. 25, 1830)

Lively, Mr. James of Maury married in Bedford County to Miss Martha
Claxton.
National Banner & Nashville Daily Advertiser (Tues., Nov. 13, 1832)

Livingston, Mr. James merchant married on Thursday the 11th inst. at
the residence of Mr. Thomas Webb by the Rev. Dr. Edgar to Miss Mary
Andrews.
The Christian Record (Sat., March 13, 1847)

Livingston, Mr. William merchant married in Nashville by Rev. Dr.
Edgar 1st. Oct. to Miss Ellen Nichol daughter of Mr. John Nichol.
National Banner & Nashville Whig (Fri., Oct. 2, 1835)

Livingston, Mr. William married in Nashville to Miss Ellen Nichol
on the 1st inst.
Nashville Republican (Sat., Oct. 3, 1835)

Lizenburg, Miss Betsey married to Mr. Samuel M'Cutchen.

Llewellen, Miss Susan married to Mr. Warren Throckmorton.

Lloyd, Mr. Lee married in Bedford County to Miss Nancy Brooks.
National Banner & Nashville Whig (Sat., Jan. 10, 1829)

Lock, Mr. Harrison married in Fayette County, Ky. to Miss Rebecca Mosby.
National Banner & Nashville Whig (Sat., March 1, 1828)

Locke, Mr. Charles C. married in Memphis to Mrs. ___ Hill.
Nashville Republican & State Gazette (Fri., Dec. 7, 1832)

Locke, Mr. Hugh S. married in LaGrange, Tenn. to Miss Martha Jane
Malone.
Nashville Republican (Sat., April 11, 1835)

Locke, Mr. Hugh S. married in La Grange, Tenn. to Miss Martha Jane
Malone daughter of the Rev. Booth Malone.
National Banner & Nashville Whig (Mon., April 13, 1835)

Locke, Mr. John W. married in this county on Wednesday last to Miss
Eliza Clark.
The Nashville Whig & Tenn. Advertiser (March 7, 1818)

Lockett, Miss Cloe married to Mr. Nicholas Welch.

Lockhart, Miss Lucy H. married to Mr. George W. Carroll.

Lockran, Mr. David married in Louisville. Ky. to Miss Mary Ann Hinkle.
National Banner & Nashville Whig (Sat., July 14, 1827)

Lockridge, Miss Jane married to Mr. Thomas R. Porter.

Lockwood, Miss Missouria M. married to Mr. John J. Porter.

Locky, Mr. W. D. merchant married at Fayetteville, Tenn. on the 13th
by the Rev. Herschell S. Porter to Miss Mary W. Hinkle daughter of
Joseph Hinkle Esq. all of Fayetteville.
Nashville Whig (Wed., Feb. 19, 1840)

Lofland, Charles Esq. of Nashville married at Russellville, Ky. on the
29th by Rev. Hooper Crews to Miss Lucy Morre daughter of the late
Henley W. Moore Esq.
National Banner & Nashville Daily Advertiser (Mon., Nov. 3, 1833)

Logan, Mr. Benjamin H. of Elkton, Ky. married in Robertson County on
the 3d inst. to Miss Martha A. R. Williamson.
National Banner & Nashville Daily Advertiser (Sat., Jan. 7, 1832)

Logan, Mrs. Mary E. married to Dr. William M. Gwin.

Loller, Mr. James married in Henderson County to Miss Elizabeth Beville.
National Banner (Sat., Sept. 19, 1829)

Lonas, Miss Sarah married to Mr. Andrew Knott.

Lonas, Miss Zalilla married to Mr. David Lyon.

London, Miss Adeline married to Mr. Willis Taylor.

London, Mr. Samuel H. married in Bedford County, Tenn. on the 1st inst.
by the Rev. Mr. Gallaway to Miss Ann C. Esselman.
National Banner & Nashville Daily Advertiser (Wed., May 23, 1832)

London, Mr. Wm. married in Fayette County, Ky. to Miss Elizabeth Ford.
National Banner (April 7, 1826)

Lones, Mr. John married in Knox County, Tenn. on the 5th inst. to Miss
Ann Tipton.
National Banner & Nashville Daily Advertiser (Mon., Feb. 18, 1833 &
March 1, 1833)

Lones, Miss Talillia married to Mr. Daniel Lyon.

Loney, Miss Jane married to Col. P. W. Porter.

Long, Col. E. M. married in Maury County to Miss Martha De graffenreid.
National Banner & Nashville Advertiser (Thurs., Jan. 19, 1832)

Long, Miss Eleanor P. married to Mr. Greenville Cook.

Long, Miss Eleanor P. married to Mr. Greenville Cook.

Long, Miss Elzira married to Dr. Robert Forbes.

Long, Mr. Gabriel B. married in Christian County, Ky. to Miss Martha
Thompson.
National Banner & Nashville Daily Advertiser (Thurs., Jan. 19, 1832)

Long, Mr. James W. married in Salem, Franklin County on Thursday evening
11th inst. to Miss Isabella Trigg daughter of the late Mr. William
Trigg.
National Banner & Nashville Whig (Tues., March 16, 1830)

Long, Capt. Jarret married in Giles County to Miss Selenda Strong.
National Banner & Nashville Whig (Fri., Jan. 29, 1830)

Long, Miss Lavinia married to James Kennedy.

Long, Miss Malvina M. married to Mr. Abner G. Petty.

Long, Medicus A. Esq. of Nashville married near Danville Warren Co.,
Ten. on Thursday Oct. 30th to Miss Mary P. Taylor.
National Banner & Nashville Whig (Mon., Nov. 3, 1834)

Long, Medicus A. Esq. of Nashville married in Warren County to Miss
Mary P. Taylor.
Nashville Republican & State Gazette (Tues., Nov. 4, 1834)

Long, Miss Nancy married to Dr. Wm. M. Thompson.

Long, Miss Nancy F. married to Mr. Isaac A. Dale.

Long, Mr. Nimrod married at Russellville, Ky. to Miss Elizabeth Curd.
National Banner & Nashville Daily Advertiser (Mon., Aug. 5, 1833)

Long, Mr. P. W. married on Monday last by the Rev. Dr. Edgar to Mrs.
Susan Ann Wills eldest daughter of George Brown, Esq. of Davidson
County.
Daily Republican Banner (Thurs., Nov. 7, 1839)

Long, Miss Paulina married to Mr. Jacob Danner.

Long, Mr. Philip W. married on Monday last by the Rev. J. T. Edgar
to Mrs Susan Wills daughter of George Brown Esq. of Davidson County.
Nashville Whig (Wed., Nov. 6, 1839)

Long, Miss Rebecca married to Lawson H. Dunaway.

Long, Miss Susan S. S. married to Mr. William H. H. West.

Long, Thomas J. married near Bowling Green, Ky. to Miss E. Irwin.
National Banner & Nashville Daily Advertiser (Mon., June 30, 1834)

Long, Capt. William married at Galveston, Texas on the 29th of April
by the American Consul to Miss Joney Ann Mays formerly of Nashville.
Nashville Whig (Mon., Aug. 6, 1838)

Longhorne, Mr. John S. formerly of Nashville married at Lynchburg,
Virginia on the 14th inst. by the Rev. William S. Reid to Miss Sarah
Elizabeth Dabney daughter of Chiswell Dabney Esq. of Lynchburg, Va.
Nashville Whig (Fri., March 1, 1839)

Longinotti, Mr. James married on 27th Sept. by Rev. Mr. McAleer of
the Catholic Church to Miss Caroline E. Jogan both of Nashville.
Nashville Whig (Fri., Oct. 1, 1841)

Longstreet, Miss Anna R. married to Doctor H. Dent.

Longust, Miss Sally married to Mr. Garret Harvey.

Looker, Miss Emmeline married to Mr. Charles E. Romeril.

Looker, Mr. James H. married at Cincinnati to Miss Rachel H. Looker.
National Banner & Nashville Whig (Sat., Jan. 10, 1829)

Looker, Miss Rachel H. married to Mr. James H. Looker.

Looney, Capt. David married in Maury County by the Rev. Dr. Stephens
to Miss Mary M'Guire daughter of Mr. Patrick M'Guire.
National Banner & Nashville Whig (Fri., Aug. 19, 1831)

Looney, Miss Jane married to Col. P. W. Porter.

Looney, Mr. Richard G. married in Maury County to Miss E. Caruthers.
National Banner & Nashville Advertiser (Fri., Jan. 27, 1832)

Looney, Mr. Wm. E. married in Paris, Tenn. to Miss Phetney M.
Frazier.
National Banner & Nashville Whig (Sat., Jan. 26, 1828)

Lorance, Miss Margaret married to Col. James Gilliam.

Lord, William S. of Huntsville, Ala. married on Thursday evening by
the Rev. D. Howell to Miss Ellen Smith of Nashville.
Nashville Whig (Sat., March 14, 1846)

Lorew, Miss Barsheba married to Mr. John G. Haskins.

Lotspeach, Mr. Felix married in Monroe City, Ten. to Miss Eliza Neal.
National Banner & Nashville Whig (Wed., Feb. 25, 1835)

Louallen, Mr. William married in Maury County to Miss Anna Gifford.
National Banner & Nashville Daily Advertiser (Thurs., May 17, 1832)

Loudermilk, Mr. George married in Knox County to Miss Polly M'Nutt.
National Banner & Nashville Whig (June 24, 1826)

Love, Mr. Charles I. of the Nashville vicinity married on the 5th inst.
by the Rev. R. B. C. Howell
Nashville Union (Mon., June 10, 1839)

Love, Mrs. Charlotte married to Mr. James P. Miller.

Love, Miss Eliza married to Dr. Robert P. Gist.

Love, Miss Elizabeth P. married to Capt. Frederick Zollicofer.

Love, Miss Francis married to Mr. James Falls.

Love, Mr. Henry of this County married on Tuesday evening last by the
Rev. Mr. Dabbs to Miss Jane N. E. Love of this town.
Nashville Whig (Aug. 23, 1824)

Love, Mrs. Jane married to Major Calvin M. Smith.

Love, Miss Jane N. E. married to Mr. Henry Love.

Love, Col. J. D. married in Maury County to Miss Elizabeth Caruthers.
National Banner (March 3, 1826)

Love, Mr. John W. married in Madison County, Ten. to Miss Martha M.
Wharton.
National Banner & Nashville Whig (Wed., Aug. 17, 1831)

Love, Mr. Joseph N. ofrmerly of Washington, Rhea County married in
Kingston to Miss Amanda Ashley of Kingston.
National Banner & Nashville Whig (Fri., May 1, 1835)

Love, Miss Martha married to Mr. Geo. Lynes.

Love, Miss Rhoda B. married to Mr. William D. Horton.

Loveitt, Mr. Joseph married in Williamson County to Miss Martha Devor.
The Western Weekly Review - Franklin, Tenn. (Fri., Dec. 23, 1831)

Lovell, Miss Bethia R. married to George F. Raworth Esq.

Lovell, Mr. M. married in Williamson County to Miss Polly Polk.
National Banner & Nashville Daily Advertiser (Thurs., May 1, 1834)

Loving, Dr. Henry T. married in Logan County to Miss Ellen Morton.
National Banner & Nashville Whig (Sat., March 10, 1827)

Loving, Miss Isabella in Haywood County married to Mr. John A. McKendree

Loving, Miss Sarah Jane married to Dr. Frederick H. Gillmore.

Loving, Gen. William H. of Brownsville married in Nashville on the
28th July by the Rev. Dr. Edgar to Miss Ruth Talbot Fletcher daughter
of Thomas H. Fletcher.
Daily Republican Banner (Fri., July 27, 1838)

Loving, Gen. William H. of Brownville, Tenn. married in Nashville on
the 26th July by the Rev. Dr. Edgar to Miss Ruth Talbot Fletcher
daughter of Thomas H. Fletcher Attorney at law.
Nashville Whig (Fri., July 27, 1838)

Loving, Mr. Willis married in Logan County, Ky. to Miss Susannah
Sterling.
National Banner & Nashville Whig (Sat., Nov. 18, 1826)

Low, Miss Margaret married to Mr. William Hill.

Low, Miss Mary married to Mr. Joseph Scott.

Lowe, Dr. Alex of Robertson County married on the 8th of Jan. to Miss
Susan Ann Boyd of Davidson County.
Nashville Republican (Thurs., Jan. 15, 1835)

Lowe, Dr. Alexander married on Thursday evening the 8th of Jan. by
Rev. William Ralston to Miss Susan Ann Boyd of Davidson County.
National Banner & Nashville Whig (Wed., Jan. 21, 1835)

Lowe, Mr. B. M. merchant of Huntsville married on the 20th ult. to
Miss Sarah Manning of Madison County, Ala.
Nashville Whig (April 9, 1823)

Lowe, Miss Elizabeth Ann married to Mr. Robert Carr.

Lowe, Mr. Lewis of Robertson County married on the 2d inst. to Miss
Mary E. Sumner of Davidson County.
Nashville Republican (Sat., April 4, 1835)

Lowe, Mr. Lewis of Robinson County married on Thursday the 2d inst. by
the Rev. Mr. Green to Miss Mary E. Sumner.
National Banner & Nashville Whig (Mon., April 6, 1835)

Lowe, Miss Martha Jane married to Mr. William H. Rogers.

Lowe, Miss Susan married to Mr. J. T. Lawrisen.

Lowe, Miss Susan F. married to Mr. J. T. Lawrison.

Lowe, Miss Tennessee married to William Woodson Esq.

Lowrey, Mr. James married in Warren County, Ky. to Miss Elizabeth
Shearley.
National Banner & Nashville Whig (Wed., Sept. 21, 1831)

Lowrie, Walter Esq. married at Springfield, Mass. to Miss Mary Childs.
Nashville Republican & State Gazette (Sat., Oct. 19, 1833)

Lowry, Mr. David married on the 2nd ult. by Rev. A. A. Mathes to Miss
Mary Tipton.
The Christian Record (Sat., Jan. 22, 1848)

Lowry, Miss Finnetta married to Mr. James Garrick.

Lowry, Miss Francis married to Mr. Jeremiah Watson.

Lowry, Miss Isabella H. married to Dr. D. M. Dobson.

Lowry, Mr. James B. married to Miss Elizabeth Meadow.

Loyd, Mr. William G. married in Giles County to Miss Jane Carter.
National Banner & Nashville Daily Advertiser (Tues., Sept. 9, 1834)

Luby, Miss Elizabeth married to Mr. J. White.

Lucas, Miss Caledonia married to Capt. William Philip.

Lucas, Mr. Fielding A. merchant married on Wednesday last by the
Rev. Mr. Hyer to Miss Sarah P. Walker all of Memphis.
Nashville Whig (Fri., Sept. 24, 1841)

Lucas, Mr. Geo. A. merchant married in Gallatin on the 4th inst. to
Miss Mary Allen.
The Nash. Whig & Tenn. Advertiser (Nov. 10, 1817)

Lucas, Miss Hannah married in Knox County to Mr. Wm. C. Armstrong.

Lucas, Miss Julia M. married to Mr. S. G. Haynie.
National Banner & Nashville Daily Advertiser (Thurs., March 29, 1832)

Lucas, Miss Louisa Ann married to Mr. Wm. Jones.

Lucas, Mr. Mark M. married in Lincoln County, Tenn. to Miss Louisa
Taylor.
National Banner & Nashville Whig (Fri., Oct. 17, 1834)

Lucas, Mr. W. married in Maury County to Miss Eliza Spurlock.
National Banner & Nashville Whig (Thurs., Nov. 18, 1830)

Luchen, Miss Eliza married to Mr. Zaccheus A. Mayhew.

Lucky, Seth J. W. Esq. married in Sullivan County to Miss Sarah Rhea.
National Banner & Nashville Daily Advertiser (Mon., Jan. 2, 1832)

Lumpkins, Mr. James married in Wilson County to Miss Sarah Dudley.
National Banner & Nashville Daily Advertiser (Wed., Aug. 29, 1832)

Lumpkins, Miss Lucinda married to Wm. Halloway.

Lunn, Mr. Eli married in Franklin to Miss Eliza Glassock.
National Banner & Nashville Whig (Sat., March 8, 1828)

Luntsford, Mr. Andrew married in McMinn County to Miss Martha C.
Terrill.
Nashville Whig (Tues., July 14, 1846)

Lusk, Miss Ann married to Mr. William Yancy.

Lusk, Miss Cynthia Ann married to Mr. James M. Graham.

Lusk, Mr. Robert married in this county on the 7th inst. to Miss
Matilda F. Fairfax.
National Banner (Sat., Oct. 17, 1829)

Lusk, Mr. Samuel B. married in Maury County to Miss Milly R. Graham.
National Banner & Nashville Daily Advertiser (Dec. 17, 1833)

Lust, Miss Ellen married to Mr. James Lust.

Lust, Mr. James married in Maury County to Miss Ellen Lust.
National Banner & Nashville Whig (Sat., Oct. 6, 1827)

Luster, Miss Chancy married to Mr. Phlegmon Beck.

Luster, Miss Louisa married to Mr. Samuel Lafever.

Luster, Miss Mary G. married to Mr. Wm. H. McNeely.

Luster, Mrs Sarah married to Dr. James H. Bacon.

Luter, Mr. married in Davidson County to Miss Rachel Smiley.
National Banner & Nashville Whig (Fri., Jan. 1st, 1830)

Luttrell, Miss Amonda M. married to Rev. George Horne.

Luttrell, Mr. James married in Knox County to Miss Ellin Bounds.
National Banner & Nashville Whig (Sat., Aug. 19, 1826)

Lyle, Miss Mary married to Mr. Isaac Pierce.

Lyles, Mr. Hillary married in this County on Thursday evening, Sept.
25th by the Rev. S. Sheppard to Miss Mary Heaton.
National Banner & Nashville Whig (Sat., Oct. 4, 1828)

Lyman, Miss Sarah P. married to Mr. Charles D. Dana.

Lynch, Miss Betsy married to Mr. Joseph Jones.

Lynch, Mr. William married on Thursday last by the Rev. Dr. Lapsley
to Miss Eliza Ann Young all of Nashville.
The Christian Record (Sat., Oct. 7, 1848)

Lynes, Mr. Geo. married in Limestone County to Miss Martha Love.
National Banner & Nashville Whig (Sat., March 31, 1827)

Lynn, Mr. James married in Louisville, Ky. to Miss Belinda Welch.
National Banner & Nashville Daily Advertiser (Fri., Sept. 7, 1832)

Lynn, Maj. Joseph married at Jackson, T. to Miss Jane Hamilton.
National Banner (Sat., May 30, 1829)

Lynn, Mr. William married in Henry County to Miss Elizabeth Lewis.
National Banner & Nashville Advertiser (Wed., April 4, 1832)

Lynne, Miss Charlotte married to Rev. Robert Baker.

Lyon, Mr. Alpheus merchant of this town married in this county on
Wednesday last to Miss Eliza Dunn.
National Banner & Nashville Whig (Sat., Feb. 10, 1827)

Lyon, Mr. Daniel married in Knoxville, Ten. to Miss Talillia Lones.
National Banner & Nashville Daily Advertiser (Mon., Aug. 26, 1833)

Lyon, Mr. David married in Knoxville, Tenn. to Miss Zalilla Lonas.
Nashville Republican & State Gazette (Tues., Aug. 27, 1833)

Lyon, Miss Susan E. married to Major Campbell Wallace.

Lytle, Miss Catherine married to Mr. Legrand H. Carney.

Lytle, Miss Jane Foster married to Mr. William B. Herring

Lytle, Miss Jean married to John Dickinson Esq.

Lytle, John S. Esq. of Cincinnati married in Nashville last evening
by the Rev. Mr. Weller to Sarah S. Biddle daughter of Charles Biddle
Esq.
National Banner & Nashville Daily Advertiser (Wed., March 14, 1832)

Lytle, Miss Martha A. married to Mr. A. C. Crawford.

Lytle, Miss Mary married to Mr. Shadrack Sills.

Lytle, Miss Sarah Jane married to Mr. J. K. Rayburn.

Lytle, Mr. W. J. married in Murfreesborough to Miss Mary Smith daughter of Col. R. Smith.
National Banner & Nashville Daily Advertiser (Mon., March 31, 1834)

Lytle, Maj. William F. of Davidson County married in Shelbyville on the 6th inst. to Miss Sophia R. Dashiell daughter of Dr. Dashiell.
Nashville Whig (Sat., Jan. 17, 1846)

Lytle, Mr. Wm. T. married in Rutherford to Miss Violet C. Henderson.
National Banner & Nashville Whig (Sat., Sept. 23, 1826)

Maberry, Miss Clara married to Mr. William Bond.

Mabry, Dr. Evans of Henderson County married in Sumner County to Miss Sally Trigg.
National Banner & Nashville Whig (Sat., April 19, 1828)

Mabry, Capt. George W. of Murfreesborough married in Sumner County to Miss Mary Seawell daughter of Benjamine Seawell Esq.
National Banner (Sat., Sept. 12, 1829)

Mabry, Miss Mary Ann married to Mr. John Cunningham Jr.

McAdoo, Mr. William married in Anderson County to Miss Nancy Hogshead.
National Banner & Nashville Daily Advertiser (Wed., Aug. 29, 1832)

M'Afae, Miss Lovy married to Mr. Tho. J. Barham.

McAfee, Miss Lovy married to Mr. Thomas J. Barham.

McAfee, Mrs. Martha E. married to Mr. James Nichol.

McAfee, Morgan Esq. married in Monticello, Miss. to Miss Selina W. Mitchell.
National Banner & Nashville Daily Advertiser (Thurs., June 28, 1832)

McAffry, Mr. Terence W. married in Knox County to Miss Seylima Stormer
National Banner & Nashville Daily Advertiser (Mon., Nov. 5, 1832)

M'Affry, Mr. Wm. P. married in Knox County to Miss Polly B. Bond daughter of Maj. Isaac Bond.
National Banner & Nashville Whig (Fri., Feb. 19, 1830)

McAifry, Miss Rosanna married to Mr. Ulysses G. Smith.

M'Alexander, Mr. Samuel married at Courtland, Ala. to Miss Judith A. Gordon.
National Banner (Sat., Sept. 19, 1829)

McAlister, Charles Esq. of East Tennessee married in Troy, Obion County, Tenn. to Miss Martha S. Harper daughter of James Harper Esq. late of S. Carolina.
National Banner & Nashville Daily Advertiser (Thurs., Feb. 28, 1833)

McAlister, Mr. Edward of Louisville married at Lexington, Ky. to Miss Eliza H. Brand daughter of John Brand Esq.
National Banner & Nashville Daily Advertiser (Fri., Feb. 17, 1832)

McAlister, Miss Frances E. married to Humphrey Marshall.

M'Alister, Miss Margaretta E. married to Mr. Henry R. W. Hill.

M'Alister, Miss Mary married to Mr. William Bradley.

McAlister, Mr. S. D. of Nashville married in Crawford County, Ar. to Miss Hane E. Knox daughter of Hugh Knox, Esq. of Crawford County, Ark.
National Banner & Nashville Whig (Feb. 13, 1835)

McAlister, Mr. William married in Davidson County on the 21st inst. by the Rev. A. H. Kerr to Miss M. A. Smith.
The Christian Record (Sat., July 1st. 1848)

McAlister, Mr. Wm. K. merchant of Nashville married at Blountsville, Tenn. to Miss Frances R. Anderson daughter of E. Anderson Esq.
National Banner & Nashville Whig (Mon., Oct. 4, 1830)

McAllister, Miss Frances married to Lieut. Humphrey Marshall.

McAlpin, R. C. Esq. of Memphis married in Shelby County, Ten. to Miss Marinda Harwichalte of Virginia.
National Banner & Nashville Whig (Fri., Jan. 9, 1835)

McAlpin, R. C. Esq. married in Memphis to Miss Marinda Warwich of Virginia.
Nashville Republican (Tues., Jan. 6, 1835)

McArthur, Col. Thomas J. married at Urbana, O. to Miss Sarah McMahan.
National Banner (Aug. 1, 1829)

McAulay, Andrew late of the firm of D. & A. McAulay married in Gallatin on Tuesday 15th inst. by Rev. Bishop Miles to Miss Laura E. May daughter of R. H. May Esq. of Mississippi.
Nashville Whig (Tues., Nov. 22, 1842)

M'Bride, Miss Mary C. married to   Wright Stanley Esq.

McBride, Mrs. Sophia married to Mr. A. J. Johnson.

McBridge, Mr. William M. of Madison County married in Trenton on the 17th ult. by the Rev. Mr. Graves to Miss Griggsby daughter of Mr. A. A. Griggsby merchant of Trenton.
The Christian Record (Sat., Dec. 4, 1847)

McBrown, Mr. Jesse married in Madison County, Ala. to Miss Nancy Medlem.
National Banner & Nashville Whig (Sat., March 17, 1827)

McCain, Mr. Arthur F. married in Haywood County on the 30th ult. by the Rev. J. Y. Taylor to Miss A. E. Cockrel.
National Banner & Nashville Whig (Fri., Dec. 10, 1830)

McCain, Mr. Ezekiel married in Bourbon County, Ky. to Miss Elizabeth Peal.
National Banner & Nashville Whig (Fri., March 6, 1835)

M'Cain, Miss Susan married to Mr. Robert H. Bell, Esq.

M'Caine, Mr. James married near Charleston, Ind. to Miss Priscilla Ann Maria Redman.
National Banner & Nashville Whig (Fri., Dec. 10, 1830)

McCaleb, Miss Lucinda Jane married to John J. Guion Esq.

M'Calf, Miss Ann married to Mr. C. H. Vandevar.

M'Call, Miss married to Mr. Joshua C. Pruitt.

M'Call, Mr. John married in Williamson County to Miss Alice Jane Andrews daughter of Rev. M. L. Andrews.
Nashville Whig (Tues., March 31, 1846)

McCall, Mr. John P. married in Russellville, Ky. to Miss Amanthis P. Hay.
National Banner & Nashville Daily Advertiser (Sat., Feb. 23, 1833)

M'Call, Miss Rhoda married to Mr. A. L. Bell.

McCall, Mr. Smith G. married Miss Cynthia Skillington.
The Western Weekly Review - Franklin, Tenn. (Fri., Nov. 11, 1831)

McCall, Mr. Smith G. married in Williamson County to Miss Cynthia Skillington.
National Banner & Nashville Whig (Mon., Nov. 14, 1831)

M'Call, Capt. William married in Sumner County to Miss Della Wood.
National Banner & Nashville Whig (Fri., Dec. 3, 1830)

McCall, Mr. William married in Nashville on the 29th ult. by the Rev. John E. McFerrin to Miss Eliza Ann Hail.
National Banner & Nashville Daily Advertiser (Thurs., March 1, 1832)

McCallen, Mr. Henry married in Memphis, Ten. to Theodosia Blythe.
National Banner & Nashville Whig (Mon., Dec. 1, 1834)

McCallie, Col. Thomas, Washington, Tenn. married in Maryville Miss Mary A. Hooks of Blount County daughter of Robert Hooks, Esq.
National Banner & Nashville Advertiser (Mon., Jan. 9, 1832)

McCammon, Miss Susan married in Henry County to Mr. William Brown.
National Banner & Nashville Advertiser (Fri., Jan. 27, 1832)

M'Campbell, Mr. Andrew married in Henry County to Miss Sarah L. Hampton.
National Banner (March 24, 1826)

M'Campbell, Miss Betsy of Knox County to Richard Nelson Esq.

McCampbell, Miss Betsy married to Mr. James Hair.

McCampbell, Hon. Thomas C. married on the 20th inst. by the Rev. Dr. Edgar to Miss Anna Gowdy daughter of Thomas Gowdy Esq. of Nashville.
Nashville Whig (Thurs., Sept. 27, 1846)

M'Can, Mr. Melvill married in Jefferson County, Ky. to Miss Polly Maddox.
National Banner (Sat., April 18, 1829)

M'Cann, Mr. James W. married at Nicholasville, Ky. to Miss Amanda F. Downing.
National Banner & Nashville Whig (Sat., Sept. 6, 1828)

McCarkle, Miss Harriett married to Andrew J. Blackmore, Esq.

M'Carley, Miss Martha married to Mr. Claiborne Acklin.

M'Carley, Miss Martha married to Mr. Gideon Childress.

M'Carley, Mr. Wm. married in Logan County, Ky. to Miss Ann Offutt.
National Banner & Nashville Whig (Sat., Dec. 30, 1826)

McCarlin, Mr. Henry married on Sunday last by E. A. Raworth, Esq. to Miss Harriett B. Harris all of Nashville.
Nashville True & Weekly Commercial Register (Fri., Oct. 25, 1850)

McCarrol, Mr. John married in Knox County, Ten. to Miss Parmela Murphy.
National Banner & Nashville Whig (Wed., Dec. 17, 1834)

McCarroll, Miss Jane B. married to Elijah Dean.

M'Carroll, Mr. John R. married in Madison County to Miss Elizabeth C. Eddings daughter of Mr. John Eddings.
National Banner & Nashville Whig (Thurs., June 24, 1830)

M'Carry, Miss Francis married to James Caruthers.

M'Carthy, Miss Elizabeth E. married to Mr. Tho's J. Weakley.

M'Cartney, Mrs. Martha H. married to Mr. George I. Weaver.

M'Carty, Mr. Benjamin married in Tazewell, Claiborne County to Miss Eunice Cogswell.
National Banner & Nashville Whig (Mon., April 11, 1831)

M'Carty, Miss Rachel married to Mr. William P. Kyle.

M'Casland, Mr. John J. married in Maury County to Miss Eleanor Vaughn.
National Banner & Nashville Whig (Wed., June 1, 1831)

McCawley, Miss Martha married to Mr. John O. Cummins.

M'Chord, Mr. Joe married in Fayette County, Ky. to Miss Polly Peacock.
National Banner (Sat., July 11, 1829)

McClain, Miss A. married to Mr. John Anderson.

McClain, Miss Isabella married to Mr. Robert Haiston.

McClanahan, Miss Elizabeth married to Mr. Robert McQuilkin.

McClanahan, Miss Isabella married to Rev. Samuel C. Davidson.

M'Clane, Mr. Rob. married in Knox County to Miss Eleanor Weaver.
National Banner (Jan. 27, 1826)

McClannahan, Mr. James married in Henderson County to Miss Eliza
Brister.
National Banner & Nashville Daily Advertiser (Jan. 4, 1832)

M'Clean, Miss Ann married to Mr. John Roach.

M'Cleary, Miss Margaret married to Mr. Joseph Hamilton.

M'Clelan, Miss Martha F. married to Mr. Benj. Haley.

M'Clellan, Mr. Albert G. married in Madison County, Ten. to Miss
Eliza Randolph formerly of Pitt County, N. C.
National Banner & Nashville Daily Advertiser (Wed., Feb. 27, 1833)

McClellan, James D. Esq. married in Jackson, Tenn. to Miss Isabella
McLean.
National Banner & Nashville Daily Advertiser (Wed., May 23, 1832)

McClellan, Mr. John married to Miss Polly Wallace of Knox County on
Wednesday 14 inst.
Knoxville Gazette (Thurs., May 22, 1794)

McClellan, Miss Mary L. married to Mr. Donald Cameron.

M'Clellan, Miss Sophia B. married to William F. Hodges, Esq.

McClellan, Uriah married in Williamson County, Ten. to Rebecca Sullivan.
National Banner & Nashville Daily Advertiser (Mon., Aug. 26, 1833)

McClellan, William of the U. S. Army married Miss Elizabeth Sevier
daughter of John Sevier late Governor of this State married on
Thursday Aug. 9, 1810 by the Rev. Samuel G. Ramsay.
Wilson's Knoxville Gazette (Aug. 11, 1810)

M'Clelland, Miss Julia A. E. married to Mr. Benjamin Y. Trotter.

McClellean, John married on Wednesday the 14th of May 1794 Mr. John
McClellan to Miss Polly Wallace, daughter of William Wallace, Esquire
of Knox County.
Knoxville Gazette (Thurs., May 22, 1794)

McClellen, Annis Miss married to Rev. Samuel Carrick.

M'Clenchan, Miss Jane married to Mr. Francis Spencer.

McClerkin, Miss Susan married to Mr. Dudley Williams.

M'Cleveland, Mr. Sampson married in Smith County to Miss Louisa Cornwall
National Banner & Nashville Daily Advertiser (Fri., Feb. 24, 1832)

M'Clung, Mr. Hugh L. of Knoxville married at Abingdon, Va. to Miss
Rachel K. T. Morgan.
National Banner (Sat., Nov. 28, 1829)

M'Clung, James W. Esq. of Huntsville, Ala. married in Madison County,
Ala. to Miss Elizabeth Spotswood.
National Banner & Nashville Daily Advertiser (Mon., July 21, 1834)

M'Clung, Mr. John married in Blount County to Miss Nancy S. Wilson.
National Banner & Nashville Whig (Sat., Feb. 23, 1828)

M'Clung, Mr. John A. of Tuscumbia married Courtland, Ala. to Miss
Susan Gray daughter of Dr. Young A. Gray.
National Banner & Nashville Whig (Fri., Dec. 10, 1830)

McClung, Miss Margaret married to Mr. Robert H. Gardner.

McClung, Miss Margaret M. married to Ebenezer Alexander Esq.

M'Clung, Miss Margaret M. married to Ebenezer Alexander Esq.

M'Clung, Miss Mary married to Mr. Pleasant M'Clung.

M'Clung, Miss Nancy married to Mr. James Humphreys.

M'Clung, Mr. Pleasant M. married in Knoxville to Miss Mary M'Clung
daughter of Col. James W. M'Clung of Huntsville.
Nashville Whig (Thurs., April 30, 1846)

McClure, Mr. Andrew married in Lexington, Ky. to Miss Rachel Barton.
National Banner & Nashville Whig (Sat., Feb. 3, 1827)

M'Clure, Miss Anna to Mr. Wm. Hudson.

McClure, Mrs. Isabella married to William H. Mitchell.

M'Clure, Miss Marian married to Gustavus A. Henry Esq.

M'Clure, Miss Nancy married to Mr. Richard D. Rankin.

M'Clure, Mrs. Susan married to Mr. Cain.

M'Clure, Mrs. Susan married to Mr. Clain.

McClure, Mr. W. C. married on the 31st ult by Rev. A. H. Kerr to
Miss Eliza J. White both of Clarksville.
Nashville Whig (Sat., April 4, 1846)

M'Clutchin, Miss Elizabeth married to Joshua D. Hill.

M'Collister, Miss Sabra married to Mr. John D. Billings.

M'Comb, Miss Nancy W. married to Rev. Cyrus W. Wilson.

McCombs, Miss Frances married to Mr. Ferguson Flemming.

McCombs, Mr. George B. of Nashville married in Giles County to Miss
Mary B. Jones.
Nashville Whig (Tues., April 14, 1846)

M'Combs, Mr. James of Nashville married on the 12th inst. by the Rev.
Mr. Cloud to Miss Elizabeth Royle of Lexington, Ky.
The Nashville Gazette (Sat., March 25, 1820)

M'Combs, Miss Maria married to Mr. John H. Smith.

McConnel, Capt. John P. of Davidson County married to Miss Martha
Kennedy of Davidson County on Thursday 12 inst.   (Sat.,June 14,1806)
Impartial Review & Cumberland Repository - published at Nashville/

M'Connell, Miss Ann married to Mr. Henry C. Walsh.

M'Connell, Miss Ann L. married to Mr. N. B. Garner.

M'Connell, Miss Myrah married to Capt. Angerean Gray.

M'Connell, Miss Sarah married to Mr. George Buchanan.

M'Connell, Miss Winniford married to Dr. William Muncooksey.

M'Conner, Mr. Newton married in Blount County to Miss Nancy Browdy.
National Banner & Nashville Daily Advertiser (Mon., April 29, 1833)

McCool, Miss Elizabeth A. married to Mr. John L. Collins.

M'Corcle, MIss Elizabeth L. married to Dr. Joel B. Houston.

M'Cord, Mr. J. E. married in Maury County to Martha Andrews.

M'Cord, Mr. John A. of Nashville formerly of Pittsburgh married in
Pittsburg on the 25th Dec. by the Rev. Mr. Hudson to Miss Letitia
Anderson of that city.
National Banner & Nashville Whig (Wed., Jan. 21, 1835)

M'Cord, Mr. William of Illinois married in Greene County to Miss
Elizabeth Rice daughter of David Rice Esq.
Nashville Whig (Thurs., March 19, 1846)

McCorkle, Miss Harriett married to Andrew J. Blackmore Esq.

M'Corkle, Dr. M. married in Wilson County on the 21st by the Rev.
D. Lowry to Miss Catherine Ann Munford.
National Banner & Nashville Daily Advertiser (Wed., April 3, 1833)

McCorkle, Mrs. Mary married to Mr. Benjamin Diggs.

McCorkel, Mr. Samuel P. married in Henry County to Miss Louisa V.
Basen.
National Banner & Nashville Daily Advertiser (Wed., Aug. 29, 1832)

M'Cormack, Miss Grace married to Mr. Hardin Campbell.

M'Cormack, Mr. William married in Anderson County to Miss Elizabeth
Butler.
National Banner & Nashville Whig (Thurs., June 3, 1830)

M'Cormick, Mr. Alexander of Washington City married in Smith County
at the residence of Col. Robert Allen to Miss Eliza Van Horn daughter
of the late Alexander Van Horn of Maryland.
National Banner & Nashville Daily Advertiser (Thurs., May 1, 1834)

M'Cormick, Mr. Samuel married at New Hromony, Ia. to Miss Adelaide
A. Lanphear.
National Banner (Feb. 24, 1826)

M'Corpen, Miss Martha of Maury County married to Mr. Enos J. Kilpatrick.

McCorry, Miss Frances married to Mr. James Caruthers.

M'Corry, Miss Susan married to James P. Clark Esq.

M'Corskry, Miss Alison Nisbet married tp Professor Charles Cleveland.

McCown, Mr. George W. of Nashville married on Feb. 8th 1848 by the
Rev. F. E. Pitts to Miss Mary Elizabeth Guy of Davidson County.
The Politician & Weekly Nashville Whig (Fri., Feb. 18, 1848)

M'Cown, Mr. Joshua W. married at Columbia to Miss Martha Shepard.
National Banner & Nashville Whig (Sat., May 17, 1828)

M'Coy, E. B. Esq. married in Madison County to Miss Nancy Ann Gillespie
National Banner & Nashville Whig (Sat., March 31, 1827)

M'Coy, Mr. Spruce married in Lincoln County to Miss Hannah Barclay.
National Banner & Nashville Whig (Sat., July 29, 1826)

McCracken, Mr. A. D. of Reynoldsburg married on the 29th Oct. to Miss
Madalina M. Williams all of Humphreys County.
National Banner & Nashville Whig (Wed., Nov. 11, 1835)

M'Cracken, Mr. Ezekiel A. married in Monroe County to Miss Nancy Shoemaker,
National Banner & Nashville Whig (Fri., Sept. 9, 1831)

M'Cracken, Miss Malinda married to Mr. William Harrell.

McCrackin, Mr. Ephraim married in Maury County, Ten. to Miss
Elizabeth A. Walker.
National Banner & Nashville Whig (Mon., Jan. 26, 1835)

M'Crackin, Mr. Ephraim married in Davidson County to Miss Elizabeth A.
Walker.
Nashville Republican (Tues., Jan. 27, 1835)

McCrady, Mr. W. M. married in Maury County to Miss Rebecca Moore.
National Banner & Nashville Daily Advertiser (Mon., Dec. 10, 1832)

McCreary, Andrew J. of Mississippi married on Thursday evening by
Rev. Doctor Wharton to Letitia C. Hagan daughter of Henry Hagan Esq.
of Nashville.
Nashville Whig (Sat., Sept. 7, 1844)

McCree, Miss Josephine late of Jackson married to Curtius H. Saunders
Esq.

McCreery, Mr. Phocion R. merchant of St. Louis married on the 8th
inst. by the Rev. Dr. Edgar to Miss Mary Jane Hynes, daughter of Col.
Andrew Hynes of Nashville.
Nashville Whig (Oct. 10, 1846)

M'Crory, Miss Hannah married to Mr. Harvey D. Parrish.

McCrory, Miss Hannah married to Mr. Thomas Hardeman.

M'Culloch, Miss Adelaide married to Mr. James Nichol.

McCulloch, Benjamin W. of Rutherford County married in Nashville on
the 19th inst. by the Rev. Mr. Hanna to Miss Ann Matilda Cannon second
daughter of the late Gov. Cannon.
Nashville Whig (Sat., Oct. 21, 1843)

McCulloch, Miss Elizabeth married to Mr. Thomas Kirkman.

McCulloch, Mr. Samuel D. of Nashville married in Murfreesboro on the
16th at the residence of D. D. Wendel by the Rev. A. L. P. Green to
Miss Sarah Ann Booker daughter of the late Richardson Booker.
Nashville Whig (Sat., Nov. 19, 1842)

M'Culloch, Miss Sarah married to Mr. John H. Smith.

M'Cullock, Miss Mary E. married to Thomas Hoard, Esq.

McCullock, Mr. Robert married in Cincinnati to Miss Ann Bowshear.
National Banner & Nashville Whig (Nov. 17, 1827)

M'Cullough, Mr. Alexander married in Henry County to Miss Louisa Bomar.
National Banner & Nashville Daily Advertiser (Wed., July 24, 1833)

McCullough, Miss Pheriba C. married to Col. James A. Crutcher.

McCullough, Mr. Samuel D. married in Maury County to Miss Harriet C. Wallis.
National Banner & Nashville Whig (Sat., Jan. 10, 1829)

McCurdy, Louisa F. married to Mr. George A. Robertson.

McCurdy, Miss Rebecca S. married to Mr. Fred Fisher.

McCurdy, Mr. Samuel M., printer of Nashville married on the 27th April in Little Rock, Arkansas by William K. Inglish, Esq. to Miss Arabella Armstrong.
Nashville Union (Mon., May 20, 1839)

M'Cutchen, Miss Eliza married to Mr. Wm. Sloss.

M'Cutchen, Mr. Samuel married in Williamson County to Miss Betsey Lizenburg.
National Banner & Nashville Whig (Thurs., Sept. 23, 1830)

M'Cutchen, Mr. William B. married in Williamson County to Miss Mary R. Edmiston.
National Banner & Nashville Whig (Mon., Oct. 4, 1830)

M'Cutcheon, Mr. Nathaniel married in West Union, Ohio to Miss Sarah Moore.
National Banner & Nashville Whig (Sat., Aug. 19, 1826)

McCutcheon, Mr. Washington C. of Williamson County married on Tuesday the 19th inst. by the Rev. John W. Ogden to Miss Martha C. Hoy of Simpson County, Ky.
The Christian Record (Sat., Sept. 23, 1848)

M'Dade, Miss Susannah married to Mr. William H. Williams.

McDaniel, Miss Charlotte married to Mr. James Brown

M'Daniel, Miss Elizabeth Jane married to Mr. G. W. Stovall.

M'Daniel, Dr. George of Clarksville married in Nashville on the 14th inst. by the Rev. Dr. Weller to Miss Susannah Diggons daughter of Mr. James Diggons of Nashville.
National Banner & Nashville Whig (Fri., July 15, 1836)

M'Daniel, Dr. George of Clarksville married in Nashville on 14th inst. by the Rev. Dr. Weller to Miss Susannah Diggons daughter of Mr. James Diggons of Nashville.
Nashville Republican (Sat., July 16, 1836)

McDaniel, Mr. Hugh married in Fayette County, Ky. to Miss Sarah Robinson.
National Banner & Nashville Whig (Fri., June 20, 1828)

McDaniel, Mr. James J. married on Sunday last by the Rev. R. B. C. Howell to Miss Rowena C. Shivers of Nashville.
The Christian Record (Sat., Oct. 28, 1848)

McDaniel, Miss Margaret married to Mr. James Triggs.

McDaniel, Mary married to Mr. Shedrick Lewis.

M'Daniel, Miss Rebecca married to Mr. Casper H. W. Pluis.

M'Daniel, Mr. Samuel married in Sumner County on the 18th ult. to Miss Ann Winchester.
National Banner & Nashville Whig (Thurs., Nov. 4, 1830)

M'Daniel, Miss Septemma married to Mr. David Carson.

McDaniel, Mr. W. S. married in Gallatin to Miss Lydia Winchester.
National Banner & Nashville Whig (Sat., Jan. 26, 1828)

M'Daniel, Mr. William P. of Franklin, Tenn. married on Friday the
1st inst. by the Rev. J. M. Driver to Miss Martha E. Scantland of
Nashville.
Nashville Whig (Fri., June 1st. 1838)

McDannold, Miss Phebe married to Mr. John Jouett.

M'Dill, Miss Jane married to Mr. Solomon V. Darman.

M'Donald, Mr. Alexander merchant married in Nashville by the Rev.
Mr. Edgar on Tuesday last to Miss Mary Harper all of Nashville.
National Banner & Nashville Daily Advertiser (Thurs., Dec. 26, 1833)

M'Donald, Mr. John N. married in Lincoln County, Ten. to Miss
Catherine H. M'Kinsie.
National Banner & Nashville Whig (Mon., April 20, 1835)

M'Donald, Dr. Jonathan married at Athens, Ala. to Miss Mary B.
Malone.
National Banner & Nashville Whig (Sat., Jan. 19, 1828)

M'Donald, Miss Lucindia W. married to Dr. Lewis Green.

McDonald, Mr. M. married in Giles County to Miss Emily C. Anderson.
Nashville Whig (Sat., April 11, 1846)

M'Donald, Miss Margaret married to Mr. Solomon Duty.

M'Donald, Miss Mary married to Mr. Charles G. Wilcox.

M'Donald, Miss Nancy C. married to Mr. William H. Baldridge.

McDonnel, Louisa married to Asbury Tarkington.

McDougal, Miss Tabitha married to Mr. L. S. Quick.

M'Dowell, Dr. Joseph N. married at Cincinnati to Miss Amanda V. Drake.
National Banner & Nashville Whig (Sat., April 14, 1827)

McDowell, Miss Nancy married to Mr. James Cochran.

M'Dowell, Miss Sarah married to Mr. James H. Allen.

M'Dowell, Miss Sarah L. married to M. L. Sullivant Esq.

M'Dowell, Mrs. Susan married to James Shannon Esq.

M'Duffie, Hon. George member of Congress married at Colubmia, S. C.
on the 27th of May to Miss Mary Rebecca Singleton Esq. daughter of
Richard Singleton Esq.
National Banner (Sat., July 4, 1829)

M'Duffy, Miss married in Maury County on the 31st ult. to Mr. Wm.
Carpenter.
National Banner & Nashville Whig (Thurs., Sept. 9, 1830)

McDuffy, Miss Rebecca married to Mr. Burrell Driver.

McElewain, Mr. James married in Warren County, Ky. to Miss Lydia
Porter.
National Banner & Nashville Advertiser (Mon., Oct. 1, 1832)

M'Elroy, Mr. Barney married in Bedford County to Miss Mary Martin.
National Banner & Nashville Daily Advertiser (Mon., Sept. 9, 1833)

M'Elwee, Miss Huldah married to Mr. Wm. Wheeler.

M'Elwee, Mr. James H. married to Miss Sa. L. Anderson daughter of
Mr. Gabriel Anderson married in Madison County.
National Banner & Nashville Whig (Jan. 1, 1830)

M'Elwee, Mr. Wm. married in Roane County to Miss Lucinda Eblen.
National Banner (Sat., April 11, 1829)

M'Ewen, Mr. C. E. married in Madison County to Miss Narcissa F. Newsom.
National Banner & Nashville Whig (Sat., June 7, 1828)

McEwen, John A. Esq. of Nashville married in Columbia on Thursday
19th inst. by Rev. James M. Arnell to Miss Elina J. Frierson daughter
of S. D. Frierson Esq. of Columbia.
The Christian Record (Sat., Nov. 4, 1848)

McEwen, Miss Margaret D. H. married to John Trimble, Esq.

McEwen, Miss Margaretta D. H. married to John Trimble Esq.

McEwen, Miss Sarah married to Mr. S. Jones Ridley.

McEwen, Miss Sarah Caroline married to Mr. John T. Jones.

M'Ewen, Miss Sarah Caroline married to Mr. John T. Jones.

McEwen, Miss W. Elizabeth married to Mr. Liston Stones.

McEwen, William Esq. merchant of Chulahoma, Miss. married on the 25th
ult. by the Rev. M. M. Marshall to Miss Tabitha V. McKinney daughter
of Dr. John V. McKinney of Fayetteville, Tenn.
National Banner & Nashville Whig (Wed., Aug. 2, 1837)

M'Ewen, Major William S. married in Kingston to Miss Matilda V. Clack
daughter of Thomas N. Clack Esq.
National Banner & Nashville Daily Advertiser (Mon., Jan. 16, 1832)

Macey, Mr. Silas N. married on Sunday last at the First Baptist Church
by the Rev. Dr. Howell to Miss Caroline A. Grady all of Nashville.
The Christian Record (Sat., Nov. 11, 1848)

McFadden, Miss Elizabeth H. married to John E. Erwin.

McFadder, Mr. C. married in Lincoln County, Ten. to Miss Minerva
Silvertooth.
National Banner & Nashville Whig (Dec. 5, 1834)

M'Farland, Benj. M. Esq. formerly of Wilson County, Ten. married Miss
Penina Dunn in Weakly County on the 7th inst.
Nashville Republican & State Gazette (Sat., August 30, 1834)

M'Farland, Miss Cynthia married to Mr R. Norman.

McFarland, Mr. George married in Jefferson County to Miss Polly Ann
Barton daughter of Wm. Barton Esq.
National Banner & Nashville Whig (Wed., Nov. 23, 1831)

McFarland, Mr. James H. married in Wilson County Nov. 1st. by the Rev.
Joseph Wynnes to Miss Charlotte Walker all of Wilson County.
Daily Republican Banner (Wed., Nov. 14, 1838)

M'Farland, Mr. John married in Henry County to Miss Nancy Ballard.
National Banner & Nashville Daily Advertiser (Thurs., March 22, 1832)

McFarland, Mr. John Jr. of Wilson County married on Wednesday last at
the residence of James Whitsett by himself to Miss Fanny Gillam
daughter of William Gillam Esq. of Nashville.
Nashville Whig (Sat., June 27, 1846)

M'Farland, Miss Maria married to Dr. Crampton G. Harris.

McFarland, Miss Nancy marroed to Mr. James H. Payton.

McFarland, Mrs. Ruth married to Mr. Anderson Hailey.

McFarland, Miss Sarah married to Mr. Joseph H. Alvord.

M'Farland, Miss Sarah married to Mr. Orange Swan.

M'Farland, Miss Saray married to Mr. Orange Swan.-

M'Ferrin, Rev. John B. of the Tennessee Conference married near Nashville on the 18th inst. by Rev. Mr. Green to Miss Almira A. Probart
of Davidson County.
National Banner & Nashville Daily Advertiser (Fri., Sept. 20, 1833)

M'Ferrin, Rev. Wm. of Tenn. married on the 23d of June to Miss Minerva
Oldham of Williamson County.
Nashville Republican (Sat., July 4, 1835)

M'Ganey, Miss married to Mr. James Miller.

McGaughey, Miss Lucinda married to Mr. Isaac B. Taylor

McGavock, Mr. David R. of Nashville married on the 23rd ult. at the
residence of Mr. F. A. Owen near Memphis, Tennessee by Rev. Moses
Brock to Miss Willie E. Harding of Memphis.
Nashville True Whig & Weekly Commercial Register (Fri., June 7, 1850

McGavock, Mr. David T. married in Nashville on the 4th by the Rev.
Mr. Weller to Miss Caroline Eliza Pugsley daughter of Charles Pugsley,
M. D., dec'd.
National Banner & Nashville Daily Advertiser (Fri., Dec. 6, 1833)

M'Gavock, Mr. David T. married in Nashville to Miss Caroline Eliza
Pugsley.
Nashville Republican & State Gazette (Sat., Dec. 7, 1833)

M'Gavock, Francis Esq. of this town married on Thursday evening last to
Miss Amanda P. daughter of Mr. John Harding of this county.
Nashville Whig (Oct. 27, 1823)

McGavock, Hugh W. Esq. married in Nashville on the 25th inst. by the
Rev. Dr. Wharton to Mary W. Hagen daughter of Henry W. Hagen Esq.
Nashville Whig (Thurs., July 27, 1843)

M'Gavock, Mr. James R. son of Randoll M'Gavock Esq. of Williamson
County married on Thursday Nov. 1st. of Gallatin by the Rev. Mr. Hume
to Miss Louisa W. Chenault.
National Banner & Nashville Daily Advertiser (Fri., Nov. 2, 1832)

M'Gavock, Mr. James R. son of Randall M'Gavock Esq. of Williamson mar-
ried on Thursday Nov. 1st. at Gallatin by the Rev. Mr. Hume. to Miss
Louisa W. Chenault.
The Western Weekly Review - Franklin, Tenn. (Fri., Nov. 9, 1832)

McGavock, John of this vicinity married on Thursday last January 25,
1820 to Miss Sally Shall of Nashville.
Nashville Gazette (Sat., Jan. 29, 1820)

McGavock, Mr. John married on the same evening Thursday last to Miss
Elizabeth Hinton both of this County.
Nashville Whig (Nov. 10, 1823)

McGavock, Col. John of Williamson County, Tennessee married in the
parish of Terrebonne on Wednesday the 6th inst. by the Rev. Mr.
McNari to Miss Caroline E. Winder daughter of Col. V. P. Winder
N. O. Delta.
The Christian Record (Sat., Dec. 23, 1848)

McGavock, Miss Lucinda married to Col. J. George Harris.

McGavock, Miss Margaret married to Mr. Hardy Bryant.

McGavock, Miss Nancy married to Mr. Eldridge Cloud.

M'Gavock, Mr. Randall jun. married in this place on Tuesday March 24, 1818 to Miss Almyra Haynes by the Rev. Mr. Wm. Hume.
The Nash. Whig & Tenn. Advertiser (Sat., March 28, 1818)

M'Gavock, Miss Sally married to Mr. Joseph L. Ewing.

McGehee, Mr. George W. married in this town last evening by the Rev. Dr. Lindsley to Mrs. Cynthia Ann Campbell.
National Banner (April 7, 1826)

McGehee, Mr. Thomas G. of Madison County, Ala. married in Lincoln County to Miss Minerva Hunt.
National Banner & Nashville Daily Advertiser (Mon., Oct. 1, 1832)

McGill, Miss Mechtileis married to Mr. O. B. Baell.

M'Gill, Miss Matilda married to O. B. Baell Esq.

McGimpsey, Miss Arey Eliza married to Doctor Joseph Kincaid.

McGinnis, Mr. Isaac N. married in Nashville at Andrew Church on Sunday the 4th inst. by the Rev. John B. McFerrin to Miss Nancy L. Johnson both of Davidson County.
The Christian Record (Sat., April 10, 1847)

M'Gonegil, Mr. John married at New Harmony, Ia. to Miss Lucy Ann Gilbert.
National Banner (Feb. 24, 1826)

M'Goodwin, David W. Esq. married in Princeton, Ky. to Miss Susan C. P. B. Wiggenton.
National Banner & Nashville Whig (Sat., April 21, 1827)

McGoodwin, Mr. John married in Warren County, Ky. to Miss Susan White.
National Banner & Nashville Whig (Sat., Feb. 24, 1827)

McGowen, Miss Melissa married to Mr. M. D. F. H. Brooks.

McGrady, Mr. W. M. married in Maury County near Springhill by the Rev. Jas. Porter to Miss Rebecca Moore.
The Western Weekly Review - Franklin, Tenn. (Fri., Dec. 7, 1832)

McGrath, Mr. James from County Donegal, Ireland married on the 26th inst. by John Wright Esq. to Miss Mary E. Harrison of Nashville.
Nashville Whig (Fri., July 27, 1838)

M'Grath, Mr. T. A. of Louisville married in Lexington, Ky. to Miss Mary Ann Roper.
National Banner & Nashville Whig (Wed., Jan. 19, 1831)

McGraw, Mr. John C. married in Nashville on 28th of June by the Rev. J. B. McFerrin to Miss S. B. Willis daughter of William L. Willis Esq.
National Banner & Nashville Daily Advertiser (Fri., June 29, 1832)

McGraw, Miss Letitia married to Mr. John Mitchell.

M'Graw, Miss Thirsa Ann married to Mr. James Varnell.

MacGregor, George MacKenzie of Ross-shire Scotland married in Nashville onthe 20th by the Rev. J. Thos. Wheat to Miss Jane Maria Christian daughter of Thomas Christian Esq. of Dublin, Ireland.
Nashville Whig (Fri., Feb. 21, 1840)

McGregor, Miss Martha M. married to Temple O. Harris Esq.

McGregory, Miss Mary Ann married to Mr. Thomas O. Tilghman.

McGregor, Mr. Ransford married in Rutherford County, Ten. to Miss
Isabella Henderson daughter of the late Col. James Henderson.
National Banner & Nashville Daily Advertiser (Sat., Sept. 6, 1834)

MacGregory, George MacKenzie of Ross-Shire, Scotland married in Nash-
ville on the 20th by the Rev. J. Thos. Wheat to Miss Jane Maria
Christian daughter of Thos. Christian Esq. of Dublin, Ireland.
Daily Republican Banner (Sat., Feb. 22, 1840)

Macguire, Edward Esq. of Nashville married in New Orleans on the 6th
inst. to Miss Fanny Brooks of New Orleans.
Nashville Whig (Sat., June 17, 1843)

M'Guire, Miss Mary married to Capt. David Looney.

M'Guire, Miss Polly married to Mr. Sharp Ray.

McGuire, Miss Sarah married to Mr. Freeman Johnson.

McHaffie, Mr. David married in Knoxville to Miss Catharine Sharod.
National Banner & Nashville Daily Advertiser (Mon., April 9, 1832)

M'Henry, Miss Elizabeth married to Mr. Samuel Gilston.

McIlwee, Mr. Thomas B. married in Point Remove township, Conway County,
Ark. on Thursday the 7th ult. to Miss Elizabeth A. Humphreys formerly
of Maury County.
National Banner & Nashville Whig (Mon., Nov. 1, 1830)

McIntosh, Miss Emeline married to Mr. David Porter.

McIntosh, Miss Locisa E. married to Mr. James W. Foster.

M'Iver, Mr. Evander of Rutherford County married in this County on the
16th inst. by the Rev. Mr. Hume to Miss Eliza N. Williams daughter
of William Williams Esq.
National Banner (March 24, 1826)

McIver, Mr. John of Rutherford County married at Lucust Grove on the
5th inst. by the Rev. Mr. Edgar to Miss Jane Martin, daughter of Major
Thomas Martin.
National Banner & Nashville Daily Advertiser (Nov. 6, 1833)

M'Iver, Mr. John of Rutherford County to Miss Jane Martin of Davidson
County on the 5th inst.
Nashville Republican & State Gazette (Thurs., Nov. 7, 1833)

M'Iver, Miss Maria married to Daniel Graham Esq.

M'Iver, Miss Matilda married to David Fentress Esq.

M'Iver, Mrs. Matilda married to David Fentress Esq.

McJilton, Miss Jane R. married to Mr. William F. Bang.

Mack, Miss Eleanor J. married to Mr. Miles P. Murphy.

Mackay, Miss Ellen married to Mr. Samuel H. Mayhall.

McKay, Mr. Felix G. merchant married on Wednesday the 22nd ult. by
the Rev. Robert A. Lapsley D. D. to Miss Jane W. Seay eldest daughter
of Samuel Seay Esq. of Nashville.
The Christian Record (Sat., Jan. 8, 1848)

McKay, Mr. J. D. formerly of Nashville married in Nashville on the
8th ult. by the Rev. John B. McFerrin to Miss Maria B. Mitchell daughter
of Asa T. Mitchell Esq. of Bowling Green, Ky.
Nashville Whig (Wed., Jan. 15, 1840)

M'Kay, Mr. Joseph L. married in Davidson County to Miss Margaret
Overton.
Nashville Republican (Tues., Jan. 27, 1835)

McKay, Dr. Samuel married in New Orleans, La. to Mrs. Ellen Daily.
National Banner & Nashville Whig (Wed., Nov. 12, 1834)

McKeage, Miss Elizabeth married to William M. Irwin Esq.

M'Kean, Miss Mary D. married to Mr. Isaac Kellough.

McKee, Mr. John Miller one of the editors of the Tribune married at
Knoxville, Tenn. on 29th by Rev. D. R. M'Anally to Miss Eliza Catherine
Havely daughter of I. B. Havely, Esq.
The Politician & Weekly Nashville Whig (Wed., Aug. 4, 1847)

McKee, Mr. Joseph H. married in Franklin County, Ky. to Miss Lucinda
Bartlett.
National Banner & Nashville Daily Advertiser (Mon., Feb. 27, 1832)

M'Kee, Miss Mary W. married to Mr. Cyrus L. Watson.

M'Kee, Miss Matilda married to Mr. Robert Patterson.

McKeirnan, Charles B., Esq. of Louisiana married in Nashville on the
18th inst. at the residence of Mr. Stephen D. Watkins by the Rev.
Dr. Edgar to Miss Rebecca Baxter, daughter of Mr. Robert Baxter of
Stewart County.
Christian Record (July 22, 1848)

McKendree, Mr. John A. married in Haywood County to Miss Isabella
Loving.
National Banner & Nashville Advertiser (Wed., Jan. 18, 1832)

M'Kenna, Miss Mary Ann married to Mr. Philip Casilly.

M'Kenney, Samuel T. Esq. of St. Louis married at Kahokia, Ill. to
Miss Jane Hays.
National Banner (May 10, 1826)

McKennie, Beverly R. publisher of the Nashville Whig married in Harde-
man County 28th to Miss Zarina H. Williams daughter of Robert F.
Williams Esq. to Hardeman County.
Nashville Whig (Wed., April 10, 1839)

McKennie, Beverly R. publisher of the Nashville Whig married in
Hardeman County 28th ult. to Miss Zarina H. Williams daughter of
Robert F. Williams Esq. of Hardeman County.
Daily Republican Banner (Fri., April 12, 1839)

McKennis, Miss Peggie married to Mr. Brentley Wilmore.

McKenzie, Mr. Hugh married in Fayetteville on the 24th ult. to Miss
Rebecca C. Cole.
National Banner & Nashville Whig (Fri., Jan. 29, 1830)

Mackey, Miss Margaret married to Mr. Linton Rogers.

M'Kiernan, Miss Susannah married to Hugh W. Dunlap Esq.

M'Kinley, Miss Elizabeth married to Mr. Donald Campbell.

M'Kinney, Charles Esq. merchant married in Lincoln County on Thursday 8th inst. by the Rev. Mr. Cowan to Miss E. Howell only daughter of Reese Howell
National Banner & Nashville Daily Advertiser (Fri., Nov. 16, 1832)

McKinney, Mr. Daniel H. married in Grainger County, Ten. to Miss Hannah West daughter of Thomas West Esq.
National Banner & Nashville Whig (Wed., Nov. 12, 1834)

M'Kinney, Rev. John B. married in Shelby County to Miss Mary H. Johnson.
National Banner & Nashville Whig (Mon., Dec. 13, 1830)

M'Kinney, Miss Mary married to Mr. Stephen C. Renfoe.

McKinney, Miss Tabitha V. married to William McEwen.

McKinnis, Miss Peggy married to Mr. Bently Wilmore.

MKinsie, Miss Catherine H. married to Mr. John N. M'Donald.

McKissick, Miss Eliza R. married to Dr. R. Dean.

M'Knight, Capt. Calvin H. married in Rutherford County to Miss Polly Z. Keys.
National Banner & Nashville Whig (Fri., Sept. 16, 1831)

M'Knight, Capt. Calvin H. married in Rutherford County to Miss Polly Z. Keys.
Nashville Republican & State Gazette (Tues., Sept. 20, 1831)

M'Knight, Eleanor M. married to Mr. David L. Sherrill.

M'Knight, Capt. William married at Pittsburgh to Miss Sarah Stockhouse.
National Banner & Nashville Whig (Sat., June 7, 1828)

McKoin, Mr. Eli married in Sumner County to Miss Sebella Walton daughter of Joshua Walton, Esq.
National Banner & Nashville Advertiser (Sat., Nov. 24, 1832)

McLain, Miss Mary married to Rev. Martin Wells.

McLain, Miss Nancy C. married to Mr. Jesse Bain.

M'Lane, Mr. John married in Logan County, Ky. to Miss Elizabeth Wiggington.
National Banner & Nashville Whig (Mon., Aug. 30, 1830)

McLane, Mr. John late of Waterloo, Ala. married in Hardin County, Ten. in the vicinity of Savannah to Mrs. Susan Pickle.
National Banner & Nashville Whig (Wed., Nov. 5, 1834)

McLaren, Mr. Alexander C. married in August 1831 to Miss Martha M. House.
The Western Weekly Review - Franklin, Tenn. (Fri., Sept. 2, 1831)

M'Laughlin, Miss Mary married to Mr. Joshua Sidwell.

M'Laughlin, Mr. William of Columbia married on Thursday evening by Rev. Dr. Howell to Miss Harriet G. Barry daughter of J. C. Barry of Nashville.
The Christian Record (Sat., Oct. 30, 1847)

M'Laughlin, William B. Esq. married in Lincoln County to Miss Sinia A. Hart.
Nashville Whig (Tues., April 21, 1846)

McLaurine, Mr. Franklin T. married in Giles County to Miss Ann Laird.
National Banner & Nashville Advertiser (Wed., Dec. 12, 1832)

McLean, Mr. A. Andrew married on 25th inst. by the Rev. A. L. P.
Green to Miss Louisa Elliston Quinn daughter of the Rev. M. H. Quinn.
National Banner & Nashville Whig (Wed., Oct. 26, 1836)

M'Lean, Mr. A. M. of Logan County, Ky. married Miss Barbara Ann Walton
daughter of Edward S. Walton Esq of Montgomery County, Tenn.
National Banner & Nashville Daily Advertiser (Mon., Aug. 12, 1833)

M'Lean, Mr. Andrew Jackson married in Logan County, Ky. to Miss Eliza
C. Ewing.
National Banner & Nashville Whig (Sat., Jan. 19, 1828)

M'Lean, Mr. C. B. married in Maury County to Miss Lucretia A. Williams.
National Banner & Nashville Whig (Wed., June 1, 1831)

McLean, Mr. Charles D. married on Tuesday evening last one of the
editors of the Recorder to Miss Marsha Searcy daughter of the Hon.
Bennett Searcy all of Clarksville.
The Nashville Whig (Feb. 21, 1816)

McLean, Hon. Charles D. of the House of Representatives of Tennessee.
Married in Nashville on Thursday evening 8th inst. by the Rev. Dr.
Jennings to Miss Jane E. Smith.
National Banner & Nashville Whig (Fri., Dec. 9, 1831)

McLean, Miss Isabella married to James D. McClellan Esq.

M'Lean, Mr. James married in Maury County, Ten. to Miss Elizabeth
Ricketts.
National Banner & Nashville Whig (Fri., April 10, 1835)

M'Lean, Mr. John of Elkton married in Christian County, Ky. to Miss
Eliza Price.
National Banner & Nashville Whig (Thurs., Oct. 28, 1830)

McLean, Mrs. L. L. of Memphis married in Nashville yesterday 17th
inst. to Marcus B. Winchester Esq. of Memphis.
Nashville Whig (Thurs., Aug. 18, 1842)

M'Lean, Miss Rebecca C. married to Mr. Augusta H. Richards.

McLean, Miss Sarah A. married to Dr. Joshua H. Hayward.

McLean, Mr. William married in Bedford County to Miss Isabella M.
Dickson daughter of Mr. Ezekiel Dickson.
National Banner & Nashville Daily Advertiser (Fri., March 28, 1834)

McLean, Mr. William A. Attorney at law of Clarkesville, Ark. married
on the 12th inst. by the Rev. J. W. Hanner to Miss Mary C. Bransford
daughter of the late Rev. John Bransford.
Nashville Whig (Mon., Nov. 15, 1841)

McLemore, Miss Catherine D. married to Thomas Gholson Esq.

M'Lemore, Miss Lucinda M. married to Mr. Daniel M'Rea.

McLemore, Miss Margaret married to Mr. Jonathan Thornberry.

McLemore, Miss Mary married to Mr. William O. Perkins.

M'Lemore, Miss Mary married to Mr. William O. Perkins.

McLemore, Miss Mary marrried to Dr. J. M. Walker.

M'Lene, Miss Margaret married to Mr. Samuel Crosby.

McLin, Miss Cary married to Mr. James Hedspeth.

Maclin, Miss Elizabeth C. married to Mr. Henry Driver.

McLin, Mr. James married in Jonesborough to Miss Sarah Clem.
Nashville Whig (Tues., July 7, 1846)

M'Lin, Miss Nancy married to Mr. R. Dobbins.

McLlroy, Miss Eliza married to Mr. Martin Everheart.

M'Llvaine, Miss Eveline married to Mr. John G. Bryan.

McLung, Mr. John A. of Tuscumbia married in Courtland, Ala. to Miss
Susan Gray.
The Nashville Republican & State Gazette (Thurs., Dec. 9, 1830)

M'Mahan, Miss Sarah married to Col. Thomas J. M'Arthur.

McMahon, Col. J. H. editor of the Memphis Enquirer married Wednesday
21st inst. at the Bay of Biloxi by Rev. Mr. Labbe to Caroline Rosalia
Morejon daughter of the late Col. Francisco Uraldo Morejon of the
Island of Cuba.
Nashville Whig (Thurs., July 6, 1843)

McMahon, Mr. Joseph F. married on Thursday last by the Rev. Jas. H.
Otey to Miss Jane L. Goff all of Williamson County.
The Western Weekly Review - Franklin, Tenn. (Fri., Feb. 3, 1832)

McMahon, Mr. Joseph F. married in Williamson County by the Rev. Mr.
Otey to Miss Jane L. Goff.
National Banner & Nashville Daily Advertiser (Mon., Feb. 6, 1832)

M'Mahon, Miss Nancy married to Mr. David Youngman.

McMannis, Mr. Samuel married on Thursday evening last by the Rev.
Mr. Craighead to Miss Julia Condon daughter of Mr. James Condon of
this place.
The Nashville Whig & Tenn. Advertiser (Oct. 27, 1817)

McMilin, Mr. J. H. of Robertson County married on the 17th inst. by
the Rev. A. G. Goodlet to Miss Lucy Jane Taylor, daughter of Robert
Taylor of Sumner County.
The Christian Record (April 3, 1847)

M'Millan, Andrew Esq. married at Knoxville to Miss Mary Littleford.
National Banner & Nashville Whig (Sat., May 24, 1828)

McMillan, Miss Eveline J. married to Capt. James L. Davis.

McMillan, Mr. James R. married in Madison County to Miss Lucinda Barnett
National Banner & Nashville Advertiser (Wed., Nov. 7, 1832)

M'Millen, Mr. Doak married in Lincoln County to Miss Madeline Davis.
Nashville Republican (Thurs., Feb. 5, 1835)

McMillen, Mr. William married in Lincoln County, Tenn. to Miss
Julia Moorehead.
National Banner & Nashville Whig (Fri., Oct. 17, 1834)

McMinn, Mr. Robert married in Bedford County to Miss Pernetti Chaffin.
National Banner & Nashville Whig (Sat., Nov. 18, 1826)

M'Mullen, Mrs. Betsey married to Mr. Silas Raymond.

M'Mullen, Miss Sarah married to Mr. Robert Atchinson.

McMurray, Miss Sarah married to Stephen S. Rash, Esq.

McMurray, Mr. William C. of the firm of McMurry & Saffarrans married in Nashville on the 31st ult. by the Rev. R. B. C. Howell to Miss H. Elizabeth Sloan daughter of J. H. Sloan late of New York.
The Christian Record (Sat., Nov. 4, 1848)

McMurry, Miss Louisa married to Mr. Robert Goodlett.

M'Murry, Miss Rachel A. married to Rev. Thomas C. Anderson.

M'Nabb, Mr. Edward married in Port Gibson, Missis. to Miss Eliza Wornel.
National Banner & Nashville Whig (Sat., Dec. 30, 1826)

M'Nairy, Miss Amanda married to Mr. James W. Porter.
National Banner & Nashville Whig (Sat., Nov. 3, 1827)

McNairy, Miss Eliza married to David Dickson Esq.

M'Nairy, Mr. John N. of Nashville married on the 8th inst. to Miss Matilda Henderson of Rutherford County.
National Banner & Nashville Daily Advertiser (Wed., Jan. 15, 1834)

M'Nairy, Mr. John N. of Nashville married Miss Matilda Henderson of Rutherford County.
Nashville Republican & State Gazette (Thurs., Jan. 16, 1834)

M'Nairy, Dr. John S. married in Nashville to Mi s Elizabeth Aloway on Thursday last.
Nashville Republican (Sat., June 20, 1835)

M'Nairy, Miss Mary Selina married to Mr. William Giles Harden.

McNairy, Mr. N. A. of Davidson County married Miss Catherine Hobson Davidson County on Sunday last.
Impartial Review & Cumberland Repository - published at Nashville March 10, 1808

McNairy, Maj. R. C. of Nashville married on the 3d by the Rev. Dr. Edgar to Miss Mary Jane Williams daughter of Col. Willoughby Williams of Davidson County.
The Politician & Weekly Nashville Whig (Fri., June 11, 1847)

McNairy, William H. of the house McNairy & Hamilton married in this vicinity on Wednesday by the Rev. Dr. Edgar to Miss Elizabeth P. Duval daughter of Major A. D. Duval.
Nashville Whig (Fri., Aug. 10, 1838)

M'Namer, Mr. Francis married in Louisville, Ky. to Miss Sally White.
National Banner (Sat., June 6, 1829)

M'Neal, Maj. E. P. of Bolivar married in Hardeman County on Thursday 22d inst. to Miss Ann Williams.
Nashville Republican (Tues., Jan. 27, 1835)

M'Neely, Miss Margaret B. married to Mr. William F. Harris.

McNeely, Mr. Wm. H. married in Blount County, Ten. to Miss Mary G. Luster.
National Banner & Nashville Whig (Mon., Nov. 10, 1834)

M'Neil, Daniel Esq. married in Lauderdale County, Ala. to Miss Jane Cunningham daughter of John P. Cunningham Esq.
National Banner & Nashville Advertiser (Mon., Aug. 27, 1832)

McNeil, Miss Elizabeth R. married to John P. Caruthers Esq.

M'Neil, Mr. Philip married in Madison County to Miss Sarah Todd daughter of George Todd, Esq.
National Banner & Nashville Daily Advertiser (Wed., Jan. 11, 1832)

McNeil, Dr. William of Nashville married in Columbia, Tennessee on
Wednesday last to Mrs. M. Hardin of Columbia
Nashville Whig (Wed., Dec. 26, 1838)

M'Neill, Mr. Archibald merchant of this place married on Tuesday
evening last to Miss Amy Greer daughter of the late And. Greer of
Smith County.
The Nashville Whig & Tenn. Advertiser (Feb. 14, 1818)

McNeill, George Esq. merchant of Nashville married on the 26th ult.
to Miss Ruth T. Greer daughter of Maj. Andrew Greer, dec'd. of Smith
County.
The Nashville Gazette (Sat., Sept. 11, 1819)

McNeill, Mary Miss married to William L. Brown, Esq.

McNeill, Mr. Philip married in Madison County to Miss Sarah Todd of
Henry County daughter of George Todd, Esq.
National Banner & Nashville Advertiser (Wed., Jan. 11, 1832)

M'Nutt, Mr. Dewitt of Cooke County married in Knox County to Miss Mary
Williams.
National Banner & Nashville Whig (Mon., April 11, 1831)

M'Nutt, Dewitt Esq. of Cooke County married in Knox County to Miss
Mary Williams.
Nashville Republican & State Gazette (Tues., April 12, 1831)

M'Nutt, Miss Dorcas E. married to Mr. Samuel Boyd.

M'Nutt, Mr. Peter married in Knox County to Miss Eleanor Callums.
National Banner & Nashville Whig (Sat., Feb. 23, 1828)

M'Nutt, Miss Polly married to Mr. George Loudermilk.

Macomb, Miss Alexandrine married to Maj. Henry Staunton.

Macon, Miss Susan Aurelia married to E. J. Williams.

M'Phail, Doctor Daniel of Franklin married on Tuesday last by the
Rev. Dr. Hicks to Miss Sarah Whitfield daughter of Wilkins Whitfield
Esq. of Williamson County.
The Western Weekly Review - Franklin, Tenn. (Fri., Oct. 14, 1831)

M'Phail, Dr. Daniel married in Williamson County to Miss Sarah Whitfield
National Banner & Nashville Whig (Mon., Oct. 17, 1831)

McPhearson, Miss Elizabeth married to Mr. Augustus Lebeaum.

M'Pherson, Mr. John married in Roane County to Miss Ethalinda Mahan
daughter of Mr. Robert Mahan.
National Banner & Nashville Whig (Tues., Feb. 2, 1830)

McQuary, Miss Martha A. M. married to Maj. W. W. Fulgham.

M'Queen, Miss Hannah married to Mr. Robert Johnson.

McQueston, Gen. William of Ky. married in Robertson County on Tuesday
the 20th by the Rev. Mr. Hume to Miss Malinda D. Clark.
National Banner & Nashville Daily Advertiser (Thurs., Nov. 22, 1832)

McQuilkin, Mr. Robert married in Rutherford County to Miss Elizabeth
McClanahan.
National Banner & Nashville Advertiser (Fri., April 27, 1832)

M'Quiston, Gen. William of Ky. married to Miss Malinda D. Clark.
Nashville Republican & State Gazette (Fri., Nov. 23, 1832)

M'Rea, Mr. Daniel married in Maury County to Miss Lucinda M. M'Lemore.
National Banner & Nashville Whig (Sat., Dec. 17, 1831)

McReynolds, Dr. D. C. of Rhea County married in Monroe County, Ten.
to Miss Mary Callaway.
National Banner & Nashville Daily Advertiser (Tues., Aug. 19, 1834)

McReynolds, Miss Eliza M. married to Mr. Cuningham Read.

M'Vay, Miss Atlantic P. married to Mr. Lewis C. Moore.

M'Vey, Mr. William married at West Union, O. married Mrs. Mary Smiley.
National Banner & Nashville Whig (Sat., July 22, 1826)

M'Whirter, Dr. Samuel C. married in Wilson County 28th ult. by the
Rev. Mr. Bradshaw to Miss Mary P. Cowan.
National Banner & Nashville Whig (Sat., June 7, 1828)

McWhorter, Miss Eliza S. married to Mr. Ralph Coffman.

McWhorter, Mr. William married in Liberty, Smith County, Tenn. by the
Rev. J. Evans to Miss Caroline Duncan eldest daughter of T. W. Duncan
Esq.
National Banner & Nashville Daily Advertiser (Tues., May 6, 1834)

M'Williams, Dr. Francis A. married in Woodville, Miss. to Miss Anetti
S. Nesmith.
National Banner & Nashville Whig (Sat., March 31, 1827)

Macy, Miss Eliza Ann married to Mr. Morgan B. Chinn.

Madden, Miss Mary J. married to Mr. J. R. A. Tomkins.

Maddin, Miss Nancy married to Mr. James Cawley.

Maddox, Miss Polly married to Mr. Melvill M'Can.

Maddox, Mr. Taply M. married in Stewart County on the 1st to Miss
Rhoda Ann Dunbar.
National Banner & Nashville Daily Advertiser (Fri., March 16, 1832)

Madeira, Miss Catherine married to Mr. Owen T. Reeves.

Mading, Miss Eliza married to Capt. Joseph Fogg.

Maffitt, Miss Eliza Jane married to T. L. Budd Esq.

Maffitt, Miss Eliza Jane married Mr. T. L. Budd.

Maffitt, Miss Henrietta married to Gen. Merabeau B. Lamar.

Maffitt, J. N. Jr., U. S. Navy married on the 18th ult. by the Rev.
Mr. Lewis to Mary Florence Murrell of Mobile City.
Daily Republican Banner (Thurs., Dec. 3, 1840)

Maffitt, J. N., Jr., of the U. S. Navy married on the 18th ulto. by
the Rev. Mr. Lewis to Mary Florence Murrell of Mobile City.
Nashville Whig (Fri., Dec. 4, 1840)

Maginas, Miss Drucilla married to Mr. William Baker.

Magness, Miss Zilpah married to Mr. William Glenn.

Magness, Miss Zilpath married to Mr. William Glenn.

Magoffin, Miss H. M. married to Charles M. Cunningham Esq.

Magors, Miss Charlotte married to Mr. Thomas Coleman.

Maguire, Miss Cornelia married to John W. Mays.

Maguire, Miss Ellen married to Mr. R. B. Mayes.

Mahaffy, Mr. Robert married at Lagrange, Ten. to Mrs. Minerva Myrick on 11th inst.
Nashville Republican (Tues., May 19, 1835)

Mahan, Miss Ethalinda married to Mr. John M'Pherson.

Mainor, Mr. Smith married in Rutherford County to Miss Parthenia Prim.
National Banner & Nashville Daily Advertiser (Tues., Nov. 20, 1832)

Mallard, Mr. J. W. married in Williamson County to Miss S. Ransom.
The Western Weekly Review (Fri., Dec. 2, 1831)

Mallard, Mr. J. W. married in Williamson County to Miss S. Ransom.
National Banner & Nashville Whig (Wed., Dec. 7, 1831)

Malone, Mr. Andrew married in Henry County to Miss Elizabeth Malone.
National Banner & Nashville Daily Advertiser (Fri., Jan. 27, 1832)

Malone, Miss Elizabeth married to Mr. Andrew Malone.

Malone, Miss Lucretia marroed to Mr. Wm. Simpson.

Malone, Miss Martha Jane married to Mr. Hugh S. Locke.

Malone, Miss Martha Jane married to Mr. Hugh S. Locke.

Malone, Miss Mary B. married to Dr. Jonathan M'Donald.

Malone, Miss Sarah married to Mr. McLin Harper.

Malone, Mr. William married in Maury County, Ten. to Miss Martha W. Zollicoffe.
National Banner & Nashville Whig (Mon., March 30, 1835)

Manahan, Miss Fanny married to Mr. Matthew Whitfield.

Manard, Mr. Micajah married in Henry County to Miss Catherine Sexton.
National Banner & Nashville Daily Advertiser (Thurs., Sept. 6, 1832)

Manchester, Mr. Willard of Murfreesboro to Miss Mary S. Taylor of this place married on Monday 31st of May 1819.
Nashville Gazette (June 5, 1819)

Maner, Mr. Richard T. aged about 70 married near Bowling Green, Ky. to Miss Eliza Richardson aged about 19.
National Banner & Nashville Whig (Wed., Nov. 19, 1834)

Maney, Miss Elizabeth M. married to Major William H. Bowman.

Maney, Miss Mary W. married to Edwin A. Keeble Esq.

Maney, Miss Mary W. married to Edwin A. Keeble, Esq.

Maney, Thomas H. Esq. married at the residence of David Dickinson, Esq. near Murfreesboro on the 12th by the Rev. G. T. Henderson to Miss Fanny M. Bell eldest daughter of the Hon. John Bell both of Rutherford County.
Nashville Whig (Wed., Oct. 20, 1841)

Mangrum, Mr. James married in Lincoln County, Ten. to Miss Averille Williamson.
National Banner & Nashville Whig (Wed., Nov. 12, 1834)

Manier, Miss J. W. married to Mr. M. L. Shelton.

Manier, Miss Malinda married to James R. Coursey.

Manire, Miss Matilda married to Charles Coursey.

Mankin, Mr. John married in Williamson County to Agnes Owen.
National Banner & Nashville Advertiser (Wed., May 16, 1832)

Mankin, John married in Williamson County to Miss Agnes Owen.
National Banner & Nashville Daily Advertiser (Wed., May 16, 1832)

Mankins, Mr. William married in Williamson County to Miss Martha
A. Dunn.
National Banner & Nashville Daily Advertiser (Thurs., May 1, 1834)

Manley, Mr. Hutchison married in Madison County, Ala. to Miss Elvira
Cannon.
National Banner & Nashville Daily Advertiser (Mon., Dec. 31, 1832)

Manley, Miss Sarah Ann married to Mr. William P. Hume.

Manley, Miss Sarah Ann married to William P. Hume.

Manly, Miss Eliza F. married to Mr. Jared Randle.

Manly, Miss Harriet F. married to Mr. Richard Hudson.

Manly, Mr. William married in Henry County, Ten. to Miss Geraldine
Randle.
National Banner & Nashville Whig (Wed., April 8, 1835)

Mann, Miss Carolina L. married to Mr. Jonathan Coleman.

Mann, Miss Eliza married to Mr. D. C. Hambaugh.

Mann, Miss Letsey married to Mr. Ramsey Vance.

Mann, Miss Lucy married to Maj. George Cassitt.

Mann, Miss Mahala married to Mr. Norman Smith.

Mannel, Prof. Henry of Cincinnati married on the 6th inst. by the
Rev. Mr. Huntington to Madame Mary T. Scho of Nashville.
The Christian Record (Sat., July 15, 1848)

Mannifee, Mary J. married to Martin S. Jones.

Manning, Mr. Benjamin married on Tuesday evening last to Miss Lucretia
Anthony, daughter of Mr. P. Anthony.
Nashville Whig (Aug. 11, 1823)

Manning, Miss Sarah married to Mr. B. M. Lowe.

Manning, Smith married in Williamson County to Frances Lazenbury.
The Western Weekly Review - Franklin, Tenn. (Fri., Feb. 10, 1832)

Manord, Mr. Micajah married in Henry County to Miss Catherine Sexton.
National Banner & Nashville Advertiser (Thurs., Sept. 6, 1832)

Mansfield, Rev. Clark married in Todd County, Ky. to Miss Beaty.
National Banner & Nashville Whig (Thurs., Oct. 28, 1830)

Mansfield, Mr. James married in Trigg County, Ky. to Miss Catherine
Jouett.
National Banner & Nashville Whig (Thurs., Oct. 28, 1830)

Manuel, Mr. John married in Little Rock, Ark. to Miss Jane M. Tooley
formerly of Nashville.
National Banner & Nashville Whig (Mon., Dec. 1, 1834)

Manus, Geo. married in Knox Co., Ten. to Miss Catherine Goddard.
National Banner & Nashville Daily Advertiser (Mon., June 30, 1834)

Marable, Miss Fredonia married to William H. Dabney Esq.

Marable, Dr. Henry H. married in Humphreys County to Miss Mary I.
Murray daughter of Mr. Francis Murry (the late)
National Banner & Nashville Whig (Mon., Feb. 28, 1831)

Marable, Dr. John H. Davidson County married to Miss Nancy J.
Watson Davidson County on Sunday last.
Impartial Review & Cumberland Repository - published at Nashville.
(Thurs., July 21, 1808)

Marable, Miss Sarah Ann married to Dr. Belfield Carter.

Marbury, Miss Elizabeth married to Mr. B. C. Dobson.

March, Miss Mary Elizabeth married to John L. Martin.

Mares, Miss Sophonia married to Dr. Joseph C. Strong.

Marine, Miss Rebecca married to Mr. William King.

Markham, Mr. James married in Jefferson County, Ky. to Miss Eliza
Keiser.
National Banner & Nashville Daily Advertiser (Mon., Aug. 19, 1833)

Marks, Mr. Nathan H. of Florence married in Lauderdale County, Ala.
to Miss Harriet Westmoreland.
National Banner & Nashville Whig (Sat., Sept. 13, 1828)

Marks, Miss Tabitha E. married to Mr. Jacob Reasonover.

Marley, Miss Margaret married to Mr. John F. Pate.

Marley, Mr. Robert married in Knox County to Miss Eliza Ann Martin.
National Banner & Nashville Advertiser (Tues., Oct. 9, 1832)

Marlin, Miss Adaline S. married to Mr. William S. Oliver.

Marlin, John L. Attorney at Law married on Thursday evening 16th inst.
by the Rev. J. B. Ferguson to Miss Mary Elizabeth March daughter of
Jesse D. March Esq. all of Nashville.
Nashville True Whig & Weekly Commercial Register (Fri., May 24, 1850)

Marquiss, Mr. Wm. married in Logan County to Miss Sarah Jane Boyce.
National Banner & Nashville Whig (Sat., Feb. 24, 1827)

Marr, Miss Agatha S. married to Mr. Robert Inge.

Marr, Mr. John of Davidson County married on Monday last of Davidson
County Miss Sally Blake.
Impartial Review & Cumberland Repository at Nashville (Sat., April 18,
1807)

Marrow, Mr. Allen married in Maury County to Miss Edney Ray.
National Banner & Nashville Whig (Wed., April 27, 1831)

Mars. Miss Elizabeth married to Mr. Samuel Murphy.

Marsh, Miss Clarissa married to Mr. William Marsh.

Marsh, Mr. Cyrus at Natchez married Miss Isabella Munce.
National Banner & Nashville Whig (Tues., March 2, 1830)

Marsh, Mr. William married in Lincoln Co. to Miss Clarissa Marsh.
National Banner (May 13, 1826)

Marshall, Miss Ann P. married to Mr. N. W. Butler.-

Marshall, Miss Catharine married to Mr. Berry Brown.

Marshall, Miss Cornelia married to Mr. Joseph Ryan.

Marshall, Miss Cornelia married to Mr. Joseph Ryan.

Marshall, Mr. David Jr. married in Carroll County to Miss Susan Barksdale.
National Banner & Nashville Whig (Sat., Sept. 13, 1828)

Marshall, Doctor Edward married in Davidson County on Wednesday 26th Feb. to Miss Mary A. Cheatham.
National Banner & Nashville Daily Advertiser (Mon., March 3, 1834)

Marshall, Mr. Elihu J. married on the 24th inst. by the Rev. Mr. T. Fanning to Miss Elizabeth Fairly both of this city.
National Banner & Nashville Whig (Mon., Dec. 28, 1835)

Marshall, Mr. Elihu S. of Nashville married on the 26th inst. to Miss Elizabeth Fairley.
Nashville Republican (Tues., Dec. 29, 1835)

Marshall, Miss Eliza married in Montgomery County to Mr. John B. Montgomery.
National Banner & Nashville Whig (Mon., March 28, 1831)

Marshall, Miss Eliza married to Mr. Jno. B. Montgomery.

Marshall, Miss Elizabeth married to Sylvanus E. Benson.

Marshall, Miss Elizabeth married to Mr. Slyvanus E. Benson.

Marshall, Gilbert married in Williamson County to Miss Louisa W. Nash.
The Western Weekly Review - Franklin, Tenn. (Fri., March 23, 1832)

Marshall, Gilbert married in Williamson County to Louisa W. Nash.
National Banner & Nashville Advertiser (Mon., March 26, 1832)

Marshall, Miss Hetty Ann married to Mr. Jacob Dobson.

Marshall, Humphrey married in Williamson County to Miss Frances E. McAlister.
The Western Weekly Review - Franklin, Tenn. (Fri., Feb. 1, 1833)

Marshall, Lieut. Humphrey of Franklin County, Ky. married in Franklin, Ten. on the 3d ult. by the Rev. J. Otey to Miss Frances McAllister of Franklin, Tenn.
National Banner & Nashville Daily Advertiser (Mon., Feb. 11, 1833)

Marshall, Mr. J. J. of Louisville, Ky. married in Cincinnati to Miss Eliza Horner.
National Banner & Nashville Daily Advertiser (Fri., March 14, 1834)

Marshall, Mr. James B. of Frankford married in Cincinnati to Miss Mary Ann S. Moore.
National Banner (Sat., Nov. 7, 1829)

Marshall, Mr. James E. married on Sunday 21st inst. by Joseph L. Jarrel, Esq. to Miss Mary E. Gray all of Davidson County.
Nashville True Whig & Weekly Commercial Register. (Fri., July 26, 1850)

Marshall, Mr. James K. married in Bourbon County, Ky. to Miss Catharine C. Hickman.
National Banner & Nashville Whig (Sat., Oct. 6, 1827)

Marshall, Miss Jane married to Mr. James D. Pucket.

Marshall, John Esq. married in Williamson County to Miss Margaret P. Campbell.
National Banner & Nashville Daily Advertiser (Mon., May 20, 1833)

Marshall, John C. merchant married in Louisville, Ky. to Miss Catherine M. Roberts.
National Banner & Nashville Daily Advertiser (Thurs., June 19, 1834)

Marshall, Miss Lucy A. married to Nicholas D. Coleman Esq.

Marshall, Miss M. married to Albert H. Winne Esq.

Marshall, Miss Mary married to John Anderson.

Marshall, Miss Sarah W. married to Mr. Edward Feltus.

Marshall, Mr. T. L. of Nashville, Ten. married on 23d inst. by the Rev. Mr. Howell to Miss Catherine Williams daughter of Mrs. Margaret Williams of Davidson County.
Daily Republican Banner (Wed., Nov. 29, 1837)

Marshall, Miss Tennessee married to Mr. Thomas Jefferson Stump.

Marshall, Miss Virginia E. married to Col. Wm. T. Lewis.

Marshall, Mr. William H. of Marshall County married on Wednesday the 5th inst. by Rev. H. B. Warren to Mrs. Delina Childress of Lincoln County daughter of Boone Wilson Esq.

Marsiliott, Miss Mary Jane married to Mr. A. G. Ewing.

Mart, Mr. Tazwell M. married in Russellville, Ky. to Miss Juliet Drew.
National Banner & Nashville Whig (Wed., Nov. 26, 1834)

Martin, Miss married to Mr. William Stewart.

Martin, Miss married to Mr. Daniel Grayson.

Martin, Miss Abigail married to Mr. T. T. Mosely.

Martin, Miss C. A. married to W. B. Matthews Esq.

Martin, Mr. Caswell married in Maury County to Miss Mary A. J. Galloway.
National Banner & Nashville Whig (Wed., June 1, 1831)

Martin, Miss Eliza married to Brown Cozzen Esq.

Martin, Miss Eliza married to John Seip Esq.

Martin, Miss Eliza Ann married to Mr. Robert Marley.

Martin, Miss Elizabeth J. married to Dr. David Barker.

Martin, Miss Elizabeth M. married to Doctor Samuel A. R. Dobbs.

Martin, Miss Emily Donelson married to Mr. G. W. J. Curry Esq.

Martin, Mr. F. of White County married in Sumner County to Miss Martha Crenshaw.
National Banner & Nashville Daily Advertiser (Mon., March 18, 1833)

Martin, Mr. George married in Hickman County, Ky. to Miss Catherine Brent Stephens of Davidson County on 12th of Oct. last.
Nashville Republican (Thurs., Jan. 1, 1835)

Martin, Mr. George married in Hickman County, Ky. to Miss Catherine Brent Stephens.
National Banner & Nashville Whig (Fri., Jan. 9, 1835)

Martin, Maj. George W. of Courtland, Ala. married in Davidson County on the 13th ult. to Miss Lucinda R. Donelson.
National Banner & Nashville Whig (Mon., Oct. 4, 1830)

Martin, Miss Harriet married to John Joyes Esq.

Martin, Mr. J. T. married in Williamson County to Miss Hannah Criswell.
Nashville Whig (Sat., July 11, 1846)

Martin, Miss Jane married to Mr. John McIver.

Martin, Miss Jane married to Mr. John M'Iver.

Martin, Mr. Jared C. married at Little Rock, A. T. to Miss Mary Douglas.
National Banner & Nashville Whig (Sat., March 10, 1827)

Martin, Mr. Jefferson married on Thursday 8th inst. to Miss Esther L. Stuart.
National Banner & Nashville Whig (Sat., Jan. 24, 1829)

Martin, Mr. John W. of the House of Martin Stevenson Co. married on the 24th by Rev. Mr. Lapsley to Miss Margaret Childress daughter of Col. Childress of Williamson County, Ten.
Nashville Whig (Wed., Dec. 25, 1839)

Martin, Mr. John W. of Nashville married on Tuesday 24th by the Rev. Mr. Lapsley to Miss Margaret J. Childress daughter of Col. William G. Childress of Pleasant Retreat, Williamson Co.
Daily Republican Banner (Fri., Dec. 27, 1839)

Martin, Mr. Joseph married in Montgomery County to Miss S. W. Adams.
National Banner & Nashville Whig (Sat., Dec. 27, 1828)

Martin, Mr. Josiah married in Rutherford County by the Rev. Thos. D. Porter to Miss Lucy Edwards.
National Banner & Nashville Whig (Tues., Dec. 27, 1831)

Martin, Mr. Joshuah L. Esq. married in Limestone County, Ala. to Miss Mary Mason.
National Banner & Nashville Whig (Sat., April 19, 1828)

Martin, Miss Julia Ann married to Mr. John Dair.

Martin, Miss Julie E. married to Mr. Benjamin D. Burch.

Martin, Miss Margaret married to Mr. J. A. Coffin.

Martin, Miss Margaret G. married to Charles Creighton Esq.

Martin, Miss Martha married to Mr. Samuel R. Rucker Esq.

Martin, Miss Martha Ann married to Mr. Clement Woodward.

Martin, Miss Martha C. married to Mr. Finney B. Gillam.

Martin, Miss Mary married to Mr. Barnett Jones.

Martin, Miss Mary married to Mr. Barnett Jones.

Martin, Miss Mary married to Mr. Barney M'Elroy.

Martin, Miss Mary married to Maj. Russell Dance.

Martin, Miss Mary Ann married to Mr. Willis L. Somerville.

Martin, Miss Mary D. married to Robert B. Currey Jr.

Martin, Miss Mary D. married to Robert B. Curry Jr.

Martin, Miss Mary J. C. married to Mr. James Ross.

Martin, Mr. Mathew married in Fayetteville, Ten. to Miss Margaret
Bright of Nashville, Tenn.
Nashville Republican & State Gazette (Thurs., April 3, 1834)

Martin, Mr. Mortimer A. Esq. married at Springfield, T. to Miss
Harriet Saunders.
National Banner & Nashville Whig (Fri., June 20, 1828)

Martin, Mr. Orville B. married at Frankfort, Ky. to Miss Sarah Ann
Sneed.
National Banner & Nashville Whig (Sat., July 8, 1826)

Martin, Miss Patsey W. married to Mr. Garnett Duncan.

Martin, Mr. Peter H. married on Thursday evening last by the Rev.
Mr. Hume to Miss Jane Bell daughter of Robin Bell, dec'd.
The Nash. Whig & Tenn. Advertiser (July 4, 1818)

Martin, Dr. Robert married in Nashville on the 1st inst. by the Rev.
Mr. Weller to Miss Priscilla Douglass eldest daughter of Col. H. L.
Douglass.
National Banner & Nashville Daily Advertiser (Fri., May 2, 1834)

Martin, Dr. Robert married in Nashville to Miss Priscilla Douglass on
1st inst.
Nashville Republican & State Gazette (Sat., May 3, 1834)

Martin, Doct. Robert married in Nashville on Tuesday last by the
Right Rev. James H. Otey to Miss E. Llewellyn Dickinson daughter of
the late Dr. William G. Dickinson.
The Politician & Weekly Nashville Whig (Fri., July 16, 1847)

Martin, Doct. Robert married in Nashville on Tuesday last by the Right
Rev. James H. Otey to Miss E. Llewellyn Dickinson daughter of the
late Dr. William G. Dickinson.
The Christian Record (Sat., July 17, 1847)

Martin, Miss Sophia Ann Josephine married to Mr. Anthony Latapie.

Martin, Miss Susan T. married to   James T. Flint, Esq.

Martin, Mr. Thomas of Pulaski, Giles County to Miss Nancy H. Topp
of Davidson County married on Tuesday evening by the Rev. Mr. Garrett.
Nashville Whig (Oct. 25, 1824)

Martin, Thomas Speaker of the House of Representatives married in
Kaskaskia to Miss Hannah Lambs.
National Banner (Jan. 6, 1826)

Martin, Capt. Thos. D. of Nashville married in Alexandria, La. on the
22nd Aug. 1850 to Miss Mary A. Brown of Louisiana.
Nashville True Whig & Weekly Commercial Register (Fri., Sept. 20, 1850)

Martin, Mr. Welcome married in Cumberland County, Ky. to Miss Elizabeth
Murphy.
National Banner & Nashville Whig (Sat., Dec. 23, 1826)

Martin, Mr. William married in Maury County to Miss Matilda Armorer.
National Banner & Nashville Whig (Mon., Oct. 4, 1830)

Martin, Mr. William married in Greenville to Miss Matilda D. Maxwell.
Nashville Republican & State Gazette (Mon., Dec. 17, 1832)

Martin, Mr. William married in Greenville, E. T. to Miss Matilda D.
Maxwell.
National Banner & Nashville Daily Advertiser (Tues., Dec. 18, 1832)

Martin, Mr. William B. Esq. married in Blount County, Tenn. to Miss Susan Montgomery.
National Banner & Nashville Advertiser (Tues., May 22, 1832)

Martin, William L. Esq. married in Wilson County on 3d inst. to Miss Emily Allcorn.
National Banner & Nashville Whig (Sat., Sept. 13, 1828)

Martin, Mr. Wilson L. married in Butler County to Miss Eleanor D. Carson.
National Banner & Nashville Whig (Mon., Sept. 26, 1831)

Mason, Miss Caroline married to Mr. David Clayton.

Mason, Miss Cyrene married to Mr. William A. Roffe.

Mason, Mr. E. C. of Russellville, Ky. married on Tuesday last at the residence of William Driver by Rev. Dr. Howell to Miss Deliah Ann Park of Nashville.
Nashville Whig (Thurs., Jan. 15, 1846)

Mason, Miss Elizabeth married to Dr. John Overton Wharton.

Mason, Miss Elizabeth Ann married to James M. Taylor.

Mason, Miss Frances married to Mr. James B. Price.

Mason, Henry E. A. Esq. married in Nashville on the 7th Dec. by the Rev. A. L. P. Green to Miss Louisa Ann Grizzard daughter of Mr. James Grizzard of Nashville.
Daily Republican Banner (Sat., Dec. 9, 1837)

Mason, Dr. James W. Mason married at Bayou de Siard, Lou. to Miss Melinda Tennell.
National Banner & Nashville Whig (Sat., March 10, 1827)

Mason, Mr. Joseph of Alabama married at Mt. Plesaant daughter of Henry Gibson, Esq. to Miss Ann Gibson.
National Banner & Nashville Advertiser (Sat., Jan. 7, 1832)

Mason, Mr. Lawrence S. married in Jackson, Madison County to Miss Sarah G. Hyde daughter of Major John H. Hyde.
National Banner & Nashville Daily Advertiser (Wed., May 22, 1833)

Mason, Mr. Lawrence S. married in Jackson, Ten. to Miss Sophia Perkins.
Nashville Republican (Thurs., July 9, 1835)

Mason, Miss Mary married to Joshuah L. Martin Esq.

Mason, Miss Mary G. married to Mr. Tyre Oldham.

Mason, Mr. Ramsey married on Monday evening last to Miss Eliza Grundy daughter of Felix Grundy Esq. of this town.
The Nashville Whig (Nov. 19, 1816)

Mason, Miss Rebecca married in Jackson, Ten. to Doctor Francis Dancy.

Mason, His Excellency Steven Governor of Michigan married in New York City to Miss Julia Elizabeth Phelps daughter of Thaddeous Phelps merchant of New York.
Nashville Whig (Wed., Nov. 14, 1838)

Mason, Mr. Sumner R. married in Nashville on the 10th inst. by Rev. Dr. Howell to Miss Mary Jane Dibble.
Nashville Whig (Thurs., Nov. 14, 1844)

Mason, Mr. William married in Knox County to Miss Cynthia Plumly.
National Banner & Nashville Whig (Sat., Sept. 15, 1827)

Mason, Miss Wuldah married to Mr. Berry Molbrey.

Masoner, Mr. John married in Greene County to Miss Nancy Kilgore.
National Banner & Nashville Whig (Mon., Dec. 6, 1830)

Massengill, Miss Mary married to James A. Whitesides, Esq.

Massengill, Miss Narcissa P. married to Mr. Benjamin F. Brideman.

Massengill, Mrs. Rebecca married to Mr. Wiley Woodall.

Massey, Manilla L. married to John Ewing Gleaves.

Massey, Mr. Thomas of Lincoln County married in this county on Thursday
last to Miss Polly Rains.
National Banner & Nashville Whig (Sat., Aug. 12, 1826)

Massey, Mr. William G. married in Rutherford County on the 12th inst.
to Miss Caroline M. Blakemore.
National Banner & Nashville Whig (Sat., July 21, 1827)

Masterson, Mr. Joseph married in Fayette County, Ky. to Miss Sarah
Webster.
National Banner (Sat., April 25, 1829)

Masterson, Mr. Thomas G. married in Nashville by Rev. J. T. Edgar on
the 3d inst. to Miss Christiana J. Roane daughter of the late Dr.
J. Roane.
National Banner & Nashville Daily Advertiser (Tues., July 8, 1834)

Masterson, Mr. Thomas G. of Nashville married on the 3d inst. to Miss
Christiana J. Roane.
Nashville Republican & State Gazette (Thurs., July 10, 1834)

Masterson, William W. Esq. of Lebanon married in Nashville on the 2nd
inst. to Miss Maria G. Grundy daughter of the Hon. Felix Grundy.
Nashville Union (Fri., Oct. 5, 1838)

Masterson, William W. Esq. married in Nashville on Tuesday by the
Rev. Dr. Edgar to Maria G. Grundy daughter of the Hon. Felix Grundy.
Nashville Whig (Fri., Oct. 5, 1838)

Mastin, Miss Mary G. married in Huntsville to Dr. Edmund Irby.
Nashville Republican & State Gazette (Wed., Jan. 30, 1830)

Mathena, Miss Sarah married to Mr. Andrew Farrell.

Mathews, Mr. Jas. married in Maury County on the 21st ult. to Miss
Surrilda L. Dooley.
National Banner & Nashville Whig (Fri., Jan. 29, 1830)

Mathews, Mr. Tennessee of Rutherford County married on 3d inst. to
Miss Priscilla W. Morton.
Nashville Republican (Tues., Dec. 22, 1835)

Mathis, Mr. Jeptha married in Hardeman County to Miss Sarah Davis.
Nashville Republican & State Gazette (Thurs., April 28, 1831)

Matlock, Miss Aleathea married to Mr. William Murry.

Matlock, Mr. Jason married in Logan County, Ky. to Miss Polly Ross.

Matlock, Mr. John of Madison County, Miss. married at Salem, Franklin
County, Tenn. to Miss Eliza Williams daughter of Richard G. Williams
Esq. of Rockcastle County, Kentucky.
National Banner & Nashville Daily Advertiser (Wed., Nov. 14, 1832)

Matthews, Mrs. married to Mr. Lewis T. Poindexter.

Matthews, Miss Alicia A. married to Mr. William G. Bakewell.

Matthews, Miss Amelia married to Mr. Ormsby Hite.

Matthews, Mr. D. of Madison married at Tuscumbia, Ala. to Miss Rebecca Herbert.
National Banner & Nashville Daily Advertiser (Thurs., Feb. 13, 1834)

Matthews, Mr. Howard married in this County to Miss Virginia Lawrence on the 27th inst.
Nashville Republican (Thurs., July 28, 1836)

Matthews, Mr. John D. married in Maury County to Miss Nancy A. Moore.
National Banner & Nashville Whig (Mon., Oct. 4, 1830)

Matthews, Miss Lucinda married to Rev. Daniel Lile.

Matthews, Miss Polly married to Mr. Henry Piper.

Matthews, W. B. Esq. married on Tuesday last at the residence of Dr. R. Martin by the Rev. John B. McFerrin to Miss C. A. Martin all of Nashville.
Nashville Whig (Thurs., Sept. 29, 1842)

Matthews, Mr. William married in Frankfort, Ky. to Miss Gabrilla Lewis.
National Banner & Nashville Whig (Mon., Oct. 17, 1831)

Matthis, Mr. Samuel married in Logan County, Ky. to Miss Fanny Curd.
National Banner & Nashville Whig (Sat., Sept. 6, 1828)

Maukin, John married in Williamson County to Miss Agnes Owen.
The Western Weekly Review - Franklin, Tenn. (Fri., May 11, 1832)

Maupin, Mr. Fountain of Campbell County married in Claiborn County, Ten. to Miss Elizabeth Rogers daughter of Maj. David Rogers.
National Banner & Nashville Whig (Fri., March 13, 1835)

Maupin, Mr. John married in Williamson County, Ten. to Miss Elizabeth Bazdell.
National Banner & Nashville Whig (Fri., Jan. 9, 1835)

Maury, Abraham P. Editor of the Nashville Republican married at Fairfield, the seat of Wm. B. Lewis, in this vicinity last evening to Miss Mary Claiborne.
National Banner (Jan. 13, 1826)

Maury, Hon. John M. married at China Grove near Natchez to Miss Carolina L. Sessions.
National Banner (Sat., June 17, 1827)

Maury, Miss Martha F. married in Williamson County on the 14th inst. by the Rev. Otey to Carey A. Farris Esq.
National Banner & Nashville Whig (Sat., Jan. 24, 1829)

Maury, Matthew F. Esq. of the U. S. Navy married in Richmond, Virginia to Miss Ann Hall Herndon of Fredericksburg.
National Banner & Nashville Daily Advertiser (Fri., Aug. 1, 1834)

Maury, Dr. R. T. married near Florence, Ala. to Miss Ellen Craig.
National Banner & Nashville Daily Advertiser (Tues., Aug. 19, 1834)

Maury, Major Robert married in this town on Wednesday evening the 19th inst. by the Rev. Mr. Hume to Miss Thedessa Thompson.
National Banner & Nashville Whig (Sat., Dec. 22, 1827)

Maxcey, Mr. Bennett of this County married in Franklin County, Ky. on the 21st of January by the Rev. Wm. Hickman to Miss Mary P. Fossee.
The Nashville Whig & Tenn. Advertiser (Feb. 7, 1818)

Maxey, Mr. Powhaten W. married in Nashville last evening by the Rev. Mr. Overall to Miss Julia Ann Hobbs.
National Banner & Nashville Daily Advertiser (Fri., Oct. 19, 1832)

Maxey, Miss Rhoda married to Mr. Frederick Ford.

Maxey, Miss Sarah married to Rev. Francis Moore.

Maxwell, Mr. married in Gibson County to Miss Martha Claiborn.
National Banner & Nashville Whig (Sat., Aug. 11, 1827)

Maxwell, Capt. Andrew married in Beechhill, Bedford County on the 4th ult. to Miss Louisa D. Watterson.
Nashville Republican & State Gazette (Sat., March 12, 1831)

Maxwell, Capt. Andrew married at Beech Grove, Bedford County on the 4th ult. to Miss Louisa D. Watterson, daughter of William S. Watterson.
National Banner & Nashville Whig (March 14, 1831)

Maxwell, Miss Catherine R. married to Mr. Joseph W. Allen.

Maxwell, Miss Mary married to Mr. Thomas B. Claiborne.

Maxwell, Miss Matilda D. married to Mr. William Martin.

Maxwell, Mr. William married in Giles County, Ten. to Miss Delila Wilkinson.
National Banner & Nashville Whig (Fri., Feb. 13, 1835)

Maxwell, Mr. William L. of Columbia married at Columbia, Tenn. on Tuesday by the Rev. Joseph Sherman to Miss Mary M. Napier.
Nashville Whig (Fri., May 21, 1841)

May, Miss Agnes married to Mr. Matthew Read.

May, Miss Catharine married to Mr. David Lawson.

May, Miss Elizabeth married to Mr. William C. Hutcheson.

May, Mr. James F. married in Davidson County on Thursday 22d inst. by the Rev. Mr. Edgar to Miss Eliza Perkins daughter of William Perkins, dec'd.
National Banner & Nashville Daily Advertiser (Tues., May 27, 1834)

May, Miss Laura E. married to Andrew McAulay.

May, Miss Mary married to Hon. John Overton.

May, Miss Mary L. married to Mr. Richard H. Barry.

May, Mr. Philip married in Madison County to Miss Caroline Dent.
National Banner & Nashville Whig (Thurs., June 3, 1830)

May, Hon. William L. married in Wilmington, Deleware on Dec. 27th Representative in Congress from Illinois to Caroline Rodney daughter of the late Caesar A. Rodney of Deleware.
Nashville Whig (Tues., Jan. 16, 1838)

Mayatt, Mr. Gordon married in Knox County to Miss Mary Hillsman.
Nashville Republican & State Gazette (Mon., April 29, 1833)

Mayes, Miss Minerva H. married to Mr. William Fields.

Mayes, Miss Minerva H. married to Mr. William Fields Jr.

Mayes, Mr. R. B. married in Columbia, Ten. to Miss Ellen Maguire.
National Banner & Nashville Whig (Fri., Jan. 9, 1835)

Mayfield, Miss Diana S. married to Mr. Edward C. Wilkerson.

Mayfield, Isaac N. married in Williamson County to Louisa Spencer.
The Western Weekly Review (Franklin, Tenn.) Fri., Feb. 10, 1832

Mayfield, Mr. Milton G. married in Giles County to Miss Mary A. Porter
daughter of David W. Porter, Esq.
National Banner & Nashville Advertiser (Fri., Dec. 21, 1832)

Mayfield, Mr. Quarles of Giles County married to Miss Elizabeth Sutton
in Bedford County.
Nashville Republican & State Gazette (Wed., January 16, 1833)

Mayfield, Mr. Quarles of Giles County married in Bedford County to
Miss Elizabeth Sutton.
National Banner & Nashville Daily Advertiser (Thurs., Jan. 17, 1833)

Mayfield, Thos. S. married in Williamson County, Ten. to Lucy Ann
Reams.
National Banner & Nashville Whig (Wed., Dec. 17, 1834)

Mayhall, Mr. Samuel H. married in Louisville, Ky. to Miss Ellen Mackey.
National Banner & Nashville Advertiser (Tues., Nov. 13, 1832)

Mayhew, Mr. Zaccheus A. married at Louisville, Ky. to Miss Eliza
Luchen.
National Banner & Nashville Whig (Sat., Jan. 10, 1828)

Maynard, Miss Emeline married to Mr. Horace P. Kezer.

Maynard, Miss Lucinda married to Mr. Henry J. Pope.

Maynard, Mr. Nelson J. married in Louisville, Ky. to Miss Gabriella
N. Walker.
National Banner & Nashville Whig (Thurs., May 20, 1830)

Mayo, Miss Maria D. married to Major General Winfield Scott.

Mayo, Miss Mary A. married to Capt. A. S. Lewis.

Mayor, Mr. William married to Miss Agnes Adams in Christian County, Ky.
National Banner & Nashville Whig (Wed., Oct. 19, 1831)

Mays, Daniel Esq. married at Lexington, Ky. to Mrs. Elizabeth Humphreys
National Banner & Nashville Daily Advertiser (Wed., June 5, 1833)

Mays, Mr. George A. married at Port Gibson, Miss to Miss Mary Ann
Montgomery.
National Banner (March 10, 1826)

Mays, Geo. G. married in Williamson County to Lavinia Davis.
National Banner & Nashville Daily Advertiser (Mon., Aug. 26, 1833)

Mays, John W. married in Maury County to Miss Cornelia Maguire.
Nashville Whig (Tues., July 14, 1846)

Mays, Miss Joney Ann married to _apt. William Long.

Mays, Miss Mary married to Mr. Samuel D. Frierson.

Mays, Miss Salina married to Mr. Albert Wingfield.

Mayson, Francis M. Esq. married at Hazlewood in this vicinity on the
8th inst. by the Rev. Mr. Howell to Ann Weston Horton second daughter
of Joseph W. Horton Esq.
Nashville Whig (Sat., Nov. 10, 1842)

Meade, Miss Seignora P. married to Dr. George N. Smith.

Meader, Mr. James Gaspard married at Trinity Chruch, Boston, by the Rev. Dr. Wainwright to Miss Clara Fisher of the Theatre.
National Banner & Nashville Whig (Mon., Dec. 29, 1834)

Meadow, Miss Angelletta married to Mr. W. S. Harris.

Meadow, Miss Elizabeth married to Mr. James B. Lowry.

Meadows, Miss Lucinda married to Mr. John H. Allen.

Meadows, Miss Angeletta married to Mr. W. S. S. Harris.

Meadows, Mary J. married to Chas. Collier.

Meany, Miss Martha H. F. married to Mr. M'William Carroll.

Mears, Mr. Isaac married at Cincinnati to Miss Abigail Raymond.
National Banner & Nashville Whig (Sat., Nov. 22, 1828)

Mebane, Mr. James B. of Williamson County married in Pulaski to Miss Louisa K. Perry.
Nashville Republican (Thurs., Aug. 13, 1835)

Mecham, Miss Francis married to Mr. Henry Dickson.

Mechan, Mr. John W. married to Miss Sarah Jane Coman.

Medlin, Miss Nancy married to Mr. Jesse McBrown.

Meek, Mr. John married in Tuscaloosa to Miss Eliza Webb.

Meeks, Miss Mary married to Mr. Wyly George.

Meese, Mr. Philip married in Maury County to Miss Harriet Butt.
National Banner & Nashville Whig (Sat., Feb. 7, 1829)

Mefford, Mr. Lilburn married in Grainger County to Miss Annette Rice.
National Banner & Nashville Whig (Fri., March 27, 1835)

Megowan, Miss Jane W. married to Mr. James Penny.

Megowan, Miss Julia C. married to Mr. Percival Gough.

Megowan, Miss Mary A. married to Mr. William P. Curd.

Meigs, Miss Theresa married to Rev. Fielding Pope.

Melaw, Miss Elizabeth married to Mr. John Speaker.

Menard, Miss Abziore married to Capt. George H. Kennerdy.

Menees, Miss Eliza married to Mr. John R. Dabbs.

Menefee, Richard H. Esq. married at Lexington, Ky. to Miss Sarah B. Jouitt daughter of the late Mr. Mathew H. Jouitt.
National Banner & Nashville Daily Advertiser (Wed., Aug. 22, 1832)

Meng, Miss Paulina married to Mr. Benjamin West.

Menifee, Mr. Jonas H. married on Thursday evening 11th by the Rev. Mr. Howell to Miss Elvira Scales all of Davidson County.
National Banner & Nashville Whig (Wed., June 17, 1835)

Menifee, Miss Mary D. married to Mr. James H. Greene.

Menifee, Miss Susanna B. married to Mr. Philip S. Stump.

Menifee, Miss Susannah B. married to Mr. Philip S. Stump.

Mercer, Miss Eliza married to Mr. John Thomas.

Mercer, Miss Patsey married to Mr. Paul Rainherd.

Meridith, Miss Isabella married to Dr. James H. Walker.

Meredith, Miss Isabella J. married to Dr. James H. Walker.

Meredith, Miss Mary married to Mr. D. C. Topp.

Meredith, Major Samuel married near Courtland, Ala. to Miss Judith Harris.
National Banner & Nashville Whig (July 8, 1826)

Meredith, Col. Samuel married in Franklin County, Ala. to Miss Louisa B. Hogan on 13th.
Nashville Republican & State Gazette (Sat., Nov. 23, 1833)

Meredith, Miss Virginia married to Mr. James H. Topp.

Meredith, Mr. W., Wholesale merchant of Nashville married on the morning of the 18th inst. by the Rev. Mr. Mack to Mrs. Mary T. Booker of Columbia, Tenn.
Nashville True Whig & Weekly Commercial Register (Wed., Dec. 25, 1850)

Meredith, Zenobia Aurelia married to Mr. Simon Sanders.

Merilie, Mr. John married in Garrered County, Ky. to Miss Lucinda Smith.
National Banner & Nashville Whig (Sat., Sept. 15, 1827)

Meritt, Miss Sarah married in Williamson Co. to Mr. R. R. Haynes.

Meritt, Miss Sarah married to Mr. R. R. Haynes.

Meriwether, Miss Caroline married to Mr. Wm. Ray.

Meriwither, Mr. David married in Madison County, Ten. to Miss Eliza Jane Deberry eldest daughter of Mathins Deberry Esq.
National Banner & Nashville Whig (Fri., Dec. 12, 1834)

Meriwether, Miss Frances married to Mr. Cobb.

Merrell, Mr. James D. of South Carolina married in Nashville on Friday the 29th ult. by the Rev. William Hume to Mrs. Mary B. Searcy relic of the late Hon. Bennett Searcy of Clarksville.
The Nashville Gazette (Wed., Nov. 3, 1819)

Merril, Miss Martha married to Mr. Oliver W. Whitmore.

Merrill, Miss Mary married to Mr. Thos. Haines.

Merriman, Miss Jane married to Mr. Harvey Norman.

Merrit, Washington married in Williamson County, Ten. to Louisa Owen.
National Banner & Nashville Daily Advertiser (Mon., Aug. 26, 1833)

Merritt, Miss Elizabeth married to Mr. R. Butterworth.

Merritt, Mr. Henry J. married in Sept. 1831 to Miss Rebecca Newsom.
The Western Weekly Review - Franklin, Tenn. (Fri., Sept. 23, 1831)

Merritt, Miss Katharine married to Mr. William Montgomery.

Merritt, Miss Narcissa married to Mr. James Johnson.

Merritt, Miss Sarah married to Mr. B. R. Haynes.

Merritt, Mr. William T. married in Williamson County to Miss Mary Shannon.
The Western Weekly Review - Franklin, Tenn. (Fri., Dec. 2, 1831)

Merritt, Mr. William T. married in Williamson County to Miss Mary Shannon.
National Banner & Nashville Whig (Wed., Dec. 7, 1831)

Merriwether, Albert G., Esq. married in Jefferson County, Ky. to Miss Edna Miller.
National Banner (June 27, 1829)

Merryman, Miss Jane married to Mr. Harvey Norman.

Mershon, Mr. James R. married on the 15th Oct. by the Rev. Dr. Howell to Miss Susan M. Atwater.
Nashville Whig (Thurs., Nov. 14, 1844)

Metcalfe, Miss Mary married to Mr. Corban Bull.

Metz, Mr. Henry of Memphis married on Tuesday the 22nd by the Rev. Jonathan Huntington to Miss Elizabeth Paulus of Nashville.
The Christian Record (Sat., Aug. 26, 1848)

Neuce, Mr. George married in Bedford County to Miss Martha Moore.
Nashville Republican & State Gazette (Wed., Jan. 16, 1833)

Mickley, Mr. James E. of Nashville married to Miss Sophia Morgan by Rev. A. L. Green.
Nashville Republican & State Gazette (Tues., Jan. 21, 1834)

Milam, Miss Eliza married to Mr. H. H. Hardin.

Miles, Miss Arrena married to Mr. William H. Renegar.

Miles, Mr. Bedford married on Tuesday June 4th by the Rev. Bartlet Barnes to Miss Narcissa Leeper all of Davidson County.
Daily Republican Banner (Fri., June 7, 1839)

Miles, Mr. John B. married in Williamson County to Miss Mary J. Edmondson.
The Western Weekly Review - Franklin, Tenn. (Fri., Dec. 23, 1831)

Miles, Miss Susanna married to Mr. Henry G. Kelvey.

Miliken, Miss Martha married to Dr. James P. Parker.

Millard, Miss Ann M. married to Maj. Francis W. Armstrong.

Millard, Miss Rebecca married to Lieut F. Britton.

Millen, Miss Elizabeth married to Mr. William Roberts.

Miller, Mr. Alexander of Davidson County married to Miss Agness Waites on Sunday last.
Nashville Republican (Tues., Sept. 8, 1835)

Miller, Miss Amanda Louisa married to Robert Morris, Esq.

Miller, Miss Ann A. married to Mr. James Gatewood.

Miller, Mr. Buckner married in Mercer County, Ky. to Miss Cook.
National Banner & Nashville Whig (Sat., Jan. 6, 1827)

Miller, Miss Catharine married to Mr. John Lindsey.

Miller, Mr. Cato married in Henry County to Miss Ann Campbell.
National Banner (Sat., Oct. 3, 1829)

Miller, Miss Christiana B. married to Mr. John W. Miller.

Miller, Miss Clara married to Dr. Richard R. Cuny.

Miller, Miss Darthula married to Major Alexander B. Bradford.

Miller, Miss Eliza married to Mr. Silas Fields.

Miller, Mrs. Elizabeth married to Mr. Daniel Weekley.

Miller, Miss Elizabeth married to Mr. William Childress.

Miller, Miss Elizabeth married to Mr. Thos. Kirkpatrick.

Miller, Mr. Henry married at Shawneetown to Miss Charlotte Ayliff.
National Banner (Feb. 24, 1826)

Miller, Miss Hetty married to Mr. David Davenport.

Miller, Mrs. J. married to Mr. George Bryan.

Miller, Mr. James married in Alleghany County, Pa. to Miss Sarah
Sterritt.
National Banner & Nashville Whig (Sat., Dec. 16, 1826)

Miller, Mr. James married in Christian County, Ky. to Miss M'Ganey.
National Banner & Nashville Whig (Sat., March 31, 1827)

Miller, Mr. James married in Madison County, Ala. to Miss Bolden.
National Banner & Nashville Whig (Mon., Sept. 12, 1831)

Miller, Mr. James married in Nashville on Thursday evening last by
the Rev. Mr. Adams to Miss Elizabeth Weller formerly of Logan County,
Ky.
National Banner & Nashville Daily Advertiser (Sat., Nov. 9, 1833)

Miller, Mr. James M. married in Maury County to Miss Amanda N. Carter.
National Banner & Nashville Whig (Sat., Jan. 10, 1829)

Miller, Mr. James P. married at Knoxville to Mrs. Charlotte Love.
National Banner (Jan. 20, 1826)

Miller, Miss Jane married to Mr. Robert Park.

Miller, Mr. John married in Adam County, Missis. to Miss Sarah A.
Davis.
National Banner & Nashville Whig (Sat., Feb. 9, 1828)

Miller, Mr. John C. of Nashville married on Tuesday 3d inst. by the
Rev. F. E. Pitts to Miss Martha A. M. Munford of Davidson County.
National Banner & Nashville Whig (Fri., March 6, 1835)

Miller, Mr. John C. Nashville married to Miss Martha A. W. Munford of
Davidson County on Tuesday evening last.
Nashville Republican (Sat., March 7, 1835)

Miller, John H. married in Maury County to Mary Ann Elizabeth Ewing.
National Banner & Nashville Whig (Wed., Feb. 25, 1835)

Miller, Mr. John S. married in Smith County to Miss Sophia Sloan.
Nashville Republican & State Gazette (Fri., Feb. 22, 1833)

Miller, Mr. John S. married in Smith County to Miss Sophia Sloan
daughter of Archibald Sloan Esq.
National Banner & Nashville Daily Advertiser (Fri., Feb. 22, 1833)

Miller, Mr. John W. married in Franklin to Miss Christiana B. Miller.
National Banner & Nashville Whig (Fri., July 25, 1828)

Miller, Miss Lucretia married to Mr. E. H. Boardman.

Miller, Miss Margaret married to Mr. E. L. Shackerford, Esq.

Miller, Miss Margaret married to Mr. Stephen Thomason.

Miller, Miss Martha married to Mr. Anderson Kincaid.

Miller, Mrs. Martha A. married to Mr. John S. Hart.

Miller, Miss Mary Ann married to Mr. William Patton.

Miller, Miss Mary E. married to Maj. Robt. B. Harney.

Miller, Miss Mary E. married to Maj. Rob. B. Harney.

Miller, Mr. Pitser of Bolivar married Miss Sarah Ann Stephens on 22d ult.
Nashville Republican (Tues., Jan. 13, 1835)

Miller, Mr. Pitser, merchant, married in Bolivar, Tenn. to Miss Sarah Ann Stephens daughter of Rev. Dr. Stephens.
National Banner & Nashville Whig (Wed., Jan. 21, 1835)

Miller, Miss Rachel married to Mr. John Bell.

Miller, Miss Rebecca married to Mr. Robert Black.

Miller, Miss Rebecca C. married to Mr. William S. Johnson.

Miller, Miss Sarah L. married to Joel H. Dyer, Esq.

Miller, Sarah Sergeant daughter of Rev. Dr. Miller married at Princeton, New Jersey on Wednesday 26th by the Rev. Dr. Miller to John F. Hageman Councellor at Law.
The Christian Record (Sat., June 18, 1847)

Miller, Sarah Sergeant married to John F. Hageman.

Miller, Mr. Thomas of Franklin married on Thursday the 5th inst. by the Rev. Thomas Madden to Miss Nancy B. Moore of Columbia.
The Western Weekly Review - Franklin, Tenn. (Fri., April 13, 1832)

Milliron, Mr. Jacob married last evening by the Rev. J. T. Wheat to Miss Sophia Langfort all of Nashville.
Nashville Whig (Wed., Sept. 9, 1840)

Mills, Astynox E. Esq. married in Sumner County to Mrs. Charlotte Pipes.
National Banner & Nashville Daily Advertiser (Sat., Sept. 13, 1834)

Mills, Mr. John F. married in Huntsville, Ala. to Miss Caledonia R. Brandon.
National Banner (Sat., May 9, 1829)

Millwater, Miss Henrietta married to Rev. Turner Saunders.

Milward, Mr. Joseph married at Lexington, Ky. to Miss Eliza Young.
National Banner (Jan. 27, 1826)

Minor, Mrs. married in Brownsville to Mr. Joseph J. Hawkins.

Minor, Capt. T. P. of the Steamboat General Green married on Tuesday evening last by the Rev. Mr. Hume to Miss Myra P. Eakin of this town (Nashville)
Nashville Whig (Aug. 4, 1823)

Minor, Miss Cordelia married to Dr. Samuel H. Dabney.

Minor, Mr. Floyd married in Morgan Co., Ala. to Miss Sarah C. Wlackwell.
National Banner & Nashville Daily Advertiser (Tues., July 15, 1834)

Minter, Miss Henrietta married to Mr. P. Owen.
Nashville Republican & State Gazette (Sat., March 12, 1831)

Minter, Mr. John T. married in this county on Tuesday evening July
22nd to Mrs. Maria White.
National Banner & Nashville Whig (Sat., Aug. 2, 1828)

Minter, Miss Sarah Ann married to Dr. R. H. Lewis.

Misser, Mr. Asa married in Lincoln County, Ten. to Miss Elizabeth
Gibson.
National Banner & Nashville Whig (Fri., Dec. 6, 1834)

Mitchell, Mr. B. G. married in Madison County to Miss Martha Wright.
National Banner (Sat., Dec. 19, 1829)

Mitchell, Miss Betsey married to Mr. Salathael Blackburn.

Mitchell, Miss Caroline V. married to Mr. Charles F. Walker.

Mitchell, Miss Christiana married to Rev. G. W. Ashbridge.

Mitchell, Mr. David married in Rutherford County to Miss Margaret
Peebles.
National Banner & Nashville Whig (Sat., Jan. 17, 1829)

Mitchell, Mr. Edward married in Hawkins County to Miss Betsey Smith.
Knoxville Gazette (Thurs., May 8, 1794)

Mitchell, Miss Eliza Ann married to Col. James H. Vaughn.

Mitchell, Miss Elizabeth married to Mr. David Sims.

Mitchell, Miss Elizabeth married to Mr. Littleton L. Ward.

Mitchell, Miss Elizabeth D. married to Mr. William M. Hargrove.

Mitchell, Mr. George married in Madison County, Ala. to Miss Emily
Peel.
National Banner & Nashville Whig (Wed., Sept. 14, 1831)

Mitchell, Dr. J. S. married at Memphis to Miss Sarah Wilson.
National Banner (Sat., May 30, 1829)

Mitchell, Col. James married in Maury County to Miss Winneford Ridley.
National Banner & Nashville Whig (Sat., Jan. 10, 1829)

Mitchell, Mr. James married at Louisville, Ky. to Miss Diana Edgerton.
National Banner & Nashville Whig (Sat., Nov. 26, 1831)

Mitchell, Miss Jane married to Mr. Samuel C. Morris.

Mitchell, John married in Giles County to Amanda N. J. Kimbrough.
National Banner & Nashville Daily Advertiser (Tues., Dec. 17, 1833)

Mitchell, Mr. John married in Madison County, Ala. to Miss Letitia
McGraw.
National Banner & Nashville Whig (Fri., Jan. 9, 1835)

Mitchell, Dr. Joseph G. Dentist of Philadelphia late of Nashville
married at Hudson, N. Y. on the 1st. Oct. to Elizabeth Skinner daughter
of H. P. Skinner Esq. of Hudson.
Nashville Whig (Wed., Oct. 24, 1838)

Mitchell, Miss Julia married to Mr. Tho. Smith.

Mitchell, Miss Lucinda L. married to Mr. Zacheus B. Phillips.

Mitchell, Miss Margaret Ann married to Samuel R. Overton, Esq.

Mitchell, Miss Maria B. married to Mr. J. D. McKay.

Mitchell, Miss Mary married to Mr. T. P. Walker.

Mitchell, Mary C. married to Mr. Walter Trimble.

Mitchell, Miss Mary L. married to Mr. Henry Satterly.

Mitchell, Miss Mary P. married to Mr. Sevier Drake.

Mitchell, Miss Myra married to Mr. Thomas G. Rucker.

Mitchell, Miss Parthena married to Mr. Robert P. Shapard.

Mitchell, Mr. Philip H. married in this town on Thursday evening to
Miss Sarah Ann Allen.
National Banner & Nashville Whig (Fri., June 20, 1828)

Mitchell, Mr. Robt. married in Russellville, Ky. to Miss Margaret
Catherine Linebaugh on the 13th inst.
Nashville Republican (Thurs., Oct. 22, 1835)

Mitchell, Mr. Robert B. married in Russellville, Ky. on the 13th by the
Rev. Mr. Hunt to Miss Margaret Catharine Linebaugh daughter of Mr.
Thomas Linebaugh.
National Banner & Nashville Whig (Mon., Oct. 26, 1835)

Mitchell, Col. Samuel married in Shelbyville to Miss Sarah Jane Jones
on the evening of the 8th inst.
Nashville Republican & State Gazette (Sat., Oct. 12, 1833)

Mitchell, Miss Sarah married to Mr. Samuel Hodge.

Mitchell, Miss Selina W. married to Mr. Morgan McAfee, Esq.

Mitchell, Miss Sophia married to Mr. Samuel Holloway.

Mitchell, Mr. Thomas married in Hawkins County to Miss Frances Dyer
on the 10 inst.
Knoxville Gazette (Thurs., April 10, 1794)

Mitchell, Mr. William of Murfreesborough married in Rutherford County
to Miss Mary Ledbetter daughter of the late Richard Ledbetter, Esq.
National Banner & Nashville Whig (Sat., Dec. 17, 1831)

Mitchell, William H. of Lexington, Tenn. married at Clarksville, Tenn.
on the 2nd inst. to Mrs. Isabella McClure.
National Banner & Nashville Daily Advertiser (Mon., Oct. 7, 1833)

Mitchell, Mr. Willis married in Maury County to Miss Rachel Gillian.
National Banner & Nashville Whig (Mon., July 12, 1830)

Mixer, Mr. Nathan married at Lexington, Ky. to Miss Eleanor Chamberlain.
National Banner (Feb. 24, 1826)

Moad, Miss Margaret married to Mr. Jacob Siler.

Moale, Miss Elizabeth married to Mr. George Cromwell.

Moberley, Mr. Ichabod married in Madison County, Ky. to Miss Pasey
Oldham.
National Banner (June 14, 1826)

Mock, Miss Mary A. E. married to Capt. Peter Wyatt.

Moffatt, Mr. James married on the 6th inst. by the Dr. Wharton to Miss Elizabeth M. Richardson all of Nashville.
Nashville Whig (Thurs., Jan. 8, 1846)

Moffatt, Mr. William married in Dandridge to Miss Nancy M. Gillespie.
National Banner & Nashville Daily Advertiser (Mon., Jan. 7, 1833)

Moffit, Miss Dolly married to Mr. Eli Smith.

Magors, Miss Charlotte married to Mr. Thomas Coleman

Molbrey, Mr. Berry married in Lauderdale County, Ala. to Miss Wuldah Mason.
National Banner & Nashville Whig (Mon., April 4, 1831)

Moman, Miss Elvira married to Mr. Thomas C. Clark.

Monohan, Mr. John married in Louisville, Ky. to Miss Margaret E. Fine.
Nashville Republican & State Gazette (Tues., June 3, 1834)

Monon, Miss Evelina married to Mr. Moses Throp.

Monroe, Miss Anna married to Richard H. Pindell, Esq.

Monroe, Miss Barbara married to Rev. Finis Harris.

Montgomery, Benjamin Rush Esq. Attorney at law married in Macon, Georgia on the 30th ult. to Miss Matilda Hardin daughter of Hon. John Hardin formerly of Augusta.
National Banner & Nashville Daily Advertiser (Mon., Dec. 2, 1833)

Montgomery, Dr. F. G. married in Hopkinsville, Ky. to Miss Anna Stiles.
National Banner & Nashville Daily Advertiser (Mon., May 28, 1832)

Montgomery, Miss Hannah married to Geo. W. Ferebee.

Montgomery, Mr. James married in Anderson County to Miss Chiles daughter of Maj. John Chiles.
National Banner & Nashville Daily Advertiser (Mon., Feb. 6, 1832)

Montgomery, Dr. Jas. P. married in Roane County, Tenn. to Miss Martha Clowney.
National Banner & Nashville Advertiser (Tues., May 22, 1832)

Montgomery, Jane Miss married to Mr. Samuel Cowan.

Montgomery, Mr. John B. married in Montgomery County to Miss Eliza Marshall.
National Banner & Nashville Whig (Mon., March 28, 1831)

Montgomery, Mr. Jno. B. of Hickman County to Miss Eliza Marshall in Montgomery County.
Nashville Republican & State Gazette (Tues., March 29, 1831)

Montgomery, Mr. Joseph married in Amite County, Miss to Miss Amelia F. Smylie.
National Banner & Nashville Whig (Sat., Feb. 21, 1829)

Montgomery, Miss Louisa married to Mr. John Bacon.

Montgomery, Miss Mary Ann married to Mr. George A. Mays.

Montgomery, Miss Mary F. married to John Brown.

Montgomery, Mary F. married to Mr. John Brown.

Montgomery, Miss Susan married to William B. Martin, Esq.

Montgomery, Mr. Thomas married in Blount County to Miss Francis Carter.
National Banner (March 17, 1826)

Montgomery, Mr. W. H. married at Memphis to Miss L. Wirt.
National Banner & Nashville Whig (Mon., April 18, 1831)

Montgomery, Mr. William of Tennessee married in Raleigh, N. C. to
Miss Matilda C. Bobbit.
National Banner & Nashville Whig (Sat., March 1, 1828)

Montgomery, Mr. William of the Steamer Tennessee married on the evening
of the 30th ult. by the Rev. Dr. Edgar to Miss Katharine Merritt
daughter of Mr. John Merritt of Nashville.
The Christian Record (Sat., Jan. 1st. 1848)

Moody, Miss Eliza married to Mr. Peter Clardy.

Moody, Mr. Francis T. married at Mt. Pleasant, Tenn. on the 30th ult.
by the Rev. William G. Cauders to Mrs. Ann W. Griffin all of Maury
County.
The Christian Record (Sat., Feb. 5, 1848)

Moody, Miss Jane married at Tuscaloosa, Ala. to Levin Powell Esq.
National Banner & Nashville Whig (Fri., March 26, 1830)

Mooney, Major Samuel P. of Indiana married in Louisville, Ky. on the
11th inst. by the Rev. Mr. Sears to Mrs. Matilda B. Hudson of Tennessee.
The Christian Record (Sat., Nov. 4, 1848)

Mooney, Miss Temperance married to Mr. Caleb B. Holcomb.

Moore, Miss married in Knox County to Mr. Nicholas Fry.

Moore, Miss Angelina married to Mr. Joseph J. S. Gill.

Moore, Mrs. Ann married to Mr. Lewis Dickson.

Moroe, Mr. Archibald married in Fayette County, Ky. to Miss Nancy
Moore.
National Banner & Nashville Whig (Fri., July 11, 1828)

Moore, Mr. Caleb married in M'Minn County to Miss Lucinda Prigmore.
National Banner & Nashville Daily Advertiser (Wed., July 31, 1831)

Moore, Miss Catherine L. M. married to Mr. Elisha Vaughn.

Moore, Mr. Charles of Nashville married in Lincoln County to Miss
Perlina Whitaker daughter of Mr. Mark Whitaker.
National Banner & Nashville Whig (Sat., Sept. 8, 1827)

Moore, Dr. Daniel of Huntsville, Ala. married to Miss Martha L.
Harrison of Brunswick County, Va.
Nashville Republican & State Gazette (Tues., Aug. 20, 1833)

Moore, Miss Eliza married to James A. Neale, Esq.

Moore, Miss Eliza married to Mr. A. B. Parsons.

Moore, Miss Elizabeth married to Mr. Enoch Gann.

Moore, Miss Elizabeth married to Mr. Willy Corbett.

Moore, Mrs. Elizabeth married to Mr. Wylly B. Corbett.

Moore, Rev. Francis of this town married in this County on Tuesday
evening last by the Rev. Mr. Paine to Miss Sarah Maxey.
National Banner (April 7, 1826)

Moore, Mr. George married in Ross Co., Ohio to Miss Rachel Umstrade.
National Banner & Nashville Whig (Sat., Sept. 15, 1827)

Moore, Mr. George W. married at Cincinnati to Miss Sarah Terry.
National Banner (Feb. 24, 1826)

Moore, Mr. Henry married in Lincoln County to Miss Fanny Cole.
National Banner & Nashville Whig (Sat., Dec. 2, 1826)

Moore, Miss Isabella married in Rutherford County to Mr. James W.
Stewart.

Moore, Mr. J. L. of Frankfort married in Fayette County, Ky. to Miss
Mary Boone.
National Banner & Nashville Daily Advertiser (Wed., July 9, 1834)

Moore, Mr. J. R. married on Thursday evening last by Rev. James Smith
to Mrs. Isabella Smith.
Nashville Republican (Sat., July 16, 1836)

Moore, Mr. James C. married in Rutherford County to Miss Martha M.
Purdy daughter of Gen. Purdy of this place.
National Banner & Nashville Whig (Sat., Nov. 18, 1826)

Moore, Mrs. Jane married to Mr. Francis R. Browning.

Moore, Miss Jane W. married to Dr. Sam S. Porter.

Moore, Mr. John married in Maury County to Miss Nancy Baugus.
National Banner & Nashville Whig (Sat., Oct. 6, 1827)

Moore, Mr. Jonathan W. married at Natchez to Miss Elizabeth Downs.
National Banner (Sat., May 9, 1829)

Moore, Major Joseph of Anderson County married in Knox County to
Miss Jane Pate.
National Banner (Sat., Aug. 29, 1829)

Moore, Miss Levisa married to Mr. Orville Green.

Moore, Mr. Lewis C. married in Lauderdale County, Ala. to Miss Atlantic
P. M'Voy daughter of Maj. Hugh M'Voy.
National Banner & Nashville Whig (Mon., Nov. 14, 1831)

Moore, Miss Louisa B. married to Mr. John Penrice.

Moore, Miss Lucindia married to Mr. H. L. Williams.

Moore, Miss Lucy married to Charles Loflan Esq.

Moore, Miss Lucy Jame M. married to Dr. Flemming Jordan.

Moore, Miss Malinda married to Mr. Wm. Thomas.

Moore, Miss Martha married to Mr. George Meuce.

Moore, Miss Martha married to Mr. George Muse.

Moore, Miss Martha A. married to Mr. Leonidas M. Bentley.

Moore, Miss Martha B. married to Mr. William B. Crawford.

Moore, Miss Mary married to Mr. David C. Ward.

Moore, Miss Mary married to Mr. Samuel Albert.

Moore, Miss Mary Ann S. married to Mr. James B. Marshall.

Moore, Miss Matilda married to Rev. Isaac Bard.

Moore, Miss Mecca married to Mr. John Holbrooks.

Moore, Miss Mecca F. married to Mr. John Holbrooks.

Moore, Miss Miry married to Mr. Bolin Chinn.

Moore, Miss Nancy married to Mr. Archibald Moore.

Moore, Miss Nancy A. married to Mr. John D. Matthews.

Moore, Miss Nancy B. married to Mr. Thomas Miller.

Moore, Miss Nancy T. married to Mr. John R. Randolph.

Moore, Miss Narcissa M. married to Mr. James Armstrong.

Moore, Parsons W. married in Williamson County to Miss Elizabeth
Nichols.
The Western Weekly Review - Franklin, Tenn. (Fri., May 11, 1832)

Moore, Parsons W. married in Williamson County to Elizabeth
Nichols.
National Banner & Nashville Advertiser (Wed., May 16, 1832)

Moore, Miss Parthena married to Mr. John Hickle.

Moore, Mr. Peter C. married in Maury County, Ten. to Miss Elizabeth
Acuff.
National Banner & Nashville Whig (Mon., Jan. 26, 1835)

Moore, Miss Rebecca married to Mr. W. M. McGrady.

Moore, Miss Rebecca R. married to Mr. P. H. Achey.

Moore, Mr. Reddick P. married in Hardeman County to Miss Mary M.
Hubbard.
National Banner & Nashville Whig (Fri., Nov. 11, 1831)

Moore, Capt. Robt. of Sumner County married Miss Nancy Green Sumner
County Thursday evening 6 inst.
Imparital Review & Cumberland Repository - Pub. at Nashville
(Sat., March 15, 1806)

Moore, Mr. Robert I. merchant of Nashville married in Hasivlle on
3d inst. by the Rev. McFerrin to Miss Martha Clay of Davidson County.
National Banner & Nashville Daily Advertiser (Tues., May 8, 1832)

Moore, Miss Ruth married to Joseph Barret, Esq.

Moore, Miss Sarah married to Mr. Nathaniel M'Cutcheon.

Moore, Miss Sarah married to Mr. Presly George.

Moore, Miss Sarah married to Mr. Presley George.

Moore, Miss Sarah E. married to Mr. Philip P. Gelchrist.

Moore, Dr. T. J. of Bowling Green married in Mercer County, Ky. to
Miss Mary Anner Thompson daughter of Mr. Richard Thompson.
National Banner & Nashville Whig (Fri., Dec. 3, 1830)

Moore, Mr. Wm. married in Crawford County, Ark. to Miss Amanda
Saunders.
National Banner & Nashville Whig (Sat., Oct. 28, 1826)

Moore, Mr. William married in Blount County to Miss Sarah Hutton.
National Banner (Sat., Nov. 21, 1829)

Moore, Mr. William of Franklin, Ky. married Miss Mary I. Duncan of
Logan Co., Ky. on Tuesday last.
Nashville Republican & State Gazette (Mon., Sept. 24, 1832)

Moore, Mr. William H. of Nashville married in Sumner County to Miss Tabithia Sanders daughter of Rev. H. Sanders.
National Banner & Nashville Whig (Sat., Jan. 10, 1829)

Moore, Mr. William S. married in Rutherford County to Miss Jane E. Henderson.
National Banner & Nashville Whig (Mon., Jan. 31, 1831)

Moorehead, Miss Julia married to Mr. William McMillen.

Moores, Mr. Eli married in Lincoln County to Miss Finetta Hynes.
National Banner & Nashville Whig (Sat., Sept. 16, 1826)

Moores, Miss Mary R. married to Capt. Thomas Hinds.

Moores, Mr. Ortho H. married in Lincoln County to Miss Frances Grizzard.
Nashville Whig (Thurs., March 19, 1846)

Moores, Miss Rhoda M. married to Mr. Francis H. Gordon.

Moores, Dr. William B. married in Smith County to Miss Nancy Gordon daughter of Mr. John Gordon.
National Banner & Nashville Daily Advertiser (Thurs., Jan. 5, 1832)

Moran, Mr. James H. of Dresden married in Carroll County to Miss Harriet Harris.
National Banner & Nashville Daily Advertiser (Sat., July 28, 1832)

Moran, Miss Margaret married to Mr. William Delany.

Morefield, Miss Ann E. married to A. J. Roberts Esq.

Morefield, Miss Ann E. T. married to Mr. A. J. Roberts.

Morefield, Miss Mary married to Mr. William Wells.

Morehead, Miss Alzira H. married to Mr. William Cameron.

Morehead, Mr. Armistead married in Todd County, Ky. to Miss Susan Crouch.
National Banner & Nashville Advertiser (Wed., June 13, 1832)

Morehead, Miss Betsy married to John H. Phelps Esq.

Morehead, Miss Caroline M. married to Mr. Lyman T. Gunn.

Morehead, Mr. Charles S. Esq. of Russellville married in Lexington, Ky. to Miss Amanda Leavy of the former place (Lexington)
Nashville Whig (July 21, 1823)

Morehead, Charles S. Esq. of Frankfort married in Lexington, Ky. to Miss Margaret Leavy daughter of Mr. William Leavy.
National Banner & Nashville Whig (Wed., Sept. 21, 1831)

Morehead, Miss Elizabeth B. married to C. Hammond Esq.

Morehead, Mr. James married in Logan County, Ky. to Miss Henrietta E. F. Poor.
National Banner & Nashville Whig (Wed., Dec. 7, 1831)

Morehead, Miss Octavia married to Mr. Samuel A. Atchison Esq.

Morejon, Caroline Rosalia married to Col. J. H. McMahon.

Morford, Miss Harriet married to Mr. John Nichol.

Morford, Josiah F. Esq. married in Warren County, T. on the 7th
inst. to Miss Jane B. Taylor.
National Banner & Nashville Whig (Sat., Sept. 16, 1826)

Morgan, Major Alexander G. of Huntsville married on the 25th ult.
to Miss America Higgins of Lexington, Ky.
Nashville Whig (Oct. 6, 1823)

Morgan, Col. Calvin G. married on the 24th ult. to Miss Henrietta
Hunt of Lexington, Ky.
Nashville Whig (Oct. 6, 1823)

Morgan, Miss Eliza married to Mr. Robert Walker.

Morgan, Mrs. Elizabeth married to Mr. H. Black.

Morgan, Miss Ellen P. married to Mr. Wm. T. Christy.

Morgan, Miss Emily married to Mr. D. O. Askew.

Morgan, F. H. married on Sunday the 4th inst. by the Rev. Dr. Edgar
to Miss Mary S. Jennings all of Nashville.
Nashville Republican (Tues., June 7, 1836)

Morgan, Mr. F. H. merchant married on the 5th inst. by the Rev. Dr.
Edgar to Miss Mary S. Jennings daughter of the late Rev. Dr. Jennings
Pastor of the Presbyterian Church.
National Banner & Nashville Whig (Fri., June 10, 1836)

Morgan, Miss Henrietta H. married to Mr. Benjamin P. Clark.

Morgan, Mr. Irby married on Thursday evening last by Rev. Dr. Howell
to Miss Julia A. Demoville all of Nashville.
Nashville Whig (Sat., Oct. 5, 1844)

Morgan, Mr. Jeremiah H. married in Henry County to Miss Lucy P. Dixon.
National Banner & Nashville Advertiser (Tues., July 3, 1832)

Morgan, Mr. John F. married in Columbia on Tuesday 29th ult. by the
Rev. Mr. Sherman to Miss Louisa J. Porter daughter of William Porter
Esq.
Nashville Whig (Fri., July 16, 1841)

Morgan, Mrs. Lucinda married to Mr. George W. Harris.

Morgan, Miss Margaret married to Dr. Robert T. Hanks.

Morgan, Miss Margaret A. W. married to Dr. Robert T. Hanks.

Morgan, Miss Martha married to Mr. William C. Scott.

Morgan, Miss Rachel K. T. married to Mr. Hugh L. M'Clung.

Morgan, Mr. Ridley married in Bedford County to Miss Lucy Ely.
Nashville Republican & State Gazette (Wed., Dec. 12, 1832)

Morgan, Mr. Samuel W. of Memphis married in Shelby County on the 15th
inst. by the Rev. F. A. Owen to Miss Elizabeth Rivers of Virginia.
National Banner & Nashville Daily Advertiser (Mon., March 26, 1832)

Morgan, Miss Sarah married to Mr. Richard Morrow.

Morgan, Mr. Simon L. married in Russellville, Ky. to Miss Nancy
Williams.
National Banner & Nashville Daily Advertiser (Sat., Feb. 16, 1833)

Morgan, Miss Sophia married to Mr. James E. Mickley.

Morgan, Miss Susan C. married to James W. Campbell, Esq.

Morgan, Mr. Thomas R. married in this county on the 4th inst. to
Miss Ann Swan.
National Banner & Nashville Whig (Sat., Oct. 7, 1826)

Morgan, Mr. William married in Williamson County to Miss Eliza Haywood.
The Western Weekly Review - Franklin, Tenn. (Fri., Dec. 2, 1831)

Morgan, Mr. Wm. married in Williamson County to Miss Eliza Haywood.
National Banner & Nashville Whig (Wed., Dec. 7, 1831)

Morine, Geo. W. married in Williamson County to Miss Sarah Bozwell.
The Western Weekly Review - Franklin, Tenn. (Fri., Dec. 14, 1832)

Morris, Miss Eleanor married to Mr. George E. Porter.

Morris, Miss Eleanor married to Mr. Geo. E. Porter.

Morris, Mr. Eli of Nashville married on Thursday last Dec. 12th by
the Rev. Mr. Brown to Miss Martha Talley daughter of Zachariah Talley
of Sumner County.
Daily Republican Banner (Tues., Dec. 17, 1839)

Morris, Mr. Eli of Nashville married on Thrusday last by the Rev. Mr.
Brown to Miss Martha N. Talley daughter of Zachariah Talley of Sumner
County.
Nashville Whig (Wed., Dec. 18, 1839)

Morris, Mr. Eli of Nashville married on Thursday by the Rev. Mr. Brown
to Miss Martha N. Talley daughter of Mr. Zachariah Talley of Sumner.
Nashville Union (Fri., Dec. 20, 1839)

Morris, Mr. Elijah married in Maury County, Ten. to Miss Elizabeth
Wadkins.
National Banner & Nashville Whig (Fri., May 8, 1835)

Morris, Miss Harriet B. married to Mr. William B. Morris.

Morris, Mr. Jacob T. married in Williamson County to Miss Jane L.
Campbell.
The Western Weekly Review - Franklin, Tenn. (Fri., Dec. 2, 1831)

Morris, Mr. Jacob T. married in Williamson County to Miss Jane L.
Campbell.
National Banner & Nashville Whig (Wed., Dec. 7, 1831)

Morris, Miss Jane married to Mr. James F. Kidrell

Morris, Mr. Joseph R. of Rutherford County married at Gallatin to
Miss Eliza S. Thomkins daughter of Capt. John Tomkins.
National Banner (Sat., Aug. 15, 1829)

Morris, Miss Mary married to Mr. Jacob Jarrett.

Morris, Miss Mary Ann married to Mr. William Withrow.

Morris, Miss Mary F. married to Mr. Wm. C. Noke.

Morris, Robert, Esq. married to Miss Amanda Louisa Miller.

Morris, Mr. Samuel C. married in Perry County to Miss Jane Mitchell.
National Banner & Nashville Whig (Sat., July 29, 1826)

Morris, Mr. William married in Knox County to Miss Frances Seay.
National Banner (Sat., Sept. 26, 1829)

Morris, Mr. William married in Williamson County to Miss Terrissa Wade.
The Western Weekly Review - Franklin, Tenn. (Fri., Dec. 2, 1831)

Morris, Mr. William married in Williamson County to Miss Terrissa Wade.
National Banner & Nashville Whig (Wed., Dec. 7, 1831)

Morris, Mr. William B. married in Rutherford County to Miss Harriet B. Morris.
National Banner & Nashville Whig (Sat., Dec. 30, 1826)

Morris, Mr. William G. married in M'Minn County to Miss Sarah Chambers daughter of Mr. Edmund Chambers.
National Banner & Nashville Whig (Thurs., June 3, 1830)

Morrison, Capt. Andrew of this place married at Pittsburgh on the 2nd inst. to Miss Elizabeth Foster of Pittsburgh.
The Nashville Whig & Tenn. Advertiser (Oct. 27, 1817)

Morrison, Mr. Charles married at Louisville, Ky. to Miss Jane Houghton.
National Banner & Nashville Whig (Sat., April 26, 1828)

Morrison, Mr. Charles married in Louisville, Ky. to Miss Mary Ann Lanning.
National Banner (Sat., Aug. 15, 1829)

Morrison, Miss Euphrosia married to Gen. George Collier.

Morrison, Mr. John married in Sumner County to Miss Mary A. Anderson.
National Banner & Nashville Daily Advertiser (Mon., March 31, 1834)

Morrison, Miss Nancy married to Mr. Hollen Thacker.

Morrison, Mr. Peter married in Jonesborough to Miss Letitia Kelly.
Nashville Republican & State Gazette (Fri., Dec. 7, 1832)

Morrison, Miss Sarah D. married to Mr. Richard M. Munford.

Morrison, Mr. Thos. married Miss Dicy Taylor in Maury County on the 24th ult.
National Banner & Nashville Whig (Fri., Jan. 29, 1830)

Morriss, Miss Sarah married to Mr. Pinkney Shaw.

Morriss, Thomas E. Esq. married at White Ash Grove, Wilson County by the Rev. John W. Brown to Miss Eliba R. Burton.
National Banner & Nashville Whig (Fri., March 13, 1835)

Morrow, Miss Jane married to Mr. Philip P. Houser.

Morrow, Mr. Richard married on the 8th inst. to Miss Sarah Morgan.
National Banner & Nashville Whig (Fri., July 18, 1828)

Morrow, Dr. Wm. J. J. married in Jefferson County, Ky. to Miss Lavinia L. Jarnagan.
National Banner & Nashville Whig (July 1, 1826)

Morton, Miss Amanda P. married to Mr. James C. Slaughter.

Morton, Miss Caroline married to Mr. John H. Smith.

Morton, Miss Caroline married to Mr. John H. Smith.

Morton, Miss Charlotte married to Samuel Watson.

Morton, Miss Charlotte married to Samuel Watson, Esq.

Morton, Mr. Elijah married on Wednesday last by Rev. Mr. Wheat to Miss Mary Angeline Humphreys.
Daily Republican Banner (Fri., May 29, 1840)

Morton, Mr. Elijah married on Wednesday by Rev. Mr. Wheat to Miss Mary Angeline Humphreys daughter of Dr. E. Humphreys of Auburn, New York.
Nashville Whig (Fri., May 20, 1840)

Morton, Miss Elizabeth married to Mr. Allen T. Gooch.

Morton, Miss Elizabeth married to Mr. Thomas S. Redd.

Morton, Miss Ellen married to Dr. Henry T. Loving.

Morton, Frances L. married to Geo. M. Gillespie.

Morten, Miss Frances W. married to Green Nolen.

Morton, Mr. George K. of Lexington, Ten. married in Henry County on the 15th ult. to Miss Nancy Caruthers.
National Banner & Nashville Whig (Thurs., July 1, 1830)

Morton, Mr. James married at Murfreesborough to Miss Amanda Smith daughter of John Smith Esq.
National Banner & Nashville Whig (Mon., Aug. 30, 1830)

Morton, Miss Jane M. married to Mr. W. M. Brown.

Morton, Mr. Joseph married in Rutherford County, Ten. to Miss Martha Sneed.
National Banner & Nashville Whig (Mon., Nov. 10, 1834)

Morton, M. B. Esq. married at Russellville, Ky. to Miss Ann Caldwell.
National Banner & Nashville Whig (Sat., Sept. 15, 1827)

Morton, Miss Martha married to William Tigner.

Morton, Miss Martha M. married to Mr. Geo. W. Smith.

Morton, Miss Mary married to Mr. John Lewis.

Morton, Miss Mary married to Mr. John Brennan.

Morton, Miss Mary married to Mr. John Brennan.

Morton, Miss Nancy W. married to Mr. Wm. Dulany.

Morton, Miss Priscilla W. married to Mr. Tennessee Mathews.

Morton, Miss Sarah married to Mr. Lewis Postlelhwait.

Morton, Miss Sarah Ann married to Mr. Oliver Hughes.

Marton, Mr. Tate of Bedford County married on Thursday the 21st to Miss Lucinda M. Hancock of Maury County.
The Western Weekly Review - Fri., June 29, 1832)

Morton, Mr. Tate of Bedford County married in Maury County to Miss Nancy Hancock.
National Banner & Nashville Advertiser (Tues., July 3, 1832)

Morton, Mr. William R. at Lexington, Ky. married to Miss Eliza J. Bradford.
National Banner & Nashville Whig (Fri., March 19, 1830)

Mosby, Miss Eliza married to Mr. Richard Smith.

Mosby, Mr. James C. married in Nashville to Miss Elizabeth P. Gwin daughter of the Rev. James Gwin.
National Banner & Nashville Daily Advertiser (Fri., Oct. 12, 1832)

Mosby, Miss Rebecca married to Mr. Harrison Lock.

Moseby, Mr. William T. married in Nashville to Miss Elizabeth A. Tilford on Thursday the 3 inst.
Nashville Republican & State Gazette (Fri., Jan. 9, 1833)

Moseby, Mr. Wm. T. married in Nashville on Thursday 3 inst. by Rev. Mr. Hume to Miss Elizabet Ann Tilford daughter of Mr. James Tilford.
National Banner & Nashville Daily Advertiser (Fri., Jan. 4, 1833)

Moseley, Hillery Mr. married in Clinton, Mi. to Miss Harriet P. Harris.
National Banner & Nashville Daily Advertiser (Tues., Aug. 5, 1834)

Moseley, Miss Laura P. married to Mr. Henry L. Brown.

Moseley, Lycurgus H. Esq. merchant of Nashville married on Wednesday morning 27th ult. in Williamson County to Miss Mary A. Starnes daughter of Dr. Starnes of Williamson.
Nashville Whig (Mon., Dec. 3, 1838)

Moseley, Miss Mary M. married to Mr. William Cowan.

Moseley, Miss Mary M. married to Mr. P. William Cowan.

Mosely, Miss Martha Ann married to Maj. Samuel A. Warner.

Mosely, Mr. T. T. married at Huntsville to Miss Abigail Martin.
National Banner (Sat., Dec. 26, 1829)

Mosely, Mr. Thomas D. of Wilson County married in Davidson County to Miss Ann Courtney W. Goodrich.
National Banner & Nashville Daily Advertiser (Thurs., Sept. 19, 1833)

Moses, Mr. Henley married in this County on Thursday evening last to Miss Evelina Carney.
National Banner & Nashville Whig (Sat., April 7, 1827)

Mosley, Mr. James married in this town to Miss Elizabeth P. Gwin daughter of the Rev. James Gwin.
National Banner & Nashville Daily Advertiser (Oct. 12, 1832)

Mosley, Miss Martha A. married in Weakley County on the 12th inst. by Rev. Mr. Dunn to S. A. Warner Esq. of Duesden.
National Banner & Nashville Whig (Sat., Aug. 30, 1828)

Moss, Mr. David T. married in Williamson County to Miss Mary W. Gideon.
National Banner & Nashville Whig (Fri., Jan. 9, 1835)

Moss, Miss Pamelia married to Mr. Abraham Irwin.

Moss, Miss Salina married to Dr. Alexander

Moss, Miss Sarah married to Mr. Benjamin W. Perry.

Moss, Miss Sophia G. married to Mr. Reuben T. Warner.

Moss, Miss Susan C. married to George W. Ewing, Esq.

Motheral, Miss Mary married to Dr. Joel Walker.

Motley, Miss Mary married to Mr. Leiws Leaver.

Moulder, Mr. William married in Knox County to Miss Nancy Davis.
Nashville Republican & State Gazette (Oct. 17, 1833)

Moulton, Mr. Payton married in Knox County to Miss Eliza Sharp.
National Banner (Sept. 5, 1829)

Mountany, Mr. Lewis married in Madison County, Ala. to Miss Nancy L.
Grant.
National Banner & Nashville Whig (Sat., Feb. 7, 1829)

Mourfield, Mr. Eli of Knox County married in Anderson County to Miss
Sarah J. Ashlock of Anderson.
National Banner & Nashville Daily Advertiser (Mon., Feb. 13, 1832)

Moyers, Miss Mary B. married to Mr. Hiram Moys.

Moyers, Miss Matilda married to Mr. John Formwalt.

Moyers, Miss Nancy Ann married to Mr. Christopher Veltineer.

Moyres, Mr. Alfred J. married in Jefferson County to Miss Jane Rheams.
National Banner & Nashville Whig (Mon., Oct. 17, 1831)

Moys, Mr. Hiram married in Jefferson County to Miss Mary B. Moyers.
National Banner & Nashville Whig (Mon., Oct. 17, 1831)

Muchmore, Miss Martha married to Mr. Thomas Batchelder.

Muir, Mr. John married at Louisville, Ky. to Miss Maria Wurts.
National Banner & Nashville Whig (Sat., May 17, 1828)

Mulder, Miss Rhoda E. married to Mr. Andrew Gassett.

Mulford, Mr. Edward A. married in Nashville on Wednesday the 4th inst.
by the Rev. Dr. Howell to Miss Catherine H. Scantland.
Nashville Whig (Sat., Nov. 7, 1846)

Mullanphy, Miss Mary Louisa married to Mr. W. Tighe.

Mulleen, Miss Cornelia A. married to Mr. William D. Fly.

Mullen, Mr. Abner married in Williamson County to Miss Mary Stanfield.
National Banner & Nashville Whig (Fri., Jan. 9, 1835)

Mullen, Miss Martha married to Mr. Giles Baker.

Muller, Mr. Frederick A. married at Louisville, Ky. to Miss Sarah
Clifton.
National Banner & Nashville Whig (Mon., July 26, 1830)

Mullikins, Miss Polly married to Mr. George Tenely.

Mullikin, Miss Polly married to Mr. George Tenely.

Mullin, Miss Marthi married to Mr. Giles Baker.

Mullins, Mr. Robert married in Grainger County to Mrs. Catherine
Dennis.
National Banner & Nashville Daily Advertiser (Tues., Oct. 9, 1832)

Mumford, Miss Alethea married to Mr. John Wright.

Mumford, Miss Mary Jane married to Mr. A. Ward.

Munce, Miss Isabella married to Mr. Cyrus Marsh.

Muncooksey, Dr. William of Monroe County married at Maryville to Miss
Winniford M'Connell.
National Banner & Nashville Daily Advertiser (Wed., Jan. 9, 1833)

Munday, Mr. William S. married on the 9th inst. at Gallatin by the
Rev. J. B. Ferguson to Miss Almira Turner of Gallatin, Tenn.
Nashville True Whig & Weekly Commercial Register (Fri., May 17, 1850)

Munford, Miss Catherine Ann married to Dr. M. M'Corkle.

Munford, Miss Martha A. M. married to Mr. John C. Miller.

Munford, Miss Martha A. W. married to Mr. John C. Miller.

Munford, Mr. Richard M. of Randolph married in Pulaski on Thursday
the 4th by the Rev. C. P. Read. to Miss Sarah D. Morrison daughter of
Mr. D. L. Morrison.
National Banner & Nashville Whig (Fri., Feb. 26, 1836)

Munford, Miss Sarah married to Mr. James Jones.

Mungall, Miss Rossella married to Mr. Enoch E. Wentzell.

Munger, Rev. John married in Roane County to Miss Nancy Young.
National Banner & Nashville Whig (Sat., Jan. 19, 1828)

Murat, Achille Esq. married in Tallahassee, Florida to Mrs. Catharine
Dangerfield Gray daughter of Maj. Byrd C. Willis.
National Banner & Nashville Whig (Sat., Aug. 26, 1826)

Murat, Prince Lucien married at Trenton, N. J. to Miss Carolina
Georgiana Frazier of South Carolina.
National Banner & Nashville Whig (Wed., Sept. 7, 1831)

Murchison, Dr. William A. of Henderson, Mi. married in Madison County,
Ten. to Miss Mary Ann Todd.
National Banner & Nashville Whig (Wed., Dec. 17, 1834)

Murdaugh, Miss Rebecca J. married to Mr. George Childress.

Murdock, Miss Eleanor married to Mr. William Dickinson.

Murfree, Miss Sally B. married to Col. David W. Dickinson.

Murfree, William L. Esq. of Nashville married on the 22nd inst. in
the vicinity of Murfreesboro by the Rev. R. B. C. Howell to Miss
Fanny Priscilla Dickinson of Rutherford County.
Nashville Whig (Sat., Nov. 25, 1843)

Murphee, Miss T. married in Bedford County to Major John Hoover.

Murphey, Miss Pormela married to Mr. John McCarrol.

Murphree, Miss Sarah married to Mr. Isaac West.

Murphey, Miss Martha married to Mr. Richard Buchanan.

Murphy, Miss Elizabeth married to Col. John Poindexter.

Murphy, Miss Elizabeth married to Mr. Welcome Martin.

Murphy, Miss Harriet Jane married to Mr. Philip D. Bell.

Murphy, Mr. John of Sartat, Miss. married to Miss Elizabeth Hickman.
Nashville Republican (Thurs., Feb. 5, 1835)

Murphy, Mr. John S. married in Davidson County to Miss Mary W.
Tinsley.
Nashville Republican (Tues., July 14, 1835)

Murphy, Miss Lucinda P. married to Mr. William Harmon.

Murphy, Miss Mary Ann married to Mr. William Yorke.

Murphy, Mr. Miles P. married in Maury County, Ten. to Miss Eleanor J. Mack.
National Banner & Nashville Whig (Wed., Feb. 25, 1835)

Murphy, Mr. Samuel married in Lauderdale County, Ala. to Miss Elizabeth Mars.
National Banner & Nashville Advertiser (Mon., Jan. 16, 1832)

Murphy, Miss Susan married to Mr. Thomas Compton.

Murray, Mr. Henry married in Smith County to Miss Francis Robinson.
National Banner & Nashville Daily Advertiser (Mon., April 2, 1832)

Murray, Capt. James D. married in Knox County to Miss Rebecca Bell.
National Banner (Sat., May 16, 1829)

Murray, Miss Jemima married to Mr. George Stephens.

Murray, Mademoiselle Mary married to Monsieur G. Ferry.

Murray, Miss Mary I. married to Dr. Henry H. Marable.

Murray, Miss Sarah married to Mr. William H. Southerland.

Murray, Mr. William married in Cincinnati to Miss Esther Barnes.
National Banner & Nashville Whig (Sat., Jan. 10, 1829)

Murrell, Miss married to Mr. Hugh Easley.

Murrell, Miss married to Mr. Hugh Easley.

Murrell, Mr. George M. of Athens, Tenn. married at the Cherokee Agency to Miss Minerva Ross.
National Banner & Nashville Daily Advertiser (Mon., July 21, 1834)

Murrell, Margaret married to Mr. Hugh Easley.

Murrell, Miss Mary married to Mr. James T. Donaldson.

Murrell, Mary Florence married to J. N. Moffitt Jr.

Murrell, Mr. Zachariah M. married in Franklin County to Miss Phebe E. White.
National Banner & Nashville Whig (Sat., Sept. 9, 1826)

Murry, Miss Mary married to Mr. James Wheeler.

Murry, Miss Mary marired to Mr. James W. Hulin.

Murry, Miss Mary I. married to Dr. Henry H. Marable.

Murry, Mr. William married in Wilson County to Miss Aleathea Matlock.
National Banner & Nashville Whig (Thurs., Oct. 21, 1830)

Muse, Mr. George married in Bedford County to Miss Martha Moore.
National Banner & Nashville Daily Advertiser (Thurs., Jan. 17, 1833)

Musgrove, Mr. Edward F. married in this town on Friday last to Miss Angelina M. Lanier.
National Banner & Nashville Whig (Sat., Jan. 10, 1829)

Musgrove, Miss Mary P. married to Mr. Robert B. Hall.

Musick, Miss Lucinda married to Mr. Samuel Willi.

Myers, Miss Anna married to Mr. William R. Spann.

Myers, Bernard, Esq. of Nashville married near Columbia on Thursday July 28th by Prof. C. D. Elliot to Margaret Bradshaw youngest daughter of the late Thomas Bradshaw of Maury County.
Nashville Whig (Fri., July 31, 1840)

Myers, Miss Madeline Barbary married to Col. James M. Parker.

Myers, Miss Martha married to Mr. Thomas C. Ingram.

Myers, Miss Nancy married to Mr. Francis N. B. Dudley.

Myers, Mr. William married in St. Louis to Miss Caroline Stevens.
National Banner & Nashville Whig (Sat., Feb. 21, 1829)

Mynatt, Mr. Gordon married in Knox County to Miss Mary Hillsman.
National Banner & Nashville Daily Advertiser (Mon., April 29, 1833)

Myrick, Dr. H. W. K. married in Maury County on the 1st inst. to Miss Elizabeth P. Hill.
National Banner & Nashville Whig (Thurs., Sept. 9, 1830)

Myrick, Mrs. Minerva married to Mr. Robert Mahaffy.

Myres, Mr. F. married in Sumner County to Miss Mary Taylor.
National Banner & Nashville Whig (Mon., Jan. 10, 1831)

Nance, Miss Caroline E. married to Mr. S. Plumlee.

Nance, Mr. Clement W. of Davidson County married in Rutherford County by the Rev. John M. Watson on the 11th to Miss Ann D. Avent of Madison County, Ala.
Nashville Republican (Sat., Feb. 20, 1836)

Nance, Miss Susan married to Mr. John C. Dobbs

Nannally, Miss Mary married to Mr. John Adams.

Napier, Mr. Leroy W. married on Sat. morning the 26th inst. by the Rev. Mr. Howell to Miss Fanny H. Robertson both of Davidson County.
Daily Republican Banner (Mon., Aug. 28, 1837)

Napier, Miss Mary Jane married to Mr. Benjamin Stones.

Napier, Miss Mary M. married to Mr. Wm. L. Maxwell.

Napier, Miss Morgiana married to Mr. William H. Johnson.

Napier, Miss Sally Fox married to Mr. Fountain Lester.

Napier, Miss Sarah C. married to Mr. James Delaunay.

Napier, Miss Susan Amanda married to Samuel B. Lee, Esq.

Nash, Miss married to Rev. John Taylor

Nash, Miss Ann married to Mr. Wm. R. Stewart

Nash, Miss Elizabeth married to Mr. Levi Johnson.

Nash, Mr. John married in Davidson Co. to Miss Lucy Jordon.
National Banner & Nashville Daily Advertiser (Tues., Aug. 19, 1834)

Nash, Maj. John B. married in Rutherford County to Miss Jane Ferguson.
National Banner & Nashville Whig (Sat., Feb. 2, 1828)

Nash, Louisa W. married to Mr. Gilbert Marshall.

Nash, Miss Louisa W. married to Gilbert Marshall.

Nash, Miss Rhoda married to Mr. Benjamin Yarbrough.

Nash, Miss Sarah married to John T. Crenshaw Esq.

Nason, Miss Mary married to Mr. John Caldwell.

Nave, Miss Phoebe married to Mr. Isaac Carriger.

Neal, Miss Ann married to Mr. L. H. Estes.

Neal, Mr. A. M. married in Williamson County to Miss Sarah G. Hayley.
The Western Weekly Review - Franklin, Tenn. (Fri., Dec. 23, 1831)

Neal, Miss Artemesia married to Mr. William W. Parker.

Neal, Miss Artemisia married to Mr. William W. Parker.

Neal, Mr. Benjamin jun. married in Jefferson County to Miss Melinda Stevenson.
National Banner & Nashville Whig (Mon., Nov. 7, 1831)

Neal, Miss Eliza married to Mr. Felix Latsspeach.

Neal, John C. married in Williamson County to Miss Ann Cahoon.

Neal, Minerva A. T. married to Thos. M. Anderson.

Neal, Miss Nancy P. married to Mr. Morris P. Williams.

Neal, Miss Patsey married to Mr. Thomas Clevinger.

Neal, Mr. William married in August 1831 to Miss Mary A. J. M. J. Parham.
The Western Weekly Review - Franklin, Tenn. (Fri., Sept. 2, 1831)

Neal, William H. married in Maury County, Ten. to Sarah A. Shaddon.
National Banner & Nashville Whig (Wed., Feb. 25, 1835)

Neale, James A. Esq. married in Bowling Green, Ky. to Miss Eliza Moore.
National Banner & Nashville Whig (Sat., Jan. 19, 1828)

Neblett, Miss Lucy Ann married to Nathaniel H. Allen Esq.

Needy, Mr. Isaac married at Shippingport, Ky. to Miss Rebecca Freburger.
National Banner & Nashville Whig (Sat., Jan. 3, 1829)

Neelands, Mr. George married at Pittsburgh to Miss Jane Holmes.
National Banner & Nashville Whig (July 1, 1826)

Neely, Miss Adelia C. married to Mr. James G. Bell.

Neely, Miss Azelia C. married to Mr. James G. Bell.

Neely, Miss Elizabeth married to Mr. Thomas Neely.

Neely, Miss Hadassah married to Mr. Samuel S. Hall.

Neely, Mr. James G. married in Bedford County to Miss Mary W. Steele daughter of Joseph Steele Esq.
National Banner & Nashville Daily Advertiser (Wed., Jan.30, 1833)

Neely, Mrs. Margaret C. married to Wm. D. Ferguson Esq.

Neely, Mr. Thomas married in Williamson County to Miss Elizabeth Neely.
National Banner & Nashville Whig (Fri., Jan. 9, 1835)

Neely, Mr. Wesley married in Maury County to Miss Mary Ann Thompson.
National Banner & Nashville Whig (Sat., Oct. 7, 1826)

Neely, William S. married in Williamson County to Miss Elizabeth Blackwell.
National Banner & Nashville Daily Advertiser (Mon., March 26, 1832)

Neely, Mr. William S. married in Williamson County to Elizabeth Blackwell.
National Banner & Nashville Advertiser (Mon., March 26, 1832)

Neely, William S. married in Williamson County to Miss Elizabeth Blackwell.
The Western Weekly Review - Franklin, Tenn. (Fri., March 23, 1832)

Negrin, Mr. Paul married in New York to Miss Maria Adele Labouisse.
National Banner & Nashville Whig (Sat., Oct. 28, 1826)

Neill, Mr. Wm. married in Jackson to Miss Jane Hughes.
National Banner & Nashville Whig (Wed., Aug. 17, 1831)

Neilson, Mr. Alexander G. married in Hardeman County to Miss Eugenia Polk.
National Banner & Nashville Whig (Sat., July 28, 1827)

Neilson, Mr. Hugh D. merchant of Trenton married in Gibson County by
the Rev. A. M. Williams to Miss Aly Jones daughter of Capt. Thos.
Jones.
National Banner & Nashville Daily Advertiser (Mon., March 18, 1833)

Neilson, Dr. Patrick D. married in Rutherford County to Miss Martha
Hoover daughter of John Hoover Esq.
National Banner & Nashville Daily Advertiser (Fri., Jan. 13, 1832)

Nelson, Mr. Abraham married in Knox County to Miss Frances Holbert.
National Banner (Sat., July 4, 1829)

Nelson, Miss Adeline married to Mr. Robert T. Walker.

Nelson, Miss Ann Elizabeth married to Mr. Joseph Hyder.

Nelson, Mr. C. W. married in Carter County to Miss Eliza Drake.
National Banner (Sat., May 16, 1829)

Nelson, Miss Eliza A. married near New Market, Tenn. Thursday 5th
Sept. by Rev. Allen H. Mathis to Mr. John Stone all of Jefferson
County.
Nashville Whig (Tues., Sept. 17, 1844)

Nelson, Mr. Horatio married in Arkansas County to Miss Harriet Darden.
National Banner & Nashville Whig (Sat., Aug. 26, 1826)

Nelson, Mr. James W. married near Jonesborough, Ten. to Miss Elizabeth
Carriger daughter of Col. Christian Carriger.
National Banner & Nashville Whig (Mon., Nov. 10, 1834)

Nelson, Miss Judith P. married to Edmund Richmond, Esq.

Nelson, Miss Judith P. married to Mr. Edmund Richmond, Esq.

Nelson, Miss Leonora N. married to Col. George H. Gordon.

Nelson, Miss Love married to Jacob Harding, Esq.

Nelson, Miss M. A. F. married to Mr. R. H. White.

Nelson, Miss Martha Ann married to Mr. L. P. Black.

Nelson, Mrs. Mary married to Mr. Joseph Caldwell.

Nelson, Miss Mary married to Mr. Hezekiah Stone.

Nelson, Miss Mary married to Capt. Thomas G. Watkins.

Nelson, Miss Mary married to Joseph Caldwell.

Nelson, Mr. Mathew married in this County on Thursday to Miss Sebela
Walker.
National Banner & Nashville Whig (Sat., Aug. 9, 1828)

Nelson, Mrs. Minerva married to Dr. Daniel Kenney.

Nelson, Miss Nancy P. married to Mr. David Taylor.

Nelson, Mr. Pezil married in Lincoln County to Miss Mary Boyles.
National Banner & Nashville Whig (Sat., Nov. 17, 1827)

Nelson, Richard Esq. of Sparta married on the 26th ult. to Miss
Betsy M'Campbell of Knox County.
Nashville Whig (July 7, 1823)

Nelson, Mr. Robert married in Montgomery County to Miss Mary A. King.
National Banner & Nashville Daily Advertiser (Mon., June 24, 1833)

Nelson, Miss Sarah married to Mr. Arthur Hamblin.

Nelson, Mr. Thomas married in Rutherford County to Miss Judith Edwards.
National Banner & Nashville Advertiser (Fri., April 27, 1832)

Nelson, Mr. Thomas married at St. Louis to Miss Margaret Patterson.
National Banner (Sat., Aug. 1, 1829)

Nesmith, Miss Annette S. married to Dr. Francis A. M'Williams.

Netherland, Miss Margaret W. married to Mr. Joseph R. Armstrong.

Neugent, Miss Mary Ann married to Gen. F. H. Bratcher.

Neugent, Miss Nancy Ann married to Gen. F. H. Bratcher.

Nevines, Mr. Wm. married in Williamson County to Belinda Nolen.
National Banner & Nashville Advertiser (Mon., March 26, 1832)

Nevins, William married in Williamson County to Miss Belinda Nolen.
The Western Weekly Review - Franklin, Tenn. (Fri., March 23, 1832)

New, Miss Emily married to Col. S. H. Boone.

Newbern, Mr. James married in Madison County to Miss Martha Jones.
National Banner & Nashville Whig (Wed., Oct. 19, 1831)

Newby, Miss Sally P. married to Mr. Ephraim Powell.

Newby, Ozwell married in Williamson County to Miss Martha Green.
The Western Weekly Review - Franklin, Tenn. (Fri., May 11, 1832)

Newby, Mr. Ozwell married in Williamson County to Martha Green.
National Banner & Nashville Advertiser (Wed., May 16, 1832)

Newcomb, Mr. Horatio D. married in Louisville on the 24th inst. to
Miss Cornelia Washington Read daughter of Thomas J. Read, Esq.
Nashville Union (Fri., June 29, 1838)

Newcomb, Mr. Horatio D. married in Louisville on the 24th inst. to
Miss Cornlia Washington Read daughter of Thomas J. Read, Esq.
Daily Republican Banner (Thurs., June 28, 1838)

Newell, Miss married to Capt. William B. Sweeny.

Newell, Mr. Albert married in Montgomery County to Miss Martha Ann
Pettus.
National Banner & Nashville Whig (Fri., May 14, 1830)

Newell, Mr. Thomas H. of Cincinnatti married on the 13 inst. to Miss
Jane Graham of Nashville.
Nashville Republican & State Gazette (Sat., March 15, 1834)

Newett, Mr. M'Nairy married in this County by Rev. Mr. Hume on the
25th ult. to Miss Lavinia Bosley daughter of John Bosley of Richland
Creek.
National Banner (Sat., July 4, 1829)

Newgent, Miss Sarah Ann married to Mr. Samuel Pattillo.

Newland, John A. Esq. married in Paris, Tenn. to Mrs. Sarah Coxx.
National Banner & Nashville Whig (Sat., May 12, 1827)

Newland, Mr. Silas married in Madison County, Ky. to Miss Emily
Broaddux.
National Banner & Nashville Whig (Sat., Sept. 9, 1826)

Newman, Miss Charity married to Mr. John W. Landrum.

Newman, Mr. Henry married at Vicksburgh, Mi. to Miss Elizabeth Sellers.
National Banner & Nashville Daily Advertiser (Fri., Sept. 20, 1833)

Newman, Mr. John married at Sparta to Miss Sally Whitley.
National Banner & Nashville Advertiser (Sat., July 7, 1832)

Newman, Miss Mary married to Allen A. Hall Esq.

Newnan, Miss Ann married to Alfred Balch Esq.

Newsom, Miss Elvira married to Mr. John Nosley.

Newsom, Miss Narcissa F. married to Mr. C. E. M'Ewen.

Newsom, Mrs. Rebecca married to Mr. Henry J. Merritt.

Newsom, Mr. Sowell of Alabama married on the 10th inst. in Jackson
County, Ten. by Richard P. Brooks Esq. to Miss Sarah Young daughter of
Capt. James Young of Jackson County.
Daily Republican Banner (Fri., Dec. 27, 1839)

Newsom, Mr. Thomas married in Bedford County to Miss Mary Reeves.
National Banner & Nashville Daily Advertiser (Wed., May 9, 1832)

Newsom, Mr. Thomas married in Bedford County to Miss Mary Reeves.
National Banner & Nashville Advertiser (Wed., May 9, 1832)

Newsome, Miss married to Mr. H. Hewett.

Newson, Miss Mary Ann married to Mr. George Skipworth.

Newson, Miss Mary Ann married to Mr. George Skipwith.

Newton, Rev. George married in Shelbyville to Miss Helen M. Cannon.
National Banner & Nashville Daily Advertiser (Mon., April 29, 1833)

Newton, Mary A. married in Bedford County to Thos. G. Flint.
National Banner & Nashville Daily Advertiser (Tues., Dec. 17, 1833)

Niblett, Mr. Francis married in Maury County to Miss Philadelphia
Ferguson.
National Banner & Nashville Whig (Mon., Sept. 26, 1831)

Nichols, Miss Maria married to Mr. Thomas A. Durham.

Nichols, John Esq. merchant of Nashville married in this vicinity on
Wednesday last 2d inst. by the Rev. J. T. Edgar, D.D. to Miss Evelina
M. Bradford.
Nashville Whig (Fri., Jan. 4, 1839)

Nichols, Miss Jane E. married to Mr. Christopher C. Williams.

Nichols, Miss Henrietta married to Charles B. Percy Esq.

Nichols, Miss Matilda married to Mr. Joseph H. Durham.

Nichols, Miss Susan married to Mr. Henry Ingram.

Nichols, Willis married in Maury County to Miss Eliza L. Pasmore.
Nashville Whig (Tues., July 14, 1846)

Nichols, Miss Elizabeth married to Parsons W. Moore.

Nichols, Mr. Christopher married in Cocke County to Miss Margaret
Allen.
National Banner & Nashville Whig (Sat., Sept. 16, 1826)

Nichol, Mr. John of Nashville married in this County on Tuesday last
to Miss Harriet Morford late of New Jersey.
National Banner & Nashville Whig (Sat., Jan. 5, 1828)

Nichol, Miss Jane married to John P. W. Brown Esq.

Nichol, Mr. James B. merchant of Nashville married on the 22nd inst.
by the Rev. Dr. Edgar to Miss Leodocia R. Hart of Davidson County.
Nashville Whig (Fri., Dec. 4, 1840)

Nichol, Mr. James of Nashville married in Rutherford County on Thursday evening 9th inst. by Rev. Mr. Hume to Miss Adelaide M'Culloch
daughter of Mr. B. M'Culloch of Rutherford.
National Banner & Nashville Whig (Mon., Sept. 13, 1830)

Nichol, Mr. James merchant of Nashville married on the 11th inst. by
the Rev. William D. Jones to Mrs. Martha E. McAfee residing near
Hopkinsville, Ky.
The Christian Record (Sat., March 27, 1847)

Nichol, Miss Henrietta married to Mr. Charles B. Percy.

Nichol, Miss Ellen married to Mr. William Livingston.

Nichol, Miss Ellen married to Mr. William Livingston.

Nichol, Miss Eliza married to Mr. James Richey.

Nicholson, Mr. Alfred O. P. married in Maury County to Miss Carolina
A. O'Reiley.
National Banner (Sat., June 27, 1829)

Nicholson, Miss Ann married to Mr. Ralph P. Smith.

Nicholson, Miss Ann married to Rev. W. A. Scott.

Nicholson, Miss Ann married to Rev. W. A. Scott.

Nicholson, Mr. Calvin H. married in Bedford County to Miss Mary B.
Jones.
National Banner & Nashville Whig (Sat., Oct. 6, 1827)

Nicholson, Miss Caroline married to H. M. Rutledge Esq.

Nicholson, Miss Caroline married to Henry A. Rutledge Esq.

Nicholson, Miss Mary Ann married to Mr. G. W. G. Payne.

Nicholson, Mr. Nathaniel married in Maury County, Ten. to Miss
Katherine Kilcrease.
National Banner & Nashville Whig (Mon., Jan. 26, 1835)

Nicholson, Mr. Nathaniel married to Miss Katharine Kilcrease.
Nashville Republican (Tues., Jan. 27, 1835)

Nicholas, Sam S. Esq. married in Louisville, Ky. to Miss Matilda
Prather.
National Banner (Sat., June 6, 1829)

Nicholson, Miss Sarah C. married to S. Owen.

Nicholson, Miss Sophia W. married to Mills Husbands.

Nichson, Miss Sarah married to Mr. Samuel Oldham.

Nickson, Miss Sarah married to Samuel Oldham.

Nidelect, Mr. Francis of Philadelphia married in St. Louis to Miss.
Celeste Pratt.   National Banner & Nashville Whig (Sat. Sept. 2,1826)

Niplett, Miss Sarah married to Mr. Perry B. Williamson.

Nix, Mr. James married near Post Gibson, Miss to Miss Eleanor Buckley.
National Banner (March 17, 1826)

Nixon, Henry Esq. married in Humphrey County on Sunday evening the
4th inst. to Miss Narcissa Pavatt.
National Banner & Nashville Whig (Sat., March 17, 1827)

Nixon, Doct. John D. married on the 22nd Oct. by the Rev. Doct. Wm. R.
Harmer to Mrs. P. Augustine all of Holmes County, Miss.
National Banner & Nashville Daily Advertiser (Mon., Nov. 4, 1833)

Nixon, Miss Priscilla A. married to Major John M. Henrie.

Noah, M. M. Esq. married in New York on the 28th ult. by Rev. Mr.
Hart to Miss Rebecca daughter of Mr. Daniel Jackson all of that city.
National Banner & Nashville Whig (Sat., Dec. 22, 1827)

Noble, Miss Margaret married to Maj. Lawrence S. Banks.

Noble, Miss Miranda married to Mr. Samuel Lidey.

Noel, Mr. Ephraim married in Maryville to Miss Jane Fleshart.
National Banner & Nashville Whig (Mon., April 11, 1831)

Noel, Mr. Ephraim married in Maryville to Miss Jane Fleshart.
National Banner & Nashville Whig (Mon., April 11, 1831)

Nofe, Miss Mary married to Capt. Colvin Bradley.

Noke, Mr. Wm. C. of this City married at New Orleans on the 10th inst.
by Rev. Abbe Bournau to Miss Mary F. Morris.
National Banner & Nashville Whig (Sat., Jan. 31, 1829)

Nolen, Miss Adelia C. married to Mr. Ben Johnson.

Nolen, Miss Adelia C. married to Mr. Benjamin Johnson.

Nolen, Miss Belinda married to Mr. Wm. Nevins.

Nolen, Miss Belinda married to William Nevins.

Nolen, Green married in Williamson County to Miss Frances W. Morten.
The Western Weekly Review - Franklin, Tenn. (Fri., Dec. 14, 1832)

Nolen, Mr. Lewis married in Dyer County, Ten. to Miss Frost.
National Banner & Nashville Whig (Wed., Dec. 17, 1834)

Nolen, Miss Malinda of Dickson County married to Mr. John Ritcherson.

Nolen, Miss Nancy married to Mr. Wilie Jones.

Noles, Miss Catherine married to Mr. John Turnbow.

Noles, Miss Catherine married to Mr. John Turnbow.

Nooe, John A. Esq. of Tuscumbia, Ala. married at the residence of
G. M. Fogg, Esq. by Rev. Charles Tomes to Miss Harriet E. Crowdus of
Simpson County, Ky.
Nashville True Whig & Weekly Commercial Register (Fri., Jan. 24, 1851)

Nooman, Mr. James D. Rutherford County married Miss Jemima M. Anderson.
National Banner & Nashville Advertiser (Mon., June 18, 1832)

Nooman, Mr. James D. married in Rutherford County, Tenn. to Miss
Jemima M. Anderson.
National Banner & Nashville Daily Advertiser (Mon., June 18, 1832)

Noon, Miss Eliza married to Mr. W. J. Dearing.

Norfleet, Mr. Edward W. of North Carolina married in Rutherford County on Tuesday 18, Oct. to Miss Elizabeth M. Read by the Rev. Payton Smith.
National Banner & Nashville Whig (Mon., Oct. 31, 1831)

Norfleet, Miss Minerva Ann of Montgomery County married in Montgomery County on the 26th inst. by the Rev. Mr. Williams to Mr. William G. M. Campbell Esq. of Davidson County.
Nashville Whig (Sat., April 29, 1843)

Norfleet, Miss Sally Elmyra married to Captain Felix Northington.

Norman, Miss Elizabeth married to Mr. Carter Clayter.

Norman, Francis married in Maury County to Miss Susan Jetton.
Nashville Whig (Tues., July 14, 1846)

Norman, Miss Frances T. married to Mr. Henry P. Gaines.

Norman, Mr. Harvey married in Nashville to Miss Jane Merryman.
Nashville Republican & State Gazette (Sat., Dec. 21, 1833)

Norman, Mr. Harvey married in Nashville on the 17th to Miss Jane Merriman.
National Banner & Nashville Daily Advertiser (Thurs., Dec. 19, 1833)

Norman, Mr. R. married in Bedford County to Miss Cynthia M'Farland.
National Banner & Nashville Daily Advertiser (Fri., Jan. 27, 1832)

Norris, Miss Cynthia married to Mr. James Sappington.

Norris, Dr. George D. married in Madison County, Ala. to Miss Martha Ragsdale of Tenn.
National Banner & Nashville Daily Advertiser (Wed., April 24, 1833)

Norris, Miss Mary Kelly married to Egbert R. Watson Esq.

Norsworthy, Mr. John of Dickson County married to Miss Nancy B. Adams on 30th.
Nashville Republican (Tues., Jan. 19, 1836)

Norsworthy, Mr. John married on 30th to Miss Nancy B. Adams.
Nashville Republican (Tues., Jan. 19, 1836)

Norsworthy, Miss Trilla married to Mr. George S. Perry.

North, Mr. Anthony married in Rutherford County to Miss Sarah P. Lawrence.
National Banner & Nashville Daily Advertiser (Tues., Nov. 20, 1832)

North, Mr. Anthony married in Rutherford County to Miss Sarah P. Lawrence.
National Banner & Nashville Advertiser (Tues., Nov. 20, 1832)

North, Mr. John married in Williamson County to Miss Mary Davis.
National Banner & Nashville Whig (Wed., Aug. 17, 1831)

North, Mr. John married on Saturday norming last to Miss Mary Davis both of Williamson County.
The Western Weekly Review - Franklin, Tenn. (Fri., Aug. 13, 1831)

North, Mr. John married in Williamson County to Miss Mary Davis.
National Banner & Nashville Whig (Wed., Aug. 17, 1831)

North, Mr. Wm. E. married in Rutherford County to Miss Purliner N. Jarratt.
National Banner (Jan. 6, 1826)

Northern, Miss Nancy Eliza married to Dr. Joseph Sandck.

Northern, Mr. William F. married in Henry County to Miss Eliza Leek.
National Banner & Nashville Daily Advertiser (Fri., March 2, 1832)

Northington, Miss Sarah married to Mr. Henry Johnson.

Norton, Miss Eliza Ellen married to Mr. John Nelson Ward.

Norton, Miss Susan G. married to Mr. Thomas C. Orear.

Norvell, Mr. C. C. married in Nashville to Miss Catherine M. Carroll
on Thursday evening last.
Nashville Republican & State Gazette. (Fri., June 28, 1833)

Norvell, C. C., Editor of the Whig - married last evening by Rev. Dr.
Edgar to Ann Jannette Gordon daughter of Capt. James Gordon of this
vicinity.
Nashville Whig (Thurs., April 25, 1844)

Norvell, Mr. Caleb C., Bookseller, married in Nashville on Thursday
evening, June 27, by Rev. P. Lindsley to Miss Catherine M. Carroll.
National Banner & Nashville Daily Advertiser (Fri., June 28, 1833)

Norvell, Miss Emeline K. married to Thomas C. Smiley.

Norvell, Mr. Henry L. married on the 6th inst. at Waverly the residence
of A. W. Putnam Esq. by Rev. Dr. Edgar to Miss Laura Sevier daughter
of Col. George Sevier all of Davidson County.
Nashville Whig (Sat., Oct. 8, 1842)

Norvell, Miss Mary married to Mr. James Walker.

Norvell, Mary Hannah married to Mr. William T. Stothart.

Norvell, Mr. Reuben B. of Philadelphia married on the 29th at the
residence of Col. William Fleming by the Rev. P. B. Robinson to Miss
George Ann Beale of Huntsville.
Nashville Whig (Tues., Dec. 6, 1842)

Norville, Miss Emeline K. married to Thos. C. Smiley, Esq.

Norwod, Miss Susannah married to Mr. Joseph Duncan.

Nosely, Mr. John, Bedford County married Miss Elvira Newsom Bedford Co.
National Banner & Nashville Advertiser (Wed., Jan. 4, 1832)

Notgrass, Thomas married in Williamson County to Miss Mary Armstrong.
The Western Weekly Review - Franklin, Tenn. (Fri., Dec. 14, 1832)

Notham, Mr. George married in Louisville, Ky. to Miss Elizabeth Cline.
National Banner & Nashville Whig (Sat., Aug. 30, 1828)

Nowland, Capt. Edward W. B. married in Nashville on Thursday evening
8th inst. by the Rev. Mr. Hume. to Miss Harriet C. Berryhill daughter
of William M. Berryhill, Esq.
National Banner & Nashville Whig (Mon., July 12, 1830)

Nowland, Miss Sarah Ann married at Indianapolis to Rev. Edwin Ray.
National Banner & Nashville Whig (Sat., Sept. 8, 1827)

Nowlen, Mr. William J. late of Nashville married on Tuesday the 17th
of Oct. by the Rev. R. Ellis to Miss Sarah Williams daughter of
William Williams Esq. of Marshall County.
Nashville Union (Tues., Nov. 14, 1837)

Nowlin, Miss Elizabeth T. married to Mr. T. A. Hall.

Noyes, Hon. Joseph C., M. C. of Maine, married in Washington City
on the 10th inst. to Miss Helen M. Alling of Salisbury, Connectcut.
Nashville Whig (Fri., July 20, 1838)

Noyes, Nat'l., Esq. married at Paris to Mrs. Rosella De Millian of
Baltimore.
Nashville Republican & State Gazette (Tues., Sept. 20, 1831)

Nugent, Miss Emiline T. married to Mr. Rufus K. Chisolm.

Nugent, Miss Emeline T. married to Mr. Rufus K. Chislom.

Nulty, Rev. Jacob married in Knox County to Miss Elizabeth Susan
Cardwell.
National Banner & Nashville Advertiser (Mon., Nov. 5, 1832)

Nulty, Rev. Jacob married in Knox County to Miss Elizabeth Susan
Cardwell.
National Banner & Nashville Daily Advertiser (Mon., Nov. 5,1832)

Nunley, Miss Elizabeth married to Mr. James Fulton.

Nunn, Miss Emily R. married to Mr. Isaac M. Philips.

Nutt, Miss Julia married to Capt. Jesse Joyner.

Oakford, Mrs. Martha C. married to Felix Parker jun. Esq.

Oakley, Mr. Martin W. married in Bedford County to Miss Elizabeth
M. Jones.
National Banner & Nashville Whig (Sat., Nov. 15, 1828)

Oats, Miss Nancy married to Mr. Albert G. Hale.

O'Brien, Miss Eliza married to Henry Hollingworth Esq.

O'Brien, Miss Sophia married to Mr. James Turnage.

O'Bryan, Miss Sophia married to Mr. James Tunnage.

Odam, Mr. Eli married on Thursday last in Sumner County to Miss
Catharine K. Phagan.
Nashville Whig (July 21, 1823)

Odam, Miss Sally married to Mr. Benj. Tarver.

Odam, Miss Sally married to Mr. John Scott.

Odel, Miss Ann married to Mr. Hardy Sellers.

O'Dell, Miss Am A. W. B. R. married to Alexander A. G. Swan Esq.

O'Dell, Miss Carolina O. R. B. W. married to Mr. John P. Bearden.

Odell, Miss Nancy married to Mr. Alexander Swan.

Odell, Mr. Samcel married in Knox County to Miss Sarah P. Arnold.
National Banner & Nashville Daily Advertiser (Mon., Sept. 10, 1832)

ODell, Mr. Thomas J. of Davidson County married to Miss Harriet
Bryant on Wednesday 16th.
Nashville Republican (Tues., Sept. 22, 1835)

Odle, Miss Ann married in Maury County to Hardy Sellers.

O'Donnell, Miss Mary married to Mr. Thomas English.

Odum, Mr. Edmund married in Weakley County on the 10th by John Henry
Moore, Esq. to Miss Mary Evans.
National Banner & Nashville Daily Advertiser (Wed., June 19, 1833)

Offutt, Miss Ann married to Mr. Wm. M'Carley.

Offutt, Mr. Fielder married in Port Gibson, Miss. to Miss Martha
Shelby.
National Banner & Nashville Whig (Sat., Aug. 19, 1826)

Offutt, Mr. Nathaniel married in Lexington, Ky. to Miss Mary Ann Payne.
National Banner & Nashville Whig (Fri., Jan. 29, 1830)

Ogburn, Miss Mary A. L. married to Mr. Samuel A. Adams.

Ogburn, Miss Mary A. L. married to Mr. Samuel Adams.

Ogden, Mr. Edward of New Orleans married at Ordoyne near Florence, Ala.
to Miss Letitia Hanna.
National Banner & Nashville Daily Advertiser (Sat., July 28, 1832)

Ogden, Miss Mary Ann married to A. C. White.

O'Hara, Mr. James married in Louisville, Ky. to Miss Isabella Whitaker.
National Banner & Nashville Daily Advertiser (Tues., June 26, 1832)

O'Hara, Miss Maria Helen married to Mr. John U. Price.

O'Hare, Miss married to Wm. Croughan Esq.

Old, Miss Eliza married to Mr. Wm. Harris.

Old, Miss Martha A. M. married to Mr. Charles B. Porter.

Old, Mr. Wm. M. married in Lincoln County to Miss Eliza Ann Edmiston.
National Banner & Nashville Whig (Mon., Jan. 5, 1835)

Oldenberg, Mr. Frederick married at Shawneetown to Mary Cook.
National Banner (Feb. 24, 1826)

Oldham, Miss Adeline married in Smith County to Mr. Levi Sholders.

Oldham, Miss Eliza married to Mr. Edward Ward.

Oldham, Miss Minerva married to Rev. Wm. M'Ferrin.

Oldham, Miss Nancy married to Mr. John Southall.

Oldham, Miss Patsey married to Mr. Ichobod Moberley.

Oldham, Mr. Samuel married in Smith County to Miss Sarah Nickson.
National Banner & Nashville Daily Advertiser (Thurs., Jan. 5, 1832)

Oldham, Mr. Tyre married in Russellville, Ky. to Miss Mary G. Mason.
National Banner & Nashville Daily Advertiser (Thurs., June 19, 1834)

Oldham, Mr. Wm. married at Lexington, Ky. to Miss Lucretia E. Elder.
National Banner & Nashville Whig (Fri., June 20, 1828)

Olinger, Miss Phebe married to Mr. Greenberry Conk.

Oliphant, Mr. Thomas J. married in this County to Miss Evelina Akin.
National Banner & Nashville Whig (Sat., March 10, 1827)

Oliver, Miss Betsy Clay married to Rev. Moses F. Rainwater.

Oliver, Mr. Edward married in Perry County, Ala. to Miss Eliza Johnson.
National Banner (Feb. 17, 1826)

Oliver, Miss Frances married to Mr. Francis H. Robinson.

Oliver, Mr. Jesse married to Miss Mary Ady, married in Lincoln County.
National Banner & Nashville Whig (Wed., Dec. 17, 1834)
Oliver, Mr. John E. married in Henry County to Miss Mary Cloys.
National Banner & Nashville Daily Advertiser (Sat., Oct. 13, 1832)

Oliver, Margaret married to Robert Whitehead.

Oliver, Miss Nancy Y. married to Mr. George F. Black.

Oliver, Miss Rosa A. married to Mr. William G. King.

Oliver, Miss Susan married to Mr. Drery Seals.

Oliver, Mr. William S. married on the 8th inst. by the Rev. Dr. Edgar
to Miss Adaline S. Marlin both of Nashville.
Nashville Whig (Fri., Sept. 10, 1841)

Omall, Mr. Elisha F. married in Williamson County, Ten. to Miss Rebecca
Lindsay.
National Banner & Nashville Whig (Mon., April 13, 1835)

On-dsa-lu-de married at the Valley Towns by the Rev. E. Jones April 12th,
1830 to Dse-go-eh.
National Banner & Nashville Whig (Mon., July 26, 1830)

O'Neal, Mr. Elijah married in Davidson County to Miss Rebecca Lindley. *Nashville Republican* (Tues., Feb. 24, 1835)

Oneal, Miss Eliza married to Mr. Fielding L. Sidebottom.

O'Neal, Miss Sarah married to Mr. William T. Wilburn.

O'Neal, Miss Sarah married to Mr. William T. Wilburn.

O'Neal, Mr. Willie married in Bedford County to Miss Phoebia Larew. *National Banner & Nashville Daily Advertiser* (Thurs., March 20, 1834)

O'Neil, Mr. Hugh Jr. Esq. married at St. Louis, Mo. to Mrs. Mary Gilhauley. *National Banner & Nashville Daily Advertiser* (Wed., May 7, 1834)

Ore, Mrs. Elizabeth married to Mr. Elias Tomlinson.

Orear, Miss Mary married to Mr. Levi Frazier.

Orear, Mr. Thomas C. married in Lexington, Ky. to Miss Susan G. Norton. *National Banner* (March 24, 1826)

O'Reilley, Miss Carolina A. married to Mr. Alfred O. P. Nicholson. *National Banner* (Sat., June 27, 1829)

O'Reilley, Doct. James C. of Maury County, Tenn. married in Philadelphia on 27th April by Rev. Philip F. Mayers, D.D. to Miss Sarah Hartley of Philadelphia. *Nashville Whig* (Mon., May 11, 1840)

Organ, Mr. Woodford married in Wilson County to Miss Jane Weir. *National Banner & Nashville Advertiser* (Wed., Aug. 29, 1832)

O'Riely, Mr. Phillip married in Lawrence County, Ala. to Miss Tralucca H. Lester. *National Banner & Nashville Whig* (Sat., Oct. 28, 1826)

O'Riley, Miss C. married to Mr. A. Crawford.

O'Riley, Dr. James of Columbia married in this town on Tuesday evening last to Miss Matilda Adams. *National Banner* (Sat., Nov. 21, 1829)

O'Riley, Miss Mary E. married to Mr. William Dale.

Orival, Miss Nancy C. L. married to Dr. Thomas J. Sneed.

Ormond, John J. Esq. married in Lawrence County, Ala. to Miss Minerva Banks. *National Banner & Nashville Whig* (Sat., Oct. 28, 1826)

Orndorff, Miss Catherine married to Mr. Ed H. Gunn.

Orndorff, Miss Catherine married to Mr. Ed. H. Gunn.

Orndoff, Mr. Eli married in Russellville, Ky. to Miss Mary Paisley. *National Banner* (Jan. 13, 1826)

Ornsby, Miss Sarah M. married to Maj. A. Phillips.

Orr, Miss Mary F. married to Mr. Winfrey Witherspoon.

Orr, William D. married in Giles County to Fanny J. Kerr. *National Banner & Nashville Daily Advertiser* (Tues., Dec. 17, 1833)

Orr, Miss Mary married to Mr. D. Draper.

Orr, Mr. Larkin B. married in Bedford County to Miss Martha Carter
daughter of William Carter, Esq.
National Banner & Nashville Daily Advertiser (Mon., June 3, 1833)

Orr, Mr. James D. married in Rutherford County to Miss Cynthia Goodloe
daughter of Henry Goodloe, Esq.
National Banner & Nashville Daily Advertiser (Mon., April 15, 1833)

Orr, Col. John married in Bedford County to Mrs. Turner.
National Banner & Nashville Daily Advertiser (Sat., Oct. 6, 1832)

Orton, Mr. May S. of Nashville married on Wednesday the 26th inst. by
the Rev. R. A. Lapsley to Miss L. A. Wingfield of Columbia, Tenn.
Nashville Whig (Thurs., Aug. 27, 1846)

Orton, Miss Nancy married to Mr. Jacob E. Guthrie.

Orton, Nancy M. married to Geo. M. Pickard.

Osborne, Mr. A. M. married on Thursday evening last to Miss Martha
Crutcher both of this place.
The Nashville Whig (Aug. 25, 1817)

Osborn, Miss Elizabeth married to Mr. John White.

Osborne, Mrs. Mary married to Thomas Washington, Esq.

Osborne, Miss Mary married to Thomas Washington Esq.

Osborne, Miss Sarah married to Mr. Thomas Hammon.

Osburn, Miss Martha married to Henry Prichitt.

Oslin, Alanson married in Williamson County to Kesiah Wood.
The Western Weekly Review - Franklin, Tenn. (Fri., Feb. 10, 1832)

Ostrander, Miss Ellen married to Mr. George Kelly.

Otey, Miss Eliza married to Paul Hildreth, Esq.

Otey, Miss Henrietta Coleman married to Rev. Charles Tomes.

Otey, Dr. Paul H. of Columbia, Tenn. married in Nashville on the 19th
inst. by the Rev. Dr. Edgar to Miss Mary Ann Bowls of Miss.
The Christian Record (Sat., March 27, 1847)

Otis, Richard W. Esq. married at Louisville, Ky. to Miss Sarah Maria
Dwyer daughter of William Dwyer, Esq.
National Banner & Nashville Whig (Fri., June 10, 1831)

Ott, Mrs. married to Mr. Boyce.

Ott, Miss Elizabeth married to Mr. Ramsey Henderson.

Outlaw, Dr. Drew A. of Stewart County married in Dickson County to
Miss Mary Ann Eliza West.
National Banner (June 3, 1826)

Outon, Mr. William married in Lincoln County, Ten. to Miss Nancy Jones.
National Banner & Nashville Whig (Mon., April 20, 1835)

Overall, Miss Parilea married to Mr. William B. Stokes.

Overall, Miss Parilea married to Wm. B. Stokes.

Overly, Miss Elizabeth married in Ross County, Ohio to Mr. John S.
Tharp.

Overton, Miss Ann married to Wm. Frazier Esq.

Overton, Anna married to R. C. Brinkley, Esq.

Overton, Miss Elizabeth married to Mr. Joshua H. Wills.

Overton, Miss Elizabeth S. married to Mr. James L. Colcate.

Overton, Miss Emma Maria married to Richard Winn, Esq.

Overton, Miss Emma Maria married to Richard Winn, Esq.

Overton, Mr. Jesse married in Summerville to Miss Matilda Beavers on Tuesday 30th ult. by the Rev. Mr. McDonald.
National Banner & Nashville Advertiser (Wed., Nov. 14, 1832)

Overton, Mr. Jesse married in Sommerville on Tuesday 30th ult. by the Rev. Mr. McDonald to Miss Matilda Beavers.
National Banner & Nashville Daily Advertiser (Wed., Nov. 14, 1832)

Overton, John, Esq. married on the 20th inst. to Mrs. May relict of Dr. May, formerly of this town.
The Clarion & Tennessee Gazette (July 25, 1820)

Overton, Hon. John of this vicinity married on the 28th ult. at Knoxville, East Tennessee to Mrs. Mary May relict of Doctor May formerly a resident of Nashville.
The Nashville Gazette. (Sat., Aug. 5, 1820)

Overton, Mr. John married on the morning of the 18th inst. by the Rev. Dr. Edgar to Miss Rachel N. Harding daughter of Mr. Thomas Harding all of Davidson County.
Nashville Whig (Wed., April 21, 1841)

Overton, Miss Margaret married in Maury County, Tenn. to Mr. Joseph L. McKay.

Overton, Miss Margaret married to Mr. Joseph L. M'Kay.

Overton, Patrick Henry Esq. late of the United States Navy married on Thursday evening the first inst. by the Rev. Mr. Craighead to Miss Rebecca Phillip daughter of the late Benjamin Phillip of this County.
Nashville Whig (April 12, 1824)

Overton, Samuel R. Esq. Navy Agent married at Pensacola on the 29th of November to Miss Margaret Ann Mitchell.
National Banner (Jan. 6, 1826)

Overton, Miss Sarah Brown married to Dr. Benjamin Wilkins.

Owen, Agnes married to Mr. John Maukin.

Owen, Everett Esq. of Williamson County married on the 28th inst. by the Rev. Dr. Howell to Mrs. Mary M. Cowen.
Nashville Whig (Thurs., Oct. 1, 1846)

Owen, Mr. Herbert married in Williamson County, Ten. to Miss Martha A.R. Thompson.
National Banner & Nashville Whig (Fri., Feb. 13, 1835)

Owen, Louisa married to Washington Merrit.

Owen, Miss Narcissa married to Mr. Joseph R. Higgins.

Owen, Mr. P. of Nashville married in Sumner County to Miss Henrietta Minter.
Nashville Republican & State Gazette (Sat., March 12, 1831)

Owen, Mr. Preston married in Jefferson County, Ky. to Miss Mary Rudy.
National Banner & Nashville Whig (Sat., March 1, 1828)

Owen, S. married in Williamson County to Miss Sarah C. Nicholson.
The Western Weekly Review - Franklin, Tenn. (Fri., Feb. 1, 1833)

Owen, Miss Susan D. married to Mr. Wm. H. Allen.

Owen, Mr. William A. married in the vicinity of Smithfield, Ky. to
Miss Rebecca Cornelius.
National Banner & Nashville Daily Advertiser (Mon., Aug. 12, 1833)

Owen, Col. William E. of Memphis married on Monday 30th inst. by the
Rev. J. T. Wheat to Miss Margaret Wilson of Nashville.
Nashville Whig (Tues., Oct. 31st. 1843)

Owen, Mr. Wm. E., merchant, married on Thursday evening last to Miss
Ann Campbell both of Franklin.
The Nashville Whig (April 30, 1817)

Owen, Maj. William E. married in Williamson County to Mrs. Catherine
James.
National Banner (Feb. 10, 1826)

Owings, Miss Eleanora N. married to Dr. George Snider.

Owsley, Miss Elizabeth married to Charles Henry Talbot, Esq.

Owsley, Mr. Erasmus Boyle of Garrard County to Miss Caroline E. Talbott
daughter of Mr. Presley Talbott in Jessamine County, Ky.
National Banner & Nashville Whig (Mon., Oct. 31, 1831)

Ozier, Mr. Joel married on the 29th Oct. to Miss Mary Carns all of
Humphreys County.
National Banner & Nashville Whig (Wed., Nov. 11, 1835)

Page, Mr. Egbert married on the 26th by John Wright Esq. to Miss Elizabeth Page all of Davidson County.
Nashville Whig (Mon., March 2, 1840)

Page, Miss Elizabeth married to Mr. Robert Franklin.

Page, Miss Frances married to Mr. Thomas Russell

Page, Mr. Jefferson married in Davidson County on the 30th ult. to Miss Louisa Quisenbury.
National Banner & Nashville Whig (Wed., Sept. 7, 1831)

Page, Mr. Jesse L. married in Logan County to Mrs. Sally Wright.
National Banner & Nashville Whig (Wed., Dec. 7, 1831)

Page, Mr. Jesse W. married in Nashville on Wednesday evening Nov. 23d inst. by the Rev. Mr. Hume to Miss Araballa Folwell.
National Banner & Nashville Whig (Thurs., Nov. 24, 1831)

Page, Mr. Jesse L. married in Logan County, Ky. to Mrs. Sally Wright.
National Banner & Nashville Whig (Wed., Dec. 7, 1831)

Page, Mr. Root married in Maury County to Miss Martha Warr.
National Banner & Nashville Whig (Sat., Dec. 17, 1831)

Page, Mr. Root married in Maury County to Miss Martha Warr.
National Banner & Nashville Whig (Sat., Dec. 17, 1831)

Page, Miss Sabina married to Mr. D. W. Cockrum.

Pageat, Alphonson Esq., Secretary to the French Legation married in Washington City on the 29th at the Presidents by the Rev. William Matthews of the Catholic Church to Miss Mary Ann Lewis daughter of William B. Lewis Esq. 2d Auditor of the Treasury.
National Banner & Nashville Daily Advertiser (Tues., Dec. 11, 1832)

Paine, Miss Amanda M. married to Mr. Francis Roach.

Paine, Miss Amanda M. married to Mr. Francis G. Roach.

Paine, Miss Ann married to Mr. Reuben Toller.

Paine, Rev. Robert of the Methodist Society married on Monday last to Miss Susannah Beck daughter of the late John E. Beck, Esq. of this place.
Nashville Whig (Nov. 15, 1824)

Paine, Miss Susan married to Collin S. Tarpley Esq.

Paine, Rev. William C. married in Paris, Ten. to Miss M. W. Gibbs daughter of Mr. John Gibbs.
National Banner & Nashville Whig (Mon., April 13, 1835)

Paine, Mr. Wirner married in Franklin County, Ala. to Miss Minarva Winston.
National Banner & Nashville Whig (Sat., July 8, 1826)

Paisley, Miss Mary married to Mr. Eli Orndoff.

Palmore, Mrs. Elizabeth W. married to James W. Bates Esq.

Palmer, Mr. Henry S. of Dixon County married in Louisville, Ky. to Mrs. Eliza Sale of Louisville.
National Banner & Nashville Whig (Sat., March 8, 1828)

Palmer, Miss Nelly married to Mr. John Christian.

Palmer, Dr. Robert C. married in Bardstown, Ky. to Miss Emily Hardin, Esq.
National Banner & Nashville Whig (Mon., Aug. 2, 1830)

Palmer, Miss Sarah married to Mr. Anderson Witt.

Palmer, Mr. Tho. married in Smith County to Miss Mary Castern.
National Banner & Nashville Advertiser (Fri., Jan. 13, 1832)

Parham, Mrs. Ann T. married to Mr. Matthew H. Quinn.

Parham, Mr. E. married at Knoxville to Miss Mary Dunn daughter of
Mr. Thomas Dunn.
National Banner & Nashville Daily Advertiser (Mon., Feb.6, 1832)

Parham, Mr. John L. married at Memphis to Miss Lucinda Runkle on the
16th inst.
National Banner & Nashville Advertiser (Mon., Oct. 29, 1832)

Parham, Miss Martha married to Mr. John Park.

Parham, Miss Mary A. J. M. J. married to Mr. William Neal.

Parham, Miss Sarah married to Mr. Philip H. Jenkins.

Parham, Mr. Thomas J. married in Maury County, Ten. to Miss Lovy
McAfee.
National Banner & Nashville Whig (Mon., Jan. 26, 1835)

Paris, Mr. Robert married in Warren County to Miss Elizabeth Perkins
daughter of Col. John B. Perkins.
National Banner & Nashville Advertiser (Thurs., Dec. 20, 1832)

Parish, Miss Catherine married to Harvey W. Ellis Esq.

Parish, Mr. David W. married in Robertson County on the 22d inst.
by the Rev. Mr. Hume to Miss Mary A. Clark.
National Banner & Nashville Daily Advertiser (Fri., Feb. 24, 1832)

Parish, Miss Sarah A. married to Mr. Felix Sherrod.

Park, Miss Deliah Ann married to Mr. E. C. Mason.

Park, Miss Elizabeth R. married to Rev. J. W. Hanner.

Park, Mr. Felding married in Lincoln County to Miss Caroline Davis.
National Banner & Nashville Whig (Sat., Dec. 30, 1826)

Park, Rev. James of Knoxville, Tennessee married at Lexington, Tennessee
married at Lexington, Va. on the 27th May by Rev. J. Skinner D.D. to
Miss Phebe C. Alexander daughter of the late William Alexander Esq. of
Rockbridge County, Va.
The Christian Record (Sat., June 26, 1847)

Park, Dr. John of Franklin married on Tuesday last, by Rev. Mr. Hanner
to Miss Mary Ann Carden daughter of Mr. A. D. Carden of Nashville.
Nashville Whig (Sat., March 12, 1842)

Park, Mr. John married in Lincoln County on the 5th inst. married
Miss Martha Parham daughter of Capt. E. Parham.
Nashville Banner & Nashville Whig (Thurs., June 24, 1830)

Park, Miss Letitia H. married to A. D. Witherspoon.

Park, Miss Louisiana married to Dr. R. M. Campbell.

Park, Mr. Robert married in Pittsburgh to Miss Jane Miller.
National Banner & Nashville Whig (Sat., Dec. 30, 1826)

Park, Miss Sarah Jane married to Capt. William Driver

Park, Miss Sophia married to George M. White, Esq.

Park, Miss Susan W. married to Dr. L. W. Baker.

Parke, Miss Sarah married to Mr. Abraham Hite.

Parker, Miss Alice married to Mr. William Wirkham.

Parker, Miss Alley married to Mr. John Hutchinson.

Parker, Mr. E. F. of Tenn. married in Madison County, Ala. to Miss
Francis E. Dyer.
National Banner & Nashville Whig (Sat., Feb. 17, 1827)

Parker, Miss Eliza E. married to Dr. Levi Ring.

Parker, Miss Elizabeth married to Mr. Richard Allen.

Parker, Felix jun. Esq. Representative from Gibson County in the
General Assembly married in Nashville on 19th Nov. by the Rev. J.
Thomas Wheat to Mrs. Martha C. Oakford late of Philadelphia.
Daily Republican Banner (Mon., Nov. 20, 1837)

Parker, Mr. George W. married on Thursday evening last to Miss
Elizabeth Ann Barry daughter of Mr. John G. Barry, Printer.
National Banner & Nashville Whig (Fri., April 10, 1835)

Parker, Col. James M. of Va. married in Lexington, Ky. to Miss
Madelina Barbary Myers of Lexington.
National Banner (April 28, 1826)

Parker, Dr. James P. married at Burlington, Ky. to Miss Martha
Miliken.
National Banner & Nashville Whig (Sat., Dec.6, 1828)

Parker, Mr. John married in Smith County to Miss Elizabeth Brown
National Banner & Nashville Daily Advertiser (Thurs., Jan. 5, 1832)

Parker, Miss Mary married to Mr. Samuel Smith.

Parker, Miss Maty Ann married to Mr. James Hague.

Parker, Mr. Milton married in Sumner County to Miss Caroline Sullivan.
National Banner & Nashville Whig (Fri., Nov. 26, 1830)

Parker, Miss Pamelia married to Mr. Isaac Litton.

Parker, Miss Pamelia married to Mr. Isaac Litton.

Parker, Mr. S. M. married on Sunday last by the Rev'd Hardy M. Cryer
to Miss Judeth Proffit both of Sumner County.
The Nashville Gazette (Wed., Nov. 3, 1819)

Parker, W. P. Esq. of Lexington, Ky. married in Bowling Green, Ky.
to Miss Camilla L. Breashear.
National Banner & Nashville Whig (Wed., Sept. 14, 1831)

Parker, Mr. William W. married in Williamson County to Miss Artemisia
Neal.
Nashville Republican & State Gazette (Mon., April 22, 1833)

Parker, Mr. William W. married in Williamson County to Miss Artemisia
Neal.
National Banner & Nashville Daily Advertiser (Mon., April 22, 1833)

Parker, Mr. William W. married on Thursday evening 18th inst. by the
Rev. J. Campbell to Miss Artemisia Neal all of Williamson County.
The Western Weekly Review - Franklin, Tenn. (Fri., April 19, 1833)

Parker, W. P. Esq. of Lexington, Ky. married Miss Camilla L. Brashear in Boling Green, Ky.
National Banner & Nashville Whig (Wed., Sept. 14, 1831)

Parker, Zelia married to Mr. Wm. Aaron.

Parkinson, Mr. John married in Washington County to Miss Rebecca Cassedy.
National Banner & Nashville Whig (Sat., July 15, 1826)

Parkinson, Miss Mary Ann married to Mr. David Beers.

Parks, Mr. Henry married in Jefferson County to Miss Sussannah Gregory.
National Banner (Sat., Nov. 28, 1829)

Parks, Mr. Joseph married in this town on Tuesday last to Miss Eliza St. Clair.
National Banner & Nashville Whig (Sat., Aug. 5, 1826)

Parks, Miss Parthana married to Capt. James Borex.

Parks, Mr. Samuel of Monroe County married in Blount County to Miss Susan Cook.
National Banner & Nashville Daily Advertiser (Tues., July 10, 1832)

Parlin, Mr. Elijah married near Port Gibson, Miss to Miss Nancy Richards.
National Banner (June 3, 1826)

Parlor, Miss Grace married to Mr. Isreal Satan.

Parlor, Miss Grace married to Mr. Isreal Statan.

Parran, Mr. Thomas O. married in Shelby County to Miss Nancy Carr.
National Banner & Nashville Whig (Sat., March 22, 1828)

Parratt, Dr. J. married in Haywood County to Miss Lucinda Waller daughter of Col. Benjamin Waller.
Nashville Whig (Tues., March 31, 1846)

Parrent, Mr. Thomas married at Louisville, Ky. to Miss Frances Harden.
National Banner & Nashville Whig (Sat., Jan. 3, 1829)

Parrish, Mrs. Catherine married to Joseph Lee.

Parrish, Mr. Eaton married in Maury County, Ten. to Miss Elizabeth H. Andrews.
National Banner & Nashville Whig (Mon., March 30, 1835)

Parrish, Mr. Frank married in this town last evening by W. Lytle Esq. to Mrs. Fanny Dismukes.
National Banner (Sat., Nov. 28, 1829)

Parrish, Mr. Harvey D. of this County married last evening to Miss Hannar M'Crory daughter of the late Col. Tho. M'Crory of Williamson County.
Nashville Whig (Jan. 29, 1823)

Parrish, Mr. James married in Woodford County, Ky. to Miss Margaret Shipp.
National Banner & Nashville Whig (Mon., Sept. 13, 1830)

Parrish, Mr. M. A. of Nashville married in Gallatin on the 16th inst. by the Rev. J. W. Hume to Miss Catherine Daughtery.
The Christian Record (Sat., Nov. 25, 1848)

Parrish, Miss Mary E. married to Mr. B. B. Pittman.

Parrish, Miss Mary E. married to Mr. Bartholomew B. Pittman.

Parrish, Miss Sally married to Mr. Robert Winser.

Parrish, Miss Sally married to Mr. Robert Winser.

Parrish, Mr. Samuel married in Christian County, Ky. to Miss Mary Garnett.
National Banner & Nashville Whig (Sat., Jan. 27, 1827)

Parrish, Mr. Samuel married in Hopkinsville to Miss Garrett.
National Banner & Nashville Whig (Sat., Feb. 3, 1827)

Parrish, Miss Sarah A. of Nashville married to Mr. Felix Sherrod in Courtland, Ala.
Nashville Republican (Thurs., June 4, 1835)

Parrish, Miss Surindia married to Mr. Moses Campbell.

Parrish, Miss Susan married to Mr. Abraham M. White.

Parrott, Miss Jane married to Rev. Stephen B. Balch.

Parrum, Miss Martha married to Mr. James Hughes.

Parrum, Miss Martha married to Mr. Jas. Hughes.

Parsley, Miss Cassandra married to Mr. Andrew Randles.

Parsons, Mr. A. B. married in Shelbyville, Tenn. to Miss Eliza Moore.
National Banner & Nashville Daily Advertiser (Sat., Aug. 24, 1833)

Parsons, Mr. B. S. of Huntingdon married in Lauderdale County, Ala. to Miss Louisa Hawkins.
National Banner & Nashville Whig (Sat., Feb. 7, 1829)

Partee, Dr. D. M. of Paris married in Smuner County to Miss Eliza A. C. Buckner.
National Banner & Nashville Whig (Sat., June 16, 1827)

Partee, Mr. Hiram married in Haywood County to Miss Louama Cherry.
National Banner (Sat., Aug. 8, 1829)

Partlow, Mr. Wm. D. married in Hardeman County to Miss Adelener H. Bolling.
National Banner & Nashville Whig (Wed., Oct. 12, 1831)

Partlow, Mr. Wm. D. married in Hardeman County to Miss Adelener H. Colling.
National Banner & Nashville Whig (Wed., Oct. 12, 1831)

Paschal, Mr. Samuel married at Carthage to Miss Susan Beloate.
National Banner & Nashville Advertiser (Fri., Feb. 10, 1832)

Pasmore, Miss Eliza L. married to Willis Nichols.

Pastlelhwait, Mr. Lewis married in Lexington, Ky. to Miss Sarah Morton.
National Banner & Nashville Whig (Sat., Jan. 3, 1829)

Pate, Miss Francis married to Mr. Henry T. Hawkins.

Pate, Jas. married in Williamson County, Ten. to Nancy Warren.
National Banner & Nashville Whig (Wed., Dec. 17, 1834)

Pate, Miss Jane married to Major Joseph Moore.

Pate, Mr. John F. married in Knox County to Miss Margaret Marley.
National Banner & Nashville Advertiser (Mon., April 23, 1832)

Pate, Miss Louisa Jane married to Mr. Thomas L. Taylor.

Pate, Mr. Thos. G. married in Madison County, Ten. to Miss Mary Butler.
National Banner & Nashville Whig (Wed., Aug. 17, 1831)

Pate, Mr. Thos. G. married in Madison County, Ten. to Miss Mary Butler.
National Banner & Nashville Whig (Wed., Aug. 17, 1831)

Paterson, Miss Margaret married to Mr. Thomas Nelson.

Pathia, Miss Nancy married to Dr. P. H. Cole.

Paton, Mr. James married in Paris, Ky. to Miss Catherine Trundell.

Paton, Mr. James married in Paris, Ky. to Miss Catherine Frindell.

Patrick, Miss Elizabeth married to Mr. Samuel Ferguson.

Patrick, Miss Elizabeth Callaway married to Mr. David Decherd.

Patrick, Miss Nancy married to Mr. Thomas Bigley.

Patrick, Miss Olive P. married to Major William Ramsey.

Patrick, Mr. Robert A. of Benton, Miss married in Madison County, Ala.
to Miss Elizabeth P. Shackelford.
National Banner & Nashville Whig (Fri., Dec. 31, 1830)

Patrick, Miss Sarah M. married to Mr. Charles L. King.

Patterson, Mr. merchant, married on Monday evening the 8th inst. to
Miss Drucilla Plumner both of Springfield.
The Nashville Whig (Sept. 15, 1817)

Patterson, Miss Ann married to Mr. Alexander Barrell.

Patterson, Miss Ann E. married to Robert P. Smith.

Patterson, Miss Ann M. married to Mr. Henry O. Dixon.

Patterson, Miss Catherine Ann married to Mr. William Yandle.

Patterson, Miss Eliza H. married to Mr. John Hallum.

Patterson, Miss Elizabeth married to Mr. Jackson C. Davis.

Patterson, Miss Elizabeth married to Mr. Jesse S. Duncan.

Patterson, Miss Elizabeth married to Mr. George Cox, jun.

Patterson, Col. George married in Montgomery County to Miss Sarah G.
Trabue.
National Banner & Nashville Whig (Wed., June 29, 1831)

Patterson, Mr. Henry married in New Orleans to Miss Biddy Kersey.
National Banner & Nashville Whig (Sat., Feb. 24, 1827)

Patterson, Mr. Jos. M. married in Williamson County to Miss Mary D.
Watkins.
The Western Weekly Review - Franklin, Tenn. (Fri., Dec. 2, 1831)

Patterson, Mr. Jos. M. married in Williamson County to Miss Mary D.
Watkins.
National Banner & Nashville Whig (Wed., Dec. 7, 1831)

Patterson, Miss Keziah married to Mr. David R. Larimore.

Patterson, Mr. N. married at St. Louis to Miss Winifred Higgins.
National Banner & Nashville Whig (Sat., Nov. 17, 1827)

Patterson, Miss Nancy F. married to Mr. J. Gilmer.

Patterson, Miss Nancy F. married to _____

Patterson, Miss Patsey married to Mr. James Bachelor.

Patterson, Mr. Richard married in Warren County, Ky. to Miss Caroline R. P. Campbell.
National Banner & Nashville Whig (Fri., July 22, 1831)

Patterson, Mr. Robert married in Monroe County to Miss Susannah Headerick.
National Banner & Nashville Whig (Fri., Sept. 9, 1831)

Patterson, Mr. Robert married in Maury County to Miss Matilda M'Kee.
National Banner & Nashville Whig (Sat., Jan. 10, 1829)

Patterson, Mr. Thomas M., Principal of Wirt College, Sumner County. Married in the vicinity of Nashville on the 19th inst. by the Rev. Dr. Edgar to Miss Mary L. S. Campbell of Davidson County.
Nashville Whig (Sat., Feb. 21, 1846)

Pattie, Miss Maria F. married to Sterling Stainback.

Pattillo, Mr. Samuel married in Rutherford County to Miss Sarah Ann Newgent.
National Banner & Nashville Advertiser (Fri., Dec. 21, 1832)

Patton, Mr. A., merchant of Jackson married in Madison County to Miss Sarah Jane Butler daughter of Col. Robert Butler of Fla.
National Banner (Sat., June 13, 1829)

Patton, Mr. A., merchant of Jackson married in Madison County to Miss Sarah Jane Butler daughter of Col. Robert Butler of Florida.
National Banner (Sat., June 13, 1829)

Patton, Miss Artemisia G. married to Ephriam G. Peyton, Esq.

Patton, Benjamin Jr. District Attorney of the U. States for the Western District of Penn. married in Dayton, O. to Miss Matilda Helfenstein.
National Banner & Nashville Daily Advertiser (Mon., May 12, 1834)

Patton, Miss Elizabeth married to Mr. John A. Dale.

Patton, Miss Elizabeth married to Mr. Charles E. Woodruff.

Patton, Mr. George married in Washington County to Miss Susan Grissum.
National Banner & Nashville Whig (Sat., July 22, 1826)

Patton, Miss Harriett B. married to Gen. Abner B. Robertson.

Patton, Mr. James married in Williamson County to Miss Narcissa Smith.
Nashville Whig (Jan. 22, 1823)

Patton, Mr. James V. of Little Rock, Ark. married in Memphis on the 15th inst. to Miss Eleanora Thaw of Washington City.
National Banner & Nashville Advertiser (Mon., March 26, 1832)

Patton, Miss Jane R. married to Mr. William H. Pope.

Patton, Miss Margaret married to Mr. Jesse Bestkinson.

Patton, Miss Margaret married to Mr. Jesse B. Atkinson.

Patton, Miss Maria married to Mr. Calvin M. Holt.

Patton, Miss Martha married to Mr. Geo. W. Smith.

Patton, Miss Mary married to Mr. Dorsey Atkerson.

Patton, Miss Mary married to Mr. Dorzey Atkinson.

Patton, Miss Mary Ann married to Mr. Orville D. Searcy.

Patton, Miss Nancy married to Walton H. Payne.

Patton, Miss Nancy married to Capt. John M. Ewen.

Patton, Mr. Robert of Florence married at Huntsville to Miss Jane
Brahan daughter of Gen. John Brahan.
National Banner & Nashville Advertiser (Mon., Feb. 6, 1832)

Patton, Mr. Samuel married in Cynthiana, Ky. to Miss Matilda Callis.
National Banner & Nashville Whig (Sat., July 22, 1826)

Patton, Mr. Sebastian married in Maury County to Miss Elizabeth Payton.
National Banner & Nashville Whig (Mon., Oct. 4, 1830)

Patton, Col. Thomas T. of North Carolina married Feb. 1st. at the
Sewanee House in Nashville by the Rev. Dr. Lapsley to Mrs. Caroline
M. Hawkins of Rutherford County.
The Christian Record (Sat., Feb. 5, 1849)

Patton, Mr. William married in Huntsville, Ala. to Miss Mary Ann Miller.
National Banner & Nashville Whig (Wed., Mar. 16, 1831)

Paul, Mr. Samuel W. married in this town on Thursday 15th inst. to
Miss Mary Jane Baird.
National Banner & Nashville Whig (Sat., Jan. 17, 1829)

Paulus, Miss Elizabeth married to Mr. Henry Metz.

Pavatt, Miss Narcissa married to Henry Nixon Esq.

Payer, Miss Mary Ann married to Mr. John Arpo.

Payne, Mr. married in Maury County, Ten. to Miss Margaret Leetch of
Bigbyville.
National Banner & Nashville Whig (Fri., Jan. 9, 1835)

Payne, Mr. Albert G. married on the 13th inst. at the residence of
Mr. James Woods by the Rev. Dr. Edgar to Miss Susan Jane Greene
eldest daughter of Robert Green Esq. all of Nashville.
The Christian Record (Sat., July 15, 1848)

Payne, Miss Ann married in Bedford County to Mr. Benj. Kimbro.

Payne, Mr. A. M. married in Lauderdale County to Miss Henrietta Wilson.
National Banner & Nashville Whig (Sat., Feb. 7, 1829)

Payne, Daniel M. Esq. of Lexington married in Harrison County, Ky. to
Miss Zelinda Ann Smith.
National Banner & Nashville Whig (Sat., Dec. 16, 1826)

Payne, Miss Elizabeth W. married to James F. Hill.

Payne, Mr. G. W. G. of Nashville married at Pittsburgh on the 10th
inst. by the Rev. G. A. Holmes to Miss Mary Ann Nicholson of Pittsburgh.
Nashville Whig (Tues., Oct. 22, 1844)

Payne, Miss Harriett married to G. G. Bole.

Payne, Harriet N. married to Jack J. Stiles.

Payne, Miss Margaret married to Mr. Jefferson Cartwright.

Payne, Miss Margaret married to Mr. Jefferson Cartright.

Payne, Miss Mary Ann married to Mr. Nathaniel Offutt.

Payne, Mrs. Mary Ann married to Mr. William Bosworth.

Payne, Mr. Spencer of Dyer married in Haywood County to Miss Matilda Thweatt.
National Banner & Nashville Whig (Sat., Aug. 11, 1827)

Payne, Mr. Walton H. married in Bedford County to Miss Nancy Patton.
National Banner (Sat., Aug. 29, 1829)

Payton, Miss Elizabeth married to Mr. Sebastian Patton.

Payton, Mr. James H. married to Miss Nancy McFarland.

Payton, Mr. James H. married to Miss Nancy McFarland.

Peach, Mr. Jonathan married in Williamson County, Ten. to Miss Jane Little.
National Banner & Nashville Whig (Fri., Feb. 13, 1835)

Peacock, Miss Polly married to Mr. Joe M'Chord.

Peacock, Mr. Wm. A. married in Bedford County to Miss Sophia Featherton.
Nashville Republican & State Gazette (Wed., Dec. 12, 1832)

Peak, Mrs. E. A. married to Mr. H. Hennenger.

Peake, Miss Sarah married to Mr. Martin Butner.

Peal, Miss Elizabeth married to Mr. Ezekiel McCain.

Pearce, Miss Elvira married to Mr. Wm. Brummitt.

Pearson, Miss Rebecca married to Mr. H. H. Harrison.

Pease, Mr. John B. of Miss. married in Nashville on the 14th Feb. by the Rev. Mr. Davis to Miss Elizabeth Dibrell daughter of Mr. Edwin Dibrell of Nashville.
National Banner & Nashville Whig (Wed., Feb. 15, 1837)

Pease, John B. of Mississippi married on the 14th by the Rev. Dr. Davis to Elizabeth Wason Dibrell daughter of Edward Dibrell Esq. of Nashville.
Nashville Republican (Thurs., Feb. 16, 1837)

Pease, Mr. John B. of Mississippi married on the 14th inst. by the Rev. Doctor Davis to Miss Elizabeth Watson Dibrell daughter of Edwin Dibrell Esq. of Nashville.
The Union (Thurs., Feb. 16, 1837)

Peay, Miss Sarah S. married to Henry T. Payne.

Peay, Mr. Thomas married in Maury County to Miss Jane Stratton.
National Banner & Nashville Whig (Wed., April 27, 1831)

Peak, Miss Eliza S. married to Mr. William B. Cuningham.

Peck, Mr. James L. married in Jessamine County, Ky. to Miss Mary Francis.
National Banner & Nashville Whig (Sat., Nov. 22, 1828)

Peck, Mr. John married in Davidson County to Mrs. Temperance B. Thompson on the 8th inst. by the Rev. A. McDowel.
National Banner & Nashville Advertiser (Fri., May 11, 1832)

Peck, Mr. John married in Davidson County on the 8th inst. by the
Rev. A. McDowel to Mrs. Temperance B. Thompson.
National Banner & Nashville Daily Advertiser (Fri., May 11, 1832)

Peck, Mr. John H. married in Jefferson County to Miss Sarah Goforth.
National Banner & Nashville Whig (Mon., Dec. 27, 1830)

Peck, Miss Maria C. married in Jefferson County to Mr. Henry Holston.

Peebles, Mr. J. B. of Williamson County, Ten. married near Florence,
Ala. to Miss Minerva Scales.
National Banner & Nashville Daily Advertiser (Mon., May 6, 1833)

Peebles, Miss Margaret married to Mr. David Mitchell.

Peebles, Thomas E. married in Williamson County to Miss Emily E.
Williams.
The Western Weekly Review - Franklin, Tenn. (Fri., March 8, 1833)

Peel, Miss Eliza married to Col. James Brickell.

Peel, Miss Emily married to Mr. George Mitchell.

Peeples, Mr. Burrell H. married on Thursday evening the 5th inst. to
Miss Elizabeth Williams daughter of Wm. E. Williams Esq. of Montgomery
County.
The Nashville Whig & Tenn. Advertiser (March 14, 1818)

Peeples, Miss Catherine married on the 25th inst. by the Rev. J. Moore
to Capt. William H. M. Lauglin all of Davidson.
The Nashville Whig & Tenn. Advertiser (Dec., 29, 1817)

Peerman, Miss Jincey married to Mr. William Combs.

Peete, Sam Esq. married in Huntsville, Ala. to Miss Susan Ann Pope.
National Banner & Nashville Daily Advertiser (Mon., Aug. 19,1833)

Pegee, Mr. Oliver married in Madison County to Miss Eliza Alston.
National Banner & Nashville Whig (Sat., Feb. 14, 1829)

Pemberton, Miss Catharine married to Mr. Christopher Hardwick.

Pemberton, Miss Frances married to Dr. R. D. Hubbard.

Pemberton, Mr. John married in Henry County, Tenn. to Miss Susan
Wimberly.
National Banner & Nashville Daily Advertiser (Mon., May 28, 1832)

Pemberton, Mr. John married in Henry County, Tenn. to Miss Susan
Winberly.
National Banner & Nashville Daily Advertiser (Mon., May 28, 1832)

Pence, Mr. Ananias married in Logan County, Ky. to Miss Martha Boyd.
National Banner & Nashville Whig (Mon, Jan. 17, 1831)

Pendleton, Mrs. Elizabeth married to Dr. M. B. Sappington.

Pendleton, Miss Elizabeth married to Dr. Mark B. Sappington.

Pendleton, Mr. Wm. married in Todd County, Ky. to Miss Harriet Frazier.
National Banner & Nashville Whig (Sat., July 14, 1827)

Penis, Miss Cassandra married to Mr. James Garrett.

Penn, Miss Virginia married to Dr. Charles Snow.

Penn, Miss Virginia Ann married to Mr. Edward R. Wallace.

Pennamaker, Miss Margaret married to Mr. John A. Perine.

Pennington, Mr. Graves married to Miss Martha Bondurant.

Pennington, Mr. John married in Davidson County on the 17th inst. to Miss Elizabeth Dotson daughrer of Timothy Dotson.
National Banner & Nashville Whig (Mon., Nov. 21, 1831)

Pennington, Dr. Jordan married at Louisville, Ky. to Miss Elizabeth A. Snethen.
National Banner & Nashville Advertiser (Mon., Jan. 30, 1832)

Pennington, Mr. Samuel married at Louisville, Ky. to Miss Mary Ann Devier.
National Banner & Nashville Daily Advertiser (Tues., July 10, 1832)

Penny, Mr. James married at Lexington, Ky. to Miss Jane W. Megowan daughter of Mr. David Megowan.
National Banner & Nashville Whig (Wed., April 27, 1831)

Pennybaker, Mr. Frederick B. married at Louisville, Ky. to Miss Margaret Ann Cooper.
National Banner & Nashville Daily Advertiser (Wed., Aug. 15, 1832)

Penrice, Mr. John editor of the Louisiana Advertiser married at New Orleans to Miss Louisa B. Moore.
National Banner (Sat., Dec. 19, 1829)

Pentecost, Miss Martha married to Mr. Wilson Dunn.

Penticost, Miss Sarah J. married to Mr. David A. Cole.

Pepin, Miss Narcissa married to Capt. William S. Wilson.

Pepper, Mr. Elkanah married in Bracken County, Ky. to Miss Lucinda King.
National Banner (March 24, 1826)

Pepper, Gen. W. W. of Springfield married at Gallatin on the 23rd inst. by the Rev. Benjamin Rawls to Miss Mary F. Solomon daughter of William Solomon Esq.
The Politician & Weekly Nashville Whig (Wed., Sept. 1st. 1847)

Percefull, Miss Amanda Malvina married to Mr. David Z. Sedan.

Percy, Charles B. Esq. of Huntsville, Ala. married in Nashville by the Rev. J. T. Edgar D. D. to Miss Henrietta Nichol the youngest daughter of Josiah Nichol.
Nashville Whig (Fri., June 5, 1840)

Percy, Dr. John Walker married by the Rev. Dr. Edgar on the 18th inst. Tuesday at the residence of John P. Erwin Esq. to Miss Fanny E. Williams daughter of the Hon. Thomas L. Williams.
Nashville Whig (Thurs., June 20, 1844)

Perine, Mr. John A. married in Louisville, Ky. to Miss Margaret N. Pennamaker.
National Banner & Nashville Daily Advertiser (Sat., Oct. 13, 1832)

Perkins, Mr. in Logan County, Ky. married to Miss Fanny Gauter.
National Banner & Nashville Whig (Fri., Feb. 11, 1831)

Perkins, Mrs. Ann married to Mr. Hezekiah Clark.

Perkins, Miss Bertheenia H. married to Thomas Hardeman Esq.

Perkins, Miss Clarissa married to Mr. Absalom Fauleover.

Perkins, Mr. Constantine B. in Maury County married to Miss Nancy R. Chears on the 28 ult. by the Rev. Robert Hardin.
National Banner & Nashville Whig (Fri., Nov. 4, 1831)

Perkins, Mrs. Eliza married to B. W. Williams Esq.

Perkins, Mrs. Eliza married to Mr. Robert Hill.

Perkins, Miss Eliza married to Mr. James F. May.

Perkins, Miss Eliza married to B. W. Williams.

Perkins, Miss Eliza M. married to Mr. Thomas H. Perkins, jun.

Perkins, Miss Elizabeth married to Mr. Robert Paris.

Perkins, Col. Jacob in Madison County, Tenn. married to Miss Mary C. Anderson.
National Banner & Nashville Whig (Wed., Oct. 19, 1831)

Perkins, Mr. James married in Logan County, Ky. to Miss Fanny Gautier.
National Banner & Nashville Whig (Fri., Feb. 11, 1831)

Perkins, Dr. James M. of Williamson County married to Miss Susannah E. Currey in Davidson County on Thursday evening June 21st by Rev. Wm. Hume.
National Banner & Nashville Advertiser (Fri., June 22, 1832)

Perkins, Dr. James M. of Williamson County married in Davidson County on Thursday 21st June by the Rev. Mr. Hume to Miss Susannah E. Curry.
National Banner & Nashville Daily Advertiser (Fri., June 22, 1832)

Perkins, Dr. Jas. Madison of William County married near Nashville to Miss Susanna E. Curry of Davidson
The Western Weekly Review - Franklin, Tenn. (Fri., June 29, 1832)

Perkins, Capt. John of Rutherford married in Wilson County to Miss Ruanna Terrill.
National Banner & Nashville Whig (Sat., March 10, 1827)

Perkins, John P. Esq. married in Haywood County to Miss Eliza H. Leigh.
National Banner (Sat., April 11, 1829)

Perkins, Mr. John S. married in Louisville, Ky. to Miss Louisa LaGrasse.
National Banner & Nashville Whig (Mon., Nov. 21, 1831)

Perkins, Mr. Joseph K. married in Butler County, Ky. to Miss Rebecca Talbot.
National Banner & Nashville Whig (Wed., May 25, 1831)

Perkins, Mr. Joseph W. married on the 18th Oct. by the Rev. Mr. Lapsley to Miss Mary R. Talbot all of Nashville.
National Banner & Nashville Whig (Mon., Oct. 19, 1835)

Perkins, Mr. Joseph W. of Nashville married to Miss Mary R. Talbot on the 18th Oct.
Nashville Republican (Tues., Oct. 20, 1835)

Perkins, Miss Lucy Ann married to Mr. Charles Lawton.

Perkins, Miss Margaret married to Mr. Robert Bradley, Jr.

Perkins, Miss Martha married to Mr. John M. Hewett Esq.

Perkins, Miss Mary A. married to Mr. John S. Claybrooks.

Perkins, Miss Mary Ann married to Mr. William Frazier.

Perkins, Mr. Nicholas of Mississippi married to Miss Polly Perkins
of Williamson County on Thursday last.
Impartial Review and Cumberland Repository - published at Nashville.
(Feb. 4, 1808)

Perkins, Mr. Nichols P. of Franklin married on Wednesday evening last
to Miss Harriet Craddock of this town.
The Nashville Whig (April 2, 1817)

Perkins, Mrs. P. of Memphis married to Dr. Dudley Dunn.

Perkins, Pawhattan Esq. married in Franklin at the residence of Capt.
B. Reece on the 12th by Rev. Dr. Edgar to Miss Catharine P. D.
Degraffenreid daughter of the late Metcolfe Degraffenreid Esq. of
Williamson County.
Nashville Whig (Sat., Jan. 15, 1842)

Perkins, Mr. Peter married on Wednesday evening last by the Rev. Mr.
Blackburn to Miss Sarah P. Camp all of Franklin.
Nashville Whig (Oct. 11, 1824)

Perkins, Miss Polly married to Mr. Nicholas Perkins.

Perkins, Miss Retta married to Mr. William Watkins.

Perkins, Samuel Esq. of Williamson County married in this county on
24th inst. to Miss Nancy Richardson.
National Banner & Nashville Whig (Sat., June 2, 1827)

Perkins, Mr. Samuel S. married in Logan County, Ky. to Miss Mary
Johnson.
National Banner & Nashville Daily Advertiser (Fri., March 9, 1832)

Perkins, Miss Sarah M. married in Williamson Co. to Dr. Charles Snaw.

Perkins, Miss Sophia married to Mr. Lawrence S. Mason.

Perkins, Mr. Thos. F. in Williamson County married to Leah A. Cannon.
National Banner & Nashville Advertiser (Wed., May 16, 1832)

Perkins, Thomas F. married in Williamson County to Miss Leah A. Cannon.
The Western Weekly Review - Franklin, Tenn. (Fri., May 11, 1832)

Perkins, Mr. Thomas H. married in Williamson County to Miss Louisa
Frast.
National Banner & Nashville Daily Advertiser (Mon., Sept. 9, 1833)

Perkins, Mr. Thomas H. in Williamson County married to Miss Louisa
Frost.
Nasvhille Republican & State Gazette (Tues., Sept. 10, 1833)

Perkins, M. Thomas H. married in Franklin on the 12th inst. to Miss
Polly Hardeman daughter of Nicholas Hardeman, Esq.
The Nash. Whig & Tenn. Advertiser (March 28, 1818)

Perkins, Mr. Thomas H. jun. in Williamson County married to Miss
Eliza M. Perkins.
National Banner & Nashville Whig (Mon., Jan. 17, 1831)

Perkins, Mr. William in Maury County married to Miss Susan D. Wilson.
National Banner & Nashville Whig (Mon., Sept. 26, 1831)

Perkins, Mr. William O. married on Wednesday last to Miss Mary
McLemore both of Williamson County.
The Western Weekly Review - Franklin, Tenn. (Fri., Nov. 4, 1831)

Perkins, Mr. William O. in Williamson County married to Miss Mary
M'Lemore.
National Banner & Nashville Whig (Mon., Nov. 7, 1831)

Perkins, Wright married in Williamson County to Mary Brown.
National Banner & Nashville Whig (Wed., Sept. 24, 1834)

Perkinson, Miss Mary married to Mr. John Stanley

Pernell, Miss Erepine H. married to Mr. John K. Yerger.

Perrell, Mr. S. married near Readyville, Rutherford County, Ten. to
Miss Mary Barkley daughter of Capt. Henry Barkley.
National Banner & Nashville Daily Advertiser (Sat., Sept. 6, 1834)

Perrin, Mr. Vaden married in Jefferson County to Miss Sarah Churchman.
National Banner & Nashville Whig (Sat., Feb. 24, 1827)

Perrine, Miss Elizabeth married to Mr. Thomas H. Armstrong.

Perry, Mr. Benjamin W. married in Gibson County to Miss Sarah Moss.
National Banner & Nashville Whig (Sat., July 28, 1827)

Perry, Miss Caroline L. married to Mr. Turner F. Jack.

Perry, Mr. George S. married at Tuscaloosa, Ala. to Miss Trilla
Norsworthy.
National Banner & Nashville Whig (Sat., July 22, 1826)

Perry, Mr. Isaac married in Smuner County on the 9th ult. to Miss
Elizabeth Franklin.
National Banner & Nashville Whig(Mon., Oct. 4, 1830)

Perry, Miss Lemantine married to Mr. James A. Shell.

Perry, Miss Louise married to Mr. Thomas L. Wiley.

Perry, Miss Louisa K. married to Mr. James B. Mebane.

Perry, Miss Malinda married to Hillard Davis.

Perry, Miss Mary Jane married to Mr. Charles S. Avery.

Perry, Mr. Mills of Kentucky married at Danville, Warren County to Miss
Frances Ann Tandy.
National Banner & Nashville Whig (Sat., Dec. 27, 1828)

Perry, Mr. Orion S. married in Franklin to Miss Nancy Edney.
National Banner & Nashville Whig (Sat., May 17, 1828)

Perry, Miss Polly married to Mr. Henry Lewis Fernival.

Perry, Royal C. D.D. Greenfield, Ohio married at Bloomingdale on the
25th by the Rev. Mr. Van Aiken to Mary Cargill of Nashville.
Daily Republican Banner (Tues., Jan. 9, 1838)

Person, Mr. Richard married in Madison County, Ala. to Miss Obedience
A. Trotman.
National Banner & Nashville Daily Advertiser (Mon., Feb. 25, 1833)

Pert, Miss Mary Ann married to Mr. Jones Campbell.

Peters, Miss Susan married to Mr. William Arthur.

Pettus, Miss Martha Ann married to Mr. Albert Newell.

Petty, Mr. Abner G. married in Madison County, Ala. to Miss Malvina
M. Long.
National Banner (Sat., April 25, 1829)

Petty, Mr. Francis G. married in Madison Co., Ala. to Miss Caroline
Waddell.
National Banner & Nashville Whig (Mon., May 23, 1831)

Petty, Mr. Hardy married in Maury County to Miss Susan Wrenn.
Nashville Republican (Thurs., March 5, 1835)

Petway, Mr. George W. married on Thursday the 10th inst. by the Rev.
John B. McFerrin to Miss Martha Susan Gaines daughter of Thomas L.
Gaines Esq. all of Nashville.
Nashville Whig (Thurs., Aug. 15, 1843)

Petway, Mr. John H. married in Davidson County on Wednesday July 3d.
by Rev. Mr. Smith to Miss Caledonia Gordon.
National Banner & Nashville Daily Advertiser (Sat., July 6, 1833)

Petway, Thos. H. married in Williamson County to Susan D. Smith.
The Western Weekly Review - Franklin, Tenn. (Fri., Feb. 10, 1832)

Petway, Mr. Thomas M. married on Thursday 2d inst. by the Rev. Mr.
Hume to Miss Susan D. Smith daughter of Mr. Alexander Smith of
Williamson County.
National Banner & Nashville Daily Advertiser (Fri., Feb. 3, 1832)

Petway, Mr. William of Davidson County married to Miss Martha Hobson
on last evening.
Nashville Republican (Sat., Feb. 28, 1835)

Petway, Mr. William married last evening 26th by the Rev. F. E. Pitts
to Miss Martha Hobson daughter of John Hobson Esq. all of Davidson
County.
National Banner & Nashville Whig (Fri., Feb. 27, 1835)

Pewit, Martha married to H. C. Duke.

Peyton, Mrs. Ann married to Hon. Hugh L. White.

Peyton, Balie Esq. married in Smith County to Miss Ann C. Smith.
National Banner & Nashville Whig (Mon., May 31, 1830)

Peyton, Ephriam G. Esq. of Gallitan married to Miss Artemisia G.
Patton near Port Gibson, Miss.
Nashville Republican & State Gazette (Thurs., April 14, 1831)

Peyton, Ephriam G. Esq. married near Post Gibson, Mi. to Miss
Artemisea G. Patton.
National Banner & Nashville Whig (Wed., April 27, 1831)

Peyton, Miss Evelina A. B. married to Dr. Edmund Anderson.

Peyton, Mr. James H. in Wilson County married to Miss Nancy M'Farland.
Nashville Republican & State Gazette (Dec. 17, 1832)

Peyton, Joseph H. Esq. married near Gallatin on Tuesday the 6th inst.
to Miss Mary Hatton daughter of the Rev. Robert Hatton.
Nashville Whig (Wed., April 14, 1841)

Peyton, Miss Sarah married to Thomas Barry, Esq.

Phagan, Miss Catharine K. married to Mr. Eli Odam.

Phatridge, Mr. C. A. married in Knox County, Ten. to Miss Eliza Seay.
National Banner & Nashville Whig (Mon., April 13, 1835)

Phelps, Mr. Burgess married in Robertson County to Miss Ellen Hensley
daughter of Mr. John Hensley.
National Banner & Nashville Advertiser (Tues., Feb. 14, 1832)

Phelps, Mr. John married in Williamson County to Miss Caroline Lea.
The Western Weekly Review - Franklin, Tenn. (Fri., Dec. 23, 1831)

Phelps, John H. Esq. married in Bowling Green, Ky. to Miss Betsy Morehead.
National Banner & Nashville Whig (Mon., Nov. 1, 1830)

Phelps, Mr. John H. married at Hopkinsville, Ky. to Miss Caroline Shipp.
National Banner & Nashville Whig (Sat., Dec. 16, 1826)

Phelps, Miss Julia Elizabeth married to His Excellency Steven Mason.

Phelps, Miss Sally married to Mr. James Walker.

Phelps, Miss Sally married to Mr. James Walker.

Phifer, Mr. Charles married in Giles County to Miss Rhoda Glover.
National Banner & Nashville Daily Advertiser (Mon., March 25, 1833)

Phifer, Miss Nancy married to Mr. William Glover.

Philips, Miss Elizabeth married to Capt. Robert Prudy.

Philips, Mr. Isaac M. married in Williamson County to Miss Emily R. Nunn daughter of Wm. R. Nunn Esq.
National Banner & Nashville Daily Advertiser (Fri., Nov. 29, 1833)

Philips, Mr. Thomas married at St. Louis to Miss Margaret Grierson.
National Banner & Nashville Advertiser (Sat., July 7, 1832)

Philips, Mr. William H. married in Franklin County, Ten. on the 13th inst. by John Thomas Slotter Esq. to Miss Elizabeth Saxton.
Nashville Whig (Tues., Jan. 27, 1846)

Philips, Maj. William J. married in Rutherford County to Miss Mary Ross.
Nashville Republican & State Gazette (Tues., Sept. 20, ___)

Phillip, Maj. A. of the U. S. Army married at Louisville, Ky. to Miss Sarah M. Ornsby.
National Banner & Nashville Whig (Sat., April 7, 1827)

Phillip, Miss Rebecca married to Patrick Henry Overton, Esq.

Phillips, Mr. Allen married in Bedford County, Ten. to Miss Francis Davis.
National Banner & Nashville Whig (Fri., March 6, 1835)

Phillips, Miss Charlotte married to Dr. Wilford D. Turner.

Phillips, Mr. David B. married at Louisville, Ky. to Miss Ann Hardin.
National Banner (Sat., Aug. 22, 1829)

Phillips, Miss Eliza married to Dr. Thomas Wells.

Phillips, Mr. Iredal married in Henry County, Ten. since the first of Jan. to Miss Vienna Wofford.
National Banner & Nashville Whig (Fri., Feb. 13, 1835)

Phillips, Capt. James married in Bedford County, Ten. to Miss Sarah Boman.
National Banner & Nashville Whig (Mon., Jan. 5, 1835)

Phillips, Miss Jane married to Mr. Grace Steward.

Phillips, Mr. Jesse married in Bedford County, Tenn. to Miss Nancy Scott.
National Banner & Nashville Daily Advertiser (Mon., July 21, 1834)

Phillips, Mr. John G. married in Louisville to Miss Elizabeth Linch.
National Banner (Sat., Aug. 1, 1829)

Phillips, Miss Lucy married to Mr. John H. Bonner.

Phillips, Captain Miles married in Bedford County to Miss Mary Harper.
National Banner & Nashville Daily Advertiser (Fri., Sept. 6, 1833)

Phillips, Miss Nancy married to Mr. John S. Williams.

Phillips, Miss Pheby married to Mr. Miller Carter.

Phillips, Capt. Richard B., Editor of the Clarksville Public Advertiser
married on Tuesday evening the 26th inst. to Miss Louisa Ann Walthall
of Christian County, Ky.
Nashville Whig (Nov. 1, 1824)

Phillips, Mr. Thomas C. married at St. Louis to Miss Margaret Grierson.
National Banner & Nashville Daily Advertiser (Sat., July 7, 1832)

Phillips, Col. Wm. married in Franklin on the 3rd inst. to Miss Elizabeth
Dwyer.
National Banner & Nashville Whig (Sat., June 14, 1828)

Phillips, Capt. William of Steamer, Daniel Webster married on Thursday
last at Stockdale, by the Rev. A. L. P. Green to Miss Caledonia Lucas.
Daily Republican Banner (Mon., Sept. 3, 1838)

Phillips, Maj. William J. married in Rutherford County to Miss Mary
Ross.
National Banner & Nashville Whig (Fri., Sept. 16, 1831)

Phillips, Mr. Zacheus B. married in Dyer County to Miss Lucinda L.
Mitchell daughter of the late Thomas Mitchell of Rutherford County.
National Banner & Nashville Whig (Mon., Aug. 30, 1830)

Philpot, MIss Emily married to Col. James A. Henslett.

Philpot, Miss Mary married to Col. John Bakewell.

Philpott, Mr. Charles T. married in Bedford County, Ten. to Miss
Rebecca Hix.
National Banner & Nashville Whig (Wed., Dec. 17, 1834)

Phipps, Miss Phebe married to Mr. Samuel Sweaney.
National Banner & Nashville Whig (Sat., Feb. 11, 18__)

Pickard, Geo. M. married in Williamson County, Ten. to Nancy M. Orton.
National Banner & Nashville Daily Advertiser (Mon., Aug. 26, 1833)

Pickering, Miss Lucia married to Mr. Charles Carman.

Pickering, William married in Williamson County to Miss Martha Whitby.
The Western Weekly Review - Franklin, Tenn. (Fri., Dec. 14, 1832)

Pickett, Mr. William married at Louisville, Ky. to Mrs. Nancy Buckner.
National Banner & Nashville Daily Advertiser (Sat., July 14, 1832)

Pickett, William S. Esq. Assistant Cashier of the Union Bank, at
Columbia, married in St. Peters Church, Columbia on 12th inst. by the
Rev. F. G. Smith to Mary Eliza Walker second daughter of James Walker
Esq. of Columbia.
Nashville Whig (Thurs., July 14, 1842)

Pickle, Mrs. Susan married to Mr. John McLean.

Pidgeon, Mr. John R. married in Hopkinsville, Ky. to Miss Sidney
Lawrison.
National Banner (May 27, 1826)

Pienovi, Mrs. Eleonore married to Mr. Francis Fernandez.

Pierce, Dr. married in Rutherford County to Miss Elizabeth Abbott daughter of David Abbott, Esq.
National Banner & Nashville Whig (Mon., Oct. 25, 1830)

Pierce, Mr. Isaac of Sumner County, Ten. married in Logan County to Miss Mary Lyle daughter of Mr. Thomas Lyle.
National Banner & Nashville Whig (Mon., May 2, 1831)

Pierce, Mr. Jacob A. married in Madison County, Ala. to Miss Charlotte Simmons.
National Banner & Nashville Whig (Sat., Aug. 30, 1828)

Pierce, Miss Mary married to Mr. Richard Vinson.

Piercy, Mr. Bryant married in Madison County, Ten. to Miss Fanny Byrn.
National Banner & Nashville Whig (Mon., Jan. 5, 1835)

Pigg, Mr. Claiborn married in Maury County to Miss Ann Holder.
National Banner & Nashville Whig (Mon., July 12, 1830)

Pigg, Mr. Joseph married in Maury County to Miss Mary Wormack.
National Banner & Nashville Whig (Mon., Aug. 8, 1831)

Piggott, Mrs. Mary A. married to James Gilliam.

Pike, Miss Emma C. married to Mr. William Crutcher.

Pike, Miss Julia Ann married to Mr. Barbee.

Pilant, Miss Francis S. married to Mr. Charles Cotton.

Pilcher, Mr. Benjamine married in Fayett County, Ky. to Miss Mary Plunket.
National Banner (April 21, 1826)

Pilcher, Miss Lucinda married to Mr. James H. Turner.

Pilcher, Mr. Mason of the House of Pilcher & Rayburn in New Orleans married on the 21st inst. by Philip Guier, Esq. to Mrs. Anna M. Bower.
Nashville Whig (Tues., Feb. 7, 1843)

Pilcher, Mr. Mason married in this town on Thursday the 26th inst. to Miss Lucretia Hubble.
National Banner (Sat., Nov. 28, 1829)

Pilcher, Mr. Merritt S. married in Nashville on Monday evening 26th Dec. to Miss Nancy Barrow by the Rev. Mr. Hume.
National Banner & Nashville Whig (Wed., Dec. 28, 1831)

Pilkinton, Mr. John M. married in Maury County, Ten. to Miss Mary A. Campbell.
National Banner & Nashville Whig (Mon., Jan. 26, 1835)

Pillow, Miss Amanda married to West H. Humphreys, Esq.

Pillow, Miss Cynthia married to Mr. John W. Saunders.

Pillow, Major Granville A. of Maury County married in Springfield on the 10th inst. to Miss Olivia D. Cheatham daughter of the late Col. Archer Cheatham.
National Banner & Nashville Daily Advertiser (Thurs., Nov. 14, 1833)

Pillow, Mr. Jerome B. married in Giles County to Miss Martha W. Harris.
Nashville Republican & State Gazette (Sat., Sept. 21, 1833)

Pillow, Miss Mary E. A. married to Mr. Nathaniel F. Smith.

Pinckard, Mr. Marshall P. of Williamsport Maury Co. married in
Williamson County on the 7th inst. by Rev. Mr. Holland to Miss Eliza
Johnson daughter of Mr. Mathews Johnson.
National Banner & Nashville Whig (Mon., July 11, 1831)

Pickney, Miss Emily married to Lieut. Richard A. Jones.

Pindell, Richard H., Esq. on 31st Dec. married Miss Anna Monroe at
Frankfort.
Nashville Republican (Tues., Jan. 13, 1835)

Pinhead, Mr. Augustine W. married in Lexington, Ky. to Miss Margaret
Yeiser.
National Banner (Sat., Nov. 28, 1829)

Pinkard, Mr. Marshall P. married in Williamson County to Miss Eliza
Johnson.
Nashville Republican & State Gazette (Tues., July 12, 1831)

Pinkard, Dr. Thomas H. married at Lawrenceburgh, Ind. to Miss Catharine
Vance.
National Banner & Nashville Whig (Sat., Dec. 23, 1826)

Pinkston, Miss Rebecca married to W. P. Lester.

Piper, Mrs. married to Dr. Combs.

Piper, Mr. Henry married in Smith County to Miss Polly Matthews.
National Banner & Nashville Whig (Fri., Nov. 18, 1831)

Pipes, Mrs. Charlotte married to Astynax E. Mills Esq.

Pipkins, Mr. Steward married on the 8th of Jan. to Miss Harrett S.
Caldwell a Daughter of Joseph Caldwell Esq. all of this County.
Nashville Whig (Jan. 15, 1823)

Pirtle, Hon. Henry married in Louisville, Ky. to Miss Jane Ann Rogers.
National Banner (Sat., June 6, 1829)

Pistol, Miss Emily Maria married to Mr. William G. Gun.

Pitchett, Miss Sarah married to Mr. James Batey.

Pitman, Mr. William married in Louisville, Ky. to Miss Nancy Cooms.
National Banner & Nashville Advertiser (Tues., June 26, 1832)

Pittman, Mr. Bartholomew B. married on the 9th inst. by W. D. F. Lowrie
to Miss Mary E. Parrish daughter of James Parrish Esq. all of Nashville.
Nashville Whig (Fri., May 10, 1839)

Pittman, Mr. William married in Louisville, Ky. to Miss Nancy Cooms.
National Banner & Nashville Daily Advertiser (Tues., June 26, 1832)

Pitts, Miss Dimeretta married to Mr. Henry Rochester.

Pitts, Rev. F. E. married in Sumner County to Miss Martha Britt.
National Banner & Nashville Whig (Sat., Aug. 25, 1827)

Platt, Miss Eulalia married to Mr. Joses Stout.

Player, Col. Thompson T. of South Carolina married in Nashville at
the residence of Col. Bell on the 6th inst. by the Rev. Dr. Edgar to
Miss Emma Yeatman daughter of the late Thomas Yeatman Esq.
Nashville Whig (Sat., Jan. 8, 1842)

Pleasanton, Miss Matilda married to Hon. John G. Watmough.

Plew, Miss Eliza married to Mr. Stephen W. Dye.

Philips, Mr. Lemuel married in Columbia to Miss Rebecca O. Cross.

Pluis, Mr. Casper H. W. married in Logan County, Ky. to Miss Rebecca M'Daniel.
National Banner & Nashville Daily Advertiser (Mon., Nov. 12, 1832)

Plumlee, Mr. S. married in Knox County to Miss Caroline E. Nance.
National Banner (April 14, 1826)

Plumly, Miss Cynthia married to Mr. William Mason.

Plummer, Miss Caroline married to Mr. William Atwood.

Plummer, Miss Drucella married to Mr. Patterson.

Plummer, Mr. Seymour merchant of Carrollsville, Tenn. married in Florence, Ala. to Miss Julia A. Boggs.
National Banner & Nashville Daily Advertiser (Mon., April 2, 1832)

Plunket, Miss Mary married to Mr. Benjamin Pilcher.

Poindexter, Hon. George U. S. Senator from Mississippi married in this town on 15th May by Rev. Dr. Hawley to Miss Ann Hewes daughter of Samuel Hewes, Esq. of Boston.
National Banner & Nashville Daily Advertiser (Fri., June 1, 1832)

Poindexter, Mr. J. of Rutherford married in Bedford County, Ten. to Miss Jane Blair.
National Banner & Nashville Daily Advertiser (Wed., July 9, 1834)

Poinsett, Hon. Joel R. of Charleston, S. C. married Mrs. Mary Pringle of Charleston, S. C.
Nashville Republican & State Gazette (Thurs., Nov. 14, 1833)

Poindexter, Major John married in Russellville, Ky. to Miss Susan Blakey.
National Banner (March 24, 1826)

Poindexter, Col. John married in Todd County, Ky. to Miss Elizabeth Murphy daughter of Jenkins Murphy.
National Banner & Nashville Advertiser (Tues., Nov. 27, 1832)

Poindexter, Mr. Lewis T. married in Montgomery County to Mrs. Matthews.
National Banner & Nashville Whig (Sat., Feb. 7, 1829)

Pointer, Miss Mary E. married to John C. Brown, Esq.

Pointer, Miss Mary W. married to Mr. St. Clair Caldwell.

Pointer, Miss Susan married to Mr. J. W. Cheairs.

Poland, Mr. John of Alabama married in Bardstown, Ky. to Miss Eliza Hayden.
National Banner & Nashville Whig (Sat., Oct. 7, 1826)

Polk, Andrew J. of Maury County married on the 14th by the Rt. Rev. James H. Otey, D.D. to Miss Rebecca Vanleer daughter of A. W. Vanleer Esq. of Nashville.
Nashville Whig (Sat., Jan. 17, 1846)

Polk, Miss Benigna married to Mr. William H. Wood.

Polk, Miss Carolina married to Mr. John Wort.

Polk, Miss Eugenia married to Mr. Alexander G. Neilson.

Polk, George W. of N. Carolina married in Williamson County by the Rt. Rev. Leonidas Polk to Miss Sally Hilliard of Williamson County.
Nashville Whig (Mon., Nov. 30, 1840)

Polk, Colonel James K. of Columbia married to Miss Sarah Childress daughter of the late Capt. Joel Childress of Murfreesboro.
Nashville Whig (Jan. 12, 1824)

Polk, Mr. John married in Davidson County to Miss Rebecca Briggs.
Nashville Republican (Tues., Jan. 27, 1835)

Polk, Lucius J. Esq. of Tennessee married in Washington City at the Mansion of the President on the 10th inst. by the Rev. Mr. Hawley to Miss Mary A. Eastin a member of the President's family.
National Banner & Nashville Daily Advertiser (Wed., April 25, 1832)

Polk, Miss Lucy N. married to Mr. William W. Leonard.

Polk, Miss Mary married to Mr. Francis L. Hodge.

Polk, Miss Mary married to Mr. Wardlow Howard.

Polk, Miss Mary married to Mr. Douglass R. Hunt.

Polk, Miss Olivia married to Mr. Daniel D. Berry.

Polk, Miss Ophelia married to Dr. John B. Hays.

Polk, Miss Polly married to Mr. M. Lovell.

Polk, Mr. William H. married in Maury County to Miss Belinda Dickinson.
Nashville Republican (Sat., April 29, 1837)

Polland, Mr. J. H. married in Maury County to Mary A. Richards.
National Banner & Nashville Advertiser (Thurs., April 5, 1832)

Pollard, Mr. Thomas married in Logan County, Ky. to Miss Mary Arnold.
National Banner & Nashville Whig (Wed., Dec. 7, 1831)

Pollard, Mr. Thomas married near Bowling Green, Ky. to Miss Emily Courts.
National Banner & Nashville Daily Advertiser (Wed., March 26, 1834)

Pollock, Miss Henrietta married to Mr. Jacob Williams.

Pollock, Mr. John of Florence married to Miss Emmeline Watson at Huntsville.
National Banner & Nashville Advertiser (Mon., Nov. 12, 1832)

Pond, Ebenezer, Esq. married in Montgomery, Ala. to Miss Carline Cleveland.
National Banner (June 3, 1826)

Pong, Mr. Robert M. married in Wayne County to Miss Esther Burgess.
National Banner & Nashville Daily Advertiser (Fri., Sept. 20, 1833)

Poor, Mr. George James married in Logan County, Ky. to Miss Berrilla Howard.
National Banner & Nashville Daily Advertiser (Mon., May 13, 1833)

Poor, Miss Henrietta E. F. married to Mr. James Morehead.

Pope, Miss Cynthia married to Newton C. Creek.

Pope, Rev. Fielding married at Athens, Tenn. to Miss Theresa Meigs.
National Banner (Sat., April 18, 1829)

Pope, Mr. Henry J. married in Tipton County on the 16th May by the Rev. Mr. Sullivan to Miss Lucinda C. Maynard daughter of Maj. F. Maynard.
National Banner & Nashville Daily Advertiser (Wed., June 12, 1833)

Pope, LeRoy Jr., Esq. of Memphis, Ten. married in Huntsville, Ala. by
the Rev. Mr. Allen to Miss Mary E. Foote daughter of P. A. Foote,
deceased.
Daily Republican Banner (Thurs., April 16, 1839)

Pope, Miss Martha married to Mr. James Howell

Pope, Miss Martha married to Mr. Alfred L. Little.

Pope, Miss Susan Ann married to Sam Peete, Esq.

Pope, Mr. William married in Rutherford County to Miss Peachy Therman.
National Banner & Nashville Daily Advertiser (Fri., March 29, 1833)

Pope, Mr. William H. married at Louisville, Ky. to Miss Mary E. Wilson.
National Banner (April 21, 1826)

Pope, Mr. William H. married in Huntsville, Ala. to Miss Jane R.
Patton daughter of Mr. William Patton.
National Banner & Nashville Whig (Thurs., Oct. 14, 1830)

Pope, Mr. William R. married in Maury County to Miss Lucy J. Grant.
National Banner & Nashville Whig (Mon., July 12, 1830)

Popin, Mr. Pierre D. married in St. Louis to Miss Catharine Cerre.
National Banner & Nashville Whig (Sat., Sept. 2, 1826)

Porter, Abner D. married in Williamson County to Miss Phoebe E.
Jordan.
The Western Weekly Review - Franklin, Tenn. (Fri., March 8, 1833)

Porter, Miss Angelina F. married to Lieut. Spencer C. Gist.

Porter, Mr. Charles B. married on the 6th inst. to Miss Martha A. M.
Old.
National Banner & Nashville Whig (Sat., Jan. 24, 1829)

Porter, Mr. David of Robinson County, Tenn. married in Logan County,
Ky. to Miss Emeline McIntosh.
National Banner & Nashville Daily Advertiser (Sat., June 1, 1833)

Porter, David M., M.D. married in Sumner County by the Rev. Mr. Saunders
to Miss Eliza A. C. Buckner.
National Banner & Nashville Whig (Sat., May 2, 1827)

Porter, Mrs. Elizabeth married in Clarksville, Tenn. to Mr. Richard
Haden.
National Banner & Nashville Daily Advertiser (Sat., June 2, 1832)

Porter, Miss Ellen married to Young J. Porter.

Porter, Mr. George E. late of Nashville married at Utica, N. Y. on
the 31st August to Miss Eleanor Morris of Utica, N. Y.
Nashville Whig (Wed., Sept. 16, 1840)

Porter, George M. married in Paris, Tenn. to Miss Elizabeth A. Crawford
both of Henry County.
Nashville Whig (Fri., Jan. 18, 1839)

Porter, Mr. James of Louisiana married Tuesdy 30th ult. at Mr. James
Moores Maury County, Tenn. by the Rev. Bishop Otey to Miss Mary T.
Walton.
Nashville Whig (Sat., June 3, 1843)

Porter, Mr. James W. married in this town last evening to Miss Amanda
M'Nairy.
National Banner & Nashville Whig (Sat., Nov. 3, 1827)

Porter, Miss Jane married to Mr. John W. Campbell, Esq.

Porter, Rev. John married on the 20th inst. to Mrs. Sumner relict of
Thomas E. Sumner Esq. formerly of Williamson County.
The Clarion & Tennessee Gazette (July 25, 1820)

Porter, Col. John, aged 76, married in Warren County, Ky. to Mrs.
Rosanna Brady aged 70.
National Banner & Nashville Daily Advertiser (Tues., Nov. 27, 1832)

Porter, Major John C. married at Sandy Hill, Ten. on the 15th of
April by Rev. J. Browning to Miss Sarah Ann Balnton of Frankfort, Ky.
National Banner & Nashville Daily Advertiser (Thurs., April 24, 1834)

Porter, Mr. John H. married in Louisville, Ky. to Miss Elizabeth White.
National Banner & Nashville Whig (Sat., March 7, 1829)

Porter, Mr. John J. of Cincinnati married at Newport, Ky. to Miss
Missouri M. Lockwood.
National Banner (Jan. 27, 1826)

Porter, Miss Louisa J. married to Mr. John F. Morgan.

Porter, Miss Lydia married to Mr. James McElewain.

Porter, Miss Mary married to Mr. George Cook.

Porter, Miss Mary A. married to Mr. Milton G. Mayfield.

Porter, Miss Penelope married to Mr. James Woods, Esq.

Porter, Col. P. W. married in Maury County on Thursday evening the
9th inst. to Miss Jane Loney daughter of A. Loney by the Rev. H. H.
Brown.
National Banner & Nashville Advertiser (Thurs., Feb. 23, 1832)

Porter, Miss Rebecca married to Memucan H. Howard, Esq.

Porter, Dr. Sam S. of S. Car. married in Fayette County, Ky. to Miss
Jane W. Moore.
National Banner (March 17, 1826)

Porter, Miss Sebina married to Mr. Alfred Holcomb.

Porter, Mr. Thomas of Logan County married in Logan County, Ky. to
Miss Jane H. Lawrence of Butler County, Ky.
National Banner & Nashville Daily Advertiser (Sat., Feb. 9, 1833)

Porter, Gen. Thomas J. of Columbia, Tenn. married at Sugar Grove
near Chilicothe, Ohio on the 22nd inst. to Miss Mary Ann Crouse
daughter of the late Col. Crouse.
Nashville Republican (Sat., July 1, 1837)

Porter, Mr. Thomas R. married in Maury County to Miss Jane Lockridge.
National Banner & Nashville Whig (Fri., March 26, 1830)

Porter, William N. Esq. married in Paris, Ten. to Miss Mary Ann
Haskell daughter of the Hon. Joshua Haskell.
National Banner & Nashville Whig (Mon., April 13, 1835)

Porter, Young J. attorney at law of Columbia married in Nashville on
27th by the Rev. Mr. Lapsley to Miss Ellen Porter of Nashville.
National Banner & Nashville Whig (Fri., Aug. 28, 1835)

Porter, Young J. Esq. of Columbia married Miss Ellen Porter of
Nashville.
Nashville Republican (Sat., Aug. 29, 1835)

Porterfield, Mr. Robert B. married on Wednesday last by the Rev.
R. B. C. Howell to Miss Mary Figuers all of Nashville.
Nashville Whig (Tues., March 29, 1842)

Porterfield, Miss Susan married to Mr. Adam G. Adams.

Posey, Mr. Dennis P. married in Rutherford County to Miss Lavinia
Dill.
National Banner & Nashville Whig (Sat., July 22, 1826)

Posey, Mr. Phares T. married in Huntsville, Ala. to Mrs. Elizabeth
Hutchings.
National Banner & Nashville Whig (Sat., Sept. 6, 1828)

Possey, Sidney C. Esq. married in Florence, Ala. to Miss Harriet
Calista Depriest.
National Banner & Nashville Daily Advertiser (Thurs., Feb. 21, 1833)

Postlethwait, Miss Emily married to David S. Cahmbers, Esq.

Postlethwait, Mr. John Jr. of Covington, Ten. married on Thursday
evening 31st ult. to Miss Sarah H. Johns daughter of Mr. John Johns
of Davidson County.
National Banner & Nashville Daily Advertiser (Sat., Feb. 2, 1833)

Postlethwait, Miss Mary married to Mr. Coleman Duncan.

Postlethwait, Miss Sally married to Mr. Tho. P. Hart.

Postlethwaite, Mr. Joseph married at Louisville, Ky. to Miss Catharine
E. Small.
National Banner & Nashville Whig (Wed., Sept. 14, 1831)

Postlethwaite, Mr. Joseph married at Louisville, Ky. to Miss Catharine
E. Small.
National Banner & Nashville Whig (Wed., Sept. 14, 1831)

Poston, Miss Elizabeth A. of Elizabethtown married in Elizabethtown,
Ky. on the 3d inst. by the Rev. Mr. Lovelace to Mr. Joseph H. Shepherd
of Nashville.
Nashville Whig (Mon., Nov. 8, 1841)

Poteete, James married in Williamson County, Ten. to Minerva Ann Fitz.
National Banner & Nashville Daily Advertiser (Mon., Aug. 26, 1833)

Pott, Mr. Joseph married in Franklin, Tenn. to Miss Jane Williamson.
National Banner & Nashville Daily Advertiser (Tues., Aug. 15, 1834)

Potter, Rev. William married in Overton County to Miss Amanda Christian
daughter of George Christian Esq.
National Banner & Nashville Whig (Mon., Nov. 1, 1830)

Potter, Mr. Wm. W. married in Pulaski to Miss Sarah H. Cokner.
National Banner & Nashville Whig (Sat., March 1, 1828)

Potts, Abner C. married to Malinda Halsted.
The Western Weekly Review - Franklin, Tenn. (Fri., Feb. 1st, 1833)

Potts, James A. married in Sumner County to Miss Jane A. Anderson.
National Banner & Nashville Advertiser (Sat., Nov. 24, 1832)

Potts, Miss Maria married in Franklin, Tenn. to Mr. George White.

Potts, Mr. Thomas married in Tuscaloosa, Ala. to Miss Lucy Hamner.
National Banner & Nashville Whig (Sat., Aug. 5, 1826)

Powell, Miss married to Mr. Jesse Lacy.

Powell, Miss Agness married to Mr. John C. Lewis.

Powell, Miss Annas R. married to Mr. Henry A. Rathbone.

Powell, Mr. Benjamin R. married on Thursday evening 13th inst. to
Miss Mary Ann Butler.
National Banner & Nashville Whig (Sat., July 22, 1826)

Powell, Mr. Birtton P. married at Louisville, Ky. to Miss Elizabeth
Birch.
National Banner & Nashville Advertiser (Tues., July 10, 1832)

Powell, Miss C. married to Maj. J. F. Powell.

Powell, Mr. Edmund married in Davidson County by the Rev. Mr. Green
to Miss Julia G. Davis.
National Banner & Nashville Whig (Wed., Jan. 21, 1835)

Powell, Mr. Edward married at Bowling Green, Ky. to Miss Eliza Ann
Cook.
National Banner (Sat., Sept. 26, 1829)

Powell, Mr. Ephraim married in Logan County, Ky. to Miss Sally P.
Newby.
National Banner & Nashville Whig (Mon., Dec. 29, 1834)

Powell, Maj. J. F. married in Maury County to Miss C. Powell.
National Banner & Nashville Daily Advertiser (Thurs., May 17, 1832)

Powell, Levin Esq. married at Tuscaloosa, Ala. to Miss Jane Moody.
National Banner & Nashville Whig (Fri., March 26, 1830)

Powell, Dr. Llewellyn married in Lauderdale County, Ala. to Miss
Sarah E. Harrison.
National Banner & Nashville Whig (Sat., March 17, 1827)

Powell, Miss Mary married to Mr. William Collins.

Powell, Miss Matilda D. married to Rev. Elbert F. Sevier.

Powell, Miss Nelly married to Mr. Obadiah Walters.

Powell, Mr. Robert B. married in St. Louis to Miss Alice Slater.
National Banner & Nashville Whig (Sat., July 22, 1826)

Powell, Mr. Seymour of Wilson County married by the Rev. James Gwin
to Mrs. Elizabeth East of Nashville.
National Banner & Nashville Whig (Mon., Oct. 26, 1835)

Powell, Mr. Seymour of Wilson County married to Mrs. Elizabeth East.
of Nashville.
Nashville Republican (Sat., Oct. 24, 1835)

Powell, Mr. S. T. late editor of the Free Press married at Shelbyville
on the 25th inst. by William Burnett, Esq. ot Miss Margaret Ruth.
Nashville Whig (Sat., Oct. 31, 1846)

Powers, Charles married in Henry County to Miss Elizabeth Rodrey.
National Banner & Nashville Daily Advertiser (Mon., April 23, 1832)

Poyner, Miss Lucy C. married to Mr. John Climer.

Poyner, Mr. Stephen S. of Tenn. married in Wilkinson County, Miss to
Miss Anne Olivia Ratcliff.
National Banner & Nashville Daily Advertiser (Mon., Feb. 17, 1834)

Poyzer, Miss married to John Stephens Esq.

Poyzer, Miss Mary M. married to Doctor James Watson.

Prather, Miss Mary J. married to Worden P. Churchill, Esq.

Prather, Miss Mary Julia married to Henry Clay, jun. esq.

Prather, Miss Matilda married to Sam S. Nicholas, Esq.

Prather, Mr. Samuel married in Blount County to Miss Mary Wright daughter of Dr. Isaac Wright.
National Banner & Nashville Daily Advertiser (Wed., May 15, 1833)

Pratt, Mr. J. married in Giles County to Miss Sarah Strong.
Nashville Whig (Tues., July 14, 1846)

Pratt, Miss Lavinia S. married to N. S. Crunk.

Pratt, Mr. Wm. S. married in Christian County, Ky. to Miss Emily Collins.
National Banner & Nashville Daily Advertiser (Tues., Feb. 5, 1833)

Prentice, Col. Charles married in Vandalia, Ill. to Miss Mary Hinds.
National Banner & Nashville Whig (June 24, 1826)

Prentice, Mr. George D. married in Louisville, Ky. to Miss Harriet Benham.
Nashville Republican (Tues., Aug. 25, 1835)

Prescott, Mr. J. married at Memphis to Miss E. Babbett.
National Banner & Nashville Whig (Wed., Nov. 2, 1831)

Prescott, Mr. James M. married in Louisville, Ky. to Miss Hannah Eaton.
National Banner & Nashville Whig (Sat., Dec. 13, 1828)

Preston, Miss Henrietta married to Lieut. Albert T. Johnson.

Preston, Miss Jane married to Mr. Frances W. Irby.

Preston, Miss Josephine married to Capt. J. Rogers.

Pretchard, J. W. married in Williamson County to Miss Joannah Ivy.
The Western Weekly Review - Franklin, Tenn. (Fri., Feb. 1, 1833)

Prewett, Miss Dolly married to Mr. John W. Guthrie.

Prewitt, Miss Dolly married to Mr. Jno. W. Guthrie.

Prewitt, Mr. Nelson married in Fayette County, Ky. to Miss Mary Ann Coleman.
National Banner (Sat., May 2, 1829)

Price, Miss Dorcas married to Mr. Samuel Humphreys.

Price, Miss Eliza married to Mr. Merryman Bradshaw.

Price, Miss Eliza married to Mr. John M'Lean.

Price, Miss Elvira H. married to Mr. Bird Smith.

Price, Mr. Isaac W. married in Monroe County to Miss Terrissa M. Kelso.
National Banner & Nashville Whig (Fri., March 26, 1830)

Price, Mr. James married in Willaimson County, Ten. to Miss Susan Vaughan.
National Banner & Nashville Whig (Fri., Feb. 13, 1835)

Price, Mr. James B. married in Lauderdale County, Ala. to Miss Frances Mason.
National Banner & Nashville Whig (Sat., Jan. 10, 1829)

Price, James Esq. married in Louisville, Ky. to Miss Sarah J. Anderson.
National Banner & Nashville Whig (Wed., Aug. 3, 1831)

Price, Miss Jane C. married to James M. Chandler.

Price, Miss J. J. married to Mr. Robert H. Jones.

Price, Miss J. J. married to Robert H. Jones, Esq.

Price, Mr. John married in Maury County to Miss Winny Taylor
National Banner & Nashville Whig (Wed., April 27, 1831)

Price, Mr. John married in Smith County to Miss Lucretia Beasly.
National Banner & Nashville Whig (Fri., Nov. 11, 1831)

Price, Mr. John U. married in Franklin County, Ky. to Miss Maria
Helen O'Hara.
National Banner & Nashville Daily Advertiser (Tues., June 26, 1832)

Price, Maj. M. A. of Virginia married to Miss Maria Barry of Sumner
County.
Nashville Republican & State Gazette (Thurs., March 17, 1831)

Price, Major M. A. of Virginia married in Sumner County on the 16th
inst. by the Rev. Mr. Hume to Miss Maria Barry.
National Banner & Nashville Whig (Fri., March 18, 1831)

Price, Mrs. M. A. married to G. W. Sweeney.

Price, Miss Mary married to Mr. Thomas Cary.

Price, Miss Mary Ann married to Mr. John S. Fullmer.

Price, Miss Mary Ann married to John S. Fullmer

Price, Miss Mary Ann married to Mr. John Dean.

Price, Miss Nancy married to Mr. Fielding Wilson.

Price, Mr. Nathaniel M. married in August 1831 to Miss Mary M. Davis.
The Western Weekly Review - Franklin, Tenn. (Fri., Sept. 2, 1831)

Price, Mr. N. M. married in Williamson County to Miss Mary Davis.
The Western Weekly Review - Franklin, Tenn. (Fri., Dec. 2, 1831)

Price, Mr. N. M. married in Williamson County to Miss Mary Davis.
National Banner & Nashville Whig (Wed., Dec. 7, 1831)

Price, Miss Pricilla married to Mr. W. Warnick.

Price, Mr. Reuben married in Garrard County, Ky. to Miss America
Cauley.
National Banner & Nashville Whig (Sat., Jan. 6, 1827)

Price, Dr. Robert C. married in Rutherford County to Miss Mary C.
Keas.
National Banner & Nashville Whig (Sat., Feb. 2, 1828)

Price, Miss Samuella married to Valerious P. Winchester, Esq.

Price, Miss Samuell married to Valerius P. Winchester, Esq.

Price, Miss Susan married to Mr. Sidney Bedford.

Price, Mr. Thomas married in Madison County, Ky. to Miss Sally Jarman.
National Banner & Nashville Whig (Sat., Jan. 10, 1828)

Price, Mr. Thos. K. of this town married in Lexington, Ky. to Miss
Eliza Robinson.
National Banner & Nashville Whig (Sat., Sept. 30, 1826)

Price, Mr. Wm. married in Knox County to Miss Mary Ann Large.
National Banner & Nashville Whig (Fri., June 27, 1828)

Prichard, Mr. William married last evening in Nashville by the Rev.
Mr. Hume to Miss Mary M. Poyzer.
National Banner & Nashville Daily Advertiser (Thurs., April 26, 1832)

Prichitt, Henry married in Williamson County to Miss Martha Osburn.
The Western Weekly Review - Franklin, Tenn. (Fri., Feb. 1, 1833)

Pride, Miss Frances Ann married to Mr. Jesse Warren.

Priest, Mr. Manoah M. married in Madison County, Ala. to Miss Nancy
Lankford.
National Banner (Feb. 3, 1826)

Priest, Miss Roaham married to Mr. Oliver Duncan.

Priest, Mr. William, aged 64 married in Jefferson County, Ten. to Miss
Mary Rosnine aged 17.
National Banner & Nashville Whig (Mon., April 13, 1835)

Priestley, Miss Sarah Ann married to Mr. Philip Hoover.

Prigmore, Miss Lucinda married to Mr. Coleb Moore.

Prim, Miss Parthenia married to Mr. Smith Mainor.

Pringle, Miss married to Mr. John Stillwell.

Pringle, Mrs. Mary married to Hon. Joel R. Poinsett.

Pritchard, Miss Elizabeth married to Mr. Henry Thompson.

Pritchard, Miss Elizabeth married to Mr. Stephen J. Hanes.

Pritchard, Miss Elizabeth married to Henry Thompson.

Pritchard, Mr. William married in Nashville to Miss Mary M. Poyzer
on last evening by Rev. Mr. Hume.
National Banner & Nashville Advertiser (Thurs., April 26, 1832)

Pritchett, Henry married in Williamson County to Miss Martha Asburn.
The Western Weekly Review - Franklin, Tenn. (Fri., March 8, 1833)

Pritchard, Mr. R. married in Williamson County to Mrs. Susan Pritchard.
Nashville Whig (Sat., July 11, 1846)

Pritchett, Mr. T. J. of Clarksville married on Wednesday the 17th inst.
by Rev. A. N. Cunningham to Miss Mary A. DeGroffinreid daughter of
Gen. DeGroffinreid of Williamson County.
Nashville True Whig & Weekly Commercial Register (Fri., April 26, 1850)

Probart, Miss Almira A. married to Rev. John B. M'Ferrin.

Probart, Miss Almira A. married to Rev. John B. M'Ferrin.

Proctor, Maj. Benjamin married in Russellville, Ky. to Miss Viers
daughter of Mr. John Viers.
National Banner & Nashville Whig (Wed., Feb. 25, 1835)

Proctor, Mr. James married in Logan County, Ky. to Miss Sally Blakey.
National Banner (Feb. 3, 1826)

Proctor, Mr. Thomas S. married in Lincoln County, Ky. to Miss Elizabeth
Craig.
National Banner (Sat., Sept. 5, 1829)

Proffit, Miss Judeth married to Mr. S. M. Parker.

Prout, H. W. Esq. married in Tuscumbia, Ala. to Miss A. C. Hogan.
National Banner & Nashville Daily Advertiser (Mon., Aug. 19, 1833)

Pruett, Mr. Jeremiah married in Maury County to Miss Unity Wilks.
National Banner & Nashville Whig (Mon., Aug. 8, 1831)

Pruitt, Mr. Joshua C. of Todd County married in Clarksville to Miss
M'Call.
National Banner & Nashville Daily Advertiser (Mon., June 24, 1833)

Pryor, Capt. Green married in Hardeman County to Miss Jane Maria
Alexander daughter of Col. Adam R. Alexander.
National Banner & Nashville Whig (Fri., July 15, 1831)

Pryor, Mr. John C. married in Winchester last week to Miss Ann E.
Bullard.
The Nashville Whig & Tenn. Advertiser (March 7, 1818)

Pucket, Mr. James D. married near Port Gibson, Miss. to Mrs. Jane
Marshall.
National Banner (June 3, 1826)

Pucket, Miss Matilda married to Mr. Patrick Sharkey.

Puckett, Miss Charlotte married to Mr. Dudley Lindsey.

Puckett, Miss Lucy married to Mr. James Bailey.

Pugh, Mr. Samuel M. married in Hempstead County, Ark. to Miss
Elizabeth White.
National Banner & Nashville Whig (Sat., Sept. 9, 1826)

Pugh, Miss Sarah W. married to Mr. James Watkins.

Pugsley, Miss Carolina Eliza married to Mr. David T. McGavock.

Pulham, Miss Eliza C. married to Mr. Thomas Shackelford.

Pully, Miss Frances married to Mr. William G. W. Seat.

Pully, Mr. Wm. married in Madison County, Ky. to Miss Elizabeth Jones.
National Banner & Nashville Whig (Sat., Oct. 28, 1826)

Purdy, Mr. John of Nashville married on Tuesday 3d inst. to Miss
Evelina Chapman.
Nashville Republican (Sat., Feb. 14, 1835)

Purdy, Mr. Josiah married in Louisville, Ky. to Miss Elizabeth Johnson.
National Banner & Nashville Daily Advertiser (Thurs., Oct. 18, 1832)

Purdy, Miss Martha M. married to Mr. James C. Moore.

Purdy, Capt. Robert of Davidson County married on Tuesday evening last
to Miss Elizabeth Philips of Davidson County.
Impartial Review & Cumberland Repository - published at Nashville
(Sat., Feb. 22, 1806)

Purdy, Mr. Thomas _? married in Bedford County, Ten. to Miss Jane C.
Yell.
National Banner & Nashville Whig (Mon., April 13, 1835)

Purris, Mrs. E. A. married to Hon. Nathen Green.

Purris, Maj. Henry S. married in Roane County to Miss Esther A. Clowney.
National Banner & Nashville Whig (Mon., 17, 1831)

Purris, Maj. Henry S. married in Roane County to Miss Esther A. Clowney.
National Banner & Nashville Whig (Mon., Oct. 17, 1831)

Pursell, Miss Nancy married to Mr. Alvin Kerron.

Pursle, Miss Lucy married to Judgematical Wright.

Purtle, Mr. John married in Warren Co., Ky. to Miss Clarissa Roberts.
National Banner & Nashville Whig (Fri., July 22, 1831)

Purvis, Mr. Allen married at Jersey Sttlement, Miss. to Miss Mary Ann
Waters.
National Banner & Nashville Whig (Sat., Aug. 4, 1827)

Puryear, Mr. Mardecai married in Williamson County on Wednesday evening
10th inst. by the Rev. T. L. Douglas to Miss Sarah A. Reese.
National Banner & Nashville Whig (Fri., Feb. 19, 1830)

Puryear, Mr. Richard married near Courtland, Ala. to Miss Maria Woodfin.
National Banner & Nashville Whig (Fri., May 7, 1830)

Putman, Miss Elizabeth married to Mr. William C. Cook.
National Banner & Nashville Whig (Wed., Dec. 7, 1831)

Putman, William married in Williamson County to Miss Delila Richardson
The Western Weekly Review - Franklin, Tenn. (Fri., June 29, 1832)

Putman, Mr. William married in Williamson County to Miss Delila
Richardson.
National Banner & Nashville Advertiser (Tues., July 3, 1832)

Putnam, A. W. Esq. of Nashville married on Wednesday 19th inst. at
Forrest Hill. The residence of Mr. E. J. Armstrong near Columbia,
Tenn. by Rev. J. M. Arnell to Mrs. Mary W. Edwards of Columbia.
The Christian Record (Sat., July 22, 1848)

Putnam, Miss Elizabeth married to Mr. William C. Cook.

Putnam, Jas. married in Williamson County, Ten. to Polly Barnett.
National Banner & Nashville Whig (Wed., Dec. 17, 1834)

Putnam, Mr. John M. of Jackson, Miss married in Huntsville, Ala. at
the residence of Col. Robert Fern on the 7th inst. to Miss Sophronia L.
Fearn daughter of Mr. George Fearn.
The Christian Record (Sat., April 17, 1847)

Putnam, Mr. John M. of Jackson, Miss married in Huntsville, Ala. at
the residence of Col. Robert Fearn, on the 7th inst. to Miss Sophronia
L. Fearn daughter of Mr. George Fearn.
The Politician & Weekly Nashville Whig (Fri., April 16, 1847)

Putney, Mr. David E. married in Hardeman Co. to Miss Elizabeth Harris.
National Banner & Nashville Whig (Wed., Oct. 5, 1831)

Pybas, Mr. Nathaniel married in Rutherford Co. to Miss Paulina A.
Vaughan.
National Banner & Nashville Advertiser (Fri., May 11, 1832)

Pybass, Miss Elizabeth married to Mr. P. G. Warren.

Pyle, Mr. Henry married inAnderson County to Miss Lucinda Clear
daughter of Mr. Peter Clear.
National Banner & Nashville Daily Advertiser (Mon., July 15, 1833)

Quarles, Miss Frances married to Mr. Thomas Little

Quarles, Col. Wm. of Arkansas married at Natchitoches to Miss
Harriet H. Combs.
National Banner & Nashville Whig (Sat., March 29, 1828)

Queener, Miss Mary A. H. married to Miss Mary A. H. Simpson??

Quick, Mr. L. S. married in Lincoln County, Ten. to Miss Tabitha
McDougal.
National Banner & Nashville Whig (Fri., Dec. 6, 1834)

Quiggles, Miss Josephine married to Mr. James Ferguson Esq.

Quinn, Miss Louisa Elliston married to Mr. A. Andrew M'Lean.

Quinn, Mr. Matthew H. married on Sunday evening last to Mrs. Ann T.
Parham both of this town.
Nashville Whig (April 9, 1823)

Quinton, Miss Sarah Ann married to Mr. Charles Wayne.

Quisenbury, Miss Louisa married to Mr. Jefferson Page.

Racine, Miss Isabella married to Mr. Charles Whistler.

Racine, Miss Janette married to Charles L. Hitchcock, Esq.

Radford, Miss Elizabeth married to Mr. Jones Watkins.

Radford, Mr. James married in Christian County, Ky. to Miss Ann P. Tandy.
National Banner & Nashville Daily Advertiser (Tues., Oct. 30, 1832)

Ragan, Mr. D. of Morganton married in Monroe County to Miss Esther Barnett.
National Banner & Nashville Whig (Wed., Nov. 2, 1831)

Ragan, Miss Elizabeth married to Mr. Robert S. Holt.

Ragan, Mr. Wm. S. married in McMinn County to Miss Mary Riddle.
National Banner & Nashville Whig (Sat., Feb. 9, 1828)

Ragland, Mr. William of Lebanon, Tenn. married in Pittsburgh, Pa. on the 18th Feb. to Miss Sarah J. Lans.
National Banner & Nashville Whig (Mon., March 13, 1837)

Ragsdale, Rev. B. H. married in Rutherford County to Miss Mary Ann Rucker.
National Banner & Nashville Whig (Sat., Feb. 3, 1827)

Ragsdale, Miss Docia married to Mr. John O. Fussell.

Ragsdale, Miss Martha married to Dr. George D. Norris.

Ragsdale, Miss Sarah married to Mr. W. P. Wright.

Railey, Miss Mary Eliza married to Rev. Frederick W. Boyd.

Rain, Miss Christiana married to Mr. Edmund Hyde.

Rainer, Mr. William R. married in Jacksborough to Miss Frances Dobney.
National Banner & Nashville Daily Advertiser (Mon., Dec. 31, 1832)

Raines, John Esq. of Davidson County to Miss Margaret Sikes daughter of Jessee Sikes Esq. married at the residence of the Brides father in Rutherford County on Tuesday afternoon 3d inst. by the Rev. Joseph H. Eaton President of Union University.
Nashville Daily Gazette. (Dec. 22, 1857)

Raines, Rolla P. Esq. married in Franklin County on the 3d day of Aug. last by the Rev. William Woods to Miss Elizabeth B. Eames.
National Banner & Nashville Whig (Mon., Sept. 6, 1830)

Rainey, Miss Elizabeth married to Mr. Wm. Smith.

Rainherd, Mr. Paul married at Louisville, Ky. to Miss Patsy Mercer.
National Banner & Nashville Whig (Sat., Jan. 19, 1828)

Rains, Miss Mary married to Mr. Preston N. Thompson.

Rains, Miss Nancy B. married to Mr. Lemuel Swearinggean.

Rains, Miss Polly married to Mr. Thomas Massey.

Rains, Miss Ursula married to Mr. Wilford B. Gowin.

Rainwater, Rev. Moses F. married in Anderson County to Miss Betsy Clay Oliver daughter of Col. Charles Y. Oliver.
National Banner & Nashville Advertiser (Thurs., Oct. 18, 1832)

Rall, Mrs. Meneda married to Mr. Robert Dunbar.

Ramey, Miss Elizabeth married to Mr. Arthur Harris.

Ramey, Mary married to Isaiah C. Gault.

Ramsey, Miss Harriet N. married to Mr. Wm. Simonton.

Ramsey, Miss Harriet N. married to Mr. William Simonton.

Ramsey, Miss Jane married to Mr. Johnson Birk.

Ramsey, Miss Lemiza A. married to Oliver M. Wozencraft.

Ramsey, Miss Sarah married to Mr. Philip J. Kearney.

Ramsey, Col. W. B. A. married in Knoxville, Ten. to Mrs. Eliza H. C. White.
National Banner & Nashville Whig (Mon., Nov. 10, 1834)

Ramsey, Major William married in Hardeman County to Miss Olive P. Patrick.
National Banner & Nashville Whig (Fri., Jan. 29, 1830)

Ramsey, Col. William B. A. of Knoxville married on the evening of the 8th inst. by the Rev. Dr. Edgar to Mrs. Susan P. Washington daughter of the late Judge Trimble of Nashville.
Nashville Whig (Tues., May 10, 1842)

Ramsom, Miss S. married to J. W. Mallard.

Randle, Miss E. K. married to Mr. Thomas P. Jarnagin.

Randle, Miss Elizabeth K. married to Mr. Thomas P. Jarnegan.

Randle, Miss Geraldine married to Mr. William Manley.

Randle, Mr. Jared married in Henry County to Miss Eliza F. Manly.
National Banner & Nashville Daily Advertiser (Fri., Feb. 15, 1833)

Randle, Miss Lucy R. married to Mr. Benjamine Travis.

Randles, Mr. Andrew married to Miss Cassandra Parsley.

Randolph, Miss Eliza married to Mr. Albert G. McClellan.

Randolph, Mrs. Elizabeth A. married to Maj. A. J. Donelson.

Randolph, Harriet married to Hon. Albert S. White.

Randolph, Mr. John R. married in Fayette County, Ky. to Miss Nancy T. Moore.
National Banner & Nashville Whig (Mon., July 19, 1830)

Randolph, Miss Lavina married to Mr. John P. Holeman.

Randolph, Miss Priscilla married to Mr. William Clark.

Randolph, Robert B. late of the U. S. Nacy married in Richmond, Va. on the 23d of March by the Rev. Mr. O'Brien to Miss Eglantine Beverly of Alexander, D. C.
National Banner & Nashville Daily Advertiser (Thurs., April 17, 1834)

Ranea, Miss Prudence married to Thomas Gills.

Raney, Miss Ann M. married to Mr. David Wells.

Ranier, Mr. William R. married in Jacksborough to Miss Francis Dabney.
National Banner & Nashville Advertiser (Mon., Dec. 13, 1832)

Rankin, Christopher Esq., Representative in Congress, from Mississippi married on the 11th ult. to Miss Julian daughter of Gen. Stricker of Baltimore.
Nashville Whig (Dec. 6, 1824)

Rankin, Mr. James O. married at West Union, O. to Miss Margaret Ruggon.
National Banner & Nashville Whig (July 1, 1826)

Rankin, Mr. Richard D. married in Monroe County to Miss Nancy M'Clure.
National Banner (Sat., Nov. 21, 1829)

Rankin, Mr. Robert married near Little Rock, Arkansas to Miss Fanny Hogan.
National Banner & Nashville Whig (Sat., Feb. 24, 1827)

Ranney, Mr. Nathan married at St. Louis to Miss Amelia Jane Shackford.
National Banner & Nashville Whig (Sat., Dec. 1, 1827)

Ransom, Miss S. married to Mr. J. W. Mallard.

Ransom, Miss S. married to Mr. J. W. Mallard.

Ransome, Mr. married in Franklin County to Miss Nancy H. Hudspeth on Thursday the 3d inst.
National Banner & Nashville Whig (Wed., Feb. 9, 1831)

Ransome, Mr. Wm. married in Franklin County on Thursday the 3d inst. by the Rev. Mr. Wood to Miss Nancy H. Hudspeth daughter of the late Robert Hudspeth.
National Banner & Nashville Whig (Wed., Feb. 9, 1831)

Rard, Mr. Henry A. married in Henry County to Miss Levina Jones.
National Banner & Nashville Daily Advertiser (Thurs., Sept. 27, 1832)

Rash, Stephen S. Esq. married in Williamson County on Thursday the 5th by Rev. Mr. Whitsell to Miss Sarah McMurray.
Nashville Whig (Mon., Aug. 9, 1841)

Ratcliff, Miss Anne Olivia married to Mr. Stephen S. Poyner.

Ratcliff, Mr. Clay M. of Franklin married in Maury County to Miss Mary W. Branch.
National Banner & Nashville Whig (Mon., Aug. 30, 1830)

Ratcliff, Rachel married to Mr. George Thompson.

Ratcliff, Mr. Wm. married in Amite County, Mississippi to Miss Abby Rice.
National Banner (Jan. 27, 1826)

Rathbone, Mr. Henry A. married in Hawkins County to Miss Annas R. Powell.
National Banner & Nashville Daily Advertiser (Wed., Jan. 18, 1832)

Rawling, Mr. Edwin married in Madison County, Ten. to Miss Eliza Tyson.
National Banner & Nashville Whig (Fri., Dec. 12, 1834)

Rawling, Miss Eliza married to Mr. Wm. Trigg.

Rawlings, Miss Ann married to Mr. Charles Sanders.

Rawlings, Miss Anna married to Dr. John Waters.

Rawlings, Miss Elizabeth married to Dr. Sims.

Rawlings, Mrs. Emily married to Major William Todd.

Rawlings, Mr. John H. married in Jackson to Miss Sarah Jane Hays.
Nashville Republican & State Gazette (Wed., Feb. 20, 1833)

Rawlings, Mr. John H. merchant of Jackson married in Madison County,
Ten. on the 14th Feb. to Miss Sarah Jane Hays daughter of the late
Col. Stokely D. Hays.
National Banner & Nashville Daily Advertiser (Thurs., Feb. 21, 1833)

Rawlins, Miss Elizabeth married to Dr. Elisha G. Syms.

Rawlins, Mrs. Emily married to Maj. Wm. Todd.

Rawlins, Miss Lucy married to Mr. Edward Steel.

Rawlins, Miss Lucy married to Mr. Edward Steel.

Rawlins, Mrs. Martha M. married to Mr. John Thompson.

Rawlins, Mr. Thomas married at Danville, Va. to Miss Emelia D. Haughton.
National Banner (Sat., April 25, 1829)

Raworth, Mr. Egbert A. married in Davidson County on the 28th ult. by
Rev. Mr. Hume to Miss Leodocia J. Boyd.
National Banner & Nashville Whig (Fri., Nov. 4, 1831)

Raworth, George F. Esq. of Dickson County, Tenn. married on Thursday
the 13th inst. by the Rev. John W. Odgen to Miss Bethia R. Lovell
of Davidson County, Tenn.
The Christian Record (Sat., Jan. 22, 1848)

Raworth, Miss Laura J. married to Doctor Augustus C. Wynne.

Ray, Miss Amelia married to Mr. J. B. Duchouquette.

Ray, Miss Cynthia married to Mr. Jefferson Alexander.

Ray, Miss Edna married to Mr. Allen Marrow.

Ray, Miss Edney married to Mr. Allen Marrow.

Ray, Rev. Edwin married at Indianapolis to Miss Sarah Ann Nawland
National Banner & Nashville Whig (Sat., Sept. 8, 1827)

Ray, Mrs. Elender married to Mr. Binom Ferrel.

Ray, Mr. Eli S. married in Williamson County to Miss Amanda Davis.
National Banner & Nashville Whig (Wed., Dec. 7, 1831)

Ray, Mr. Eli S. married in Williamson County to Miss Amanda Davis.
The Western Weekly Review - Franklin, Tenn. (Fri., Dec. 2, 1831)

Ray, Mr. James M. married in Bedford County, Ten. to Miss Nancy Brown.
National Banner & Nashville Whig (Fri., June 10, 1836)

Ray, Miss Lucinda married to Mr. David Ethridge.

Ray, Mr. Sharp married in Bedford County on the 18th inst. to Miss
Polly M'Guire.
National Banner (Jan. 27, 1826)

Ray, Mr. Wm. married at Louisville, Ky. to Miss Caroline Meriwether.
National Banner & Nashville Whig (Sat., Dec. 30, 1826)

Rayburn, French married on the 19th inst. at Cumberland Iron Works by
the Rev. A. A. Muller D. D. to Catherine E. Stacker daughter of
Samuel Stacker.
Nashville Whig (Mon., May 24, 1840)

Rayburn, Mr. J. K. married in this town on Thursday evening last to
Miss Sarah Jane Lytle daughter of Wm. Lytle, Esq.
National Banner & Nashville Whig (Sat., June 7, 1828)

Rayburn, Mr. Samuel S. married in Nashville on Sun. evening last to
Miss Susan P. Davis.
National Banner & Nashville Whig (Thurs., July 16, 1830)

Raymond, Miss Abigail married to Mr. Isaac Raymond.

Raymond, Nelson T. of Nashville married on Wednesday 2nd inst. by the
Rev. Mr. Evans to Miss Providence Levition of Sumner County
Nashville Whig (Mon., Dec. 7, 1840)

Raymond, Mr. Silas married in Louisville, Ky. to Mrs. Betsey M'Mullin.
National Banner & Nashville Whig (Sat., Oct. 28, 1826)

Rayse, Mr. Vera married at Cincinnati to Miss Ann Maria Tenmer.
National Banner (April 28, 1826)

Razor, Mr. George F. married at Hopkinsville, Ky. to Miss Julia Ann
Gravens.
National Banner & Nashville Daily Advertiser (Tues., May 8, 1832)

Read, Miss Cornelia Washington married to Mr. Horatio D. Newcomb.

Read, Miss Cornelia Washington married to Mr. Horatio D. Banner.

Read, Mr. Cuningham married in Logan County, Ky. to Miss Eliza M.
McReynolds.
National Banner & Nashville Whig (Sat., Feb. 9, 1828)

Read, Miss Eliza J. married to Mr. Phineas Holmes.

Read, Miss Elizabeth C. married to Mr. Jacob Bondurant.

Read, Miss Elizabeth M. married to Mr. Edward W. Norfleet

Read, Miss Elizabeth M. married to Mr. Edward W. Norfleet.

Read, Miss Elmira married to Mr. Ed. H. Childress.

Read, Mr. John Allen married in Columbia to Miss Oliva Harris on
Wednesday evening last.
Nashville Republican & State Gazette (Fri., July 19, 1833)

Read, Mr. John W. married in Maury County to Miss Ann D. Journey.
National Banner & Nashville Whig (Fri., Dec. 10, 1830)

Read, Miss Laura C. married to Harrison Barksdale.

Read, Gen. Leigh married in Florida to Miss Eliza M. Branch daughter
of Hon. John Branch.
Daily Republican Banner (Mon, June 25, 1838)

Read, Miss Martha E. married to Mr. John G. Brown.

Read, Miss Mary Jane married to Dr. German Baker.

Read, Mr. Mathew married in Franklin County, Ala. to Miss Agnes May.
National Banner (Sat., April 25, 1829)

Read, Mr. Noel married in Smith County to Miss Amanda Beasley.
National Banner & Nashville Whig (Tues., Dec. 13, 1831)

Read, Dr. Thomas H. of Rutherford County, Ten. married in Decatur,
Macon County, Illinois on the 24th August to Miss Elizabeth Allen of
Loudon County, Virginia.
Nashville Republican (Thurs., Sept. 15, 1836)

Read, Doctor Thomas H. of Rutherford County, Tennessee married in Decatur, Macon County, Illinois on the 24th Aug. to Miss Elizabeth Allen of Loudon County, Virginia.
The Union (Tues., Sept. 13, 1836)

Reader, Nancy L. married to Johnson D. Williams.

Reader, Mr. Samuel P. of New Orleans married at Louisville, Ky. to Miss Catherine Boggs.
National Banner & Nashville Whig (Sat., Oct. 25, 1828)

Ready, Aaron Esq. married at Tuscaloosa, Ala. to Miss Jerusha Sims.
National Banner & Nashville Whig (Tues., Feb. 23, 1830)

Ready, Miss Mary married to Mr. James Holmes.

Ready, Mr. William F. of Rutherford County married in Franklin to Miss Isabel C. Burkley.
National Banner & Nashville Advertiser (Mon., Dec. 17, 1832)

Ready, Mr. William F. of Readyville, Rutherford County married in Franklin on Thursday last by the Rev. Jas. H. Otey to Miss Isabel C. Burkley of Williamson County.
The Western Weekly Review - Franklin, Tenn. (Dec. 14, 1832)

Ready, Mr. William F. of Readyville married to Miss Isabel C. Burkley.
Nashville Republican & State Gazette (Mon., Dec. 17, 1832)

Reams, Lucy Ann married to Thos. S. Mayfield.

Reams, Robert. married in Williamson County to Miss Mary F. Womac.
The Western Weekly Review - Franklin, Tenn. (Fri., Feb. 1, 1833)

Reasons, Mr. Jsoeph married in Montgomery County to Miss Amanda N. Brown daughter of Mr. James Brown.
National Banner (Sat., Sept. 19, 1829)

Reasonover, Mr. Jacob married in Giles County to Miss Tabitha E. Marks.
Nashville Republican & State Gazette (Mon., Feb. 4, 1833)

Reasor, Mr. William married at Cincinnati to Miss Mary T. Burnet daughter of Isaac Burnet Esq.
National Banner & Nashville Daily Advertiser (Fri., March 9, 1832)

Reaves, Mr. Henry W. married in Williamson County, Ten. to Miss Eliza Baker.
National Banner & Nashville Whig (Mon., April 13, 1835)

Reaves, Miss Sarah W. married to Mr. Anderson A. Latta.

Record, Mr. James B. married in Maury County to Miss Rachel Tillmen.
National Banner & Nashville Whig (Mon., Aug. 8, 1831)

Redd, Mrs. married to Capt. Edwin Kelly.

Redd, Mr. Waller B. in Fayette County, Ky. married to Miss Rebecca Allen.
National Banner & Nashville Whig (Wed., July 27, 1831)

Reddick, Mr. J. of Nashville married to Miss Martha Langford on 3d. inst.
Nashville Republican & State Gazette (Mon., March 4, 1833)

Reddick, Mr. John married in Nashville on the 3d inst. by John Wright Esq. to Miss Martha Langford.
National Banner & Nashville Daily Advertiser (Mon., March 4, 1833)

Redding, Miss Elizabeth H. married to Mr. William H. Redding.

Redding, Mr. William H. married in Bedford County to Miss Elizabeth Hester.
National Banner & Nashville Whig (Sat., Nov. 15, 1828)

Redman, Mr. Allen married at Shawneetown to Miss Ann Sidwell (Sedivell)
National Banner (March 10, 1826)

Redman, Miss Priscilla Ann Maria married to Mr. James M'Cain.

Reece, Mr. Joel married in Fayetteville on the 24th ult. to Miss Polly R. Leftwich.
National Banner & Nashville Whig (Fri., Jan. 29, 1830)

Reed, Miss Ann S. married to Mr. John H. Ward.

Reed, Mr. Charles married in Lexington, Ky. to Miss Lucy Sharp.
National Banner & Nashville Whig (Sat, March 10, 1827)

Reed, Miss Emeline married to Mr. George Timberlake.

Reed, Miss Emily J. married to Mr. John W. Smith.

Reed, Mr. Finis married in Hardeman County to Miss Luzena Hopkins.
National Banner & Nashville Whig (Fri., Aug. 13, 1831)

Reed, Mr. Griffin married at Florence, Ala. to Miss Jane Smith.
National Banner (Sat., Nov. 28, 1829)

Reed, Mr. Henry married at Danville, Ky. to Miss Martha Thorn.
National Banner & Nashville Whig (Sat., Feb. 23, 1828)

Reed, Isaac Shelby Esq. of Mississippi married at Washington to Miss Ann Laura Green daughter of Gen. Duff Green editor of the U. S. Telgraph.
National Banner & Nashville Daily Advertiser (Tues., July 10, 1832)

Reed, Mr. John A. married at Columbia to Miss Olivia Harris.
National Banner & Nashville Daily Advertiser (Wed., July 31, 1833)

Reed, Margaret M. married to Thomas M. Garrett.

Reed, Miss Mary J. married to Mr. John W. Steele.

Reed, Miss Mary L. married to Mr. James Riddle.

Reed, Miss Olivia F. married to Mr. Wm. Andrews.

Reed, Madam Theresa married to Mr. S. Cole.

Reel, Miss Hudley Ann Eliza married to Mr. Charles Jabine.

Reese, Miss Sarah A. married to Mr. Mordicia Puryear.

Reese, Hon. Wm. B. of Knoxville, Ten. married to Miss Henrietta Brown in Franklin, Ky.
Nashville Republican & State Gazette (Tues., Feb. 18, 1834)

Reese, Hon. W. B. of Knoxville, Ten. married in Frankfort, Ky. on the 30th Jan. to Miss Henrietta Brown of Frankfort.
National Banner & Nashville Daily Advertiser (Mon., Feb. 17, 1834)

Reeves, Miss married to Mr. Cross.

Reeves, Mr. John married in Bedford County to Miss Mary Holt daughter of Mr. Michael Holt.
National Banner & Nashville Daily Advertiser (Tues., Nov. 27, 1832)

Reeves, Miss Mary married to Mr. Thomas Newsom.

Reeves, Maj. Moses G. married in Murfreesborough to Miss Catharine
Shields.
National Banner & Nashville Whig (Sat., March 1, 1828)

Reeves, Mr. Owen T. married at Chillicothe, O. to Miss Catherine
Madeira.
National Banner (Sat., Aug. 1, 1829)

Reeves, Willis L. Esq. of Elkton married in Warren County, Ky. to
Mrs. Margaret Harrison.
National Banner & Nashville Whig (Mon., Dec. 6, 1830)

Regan, Rev. Mr. married in Knoxville to Miss Catherine Webb.
National Banner & Nashville Whig (Mon., Oct. 17, 1831)

Reid, Miss Florida Forsyth married to Lieut H. L. Dancy.

Reid, John Esq. Attorney at law married in Loudon Hill the mansion of
Col. W. B. A. Ramsey in the vicinity of Knoxville the 15th inst. by
the Rev. Dr. Anderson to Miss M. Louisa Trimble daughter of the late
Judge Trimble all of Nashville.
Nashville Whig, Tues., May 21, 1844)

Reid, Miss Sophia married to Mr. Lafayette Searcy.

Reily, Mr. Jesse M. married in Winchester, Ky. to Miss Mary Lampton.
National Banner & Nashville Whig (Sat., Oct. 7, 1826)

Reinhardt, Mr. Ephraim married in M'Minn County to Miss Julian Duke.
National Banner (Sat., June 13, 1829)

Remington, Miss Eliza married to Mr. James Bell.

Remington, Mr. Greenberry married in Harrison County, Ky. to Miss
Lucinda Hamilton.
National Banner (March 17, 1826)

Renegar, Mr. William H. married in Lincoln County, Ten. to Miss
Arrena Miles.
National Banner & Nashville Whig (Fri., Jan. 23, 1835)

Renfoe, Mr. Stephen C. married in Grainger County to Miss Mary M'Kinney
daughter of Mr. Seth M'Kinney.
National Banner & Nashville Daily Advertiser (Mon., Sept. 10, 1832)

Renfoe, Mr. Jesse married in Maury County to Miss Sina Roper.
National Banner & Nashville Whig (Mon, Aug. 8, 1831)

Renfro, Miss Paulina married to Mr. James Jones.

Renish, Mr. W. married in Ross County, Ohio to Miss Jane Boggs.
National Banner & Nashville Whig (Sat., May 26, 1827)

Reno, Mr. James G. of Cincinnati married on the 21st inst. by the Rev.
Dr. Edgar to Miss Mary C. Glenn daughter of S. Glenn Esq. of Nashville.
Nashville Whig (Fri., Oct. 22, 1841)

Reno, Miss Martha Jane married to Mr. Thomas J. Terrice.

Renshaw, Miss Henrietta married to Mr. Wallis Willoughby.

Rensselaer, Henry Van of Albany married at Jamaica, L. Island to Miss
Elizabeth Ray King daughter of John A. King Esq.
National Banner & Nashville Daily Advertiser (Thurs., Sept. 19, 1833)

Revis, Miss Lucy Ann J. married to Mr. K. Holliday.

Reyburn, Dr. Wm. P. married near Little Rock, Ark. to Miss Elizabeth Hane Trotter daughter of Mr. B. Trotter late of Williamson County.
National Banner & Nashville Whig (Wed., May 16, 1831)

Reyburn, Dr. Wm. P. married in Arkansas to Miss Elizabeth Jane Trotter of Williamson County, Tenn.
Nashville Republican & State Gazette (Thurs., May 12, 1831)

Reynolds, Miss Amanda F. of Smith Co. married to Mr. L. B. Fite.

Reynolds, Mr. Benj. B. married at Cincinnati to Miss Elizabeth Guest.
National Banner (March 24, 1826)

Reynolds, Miss Catherine married to Mr. Alexander Dugger.

Reynolds, Miss Charlotte married to Mr. James O. Gentry.

Reynolds, Miss Eliza E. married to Mr. Jesse Conn.

Reynolds, Mr. George F. married in Knox County to Miss Elizabeth Gentry.
National Banner (Feb. 17, 1826)

Reynolds, James B. Esq. late member of Congress married at Clarksville to Mrs. Elder.
National Banner & Nashville Whig (Sat., Feb. 21, 1829)

Reynolds, Dr. J. Houston of Memphis married on 26th inst. by the Rev. R. A. Lapsley D.D. to Miss Jane W. Trabue daughter of Charles C. Trabue of Nashville.
Nashville True Whig & Weekly Commercial Register. (Fri., Oct. 4, 1850)

Reynolds, Mr. John married in Warren County, Ky. to Miss Susan Harney.
National Banner & Nashville Whig (Mon., Aug. 1, 1831)

Reynolds, Mr. John married in Warren County to Miss Susan Harney.
National Banner & Nashville Whig (Mon., Aug. 1, 1831)

Reynolds, Miss Letitia married to Mr. John L. Henderson.

Reynolds, Miss Rachel married to Mr. W. E. Farran.

Reynolds, Mr. Silas married in Rutherford County to Miss Nancy Keele daughter of Rev. Wm. Keele.
National Banner & Nashville Advertiser (Thurs., Aug. 23, 1832)

Reynolds, Miss Virginia married to Mr. Anthony S. Camp.

Reynolds, Mr. William married in Bolivar to Miss Tabitha Cookburn.
National Banner & Nashville Whig (Thurs., Nov. 8, 1830)

Reynolds, Miss Williamina married to Mr. William S. Davenport.

Rhea, Miss Frances married to Dr. Thomas P. Hawkins.

Rhea, James C. Esq. married in Elizabethton to Miss Elizabeth Carter daughter of Alfred Carter Esq.
National Banner & Nashville Daily Advertiser (Mon., Jan. 2, 1832)

Rhea, Col. Joseph C. married in Pulaski to Miss Margaret Y. Field.
National Banner & Nashville Daily Advertiser (Wed., Dec. 10, 1832)

Rhea, Miss Sarah married to Seth J. W. Lucky Esq.

Rheams, Miss Jane married to Mr. Alfred J. Moyers.

Rhemes, Miss Jane married to Mr. Alfred J. Moyers.

Rhems, Miss Mary Jane married to Mr. James M. Gault.

Rhoads, Miss Rachel married to Mr. George Harrison.

Rhodes, Miss Ann R. married to Mr. James H. M. Hall.

Rhoten, Rev. Josiah married at Newport to Miss Juliet Garrett.
National Banner & Nashville Whig (Sat., Oct. 6, 1827)

Rice, Miss Abby married to Mr. Wm. Ratcliff.

Rice, Miss Agatha married to Mr. Jesse Scott.

Rice, Miss Agatha P. married to Mr. Jesse G. Scott.

Rice, Miss Amanda M. married to Mr. William Wilson.

Rice, Miss Ann Maria married to Mr. Phinchas C. Lindsey.

Rice, Miss Annette married to Mr. Lilburn Mefford.

Rice, Miss Elizabeth married to Mr. William M'Cord.

Rice, Mr. James married at Tuscaloosa, Ala. to Miss Maria T. Files.
National Banner & Nashville Whig (June 17, 1826)

Rice, Miss Mary Ann married to Mr. Hugh Brown Esq.

Rice, Mr. R. R. married in Nashville on Tuesday last by the Rev.
Mr. Edgar to Miss Mary Ann Shirley daughter of the late Paul Shirley
Esq.
The Union (Sat., Oct. 15, 1836)

Rice, Mr. R. R. married in Nashville on 11th Oct. by the Rev. Mr.
Edgar to Miss Mary Ann Shirley both of Nashville.
National Banner & Nashville Whig (Wed., Oct. 12, 1836)

Richards, Miss married to Maj. John Sevier.

Richards, Mr. Augusta H. married at Washington City to Rebecca C.
M'Lean.
National Banner & Nashville Whig (Sat., Feb. 14, 1829)

Richards, Mr. C. married in Smith County to Miss B. Kemp.
National Banner & Nashville Daily Advertiser (Thurs., Jan. 5, 1832)

Richards, Mr. Gustavus U. of New York married July 31st in Bolton to
Miss Elextoria B. Wilder.
Nashville Republican & State Gazette (Sat., Oct. 5, 1833)

Richards, Miss Mary A. married to J. H. Polland.

Richards, Miss Nancy married to Mr. Elijah Parlin.

Richards, Mr. Thomas married in Logan County, Ky. to Miss Ann Duvall.
National Banner & Nashville Whig (Sat., May 17, 1828)

Richards, Mr. William, merchant of Line Port, Tenn. married on the
16th inst. by the Rev. J. H. Bristone to Miss Martha L. White daughter
of the Rev. Samuel White of Christian County, Ky.
The Politician & Weekly Nashville Whig (Fri., March 3, 1838)

Richards, Dr. Wm. L. married at Georgetown, Ky. to Miss Eleanor E. S.
Keane.
National Banner & Nashville Whig (Sat., Oct. 28, 1826)

Richardson, Mr. Chauncy married in Tuscumbia, Ala. to Miss Martha
Goodwin.
National Banner & Nashville Daily Advertiser (Mon., July 15, 1833)

Richardson, Mr. David M. married in this County on Thursday evening last to Miss Paul na Sergeant.
National Banner & Nashville Whig (Sat., April 7, 1827)

Richardson, David P. Esq. of La. married in Nashville on the 18th inst. by Rev. Mr. McFerrin to Miss Ellen M. Bosworth.
National Banner & Nashville Whig (Wed., Jan. 20, 1836)

Richardson, Miss Delila married to William Putnam.

Richardson, Miss Eliza married to Mr. Richard T. Maner.

Richardson, Miss Elizabeth M. married to Mr. James Moffatt.

Richardson, Miss Elizabeth married to Mr. Richardson Eubanks.

Richardson, James N. T. Esq. married in vicinity of Nashville on the 10th inst. by Rev. A. L. P. Green to Mrs. Emma M. Winn both of Louisiana.
Nashville Whig (Wed., Aug. 11, 1841)

Richardson, Miss Mary Ann married to Col. George Wilson.

Richardson, Miss Mary C. married to Rev. Absolom Adams.

Richardson, Miss Nancy married to Samuel Perkins Esq.

Richardson, Miss Sarah Jane married to Mr. Nathaniel Evans.

Richardson, Miss Peggy married to Mr. Notley Wilkinson.

Richardson, Mr. Richard married in Cincinnati to Miss Mary Ann Knox.
National Banner & Nashville Whig (Sat., April 12, 1828)

Richey, Mr. James married in Christian County, Ky. to Miss Eliza Nichol.
National Banner (Jan. 20, 1826)

Richie, Mr. H. married in Lexington, Ky. to Miss Elizabeth Smeads.
National Banner & Nashville Whig (Wed., June 1, 1831)

Richmond, Miss Ann Elizabeth married to Mr. George Thomas.

Richmond, Mr. Braddock merchant of Nashville married on Thursday evening last by the Rev. Mr. Whitsett to Mrs. Winny Garrett of its vicinity.
The Clarion & Tennessee Gazette (Jan. 30, 1821)

Richmond, Edmund Esq. of Brownville married in Haywood County to Miss Judith P. Nelson.
National Banner & Nashville Daily Advertiser (Thurs., Jan. 17, 1833)

Richmond, Edmund, Esq. of Brownsville married in Haywood County to Miss Judith P. Nelson.
Nashville Republican & State Gazette (Wed., Jan. 16, 1833)

Richmond, Mr. Ezehiel married in Hardeman County to Miss Margaret Alexander.
National Banner & Nashville Advertiser (Sat., March 3, 1832)

Richmond, Miss Harriet married to Mr. Joseph H. Johnson.

Ricket, Mr. Wm. married in Madison County to Miss Cynthia Frazier.
National Banner & Nashville Advertiser (Wed., Aug. 29, 1832)

Ricketts, Miss Elizabeth married to Mr. James M'Lean.

Ricks, Mr. Benjamin S. married at Tuscumbia, Ala. to Miss Catherine F. Winter.   National Banner (Sat., Aug. 1, 1829)

Ricks, Miss Oliva married to Dr. Daniel M. Gwinn.

Riddle, Miss Eleanor married to Mr. Henry Forsyth.

Riddle, Mrs. Frances married to Capt. Pleasent Crew.

Riddle, Mr. James married in McMinn County to Miss Mary L. Reed.
Nashville Whig (Tues., July 14, 1846)

Riddle, Miss Jeanett married to Mr. T. Chaffen.

Riddle, Mr. Madison married at Pulaski to Miss Mary Wilkinson daughter
of Maj. Thomas Wilkinson.
National Banner & Nashville Whig (Fri., June 2, 1831)

Riddle, Miss Mary married to Mr. Wm. S. Ragan.

Riddle, Robert S. married in Giles County to Teresa W. Barnett.
National Banner & Nashville Daily Advertiser (Tues., Dec. 17, 1833)

Riddle, Miss Sarah married to Mr. John J. Bingham.
National Banner (Feb. 10, 1826)

Riddle, Susan married to Thomas Jones.

Ridge, Miss Mary Ann married to Mr. Thomas T. Dunn.

Ridgeway, Miss Ann married to Mr. J. Kugkendall.

Ridgley, Miss Lucy E. married to Dr. John F. Henry.

Ridley, Miss married to Mr. Elisha Williams.

Ridley, Miss married to Mr. Elisha Williams.

Ridley, Mr. George of Williamson County married on Thursday evening
by Thomas Williamson Esq. to Miss Mary Vaughn of Nashville.
The Nashville Gazette (Wed., March 15, 1820)

Ridley, Mr. Hanse H. married in Davidson County on the 11th inst. by
Rev. Peter Fuqua to Miss Sarah A. B. Everett both of Davidson County.
National Banner & Nashville Whig (Mon., June 21, 1830)

Ridley, Mr. James Jr. married in this county to Miss Hannah H.
Williams of Rutherford County on Wednesday 6th inst.
Nashville Republican (Thurs., July 7, 1836)

Ridley, Mr. James Jr. of Davidson County married on Wednesday the
6th inst. by Rev. Mr. Fuqua to Miss Hannah H. Williams daughter of
John Williams Esq. of Rutherford County.
Nashville Republican (Thurs., July 7, 1836)

Ridley, Mr. S. Jones of Mississippi married in Williamson County on
Tuesday the 8th inst. by the Rev. Mr. Cunningham to Miss Sarah
McEwen daughter of C. E. McEwen.
Nashville Whig (Sat., Sept. 12, 1846)

Ridley, Miss Winneford married to Col. James Mitchell.

Rieves, Thomas E. married in Williamson County to Miss Martha Turner.
The Western Weekly Review - Franklin, Tenn. (Fri., Feb. 10, 1832)

Rife, Mr. Sylvester married in Lincoln County to Miss Catharine Baker.
National Banner & Nashville Whig (Sat., Dec. 30, 1826)

Rigg, Elizabeth married to Charles Humphreys, Esq.

Rigglesworth, Miss Sarah married to Robert C. Thompson, Esq.

Riggs, Mr. Gideon of Williamson County married on Thursday 8th ult.
by the Rev. J. J. Dobson to Miss Catharine Holdin of Chapel Hill
Marshall County, Tenn.
Daily Republican Banner (Mon., March 19, 1838)

Riggs, Mr. Gideon married in Bedford County to Miss Sophia Campbell.
National Banner & Nashville Whig (Sat., Jan. 3, 1829)

Riggs, Samuel J. Esq. of Philadelphia married on Thursday last by the
Rev. Dr. Edgar to Miss Medora Cheatham daughter of Leonard P. Cheatham
Esq. of Davidson County.
National Banner & Nashville Whig (Mon., Sept. 28, 1835)

Riggs, Samuel J. Esq. of Philadelphia married to Miss Medora Cheatham
of Davidson County on Thursday last.
Nashville Republican (Sat., Sept. 26, 1835)

Riggus, Mr. Daniel married in Williamson County to Miss Ann N.
Sudbury.
National Banner & Nashville Advertiser (Mon., March 26, 1832)

Riggus, Daniel married in Williamson County to Miss Ann N. Sudbury.
The Western Weekly Review - Franklin, Tenn. (Fri., March 23, 1832)

Riley, Miss married in Lagrange, Ala. to Doctor W. H. Harrington.
National Banner & Nashville Daily Advertiser (Mon, May 28, 1832)

Riley, Miss Mary Ann married to Mr. Jacob Smith.

Ring, Dr. Levi married on the 29th ult. to Miss Eliza E. Parker both
of Haysboro.
Nashville Whig (Nov. 10, 1823)

Ripley, Gen. E. W. married at Francisville, La. to Miss Aurelia Davis.
National Banner & Nashville Whig (Mon., Aug. 30, 1830)

Riprogle, Miss Catherine married to Mr. Ivey Tilman.

Rison, Mr. James of Smith married in Lebanon to Miss Mary Ann Sypert.
National Banner & Nashville Daily Advertiser (Mon., Dec. 10, 1832)

Ritcherson, Mr. John od Dickson County married Miss Malinda Nolen on
19th Nov.
Nashville Republican (Tues., Jan. 19, 1836)

Ritchie, Miss Rebecca married to Mr. Henry Sweeny.

Ritchie, Miss Rebecca married to Mr. Henry Sweeny.

Rivers, Miss Elizabeth married to Mr. Samuel W. Morgan.

Rivers, Mr. John married in Montgomery County to Miss Mildred Dabney
daughter of the late Dr. Samuel Dabney.
National Banner & Nashville Whig (Fri., Feb. 26, 1830)

Rivers, Miss Peggy married to Mr. John Erwin.

Rivers, Robert J. Esq. married at Springfield, Ten. to Miss Amanda
Cheatham.
National Banner & Nashville Whig (Fri., June 20, 1828)

Rivers, Thomas Esq. of Sommerville, Tenn. married on Monday the 13th
by the Rev. R. H. Rivers to Miss Mary Ann Trigg of Franklin, Tenn.
Nashville Whig (Sat., Nov. 25, 1843)

Rivers, Mr. Thomas M. married in Haywood County to Miss Sarah S. Groves
National Banner & Nashville Daily Advertiser (Wed., Jan. 18, 1832)

Rives, Miss Emeline C. married to Mr. Wm. B. Grove.

Roach, Mrs. married to Mr. Joseph Gentry.

Roach, Mr. Francis G. married in Giles County to Miss Amanda M.
Paine.
Nashville Republican & State Gazette (Dec. 9, 1834)

Roach, Mr. Francis G. of Nashville married in Giles County, Ten. on
Dec. 4th by Rev. J. B. McFerrin to Miss Amanda M. Paine daughter of
James Paine Esq. of Giles.
National Banner & Nashville Whig (Mon., Dec. 16, 1834)

Roach, Mr. John of Elkton, Ky. married Miss Ann M'Clean of Logan County
Ky.
National Banner & Nashville Daily Advertiser (Mon., Aug. 12, 1833)

Roach, Miss Matilda married to Mr. William Kingston.

Roades, Miss Eliza married to Mr. Evon Shelby.

Roads, Mr. George W. married in Henry County to Miss Elizabeth
Copeland.
National Banner & Nashville Advertiser (Wed., Jan. 11, 1832)

Roane, Miss Christiana J. married to Mr. Thomas G. Masterson.

Robb, Mr. John H. married in Lexington, Ky. to Miss Nancy S. Smith.
National Banner & Nashville Whig (Fri., July 11, 1828)

Robb, Joseph M. Esq. married in Gallatin to Miss Martha K. Calhoun.
Nashville Whig (Wed., Oct. 7, 1840)

Robberts, Mrs. Eleanor married to Mr. Wm. Asaley.

Robert, Mr. Alexis J. of Nashville married on Tuesday the 16th by the
Rev. Mr. Elliott to Miss Mary Anna Ann Stevens formerly of Nashville,
North Carolina.
Nashville Whig (Sat., May 20, 1843)

Robert, Miss Catherine M. married to John C. Marshall.

Robert, Mr. Sanderson married in Philadelphia to Miss Sarah Baker.
National Banner & Nashville Whig (Sat., Jan. 31, 1829)

Roberts, Miss A. married to Mr. John H. Christy.

Roberts, Miss Abiah married to Mr. Clark G. Crozier.

Roberts, Mr. A. J. married in Nashville on the 29th by the Rev. Mr.
Green to Miss Ann E. T. Morefield.
National Banner & Nashville Whig (Wed., Jan. 4, 1837)

Roberts, A. J. Esq. of Memphis married in Nashville on the 29th ult.
by the Rev. Mr. Green ot Miss Ann E. Morefield of Nashville.
The Union (Sat., Jan. 7, 1837)

Roberts, Mr. Charles L. married in Madison County, Ala. to Miss Sarah
Beville daughter of Col. Woodliff Beville.
National Banner & Nashville Whig (Mon., June 7, 1830)

Roberts, Miss Clarissa married to Mr. John Purtle.

Roberts, Miss Clarissa R. married to Mr. John Purtle.

Roberts, Miss Emily M. married to Mr. Milton J. Hamer.

Roberts, Miss Frances E. married to Mr. James A. Grant.

Roberts, Mr. Henry merchant of Elkton married in Todd County, Ky. on the 22d ult. to Miss Minerva Greenfield youngest daughter of Thos. Greenfield Esq.
National Banner & Nashville Whig (Fri., Oct. 2, 1835)

Roberts, Miss Icy married to Henry Dishon.

Roberts, Mr. James married in Bedford County, Tenn. to Miss Nancy Haley.
National Banner & Nashville Daily Advertiser (Mon., July 21, 1834)

Roberts, Mr. James F. of Coinsville married on the 10th inst. at the residence of H. Legon by Thomas C. Cawthorn Esq. to Miss Sarah E. Jenkins daughter of Mr. John H. Jenkins all of Wilson County.
Nashville Union (Sat., May 16, 1846)

Roberts, Jesse married in Williamson County to Miss Nancy Trimble.
The Western Weekly Review - Franklin, Tenn. (Fri., Dec. 14, 1832)

Roberts, Mr. John B. married in Maury County to Miss Martha S. Williams daughter of John Williams Esq.
National Banner & Nashville Whig (Mon., Sept. 6, 1830)

Roberts, Miss Letty married to Mr. Jas. B. Baucanan.

Roberts, Miss Mahala married to Mr. Wm. A. Clarke.

Roberts, Miss Marion C. married to Mr. William Harding.

Roberts, Miss Martha married to Mr. Charles Root.

Roberts, Miss Mary married to Col. Thomas W. Townsend.

Roberts, Miss Mary G. married to Mr. James M. Shepard.

Roberts, Miss Nancy married to Maj. Austin A. King.

Robertson, Gen'l Abner B. of Nashville married in Bedford County on the 15th inst. to Miss Harriett B. Patton daughter of John Patton Esq.
Nashville Republican (Mon., Nov. 21, 1836)

Robertson, Dr. Benj. F. married on Tuesday evening last to Miss Eliza Martha Goodloe both of Columbia.
Nashville Whig (Oct. 6, 1823)

Robertson, Mr. Drury married in September 1831 to Miss Emily O. Davis.
The Western Weekly Review - Franklin, Tenn. (Fri., Sept. 23, 1831)

Robertson, Mr. Drury of Murfreesborough married in Williamson County on the 29th ult. to Miss Emily O. Davis daughter of Holland Davis Esq.
National Banner & Nashville Whig (Wed., Oct. 12, 1831)

Robertson, Miss Eleanor R. married to Mr. Duncan N. Hennen.

Robertson, Miss Eleanora married to Mr. Duncan N. Hennen.

Robertson, Miss Elizabeth married to Mr. Leyton Hunter Esq.

Robertson, Miss Elizabeth married to Mr. Leonard Cheatham Esq.

Robertson, Miss Elizabeth A. married to Thomas Smith Esq.

Robertson, Miss Fanny H. married to Mr. Leroy W. Napier.

Roberts, Mr. Nathan near Bolivar married to Miss Mary P. Roper.
Nashville Republican & State Gazette (Sat., Oct. 29, 1831)

Roberts, Miss Obiah married to Mr. Clark G. Crozier.

Roberts, Miss Pamelia married to Mr. Wilham Thornhill.

Roberts, Miss Rachel married to Mr. John C. Gilbert.

Roberts, Mr. T. B. of Jackson County married in Smith County to Miss Jane Trousdale.
National Banner & Nashville Daily Advertiser (Fri., March 23, 1832)

Roberts, Mr. William married in the vicinity of Russellville, Ky. to Miss Elizabeth Millen both of South Union, Ky.
National Banner & Nashville Daily Advertiser (Sat., Feb. 2, 1833)

Roberts, Mr. William married in Davidson County on Wednesday 17th inst. by the Rev. Mr. Whitsett to Miss Sarah J. Chowning.
National Banner & Nashville Whig (Fri., Feb. 26, 1830)

Roberts, Mr. Zachariah H. married in Madison County to Miss Sarah Fly.
National Banner & Nashville Whig (Mon., Aug. 30, 1830)

Robertson, Dr. Felix Nashville married on Sunday last to Miss Lydia Waters.
Impartial Review & Cumberland Repository - published at Nashville (Thurs., Oct. 13, 1808)

Robertson, Dr. F. J. of Nashville married on Thursday evening at Melrose in Nashville vicinity by C. D. Elliott to Miss Laura L. Brown eldest daughter of Gov. Aaron V. Brown.
Nashville Truly Whig & Weekly Commercial Register (Fri., June 28, 1850)

Robertson, Miss Frances N. married to Mr. Frederick Christian.

Robertson, Mr. George A. of Stanford married in Frankfort, Ky. to Miss Louisa F. M'Curdy daughter of Dr. A. F. M'Curdy.
National Banner & Nashville Whig (Mon., May 2, 1831)

Robertson, James W. Esq. married on the 18th inst. by the Rev. Mr. Lapsley to Miss Margaret Graham all of Nashville.
Nashville Whig (Fri., May 21, 1841)

Robertson, Miss Jane T. married to Dr. Baker Walsh.

Robertson, Mr. John married in Nashville to Miss Nancy Allen.
National Banner & Nashville Daily Advertiser (Tues., March 25, 1834)

Robertson, Miss L. married to Mr. Leonard J. Caldwell.

Robertson, Miss Levinia marroed to John E. Beck, Esq.

Robertson, Miss Lucinda married to Mr. Creenbury Greer.

Robertson, Miss Martha A. married to Addison H. Douglas, Esq.

Robertson, Miss Martha Ann married to Mr. Abram Stevens.

Robertson, Miss Mary married to Franklin Sullivan Esq.

Robertson, Miss Mary married to Franklin Sullivan Esq.

Robertson, Miss Mary Ann married to Mr. James B. Anderson.

Robertson, Miss Mary E. married to James Thomas Craig.

Robertson, Mr. Nathaniel B. married in Vandalia, Illinois to Miss Evelina Wakefield.
National Banner & Nashville Whig (July 8, 1826)

Robertson, Mr. Wm. B. Davidson Co. married Miss Leodocia Erwin Davidson County on Sunday last. Impartial Review & Cumberland Repository - published at Nashville (Sat., April 11, 1807)

Robeson, Mr. Bartaram married near Cahawba, Ala. to Miss Temperance Thurman.
National Banner (March 17, 1826)

Robeson, Miss Susan W. married to Mr. H. H. Hills.

Robin, Miss Madgelaine married to Mr. Henry Weaver.

Robins, Ephraim Esq. of Cincinnati married in Zanesville to Miss Jane Hussey daughter of Asahel Hussey Esq. of Baltimore.
National Banner & Nashville Daily Advertiser (Mon., Feb. 6, 1832)

Robins, Ephraim Esq. of Cincinnati married in Zanesville to Miss Jane Hussey of Baltimore.
National Banner & Nashville Advertiser (Mon., Feb. 6, 1832)

Robins, Miss Mary J. married to Mr. Lewis D. Barham.

Robins, Miss Mary J. married to Mr. Lewis D. Barham.

Robinson, Miss Amonda married to Mr. Owen D. Winn.

Robinson, Miss Ann M. married to Mr. Wm. P. Kern.

Robinson, Miss Anne married to Mr. W. Bartley.

Robinson, Miss B. married in Russellville, Ky. to Mr. James Alexander.
National Banner & Nashville Advertiser (Tues., June 26, 1832)

Robinson, Miss Catherine married to Mr. William Fothergill.

Robinson, Mr. David V. married in Logan County to Miss Susan H. Carr.
National Banner & Nashville Whig (Sat., Dec. 6, 1828)

Robinson, Mr. Dawson H. of Savannah, Hardin County married in Wayne County on the 5th inst. to Miss Kitturah daughter of James Elliot.
National Banner & Nashville Whig (Mon., Aug. 16, 1830)

Robinson, Miss Eliza married to Mr. Thos K. Price.

Robinson, Miss Elizabeth Jane married to Alexander M. Hardin Esq.

Robinson, Miss Elizabeth Jane married to Mr. Alexander M. Hardin Esq.

Robinson, Miss Elizabeth M. married to Mr. James B. Ferguson Jr.

Robinson, Mr. Enus married in Maury County, Ten. to Miss Sarah W. Hart.
National Banner & Nashville Whig (Wed., Feb. 25, 1835)

Robinson, Miss Frances married to Mr. Henry Murray.

Robinson, Miss Frances married to Mr. Samuel Lane.

Robinson, Mr. Francis H. married in Anderson County to Miss Frances Oliver daughter of Douglas Oliver Esq.
National Banner & Nashville Daily Advertiser (Wed., May 22, 1833)

Robinson, Mr. Hardy, Williamson County married to Matilda Case.
National Banner & Nashville Advertiser (Mon., March 26, 1832)

Robinson, Hardy married in Williamson County to Miss Matilda Cate.
The Western Weekly Review - Franklin, Tenn. (Fri., March 23, 1832)

Robinson, J. B, merchant married on Tuesday evening 14th inst. by the Rev. A. L. P. Green to Miss Marie A. Hewlett both of Nashville
Daily Republican Banner (Fri., Nov. 17, 1837)

Robinson, Mr. James married in Smith County to Miss Fanny Hensley.
National Banner & Nashville Daily Advertiser (Sat., March 3, 1832)

Robinson, James Esq. merchant of Winchester married at Winchester
on the 17th Feb. by the Rev. T. C. Anderson to Miss Eliza Hutchens
of Paris, Ky.
Nashville Whig (Wed., Feb. 26, 1840)

Robinson, Mr. James C. married in this town on Wednesday evening last
by the Rev. Mr. Hume to Miss Susan Litton.
National Banner & Nashville Whig (Sat., Feb. 9, 1828)

Robinson, Mr. John married in Vandalia, Ill. to Miss Piety Wakefield.
National Banner & Nashville Whig (June 24, 1826)

Robinson, Mr. John married at Marshall's Ferry to Miss Ann Bentley.
Nashville Republican & State Gazette (Mon., Jan. 21, 1833)

Robinson, Mr. John married in Nashville to Miss Nancy L. Allen on
Friday 21, in st.
Nashville Republican & State Gazette (Tues., March 25, 1834)

Robinson, Mr. John of Manchester, England married to Miss Rebecca
Williams of Boston.
Nashville Republican & State Gazette (Thurs., Aug. 29, 1833)

Robinson, Mr. John R. married in Cumberlandtown to Miss Sally Watkins
of Richmond, Va.
National Banner & Nashville Whig (Sat., Sept. 13, 1828)

Robinson, Miss L. married to Mr. Leonard Caldwell.

Robinson, Miss Lydia married to John C. Avery, Esq.

Robinson, Miss Martha B. married to Mr. Christopher Guinn.

Robinson, Miss Mary married to J. C. Sumner, Esq.

Robinson, Miss Mary G. married to Mr. Wm. M. Coleman.

Robinson, Mary Stuart married to Hugh Elliot, Esq.

Robinson, M. S. married to Mr. James H. Gilis.

Robinson, Miss Prudence F. married to Mr. William Tatum.

Robinson, Mr. Robert of Hartsville married in Smith County to Miss
Eliza Goodall.
National Banner & Nashville Whig (Sat., Nov. 17, 1827)

Robinson, Mr. Samuel W. married in Pikeville, Tenn. on Thursday 13th
inst. by the Rev. John Heminger to Miss Eliza C. Bridgmon eldest
daughter of John Bridgmon, Esq.
National Banner & Nashville Daily Advertiser (Tues., March 25, 1834)

Robinson, Miss Sarah married to Mr. Hugh McDaniel.

Robinson, Miss Sarah married to Mr. Andrew Christopher.

Robinson, Miss Serena G. married to Mr. L. A. Kincannon.

Robinson, Miss Susan married to Mr. Benjamin Hilderbrand.

Robinson, Dr. William married in Smith County to Miss Martha Lack.
National Banner & Nashville Daily Advertiser (Mon., April 2, 1832)

Robinson, Mr. William M. married in Washington County to Miss Rachel
Thomas.
National Banner (May 20, 1826)

Robison, Miss Mary Ann married to Mr. H. Kerr.

Roby, Miss Ann married to Dr. Charles Humphreys.

Roche, John Esq. married in Lexington, Ky. to Miss Sarah Ann Elizabeth Smith.
National Banner & Nashville Whig (Sat., Dec. 16, 1826)

Rochelle, Mr. Robert merchant of Humphreys County married on 18th December to Miss Phoebe Anderson of Stewart County.
National Banner & Nashville Whig (Fri., Jan. 8, 1836)

Rochester, Mr. Henry married in Scott County, Ky. to Miss Dimeretta Pitts.
National Banner & Nashville Whig (Sat., Jan. 12, 1828)

Rockhold, Mr. Hezekiah married in Montgomery County to Miss Elizabeth Wilkerson.
National Banner & Nashville Daily Advertiser (Sat., Feb. 11, 1832)

Rodery, Miss Nancy married to Mr. Perser Yates.

Rodes, Miss Cynthia married to Peter R. Booker Esq.

Rodes, Mr. Robert of Giles Co. married on the 20th inst. by the Rev. Mr. Kendrick to Miss Sarah Elizabeth Carter daughter of Dr. Ben Carter of Pulaski, Tenn.
Daily Republican Banner (Sat., Oct. 24, 1840)

Rodes, Dr. Tyree married in Tipton County to Miss Eliza Tipton daughter of Gen. Jacob Tipton.
National Banner & Nashville Advertiser (Wed., Jan. 18, 1832)

Rodgers, Miss Elizabeth married to Capt. Lawson D. Franklin.

Rodgers, Miss Margaret married to Mr. Moses Woodfin.

Rodgers, Miss Nancy married to Mr. John Cameron.

Rodgers, Miss Sarah W. married to Capt. George Hays.

Rodney, Caroline married to Hon. William L. May.

Rodrey, Miss Elizabeth married to Charles Powers.

Roe, Mr. John Jr. married in Lewis County, Ky. to Miss Louisa Everett.
National Banner (April 7, 1826)

Roffe, Mr. William A. married in Lauderdale County, Ala. to Miss Cyrene Mason.
National Banner & Nashville Whig (Mon., April 4, 1831)

Rogers, Mrs. Ann married Monday evening last by Rev. Lewis Garrett to Mr. Peter Higgins.

Rogers, Dr. Archibald married at Kingston to Miss Sally S. Clark.
National Banner & Nashville Whig (Sat., Feb. 21, 1829)

Rogers, Miss Eliza Ann married to Mr. Thomas T. Shreve.

Rogers, Miss Elizabeth married to Mr. Fountain Maupin.

Rogers, Miss H. A. married to Mr. John Johnson.

Rogers, Mr. Henry B. of Dickson County married Miss Crissy H. Burton on 20th.
Nashville Republican (Tues., Jan. 19, 1836)

Rogers, Capt. J. of the U. S. Army married at Louisville, Ky. to Miss Josephine Preston daughter of the late Major William Preston.
National Banner & Nashville Whig (Fri., Oct. 21, 1831)

Rogers, Mr. James married in Sumner County to Miss Polly Brazil.
National Banner & Nashville Daily Advertiser (Mon., May 13, 1833)

Rogers, Miss Jane Ann married to Hon. Henry Pirtle.

Rogers, Col. John B. of McMinnville married in Knox County to Miss Louisa Clark.
National Banner & Nashville Whig (Sat., Nov. 4, 1826)

Rogers, Mr. Joseph married in Logan County, Ky. to Miss Emily Haden.
National Banner & Nashville Whig (Sat., Sept. 20, 1828)

Rogers, Mr. Leonard married at Louisville, Ky. to Miss Minerva Bronson.
National Banner & Nashville Whig (Mon., April 4, 1831)

Rogers, Mr. Linton married at Chambersburg on Tuesday morning Aug. 5, by the Rev. Mr. Upford to Miss Margaret Mackey daughter of Mr. William Mackey all of Pittsburg.
National Banner & Nashville Daily Advertiser (Sat., Sept. 6, 1834)

Rogers, Miss Mary married to Mr. Edward Trabue.

Rogers, Miss Mary C. married to Mr. Rowland Ellis.

Rogers, Mr. Robert married in Madison County to Miss Elizabeth Tilman.
National Banner & Nashville Whig (Fri., Oct. 17, 1834)

Rogers, Mr. Thomas of Dubuque, Iowa married on the 21st inst. at the residence of Mr. John Finn to Miss Ann W. Burton of Nashville.
Nashville True Whig & Weekly Commercial Register (Fri., Oct. 25, 1850)

Rogers, Mr. W. C. of Virginia married at Louisville, Ky. to Miss Josephine D. Rowan daughter of Hon. John Rowan.
National Banner & Nashville Daily Advertiser (Mon., July 21, 1834)

Rogers, Dr. William married in Tazewell, Claiborne County, Tenn. to Miss Malinda Sewell daughter of Benjamin Sewell, Esq.
National Banner & Nashville Whig (Mon., Jan. 5, 1835)

Rogers, Mr. William H. married in Florence, Ala. to Miss Martha Jane Lowe.
National Banner & Nashville Whig (Thurs., May 20, 1830)

Roister, Mr. G. W. married in Smith County to Mrs. Mary Baker.
National Banner & Nashville Advertiser (Fri., Jan. 13, 1832)

Roister, Mr. G. W. married in Smith County to Miss Mary Baker.
National Banner & Nashville Daily Advertiser (Fri., Jan. 13, 1832)

Roling, Mr. John married on the 22nd of Aug. by the Rev. H. D. Comming to Miss Mary Eliza Dickerson daughter of John B. Dickerson Esq. of Covington, Tipton County, Tenn.
Nashville Whig & Weekly Commercial Register (Fri., Sept. 6, 1850)

Rolling, Miss Jane married to Mr. James Johnson.

Rollings, Mr. H., merchant of this city married on Wednesday evening last by the Rev. Mr. Hume to Miss Martha Ann daughter of M. C. Dunn Esq. of this county.
National Banner & Nashville Whig (Sat., Nov. 3, 1827)

Rolling, Miss Jane married to Mr. James Johnson.

Rollings, James S. of Sumner County married Thursday last to Miss Rachel Hutchins of Davidson County.
Impartial Review & Cumberland Repository. (Aug. 9, 1806)

Root, Mr. Charles married in Shelby County to Miss Martha Roberts.
National Banner & Nashville Whig (Wed., Oct. 12, 1831)

Roots, Miss Honora G. married to Mr. James Drake.

Roper, Miss Mary Ann married to Mr. T. A. M'Grath.

Roper, Miss Mary P. married to Mr. Nathan Roberts.

Roper, Miss Matilda married to Mr. Geo. Harris Esq.

Roper, Miss Sina married to Mr. Jesse Renfro.

Ropes, Mr. Nath'l. married in Anderson, O. to Miss Sarah E. Brown.
National Banner & Nashville Whig (Sat., July 22, 1826)

Roscoe, Miss Sarah A. married to Mr. Alexander S. Villeplait.

Rose, Miss Elizabeth married to Mr. Jesse Sykes.

Rose, Miss Esther married to Mr. Charles B. Devinny.

Rose, Miss Luritta married to Hon. Thomas D. Arnold.

Rose, Miss Margaret Jane married to Mr. John W. Bobbett.

Rose, Miss Rebecca married to Mr. John Cooxey.

Rose, Mr. Sidney married in Louisville, Ky. to Miss Susan Kelly.
National Banner & Nashville Daily Advertiser (Sat., Aug. 17, 1833)

Rosenhaur, Miss Jane D. married to Lewis S. Ullman.

Rosnine, Miss Mary married to Mr. William Priest.

Ross, Mr. Allen of Wilson County married near Cairo, Sumner County, Ten. to Miss ___ Taylor.
National Banner & Nashville Whig (Fri., March 13, 1835)

Ross, Miss Angeline S. married to Solomon H. Shaw.

Ross, Mr. Christopher married in Chillicothe to Miss Mary Dresback.
National Banner & Nashville Whig (Sat., Aug. 12, 1826)

Ross, Mr. James of Anderson County married at the residence of Mrs. Martin in Roane County, Tenn. by the Rev. Thomas Brown on Tuesday the 28th April to Miss Mary J. C. Martin.
Nashville Whig (Tues., May 19, 1846)

Ross, James F. married in Williamson County to Miss Elizabeth M. Sharp.
The Western Weekly Review - Franklin, Tenn. (Fri., Dec. 14, 1832)

Ross, Miss Lucinda married to Mr. Isaac Smith.

Ross, Miss Margaret married to James C. Herrison, Esq.

Ross, Miss Martha married to Mr. Fielding Travis.

Ross, Miss Martha married to Mr. Fielden Travis.

Ross, Miss Mary married to Maj. William J. Philips.

Ross, Miss Mary married to Capt. Cornelius Slater.

Ross, Miss Minerva married to Mr. George M. Murrell

Ross, Nathan Jr., Esq. married in Shelby County on the 11th June by the Rev. Williamson to Miss Ann Eliza Jones.
National Banner & Nashville Daily Advertiser (Wed., July 3, 1833)

Ross, Miss Polly married to Mr. Jason Matlock.

Ross, Miss Sophia W. married to Mr. Stephens Fuqua Jr.

Rossell, Mr. Fielding married in Fayette County, Ky. to Miss Polly Rossell.
National Banner & Nashville Whig (Sat., Aug. 30, 1828)

Rothrock, Mr. Jonathan married in Giles County to Miss Margaret A. Gordan.
National Banner & Nashville Whig (Mon., Nov. 21, 1831)

Rothrock, Mr. Jonathan married on Thursday the 10th inst. to Miss Margaret A. Gordon both of Giles County.
The Western Weekly Review - Franklin, Tenn. (Fri., Nov. 18, 1831)

Rounsavall, Miss Elizabeth married to Mr. Daniel German.

Rounsaville, Amos married in Williamson County to Susan F. Walker.
National Banner & Nashville Daily Advertiser (Mon., Aug. 26, 1833)

Roup, Miss Elizabeth married to Mr. James Watkins.

Rourke, Mr. John O. married at St. Louis to Miss Theresa Welsh.
National Banner & Nashville Whig (Sat., May 19, 1827)

Rowen, Mr. John married in Bledsoe County, Tenn. to Miss Keturak M. Worthington.
National Banner & Nashville Daily Advertiser (Mon., June 18, 1832)

Rowan, Miss Josephine D. married to Mr. W. C. Rogers.

Rowan, Mr. Wm. married in Mercer County, Ky. to Miss Eliza Boice.
National Banner & Nashville Whig (Sat., Oct. 7, 1826)

Rowark, Miss Nancy married to Mr. Thomas Simpson.

Rowe, Miss Charity married to Mr. Westley W. Jones.

Rowe, Miss Mary Ann married to Mr. Marcus H. Baynes.

Rowell, Dr. Neil married in Florence to Miss Martha Ann Cheatham.
National Banner & Nashville Advertiser (Tues., Dec. 18, 1832)

Rowell, Dr. Niel married in Florence to Miss Martha Ann Cheatham.
Nashville Republican & State Gazette (Mon., Dec. 17, 1832)

Rowell, Mr. John M. married in Lincoln County to Miss Lucinda Shuffield
National Banner & Nashville Whig (Mon., Jan. 5, 1835)

Rowland, Mr. Christopher married in Madison County, Ky. to Miss Jane Broaddus.
National Banner & Nashville Whig (Sat., Feb. 17, 1827)

Rowles, George W. Esq. late Representative in the Legislature from Bradley County married in Cleveland, Tenn. to Miss Mary A. Stout daughter of the late Dr. Stout of Cleveland.
Nashville Whig (Thurs., Jan. 26, 1843)

Rowlett, Miss Ann married to Mr. Drury Floyd.

Rowlins, Mr. Eldred married at Athens, Ala. to Miss Sarah Jane Bass.
National Banner (Sat., Sept. 5, 1829)

Roy, Miss Amelia married to Mr. J. B. Couchauquette.

Roy, Mr. Eli S. married in Williamson County to Miss Amanda Davis.
National Banner & Nashville Whig (Wed., Dec. 7, 1831)

Royister, Miss Mary E. P. married to Mr. John H. Coussens.

Royle, Miss Elizabeth married to Mr. James M'Combs.

Royster, Miss married to Mr. John T. Dismukes.

Royster, Dr. John S. of Franklin, Ky. married at Gallatin on Wednesday
the 30th ult. by the Rev. J. B. Ferguson to Miss Josephine Turner of
Gallatin.
Nashville True Whig & Weekly Commercial Register (Fri., May 17, 1850)

Rozier, Miss Jane married to Mr. Samuel G. Burrow.

Rubel, Dr. P. married in Jefferson County to Miss Jane Shelby.
National Banner & Nashville Whig (Sat., April 21, 1827)

Rucker, Mr. Benjamin of Rutherford married Mrs. Eliza Welch of Nashville.
Nashville Republican (Thurs., Oct. 15, 1835)

Rucker, Mr. Benjamin of Rutherford married in Nashville on Tuesday
13th Oct. by the Rev. Simpson Sheppard to Miss Eliza Welch of Nashville.
National Banner & Nashville Whig (Wed., Oct. 14, 1835)

Rucker, Miss Joice R. married to Mr. Thomas S. Rucker.

Rucker, Miss Lucy W. married to Mr. Lewis Garner.

Rucker, Miss Rebecca T. married to Dr. Richard L. Thompson.

Rucker, Samuel R. Esq. married in Bedford County to Miss Martha Martin.
National Banner & Nashville Whig (Sat., Feb. 23, 1828)

Rucker, Mr. Thomas G. merchant of that place to Miss Myra Mitchell
daughrer of Mr. T. Mitchell of Jefferson married on the 9th inst.
Friday evening at Murfreesborough.
The Nash Whig & Tenn. Advertiser (Jan. 24, 1818)

Rucker, Mr. Thomas S. married in Rutherford County to Miss Joice R.
Rucker.
Nashville Whig (April 9, 1823)

Rucks, Miss Elizabeth married to Jacob Halfacre.

Rucks, James Esq. Counsellor at law married on Wednesday evening last
in this town by the Rev. Mr. Lindley to Miss Louisa V. Brown daughter
of the late Dr. Preston Brown of Ky.
National Banner & Nashville Whig (Sat., May 19, 1827)

Rucks, Miss Malvina married to William Yerger.

Rucks, Miss Malvina married to William Yerger Esq.

Rucks, Miss Prudence B. married to Obadiah R. Hubbard.

Rucks, Mr. Warner T. married at Carthage to Miss Dorothy J. Cardwell.
National Banner & Nashville Whig (Fri., Nov. 11, 1831)

Rudy, Miss Mary married to Mr. Preston Owen.

Ruffin, Mr. James D. married in Valmont, Tenn. to Miss Rosina Ruffin
daughter of Maj. James Ruffin all of Hardeman County.
National Banner & Nashville Daily Advertiser (Tues., Aug. 5, 1834)

Ruffin, James F. Esq. of Sommerville, Tenn. married on the 29th
July to Miss Eliza A. Wood daughter of Capt. Drury Wood of Alber-
marle, Val.
Nashville Republican (Tues., Sept. 27, 1836)

Ruffin, Miss Lucy Ann married to Mr. Charles W. Hunt.

Ruffin, Miss Rosina married to Mr. James Ruffin.

Rufty, Mr. Littleton married in Stewart County, Ten. to Miss Martha
Throgmorton.
National Banner & Nashville Daily Advertiser (Mon., Aug. 12, 1833)

Ruggon, Miss Margaret married to Mr. James O. Rankin.

Ruland, Miss Ann married to Mr. M. Anderson.

Rumbly, Miss Louisa married to Mr. Edward Lindsay.

Rundell, Miss Phebe married to Mr. John T. Leggitt.

Runkle, Miss Elizabeth L. married to Mr. William L. Coates.

Runkle, Miss Lucinda married to Mr. John L. Parham.

Runkle, Miss Lucinda married to Mr. John L. Parham.

Runnels, Howell W. Esq. married in Marion County, Miss. to Miss Cary
D. Collins.
National Banner & Nashville Whig (Sat., Jan. 27, 1827)

Runyen, Mr. B. M. married in Nashville on Wednesday last by the Rev.
Dr. Wharton to Miss Mary E. Dunkin.
Nashville Whig (Sat., June 3, 1843)

Rupe, Miss Elizabeth married to Mr. W. N. Crutcher.

Rush, Mr. Elijah married in Henry County to Miss Elizabeth Hatler.
National Banner & Nashville Daily Advertiser (Fri., April 12, 1833)

Rush, Miss Jane married to Mr. James Gilbert.

Rush, Mr. John W. married in Rose County, Ohio to Miss Sarah C. Brown.
National Banner & Nashville Whig (Sat., Oct. 28, 1826)

Rush, Miss Sarah C. married to Mr. Urban Campbell.

Rush, Mr. William married in Logan County, Ky. to Miss Harriet Campbell.
National Banner & Nashville Whig (Thurs., Oct. 28, 1830)

Russell, Mr. Alfred H. married in the Baptist Church on the 1st day
of Jan. by the Rev. Mr. Howell to Miss Elizabeth Baird all of Nashville.
Nashville Whig (Thurs., Jan. 4, 1844)

Russell, Miss Ann married to Mr. William Carty.

Russell, Miss Elizabeth married to Mathew Wilson.

Russell, Mr. Haley married in Williamson County, Ten. to Miss Mary
Tweatt.
National Banner & Nashville Whig (Fri., Feb. 13, 1835)

Russell, Mr. Jacob married in Monroe County, Tenn. to Miss Wyly.
National Banner & Nashville Daily Advertiser (Tues., May 22, 1832)

Russell, Mr. Joseph married in Knox Co. to Miss Mildred Scott.
National Banner & Nashville Whig (Sat., Sept. 8, 1827)

Russell, Miss Mary married to Horatio Wade.

Russell, Mrs. Mary O. married to Robert Wickliffe.

Russell, Mr. Matthew C. married in Giles County to Miss Nancy Ada.
Nashville Whig (Tues., July 14, 1846)

Russell, Mr. Thomas married in Logan County, Ky. to Miss Frances Page
daughter of Samuel Page.
National Banner & Nashville Whig (Mon., Dec. 29, 1834)

Russell, Hon. W., Judge of the U. S. District Court married in Auburn,
New Jersey to Miss Jane P. Balch late of Georgetown, D. C.
The Union (Sat., June 18, 1836)

Russhing, Mr. Enoch married in Bedford County to Miss Mary A. Dwiggins.
National Banner & Nashville Whig (Mon., Oct. 31, 1831)

Russworm, Miss Virginia married to Maj. Wiley Gordon.

Russworm, Miss Virginia A. married to Major W. B. Gordon.

Rust, Mr. Peter H. of Loudon County, Va. married in Lexington, Ky. to
Miss Ann E. Villars.
National Banner & Nashville Whig (Sat., Nov. 15, 1828)

Ruth, Miss Margaret married to Mr. S. T. Powell.

Rutherford, Mrs. married to Mr. Aker.

Rutherford, Miss Clarissa married to Mr. Jesse Garner.

Rutherford, Miss Elizabeth married to Mr. John Cloud.

Rutherford, Mr. Joseph of Little Rock married in Arkansas to Miss
Malinda Bland of Saline Township.
National Banner & Nashville Daily Advertiser (Fri., Aug. 16, 1833)

Rutherford, Mr. Loyd married in Knoxville to Miss Elizabeth Hill
daughter of Mr. Anderson Hill.
National Banner & Nashville Whig (Wed., Sept. 24, 1834)

Rutherford, Mr. Thomas S. Esq. merchant formerly of Nashville married
in St. Louis, Mo. to Miss Lucille Tisson of St. Louis.
Nashville Whig (Wed., Dec. 30, 1840)

Rutland, James B. Esq. married on Wednesday 19th inst. by the Rev.
George Donnell to Miss Asenath A. Abbe all of Lebanon.
Nashville Whig (Sat., Oct. 22, 1842)

Rutledge, Miss Emma married to Mr. Daniel Blake.

Rutledge, Miss Emma P. married to Daniel Blake Esq.

Rutledge, Henry A. Esq., Nashville, married Miss Caroline Nicholson
on last evening married last evening by the Rev. Mr. Weller.
National Banner & Nashville Whig (Fri., Nov. 25, 1831)

Rutledge, H. M. Esq. married in Nashville to Miss Caroline Nicholson.
The Western Weekly Review - Franklin, Tenn. (Fri., Dec. 2, 1831)

Rutledge, Miss Mary married to Mr. Elijah Sparks.

Rutledge, Miss Mary married to Francis H. Fogg Esq.

Rutledge, Mrs. Martha M. married to Dr. Isaac J. Thomas.

Rutter, Mr. Solomon married in Lincoln County, Tenn. to Miss Elizabeth Elzy.
National Banner & Nashville Whig (Fri., Jan. 23, 1835)

Ryall, Mr. Thomas C. of N. Jersey married on 21st inst. by the Rev. Mr. Wheat to Miss Elizabeth S. Scudder of Nashville.
Daily Republican Banner (Mon., Dec. 25, 1837)

Ryan, Mr. of North Carolina married in Robertson County to Miss Emily Turner.
National Banner & Nashville Whig (Fri., July 22, 1831)

Ryan, Miss Elizabeth married to Mr. John Cheek.

Ryan, Mr. Joseph married in Nashville on the 5th to Miss Cornelia Marshall.
National Banner & Nashville Whig (Mon., March 9, 1835)

Ryan, Mr. Joseph of Nashville married on Thursday last to Miss Cornelia Marshall.
Nashville Republican (Sat., March 7, 1835)

Ryburn, Major Washington married in Robertson County on Thursday 24th July to Miss Amanda Washington.
National Banner & Nashville Whig (Sat., Aug. 2, 1828)

Saddler, Mr. Albert J. married in Triana, Ala. to Miss Pocahontas Franklin.
National Banner & Nashville Whig (Fri., Dec. 17, 1830)

Saddler, Miss Martha married to Mr. Daniel Wilkerson.

Sadler, Miss Mary Ann Elizabeth married to Mr. William W. Allen.

Saffarans, Miss Elizabeth married to Mr. William A. Garth.

Safferans, Mr. David married in Sumner County on the 12th to Miss Malvina Gardner.
National Banner (Sat., May 30, 1829)

Sale, Mrs. Eliza married to Mr. Henry S. Palmer.

Sale, Miss Mary Louisa married to Dr. Alfred W. Harris.

Salisbury, Mr. Josiah O. married at Louisville, Ky. to Miss Laura Turner.
National Banner & Nashville Whig (Sat., Dec. 30, 1826)

Salle, Dominibue married at Mobile, February 1st. to Miss Nathalie Herpin.
The Nashville Gazette (Sat., March 31, 1821)

Sample, Miss Mary married to Mr. Benjamin Kirby

Sampson, Mr. Johnson married in Smith County to Miss Susannah Snoddy.
National Banner & Nashville Advertiser (Fri., May 4, 1832)

Sampson, Mr. William S. married at Cincinnatti to Miss Ann Maria Coolidge.
National Banner & Nashville Whig (Fri., Sept. 9, 1831)

Samuel, Miss Sarah E. married to Mr. Samuel Brown.

Sandck, Dr. Joseph of Williamson County married by the Rev. William B. Carpenter to Miss Nancy Eliza Northern of Davidson County.
Nashville Whig (Fri., Dec. 3, 1841)

Sanders, Miss Ann T. married to Edward B. Bartlett Esq.

Sanders, Mr. Charles married in Nashville on Wednesday 29th Aug. by the Rev. William Hume to Miss Ann Rawlings all of Nashville.
National Banner & Nashville Daily Advertiser (Fri., Aug. 31, 1832)

Sanders, Capt. Daniel T. of Memphis married on Tuesday 22nd inst. by the Rev. J. W. Hall to Miss Elizabeth Iradale of Davidson County.
Daily Republican Banner (Fri., Jan. 25, 1839)

Sanders, Miss Elizabeth married to Mr. T. Smith.

Sanders, John W. Esq. married at Louisville, Ky. to Miss Anna T. Blake.
National Banner & Nashville Whig (Wed., July 27, 1831)

Sanders, LaFayett, Esq. Attorney at law, married in Sumner County on Thursday last to Miss Mary Smith daughter of Col. George Smith.
The Nashville Whig & Tenn. Advertiser (April 4, 1818)

Sanders, Miss Mary Ann married to Mr. M. M. Dill.

Sanders, Miss Mary M. married to Col. Robert H. Lake.

Sanders, Miss Matilda married to Mr. John Slaughter.

Sanders, Mr. Robert A. married on the 12th inst. by the Rev. A. G.
Goodlett to Miss Alison E. Doom all of Nashville.
Nashville Whig (Sat., Dec. 14, 1844)

Sanders, Miss Sarah G. married to Col. Robert Wier.

Sanders, Mr. Simon T. of Denmark married in Haywood County to Zenobia
Aurelia Meredith.
National Banner & Nashville Whig (Thurs., June 24, 1830)

Sanders, Miss Tabitha married to Mr. Williams H. Moore.

Sanders, Mr. Uriah R. married in White County to Miss Nancy Simpson.
National Banner (Sat., April 18, 1829)

Sanderson, Mrs. Charlotte married to Mr. Sidney Tines
National Banner (Sat., June 27, 1829)

Sanderson, Mr. John F. of Gallatin married on the evening of the 8th
by the Rev. Mr. Bryant to Miss Mary Catharine Douglass of Sumner
County.
The Christian Record (Sat., July 17, 1847)

Sanderson, Mr. John F. of Gallatin married on the 8th inst. by the
Rev. Mr. Bryant to Miss Mary Catharine Douglass daughter of Mr. Isaac
C. Douglass of Sumner County.
The Politician & Weekly Nashville Whig (Fri., July 16, 1847)

Sanderson, Miss Mary M. married to Mr. Zebuton P. Cantrill.

Sanderson, Mr. Robert of this town (Nashville) married on Friday
evening to Miss Mary M. Franklin of Sumner County.
Nashville Whig (July 7, 1823)

Sanderson, Mr. Timothy married in Madison County, Ala. to Miss Susan
Grant.
National Banner & Nashville Whig (Thurs., July 29, 1830)

Sandford, Miss Ann H. married to Dr. Hiram Glasscock.

Sandford, Mr. Robert W. married in Tipton County to Miss Francis D.
Small.
National Banner & Nashville Whig (Sat., Jan. 6, 1827)

Sandy, Mr. William of Davidson County married on the 5th inst. to Miss
Floridia Howlett.
Nashville Republican (Sat., Aug. 8, 1835)

Sandy, Mr. William married on Wednesday evening 5th inst. to Miss
Florida Howlett both of Davidson County.
National Banner & Nashville Whig (Mon., Aug. 10, 1835)

Sanford, Miss Ann H. married to Dr. Hiram Glascock.

Sangester, Miss Mary married to Mr. Thomas Callender.

Sans, Miss Polly married to Mr. W. P. Brown.

Sappington, Mr. James married in Lincoln County to Miss Cynthia Norris.
National Banner & Nashville Whig (Thurs., June 24, 1830)

Sappington, Miss Lucy H. married to Mr. Walter D. Dabney.

Sappington, Dr. Mark B. married at Memphis to Mrs. Elizabeth Pendleton.
National Banner & Nashville Daily Advertiser (Wed., Jan. 9, 1833)

Sappington, Dr. M. B. married in Memphis to Mrs. Elizabeth Pendleton.
Nashville Republican & State Gazette (Fri., Jan. 9, 1833)

Sappington, Mr. Thomas S. married in September 1831 to Miss Sophronia Barnett.
The Western Weekly Review - Franklin, Tenn. (Fri., Sept. 23, 1831)

Sassee, Mr. Stephens married in Williamson County to Miss Elizabeth Wilson.
Nashville Whig (Aug. 11, 1823)

Satan, Mr. Israel journeyman cabinet maker married in Marilda U. C. 13th inst. to Miss Grace Parlor.
National Banner & Nashville Whig (Wed., May 18, 1831)

Satterfield, Miss Sarah A. married to Mr. J. M. Church.

Satterly, Mr. Henry married in Shippingport, Ky. to Miss Mary L. Mitchell.
National Banner & Nashville Whig (Sat., Dec. 13, 1828)

Satterwhite, Miss Eliza J. married to Capt. Edwin A. Turpin.

Satterwhite, Miss Sarah V. married to Mr. James M. Holloway.

Satterwhite, Dr. Thomas P. married in Lexington, Ky. to Miss Mary C. Breakinridge daughter of the late Joseph Cabell Breakinridge, Esq.
National Banner & Nashville Advertiser (Fri., Jan. 27, 1832)

Saunders, Miss Alethia married to Dr. R. P. Allison.

Saunders, Miss Almedia married to Col. Joseph H. Talbot.

Saunders, Miss Amanda married to Mr. Wm. Moore.

Saunders, Miss Ann married to Hon. Terry H. Cahal.

Saunders, Mr. Benj. R. married in Madison County, Ala. to Miss Mary R. Carter.
National Banner (March 31, 1826)

Saunders, Mr. C. C. married in Columbus, Ohio to Miss Susan F. Wright.
National Banner & Nashville Daily Advertiser (Thurs., Sept. 12, 1833)

Saunders, Curtius H. Esq. married at Ripley, Miss. on the 19th ult. to Miss Josephine McCree late of Jackson.
Nashville Whig (Fri., March 8, 1839)

Saunders, David M. Esq. married in Gallatin on the 11th inst. to Miss Jane Dwyer daughter of Jeremiah Dwyer.
National Banner & Nashville Whig (Fri., June 27, 1828)

Saunders, Miss Elizabeth married to Mr. W. N. Hawkins.

Saunders, Miss Elizabeth married to Mr. W. N. Hawkins.

Saunders, Miss Emily married to Col. Meredith P. Gentry.

Saunders, Miss Eugenia Cathesine married to John S. Simpson Esq.

Saunders, Miss Harriet married to Mortimer A. Martin Esq.

Saunders, Mr. James married at Frankfort, Ky. to Miss Nancy Jane Hardin.
National Banner & Nashville Whig (Fri., Feb. 19, 1830)

Saunders, Mr. John W. merchant of Springfield, Robertson County married in Maury County on the 30th ult. to Miss Cynthia H. Pillow daughter of the late Mr. Gideon Pillow.
National Banner & Nashville Daily Advertiser (Mon., Nov. 19, 1832)

Saunders, Miss Julian Maria married at Baton Rogue, La. to William R. Keepers.

Saunders, Miss Levinia married to Mr. Theadore Fagundus.

Saunders, Miss Martha married to Benjamin M. Bradford, Esq.

Saunders, Miss Mary Ann married to Dr. James W. Hoggart.

Saunders, Miss Mary P. married to Mr. Peter Tardiff, junior.

Saunders, Miss Sarah married to Robert L. Caruthers, Esq.

Saunders, Rev. Turner married in Lawrence County, Ala. to Miss Henrietta Millwater.
National Banner & Nashville Whig (Sat., July 22, 1826)

Saunders, Dr. Pascal W. formerly of Davidson County married in Dyer County, on the 21st inst. to Miss Susan Catherine Kinley daughter of John Kenley Esq.
National Banner & Nashville Daily Advertiser (Wed., March 20, 1833)

Saunders, Miss Susan married to Mr. David Allen.

Saunders, Miss Susannah married to Mr. Richard Cheatham.

Saunderson, Mr. Leonard married in Smith County to Miss Mary D. Duncan.
National Banner & Nashville Whig (Sat., June 16, 1827)

Savage, Miss Sarah N. married to Major John B. Dillahunty.

Savage, Wm. H. Esq. married at St. Louis to Miss Adelaida Hay of Cakakia, Ill.
National Banner (April 28, 1826)

Sawyer, Lieut. H. B. of the U. S. Nanvy married in Burlington, Vt. to Miss Rozelana Wadesworth.
National Banner & Nashville Daily Advertiser (Tues., Nov. 19, 1833)

Sawyer, Miss Lucinda married to Mr. William Sawyer.

Sawyer, Miss Polly married to Mr. Amos P. Balch.

Sawyer, Mr. William married in Warren County, Ky. to Miss Lucinda Sawyer
National Banner (March 10, 1826)

Saxton, Miss Elizabeth married to Mr. William H. Philips.

Sayer, Mr. Henry married in Williamson County to Miss Elizabeth Underwood.
National Banner & Nashville Whig (Wed., Dec. 7, 1831)

Sayer, Mr. Henry married in Williamson County to Miss Elizabeth Underwood.
National Banner & Nashville Whig (Wed., Dec. 7, 1831)

Saylar, Mr. John married at Little Rock, Ark. to Miss Charlotte Fowler.
National Banner (April 14, 1826)

Sayles, Dr. Wm. P. of Henderson County married in Wilson County on the 9th inst. to Miss Agnes Watkins.
National Banner & Nashville Daily Advertiser (Wed., Jan. 15, 1834)

Scales, Miss Ann B. married to Mr. Wm. Clark.

Scales, Miss Caledonia M. married to Mr. Herekiah F. Hamner.

Scales, Miss Elvira married to Mr. Jonas H. Menifee.

Scales, Mr. Jeremiah of Davidson County married on the 13th inst. to Miss Delilah Bosley.
Nashville Republican & State Gazette (Fri., June 14, 1833)

Scales, Mr. Jeremiah married in Davidson County to Miss Delilah Bosley.
National Banner & Nashville Daily Advertiser (Sat., June 15, 1833)

Scales, Miss Minerva married to Mr. J. B. Peebles.

Scales, William P. Esq. of Miss. married on Tuesday 24th inst. by Rev. R. W. January to Miss Mary Hardeman daughter of Constant Hardeman of Rutherford County.
Nashville Whig (Sat., Oct. 28, 1843)

Scantland, Miss Catharine H. married to Mr. Edward A. Mulford.

Scantland, Miss Martha E. married to Mr. William P. M. Daniel.

Scarborough, Mr. Wm. married in Wullivan County to Miss Sarah Gains.
Nashville Republican & State Gazette (Sat., Oct. 19, 1833)

Scheider, Miss Catharine of Nashville married to Mr. Christian Hofstetter of Fountain of Health.
The Christian Record (Sat., July 1st. 1848)

Schenck, Mr. John B. of New York married on 12th Sept. in Robertson County by the Rev. John Thomas Wheat to Miss Caroline Almira Bucknell daughter of Mr. D. D. Bucknell of Tenn.
Nashville Whig (Sat., Oct. 15, 1842)

Schetter, Mr. Philip of Giles County married Miss Virginia A. Wharton on Thursday May 10 by the Rev. Mr. Hume.
National Banner & Nashville Advertiser (Fri., May 11, 1832)

Schilderknect, Mr. Peter married at Unterwalden, Penn. by the Rev. Dietrich Schleichevelder to Miss Christiana Schiechtwood.
National Banner (Feb. 3, 1826)

Schingig, Mr. Napoleon married in Louisville, Ky. to Miss Barbara Bowen.
National Banner & Nashville Whig (Fri., March 13, 1835)

Scho, Madame Mary T. married to Prof. Henry Mannel.

Schooler, Miss Nancy married to Mr. Robert Winsett.

Schwing, Miss Maria S. married to Mr. William Kendrick.

Scoggins, Miss Mary married to Mr. Turner Lane, Jun.

Scott, Miss Arabella married to Maj. William M. Davis.

Scott, Miss Catherine married to Mr. W. Johnson.

Scott, Miss Catherine married to Mr. Richard Bearden Jr.

Scott, Charles Esq. of Vicksburg, Miss married on the 19th inst. by the Rev. J. T. Wheat at the residence of Dr. J. Shelby to Miss Elizabeth M. Bullus daughter of the late Joseph M. Bullus of Gallatin.
Nashville Union (Mon., Sept. 23, 1839)

Scott, Charles Esq. of Vicksburg, Miss. married last evening in Nashville by the Rev. J. T. Wheat to Miss Elizabeth M. Bullus daughter of the late Joseph M. Bullus of Gallatin.
Nashville Whig (Fri., Sept. 20, 1839)

Scott, Dr. David T. of Clarksville married in Winchester, Ten. to Miss Charity Ann Slatter of Winchester.
National Banner & Nashville Whig (Mon., Oct. 20, 1834)

Scott, Doctor David T. married in Franklin County, Tenn. on the 11th to Miss Charity Ann Slatter formerly of Hopkinsville, Ky.
National Banner & Nashville Daily Advertiser (Tues., Sept. 16, 1834)

Scott, Miss Eliza married to Preston W. Farrer Esq.

Scott, Miss Elizabeth married to Mr. Henry Clay, Jr.

Scott, Mr. George married in Davidson County to Miss Margaret Speece.
National Banner & Nashville Whig (Fri., July 29, 1831)

Scott, Mr. Hamden S. of Knox County married in Bledsoe County, Ten. to Miss Rebecca Kimmer.
National Banner & Nashville Whig (Fri., Jan. 23, 1835)

Scott, Mr. Harden married in Fayette County to Miss Elizabeth Smith.
National Banner & Nashville Whig (Mon., Dec. 13, 1830)

Scott, Jacob Jr. married in Williamson County, Ten. to Mary Dyer.
National Banner & Nashville Daily Advertiser (Mon., Aug. 26, 1833)

Scott, Mr. James married near Bolivar to Miss Eliza Land.
National Banner & Nashville Whig (July 28, 1827)

Scott, Mr. James A. married at Columbus, Crawford County to Miss Frances Thompson eldest daughter of Mr. David Thompson.
National Banner & Nashville Whig (Mon., March 20, 1837)

Scott, Mr. Jesse G. married in Madison County, Ala. to Miss Agatha P. Rice.
National Banner & Nashville Whig (Fri., May 20, 1831)

Scott, Mr. Jesse G. married in Madison County, Ala. to Miss Agatha P. Rice.
Nashville Republican & State Gazette (Thurs., May 19, 1831)

Scott, Mr. John married in Smith County, Ten. to Miss Sally Odom.
National Banner & Nashville Advertiser (Fri., May 4, 1832)

Scott, Mr. John of Pope County married in Johnson Cty, Ark. to Miss Nancy E. Jemison daughter of Judge Jemison.
National Banner & Nashville Whig (Wed., Feb. 25, 1835)

Scott, Mr. John married in Smith County, Tenn. to Miss Sally Odam.
National Banner & Nashville Daily Advertiser (Fri., May 4, 1832)

Scott, John N. Esq. married on Thursday evening the 26th ult. to Miss Betsey M. White daughter of Mr. L. White Esq. all of Knoxville.
Dec. 1818 - 12. Volumen, number & name of paper torn off

Scott, Mr. Joseph married in Knox County to Miss Mary Loew.
National Banner & Nashville Whig (Sat., Nov. 15, 1828)

Scott, Mr. Joshua married in Bedford County to Miss Mary Green.
National Banner & Nashville Daily Advertiser (Thurs., Aug. 23, 1832)

Scott, Miss Judith D. married to Mr. Josiah G. Brown.

Scott, Miss Lydia married to Mr. Jas. M. Barbour. -

Scott, Miss Martha married to Mr. Peter Wilson.

Scott, Miss Mary married to Mr. John Knight.

Scott, Miss Mary Ann married to William Swan Esq.

Scott, Miss Mary Jane married to Mr. Calvin M. Hickey.

Scott, Miss Matilda married to Mr. William Kerley.

Scott, Miss Mildred married to Mr. Joseph Russell.

Scott, Miss Nancy married to Mr. Jesse Phillips.

Scott, Robert W. Esq. married at Frankfort, Ky. to Miss Elizabeth
Brown daughter of Dr. Preston Brown.
National Banner & Nashville Whig (Mon., Oct. 31, 1831)

Scott, Miss Sarah married to Mr. William Bizzell.

Scott, Miss Sarah married to Mr. Wm. Bizzell.

Scott, Mr. S. M. of the City Hotel married on Tuesday the 25th inst.
by the Rev. H. R. Puryear to Miss Mary J. Waggoner of Ballard Co., Ky.
Nashville True Whig & Weekly Commercial Register (Fri., April 4, 1850)

Scott, Rev. W. A. of Louisiana married on the 19th by the Rev. Mr.
Lapsley to Miss Ann Nicholson of Nashville.
The Union (Thurs., Dec. 21, 1836)

Scott, Rev. W. A. of Louisiana married in Nashville, Jan. 19th by the
Rev. Mr. Lapsley to Miss Ann Nicholson of Nashville.
Nashville Republican (Thurs., Jan. 21, 1836)

Scott, Rev. W. A. of Louisiana married on the 19th inst. by the Rev.
Mr. Lapsley to Miss Ann Nicholson of Nashville.
National Banner & Nashville Whig (Wed., Jan. 20, 1836)

Scott, Mr. Walter of Springfield married on the 15th at McMinnville
by the Rev. Mr. Stone to Miss Mary E. Grundy of McMinnville.
Nashville Whig (Tues., Dec. 22, 1846)

Scott, Mr. Walter of Springfield married on the 15th inst. at McMinnville by the Rev. Mr. Stone to Miss Mary E. Grundy of the former place.
The Christian Record (Sat., Dec. 26, 1846)

Scott, Mr. William married in Maury County to Miss Martha Morgan.
National Banner & Nashville Whig (Wed., June 1, 1831)

Scott, Mr. William C. married in Maury County to Miss Martha Morgan.
National Banner & Nashville Whig (Wed., June 1, 1831)

Scott, Mr. Wm. G. married in Maury County to Miss Elizabeth Stratton.
National Banner & Nashville Daily Advertiser (Wed., March 6, 1833)

Scott, Mr. William P. married in Somerville, Morgan County, Ala. to
Miss Eliza R. Van Dyke.
National Banner & Nashville Whig (June 24, 1826)

Scott, Mr. William Parker married in Jackson, Miss. to Miss Fanny
May Bibb daughter of the late Judge Bibb of Ala.
Nashville Whig (Thurs., June 25, 1846)

Scott, Major General Winfield of the United States Army married near
Richmond, Va. to Miss Maria D. Mayo.
The Nashville Whig (April 2, 1817)

Scovel, Miss Sophia P. married to Mr. Thomas C. Webb.

Scruggs, Miss Mary married to Mr. Samuel Jarred.

Scudder, Miss Elizabeth S. married to Mr. Thomas C. Ryall.

Seals, Mr. Drery married on Thursday the 21st to Miss Susan Oliver daughter of James Oliver all of Dickson County.
Nashville Union (Fri., Nov. 29, 1839)

Searcy, Miss Elizabeth H. married to Dr. William A. East.

Searcy, Miss Elvira J. married to Mr. Andrew Erwin Jr.

Searcy, Granville D. Esq. married in Tipton County to Miss M. A. Booker.
National Banner & Nashville Advertiser (Wed., Feb. 15, 1832)

Searcy, Mr. John O. of Ky. married at Port Gibson, Miss to Miss Mary Ann Vandorn.
National Banner & Nashville Whig (Sat., May 12, 1827)

Searcy, Miss Julia Ann married to Capt. James H. Dearing.

Searcy, Mr. Lafayette married in Henry County to Miss Sophia Reid.
National Banner & Nashville Whig (Fri., Feb. 26, 1830)

Searcy, Miss Marsha married to Mr. Charles D. M'Lean.

Searcy, Mrs. Mary B. married to Mr. James D. Merrell.

Searcy, Mr. Orville D. of this city married on the 25th ult. by the Rev'd George Newton to Miss Mary Ann Patton of Bedford County.
The Nashville Clarion (March 7, 1821)

Searcy, Miss Sarah H. married to Mr. Charles Slater.

Seat, Mr. William G. W. married on Tuesday 14th inst. by Joseph L. Jarrell Esq. at his residence to Miss Frances Pully all of Davidson County.
Nashville True Whig & Weekly Commercial Register (Fri., Jan. 17, 1851)

Seawell, Mr. John H. married in Fayette County to Miss Louisa A. Hendon.
National Banner & Nashville Whig (Sat., May 17, 1828)

Seawell, Miss Mary married to Capt. George W. Mabry.

Seay, Miss Eliza married to Mr. C. A. Phatridge.

Seay, Miss Frances married to Mr. William Morris.

Seay, Miss Jane W. married to Mr. Felix G. McKay.

Seay, John M. D. of Ala. married in Nashville on the 21st ult. by the Rt. Rev. James H. Otey D. D. Bishop of Tennessee to Salina Patten Wheat daughter of Rev. J. T. Wheat D.D. Rector of Christ Church, Nashville.
The Christian Record (Sat., Jan. 8, 1848)

Seay, John M. D. of Ala. married on the 21st inst. by the Rt. Rev. James Harvey Otey, D.D. Bishop of Tennessee to Salina Patten Wheat daughter of Rev. J. T. Wheat, D.D.
The Politician & Weekly Nashville Whig (Fri., Dec. 31, 1847)

Seay, Mr. Joseph married in Knoxville to Miss Christiana Jent.
National Banner & Nashville Whig (Sat., Aug. 18, 1827)

Seay, Miss Matilda married to Mr. Edward C. Eggleson.

Seay, Miss Nancy married to Mr. Anderson Hill.

Sebree, Maj. Wm. married in Pensacola to Mrs. Ann S. Clark.
National Banner & Nashville Whig (Sat., Sept. 2, 1826)

Secrest, Miss Martha married to Mr. Thomas Holloway.

Sedan, Mr. David Z. of Cincinnati married at Elizabethtown, Ky. to Miss Amanda Malvina Percefull.
National Banner (Sat., July 4, 1829)

Sedwell, Miss Ann married to Mr. Allen Redman.

See, Miss Martha married to Mr. Joseph R. Carty.

Seigler, Miss Elizabeth S. married to Mr. James M. Hawkins.

Seip, John Esq. of Louisiana married on the evening of the 17th inst. by the Rev. Dr. Edgar to Miss Eliza Martin daughter of the late Thomas Martin Esq. of Davidson County.
Nashville Whig (Fri., Oct. 18, 1839)

Sellers, Miss Elizabeth married to Mr. Henry Newman.

Sellers, Mr. Hardy married in Maury County to Miss Ann Odle.
National Banner & Nashville Whig (Sat., Dec. 17, 1831)

Sellman, Miss Julia A. E. married to James F. Conover, Esq.

Senter, Miss Catherine married to Mr. Isaac Crow.

Senter, Miss Susan M. married to Mr. William B. Hall.

Senter, Miss Susanna M. married to Mr. Wm. B. S. Hall.

Sergeant, Miss Paulna married to Mr. David M. Richardson.

Serginer, Mr. Jesse married in Limestone County, Ala. to Miss Mary Ann Bell.
National Banner & Nashville Daily Advertiser (Tues., Sept. 3, 1832)

Sessions, Miss Carolina married to John Baynton Esq.

Sessions, Mr. J. P. married in Williamson County to Miss Anna G. Hardeman.
Nashville Whig (Sat., July 11, 1846)

Sessoms, Miss Martha married to Mr. Hugh H. Shaw.

Settle, Miss Charity married to Mr. John Bond.

Settle, Mr. Cooper one of the editors of the Louisville Examiner married in Louisville, Ky. to Miss Sarah Ann Cornell.
National Banner & Nashville Daily Advertiser (Fri., March 1, 1833)

Seudder, Phillip I, Esq. married on the 11th inst. at Shelbyville to Miss Harriett Whitney both of that town.
Nashville Whig (Feb. 26, 1823)

Sevier, Miss Ann married in Harden County to Mr. James Irwin.

Sevier, Mr. E. G. married in Roan County to Miss Mary C. Brown.
National Banner & Nashville Whig (Sat., Dec. 15, 1827)

Sevier, Rev. Elbert F. of Washington County, Tenn. married in Shelby County, Ala. to Miss Matilda D. Powell.
National Banner & Nashville Daily Advertiser (Thurs., Aug. 23, 1832)

Sevier, Miss Eliza M. married to John T. Donald, Esq.

Sevier, Col. George W. of Davidson County married on the 17th inst. by the Rev. Dr. Edgar to Miss Sarah Shirley of Nashville.
Nashville Whig (Tues., Nov. 22, 1842)

Sevier, John Major married lately, of Jonesborough to Miss Richards of Batstoe, New Jersey.
Knoxville Gazette (Thurs, April 10, 1794)

Sevier, Miss Laura married to Mr. Henry L. Norvell.

Sevier, Miss Mary married to Mr. James Stewart.

Sevier, Nancy Miss married to Mr. Walter King.

Sewell, Rev. Benjamin H. of Williamson County married in Madison County to Miss Lucy H. Brown.
National Banner (March 24, 1826)

Sewell, Miss Malinda married to Dr. William Rogers.

Sewell, Mr. William married on the 8th of Oct. to Miss Ann Baker.
Nashville Republican (Tues., Jan. 19, 1836)

Sexton, Miss Catherine married to Mr. Micajah Manard.

Shackelford, E. L. Esq. married in Madison County, Ky. to Miss Margaret Miller.
National Banner (March 3, 1826)

Shackelford, Miss Elizabeth married to Mr. Robert A. Patrick.

Shackelford, Mr. Thomas married on Wednesday evening last to Miss Eliza C. Pulham of Williamson County.
The Nashville Whig (April 30, 1817)

Shackford, Miss Amanda Jane married to Mr. Nathan Ranney.

Shacklford, Miss Caroline A. married to Mr. John M. Shannon.

Shaddon, Sarah A. married to William H. Neal.

Shaddy, Miss Mary married to Mr. William Delk.

Shaffer, Mr. Christian married at Louisville, Ky. to Miss Julia Hoke.
National Banner & Nashville Whig (Sat., April 26, 1828)

Shaffer, Mr. James married near Cairo to Miss Giles.
National Banner & Nashville Whig (Sat., Jan. 6, 1827)

Shalders, Mr. Levi married in Smith County to Miss Adeline Oldham.
National Banner & Nashville Whig (Tues., Dec. 13, 1831)

Shall, Mr. Ephraim P. married in Nashville last evening by the Rev. Mr. Hume to Miss Ann B. Spence.
National Banner & Nashville Whig (Fri., Sept. 16, 1831)

Shall, Mr. Ephraim P. of Nashville married Miss Ann B. Spence.
Nashville Republican & State Gazette (Sat., September 17, 1831)

Shall, Mr. Jacob merchant of Pulaski married on Monday evening last to Miss Ann James of this vicinity.
Nashville Whig (Dec. 15, 1823)

Shall, Mrs. J. J. married to Dr. David Holt.

Shall, Miss Margaret Jane married to Thomas B. Winston Esq.

Shall, Miss Sally married to Mr. John M'Gavock.

Shallcross, Mr. John E. married in Louisville, Ky. to Miss Louisa W. Taylor.
National Banner & Nashville Daily Advertiser (Thurs., Oct. 18, 1832)

Shannon, Mr. Thomas S. married on Thursday evening last to Miss
Catharine Waters both of this town.
The Nashville Whig (Feb. 26, 1817)

Shannon, Mr. Pierce married at Louisville, Ky. to Miss Elmira J.
Taylor.
National Banner & Nashville Whig (Wed., July 6, 1831)

Shannon, Miss Mary married to Mr. William T. Merritt.

Shannon, Mr. John M. formerly of Davidson County married Miss Caroline
A. Shacklford both of Loundes County, Miss. on 9th ult.
Nashville Republican & State Gazette (Tues., Feb. 11, 1834)

Shannon, Mr. John A. married in Wilson County on the 8th of Jan. to
Miss Winey Clemmons.
National Banner & Nashville Daily Advertiser (Fri., Jan. 17, 1834)

Shannon, Miss Jane married to Mr. William Shaw.

Shannon, Mr. James Esq. of Wheeling, W. Va. married in Kentucky to
Mrs. Susan M'Dowell
Nashville Whig (May 31, 1824)

Shannon, Mr. Francis married in Madison County to Miss Mary Ewing.
National Banner & Nashville Whig (Sat., June 23, 1827)

Shamon, Mr. Wm. married at Lexington, Ky. to Miss Lucy Jane Hawkins.
National Banner & Nashville Whig (Sat., April 14, 1827)

Shankle, Mr. Elias married in Henry County to Miss Matilda Swor.
National Banner & Nashville Advertiser (Wed., Jan. 18, 1832)

Shanklin, Mr. Geo. W. married in Bedford County to Miss Eleanor Wilson.
National Banner & Nashville Whig (Sat., Aug. 26, 1826)

Shapard, Mr. Robert P. married in Rutherford County to Miss Parthena
Mitchell.
National Banner (Sat., Nov. 21, 1829)

Shappard, Miss Matilda married to Mr. A. S. Caldwell.

Sharkey, Mr. Patrick married in Hinds County, Miss. to Miss Matilda
Pucket.
National Banner & Nashville Whig (Sat., Feb. 3, 1827)

Sharod, Miss Catherine married to Mr. David McHoffie.

Sharod, Miss Catharine married to Mr. David McHaffie.

Sharp, Miss Ann married to Mr. Caswell Lea.

Sharp, Miss Eliza married to Mr. Payton Moulton.

Sharp, Miss Elizabeth C. married to Mr. Alansin Cannon.

Sharp, Miss Elizabeth M. married to James F. Ross.

Sharp, Mr. Hiram of M'Minn County married to Miss Catherine Herring
in Anderson County.
National Banner & Nashville Daily Advertiser (Mon., July 15, 1833)

Sharp, Miss Jemima C. married to Mr. Charles T. Hogsett.

Sharp, Miss Lucy married to Mr. Charles Reed.

Sharp, Mr. Samuel M. married in Williamson County to Miss Ann Henderson.
National Banner & Nashville Whig (Sat., Aug. 4, 1827)

Sharp, Mr. Wm., aged 18, married in Hawkins County to Mrs. Rebecca Varnel aged 64.
National Banner & Nashville Whig (Sat., Oct. 28, 1826)

Sharpe, Miss Eleanor E. married to Mr. John M. Becton.

Shaw, Miss Elizabeth married to Mr. James Crawford.

Shaw, Mr. George married in Bedford County to Miss Sophia Armstrong daughter of Dr. James L. Armstrong.
National Banner & Nashville Advertiser (Thurs., Sept. 6, 1832)

Shaw, Mr. George married in Bedford County to Miss Sophia Armstrong daughter of Dr. James L. Armstrong.
National Banner & Nashville Daily Advertiser (Thurs., Sept. 6, 1832)

Shaw, Mr. Hugh H. married in Maury County to Miss Martha Sessoms.
National Banner & Nashville Whig (Fri., Feb. 12, 1830)

Shaw, Isaac married in Williamson County to Miss Sarah Gatlin.
The Western Weekly Review - Franklin, Ten. (Fri., Dec. 14, 1832)

Shaw, Mr. James G. married in Bedford County to Miss Sarah Koance.
National Banner & Nashville Daily Advertiser (Fri., Jan. 27, 1832)

Shaw, Mr. James S. married at New Orleans to Miss Virginia Hopp.
National Banner & Nashville Whig (Sat., Jan. 6, 1827)

Shaw, Mr. Pinkney married in Rutherford County, Ten. to Miss Sarah Morriss daughter of Capt. George Morriss.
National Banner & Nashville Whig (Mon., Nov. 10, 1834)

Shaw, Miss Priscilla married to Mr. Wm. B. Swain.

Shaw, Mr. Samuel E. of Louisville married in Scott County, Ky. to Miss Catherine S. Glass.
National Banner & Nashville Whig (Mon., Dec. 13, 1830)

Shaw, Mr. S. H. of Trenton married in Fayette County to Miss Caroline Douglass.
Nashville Whig (Thurs., April 30, 1846)

Shaw, Solomon H. of Trenton, T. married in Dixon County on the 18th inst. by the Rev. Samuel H. Peak to Miss Angeline S. Ross daughter of James Ross, Esq.
National Banner & Nashville Daily Advertiser (Fri., Dec. 27, 1833)

Shaw, Mr. William married in Jefferson County, Ky. to Miss Jane Shannon.
National Banner & Nashville Daily Advertiser (Fri., Feb. 15, 1833)

Shealds, Mr. William married in Davidson County to Miss Maria Clay on Thursday evening 27th inst.
National Banner & Nashville Whig (Fri., Jan. 28, 1831)

Shearley, Miss Elizabeth married to Mr. James Lowrey.

Shearon, Miss E. B. married to Col. J. C. Tipton.

Shearon, Miss Rebecca married to Mr. George Fisher.

Shearon, Mr. Thomas W. married on Wednesday evening the 12th in Dickson County to Miss Elizabeth Brewer.
National Banner & Nashville Whig (Sat., Dec. 15, 1827)

Shearon, Mr. Thomas W. married in Nashville on the 17th inst. by the Rev. Mr. Gwyn to Miss Laetitia H. Brewer.
National Banner & Nashville Whig (Fri., Nov. 18, 1831)

Sheerman, Miss Martha married to Mr. James B. Davis.

Shelburn, Miss Elizabeth married to Mr. Joseph Tennison.

Shelby, Miss Ann married to Washington Barrow, Esq.

Shelby, Miss Caroline Laura married to Mr. Henry Blood.

Shelby, Mr. Evon married in Maury County, Ten. to Miss Eliza Roades.
National Banner & Nashville Whig (Fri., April 10, 1835)

Shelby, Miss Jane married to Dr. P. Rubel.

Shelby, Mr. Joe of Texas married on the 9th inst. by the Rev. Mr.
Slater to Miss R. S. Cahmbers daugther of J. Chambers Esq. of Gallatin,
Tennessee.
Nashville Whig (Thurs., Sept. 17, 1846)

Shelby, Miss Levisa married to Mr. J. E. Brunson.

Shelby, Orville Esq. of this state married at Lexington, Ky. on the
12th inst. to Miss Ann Maria Boswell daughter of Dr. Joseph Boswell.
National Banner (Sat., Nov. 21, 1829)

Shelby, Miss Priscilla married to Mr. David Williams.

Shelby, Miss Sarah B. D. married to Dr. Miles S. Watkins.

Shelby, Miss Sarah M. married to Mr. Richard Higgins Jun.

Shell, Miss Amanda married to Mr. William Thompson.

Shell, Mr. James A. married in Giles County to Miss Lemantine Perry.
National Banner (Sat., April 18, 1829)

Shelton, Mr. Abram married in Paris, Ten. to Miss Susan Lewis.
National Banner & Nashville Whig (Sat., April 26, 1828)

Shelton, Miss America married to Mr. N. Bond.

Shelton, Miss Charlotte married to Mr. Elisha Jones.

Shelton, Mr. Geo. W. married in Maury County to Nancy Fitzgerald.
National Banner & Nashville Advertiser (Thurs., April 5, 1832)

Shelton, Mr. M. L. married on the 7th inst. by Rev. J. B. McFerrin to
Miss I. W. Manier all of Nashville.
Nashville True Whig & Weekly Commercial Register (Fri., Aug. 9, 1850)

Shelton, Mr. Thomas of Giles married in Lauderdale County, Ala. to Miss
Blanche C. Chambers.
National Banner & Nashville Whig (Sat., Sept. 6, 1828)

Shepard, Mr. James M. married on Sunday the 11th inst. at the residence
of Henry Ligon by Thomas H. Cawthon, Esq. to Miss Mary G. Roberts
daughter of Samuel Rogers Esq. all of Wilson County.
Nashville Whig (Tues., Jan. 20, 1846)

Shepard, Miss Martha married to Mr. Joshua W. M'Cown.

Shepherd, Miss Catherine married to Mr. John H. Trigg.

Shepherd, Mr. Charles married in Christian County, Ky. to Miss Susan
Hobson.
National Banner (Jan. 20, 1826)

Shepherd, Mr. James M. of Granville, Jackson County to Miss Eliza J.
Strother married on 9th inst. by Rev. Jesse Moreland daughter of Judd

Strother Esq. of Smith County.
Nashville Whig (Thurs. Feb. 23, 1843)

Shepherd, Mr. Joseph H. of Nashville married in Elizabethtown, Ky.
on the 3d inst. by the Rev. Mr. Lovelace to Miss Elizabeth A. Poston
of Elizabethtown.
Nashville Whig (Mon., Nov. 8, 1841)

Shepherd, Miss Mary married to Mr. James S. Garbra.

Shepherd, Sarah married to Danl. L. White.

Shepherd, Mr. William B. married on Yesterday evening 20th inst. by
the Rev. Dr. Edgar to Miss Eliza J. Ferguson all of Nashville.
Nashville True Whig & Weekly Commercial Register. (Fri., June 28, 1850)

Sheppard, B. Harper Attorney at law of Jackson, Tenn. married in Nash-
ville on the 2d inst. by the Rev. A. H. Dashiell to Miss Phereby
E. R. Donelson of Williamson County.
Nashville Union (Fri., Aug. 3, 1838)

Sheppard, B. Harper, Attorney at law of Jackson, Tenn. married in
Nashville on the 2d inst. by the Rev. A. H. Dashiell to Miss Phererey
E. R. Donelson daughter of the late Lemuel Donelson of Williamson
County.
Nashville Whig (Fri., Aug. 3, 1838)

Sheppard, Miss Martha married to Mr. Henry Cook.

Sheppard, Miss Martha M. married to Mr. A. S. Caldwell.

Sheppard, Miss Matilda N. married to Mr. A. S. Caldwell

Sherrell, Mr. David L. of Lincoln County, N. C. married in Iredell
County, N. C. to Eleanor M. M'Knight of Fayette County, Tenn.
National Banner & Nashville Whig (Mon., Nov. 7, 1831)

Sherrell, Miss Martha married to Mr. William F. Thorp.

Sherrod, Mr. Felix married in Courtland, Ala. to Miss Sarah A. Parish
daughter of the late Colonel Joel Parish.
National Banner & Nashville Whig (Fri., June 5, 1835)

Sherrod, Mr. Felix married in Courtland, Ala. to Miss Sarah A. Parrish
of Nashville.
Nashville Republican (Thurs., June 4, 1835)

Shewell, Thomas Esq. of Philadelphia married in Nashville on Saturday
evening last. by the Rev. Dr. Lindsley to Miss Augusta Anderson of
that city.
National Banner & Nashville Whig (Thurs., Nov. 11, 1830)

Shider, Mr. A. B. of Nashville married on Thursday last to Miss
Elizabeth Garner.
Nashville Republican & State Gazette (Sat., April 26, 1834)

Shields, Mr. Benjamin Franklin married in Montgomery County, Ten.
to Miss Susan A. Bowls.
National Banner & Nashville Daily Advertiser (Tues., Aug. 20, 1833)

Shields, Miss Catharine married to Maj. Moses G. Reeves.

Shields, Mr. John S. married in Roane County to Miss Sarah Haggard
daughter of John Haggard, Esq.
National Banner (Sat., Oct. 3, 1829)

Shields, Miss Rebecca married to Mr. John S. Ustick.

Shields, Miss Unity married to Zebulon Hassell.

Shillington, Miss Cynthia married to Mr. Smith G. McCall.

Shindlebower, Mr. Abner married in Franklin Co., Ky. to Miss. Nancy Beaver.
National Banner & Nashville Daily Advertiser (Fri., July 18, 1834)

Shipp, Miss Caroline married to John H. Phelps, Esq.

Shipp, Miss Margaret married to Mr. James Parrish.

Shipp, Mr. William married in Knox County to Miss Martha Barnwell.
National Banner & Nashville Whig (Mon., Oct. 11, 1830)

Shirley, Mr. Lewis married in Oldham County, Ky. to Miss Paulina Keller.
National Banner & Nashville Whig (Mon., July 26, 1830)

Shirley, Miss Mary Ann married to Mr. Alfred Herr.

Shirley, Miss Mary Ann married to Mr. R. R. Tice.

Shirley, Miss Mary Ann married to Mr. R. R. Rice.

Shirley, Paul merchant of this place (Nashville) married on Tuesday evening last (Dec. 6th, 1814) by Rev. Mr. Blackburn to Miss Sarah C. Gibson of Jefferson.
Nashville Whig (Tues., Dec. 13, 1814)

Shirley, Miss Sarah married to Col. George W. Sevier.

Shivers, Miss Rowena C. married to Mr. James J. McDaniel.

Shmidt, Mr. Andrew married at Tuscaloosa, Ala. to Mrs. Polly Wier.
National Banner & Nashville Whig (June 17, 1826)

Shockley, Miss married to Mr. D. B. Crawford.

Shockley, Miss Algeline married to Mr. D. B. Crawford.

Shockley, Miss Nancy married to Col. Jonathan Webster.

Shockley, Miss Nancy C. married to Col. Jonathan Webster.

Shoemake, Miss Lydia married to Mr. Henry Beasley.

Shoemaker, Miss Nancy married to Mr. Ezekiel A. M'Crackin.

Shores, Miss Mary Ann married to Co. Watson M. Cooke.

Short, Miss Lillian married to Mr. Samuel Talley.

Short, Miss Milly married to Mr. John Goodrich.

Short, Thomas married in Williamson County to Unice T. Brown.
National Banner & Nashville Daily Advertiser (Mon., Aug. 26,1833)

Shotwell, Miss Edith married to Mr. O. D. Sledge.

Shotwell, Mr. Robert married in Madison County, Ala. to Miss Mary E. H. Taliaferro.
National Banner & Nashville Whig (Sat., Dec. 9, 1826)

Showard, Miss Ann O. married to Mr. Joseph C. Irwin.

Shreve, Miss Sarah Ann married to Rev. T. Fanning.

Shreve, Mr. Thomas T. married in Bath County, Ky. to Miss Eliza Ann Rogers.
National Banner (Jan. 27, 1826)

Shreve, Dr. William M. married in Lexington, Ky. to Miss Caroline
Boyce.
National Banner & Nashville Whig (Sat., Jan. 17, 1829)

Shrewsbury, Miss J. L. E. of Nashville married to Mr. Charles I. Love.

Shrewsbury, Miss Mary D. married to Mr. Hezekeah Bradbury Esq.

Shropshire, Miss Sarah married to Mr. H. P. Dorris.

Shryock, Miss Elizabeth married to Mr. Thomas Hickman.

Shryock, Mr. Gideon of Lexington married in Frankfort, Ky. to Miss
Elizabeth Bacon.
National Banner (Sat., July 11, 1829)

Shuffield, Miss Lucinda married to Mr. John M. Rowell.

Shuford, Mr. Jacob R., merchant, married in Ashville, N. C. to Miss
Mary E. Smith daughter of Col. J. M. Smith.
National Banner & Nashville Daily Advertiser (Wed., July 9, 1834)

Shull, Miss Sally married to Mr. William C. Grimes.

Shultz, Mr. C. F. of Nashville married on the 4th inst. by the Rev.
J. Thomas Wheat to Miss Petronille Mary Lavisson of Mobile, Ala.
Nashville Whig (Fri., Nov. 5, 1841)

Shumaker, Mr. Wm. C. married in Rutherford County to Miss Elizabeth
Stator.
National Banner (Sat., Oct. 10, 1829)

Shutmate, Miss Margaret J. married to Rev. William J. Keith.

Shute, Miss Elizabeth married to Mr. B. Spence.

Shute, Mr. Lee married in Davidson County to Miss Margaret Dunn on
Wednesday 12th inst.
National Banner & Nashville Whig (Mon., Jan. 17, 1831)

Shute, Mr. Lee married to Miss Margaret Dunn of this County.
Nashville Republican & State Gazette (Sat., Jan. 15, 1831)

Shute, Miss Louisa V. married to Mr. John C. Wilson.

Shute, Miss Martha married to Andrew J. Hoover, Esq.

Shute, Miss Martha married to J. Hoover Esq.

Shute, Mr. Philip S. married Miss Hannah P. Demoss both of this County.
National Banner & Nashville Daily Advertiser (Sat., Jan. 21, 1832)

Shute, Mr. Philip S. married in Davidson County to Miss Hannah De Moss.
Nashville Republican & State Gazette (Sat., Jan. 21, 1832)

Shute, Miss Sussannah married to Mr. James Harden.

Shute, Mr. Thomas married on the 6th inst. by the Rev. Dr. Edgar to
Miss Tennessee Demoss daughter of Abraham Demoss, Esq. all of
Davidson County.
Daily Republican Banner (Thurs., Feb. 13, 1840)

Shute, Mr. Thomas married on the 6th inst. by the Rev. Dr. Edgar to
Miss Tennessee Demoss daughter of Abram Demoss, Esq. all of Davidson
County.
Nashville Whig (Mon., Feb. 10, 1840)

Shibley, Lieut E. Sproat married at Detroit to Miss Harriet L. Hunt.
National Banner & Nashville Whig (Fri., June 17, 1831)

Sibley, Lieut. E. Sproat of the U. S. Army married at Detroit to Miss Harriet L. Hunt daughter of Col. Henry J. Hunt.
National Banner & Nashville Whig (Fri., June 17, 1831)

Sidebottom, Mr. Fielding L. of Dover married in Stewart County to Miss Eliza Oneal.
National Banner & Nashville Advertiser (Mon., March 5, 1832)

Sides, Mr. Nelson married in Henry County to Miss Elizabeth Bose.
National Banner & Nashville Advertiser (Mon., April 23, 1832)

Sides, Nelson married in Henry County to Miss Elizabeth Bose.
National Banner & Nashville Daily Advertiser (Mon., April 23, 1832)

Sidwell, Mr. Joshua married in Bourbon County, Ky. to Miss Mary M'Laughlin.
National Banner (March 10, 1826)

Siler, Mr. Jacob married on the 31st to Miss Margaret Moad both of Campbell County.
National Banner & Nashville Daily Advertiser (Mon., Feb. 11, 1833)

Sill, Mr. Shadrock married at Cincinnati to Miss Mary Lytle.
National Banner & Nashville Whig (Mon., Sept. 6, 1830)

Sills, Miss Mary of Rutherford married to Mr. Joseph B. Turner.

Silsbee, Miss Mary C. married to Jared Sparks, Esq.

Silvertooth, Miss Minerva married to Mr. C. McFadder.

Silvey, Mr. Jacob married in Madison County, Ala. to Miss Sarah Ann Scruggs.
National Banner & Nashville Whig (Wed., Aug. 3, 1831)

Simmons, Mr. Benjamin D. married in Logan County, Ky. to Miss Jane Webb.
National Banner & Nashville Daily Advertiser (Mon., May 13, 1833)

Simmons, Miss Charlotte married to Mr. Jacob A. Pierce.

Simmans, Mr. Hawkins married in Williamson County to Miss Mary T. Jackson.
National Banner & Nashville Whig (Wed., Dec. 7, 1831)

Simmans, Mr. Hawkins married in Williamson County to Miss Mary T. Jackson.
The Western Weekly Review - Franklin, Tenn. (Fri., Dec. 2, 1831)

Simmons, Capt. John married in Franklin County, Ten. on the 15th inst. to Miss Nancy Hudnall.
National Banner & Nashville Whig (Sat., Feb. 16, 1828)

Simmons, Miss Mary married to Mr. Thomas Thompson.

Simmons, Mr. Yancy married to Miss Eliza R. Hiter in Franklin on the 14th.
National Banner & Nashville Whig (Fri., Jan. 29, 1830)

Simms, Mr. Douglass R. married in Shelbyville on the 2d inst. to Miss Barbary Jane Brooks.
Nashville Whig (Mon., Aug. 6, 1838)

Simms, Miss Jerusha married to Aaron Ready, Esq.

Simons, Mr. Joel married in Hardeman County to Miss Elizabeth Green.
National Banner & Nashville Whig (Fri., July 18, 1828)

Simonton, Mr. William married in Maury County on the 16th of May to
Miss Harriet N. Ramsey.
National Banner & Nashville Whig (Fri., June 10, 1831)

Simonton, Mr. Wm. married in Maury County to Miss Harriet N. Ramsey
in Maury County.
Nashville Republican & State Gazette (Thurs., June 9, 1831)

Simpson, Mr. Andrew married in Henry County to Miss Polly Williams.
National Banner & Nashville Whig (Fri., Nov. 18, 1831)

Simpson, Mr. Elias married in Warren County, Ky. to Miss Nancy Biggs.
National Banner & Nashville Whig (Wed., Sept. 21, 1831)

Simpson, Mr. Elias H. married in this town on the 8th inst. by the
Rev. Mr. Hume to Miss Adeline Fisher.
National Banner & Nashville Whig (Sat., May 17, 1828)

Simpson, Mr. Elias married to Miss Nancy Biggs married in Warren Co.,Ky.
National Banner & Nashville Whig (Wed., Sept. 21, 1831)

Simpson, Mr. Francis married in Jonesborough, Ten. to Miss Mary C.
Blair daughter of the Hon. Jno. Blair.
National Banner & Nashville Daily Advertiser (Fri., Sept. 19, 1834)

Simpson, Mr. George married in Henry County to Miss Martha Davis.
National Banner & Nashville Advertiser (Mon., April 23, 1832)

Simpson, John S. Esq. married at the fountain of health, Davidson
County by the Rev. Mr. Weller to Miss Eugenia Catherine Saunders
daughter of William Saunders Esq.
National Banner & Nashville Whig (Thurs., Nov. 11, 1830)

Simpson, Miss Mary married to Mr. Jefferson Griffin.
National Banner & Nashville Advertiser (Mon., Feb. 6, 1832)

Simpson, Miss Mary married to Mr. James Anderson.

Simpson, Miss Mary married to Mr. Jefferson Griffin.

Simpson, Miss Mary married to Mr. D. S. Cheatham.

Simpson, Miss Mary Ann married to Mr. James G. Guthrie.

Simpson, Miss Mary A. H. married to Mr. John Queener.

Simpson, Miss Mary H. married to Mr. John S. Van De Graff.

Simpson, Miss Mary M. married to Mr. Daniel D. Jones.

Simpson, Miss Mary Selina married to John B. Cook, Esq.

Simpson, Miss Nancy married to Mr. Uriah R. Sanders.

Simpson, Mr. Thomas married in Lincoln County to Miss Nancy Rowark.
National Banner & Nashville Daily Advertiser (Tues., May 20, 1834)

Simpson, Mr. Washington H. married in Nashville on the 23d inst. by
the Rev. J. B. McFerrin to Miss Leathy Elizabeth Bolton.
Nashville Whig (Tues., June 28, 1842)

Simpson, Mr. Wm. married in Henry County to Miss Lucretia Malone.
National Banner & Nashville Daily Advertiser (Fri., Feb. 8, 1833)

Sims, Dr. of Rutherford County married in Winchester on the 11th
inst. to Miss Elizabeth Rawlings.
National Banner & Nashville Whig (Sat., Nov. 15, 1828)

Sims, Dr. David of Giles County married to Miss Nancy Adams.
Nashville Republican & State Gazette (Thurs., May 5, 1831)

Sims, Mr. David of Davidson County married in Sumner County on the
16th ult. to Miss Elizabeth Mitchell daughter of James Mitchell Esq.
The Nashville Whig & Tennessee Advertiser (Aug. 8, 1818)

Sims, Miss Frances L. married to Mr. John P. Smith.

Sims, Miss Jane H. married to Mr. Rob. C. Foster.

Sims, John G. Esq. married on Thursday evening the 10th inst. November
10, 1814, Nashville, to Miss A. Hightower of Williamson County daughter
of Capt. Richard Hightower.
Nashville Whig (Tues., Nov. 22, 1814)

Sims, Rebecca Watson married to Col. J. P. Campbell.

Sims, Mr. Robert L. married in Rutherford County to Miss Catherine
C. Hawkins.
National Banner & Nashville Whig (Fri., May 27, 1831)

Sims, Thomas married in Williamson County to Miss Mary S. Yeargin.
National Banner & Nashville Daily Advertiser (Wed., May 16, 1832)

Sims, Thomas married in Williamson County to Miss Mary S. Yeargin.
The Western Weekly Review - Franklin, Tenn. (Fri., May 11, 1832)

Sinclair, Catherine married to Edwin Forrest, Esq.

Sinclair, Miss Sarah married to Mr. Joseph Hukill.

Singleton, Miss Catherine C. married to Mr. Henry B. Champion.

Singleton, Miss Emily J. married to Mr. Robert P. Champ.

Singleton, Miss Mary Rebecca married to Hon. George M'Duffie.

Singleton, Miss Sarah Angelica married to Maj. Abraham Van Buren.

Sires, Mr. Bennett married in Williamson County to Miss Nancy Hamlet.
The Western Weekly Review - Franklin, Tenn. (Fri., Dec. 2, 1831)

Siris, Mr. Bennett married in Williamson County to Miss Nancy Hamlet.
National Banner & Nashville Whig (Wed., Dec. 7, 1831)

Sittler, Miss Caroline married to Mr. Gilbert Haaen.

Sivley, Miss Eliza married to Capt. John B. Cooper.

Sivley, Mr. Jacob married in Madison County, Ala. to Miss Sarah Ann
Scruggs.
National Banner & Nashville Whig (Wed., Aug. 3, 1831)

Skeggs, Mr. Thomas L. married in Nashville to Miss Mary Jane Boyd.
National Banner & Nashville Daily Advertiser (Sat., June 15, 1833)

Skeggs, Mr. Thos. L. of Nashville married on 12 inst. to Miss Mary Jane
Boyd of Nashville.
Nashville Republican & State Gazette (Fri., June 14, 1833)

Skillington, Miss Cynthia married to Mr. Smith G. McCall.

Skinkle, Miss Eliza married to Stephen M. Van Wyck, Esq.

Skinner, Elizabeth married to Dr. Joseph G. Mitchell.

Skipwith, Mr. George married in Maury County to Miss Mary Ann Newsom daughter of Maj. Wm. Newsom.
National Banner (Jan. 13, 1826)

Skyles, Mr. of Bowlingreen, Ky. married on Thursday evening last at Judge M'Nairys by the Rev. Mr. Lapsely to Miss Elizabeth Bell niece of Judge M'Nairy.
The Nashville Gazette (Sat., March 18, 1820)

Slater, Miss Alice married to Mr. Robert B. Powell

Slater, Mr. Charles married at Mount Pinson to Miss Sarah H. Searcy.
National Banner & Nashville Whig (Sat., April 19, 1828)

Slater, Capt. Cornelius married in Lincoln County to Miss Mary Ross.
National Banner & Nashville Whig (Sat., Aug. 26, 1826)

Slater, Miss Sarah married to Mr. Thomas Holt.

Slatery, Miss Margaret married to Mr. William Coulson.

Slatter, Miss Charity Ann married to Doctor David T. Scott.

Slatter, Mr. James R. married in Winchester on 22d July by the Rev. Joseph A. Copp to Miss Rebecca Estill.
National Banner & Nashville Daily Advertiser (Wed., July 31, 1833)

Slaughter, Miss Ann married to John F. Worthington, Esq.

Slaughter, Mr. James C. married at Russellville, Ky. to Miss Amanda P. Morton.
National Banner (Sat., July 4, 1829)

Slaughter, Miss Jane O. married to Mr. William E. Collier.

Slaughter, Mr. John married at Louisville, Ky. to Miss Matilda Sanders.
National Banner & Nashville Whig (Sat., Feb. 2, 1828)

Slaughter, Mr. John B. married in Russellville, Ky. to Miss Mary Edwards daughter of Presly Edwards Esq.
National Banner & Nashville Daily Advertiser (Thurs., Jan. 19, 1832)

Slaughter, Miss Lucy B. B. married to Mr. Joseph B. Bigger.

Slaughter, Richard B. Esq. married in Logan County, Ky. to Miss Sinia Bagwell.
National Banner & Nashville Whig (Sat., Sept. 6, 1828)

Slaughter, Miss Sally married to Mr. Wm. Whitsitt.

Slauter, A. G. Esq. married in Todd County, Ky. to Miss Helen Coleman.
National Banner & Nashville Whig (Sat., Aug. 25, 1827)

Slayton, Mr. Hickman married in Jackson to Miss Caroline Clark.
National Banner & Nashville Daily Advertiser (Thurs., July 12, 1832)

Slealey, Mr. John M. married in Sumner County on the 8th inst. to Miss Derinda Gibson.
National Banner & Nashville Whig (Sat., Aug. 26, 1826)

Sledge, Mrs. Mary Ann married to L. C. Lishy.

Sledge, Miss Mary E. married to Capt. John H. Harris.

Sledge, Mr. O. D. married in Madison City, Ala. to Miss Edith Shotwell.
Nashville Republican & State Gazette (Thurs., March 3, 1831)

Sledge, Mr. Robert married in Williamson County to Miss Catherine Smithson.
National Banner & Nashville Daily Advertiser (Mon., April 1, 1833)

Sledge, Mr. Robt. married in Williamson County to Miss Catharine K. Smithson.
The Western Weekly Review - Franklin, Tenn. (Fri., March 29, 1833)

Sledge, Zebulon L. married in Williamson County, Ten. to Sarah O. N. Warren.
National Banner & Nashville Whig (Wed., Dec. 17, 1834)

Sloan, Miss H. Elizabeth H. married to Mr. William C. McMurray.

Sloan, Miss Sophia married to Mr. John L. Miller.

Sloan, Miss Sophia married to Mr. John S. Miller.

Slocumb, Miss Francis T. married to Mr. W. Goode.

Sloo, Albert G. Esq. married at Vincennes to Miss Harriet White.
National Banner (Feb. 24, 1826)

Sloss, Mr. Wm. married in Logan County, Ky. to Miss Eliza M'Cutchen.
National Banner & Nashville Whig (Sat., April 7, 1827)

Sluder, Mr. A. B. married on Thursday 24th inst. by the Rev. Mr. Pitts to Miss Elizabeth Garner all of this city.
National Banner & Nashville Daily Advertiser (Sat., April 26, 1834)

Small, Miss Catharine E. married to Mr. Joseph Postlethwaite.

Small, Miss Francis D. married to Mr. Robert W. Sandford.

Small, Mr. John married in Russellville, Ky. to Miss Patsy Curd.
National Banner & Nashville Whig (Sat., Oct. 28, 1826)

Small, Mr. Vincent married at Huntsville, Ala. to Miss Elizabeth Day.
National Banner (Sat., May 2, 1829)

Smart, Mr. James R. married in Knox County to Miss Martha Cobb.
National Banner (Sat., Aug. 1, 1829)

Smeads, Miss Elizabeth married to Mr. H. Richie.

Smetson, Miss Sarah married to Mr. James Johnson.

Smiley, Dr. Alexander H. of Trenton married at Mt. Holyoke on the 13th inst. by the Rev. C. H. Gillaspy to Miss Ann E. Cowan daughter of James Cowen, Esq. of Henry Co.
Nashville Whig (Sat., May 23, 1846)

Smiley, Miss Catherine married to Mr. Samuel H. Bugg.

Smiley, Miss Emily married to Ashiel Brunson Esq.

Smiley, Miss Louisa Jane married to Mr. Charles M. Hays.

Smiley, Mrs. Mary married to Mr. William M'Vey.

Smiley, Miss Rachel married to Mr. Luter.

Smiley, Robert G. Esq. married yesterday morning by the Rev. Dr. R. A. Lapsley to Miss Rachel Douglass Boyd both of Nashville.
Nashville Whig (Thurs., Sept. 17, 1846)

Smiser, Miss Ellen married to Mr. James Gray Booker.

Smith, Miss married to Mr. Hugh R. Lacy.

Smith, Mrs. married to Major Ulysses Spalding.

Smith, Mr. Abiel married at Cincinnati to Miss Ann Hall.
National Banner & Nashville Whig (Sat., June 7, 1828)

Smith, Mr. Abraham married Miss Mary E. B. Hendley in Lexington, Ky.
National Banner & Nashville Whig (Fri., Jan. 29, 1830)

Smith, Miss Agnes married to Mr. Winslow Hart.

Smith, Mr. Alexander W. married in Rutherford County on Thursday
evening 2nd inst. to Miss Martha C. Smith daughter of the Rev. Peyton
Smith.
National Banner & Nashville Whig (Mon., Sept. 6, 1830)

Smith, Miss Amanda married to Mr. James Morton.

Smith, Mr. Ananias B. married in Logan County, Ky. to Miss Elizabeth
Hughes.
National Banner & Nashville Whig (Wed., Feb. 4, 1835)

Smith, Mr. Andrew J. of Nashville married on Thursday 10th inst. by
the Rev. Dr. Lapsley to Miss Patricia S. Young of Albany, N. Y.
The Christian Record (Sat., Aug. 12, 1848)

Smith, Miss Ann married to Wm. P. Booker, Esq.

Smith, Mrs. Ann married to Mr. Thomas Jokes.

Smith, Miss Ann C. married to Balie Peyton, Esq.

Smith, Mr. Benjamin B. Smith of Columbia (Maury County) married in
Murry County to Catharine Jenkins.
Nashville Whig (Jan. 22, 1823)

Smith, Benjamin D. Esq. of Williamson County married in Nashville on
3d inst. by the Rev. Mr. Hume to Miss Harriet S. Criddle of Davidson
County.
National Banner & Nashville Daily Advertiser (Fri., May 4, 1832)

Smith, Miss Betsey married to Mr. Edward Mitchell.

Smith, Mr. Bird of Lexington married in Woodford County, Ky. to Miss
Elvira H. Price.
National Banner (Feb. 10, 1826)

Smith, Major Calvin M. of Columbia married in this County to Mrs. Jane
Love.
National Banner & Nashville Whig (Sat., Jan. 27, 1827)

Smith, Mrs. Caroline married to Mr. Leroy C. Coleman.

Smith, Mrs. Caroline married to Mr. Hiram Dunham.

Smith, Miss Caroline M. married to Mr. James M. Chelton.

Smith, Miss Catherine married to Mr. Jacob Butts.

Smith, Catharine M. married to Rev. Neal M. Gordan.

Smith, Mr. Champion E. of Lincoln County, Tenn. married in Lawrence
County, Ala. to Miss Mary Walton.
National Banner & Nashville Whig (Mon., April 4, 1831)

Smith, Mr. Charles Maury Co. married in Gallatin to Miss Francis
Whitehead.
National Banner & Nashville Whig (Sat., Aug. 25, 1827)

Smith, Mr. Charles married in Knox County to Miss Ann Tabler.
National Banner & Nashville Whig (Sat., Nov. 22, 1828)

Smith, Mr. Charles M. married in Cincinnati to Miss Cedonia Highland.
National Banner & Nashville Whig (Sat., Jan. 10, 1829)

Smith, Rev. Cyrus, Professor of Languages in the University of Tennessee
Murfreesboro married in Nashville on 7th inst. by the Rev. Mr. Howell
to Miss Dorinda Lamsden daughter of Charles Lamsden of Sterling, Mass.
Nashville Whig (Fri., Oct. 8, 1841)

Smith, David A. Esq. at Huntsville, Ala. married Miss Eliza E. Allen.
National Banner & Nashville Whig (Tues., Aug. 10, 1831)

Smith, Col. Davis married in Lincoln County to Miss Ruth Davis.
National Banner & Nashville Whig (Sat., Feb. 23, 1828)

Smith, Mr. E. H. married in Madison County to Miss Nancy Spratt.
National Banner & Nashville Whig (Wed., Dec. 1, 1830)

Smith, E. H. Esq. of Madisonville married in Madison County, Tenn. to
Miss Nancy Sprat.
Nashville Republican & State Gazette (Thurs., Dec. 16, 1830)

Smith, Mr. Eli Hardeman County married Miss Dolly Moffit daughter of
John Moffit Esq.
National Banner & Nashville Advertiser (Sat., Jan. 7, 1832)

Smith, Mr. Elias P. married at Huntsville, Ala. to Mrs. Margaret
Glascock.
National Banner & Nashville Whig (Wed., March 23, 1831)

Smith, Miss Eliza married to Mr. L. D. Wallis.

Smith, Miss Eliza P. married to Mr. Samuel Ewalt.

Smith, Miss Eliza P. married to Henry B. Brickell, Esq.

Smith, Miss Elizabeth married to Mr. Burrell Bender.

Smith, Miss Elizabeth married to Mr. Isaac Joseph.

Smith, Miss Elizabeth married to Mr. Julius Fagg.

Smith, Miss Elizabeth married to Mr. John G. Talbot.

Smith, Miss Elizabeth married to Mr. Harden Scott.

Smith, Miss Elizabeth Caldwell married to Hon. Joseph Duncan.

Smith, Miss Elizabeth S. married to John Vandyke.

Smith, Miss Ellen married to William S. Lord.

Smith, Miss Emeline married to Mr. Richard Christmas.

Smith, Miss Evelina married to Mr. Pleasant T. Cunningham.

Smith, Miss Eveline P. married to Mr. Sidney Smith.

Smith, Miss Fanny married to Mr. John Todd Edgar.

Smith, Miss Frances married to Mr. Robert S. Cummings.

Smith, Mr. George A. married to Mrs. Sarah Wilkinson.

Smith, Maj. George H. married in Sumner on Sunday 21st ult. to Miss
Louisa B. Turner both of that County.
National Banner (June 3, 1826)

Smith, Mr. George M. of Sommerville married in Fayette County to Miss Elizabeth Hatch.
National Banner & Nashville Daily Advertiser (Wed., Feb. 27, 1833)

Smith, Dr. George N. married in Greene County, Ala. to Miss Seignora P. Meade.
National Banner & Nashville Daily Advertiser (Mon., Sept. 10, 1832)

Smith, Mr. Geo. R. married in Scott County, Ky. to Miss Mileta Ann Thompson.
National Banner & Nashville Whig (Sat., May 19, 1827)

Smith, Mr. George W. married in Nashville last evening on the 22d inst. by the Rev. Mr. Hume to Miss Susan Sneed.
National Banner & Nashville Daily Advertiser (Fri., Feb. 24, 1832)

Smith, Mr. Geo. W. married at Huntsville, Ala. on the 3d inst to Miss Martha Patton.
National Banner & Nashville Whig (Sat., Feb. 14, 1829)

Smith, Mr. Geo. W. of Rutherford County married Miss Martha M. Morton on the 2d inst.
Nashville Republican (Tues., Dec. 22, 1835)

Smith, Mr. Gransford P. married Miss Mary Webster in Lexington, Ky.
National Banner & Nashville Whig (Sat., Sept. 2, 1826)

Smith, Granville P. of Nashville married in the Parish Rapides, La. to Donora C. Cheney daughter of the late Hampton J. Cheney of Louisiana.
Nashville Whig (Fri., Dec. 4, 1840)

Smith, Miss Harriet married to George C. Barfield Esq.

Smith, Miss Harriet E. married to Mr. Marcus L. Hohe.

Smith, Mr. Henry married in Lincoln County to Miss Mary Hannah.
National Banner & Nashville Whig (Sat., Dec. 30, 1826)

Smith, Mr. Henry married in Fayette County to Miss Caroline Hatch.
National Banner & Nashville Daily Advertiser (Wed., Feb. 27, 1833)

Smith, Mr. Henry F. married in Wilson County on the 6th inst. by the Rev. Thos. Calhoun to Miss Missouri Gleaves.
National Banner & Nashville Whig (Sat., March 31, 1827)

Smith, Mr. Hugh married in Athens to Mrs. Elizabeth Jane Fyffe.
National Banner & Nashville Whig (Fri., Jan. 22, 1830)

Smith, Mr. Isaac married in Davidson County to Miss Lucindia Ross.
Nashville Republican (Tues., Jan. 27, 1835)

Smith, Mrs. Isabella married to Mr. J. R. Moore.

Smith, Mr. Jacob married in Louisville, Ky. to Miss Mary Ann Riley.
National Banner (Sat., April 18, 1829)

Smith, Mr. James D. of Carthage married in Knoxville to Miss Eliza E. Hamilton.
National Banner & Nashville Daily Advertiser (Mon., Jan. 14, 1833)

Smith, Mr. James G. married in Lincoln County to Miss Margaret Beard.
National Banner (May 27, 1826)

Smith, Mr. James T. married in Madison County, Ky. to Miss Jane Grimes.
National Banner (March 24, 1826)

Smith, Miss Jane married to Mr. Smith Grant.

Smith, Miss Jane married to Mr. Griffin Reed.

Smith, Miss Jane E. married to Hon. Charles D. McLean.

Smith, Miss Jemima married to Mr. Jesse G. Lindell.

Smith, Mr. Jeremiah L. married in Garrard County, Ky. to Miss Sarah Ann Hughes.
National Banner & Nashville Whig (Sat., Sept. 15, 1827)

Smith, Mr. Jesse L. of this town married on the 26th ult. to Miss Mary West of Robertson County.
Nashville Whig (March 19, 1823)

Smith, Mr. Joel M. (of Nashville) married on Wednesday evening last to Miss Charlotte Bareman of this County (Davidson).
Nashville Whig (June 11, 1823)

Smith, Joel R. of Columbia married to Miss Nancy J. Grizzard of this County.
The Clarion & Tennessee Gazette (Oct. 31, 1820)

Smith, Mr. John B. of Davidson County married in Nashville Wednesday evening 23d inst. by the Rev. Jno. Holland to Miss Louisa J. Scruggs.
National Banner & Nashville Whig (Fri., Nov. 25, 1831)

Smith, John C. married in Henry County to Miss Nancy Dixon (Dickson)
National Banner & Nashville Daily Advertiser (Mon., April 23, 1832)

Smith, Mr. John H. merchant of this town married on Thursday last to Miss Maria M'Combs of this County.
The Nashville Whig (Dec. 28, 1815)

Smith, Mr. John H. married in Rutherford County to Miss Sarah M'Culloch.
National Banner & Nashville Daily Advertiser (Sat., June 22, 1833)

Smith, Mr. John H. of Nashville married on the 13th inst. to Miss Caroline Morton.
Nashville Republican & State Gazette (Sat., Feb. 15, 1834)

Smith, Mr. John P. formerly of Jefferson M. T. married on the same evening (Friday) by the Rev. Edmund Jones to Miss Francis L. Sims daughter of Doctor S. Sims of Rutherford County.
The Nashville Whig & Tenn. Advertiser (Jan. 24, 1818)

Smith, Mr. John P. of Little Rock, Arkansas married on the 16th ult. by the Rev. John Bransford to Miss Mary Langsdon of Nashville.
Little Rock Times
Nashville Republican (Mon., Dec. 5, 1836)

Smith, Mr. John W. married in Nashville on Sunday morning last by the Rev. R. B. C. Howell to Miss Emily J. Reed.
Daily Republican Banner (Tues., Jan. 8,1839)

Smith, Mr. John W. married in Henry County to Miss Elizabeth Haynes.
National Banner & Nashville Daily Advertiser (Fri., Feb. 8, 1833)

Smith, Dr. Joseph married in Gallatin to Miss Margaret Allen.
National Banner & Nashville Whig (Mon., July 19, 1830)

Smith, Mr. Joseph C. of Condia aged 80 years married in Hooksett to Mrs. Sarah King of Hooksett aged 88 years.
Daily Republican Banner (Wed., Aug. 8, 1838)

Smith, Rev. Josiah R. married in Tazwell to Miss Bartheny Cloud.
National Banner & Nashville Whig (Sat., Nov. 18, 1826)

Smith, Capt. Lee married in Lincoln County to Miss Elizabeth Cliff.
National Banner & Nashville Whig (Sat., Dec. 30, 1826)

Smith, Col. Lemuel of Hardeman County married in Jackson County, Tenn.
to Miss Amelia Wilkinson of Jackson.
National Banner & Nashville Whig (Wed., Nov. 26, 1834)

Smith, Miss Lucinda married to Mr. John Merilie.

Smith, Miss Lucinda married to Lieut. Lawrence F. Carter.

Smith, Miss M. A. married to Mr. William McAlister.

Smith, Miss Malvina D. married to Mr. Nathaniel D. Terry.

Smith, Miss Margaret married to Mr. William Christopher.

Smith, Miss Margaret J. married to Edward S. Butler.

Smith, Miss Maria married to Mr. James Bostick.

Smith, Mrs. Mariah A. H. married to John Bellamy Esq.

Smith, Miss Martha married to Mr. Thomas Smith.

Smith, Miss Martha C. married to Mr. Alexander W. Smith.

Smith, Miss Mary married to Mr. William B. Lillard.

Smith, Miss Mary married to Mr. Hubbard H. Fennell.

Smith, Miss Mary married to Mr. William B. Lillard.

Smith, Miss Mary married to Mr. William Brantly.

Smith, Miss Mary married to Mr. W. J. Lytle.

Smith, Miss Mary Ann married to Samuel R. Wackett, Esq.

Smith, Miss Mary E. married to Mr. Hampton J. Chaney.

Smith, Miss Mary E. married to Mr. Jacob R. Shuford.

Smith, Miss Mary M. married to Mr. Robert Church.

Smith, Prof. N. B. of Franklin College married on the 31st March in
Franklin County, Tenn. by the Rev. S. E. Jones to Miss Keren C.
Lipscomb daughter of Mr. Graville Lipscomb of Franklin Co.
Nashville True Whig & Weekly Commercial Register (Fri., April 12, 1850)

Smith, Miss Nancy S. married to Mr. John H. Robb.

Smith, Miss Narcissa married to Mr. James Patton.

Smith, Mr. Nathaniel F. married in Maury County to Miss Mary E. A.
Pillow on the 14th Jan.
Nashville Republican (Tues., Jan.27, 1835)

Smith, Mr. Norman married in Louisville to Miss Mahala Mann.
National Banner (Sat., Aug. 1, 1829)

Smith, Miss Patsey married to Thomas Foster, Esq.

Smith, Dr. Peter married on Tuesday Nov. 7th by the Rev. Dr. Lapsley
at the residence of Simon Glenn, Esq. to Miss Mary Earthman all of
Nashville
The Christian Record (Sat., Nov. 11, 1848)

Smith, Mr. Pleasant of Nashville married on the 16th inst. by the
Rev. Dr. Edgar to Miss Mary Jane Ewing daughter of William Ewing, Sen.
of Nashville.
Nashville Republican (Tues., Feb. 21, 1837)

Smith, Mr. Ralph P. married in this town on 1st inst. by the Rev.
Mr. Lindsley to Miss Ann Nicholson.
National Banner & Nashville Whig (Sat., Jan. 3, 1829)

Smith, Miss Rebecca married to Mr. Isaac Litton.

Smith, Miss Rebecca married to Mr. Willis Snell.

Smith, Miss Susan D. married to Mr. Thomas M. Petway.

Smith, Mr. Richard of Elkton married Miss Eliza Mosby.
National Banner & Nashville Advertiser (Sat., July 28, 1832)

Smith, Mr. Robert married in Nashville the 31st ult. by James L.
Jarrell Esq. to Miss Martha Baker all of Davidson County.
Nashville True Whig & Weekly Commercial Register (Fri., Jan. 3, 1851)

Smith, Mr. Robert P. married in Maury County to Miss Ann E. Patterson.
National Banner & Nashville Whig (Mon., Oct. 4, 1830)

Smith, Miss Sally married to Mr. Thomas Watson Jr.

Smith, Mr. Samuel married in Louisville, Ky. to Miss Mary Parker.
National Banner & Nashville Daily Advertiser (Mon., July 28, 1834)

Smith, Mr. Samuel married in Henry County, Ten. since the first of
Jan. to Miss Martitia Smoot.
National Banner & Nashville Whig (Fri., Feb. 13, 1835)

Smith, Miss Sarah married to Mr. Josiah Goodnough.

Smith, Miss Sarah Ann married to Mr. Samuel Warner.
National Banner & Nashvile Daily Advertiser (Tues., March 11, 1834)

Smith, Miss Sarah Ann Elizabeth married to Mr. John Roche Esq.

Smith, Miss Sarah B. married to Mr. William H. Girard.

Smith, Doct. Sidney of Nashville married in Nashville on Thursday
evening 10th inst. by the Rev. Mr. Hume to Miss Eliza Jane Wharton
daughter of Jesse Wharton, Esq. of Davidson County.
National Banner & Nashville Daily Advertiser(Fri., Jan. 11, 1833)

Smith, Mr. Sidney married in Fayette County to Miss Evelina P. Smith.
National Banner & Nashville Whig (Mon., July 4, 1831)

Smith, Mr. Sidney P. married in Giles Co., Ten. to Miss Margaret
Dabney.
National Banner & Nashville Daily Advertiser (Tues., July 15, 1834)

Smith, Miss Susan married to Mr. Thomas J. Waters.

Smith, Miss Susan P. married to Mr. Isaac H. Wall.

Smith, Miss Susanna married to Mr. Myers Suggs.

Smith, Dr. Sydney married to Miss Eliza Jane Wharton on Thursday
evening 10 inst.
Nashville Republican & State Gazette (Fri., Jan. 11, 1833)

Smith, Miss Synthia J. married to Mr. Silas Hindman.

Smith, Mr. T. married in Franklin, Ten. to Miss Elizabeth Sanders.
National Banner & Nashville Whig (Sat., Sept. 9, 1826)

Smith, Mr. Tho. married in Florence, Ala. to Miss Jula Mitchell.
National Banner & Nashville Whig (Mon., Nov. 14, 1831)

Smith, Thomas Esq. of Gainsboro, Ten. married in Nashville daughter
of Dr. Felix Robertson on Thursday 17, inst. to Miss Elizabeth A.
Robertson.
Nashville Republican & State Gazette (Sat., July 19, 1834)

Smith, Mr. Thomas F. of Nashville married on Thursday the 19th inst.
by the Rev. Mr. Lapsley to Miss Elizabeth W. Wood youngest daughter
of Capt. Wood of the Nashville vicinity.
Nashville Whig (Tues., Dec. 24, 1844)

Smith, Mr. Thomas H. manager for Col. Tom Smith married on Thursday
June 29, by Obediah Smith Esq. J. P. to Miss Martha Smith daughter
of Stephen Smith all of Arkansas County, Ark.
Nashville Whig (Thurs., Aug. 10, 1843)

Smith, Mr. Ulysses G. married at Knoxville to Miss Rosanna McAifry.
National Banner & Nashville Whig (Sat., Feb. 17, 1827)

Smith, Mr. W. married in Davidson County, Tenn. to Miss Julia Davis.
National Banner & Nashville Whig (Wed., Nov. 12, 1834)

Smith, Mr. Walter C. married in Logan County, Ky. to Miss Angelina
Foster.
National Banner & Nashville Whig (Sat., Nov. 18, 1826)

Smith, Mr. Wm. of Nashville married to Miss Elizabeth Rainey on the
4th inst.
Nashville Republican & State Gazette (Fri., April 5, 1833)

Smith, Rev. William of Wilson County married on the 31st ult. by the
Rev. Samuel Casley to Miss Rebecca Ann Frazor of Davidson County.
Nashville Union (Mon., Nov. 4, 1839)

Smith, Capt. William Dudley married in Wilson County on the 9th ult.
to Miss Caroline Figuers.
National Banner & Nashville Whig (Fri., Oct. 3, 1834)

Smith, Mr. Wm. M. married in Williamson County to Miss Margaret M.
Wilson.
National Banner & Nashville Whig (Fri., Jan. 9, 1835)

Smith, Miss Zelinda Ann married to Daniel M. Payne, Esq.

Smithers, Miss Mary married to Dr. T. J. Kilpatrick.

Smithson, Miss Catharine K. married to Robt. Sledge.

Smithson, Horatio H. married in Williamson County to Miss Lydia
Andrews.
The Western Weekly Review - Franklin, Tenn. (Fri., Dec. 14, 1832)

Smithson, Martha married to Mr. William H. Vaden.

Smithson, Mr. Wm. O. married in Williamson County, Tenn. to Miss Lucy
W. Giles.
National Banner & Nashville Whig (Fri., Jan. 9, 1835)

Smoot, Miss Martitia married to Mr. Samuel Smith.

Smylie, Miss Amelia F. married to Mr. Joseph Montgomery.

Sneed, Mr. Charles E. married near Tuscaloosa, Ala. to Miss Ann T.
Beams.
National Banner & Nashville Whig (Sat., Jan. 6, 1827)

Sneed, Miss Martha married to Mr. Joseph Morton.

Sneed, Miss Mary married to Mr. William Bennett.

Sneed, Rev. Samuel K. married in Lincoln County, Ky. to Miss Nancy W. Green.
National Banner & Nashville Whig (Sat., July 14, 1827)

Sneed, Miss Sarah Ann married to Mr. Orville B. Martin.

Sneed, Miss Susan married to Mr. George W. Smith.

Sneed, Dr. Thomas J. married in Smith County to Miss Nancy C. L. Orival.
National Banner & Nashville Whig (Sat., April 26, 1828)

Snell, Mr. George R. married in Wilson County, Ten. to Miss Harriet Bettes.
National Banner & Nashville Daily Advertiser (Mon., May 28, 1832)

Snell, Mr. James married at St. Louis, Mo. to Miss Julia Bellesseme
National Banner (June 3, 1826)

Snell, Miss Mary married to Mr. John Burrow.

Snell, Mr. Willis married in Rutherford County, Ten. to Miss Rebecca Smith.
National Banner & Nashville Whig (Wed., Sept. 24, 1834)

Snethen, Miss Elizabeth A. married to Dr. Jordan Pennington.

Snider, Miss Christa married to Mr. Squire Embry.

Snider, Miss Emilie L. married to Mr. Edward King.

Snider, Miss Eve married to Mr. F. Knoepple.

Snider, Dr. George married at Jackson to Miss Eleanora M. Owing late of Baltimore.
National Banner & Nashville Advertiser (Fri., Jan. 27, 1832)

Snider, Mr. James married on the 9th inst. by Joseph L. Jarrell, Esq. to Miss Rosanna Baker all of Mill Creek Valley.
The Politician & Weekly Nashville Whig (Fri., March 17, 1848)

Snider, Mr. Jonas married in Henry County, Ten. to Miss Alpha Upchurch.
National Banner & Nashville Whig (Fri., March 6, 1835)

Snider, Miss Louisa married to Mr. Thomas Judy.

Snoddy, Miss Susannah married to Mr. Johnson Sampson.

Snow, Dr. Charles married in Tuscaloosa, Ala. to Miss Virginia Penn.
National Banner & Nashville Whig (Fri., June 10, 1831)

Snow, Dr. Charles of Ala. married in Williamson County to Miss Sarah M. Perkins.
National Banner & Nashville Whig (Sat., Oct. 25, 1828)

Snow, Miss Hannah Amanda married to Mr. Henry M. Stratton.

Snow, Miss Mary Ann married to Mr. Madison Stratton.

Snowden, Mr. Arthur H. Nashville married Miss L. A. Bogardus (dau. of Gen. Bogardus) New York.
National Banner & Nashville Whig (Wed., April 6, 1831)

Snowden, Miss Cornelia C. married to Rosewell P. Hayes, M.D.

Snowden, Mr. J. Baynard married in the City of New York on the 26th
Feb. by the Right Reverend Bishop Onderdonk to Miss Aspasia S. J.
Bogardus daughter of Gen. Robert Bogardus.
National Banner & Nashville Whig (Mon., March 16, 1835)

Snowden, Mr. James A. married in Franklin County, Tenn. on the 24th
March by the Rev. Mr. Steele to Miss Sophia Holder daughter of John
W. Holder Esq.
National Banner & Nashville Whig (Fri., April 3, 1835)

Sommerville, John married last evening, Wednesday, May 21, 1794
Mr. John Sommerville, merchant of his town, to Miss Elizabeth Chisolm
daughter of John Chisolm, Esquire.
Knoxville Gazette (Thurs., May 22, 1794)

Savy, Mr. Maleca age about 70 years married a few weeks since in New
York, Montgomery County by James Bowers, Esq. to Miss Mary Cockran
age about 50 years.
Nashville Whig (April 12, 1824)

Snowden, Mr. Samuel B. married in this town last evening to Miss Jane
W. Hume daughter of Rev. Wm. Hume.
National Banner (Sat., Dec. 19, 1829)

Snyder, Miss Maria married to Mr. John Wallace.

Solms, Elizabeth Catharine married to Mr. Robert A. Little.

Solomon, Miss Mary F. married to Gen. W. W. Pepper.

Somers, Mr. George married in Weakley County to Miss Elizabeth Tomlinson
National Banner & Nashville Daily Advertiser (Mon., May 13, 1833)

Sommerville, Miss Caroline married to Capt. John Young.

Somerville, Mr. Willis L. married at Bunker Hill (Hardeman County) to
Miss Mary Ann Martin on 16th inst.
Nashville Republican & State Gazette (Sat., Jan. 25, 1834)

Southall, Mr. John married in Williamson County to Miss Nancy Oldham.
National Banner & Nashville Whig (Sat., Dec. 30, 1826)

Southall, Miss Martha E. married to Dr. Charles G. English.

Southerland, Mr. William H. married on Wednesday Jan. 20th by Rev.
Dr. Lemerick to Miss Sarah Murray daughter of Mr. John Murray all of
Wheeling from the Wheeling Times, Dec. 28.
National Banner & Nashville Whig (Fri., Jan. 22, 1836)

Southgate, Miss Frances married to Mr. John N Talioferro.

Southgate, James Esq. married in Cincinnati to Miss Cornelia S. T.
Brigham.
National Banner & Nashville Whig (Fri., May 20, 1831)

Spackman, William, merchant of Philadelphia, married at Christ Church
in the City of Philadelphia on the 9th inst. by the Rev. Dr. Dorr to
Mrs. Susan Washington formerly of Nashville
Nashville Whig (Mon., Sept. 20, 1841)

Spain, Mr. John N. married in Nashville on the 31st Dec. by the
Rev. A. L. P. Green to Miss Eliza Ann Hartley both of Nashville.
The Union (Sat., Jan. 2, 1836)

Spain, Mr. Littlebury K. married on Thursday the 30th inst. by the Rev.
A. L. P. Green to Miss Sarah G. Spain all of Nashville.
Nashville Whig (Fri., July 31, 1840)

Spain, Miss Martha Ann married to Mr. George J. Johnson.

Spain, Miss Sarah G. married to Mr. Littlebury K. Spain.

Spalding, Major Ulysesses married in Williamson County on Tuesday last to Mrs. Smith.
National Banner & Nashville Whig (Sat., Sept. 8, 1827)

Spangler, Miss Mary M. married to Mr. Ashton Garrett.

Spann, Hon. C. S. married in Brownville, Hinds County, Mississippi on the 18th Dec. last by the Rev. N. R. Granberry to Miss Henritta W. Lanier all of Hinds County, Mississippi.
Nashville Whig (Tues., Feb. 10, 1846)

Spann, Rev. Wm. F. married in Franklin, Ten. to Miss Susanna L. Johnson daughter of Mr. Andrew Johnson.
National Banner & Nashville Daily Advertiser (Tues., Aug. 5, 1834)

Spann, Mr. William R. married in Williamson County to Miss Anna Myers.
National Banner & Nashville Whig (Fri., Jan. 9, 1835)

Sparkman, Mr. Samuel married in Nashville on the 19th inst. to Miss Sarah Eastis all of Nashville.
The Union (Sat., Nov. 21, 1835)

Sparks, Mr. Elijah married in Rutherford County to Miss Mary Rutledge daughter of Mr. William Rutledge.
National Banner & Nashville Whig (Sat., Dec. 17, 1831)

Sparks, Jared Esq. married at Salem, Mass. on Tuesday last by the Rev. Dr. Flint to Miss Mary C. Silsbee daughter of Hon. Nathaniel Silsbee.
Daily Republican Banner (Thurs., June 6, 1839)

Sparks, Dr. Jos. K. married at Cincinnati to Miss Elizabeth Goodwin.
National Banner & Nashville Whig (Sat., May 19, 1827)

Sparks, Miss Louisa married to Mr. Henry Stephenson.

Speaker, Mr. John married in Louisville, Ky. to Miss Elizabeth Melow.
National Banner & Nashville Whig (Sat., April 7, 1827)

Speck, Mr. David married at Huntsville, Ala. to Miss Martha Humes.
National Banner & Nashville Whig (Sat., May 3, 1828)

Speckernagle, Mr. John M. married in Memphis to Miss Mary Jane Davis daughter of Thomas Davis, Esq.
National Banner & Nashville Advertiser (Sat., March 3, 1832)

Speece, Miss Eliza married to Mr. Joseph Francis.

Speece, Miss Elizabeth married to Mr. Henry Alley.

Speece, Miss Margaret married to Mr. George Scott.

Spence, Miss Anna B. married to Mr. Ephriam P. Shall.

Spence, Mr. B. of this city, married on Wednesday evening the 28th inst. by the Rev. Mr. Campbell to Miss Elizabeth Shute daughter of John Shute Esq. of this County.
Nashville Whig (May 3, 1824)

Spence, Miss Catherine married to Mr. Lewis M. Kennard.

Spence, Miss Elizabeth married to Mr. John Spence.

Spence, Mr. John of Somersville, Ten. married in Rutherford County, Ten. to Miss Elizabeth Spence of Murfreesborough.
National Banner & Nashville Whig (Wed., Sept. 24, 1834)

Spence, Mr. Marmon married in this town on Thursday evening 23d ult. to Miss Sarah Wasson both of Murfreesborough.
National Banner (March 3, 1826)

Spence, Miss Mary married to Mr. John Kirk.

Spence, Miss Mary A. married to Mr. Daniel Hews.

Spence, Miss Mary S. married to Mr. John Kirk.

Spence, Miss Nancy married to Mr. Isaac Ivy.

Spencer, Mr. Francis married in Maury County to Miss Jane M'Clenchan.
National Banner & Nashville Whig (Mon, Sept. 26, 1831)

Spencer, Mr. John married in Madison County to Miss Emily Greer.
National Banner & Nashville Daily Advertiser (Thurs., Aug. 16, 1832)

Spencer, Mr. John of McMinn County married on the 16th of April to Miss Martha A. Likins of Monroe County.
National Banner & Nashville Whig (Fri., May 1, 1835)

Spencer, Louisa married to Isaac N. Mayfield.

Spencer, Miss Martha Maria married to Mr. Ariel Draper.

Spencer, Mr. Samuel married in Huntsville to Miss Caroline R. H. Cain daughter of Thomas Cain Esq.
National Banner (Sat., Oct. 10, 1829)

Spencer, Mr. Samuel married in Huntsville to Miss Caroline R. R. Cain.
Nashville Republican & State Gazette (Thurs., Oct. 17, 1833)

Spider, Miss Mary married to Mr. William Crabb.

Spillers, Mr. William married in Newport, E. Tenn. to Miss Jane Brooks.
National Banner & Nashville Whig (Sat., Dec. 9, 1826)

Spivey, Mr. Thomas W. married in Smith County to Miss Nancy Banks.
National Banner & Nashville Daily Advertiser (Fri., Feb. 10, 1832)

Spivy, Miss Louivisy married to Mr. Daniel D. Walker.

Spotswood, Miss Elizabeth married to Mr. James W. M'Clung Esq.

Sprague, Miss Lucrettia O. married to Mr. John Thomson.

Spratt, Miss Nancy married to Mr. E. H. Smith.

Sprawl, Miss Susan married to Mr. Samuel Dun.

Springer, John Esq. married in Madison County, Illinois to Miss Elizabeth Biggs.
National Banner (April 21, 1826)

Springle, Miss Sarah married to Mr. Jonathan B. Hager.

Sprinkle, Miss Sarah married to Mr. James Briant.

Sprowl, Mr. Alexander married in Lexington, Ky. to Miss Margaret Weems.
National Banner & Nashville Whig (Sept. 2, 1826)

Spurlock, Miss Eliza married to Mr. W. Lucas.

Spyker, Miss Maria Catherine married to Mr. Joseph H. Bradford.

Stacker, Catherine E. married to French Rayburn.

Stackhouse, Miss Sarah married to Capt. William M'Knight.

Stacks, Mr. Demarcus G. married at Knoxville to Miss Margaret Dardis.
National Banner (Sat., May 2, 1829)

Staden, Mr. Travice of Dickson County married to Miss Lovy Council on
27th.
Nashville Republican (Tues., Jan. 19, 1836)

Stagg, Miss married to Mr. James Crittenden.

Staggs, Mr. E. B. married in Williamson County to Miss Mary Winstead.
National Banner & Nashville Whig (Sat., Feb. 16, 1828)

Staggs, Miss Mary married to Mr. Joseph Brown

Staggs, Miss Mary D. married to Mr. John Q. Stanbrough.

Staggs, Miss Narcissa married to Mr. James G. Crittenden.

Stainback, Mr. James W. married in the Nashville vicinity on the
16th inst. by the Rev. F. E. Pitts to Miss Martha C. Epps.
National Banner & Nashville Whig (Mon., Oct. 20, 1834)

Stainback, Mr. Sterling married in Madison County, Ala. to Miss
Maria F. Pattie.
National Banner & Nashville Whig (Wed., Nov. 23, 1831)

Staley, Mr. Oscar of Gallatin married in Scottsville, Ky. to Miss
Sophia Griggs.
National Banner & Nashville Daily Advertiser (Tues., April 9, 1833)

Staley, Mr. Theodore married in Cairo to Miss Brown.
National Banner & Nashville Whig (Sat., Sept. 20, 1828)

Stall, Miss Frances H. married to Mr. William Beard.

Stall, Miss Francis H. married to Mr. William Beard.

Stamer, Mr. Geo. married in Knox County to Miss Frances England.
National Banner & Nashville Whig (Sat., Sept. 15, 1827)

Stamper, Mr. R. W. married in Louisville, Ky. to Miss Mary E. Tewells.
National Banner & Nashville Whig (Fri., March 12, 1835)

Stanback, Mr. James H. W. married in this vicinity to Miss Martha C.
Epps on Thursday last.
Nashville Republican & State Gazette (Sat., Oct. 18, 1834)

Stanbrough, Mr. John O. late of Massach'ts. married on Thursday by
the Rev. Mr. Ferguson to Miss Mary D. Staggs of Nashville.
The Politician & Weekly Nashville Whig (Wed., Sept. 15, 1847)

Stanfield, Mr. Hosea married in Williamson County, Ten. to Miss Mary
Griggs.
National Banner & Nashville Whig (Fri., Feb. 13, 1835)

Stanfield, Miss Mary married to Mr. Abner Mullen.

Stanford, Miss Harriett married to Edwin T. Clark, Esq.

Stanley, Miss Eliza married to Mr. James H. Butler.

Stanley, Mr. James married on Thursday the 19th inst. by John
Billingly Esq. to Miss Jane Temple all of Davidson County.
Nashville Union (Mon., Dec. 23, 1839)

Stanley, Mr. John married in Shelby County to Miss Mary Perkinson.
National Banner & Nashville Whig (Sat., Aug. 18, 1827)

Stanley, Miss Levina married to Mr. James L. Atcheson.

Stanley, Mr. Martin married on the 10th inst. to Miss Eliza Little.
National Banner & Nashville Whig (Sat., Jan. 24, 1829)

Stanley, Mr. N. Y. of Kentucky married in Nashville on Thursday the
10th inst. by the Rev. J. Morrow to Miss Harriett A. Jonte of Nashville.
Nashville Whig (Sat., Sept. 12, 1846)

Stanley, Wright Esq. of Williamson married in this County to Miss
Mary C. M'Bride.
National Banner (Sat., July 18, 1829)

Stanton, Miss Gracy Arrington Howell married to Mr. Nathan Adams.
National Banner & Nashville Daily Advertiser (Fri., June 21, 1833)

Stark, Mr. John C. married in Nashville on Thursday the 23d inst. by the
Rev. Thos. Springfield to Miss Burchel Williams daughter of Thomas
Williams, Esq. all of Montgomery County.
Daily Republican Banner (Sat., May 25, 1839)

Stark, Mr. John C. married in Nashville on the 23d inst. by the
Rev. Thomas Stringfield at the house of W. Lowe to Miss Burchet
Williams daughter of Thomas Williams all of Montgomery County.
Nashville Union (Fri., May 24, 1839)

Stark, Mr. John C. married in Nashville on Thursday the 23d inst.
by the Rev. Thomas Stringfield to Miss Barchet William daughter of
Thomas Williams all of Montgomery County.
Nashville Whig (Fri., May 24, 1839)

Stark, Miss Nancy married to Mr. Edward Wollen.

Starkey, Mr. George married in Louisville, Ky. to Miss Eleanor E.
Ferguson.
National Banner & Nashville Whig (Sat., Nov. 17, 1827)

Starkey, Miss Martha married to Mr. Charles Whittingham.

Starnes, Miss Mary A. married to Lycurgus H. Moseley Esq.

Starr, Mr. John married in Louisville, Ky. to Miss Rebecca Estlin.
National Banner & Nashville Daily Advertiser (Fri., Aug. 30, 1833)

Starr, Richard D. formerly of Nashville married on the 18th Feb. to
Miss Charlotte Williams of Boonville, Mo.
National Banner & Nashville Whig (Mon., March 21, 1836)

Starr, Mr. Wm. E. married at Edwardsville, Ill. to Miss Elvira Amanda
Stephenson.
National Banner & Nashville Whig (Sat., May 19, 1827)

Statan, Mr. Isreal married in Matilda U. C. to Miss Grace Parlor.
National Banner & Nashville Whig (Wed., May 18, 1831)

Staton, Mr. George W. of Wilson County married in Rutherford County
to Miss Nancy Walls.
National Banner & Nashville Whig (Mon., Jan. 31, 1831)

Stator, Mr. Elizabeth married to Mr. Wm. C. Shumaker.

Staunton, Maj. Henry of U. S. Army married in Washington City to Miss Alexandrine Macomb daughter of Maj. Gen. A. Macomb.
National Banner & Nashville Daily Advertiser (Mon., March 3, 1834)

St. Clair, Miss Eliza married to Mr. Joseph Parks.

Stedman, Miss Maria N. married to Dr. Owen C. Blount.

Steed, Miss Elizabeth married to Mr. John Howard.

Steel, Mr. Edward married in Nashville to Miss Lucy Rawlins on Saturday, Nov. 24, by the Rev. Mr. Hume.
National Banner & Nashville Advertiser (Wed., Nov. 28, 1832)

Steel, Mr. James A. married in Haywood County to Miss Mary H. Harlson.
National Banner & Nashville Whig (Sat., Feb. 14, 1829)

Steel, Miss Rebecca married to Mr. W. M. Turpin.

Steel, Miss Sina married to Mr. Meredith Brewer.

Steel, Volney H. married in Bedford County to Eliza Houston.
National Banner & Nashville Daily Advertiser (Tues., Dec. 17, 1833)

Steel, Mr. William married in Knox County to Miss Elizabeth Jane Dudley.
National Banner & Nashville Daily Advertiser (Mon., Nov. 5, 1832)

Steel, Mr. John W. married on the 4th July by the Rev. R. B. C. Howell to Miss Mary J. Reed all of Nashville.
Nashville Whig (Fri., July 6, 1838)

Steele, Miss Lucy Ann married to Mr. Henry L. Claiborne.

Steele, Miss Margaret H. married to Mr. William M. Carlisle.

Steele, Miss Mary P. married to Mr. Valentine E. Cuningham.

Steele, Miss Mary W. married to Mr. James G. Neely.

Steele, Miss Rebecca married to Mr. William Turpin.

Stein, Mr. Albert married on Thursday the 22d by the Rev. Dr. Lindsley to Miss Caroline Troost daughter of Dr. Gerard Troost all of Nashville.
National Banner & Nashville Daily Advertiser (Fri., Nov. 22, 1833)

Step, Miss Cerinda married to Mr. David Wood.

Stephen, Miss Mary married to Mr. Wm. Finch.

Stephens, Rev. A. married in Nashville to Miss Caroline M. Lawrence daughter of Dr. William P. Lawrence.
Daily Republican Banner (Mon., April 11, 1838)

Stephens, Mr. A., Professor of Modern Language in the University of Nashville married last eveing by the Rt. Rev. Bishop Otey to Miss Minerva Lawrence daughter of Dr. W. P. Lawrence of Nashville.
Nashville Whig (Fri., April 6, 1838)

Stephens, Miss Catherine Brent married to Mr. George Martin.

Stephens, Miss Charlotte married to Mr. Joseph C. Hensley.

Stephens, Mr. George married in Monroe County to Miss Jemima Murray.
National Banner & Nashville Whig (Fri., Sept. 9, 1831)

Stephens, Jas. married in Williamson Co., Ten. to Harriett Goodwin.
National Banner & Nashville Daily Advertiser (Mon., Aug. 26, 1833)

Stephens, Mr. James married in Bledsoe County, Ten. to Miss Isabella
H. Batty.
National Banner & Nashville Whig (Fri., July 15, 1831)

Stephens, Mr. John married in Cynthiana, Ky. to Mrs. Mary Glenn.
National Banner & Nashville Whig (Sat., July 22, 1826)

Stephens, John Esq. married on Thursday evening last by the Rev. Mr.
Hume to Miss Payzer daughter of Mr. B. Payzer of Nashville.
The Nashville Gazette (Sat., June 10, 1820)

Stephens, Mr. Luther married at Lexington, Ky. to Miss Ann Stillman.
National Banner (Jan. 27, 1826)

Stephens, Miss Margaret M. married to James H. Thomas Esq.

Stephens, Miss Mary married to Mr. William Finch.

Stephens, Miss Mary Ann married to Mr. Anderson Andres.

Stephens, Miss Sarah Ann married to Mr. Pitser Miller.

Stephens, Miss Sarah Ann married to Mr. Pitser Miller.

Stephens, William married in Williamson County to Martha Chrisman.
National Banner & Nashville Whig (Wed., Sept. 24, 1834)

Stephenson, Miss Elvira Amanda married to Mr. Wm. E. Starr.

Stephenson, Mr. Henry married in Jonesborough to Miss Louisa Sparks.
National Banner & Nashville Whig (Wed., Aug. 17, 1831)

Stephenson, Miss Jane E. married to Mr. Robert M. Frierson.

Stephenson, Mr. John B. married in Washington, Tenn. to Miss Elizabeth
B. Ustick.
National Banner & Nashville Daily Advertiser (Mon., March 18, 1833)

Stephenson, Miss Martha married to Maj. William Strain.

Stepheson, Mr. Henry married in Jonesborough to Miss Louisa Sparks.
National Banner & Nashville Whig (Wed., Aug. 17, 1831)

Sterling, Miss Susannah married to Mr. Willis Loving.

Sterritt, Miss Sarah married to Mr. James Miller.

Stevens, Mr. Abram of Nashville married on Thursday June 29th by Rev.
Dr. Lapsley to Miss Martha Ann Robertson of Davidson County.
The Christian Record (Sat., July 15, 1848)

Stevens, Miss Caroline married to Mr. William Myers.

Stevens, Edward Jr. married in Williamson County to Miss Paulina Lamb.
National Banner & Nashville Daily Advertiser (Mon., March 26, 1832)

Stevens, Edwards Jr. married in Williamson County to Miss Paulina
Lamb.
The Western Weekly Review - Franklin, Tenn. (Fri., March 23, 1832)

Stevens, Miss Julia M. married to Maj. N. Lawrence Lindsley.

Stevens, Miss Mary Ann Anna married to Mr. Alexis J. Robert.

Stevens, Miss Mary P. married to Rev. John Trotter.

Stevens, Mr. Samuel married in Miss. on the 20th Dec. last by Esq.
Smith to Miss Sophronia Macon Jones.
The Union (Tues., Feb. 2, 1836)

Stevens, Capt. Thomas L. married on Wednesday last by the Rev. D. A. Penick to Miss Martha J. Farley daughter of Mr. James Farley (From the Milton, N. C. Spectator, Aug. 1)
The Western Weekly Review (Fri., Aug. 17, 1832)

Stevenson, Miss Eliza married to Thomas Davis Esq.

Stevenson, Miss Ellen married to Godfrey M. Fogg Esq.

Stevenson, Miss Ellen married to Godfrey M. Fogg Esq.

Stevenson, Miss Juliet married to Dr. John A. Crawdus.

Stevenson, Miss Melinda married to Mr. Benjamin Neal, Jr.

Stevenson, Miss Rebecca married to Doctor Thomas Lipscomb.

Stevenson, Miss Sarah married to Mr. John Wiley.

Stevenson, Miss Sidney Ann married to Mr. William Gordley.

Stevenson, Mr. V. K. married in Nashville to Miss Elizabeth Childress.
Nashville Republican & State Gazette (Sat., Feb. 1, 1834)

Stevenson, Vernon K. Esq., President of the Nashville & Chattanooga Railroad married on Wednesday by Rev. Dr. Edgar to Miss Elizabeth S. Brown daughter of Judge M. W. Brown all of Nashville.
Nashville True Whig & Weekly Commercial Register (Fri., April 12, 1850)

Steward, Mr. Grace married in Bedford County to Miss Jane Phillips.
National Banner & Nashville Daily Advertiser (Wed., Jan. 4, 1832)

Steward, Miss Sally married to Mr. Allen M. Butler.

Steward, Miss Susan married to Mr. Samuel W. Athey.

Stewart, Mr. A. married at Huntsville, Ala. to Miss Mary M. Walker.
National Banner & Nashville Whig (Sat., June 2, 1827)

Stewart, Miss Alvira married to Elijah Hise Esq.

Stewart, Miss Elizabeth married to Mr. Robert Dean.

Stewart, Mr. J. married in Davidson County to Miss Mahala Corbitt.
National Banner & Nashville Whig (Mon., Sept. 22, 1834)

Stewart, James married in Williamson County to Francis Warren.
The Western Weekly Review - Franklin, Tenn. (Fri., March 8, 1833)

Stewart, Mr. James married at Jonesborough to Miss Mary Sevier.
National Banner (Sat., July 18, 1829)

Stewart, Capt. James of Jonesborough E. T. married Miss Emily Rosanna Deaderick of this town on Tuesday evening last by the Rev. Mr. M'Mahan.
The Nashville Whig (Sept. 1st. 1817)

Stewart, Mr. James W. married in Rutherford County to Miss Isabella Moore.
National Banner & Nashville Whig (Fri., Nov. 11, 1831)

Stewart, Mr. John G. married in Logan County, Ky. to Miss Sarah R. Wood daughter of Mr. Lewis Wood.
National Banner & Nashville Whig (Mon., June 20, 1831)

Stewart, Miss Launno married to Mr. John Watson.

Stewart, Miss Mary married to Mr. Silas C. Goodrich.

Stewart, Mr. William married in Todd County, Ky. to Miss Martin.
National Banner & Nashville Whig (Wed., Oct. 19, 1831)

Stewart, Mr. Wm. R. married in Rutherford County to Miss Ann Nash.
National Banner & Nashville Whig (Sat., Aug. 30, 1828)

Stewart, Mr. Willis married in Jefferson County, Ky. to Miss Patsey
P. Taylor.
National Banner & Nashville Whig (Sat., Jan. 6, 1827)

Stichies, Mr. Andrew aged 16 married at Claverak, N. J. to Miss
Catherine Holsapple aged 14.
National Banner & Nashville Daily Advertiser (Thurs., Sept. 12,1833)

Stikes, Miss Nancy married to Mr. Elza Dunbar.

Stiles, Mr. Squire married in St. Clair County, Illinois to Miss
Abigail Cravens.
National Banner (May 27, 1826)

Stiles, Miss Anna married to Dr. F. G. Montgomery.

Stiles, Jack J. married in Giles County to Harriet N. Payne.
National Banner & Nashville Daily Advertiser (Tues., Dec. 17, 1833)

Stillman, Miss Ann married to Mr. Luther Stephens.

Stillwell, Mr. John married in Arkansas County, A. T. to Miss Pringle.
National Banner (March 31, 1826)

Stimball, Miss Sophia married to Mr. George Lischer.

Stinson, Mr. John married in Jefferson County, Ky. to Miss Elizabeth
Baker.
National Banner (Sat., April 18, 1829)

Stith, Miss Adeline A. married to Mr. Edward L. Travis.
National Banner & Nashville Whig (Wed., Dec. 28, 1831)

Stoaks, MIss Elizabeth married to Mr. Thomas J. Brown.

Stockard, Col. Samuel S. of Maury County married in Pulaski, Ten. to
Miss Maria Louisa Lester daughter of Mr. Fountain Lester of Pulaski.
National Banner & Nashville Whig (Wed., March 4, 1835)

Stockart, Col. Samuel S. of Maury County married on 25 Feb. to Miss
Maria Louisa Lester Nashville.
Nashville Republican (Tues., March 3, 1835)

Stoddard, Miss L. M. married to Mr. Abraham S. Davidson.

Stokes, Edward married in Williamson County to Miss Mary Tatum.
The Western Weekly Review - Franklin, Tenn. (Fri., Dec. 14, 1832)

Stokes, Mrs. Elizabeth married to Maj. S. Muel Elam.

Stokes, Mr. John M. married at Cincinnati to Miss Sophia Ward.
National Banner & Nashville Whig (Sat., June 14, 1828)

Stokes, Jordan Esq. from the County of Smith married at Carthage, Feb.
11 by Rev. Mr. Brown to Miss Penelope Williams daughter of the late
Hon. Nathaniel Williams. of Smith County.
Nashville Whig (Wed., Feb. 19, 1840)

Stokes, Jordan Esq. married on the 10th inst. at Lebanon by the Rev.
F. E. Pitts to Miss Martha Jane Frazer of Lebanon.
Nashville Whig (Tues., Oct. 18, 1842)

Stokes, Miss Mary married to Mr. John Arnold.

Stokes, Miss Nancy married to Mr. Elza Dunbar.

Stokes, Philadelphia married to Mr. Benj. L. Tatum.

Stokes, Mr. Wm. B. married in Smith County to Miss Parilea Overall.
National Banner & Nashville Advertiser (Fri., Jan. 27, 1832)

Stokes, Mr. William B. married in Smith County on the 18th inst. to
Miss Parelia Overall.
National Banner & Nashville Daily Advertiser (Fri., Jan. 27, 1832)

Stone, Miss Abenica married to Mr. Thorton Wright.
National Banner & Nashville Whig (Fri., March 6, 1835)

Stone, Mrs. Amelia married to Mr. Nathaniel H. Banister.

Stone, Maj. Ebenezer married in Smith Co., Tenn. May 30 by the Rev.
Malen A. Marlone to Miss Julia Derickson all of Smith County.
Nashville True Whig & Weekly Commercial Register (Fri., June 21, 1850)

Stone, Miss Eliza married to Mr. William H. Crouch.
National Banner & Nashville Advertiser (Mon., Dec. 10, 1832)

Stone, Miss Eliza married to Mr. William H. Crouch.

Stone, Gregory D. Esq. married in Russellville, Ala. to Miss Eliza F.
Faris.
National Banner & Nashville Whig (Sat., Sept. 23, 1826)

Stone, Mr. George W. married in Lincoln County, Ten. to Miss Mary
Gillespie.
National Banner & Nashville Whig (Mon., Jan. 5, 1835)

Stone, Mr. Hezekiah married in Jefferson County on the 18th January,
by the Rev. William Cates to Miss Mary Nelson.
Nashville Whig (Thurs., Feb. 24, 1842)

Stone, Mr. John married near New Market, Tenn. on Thursday 5th Sept.
by the Rev. Allen H. Mathis to Miss Eliza A. Nelson all of Jefferson
County.
Nashville Whig (Tues., Sept. 17, 1844)

Stone, Mr. L. L. of Lincoln County, Ten. married in Madison County, Ala.
to Miss Eveline Drake.
National Banner & Nashville Whig (Thurs., June 3, 1830)

Stone, Miss Mary married to Mr. Charles Campbell.

Stone, Miss Mary married to Mr. William Jopland.

Stone, Miss Mary married to Mr. William Jopland.

Stone, Mr. Michael H. married in Grainger County to Miss Sarah Campbell.
National Banner & Nashville Whig (Sat., April 7, 1827)

Stone, Mr. Robert married in Maury County to Miss M. Gentry.
National Banner & Nashville Daily Advertiser (Thurs., May 17, 1832)

Stone, Miss Sarah married to Mr. Pleasant Wilson.

Stone, Miss Sarah E. married to Mr. H. B. Cleaveland.

Stone, Miss Susan married to Mr. Churchhill Yager.

Stone, Mr. Thomas married in Sumner County to Miss Matilda H. Walker.
National Banner & Nashville Whig (Mon., Aug. 9, 1830)

Stoner, Mr. Porter J. married near Bardstown, Ky. to Miss Mary Ann Hall daughter of Mr. S. Hall.
National Banner & Nashville Whig (Wed., Nov. 19, 1834)

Stones, Mr. Benjamin of Nashville married in Dickson County on the 8th inst. by T. Parma, Esq. to Miss Mary Jane Napier daughter of H. C. Napier Esq. of Dickson County, Tennessee.
Nashville Whig (Tues., Feb. 14, 1843)

Stones, Mr. Liston of Nashville married on the 25th inst. by the Rev. Dr. Edgar to Miss W. Elizabeth McEwen daughter of Mr. Joseph H. McEwen of Davidson County.
Nashville Whig (Mon., March 25, 1839)

Stormer, Miss Seylima married to Mr. Terence W. McAffry.

Story, Miss Maria married to Mr. Judiah Hockersmith.
National Banner (April 14, 1826)

Story, Mr. Thomas J. married in Vernon, Ia. to Miss Jane Vawter.
National Banner (Jan. 13, 1826)

Stothart, Dr. Alexander H. married in Davidson County on Thursday evening the 27th June by the Rev. Mr. Gwin to Miss Sarah Ann Bosley
National Banner & Nashville Daily Advertiser (Sat., June 29, 1833)

Stothart, Dr. Alexander H. married in Davidson County to Miss Sarah Ann Bosley on Thursday evening last.
Nashville Republican & State Gazette (Fri., June 28, 1833)

Stothart, Mr. William T. married in this vicinity on Thursday 10th inst. by the Rev. Dr. Wharton to Mary Hannah Norvell daughter of Moses Norvell Esq.
Nashville Whig (Sat., Aug. 12, 1843)

Stout, Miss Catherine married to Mr. Robert T. Hill.

Stout, Miss Frances married to Capt. Leander Knowles.

Stout, Mrs. Harriet married to Mr. Wm. Kiser.

Stout, Capt. Ira A. married on Wednesday 26th inst. by the Rev. C. D. Elliott to Miss Sarah A. Graham all of Nashville.
Nashville Whig (Sat., Oct. 29, 1842)

Stout, Mr. Jesse married in Spencer County, Ky. to Miss Peggy Carter.
National Banner & Nashville Whig (Sat., Aug. 11, 1827)

Stout, Miss Margaret J. married to Mr. Daniel B. Hill.
National Banner & Nashville Daily Advertiser (Fri., Feb. 24, 1832)

Stout, Miss Mary A. married to Mr. George W. Rawles, Esq.

Stout, Mr. Moses married at St. Louis to Miss Eulalia Platt.
National Banner & Nashville Whig (Fri., Nov. 26, 1830)

Stout, Miss Rebecca A. married to Mr. Zachariah Blackman.

Stovall, Miss Fanny married to Mr. James Brittan.

Stovall, Mr. G. W. married in Madison County, Ala. to Miss Elizabeth Jane M'Daniel.
National Banner & Nashville Whig (Mon., Dec. 6, 1830)

Stovall, Mr. John D. of Rutherford County married in Bedford County to Miss Mary Drake of Bedford County.
National Banner (Jan. 6, 1826)

Stovall, Miss Mary Ann married to Maj. Alfred Gardner.

Stow, Miss Edy married to Mr. George J. G. Dunn.

Stowell, Mr. Seth married in Louisville to Miss Rachel Hynes.
National Banner & Nashville Whig (Sat., March 31, 1827)

Strader, Capt. J. married at Cincinnati to Miss Julia Dunseth.
National Banner & Nashville Whig (Sat., June 2, 1827)

Strain, Mr. John married in Henry County to Miss Mahala Dobbs.
National Banner & Nashville Advertiser (March 2, 1832)

Strain, Maj. William married in Washington County to Miss Martha
Stephenson.
National Banner & Nashville Daily Advertiser (Sat., Sept. 22, 1832)

Strain, Maj. William married in Washington County to Miss Martha
Stephenson.
National Banner & Nashville Advertiser (Sat., Sept. 22, 1832)

Strange, Miss Jamima married to Mr. William Elam.

Stratton, Mr. Edward merchant of Gallatin, Sumner County married on
Tuesday the 2nd inst. to Miss Lavenia Walton of Sumner County.
The Union (Sat., Aug. 20, 1836)

Stratton, Mr. Edward married in Sumner County to Miss Sarah C. Tyree.
National Banner (Sat., Aug. 1, 1829)

Stratton, Miss Elizabeth married to Mr. Wm. G. Scott.

Stratton, Miss Helen M. married to Mr. Albert B. Burgess.

Stratton, Miss Jane married to Mr. Thomas Peay.

Stratton, Mr. John married in Sumner County to Miss Frances Clay.
National Banner & Nashville Daily Advertiser (Wed., Feb. 8, 1832)

Stratton, Miss Helen M. married to Mr. Albert B. Burgess.

Stratton, Mr. Henry M. of Sumner County married in Nashville on Wed.
evening last to Miss Hannah Amanda Snow daughter of Mr. David Snow.
National Banner & Nashville Whig (Fri., Nov. 26, 1830)

Stratton, Mr. Madison married in Davidson County on Wednesday evening
last by the Rev. Mr. Green to Miss Mary Ann Snow.
National Banner & Nashville Daily Advertiser (Sat., May 24, 1834)

Stratton, Mr. Thomas E. married on the 6th inst. by Rev. Dr. Howell
to Miss Sarah M. Morris all of Nashville.
Nashville Whig (Thurs., Nov. 14, 1844)

Street, Rev. O. D. of Winchester, Ten. married in Madison County, Ala.
to Miss Mary Ann Atkins.
National Banner & Nashville Daily Advertiser (Sat., Sept. 6, 1834)

Stribling, Miss Mary M. married to William P. Horne, Esq.

Stricker, Miss Julian married to Christopher Rankins Esq.

Stringfield, Rev. Thomas married in Jefferson County to Miss Sarah
Williams.
National Banner & Nashville Whig (Sat., Oct. 28, 1826)

Strong, Miss Amelia married to Mr. Stephen Gibson.

Strong, Miss Catherine married to Maj. Barkley M. Wallace.

Strong, Mr. D. E. A. married in Cincinnati to Mrs. Olivia E. Drake.
National Banner & Nashville Daily Advertiser (Wed., Aug. 15, 1832)

Strong, Dr. Joseph C. married in Shelbyville to Miss Sophonia Mares.
National Banner & Nashville Advertiser (Sat., Oct. 6, 1832)

Strong, Miss Martha married to Mr. Molton Dickson.

Strong, Miss Mary married to Mr. Gideon M. Hazen.

Strong, Miss Sarah married to Mr. J. Pratt.

Strong, Miss Selenda married to Capt. Jarret Long.

Strother, Miss Amanda married to Mr. William A. Cook.

Strother, Miss Eliza J. married to Mr. James M. Sheppard.

Strother, Mr. William married in Louisville, Ky. to Miss Maria Jones.
National Banner & Nashville Advertiser (Tues., June 26, 1832)

Stroud, Miss Elizabeth M. married to Mr. James Carson.

Stuart, Miss Esther L. married to Mr. Jefferson Martin.

Stuart, Mr. S. E. married in Sullivan Co., Ten. to Miss Jane G.
Gammon daughter ofGeorge Gammon, Esq.
National Banner & Nashville Daily Advertiser (Mon., June 30, 1834)

Stubblefield, Mr. Flemming married near Hartsville on the 18th ult. by
the Rev. J. Dillard to Miss Elmyra Britton daughter of Mr. Richard
Britton.
National Banner & Nashville Whig (Fri., March 12, 1830)

Stubbs, Miss Rachel R. married to Mr. John F. Bowls.

Stubbs, Miss Rachel R. married to Mr. John Bowls.

Studervant, Mrs. Nancy married to William Bryant.

Stump, Mrs. Anna B. married to Henry Hollingsworth Esq.

Stump, Mr. Philip S. married on Thursday Oct. 1st. by Rev. Mr. Howell
to Miss Susanna B. Menifee all of Nashville.
National Banner & Nashville Whig (Fri., Oct. 2, 1835)

Stump, Mr. Philip S. of Davidson County married to Miss Susannah B.
Menifee of Davidson County.
Nashville Republican (Sat., Oct. 3, 1835)

Stump, Mr. Thomas Jefferson married on Wednesday evening last to Miss
Tennessee Marshall daughter of Mr. Elihu Marshall.
National Banner (Fri., Dec. 23, 1825)

Sturdivant, Miss Mary married to Mr. Adam Earhart.

Suares, Miss Judith married to Mr. Wm. H. Limbert.

Sublett, Mr. A. C. married in Rutherford County to Mrs. Louisa Lewis.
National Banner & Nashville Whig (Sat., Jan. 17, 1829)

Sublett, Miss Sarah C. married to Mr. John D. Black.

Sudberry, Miss Ann N. married to Daniel Riggus.

Suddeth, Mr. John married in Roane County to Miss Eveline Center.
National Banner (Sat., May 9, 1829)

Suel, Miss Eliza M. married to Mr. Simeon W. Johnson.

Sugg, Dr. H. H. of Robertson County married to Mary Ann R. Grimes of
Montgomery County on the 2d May.
National Banner & Nashville Advertiser (Wed., May 9, 1832)

Suggs, Mr. Myers married in Bedford County to Miss Sussana Smith.
National Banner & Nashville Whig (Sat., Feb. 17, 1827)

Sullinger, Miss Penelope married to Mr. Henry Inis.

Sullivan, Miss Caroline married to Mr. Milton Parker.

Sullivan, Franklin Esq. merchant of Baltimore married on Wednesday
evening by the Rev. Philip Lindsley to Mary Robertson daughter of
Dr. Felix Robertson of Nashville.
Nashville Whig (Mon., Jan. 20, 1840)

Sullivan, Franklin Esq. merchant of Baltimore married on Wednesday
evening by the Rev. Philip Lindsley to Mary Robertson daughter of
Dr. Felix Robertson of Nashville.
Daily Republican Banner (Tues., Jan. 21, 1840)

Sullivan, Rev. Isaac married in Madison, Ala. to Miss Mary B. Harris.
National Banner & Nashville Whig (Sat., July 8, 1826)

Sullivan, Mr. Layton married in Madison County, Ten. to Miss Mary
Anderson.
National Banner & Nashville Whig (Sat., May 3, 1828)

Sullivan, Rebecca married in William County, Ten. to Uriah McClellan.
National Banner & Nashville Daily Advertiser (Mon., Aug. 26, 1833)

Sullivan, Mr. R. F. married in Tipton County to Miss Julian Davis.
National Banner (Sat., Oct. 10, 1829)

Sullivan, Mr. Richard Fox married in Tipton County to Miss Julia
Ann Davis.
National Banner (Sat., Sept. 19, 1829)

Sullivant, M. L. Esq. married in Mercer County, Ky. to Miss Sarah L.
M'Dowell
National Banner & Nashville Whig (Sat., July 14, 1827)

Summers, Miss Emelia married to Mr. David Farwater.

Sumner, Mrs. married to Rev. John Porter.

Sumner, J. C. Esq. married in Crawford County, Ark. married to Miss
Mary Robinson.
National Banner & Nashville Whig (Sat., Oct. 28, 1826)

Sumner, Miss Mary E. married to Mr. Lewis Lowe.

Sumner, Miss Temperance A. married to Mr. John Boss.

Sumner, Thomas J. Esq. Editor of the Democrat at Huntsville, Ala.
married Miss Louisa A. Lanier.
National Banner & Nashville Whig (Thurs., May 20, 1830)

Sumner, Mr. Thomas R. of Williamson County married to Miss Mary
Hughlett of Overton County on 15 ult.
Impartial Review & Cumberland Repository - published at Nashville
(Thurs., Sept. 3, 1807)

Sumners, Miss Mary E. married to Mr. Lewis Loewe.

Sumners, Mr. Noah C. married in Jessamine County, Ky. to Miss
Margaret C. Harrison.
National Banner & Nashville Whig (Sat., Dec. 30, 1826)

Summers, Miss Polly married to Mr. Peter Varner.

Summerville, Mr. John of Knoxville married Miss Elizabeth Chisolm.
Knoxville Gazette (Thurs., May 22, 1794)

Summerville, Mr. John H. married in this County on Friday night last to Miss Evelina Hewitt.
National Banner & Nashville Whig (Sat., Oct. 28, 1826)

Sutton, Miss Laurel married to Mr. G. W. Humphreys.

Suttin, Miss Elizabeth married to Mr. Richard Baresford.

Sutton, Miss Caroline married to Mr. Fountain Lester.

Sutton, Miss Caroline married to Mr. Fountain C. Lester.

Sutton, Miss Elizabeth married to Mr. Quarels Mayfield.

Sutton, Mr. George Washington married in Lexington, Ky. to Miss Laura C. Grosoenor.
National Banner & Nashville Whig (Sat., March 1, 1828)

Sutton, Miss S. married to Mr. Silas B. Wakefield.

Swor, Miss Matilda married to Mr. Elias Shankle.

Tabler, Miss Ann married to Mr. Chas. Smith.

Tabler, Mr. William at Huntsville married Miss Ann Eversoll.
National Banner & Nashville Whig (Tues., April 27, 1830)

Taff, Dr. W. (of the Alabama Territory) married on Thursday evening
last by the Rev. Mr. Hume to Miss Julia M. Coleman daughter of Joseph
Coleman Esq. of this vicinity.
Nashville Whig & Tennessee Advertiser (June 20, 1818)

Taggart, Dr. James married in Clark County, Ky. to Miss Chiles.
National Banner (Feb. 17, 1826)

Talbert, Mr. Lewis, Louisville, Ky. married to Mrs. Nancy Ferguson.
National Banner & Nashville Advertiser (Mon., Jan. 30, 1832

Talbert, Miss Rebecca W. married to Mr. Anthony P. Bodley.

Talbot, Mr. Albert G. married in Jessamine County, Ky. to Miss Elizabeth
Caldwell daughter of Capt. Wm. Caldwe..
National Banner & Nashville Whig (Mon., Jan. 31, 1831)

Talbot, Miss Ann R. married to Mr. J. B. Danforth.

Talbot, Capt. Benjamin of Shawneetown, I. T. married last evening to
Miss Maria Williams of this town.
The Nashville Whig (March 5, 1817)

Talbot, Miss Caroline married to Mr. William Talbot.

Talbot, Charles Henry Esq. married in Garrard County, Ky. to Miss
Elizabeth Owsley daughter of Judge Owsley.
National Banner & Nashville Whig (Sat., Dec. 6, 1828)

Talbot, Miss Cordelia married to Mr. Erasmus T. Talbot.

Talbot, Mr. Courtney of Bourbon County married in Fayette County, Ky.
to Miss Elizabeth Harp.
National Banner & Nashville Whig (Mon., Dec. 27, 1830)

Talbot, Miss Eliza married to Mr. Abram B. Taylor.

Talbot, Miss Eliza married to Mr. Abraham B. Taylor.

Talbot, Mr. Erasmus T. of Louisville, Ky. married on the 24th Jan. to
Miss Cordelia Talbot of Henderson County, Ky.
National Banner & Nashville Daily Advertiser (Sat., Feb. 9, 1888)

Talbot, James L. Esq. one of the Editors of the District Telegraph
married near Jackson, Tennessee on the 16th inst. to Miss Ann P.
Dickens of Madison County.
Nashville Whig (Tues., Jan. 23, 1838)

Talbot, Mr. John G. of Jessamine County, Ky. married in Garrard County,
Ky. to Miss Elizabeth Smith daughter of Mr. Edmund Smith.
National Banner (Sat., Sept. 5, 1829)

Talbot, Col. Joseph H. married at Jackson on Thursday evening last to
Miss Almedia Saunders daughter of the late Frances Saunders, Esq.
National Banner & Nashville Whig (Sat., March 17, 1827)

Talbot, Miss Margaret married to Mr. Edward A. Dudley.

Talbot, Miss Mary R. married to Mr. Joseph W. Perkins.

Talbot, Miss Polly married to Dr. Samuel Hogg.

Talbot, Miss Priscilla S. H. married to Dr. Cyrus M. Goodlin.

Talbot, Miss Rebecca married to Mr. Joseph K. Perkins.

Talbot, Miss Sophia married to Mr. E. S. Hall.

Talbot, Mr. William of Georgia married on Thursday evening last by the
Rev. Mr. Hume to Miss Caroline Talbot daughter of Thomas Talbot Esq.
of Davidson County.
The Nashville Gazette (Sat., Jan. 8, 1820)

Talbot, Miss Hester Ann married to Mr. James Gillespie.

Taliaferro, Miss Ann married to Mr. James J. Sayer.

Taliaferro, Miss Elizabeth married to Mr. Charles Drummond.

Taliaferro, Miss Harriet D. married to Mr. Jacob R. Hogan.

Talliaferro, John A. of Trenton, Ten. married on Sept. 28th by the Rev.
Mr. Howell to Miss Mary Talliaferro daughter of Baldwin Talliaferro
Esq. of Williamson County, Ten.
Daily Republican Banner (Tues., Oct. 3,1837)

Talliaferro, Mr. John N. married in Newport, Ky. to Miss Frances M.
Southgate daughter of Richard Southgate Esq.
National Banner & Nashville Whig (Fri., Dec. 10, 1830)

Talliaferro, Miss Mary married to John A. Talliaferro.

Taliaferro, Miss Mary E. H. married to Mr. Robert Shotwell.

Taliaferro, Miss Sarah Ann married to Mr. Jack Taylor.

Taliaferro, Mr. William B. married in Franklin County, Tenn. on the
7th by the Rev. Robert Dougan to Miss Keren Happuch Hendon.
National Banner & Nashville Daily Advertiser (Fri., Aug. 22, 1834)

Talley, Miss Martha N. married to Mr. Eli Morris.

Talley, Miss Pamelo married to Mr. Lorezo Watkins.

Talley, Mr. Samuel of Lincoln County married in Williamson County to
Miss Lillian Short daughter of Isaac Short, Esq.
National Banner & Nashville Daily Advertiser (Mon., Nov. 29, 1833)

Talley, Miss Sarah Ann married to Mr. Thomas Hobson.

Talley, Mr. Thomas J. of Sumner married on Tuesday the 14th by the Rev.
Mr. Gray to Miss Permelia Butterworth of Davidson County.
Nashville Whig (Sat., Feb. 18, 1843)

Tandy, Mr. married in Hopkinsville, Ky. to Miss Woodfolk.
National Banner & Nashville Whig (Sat., Dec. 16, 1826)

Tandy, Miss Ann married to Mr. James Radford.

Tandy, Miss Ann P. married to Mr. James Radford.

Tanner, Mr. Edward married in Shippingport to Miss Sarah W. Elder Jr.
National Banner & Nashville Whig (Sat., Aug. 19, 1826)

Tandy, Miss Frances Ann married to Mr. Mills Perry.

Tandy, Mr. John H. of Ky. married on the 19th inst. by the Rev. R. B. C.
Howell to Miss Sarah Trice daughter of Thomas A. Trice Esq. of Nash-
ville.
The Politician & Weekly Nashville Whig (Fri., Oct. 22, 1847)

Taney, Miss Anna Arnold married to James Mason Campbell, Esq.

Tannehill, Miss Ann Maria married to Mr. William B. Bayless.

Tannehill, Miss Mary Margaret married to Mr. William T. Berry.

Tannehill, Mr. Z. H. of Mobile, formerly of Nashville married at
Louisville, Ky. on the 27th ult. to Miss Mary E. Albert of Louisville.
Nashville Whig (Tues., July 9, 1844)

Tanner, Miss Mary married to R. H. Burton.

Tansil, Mr. Eramus D. married in Weakley County to Miss Mary Ann Allen.
National Banner & Nashville Daily Advertiser (Wed., June 12, 1833)

Tappan, Col. B. S. married in Williamson County to Miss Margaret B.
Wood on Thursday evening 22d inst. by the Rev. James H. Otey.
National Banner & Nashville Advertiser (Mon., March 26, 1832)

Tappan, Capt. E. S., merchant of Brownsville, Tenn. married in Somer-
ville on the 4th inst. by the Rev. James Hamilton to Miss Sarah Jane
Williamson.
The Western Weekly Review - Franklin, Ten. (Fri., July 27, 1832)

Tarascon, Miss Nanine married to Mr. Edmund H. Taylor.

Tardiff, Mr. Peter junior publisher of the National Banner & Whig
married at the Fountain of Health, Davidson County, Ten. 30th Sept. by
the Rev. Mr. Edgar to Miss Mary P. Saunders daughter of William Saunders
Esq.
National Banner & Nashville Whig (Fri., Oct. 2, 1835)

Tarlton, Mr. Robert M. married in Arkansas County to Miss Mary Ann
Holland.
National Banner & Nashville Whig (Sat., Aug. 26, 1826)

Tarpley, Collin S. Esq. married in Giles County on Tuesday 10th inst.
by Rev. H. H. Brown to Miss Susan Paine, daughter of James Paine Esq.
National Banner & Nashville Whig (Sat., Oct. 4, 1828)

Tarpley, Mr. Ezra married in Columbia to Miss Eliza Voorhies.
National Banner & Nashville Daily Advertiser (Wed., Aug. 21, 1833)

Tarpley, Miss Susan married to Mr. F. A. Westmoreland.

Tarrant, Mr. Larkin married at Cincinnati to Miss Emeline Tunis.
National Banner (Feb. 10, 1826)

Tart, Mr. James married in Henry County, Ten. since the first of Jan.
to Miss Jubitha Wade.
National Banner & Nashville Whig (Fri., Feb. 13, 1835)

Tarver, Mr. Benj. of Wilson County married Miss Sally Odam of Sumner
County on Sunday 17, inst.
Impartial Review & Cumberland Repository - published at Nashville
(Sat., Aug. 30, 1806)

Tarver, Miss Elizabeth H. married to Mr. John S. Brown.

Tary, Rev. Thomas W., Missionary to China, married at Kilmarnock,
Lancaster County, Virginia on the 3d inst. by the Rev. J. Lewis Shuck
to Miss Isabell Hall, third daughter of the Rev. Addison Hall.
Nashville Whig (Tues., Dec. 29, 1846)

Tate, Mr. James R. married in Frankfort, Ky. to Miss Eliza Hampton.
National Banner & Nashville Daily Advertiser (Thurs., June 19, 1834)

Tate, Miss Jane E. married to William M. C. Gambell.

Tate, Col. J. P. of N. Carolina married in Maury County to Miss Mary Webster.
National Banner (Jan. 27, 1826)

Tate, Rev. John married in M'Minn County to Miss Jane Weir daughter of Mr. George Weir.
National Banner (Sat., Sept. 12, 1829)

Tate, Miss Margaret married to Mr. Nelson Eli.

Tate, Miss Mary J. married to Col. James Camp.

Tate, Capt. Samuel B. married in Grainger County to Miss Caroline Center.
National Banner & Nashville Whig (Sat., May 24, 1828)

Tate, Mr. William married in Madison County, Ala. to Miss Lucy Bronough.
National Banner & Nashville Whig (Fri., Feb. 12, 1830)

Tatum, Benjamin L. married in Williamson County to Miss Philadelphia Stokes.
National Banner & Nashville Daily Advertiser (Mon., March 26, 1832)

Tatum, Miss Mary married to Edward Stokes.

Tatum, Mr. William married in Logan County, Ky. to Miss Prudence F. Robinson.
National Banner & Nashville Whig (Mon., Dec. 29, 1834)

Taul, Miss Louisiana married to Mr. Tipton Bradford.

Taul, Maj. Thomas P. married in Franklin County on the 7th inst. by the Rev. Mr. Witter to Miss Caroline P. Anderson daughter of Col. Wm. P. Anderson.
National Banner & Nashville Whig (Sat., March 17, 1827)

Taws, Capt. Charles married at Louisville, Ky. to Miss Celia Duncan.
National Banner & Nashville Whig (Mon., Nov. 22, 1830)

Taylor, Miss married to Mr. Allen Ross.

Taylor, Mr. Abraham B. of Hartsville married Miss Henrietta T. Bryan of Robertson County on the 21st.
Nashville Republican & State Gazette (Thurs., Dec. 23, 1830)

Taylor, Mr. Abraham B. of Raleigh, Ten. on the 8th inst. married Miss Eliza Talbot of Jackson, Ten.
Nashville Republican (Tues., Jan. 13, 1835)

Taylor, Mr. Abram B., merchant of Raleigh, Ten. married in Jackson, Ten. to Miss Eliza Talbot of Jackson.
National Banner & Nashville Whig (Wed., Jan. 21, 1835)

Taylor, Mr. Allen married in Spencer County, Ky. to Miss Mary Gilleland.
National Banner (Feb. 3, 1826)

Taylor, Miss Amanda married to Rev. Simeon N. Crane.

Taylor, Miss Ann married to Rev. Alexander Downey.

Taylor, Miss Ann America married to Mr. Uriah Taylor.

Taylor, Mr. Bailey W. married in this County on Thursday evening last to Miss Delila Austin.
National Banner & Nashville Whig (Sat., April 7, 1827)

Taylor, Miss Betsy married to Mr. Joseph Jones.

Taylor, Miss Courtney Ann married to Mr. John D. Colmisnil.

Taylor, Mr. David married at Columbus, Ohio to Miss Nancy P. Nelson.
National Banner & Nashville Whig (Fri., Oct. 20, 1826)

Taylor, Mr. David married in Sumner County to Miss Louisa Durham on
the 10 inst.
National Banner & Nashville Whig (Mon., March 21, 1831)

Taylor, Mr. David married in Rutherford County on the 12th inst. to
Miss Rachel Witherspoon.
National Banner & Nashville Daily Advertiser (Mon., March 25, 1833)

Taylor, Miss Dicy married to Mr. Thos. Morrison.
National Banner & Nashville Whig (Fri., Jan. 29, 1830)

Taylor, Mr. Edmund H. married at Louisville, Ky. to Nanine Tarascon.
National Banner & Nashville Whig (Sat., Aug. 9, 1828)

Taylor, Miss Elizabeth married to Mr. Addison Boyd.

Taylor, Miss Elizabeth married to Mr. John B. Cardwell.

Taylor, Miss Elizabeth married to Col. William Wallace Smith Bliss.

Taylor, Miss Elmira J. married to Mr. Pierce Shannon.

Taylor, Miss Emelie V. married to Mr. Robert W. Walker.

Taylor, Miss Emily married to Mr. J. P. Coleman.

Taylor, Miss Evelina E. C. married to Ch. K. Gillespie.

Taylor, Miss Francis T. G. married to Mr. James S. Crutchfield.

Taylor, Mr. Grizell married in Williamson County to Mr. John Jordan.
The Western Weekly Review - Franklin, Tenn. (Fri., Dec. 23, 1831)

Taylor, Mr. Isaac B. married in Sumner County, Ten. to Miss Lucinda
McGaughey.
National Banner & Nashville Daily Advertiser (Tues., Nov. 19, 1833)

Taylor, Mr. Jack married at Louisville, Ky. to Miss Sarah Ann Taliaferro
National Banner & Nashville Whig (Sat., Dec. 6, 1828)

Taylor, Mr. James Jr. of Newport married in Kentucky to Wm. T. Barry.
Nashville Whig (May 31, 1824)

Taylor, Dr. James H. of Haywood County married in Brownsville, Tenn.
on the 15th inst. by the Rev. Peter R. Bland to Miss Mary T. Bond
daughter of Mr. W. S. Bond.
National Banner & Nashville Daily Advertiser (Tues., Oct. 29, 1833)

Taylor, Mr. James M. married at Knoxville to Miss Elizabeth Ann Mason.
National Banner & Nashville Daily Advertiser (Fri., March 1, 1833)

Taylor, Miss Jane B. married to Mr. Josiah F. Morford, Esq.

Taylor, Rev. John aged 80 married in Frankfort, Ky. to Miss Nash aged
40 years.
National Banner & Nashville Daily Advertiser (Mon., Aug. 26, 1833)

Taylor, Mr. John married in Maury County to Miss Mary Baily.
National Banner & Nashville Whig (Thurs., Nov. 18, 1830)

Taylor, Mr. Joseph married in Cincinnati to Miss Elizabeth Chamberlain.
National Banner & Nashville Whig (Sat., April 12, 1828)

Taylor, Mr. Joseph F. married in Bourbon County, Ky. to Miss Louisa Eales.
National Banner & Nashville Whig (Fri., March 6, 1835)

Taylor, Miss Louisa married to Mr. Mark M. Lucas.

Taylor, Miss Louisa W. married to Mr. John E. Shallcross.

Taylor, Miss Lucy Jane married to Mr. J. H. McMilen.

Taylor, Martha Ella married to Charles D. Drake, Esq.

Taylor, Miss Mary married to Mr. Timothy Walton.

Taylor, Miss Mary married to Mr. F. Myers.

Taylor, Miss Mary Ann married to Mr. Thomas Coleman.

Taylor, Miss Mary P. married to Medicus A. Long, Esq.

Taylor, Miss Mary S. married to Mr. Williard Manchester.

Taylor, Miss Mary Smythe married to Meredith Calhoun Esq.

Taylor, Miss Nancy married to Mr. Lemuel A. Wilson.

Taylor, Mr. Nathaniel P. of Jefferson County, Ky. married at St. Louis to Mrs. Matilda Walker daughter of Major William Christy.
National Banner & Nashville Daily Advertiser (Sat., July 7, 1832)

Taylor, Miss Patsey P. married to Mr. Willis Stewart.

Taylor, Mrs. Polly married to Mr. William P. Hackett.

Taylor, Mrs. Sarah married to Mr. French Doores.

Taylor, Miss Sarah married to Mr. Wm. Grider.

Taylor, Miss Sarah married to Mr. Joseph Bell.

Taylor, Sarah married to John King.

Taylor, Miss Susan married to Mr. Samuel M. Lewis.

Taylor, Miss Susan Y. married to Dr. Allen J. Barbee.'

Taylor, Mr. Thomas L. married in Williamson County near Versaillies on the 24th inst. to Miss Louisa Jane Pate daughter of Mr. K. Pate.
National Banner & Nashville Daily Advertiser (Fri., Nov. 1, 1833)

Taylor, Mr. Uriah married in Warren County, Ky. to Miss Ann America Taylor.
National Banner & Nashville Whig (Wed., Sept. 21, 1831)

Taylor, Mr. William married in Jackson, Ten. on the 6th Oct. to Miss Hester C. Lee.
National Banner & Nashville Whig (Mon., Oct. 17th, 1836)

Taylor, Mr. Wm. married in Lincoln County, Ky. to Miss Fanny Warren.
National Banner & Nashville Whig (Sat., Feb. 9, 1828)

Taylor, Mr. William D. S. of Jefferson County married in Oldham County, Ky. to Miss Jane P. Barbour daughter of P. G. S. Barbour, Esq.
National Banner (Sat., Sept. 5, 1829)

Taylor, Mr. Willie married in Franklin County to Miss Adeline London of Jackson County, Ala.
National Banner & Nashville Whig (Sept. 2, 1826)

Taylor, Miss Winny married to Mr. John Price.

Tear, Mr. Richard married in Sumner County to Elizabeth Dunigan.
National Banner & Nashville Daily Advertiser (Fri., Aug. 16, 1833)

Tedford, Miss Mary married to Col. Andrew Cambell

Temple, Miss Agnes E. married to Col. B. F. Foster.

Temple, Mr. Edward M., merchant of Randolph, married on the 3d inst.
by the Rev. Marcus C. Henderson to Miss Sarah Dunham daughter of Daniel
A. Dunham, Esq. all of Tipton County, Ten.
National Banner & Nashville Advertiser (Tues., May 13, 1834)

Temple, Miss Ellen married to Mr. T. Kezer.

Temple, Mr. J. C. of Logan County, Ky. married near Bardstown, Ky.
to Miss Sarah F. Brashear.
National Banner & Nashville Whig (Mon., Nov. 10, 1834)

Temple, Miss Jane married to Mr. James Stanly.

Temple, Mr. Llewellen A. married in Williamson County to Miss Susan T.
Hughes.
National Banner & Nashville Daily Advertiser (Mon., Feb. 25, 1833)

Tenely, Mr. George married in Louisville, Ky. to Miss Polly Mullikin.
National Banner & Nashville Whig (Mon., April 4, 1831)

Tennant, Miss Avon married to Mr. Thomas P. Adams.

Tennell, Miss Melinda married to Dr. James W. Mason.

Tenner, Miss Ann Maria married to Mr. Vera Roysa.

Tennison, Mr. Joseph married in Williamson County to Miss Elizabeth
Shelburn.
National Banner & Nashville Daily Advertiser (Mon., Jan. 7, 1833)

Terraus, Miss Louisa married to Mr. Ezra Webb.

Terrel, Mr. married in Stewart County to Miss Penelope Yarbro.
National Banner & Nashville Advertiser (Mon., Feb. 20, 1832)

Terrell, Miss Courtney Ann married to Ferdinand L. Claiborne.

Terrell, Mr. John L. married at Clarksville to Miss Jones.
National Banner & Nashville Whig (Mon., July 12, 1830)

Terrell, Mr. William married in Williamson County, Ten. to Miss Sally
Tyner.
National Banner & Nashville Whig (Fri., Feb. 13, 1835)

Terrice, Mr. Thomas J. married in Louisville, Ky. to Miss Martha Jane
Reno.
National Banner & Nashville Whig (Fri., March 13, 1835)

Terrill, Mr. married in Stewart County to Miss Penelope Yarbro.
National Banner & Nashville Daily Advertiser (Mon., Feb. 20, 1832)

Terrill, Mr. of Shelbyville married in Columbia to Miss Louisa Laird.
National Banner & Nashville Whig (Mon., July 12, 1830)

Terrill, Miss Martha C. married to Mr. Andrew Luntsford.

Terrill, Miss Ruanna married to Capt. John Perkins.

Terry, Miss Elizabeth married to Rev. Thomas P. Davidson.

Terry, Miss Jane married to Mr. John Crews.

Terry, Miss Mary M. married to Mr. Lawrence H. Hall.

Terry, Miss Nancy married to Mr. William Terry.

Terry, Mr. Nathaniel D. of Davidson County married on Sunday 15th Nov. by the Rev. Jonathan Wisener to Miss Malvina D. Smith of Sumner County. Daily Republican Banner (Wed., Nov. 25, 1840)

Terry, Miss Sarah married to Mr. George W. Moore.

Terry, Mr. William married in Courtland, Ala. to Miss Nancy Terry. National Banner & Nashville Whig (Fri., Dec. 10, 1830)

Tevis, Miss Emily married to Mr. Thos. Fowler.

Tewells, Miss Mary E. married to Mr. R. W. Stamps.

Thacker, Mr. Hollen married in Louisville, Ky. to Miss Nancy Morrison. National Banner & Nashville Whig (Fri., Feb. 18, 1831)

Thacker, Mr. Joel married in McMinn County to Miss Edy West. National Banner & Nashville Whig (Wed., Nov. 2, 1831)

Thatcher, Mr. James C. married in Campbell County to Miss Harriet D. Wheeler. National Banner & Nashville Whig (Mon., Sept. 13, 1830)

Thatcher, Mr. Samuel married in Knox County to Miss Malinda Craighead. National Banner & Nashville Whig (Sat., Oct. 6, 1827)

Thaw, Miss Eleanor married to Mr. James V. Patton.

Thaw, Miss Eliza Jane married to Col. A. W. Goodrich.

Theobald, Miss Adeline married to Mr. Robert H. Crittenden.

Therman, Miss Peachy married to Mr. William Pope.

Thomas, Mr. of Marion City, Missouri married on last evening by the Rev. Dr. Edgar to Miss Lucretia O. Sprague of Nashville. The Union (Sat., March 11, 1837)

Thomas, Mr. Adam married in Knox County to Miss Lydia Yearout. National Banner & Nashville Daily Advertiser (Mon., June 24, 1833)

Thomas, Miss Caroline A. married to Dr. J. B. Duke.

Thomas, Miss Elizabeth married to John E. Garner.

Thomas, Miss Elizabeth H. married to Mr. Horace G. Bledsoe.

Thomas, Mr. George, Dentist, married on Thursday, Sept. 15th by Dr. Davis to Miss Ann Elizabeth Richmond all of Nashville. Nashville Republican (Tues., Sept. 20, 1836)

Thomas, Dr. Isaac J. married in Maury County to Mrs. Polly Kimbell. National Banner (Sat., April 25, 1829)

Thomas, Dr. Isaac J. married in Maury County, Ten. to Mrs. Martha M. Rutledge. National Banner & Nashville Daily Advertiser (Wed., July 10, 1834)

Thomas, James H. Esq. married in Columbia to Miss Margaret M. Stephens daughter of the Rev. Daniel Stephens. National Banner & Nashville Daily Advertiser (Thurs., Dec. 27, 1832)

Thomas, Hon. James H. of Tenn. married at Graysboro, Ga. on the 19th inst. by the Rev. T. F. Scott to Miss Avarella Harper daughter of H. G. Harper of Graysboro, Ga.
Nashville True Whig & Weekly Commercial Register (Fri., Dec. 6, 1850)

Thomas, Mr. Jesse of the firm of Kay & Thomas married on the 20th Jan. by Rev. J. B. McFerrin to Miss Elizabeth Litton daughter of Mr. Joseph Litton all of Nashville.
National Banner & Nashville Whig (Fri., Jan. 22, 1836)

Thomas, Mr. Jesse, merchant, married in Nashville on Tuesday 20th inst. by Rev. John B. McFerrin to Miss Elizabeth Litton daughter of Mr. Joseph Litton.
The Union (Thurs., Jan. 21, 1836)

Thomas, Miss Jincy W. married to John Joslin.

Thomas, Miss Joanna married to Mr. George Cammack.

Thomas, Mr. John married at Louisville, Ky. to Miss Eliza Mercer.
National Banner & Nashville Whig (Sat., Aug. 9, 1828)

Thomas, Mr. John married in Louisville, Ky. to Miss Eliza Mercer.
National Banner & Nashville Whig (Fri., July 25, 1828)

Thomas, Mr. John E. married on the 11th inst. by the Rev. Mr. Howell to Miss Sarah Elizabeth Coleman daughter of George W. Coleman Esq. all of Nashville.
Nashville Whig (Thurs., July 13, 1843)

Thomas, Miss Lucy Ann married to Mr. George D. Blakey.

Thomas, Miss Margaret J. married to Mr. Aaron Wright.

Thomas, Mr. Peter married in Nashville on the evening of the 23rd. by T. J. Read Esq. to Miss Margaret Ballentine.
National Banner & Nashville Daily Advertiser (Fri., July 25, 1834)

Thomas, Miss Rachel married to Mr. William M. Robinson.

Thomas, Miss Sally married to Mr. David Vaughn.

Thomas, Mr. Smith married in Russellville, Ky. to Miss Mary Ann Wright.
National Banner & Nashville Daily Advertiser (Sat., Feb. 15, 1833)

Thomas, Mr. Wm. married at Tuscaloosa, Ala. to Miss Malinda Moore.
National Banner & Nashville Whig (July 1, 1826)

Thomas, Mr. William G. married in Weakley County to Miss Elizabeth Vincent.
National Banner & Nashville Daily Advertiser (Mon., May 13, 1833)

Thomas, Mr. William H. married in Nashville on Tuesday last by the Rev. Mr. McFerrin to Miss Jane Bailey.
National Banner & Nashville Daily Advertiser (Thurs., Feb. 2, 1832)

Thomas, Mr. Theophilus R. married at Courtland, Ala. to Miss Eliza A. M. Blocker.
National Banner (Sat., Sept. 26, 1829)

Thomason, Mr. James married in Maury County to Miss Tata Thomason.
National Banner & Nashville Whig (Mon., Aug. 8, 1831)

Thomason, Miss Tate married to Mr. James Thomason.

Thomason, Mr. Stephen married in Scott County to Miss Margaret Miller.
National Banner (Sat., April 25, 1829)

Thompson, Mr. married in Fayette County to Miss Martha Hayes
National Banner & Nashville Whig (Mon., April 18, 1831)

Thompson, Miss Adelia married to Mr. Nathan S. Drake.

Thompson, Mr. Alexander merchant of Nashville married in Springhill
on Tuesday 16th inst. by Dr. Hardin to Miss Lucy P. Jeffreys of Maury.
Daily Republican Banner (Tues., April 23, 1839)

Thompson, Miss Angelica Charlotte married to Mr. James E. Yeatman Esq.

Thompson, Miss Angelica Charlotte married to James E. Yeatman Esq.

Thompson, Miss Ann married to Dr. Colbert Blair.

Thompson, Miss Catharine married to Mr. A. L. Lamb.

Thompson, Miss Catharine R. married to Mr. Eugene Underwood.

Thompson, Mr. Charles married in Smith County to Miss Margaret Black.
on 18th inst.
National Banner & Nashville Advertiser (Fri., Jan. 27, 1832) .

Thompson, Mr. Charles A. R. of the firm of Thompson & Co. married on
Tuesday the 27th ult. by the Rev. Dr. Edgar to Miss Margaret Ann Edgar
all of Nashville.
The Christian Record (Sat., Nov. 14, 1846)

Thompson, Mr. Charles A. R. of the firm of Thompson & Co. married on
Tuesday evening, by the Rev. Dr. Edgar to Miss Margaret Anne Edgar
all of Nashville.
Nashville Whig (Thurs., Oct. 29, 1846)

Thompson, Miss Eliza Ann married to Mr. William White.

Thompson, Miss Frances married to Mr. Valentine Jenkins.

Thompson, Miss Francis married to Mr. James A. Scott.

Thompson, Rev. Frederick A. married in Maury County to Miss Sarah M.
Holland.
Nashville Whig (Tues., March 31, 1846)

Thompson, Dr. George married in Rutherford County to Miss Eliza Keeble.
National Banner & Nashville Whig (Sat., Nov. 18, 1826)

Thompson, Mr. Geo. married in Williamson County to Rachel Ratcliffe.
National Banner & Nashville Advertiser (Wed., May 16, 1832)

Thompson, Geo. married in Williamson County to Miss Rachel Ratcliffe.
The Western Weekly Review - Franklin, Tenn. (Fri., May 11, 1832)

Thompson, Mr. George L. married in Weakley County to Miss Nancy Higgs.
National Banner & Nashville Daily Advertiser (Mon., May 13, 1833)

Thompson, Dr. Gideon B. of Washington, Rhea County married in M'Minn
County to Miss Mira Waterhouse daughter of the late Mr. Richard C.
Waterhouse.
National Banner & Nashville Whig (Thurs., May 27, 1830)

Thompson, Henry married at Louisville, Ky. to Miss Elizabeth A.
Pritchard.
National Banner & Nashville Daily Advertiser (Mon., Jan. 30, 1832)

Thompson, Dr. Wm. M. married in Logan County, Ky. to Miss Nancy Long.
National Banner & Nashville Whig (Sat., Dec. 30, 1826)

Thompson, Miss Isaphaena P. married to Dr. John Bassett.

Thompson, Miss Isaphoena P. married to Dr. John G. Bassett.

Thompson, Mr. James H. married in Davidson County to Miss Rosini C. Harris.
Nashville Republican (Thurs., Dec. 10, 1835)

Thompson, Miss Jane married to Mr. Mr. Samuel Graham.

Thompson, Mr. John married in Davidson County on Sunday morning 25th inst. by the Rev. Mr. Baker to Miss Elizabeth N. Buchanan.
National Banner & Nashville Whig (Mon., July 26, 1830)

Thompson, Mr. John married in Franklin County, Ala. to Miss Eusebia Hodges.
National Banner & Nashville Advertiser (Thurs., Aug. 17, 1832)

Thompson, Mr. John formerly of Nashville married in La Grange, Tenn. on the 15th inst. by the Rev. S. M. Williamson to Miss Miss Mary Jane Wilkins formerly of Petersburg, Va.
Nashville Whig (Tues., Nov. 28, 1843)

Thompson, Mr. John married on the same evening (Wednesday) to Miss Mary Washington both of this County.
Nashville Whig (April 30, 1823)

Thompson, Mr. John married in Davidson County to Mrs. Martha M. Rawlins on the 27th Nov. by the Rev. Mr. Hume.
National Banner & Nashville Advertiser (Wed., Nov. 28, 1832)

Thompson, Mr. Joseph P. married in Shelbyville, Tenn. to Miss Prudence Allison.
National Banner & Nashville Daily Advertiser (Sat., Aug. 24, 1833)

Thompson, Miss Maria married to Capt. James Brittain.

Thompson, Miss Martha married to Mr. Gabriel B. Long.

Thompson, Miss Martha, Richland Creek, married Mr. R. W. Hart of Nashville on Thursday last.
Impartial Review & Cumberland Repository - published at Nashville (Thurs., Sept. 29, 1808)

Thompson, Miss Martha A. R. married to Mr. Herbert Owen.

Thompson, Miss Martha B. married to Mr. Abel Breeden.

Thompson, Miss Mary Amner married to Dr. T. J. Moore.

Thompson, Miss Mary Ann married to Mr. Wesley Neely.

Thompson, Miss Mary Ann married to Mr. James A. Hunter.

Thompson, Miss Mary J. married to Mr. J. Haggard.

Thompson, Mr. Matthew married in Knox County to Miss Mahana Kidd.
National Banner & Nashville Daily Advertiser (Mon., Sept. 10, 1832)

Thompson, Miss Mileta Ann married to Mr. Geo. R. Smith.

Thompson, Miss Miranda married to Mr. Henry Wade.

Thompson, Mr. Preston N. married in Maury County to Miss Mary Rains.
National Banner & Nashville Whig (Mon., July 12, 1830)

Thompson, Miss Rhoda Dorcus married to Mr. Alfred Goin.

Thompson, Dr. Richard L. married in Rutherford County to Mrs. Rebecca T. Rucker.
National Banner & Nashville Whig (Sat., May 17, 1828)

Thompson, Mr. Robert married in Somerville, Ala. to Miss Sarah
Elizabeth Humphreys daughter of Dr. Carlisle Humphreys.
National Banner & Nashville Whig (Wed., Feb. 25, 1835)

Thompson, Mr. Robert B. married in Knox County, Ten. to Miss Jane
Earwood.
National Banner & Nashville Whig (Mon., Jan. 5, 1835)

Thompson, Robert C. Esq. married in Louisville, Ky. on Tuesday evening
20th inst. to Miss Sarah Wrigglesworth.
National Banner & Nashville Whig (Wed., Sept. 28, 1831)

Thompson, Miss Rosella G. married to Mr. John Coleman.

Thompson, Mr. Samuel married in Coffee County on the 16th inst. by the
Rev. Joseph Crawford to Miss Eliza M. Hickerson daughter of John
Hickerson.
Daily Republican Banner (Fri., Jan. 24, 1840)

Thompson, Mrs. Susan married to Mr. Isom R. Thweat.

Thompson, Miss Tabitha A. married to Mr. Samuel B. Briant.

Thompson, Mrs. Temperence B. married to Mr. John Peck.

Thompson, Miss Thedessa married to Major Robert Maury.

Thompson, Mr. Thomas married in Logan County, Ky. to Miss Mary Simmons.
National Banner & Nashville Whig (Thurs., June 17, 1830)

Thompson, Dr. William married in Rutherford County to Miss Martha Johns.
National Banner & Nashville Whig (Sat., April 26, 1828)

Thompson, Mr. William married on the 24th inst. by John Wright, Esq.
to Miss Amanda Shell all of Davidson County.
Nashville Whig (Wed., Dec. 25, 1839)

Thompson, Wm. D. Esq. married in Fayetteville to Miss Hetty E. K.
Greer.
National Banner & Nashville Whig (Sat., Feb. 2, 1828)

Thompson, Dr. William L. married in Rutherford County to Miss Martha
Johns.
National Banner & Nashville Whig (Sat., May 17, 1828)

Thompson, Dr. Wm. M. married at Hopkinsville, Ky. to Miss Nancy Long.
National Banner & Nashville Whig (Sat., Dec. 16, 1826)

Thomson, Miss Emerine married to Mr. Elijah H. Drake.

Thomson, Rev. Herbert C. of the city of New York married in Franklin,
Simpson County, Ky. on 24th inst. by Rev. Richard Owings to Miss
Louisa Walker Hail eldest daughter of Durham Hail Esq.
National Banner & Nashville Whig (Mon., Oct. 31, 1831)

Thomson, Mr. John of Marion City, Mo. married on last evening at
Westwood by the Rev. Dr. Edgar to Miss Lucrettia O. Sprague of Nashville.
National Banner & Nashville Whig (Fri., March 10, 1837)

Thorn, Miss Martha married to Mr. Henry Reed.

Thornberry, James W. Esq. married in Louisville to Miss Malinda
Berkley.
National Banner & Nashville Whig (Sat., Aug. 19, 1826)

Thornberry, Mr. Jonathan married near Florence, Ala. to Miss Margaret
McLemore.
National Banner & Nashville Whig (Wed., Jan. 21, 1835)

Thornberry, Miss Susan S. married to Mr. Jonathan Davis.

Thornhill, Miss Matilda married to Robert Wilson.

Thornhill, Mr. Wilham married in Gallatin on the night of the 21st.
inst. by James L. M'Koin, Esq. to Miss Pamelia Roberts.
National Banner & Nashville Daily Advertiser (Wed., Jan. 30, 1833)

Thornton, Miss Eleanor married to Mr. Edward Dannaby.

Thornton, Miss Lucy Ann married to Capt. John F. Busby

Thornton, Miss Mary Ann married to Mr. George W. Grisham.

Thorp, Mr. G. C. married on the 16th inst. by the Rev. Mr. Smith to
Miss Mary Wells.
The Union (Thurs., Aug. 17, 1837)

Thorp, Mr. Harris D. married at Knoxville to Miss Solina Aryes.
National Banner & Nashville Whig (Sat., June 23, 1827)

Thorp, Mr. John S. married in Ross County, Ohio to Miss Elizabeth
Overly.
National Banner & Nashville Whig (Sat, Sept. 15, 1827)

Thorp, Mr. William F. married in Giles County to Miss Martha Sherrell.
National Banner & Nashville Whig (Fri., Feb. 26, 1830)

Thorpe, Mr. George W. married on Wednesday the 16th inst. by the Rev.
Mr. Smith to Miss Mary Wells late of London.
National Banner & Nashville Whig (Fri., Aug. 18, 1837)

Threatt, Miss Fanny married to Mr. Peter Thrett.

Thrett, Mr. Peter married in Williamson County to Miss Fanny Threatt.
National Banner & Nashville Daily Advertiser (Mon., May 20, 1833)

Throckmorton, Mr. Warren married at Louisville, Ky. to Miss Susan
Llewellen.
National Banner & Nashville Whig (Sat., May 17, 1828)

Throgmorton, Miss Martha married to Mr. Littleton Rufty.

Throp, Mr. Moses married in Louisville, Ky. to Miss Evelina Monon.
National Banner & Nashville Whig (Sat., July 8, 1826)

Thurman, Miss Temperance married to Mr. Bartram Robeson.

Thweat, Miss Emeline married to Mr. Hugh Haffy.

Thweat, Mr. Isom R. of Franklin, Tenn. married at Columbus, Miss. on
the 18th inst. by the Rev. O. L. Nash to Mrs. Susan Thompson of
Columbus, Miss.
Nashville Whig (Fri., Nov. 2, 1838)

Thweatt, Miss Matilda married to Mr. Spencer Payne.

Thweatt, Mr. William H. married in August 1831 to Miss Mary Allen.
The Western Weekly Review - Franklin, Tenn. (Fri., Sept. 2, 1831)

Tideman, Miss Margaret P. H. married to W. R. Campbell, Esq.

Tierman, Miss Catherine married to Mr. Frederick Chatard.

Tierney, Miss Mary C. married to Mr. John Dwyer.

Tighe, Mr. W. married at St. Louis, Mo. to Miss Mary Louisa Mullanphy.
National Banner & Nashville Daily Advertiser (Fri., Nov. 15, 1833)

Tigner, William married in Williamson County to Miss Martha Morton.
The Western Weekly Review - Franklin, Tenn. (Fri., Feb. 1, 1833)

Tilford, Miss Elizabeth A. married to Mr. William T. Moseby.

Tilford, Miss Elizabeth Ann married to Mr. Wm. T. Moseby.

Tilford, Miss Martha L. married to Uriah S. Cummins Esq.

Tilford, Miss Mary Jane married to Mr. Warren Walker.

Tilghman, Mr. Thomas O. of New Orleans married on the 26th May by the
Rev. E. Sweat to Miss Mary Ann McGregor daughter of the late Capt.
Flowers McGregor of Wilson County.
The Politician & Weekly Nashville Whig (Fri., June 4, 1847)

Tillay, Mr. Frances B. married at Louisville, Ky. to Miss Mary
Eliza Gwathmey.
National Banner & Nashville Whig (Sat., Dec. 16, 1826)

Tillett, Mr. Wm. married in Jefferson County to Miss Sarah Breeden.
National Banner & Nashville Whig (Mon., April 25, 1831)

Tilly, Miss Mary married to Mr. John Washington Hudson.

Tilman, Miss Elizabeth married to Mr. Robert Rogers.

Tilman, Mr. Ivey married in Madison County, Ten. to Miss Catherine
Riprogle.
National Banner & Nashville Whig (Wed., March 11, 1835)

Tillman, Rachel married to Mr. James B. Record.

Tilmon, Miss Sarah married to Mr. Henry Cannon.

Timberlake, Mr. George married at Lexington, Ky. to Miss Emeline
Reed.
National Banner (Sat., Oct. 10, 1829)

Timberlake, Mrs. Margaret married to Hon. John H. Eaton.

Timmerman, Mr. John T. married in Georgetown, Ky. to Miss Lucy C.
Finnell.
National Banner & Nashville Whig (Mon., Oct. 4, 1830)

Timmons, Mr. Elisha married at Cincinnati to Miss Elizabeth Williams.
National Banner & Nashville Whig (Sat., June 7, 1828)

Tims, Mr. Sidney married in Madison County to Mrs. Charlotte Sandrun.
National Banner (Sat., June 27, 1829)

Tindal, Miss Martha Jane married to Mr. Bushrod T. Daughty.

Tindall, Miss Susan C. married to Mr. Willis Jones.

Tinsley, Miss Mary W. married to Mr. John S. Murphy.

Tipton, Miss Ann married to Mr. John Lones or (Jones)

Tipton, Miss Eliza married to Dr. Tyree Rodes.

Tipton, Col. J. C. of East Tenn. married on Thursday the 19th inst. at
the residence of Thomas W. Shearon Esq. by Rev. J. B. Ferguson to Miss
E. B. Shearon of Davidson.
Nashville True Whig & Weekly Commercial Register (Fri., Jan. 3, 1851)

Tipton, Mr. Jonathan married in Wilson County to Miss Martha Cox.
National Banner & Nashville Daily Advertiser (Mon., March 18, 1833)

Tipton, Miss Mary married to Mr. David Lowery.

Tipton, Miss Minerva Jane married to Mr. Solomon Clayton.

Tipton, Miss Minerva Jane married to Mr. Solomon Clayton.

Tipton, Miss Rebecca married to Capt. Valentine Davis.

Tisson, Miss Lucille married to Thomas S. Rutherford, Esq.

Titus, Miss Isabella married to Mr. Wiley Kimbrough.

Toca, Mr. Joseph married in Mobile on the 3d day of December, 1833 to Miss Catherine Jacobs of Kentucky.
National Banner & Nashville Daily Advertiser (Tues., June 24, 1834)

Todd, Miss Ann Jane married to Mr. J. B. Wallace.

Todd, Dr. Charles W. of Maryville married in Telico to Miss Blackburn daughter of Mr. Samuel Blackburn.
National Banner (Sat., Sept. 26, 1829)

Todd, Miss Eliza married to Major William O. Butler.

Todd, Miss Elizabeth married to N. W. Edwards Esq.

Todd, Miss Elizabeth married to Adam Huntsman Esq.

Todd, Miss Elizabeth S. married to Mr. Albert G. Hodges.

Todd, Mrs. Maria K. married to John J. Crittenden Esq.

Todd, Miss Mary Ann married to Dr. William A. Murchison.

Todd, Robert S. Esq. married in Frankfort, Ky. to Miss Elizabeth Humphreys.
National Banner & Nashville Whig (Dec. 2, 1826)

Todd, Maj. Wm. married in Hardeman County to Mrs. Emily Rawlins near Bolivar on 27th Nov.
National Banner & Nashville Advertiser (Mon., Dec. 3, 1832)

Todd, Miss Rebecca married to Mr. S. H. Lester.

Todd, Robert S. Esq. married in Frankford, Ky. to Miss Elizabeth Humphreys.
National Banner & Nashville Whig (Sat., Dec. 2, 1826)

Todd, Miss Sarah married to Mr. Philip McNeill.

Tolbert, Miss Amanda married to Mr. E. Castons.

Tolwell, Miss Arabella married to Mr. Jesse W. Page.

Tomes, Rev. Charles married in St. Peters Church Columbia on 24th ult. by Rev. F. G. Smith to Miss Henrietta Coleman Otey daughter of Rt. Rev. Bishop Otey.
Nashville Whig (Tues., Dec. 8, 1846)

Tomkins, Miss Eliza S. married to Mr. Joseph R. Morris.

Tomkins, Mr. J. R. A. of Gallatin married in Smith County to Miss Mary J. Madden.
National Banner & Nashville Whig (Thurs., July 29, 1830)

Tomlinson, Mr. Elias married in Weakley County on the 10th inst. by John Henry Moore, Esq. to Mrs. Elizabeth Ore widow of the late William C. Ore.
National Banner & Nashville Daily Advertiser (Wed., June 19, 1833)

Tomlinson, Miss Elizabeth married to Mr. George Somers.

Tompkins, Miss Frances married to Mr. Moses Alexander.

Tompkins, Hon. George Judge of the Supreme Court married in Boone Co. on Thursday last by the Rev. Justinian Williams to Elizabeth Lientz eldest daughter of William Lientz Esq.
Nashville Whig (Oct. 18, 1824)

Toncry, Miss Lucinda married to Mr. Hilton Humphreys.

Toney, Mr. Henry married in Maury County to Miss Marinda Dorch.
National Banner & Nashville Whig (Mon., Sept. 26, 1831)

Tooley, Miss Jane M. married to Mr. John Manuel.

Tooley, Mrs. Mary married to John Chambers, Esq.

Topp, Mr. D. C. married in Greensboro, Ala. on the 3d inst. by the Rev. Mr. Goodman to Miss Mary Meredeth both of Greensboro, Ala.
Daily Republican Banner (Tues., Jan. 16, 1838)

Topp, Mr. James H. married in Giles County to Miss Virginia Meredith.
Nashville Republican & State Gazette (Tues., May 13, 1834)

Topp, Miss Nancy H. married to Mr. Thomas Martin.

Topp, Mr. Robertson of Memphis married on Thursday evening last by the Rev. J. T. Edgar to Miss Elizabeth Vance of Nashville.
Nashville Republican (Thurs., May 2, 1837)

Torbitt, Granville C. member of the Legislature from Monroe County married on Tuesday 22nd by the Rev. R. B. C. Howell to Miss Louisa Barrow daughter of Matthew Barrow Esq. of this vicinity.
Nashville Whig (Thurs., Nov. 24, 1842)

Torian, Miss Sarah F. married to Milton Brown Esq.

Toryann, Miss Sarah Ann married to Mr. Milton Brown, Esq.

Totten, Mr. James L. Esq. married in Gibson County by the Rev. N. J. Hess on Thursday 20th ult. to Miss Sarah E. Dyer daughter of the late Col. R. H. Dyer.
National Banner & Nashville Daily Advertiser (Sat., July 13, 1833)

Totten, Rev'd Silas Professor of Mathematics, Washington College, Hartfort City married at Albany, N. Y. to Miss Mary Isham.
National Banner & Nashville Daily Advertiser (Thurs., Sept. 12, 1833)

Towell, Miss Peggy married to Mr. Robert West.

Townes, Miss Frances married to Mr. Will M. Gregg.

Towns, Miss C. C. married to Mr. J. W. Grizzard.

Townsend, Miss Eliza Ann married to Mr. John W. Judkins.

Townsend, Miss Elizabeth married to Mr. Eli Crumbaugh.

Townsend, Jabez R. Esq. married in Springfield, Green County, Mo. on the 20th ulto. to Miss Susannah S. V. Crenshaw daughter of William T. Crenshaw late of Nashville, Tenn.
Nashville Whig (Sat., April 13, 1844)

Townsend, Col. Thomas W. married in Logan County, Ky. to Miss Mary Roberts.
National Banner & Nashville Advertiser (Mon., April 30, 1832)

Townsent, Mr. Benjamin married in Logan County, Ky. to Miss S. H. Allen.
National Banner & Nashville Whig (Mon., May 22, 1831)

Townsent, Miss Elizabeth married to Mr. Eli Crumbaugh.

Trabue, Mr. Charles C. married on Wednesday evening last to Miss
Agnes Woods both of Nashville.
The Nashville Gazette (Sat., July 8, 1820)

Trabue, Mr. Edwards married in Logan County, Ky. to Miss Mary Rogers.
National Banner & Nashville Whig (Sat., March 17, 1827)

Trabue, Mr. James married in Todd County, Ky. to Miss Judith Wooldridge.
National Banner & Nashville Whig (Sat., March 10, 1827)

Trabue, Miss Jane W. married to Dr. Houston Reynolds.

Trabue, Miss Sarah G. married to Col. George Patterson.

Travis, Mr. Benjamin W. married in Henry County to Miss Lucy R. Randle.
National Banner & Nashville Whig (Fri., Dec. 9, 1831)

Travis, Mr. Edward L. married in Henry County to Miss Adeline A.
Stith.
National Banner & Nashville Whig (Wed., Dec. 28, 1831)

Travis, Miss Eliza married to Mr. James Allen.

Travis, Mr. Fielden married in Weakley County on the 23d May by Henry
Moore, Esq. to Miss Martha Ross.
National Banner & Nashville Daily Advertiser (Fri., May 31, 1833)

Travis, Mr. Fielding married in Weakley County to Miss Martha Ross.
National Banner & Nashville Daily Advertiser (Wed., June 12, 1833)

Travis, Mr. Robert married in Henry County to Miss Amanda Hicks.
National Banner & Nashville Advertiser (Wed., Jan. 11, 1832)

Traywich, Mr. Henry L. married in Smith County to Miss Peggy Dillard.
National Banner & Nashville Advertiser (Fri., May 4, 1832)

Tribble, Mr. Alfred of Dickson Co. married in Henderson County to Miss
Rebecca Coffee.
National Banner (Sat., Aug. 15, 1829)

Tribble, Dr. George married in Madison County, Ky. to Miss Patsy Embry.
National Banner & Nashville Whig (Sat., Sept. 20, 1828)

Tribby, Miss Rebecca married to Mr. James Turner.

Trice, Miss Elizabeth married to Mr. Thomas Gaitwood.

Trice, Miss Sarah married to Mr. John H. Tandy.

Trice, Mr. Thomas J. married in Paris, Ten. to Miss Sarah W. Lewis.
National Banner & Nashville Whig (Sat., May 17, 1828)

Trier, Miss Margaret Ann married to Mr. William W. Floyd.

Trigg, Mr. Harden S. married in Sumner County, Ten. to Miss Elizabeth
J. Wilson daughter of Stephen Wilson Esq.
National Banner & Nashville Daily Advertiser (Tues., Aug. 5, 1834)

Trigg, Miss Isabella married to Mr. James W. Long.

Trigg, Miss Jane married to Mr. Joseph K. Kent.

Trigg, Mr. John H. married in Sumner County to Miss Catharine Shepherd.
National Banner & Nashville Whig (Mon., Sept. 12, 1831)

Trigg, Miss Margaret B. married to Henry C. Walker Esq.

Trigg, Miss Mary Ann married to _____?

Trigg, Miss Sally married to Dr. Evan Mabry.

Trigg, Thomas B. Esq. of the firm of Chester & Trigg, Memphis, married in Rutherford County on the 24th inst. by the Rev. Dr. Lapsley to Miss Susan N. Weakley second daughter of Col. R. L. Weakley.
The Politician & Weekley Nashville Whig (Fri., July 2, 1847)

Trigg, Mr. Wm. married in Madison County to Miss Eliza Rawling.
National Banner & Nashville Whig (Sat., Nov. 17, 1827)

Triggs, Mr. James married in Davidson on the 9th to Miss Margaret M'Daniel all of Nashville.
Nashville Union (Monday 14 _____)

Triggs, Mr. James married in Davidson County on the 9th inst. to Miss Margaret McDaniel both of Nashville.
Nashville Whig (Mon., Nov. 11, 1839)

Triggs, Mr. John H. married in Sumner County to Miss Catherine Shepherd.
National Banner & Nashville Whig (Mon., Sept. 12, 1831)

Trimble, Miss Eliza M. married to A. V. S. Lindsley Esq.

Trimble, Miss Eliza married to A. V. S. Lindsley Esq.

Trimble, John Esq. of Nashville married on 17th inst. to Miss Margaret D. H. McEwen.
Nashville Republican (Sat., Sept. 19, 1835)

Trimble, Miss M. Louisa married to John Reid Esq.

Trimble, Miss Mary married to Mr. James C. Ford.

Trimble, Miss Mary Ann married to Neil S. Brown Esq.

Trimble, Miss Nancy married to Jesse Roberts.

Trimble, Miss Rebecca married to Garret Davis Esq.

Trimble, Miss Susan P. married to Mr. William L. Washington Esq.

Trimble, Thomas C. Esq. Attorney at law married on May 23d at the residence of James Rucks Esq. of Nashville to Miss Fanny E. Williams daughter of the late Judge Nathaniel L. Williams.

Trimble, Thomas C. married on Tuesday 23d inst. by the Rev. J. T. Edgar to Miss Fanny Williams daughter of the late Judge N. L. Williams of Winchester, Ten.
The Union (Sat., May 27, 1837)

Trimble, Mr. Walter of Kenhawa, Virginia married on Wednesday evening last to Mary C. Mitchell of Gallatin.
Nashville Whig (March 19, 1823)

Triplet, Miss Nancy married to Mr. Ira Doan.

Triplett, Mr. Charles married in Fleming County, Ky. to Miss Clarissa Dawkins.
National Banner & Nashville Whig (Sat., Jan. 20, 1827)

Tripplin, Miss Martha R. married to Mr. John P. Crittenden.

Troost, Miss Caroline married to Mr. Albert Stein.

Trotman, Miss Obedience A. married to Mr. Richard Person.

Trott, Miss Sarah married to Mr. Isaac W. Brashears.

Trotter, Mr. Benjamin Y. married in Sommerville, Fayette County to Miss Julia A. E. M'Clelland.
National Banner & Nashville Daily Advertiser (Mon., April 15, 1833)

Trotter, Mr. David married at Cincinnati to Miss M. L. Hamilton.
National Banner & Nashville Daily Advertiser (Thurs., Oct. 11, 1832)

Trotter, Miss Elizabeth Jane married to Dr. Wm. P. Reyburn.

Trotter, Isham G. Esq. of Franklin, Tenn. married in Woodford County, Ky. to Miss Mary Humphreys.
National Banner & Nashville Whig (Sat., Dec. 1, 1827)

Trotter, Rev. John married in Monroe County to Miss Mary P. Stevens.
National Banner & Nashville Whig (Mon., May 9, 1831)

Trotter, Rev. John P. of Lexington married Miss Pamela Brashear of Mercer County.
National Banner & Nashville Whig (Fri., Feb. 19, 1830)

Trotter, Miss Martha married to Mr. John Baugh.

Trotter, Miss Mary Ann married to William A. Leavy Esq.

Trotter, Mr. Thomas married in Louisville, Ky. to Miss Sarah Buchanan.
National Banner & Nashville Daily Advertiser (Sat., Aug. 17, 1833)

Troup, Capt. J. V. married at Smithland, Ky. on the 12th inst. to Miss Maria Johnston of Smithland, Ky.
Nashville Whig (Tues., April 19, 1842)

Trousdale, Mr. B. B., merchant, married lately in Springfield to Mrs. Susan Harwell.
The Nashville Whig & Tenn. Advertiser (March 28, 1818)

Trousdale, Miss Jane married to Mr. T. B. Roberts.

Trower, Miss Edna A. married to Maj. Thomas A. Brown.

Trower, Miss Edna A. married to Maj. Thomas A. Brown.

Trundell, Miss Catherine married to Mr. James Paton.

Tucker, Miss Annis married to Mr. Benjamin N. Bugg.

Tucker, Mr. George W. married in Franklin Co., Ten. by the Rev. J. Dougan to Miss Mary Foster.
National Banner & Nashville Daily Advertiser (Thurs., June 19, 1834)

Tucker, Mr. John married in Davidson County on the 4th ult. to Miss Sarah Hughes.
National Banner & Nashville Whig (Mon., Nov. 8, 1830)

Tucker, Miss Julia Ann married to Shadrock Weaver.

Tucker, Mr. Philip G. of Jackson married Montgomery County to Miss Martha Williams.
National Banner (March 10, 1826)

Tucker, Miss Violet married to Mr. Alexander Graham.

Tudor, Miss Elizabeth married to Mr. Oliver Wells.

Tuirer, Mr. George married near Port Gibson, Miss. to Miss Mary Lenner.
National Banner & Nashville Whig (Sat., Oct. 28, 1826)

Tunis, Miss Emeline married to Mr. Larkin M. Torrant.

Tunnage, Mr. James married on Oct. 1st. by John Wright Esq. to Miss Sophia O'Brian all of Nashville.
National Banner & Nashville Whig (Fri., Oct. 2, 1835)

Turley, Miss Elizabeth married to Mr. Robert Buchanan.

Turley, Miss Mary E. married to Dr. Thomas W. Harris.

Turman, Mr. J. M. of Aberdeen, Miss married on the 23d inst. by the Rev. Dr. Lindsley to Miss Mary Hume of Nashville.
Daily Republican Banner (Fri., April 26, 1839)

Turnage, Mr. James of Nashville married on the 1st inst. to Miss Sophia O'Brien.
Nashville Republican (Sat., Oct. 3, 1835)

Turnage, Miss Mary M. married to Mr. John Wallard.

Turnbow, Mr. John married in Maury County to Miss Catherine Noles.
National Banner & Nashville Whig (Sat., Dec. 17, 1831)

Turnbull, Miss Gracie C. married to Mr. William Izard Bull.

Turner, Mrs. married to Col. John Orr.

Turner, Miss Almira married to Mr. William S. Munday.

Turner, Mr. Andrew married in Bourbon County, Ky. to Miss Barthena Coons.
National Banner & Nashville Whig (Sat., Dec. 23, 1826)

Turner, Mr. Benjamin of Ala. married in Maury County, Ten. to Miss Caroline Webster.
National Banner & Nashville Daily Advertiser (Mon., Nov. 4, 1833)

Turner, Miss Elizabeth married to Mr. John A. Fackler.

Turner, Miss Emily married to Mr. Ryan.

Turner, Mr. George married in Maury County to Miss Rebecca Fausett.
National Banner & Nashville Whig (Thurs., Sept. 16, 1830)

Turner, Miss Isabella married to Mr. Harrison Boyd Hinton.

Turner, Mr. James married in Cincinnati to Miss Rebecca Tribby.
National Banner & Nashville Whig (Sat., Jan. 10, 1829)

Turner, Mr. James H. married in this town last evening to Miss Lucinda Pilcher.
National Banner (Sat., Sept. 17, 1829)

Turner, Mr. John married in Williamson County to Miss Jane Brown.
National Banner & Nashville Advertiser (Tues., July 3, 1832)

Turner, John married in Williamson County to Miss Jane Brown.
The Western Weekly Review - Franklin, Tenn. (Fri., June 29, 1832)

Turner, John B. married on the 1st inst.[Dec. 4, 1857] by Rev. W. M. Reid to Miss Ellen M. Wilkinson all of Davidson County.
Nashville Daily Gazette (Dec. 4, 1857)

Turner, Maj. John E. of Turnerville married on the ult. to Miss Wealthy S. Bryan daughter of James H. Bryan Esq. of Robinson County.
Nashville Whig (April 2, 1823)

Turner, Mr. John H. married in Sumner County to Miss Sarah M. Wiseman daughter of the Rev. John Wiseman.
National Banner & Nashville Whig (Mon., June 13, 1831)

Turner, Mr. Jno. H. married in Sumner County to Miss Sarah M. Wiseman.
Nashville Republican & State Gazette (Tues., June 14, 1831)

Turner, Mr. Joseph B. married on Tuesday evening las to Miss Mary Sills of Rutherford.
The Nashville Whig (May 19, 1817)

Turner, Miss Josephine married to Dr. John S. Royeston.

Turner, Miss Julia A. married to John H. Gee.

Turner, Miss Laura married to Jasiah O. Salisbury.

Turner, Mr. Lorenzo D. married in Maury County to Miss Evaline E. Hill.
National Banner & Nashville Whig (Mon., Aug. 8, 1831)

Turner, Miss Louisa B. married to Maj. George H. Smith.

Turner, Miss Maria W. married to Mr. Chs. H. Dickinson.

Turner, Martha married to Thomas E. Rieves.

Turner, Miss Martha married to Doctor H. C. Bradford.

Turner, Mr. Martin married in Madison County, Ky. to Miss Judith Walker.
National Banner (March 31, 1826)

Turner, Miss Mary married to Mr. R. H. Burton.

Turner, Miss Minerva married to Col. Joel L. Jones.

Turner, Miss Nancy married to Mr. John B. Armstrong.

Turner, Miss Nancy M. J. P. married to Dr. Robert Bedford.

Turner, Mr. Richard Ambrose of Wilson married on Wednesday evening 18th Dec. to Mrs. Anne Drake of Davidson County.
National Banner & Nashville Daily Advertiser (Sat., Dec. 21, 1833)

Turner, Miss Sally married to Mr. James M. Cook.

Turner, Miss Sarah married to Mr. James D. Cuningham.

Turner, Dr. Wilford D. married in Stewart County to Miss Charlotte Phillips.
National Banner & Nashville Whig (Sat., July 29, 1826)

Turner, Mr. William D. married in Madison County to Miss Maria Espy.
National Banner & Nashville Whig (Sat., Jan. 10, 1829)

Turner, Mr. William K. married in Robertson County to Miss Elizabeth Cheatham.
National Banner & Nashville Whig (Sat., Aug. 12, 1826)

Turney, Hopkins L. Esq. of Jasper married at Washington, Rhea County to Miss Theresa Francis daughter of Miller Francis Esq.
National Banner (June 10, 1826)

Turney, Sam Esq. married in White County, Ten. to Miss Caroline Fisk.
Nashville Republican & State Gazette (Tues., May 24, 1831)

Turney, Samuel Esq. married in White County to Miss Caroline Fisk.
National Banner & Nashville Whig (Wed., May 25, 1831)

Turpin, Capt. Edwin A. married in Louisville, Ky. to Miss Eliza J. Satterwhite.
National Banner & Nashville Whig (Mon., July 18, 1831)

Turpin, Miss Elizabeth married to Mr. James Lane.

Turpin, Mr. William marriedin Henry County to Miss Rebecca Steele.
National Banner & Nashville Daily Advertiser (Wed., Jan. 11, 1832)

Tutt, Miss Ann married to Mr. Charles Bonnycastle.

Tweatt, Miss Mary married to Mr. Haley Russell.

Twomey, Mr. James E. married in McMinn County to Miss Jane M. Alexander.
National Banner & Nashville Whig (Sat., Jan. 26, 1828)

Twyman, Mr. Stephen T. married in Scott County, Ky. to Miss Julian Greenwell.
National Banner & Nashville Daily Advertiser (Tues., July 3, 1832)

Tyffe, Mrs. Margaret L. married to Mr. Randolph Eason.

Tyner, Miss Sally married to Mr. William Terrell.

Tyree, Miss Jane M. married to Col. William Walton.

Tyree, Miss Jane M. married to Col. William Walton.

Tyree, Miss Mary L. married to Col. David Gillespie.

Tyree, Miss Mary L. married to Col. David Gillespie.

Tyree, Miss Sarah C. married to Mr. Edward Stratton.

Tyson, Miss Eliza married to Mr. Edwin Rawling.

Tyson, Miss Eliza Ann married to John Fly, Esq.

Uliss, Miss Mary married to Rev. William Jenkins.

Ullman, Lewis S. married in Nashville on the 25th ulto. by the E. A. Raworth Esq. to Miss Jane D. Rosenhaur.
Nashville True Whig & Weekly Commercial Register (Fri., May 17, 1850)

Umstrade, Miss Rachel married to Mr. George Moore.

Underwood, Mr. Albert G. married in Pulaski to Miss Joanna Holden.
National Banner & Nashville Whig (Mon., May 31, 1830)

Underwood, Mr. Elias married in Maury County to Miss Martha Willis.
National Banner & Nashville Whig (Wed., April 27, 1831)

Underwood, Miss Elizabeth married to Mr. Henry Sayer.

Underwood, Miss Elizabeth married to Mr. Thompson Fruit.

Underwood, Mr. Eugene of Bowling Green, Ky. married on the 13th inst. by the Rev. Dr. Edgar to Miss Catharine R. Thompson daughter of William Thompson Esq. of Nashville.
Nashville Whig (Thurs., Oct. 15, 1846)

Underwood, Warren L. Esq. married in Bowling Green, Ky. to Miss Lucy Henry daughter of Mr. Matthew Henry.
National Banner & Nashville Whig (Wed., Sept. 7, 1831)

Upchurch, Miss Alpha married to Mr. Jonas Snider.

Upshaw, Col. A. M. M. of Pulaski married Miss Nancy Crocket in Columbia.
National Banner & Nashville Whig (Thurs., May 27, 1830)

Upshaw, Mr. Arther H. W. of Giles County married on Wednesday last, in this vicinity to Miss Martha Ann Jones of this vicinity.
Nashville Whig (Feb. 23, 1824)

Upton, Miss Eliza married to Mr. Samuel Kelly.

Usher, Miss Elizabeth H. married to Rev. James G. Barnett.

Ustick, Miss Elizabeth B. married to Mr. John B. Stephenson.

Ustick, Mr. John S. of this town married in Washington City to Miss Rebecca Sheilds daughter of the late Captain Robert Shields of Philadelphia.
Nashville Whig (Sept. 27, 1824)

Utley, Mr. James married in Logan County, Ky. to Miss Mary E. Acock.
National Banner & Nashville Daily Advertiser (Tues., Feb. 14, 1832)

Vacaro, Mr. Philip married at Louisville, Ky. to Miss Nancy Holt.
National Banner & Nashville Whig (Mon., Nov. 8, 1830)

Vaden, William H. married in Williamson County to Miss Martha Smithson.
National Banner & Nashville Daily Advertiser (Wed., May 16, 1832)

Vaden, William H. married in Williamson County to Miss Martha Smithson.
The Western Weekly Review - Franklin, Ten. (Fri., May 11, 1832)

Valcourt, Mr. T. De, editor of Attakapas Gazette. Married at St.
Martinsville, La. to Miss Felonist Guidry.
National Banner & Nashville Whig (Sat., May 12, 1827)

Valentine, Mrs. Martha married to Dr. Wilson Faulk.

Valiant, Mr. Wm. married in Madison County, Ala. to Miss Margaret Hussey.
National Banner & Nashville Daily Advertiser (Thurs., Feb. 21,1833)

Van, Miss Mary married to Mr Augustus Edwards.

Van Antwerp, Miss Eliza married to Rev. H. B. Bascom, D.D.

Van Buren, Maj. Abraham oldest son to the President married on the 17th
Nov. by the Rev. Mr. Converse to Miss Sarah Angelica Singleton daughter
of Mr. Richardsin Singleton in Sumpter District, S. C.
Daily Republican Banner (Fri., Dec. 28, 1838)

Vance, Miss Catharine married to Dr. Thomas H. Pinkard.

Vance, Mr. Elisha Q. of Nashville married on the 7th inst. to Miss
Cyprissa Brooks.
Nashville Republican (Tues., May 26, 1835)

Vance, Miss Eliza married to Mr. Dickenson Lenderman.

Vance, Miss Elizabeth married to Mr. Robertson Topp.

Vance, Miss Heziah married to Mr. O. P. Henderson.

Vance, Miss Margaret married to Geo. C. Childress, Esq.

Vance, Mr. Ramsey married in Smith County to Miss Letsey Mann.
National Banner & Nashville Daily Advertiser (Fri., Jan. 13, 1832)

Van Court, Rev. Alexander of Mississippi married on last evening by
the Rev. Mr. Lapsley at the residence of R. Lusk, Esq. of Nashville to
Miss Harriet Overton eldest daughter of Robt. C. Hynson, Esq.
Nashville Whig (Tues., Dec. 13, 1842)

Vancourt, Rev. John H. married at Natchez to Miss Catherine Swayze.
National Banner & Nashville Whig (July 1, 1826)

Van De Graff, Mr. John S. married in Fayette County, Ky. to Miss Mary
H. Simpson.
National Banner & Nashville Whig (Sat., Oct. 25, 1828)

Vanderpool, Miss Adareen married to Mr. Ralph P. Hunt.

Vandevar, Mr. C. H. of New Orleans married in Natchez to Miss Ann M'Calf.
National Banner & Nashville Whig (June 24, 1826)

Vanderwoort, Mr. Peter Jun., married in Nashville on Tuesday evening
last by Rev. Mr. Weller to Miss Mary Biddle daughter of Mr. Charles
Biddle Esq.
National Banner & Nashville Whig (Thurs., Sept. 16, 1830)

Vandorn, Miss Mary Ann married to Mr. John O. Searcy.

Van Dyke, Miss Eliza R. married to Mr. William P. Scott.

Vandyke, John married on Tuesday 25th inst. by the Rev. Mr. Elliott to Miss Elizabeth S. Smith second daughter of John T. & Elizabeth Smith all of Nashville.
Nashville Whig (Thurs., Jan. 27, 1842)

Van Dyke, Miss Sally married to Mr. Nelson Davy.

Vanhook, Miss Margaret married to Mr. James M. Williams.

Van Horn, Miss Eliza married to Mr. Alexander M'Cormick.

Vanhouton, Miss Phebe L. married to Mr. John H. Lewis.

Vanleer, Miss Eleanora married to Hugh Kirkman, Esq.

Vanleer, Miss Rebecca married to Andrew J. Polk.

Vanleer, Mr. Samuel of this vicinity married at Florence, Ala. to Miss Ameila W. Terrass.
National Banner (April 7, 1826)

Vanmeter, Miss Mary Jane married to Mr. William Cooke.

Vannerson, Mr. Francis married in Rutherford County to Miss Elizabeth W. Elam.
National Banner & Nashville Daily Advertiser (Sat., July 14, 1832)

Vannoy, Miss Eliza married to Mr. Joseph H. Dickson.

Vannoy, Rev. William of Ky. married in Campbell County to Miss Kitty C. Wheeler daughter of Thomas Wheeler Esq.
National Banner (Sat., Dec. 26, 1829)

Van Pelt, Mr. James married at Poplar Corner, Madison County, Ten. to Miss Chaney Edwards both formerly of Edgecomb County, N. C.
National Banner & Nashville Whig (Wed., Dec. 28, 1831)

Vansant, Miss Ann Maria married to Mr. John W. Deniston.

Varnel, Miss Rebecca married to Mr. Wm. Sharp.

Varnell, Mr. James married in Wilkinson County, Missis. to Miss Thirsa Ann M'Graw.
National Banner & Nashville Whig (Sat., Feb. 10, 1827)

Varner, Mr. Peter married in Knox County to Miss Polly Summers.
National Banner & Nashville Whig (Mon., Oct. 31, 1831)

Vaughan, Miss Eliza D. married to Mr. Osevy Daniel.

Vaughan, Mr. Hiram married on Wednesday evening last in Nashville by the Rev. Mr. Slater to Miss Catharine C. Hobbs.
The Christian Record (Sat., Feb. 5, 1848)

Vaughan, Miss Jane M. married to Dr. Joseph Cloud.

Vaughan, Mr. Lemuel married in Williamson County, Ten. to Miss Mary Wall.
National Banner & Nashville Whig (Fri., Feb. 13, 1835)

Vaughan, Miss Paulina A. married to Mr. Nathaniel Pibes.

Vaughan, Miss Susan married to Mr. James Price.

Vaughn, Dr. A. G. married in Madison County, Ala. to Miss Mary O. Walton.
Nashville Republican & State Gazette (Thurs., June 9, 1831)

Vaughn, Mr. Asa N. married in Franklin to Miss Araminta Craig.
National Banner & Nashville Daily Advertiser (Mon., Jan. 16, 1832)

Vaughn, Mr. Asa N. married on Wednesday the 11th inst. to Miss Araminta
Craig daughter of Mr. Jas. Craig.
The Western Weekly Review - Franklin, Ten. (Fri., Jan. 13, 1832)

Vaughn, Mr. David married on Thursday evening by the Rev. Mr. Hume to
Miss Sally Thomas all of this County.
Nashville Whig (Sept. 13, 1824)

Vaughn, Miss Eleanora married to Mr. John J. McCasland.

Vaughn, Miss Eleanor married to Mr. John J. M'Casland.

Vaughn, Mr. Elisha married in Sumner County on the 25th ult. to Miss
Catherine L. M. Moore.
National Banenr & Nashville Whig (Fri., Oct. 3, 1834)

Vaughn, Mr. Elisha B. married in Rutherford County to Miss Mahala
Wade.
Nashville Whig (April 9, 1823)

Vaughn, Mr. H. married on Wednesday last by the Rev. Mr. Slater to Miss
Catharine Hobbs all of Nashville.
The Politician & Weekly Nashville Whig (Fri., Feb. 4, 1848)

Vaughn, Col. James H. married at Dixon's Springs, Smith County on the
25th to Miss Eliza Ann Mitchell.
National Banner & Nashville Daily Advertiser (Mon., Aug. 5, 1833)

Vaughn, Miss Jane M. married to Dr. Joseph Cloud.

Vaughn, Miss Mary married to Mr. George Ridley.

Vaughn, Miss Nancy married to Mr. James A. Hudgins.

Vaughn, Miss Sarah married to Mr. Osborne Henley.

Vaughn, Miss Virginia married to Mr. O. C. Beech.

Vaughn, William married in Williamson County to Miss Milissa Craig.
National Banner & Nashville Advertiser (Mon., March 26, 1832)

Vaughn, William married in Williamson County to Miss Melissa Craig.
The Western Weekly Review - Franklin, Tenn. (Fri., March 23, 1832)

Vaught, Mr. Nathan married in Maury County to Miss Lucretia Journey.
National Banner (Feb. 3, 1826)

Vaugine, Mr. Etienne married in Vaugine Township, Ark. to Miss Matilda
Dereusseaux.
National Banner & Nashville Whig (Sat., Feb- 24, 1827)

Vaugine, Mr. Francis Jr. married in Arkansas to Miss Matilda de Villemon.
National Banner & Nashville Whig (Sat., Sept. 9, 1826)

Vaulx, Miss Ann C. married to Mr. Samuel J. Carter.

Vaulx, Mr. James married in Madison County to Miss Eliza Fenner.
National Banner & Nashville Whig (Sat., Feb. 3, 1827)

Vaulx, Mr. Joseph married in this town on Thursday evening last to
Miss Susan Hobson.
National Banner & Nashville Whig (Sat., Dec. 23, 1826)

Vaulx, Joseph married in Nashville on the 27th ult. to Miss Eleanor
N. A. Armstrong daughter of Gen. A. Armstrong.
Daily Republican Banner (Sat., Aug. 29, 1840)

Vaulx, Joseph Esq. married on the 27th inst. by Rev. Dr. Edgar to Miss
Eleanor N. A. Armstrong eldest daughter of Gen. R. Armstrong all of
Nashville.
Nashville Whig (Fri., Aug. 28, 1840)

Vawter, Miss Jane married to Mr. Thomas J. Story.
National Banner (Jan. 13, 1826)

Veal, Miss Minerva T. married to Mr. Edward Laverty.

Veal, Miss Susan W. married to Dr John Cooper.

Veitch, Miss Maria married to Mr. Peyton H. Wheeler.

Veltineer, Mr. Christopher married in Woodford County, Ky. to Miss
Nancy Ann Moyers.
National Banner (March 3, 1826)

Vernon, Mr. Miles C. married in Knox County to Miss Catharine Karnes.
National Banner & Nashville Whig (Mon., Oct. 11, 1830)

Vick, Miss Amanda married to Mr. William L. Anderson.

Vick, Miss Ann A. married to Dr. Robert A. Irion.

Vick, Mr. E. S. married in Russellville, Ky. to Miss Mary Ann Drew.
National Banner & Nashville Whig (Mon., Aug. 1, 1831)

Viers, Miss married to Maj. Benjamin Proctor.

Vigus, Miss Mary married to Col. John W. Byrn.

Villars, Miss Ann E. married to Mr. Peter H. Rust.

Villemon, Miss Matilda De married to Mr. Francis Vaugine Jr.

Valleplait, Mr. Alexander S. married in Nashville on 28th Dec. by the
Rev. J. Thomas Wheat to Miss Sarah A. Roscoe.
Daily Republican Banner (Fri., Dec. 29, 1837)

Valliplait, Mr. Alexander S.. married at the residence of W. Hasell
Hunt, Esq. in Nashville on 28th Dec. by Rev. J. Thomas Wheat to Miss
Sarah A. Roscoe.
Nashville Union (Sat., Dec. 30, 1837)

Vincent, Miss Elizabeth married to Mr. William G. Thomas.

Vincent, Mr. William B. of Covington, W. D. married at Gallatin on
the 15th inst. by Rev. Dr. Edgar to Miss Elizabeth Henderson daughter
of the late Charles Henderson fo Sumner County.
Nashville Whig (Fri., Jan. 15, 1841)

Vinson, Mr. Richard married in Warren County to Miss Mary Pierce.
National Banner (March 10, 1826)

Violett, Mr. John of Nashville married to Miss Winniford Y. Young
in Logan County, Ky.
National Banner & Nashville Whig (Fri., Jan. 29, 1830)

Virden, Mr. Daniel married in Lexington, Ky. to Miss Caroline Barnet.
National Banner & Nashville Whig (Sat., Sept. 20, 1828)

Voorhies, Miss Amanda married to Mr. James F. Henderson.

Voorhies, Miss Eliza married to Mr. Ezra Tarpley.

Voorhies, Miss Sarah Maria married to Mr. Hugh F. Bell.

Voorhies, Miss Susan married to Dr. John P. Wortham.

Waler, Mr. Richard D. married in Campbell County, T. to Miss Charlotte S. Bridgeman.
National Banner & Nashville Whig (Sat., Sept. 16, 1826)

Walker, Mrs. of Giles married in Giles County to Mr. Josiah Alderson of Columbia.
National Banner (March 24, 1826)

Walker, Miss Amanda F. married to Mr. Abraham S. Hoggatt.

Walker, Mr. Barkley V. married in Knox County to Miss Peggy Ann Douglass
National Banner (Sat., Dec. 26, 1829)

Walker, Miss Bethenia married to J. W. Clay Esq.

Walker, Mr. Leroy P. of Huntsville, Ala. married to Miss Elizabeth Hudnell of Miss.
Nashville Republican (Thurs., June 23, 1836)

Walker, Miss Levina married to Mr. Bartlet Eves.

Walker, Miss Lucindia married to Mr. Thomas J. Childress.

Walker, Miss Marie Jane married to Dr. Richard L. Fearn.

Walker, Mary Eliza married to William S. Pickett Esq.

Walker, Miss Mary M. married to Mr. A. Stewart.

Walker, Miss Mary R. married to Mr. Walker A. Hoffar.

Walker, Capt. Mathew P., Davidson County married to Miss Nancy Hope of Davidson County on last Wednesday.
Impartial Review and Cumberland Repository - published at Nashville Sat., March 21, 1807)

Walker, Mrs. Matilda married to Mr. Nathaniel P. Taylor.

Walker, Miss Rebecca married to Mr. Gray Andrews.

Walker, Mr. Robert of Haywood County, Tenn. married to Miss Eliza Morgan in Florence, Ala.
National Banner & Nashville Whig (Mon., Nov. 28, 1831)

Walker, Mr. Robert W. of Pine Bluff, Ark. formerly of Nashville married on the 27th at Napoleon, Ark. to Mi-s Enlelie V. Taylor daughter of Creed Taylor of Napoleon.
Nahsville Whig (Thurs., Feb. 10, 1842)

Walker, Mr. Samuel P. married in Maury County, Tenn. to Miss Eleanor Wormley.
National Banner & Nashville Whig (Wed., Nov. 12, 1834)

Walker, Miss Sarah P. married to Mr. Feilding A. Lucas.

Walker, Miss Sebela married to Mr. Matthew Nelson.

Walker, Miss Susan married to Richard Hay.

Walker, Susan F. married to Amos Rounsaville.

Walker, Mr. T. P. in Dyersburg, Tenn. married to Miss Mary Mitchell.
Nashville Republican & State Gazette (Thurs., April 21, 1831)

Walker, Mr. Warren married on the 14th inst. by the Rev. James Whitsett to Miss Mary Jane Tilford of this vicinity.
Nashville Whig (Sat., March 18, 1843)

Walker, Mr. William A. of Knox County married in M'Minn County to Miss Margaret Weir.
National Banner & Nashville Whig (Thurs., July 22, 1830)

Walkly, Mr. Nelson married in Tuscaloosa, Ala. on the 15th Aug. to Miss Elvira M. Barnett.
National Banner & Nashville Daily Advertiser (Wed., Aug. 28, 1833)

Wall, Mr. Isaac H. of Huntsville married in Lincoln County to Miss Susan P. Smith.
National Banner & Nashville Whig (Sat., April 7, 1827)

Wall, Miss Mary married to Mr. Lemuel Vaughan.

Wallace, Maj. Barkley M. at Knoxville married to Miss Catherine Strong.
National Banner & Nashville Whig (Mon., Dec. 19, 1831)

Wallace, Mr. Benjamin in McMinn, County married to Miss Mary Anderson McMinn County daughter of Mr. Isaac Anderson.
National Banner & Nashville Advertiser (Jan. 4, 1832)

Wallace, Olivar married on Thursday, February 5, 1795 in Jefferson County, Mr. Olivar Wallace to Miss Thankful Harris.
Knoxville Gazette (Fri., Feb. 27, 1795)

Wallace, Polly Miss married to Mr. John McClellan.

Walter, Mr. Alpha married at Louisville, Ky. to Miss Margaret Lindsey.
National Banner & Nashville Whig (Sat., March 1, 1828)

Watkins, Claiborne, Esquire married on the 15th of May, 1794 in Washington County, Virginia, Claiborne Watkins, Esquire of Abingdon to Miss Elizabeth Craig daughter of Capt. Robert Craig.
Knoxville Gazette. (Thurs., June 5, 1794)

Webster, Mr. Jonathan married in Maury County to Miss Lucy Gant.
National Banner & Nashville Whig (Wed., June 1, 1831)

Webster, Col. Jonathan married in Bedford County by the Rev. Richard Cuningham to Miss Nancy C. Shockley.
National Banner & Nashville Whig (Fri., Aug. 21, 1835)

Wackett, Samuel R. Esq. of Rhea County married on the 22nd ult. to Miss Mary Ann Smith daughter of Mr. Wright Smith.
National Banner & Nashville Daily Advertiser (Mon., Feb. 11, 1833)

Waddel, Mr. Joseph P. married in Florence, Ala. to Miss Lucinda R. Bryn.
National Banner & Nashville Daily Advertiser (Mon., Jan. 16, 1832)

Waddel, Miss Lucy married to Mr. John L. Cole.

Waddell, Miss Caroline married to Mr. Francis G. Petty.

Waddell, Miss Eliza married to Mr. Allen H. Irwin.

Wade, Mr. Charles of Wilson County married in Smith County to Miss Charlotte Carter.
National Banner & Nashville Daily Advertiser (Wed., May 1, 1833)

Wade, David S. Esq. married at Cincinnati to Miss Ann Bartow.
National Banner (April 14, 1826)

Wade, Miss Eliza A. married to Mr. Benjamin Elder.

Wade, Miss Elizabeth C. married to Mr. Isaiah Brasfield.

Wade, Mr. George married in Rutherford County to Miss Francis Basey.
National Banner (Jan. 6, 1826)

Wade, Mr. Henry of this city married on Thursday evening last by the Rev. G. Blackburn to Miss Miranda Thompson daughter of Robt. Thompson of this County.
The Nashville Whig (June 9th, 1817)

Wade, Horatio married in Maury County to Miss Mary Russell.
National Banner & Nashville Daily Advertiser (Thurs., April 5, 1832)

Wade, Miss Jane married to Mr. Isaac Brown.

Wade, Miss Jubitha married to Mr. James Tart.

Wade, Miss Mahala married to Mr. Elisha B. Vaughn.

Wade, Miss Terrissa married to Mr. William Morris.

Wadkins, Miss Elizabeth married to Mr. Elizah Morris.

Wadsworth, Miss Roxelana married to Lieut. H. B. Sawyers.

Wafford, Miss Vienna married to Mr. Iredal Phillips.

Waggoner, Mr. H. G. married in Harden County to Mrs. Best.
National Banner & Nashville Whig (Sat., Aug. 11, 1827)

Waggoner, Miss Mary J. married to Mr. S. M. Scott.

Waggoner, Dr. R. J. of Elkton married in Logan County, Ky. to Miss Margaret E. B. Whitaker.
National Banner & Nashville Whig (Thurs., July 29, 1830)

Waind, Mr. William married in Davidson County on Tuesday 26th May to Miss Margaret Harris daughter of Mr. A. G. Harris.
National Banner & Nashville Whig (Fri., May 29, 1835)

Waites, Miss Angess married to Mr. Alexander Miller.

Wakefield, Miss Evelina married to Mr. Nathaniel B. Robertson.

Wakefield, Miss Piety married to Mr. John Robinson.

Wakefield, Mr. Silas B. married in Smith County to Miss S. Sutton.
National Banner & Nashville Advertiser (Fri., Feb. 24, 1832)

Walden, Mr. William of Lexington married in Lexington, Ky. to Mrs. Margaret Haydon of Jessamine County daughter of Peter Higbee of Lexington.
National Banner & Nashville Whig (Fri., Jan. 23, 1835)

Waldin, Mr. A. S. married in Knox County to Miss Isabella J. White.
Nashville Whig (Tues., July 14, 1846)

Walker, Mr. Charles F. of Taledega, Ala. married on the 2d inst. to Miss Caroline V. Mitchell of Rutherford.
Nashville Republican (Sat., Sept. 12, 1835)

Walker, Miss Charlotte married to Mr. James H. McFarland.

Walker, Mr. D. of Arkansas Territory married in Logan County, Ky. to Miss Jane Washington.
National Banner & Nashville Daily Advertiser (Sat., Feb. 9, 1833)

Walker, Mr. Daniel D. married in Maury County to Miss Louivisy Spivey.
National Banner & Nashville Whig (Fri., Dec. 10, 1830)

Walker, Miss Elizabeth C. married to Mr. John B. Carson.

Walker, Miss Elizabeth A. married to Mr. Ephraim McCrackin.

Walker, Miss Elspa M. married to Mr. Reuben L. Kay.

Walker, Mr. Eramus, editor of the Intelligener married at Tuscaloosa, Ala. to Miss Ann P. Childress.
National Banner (Sat., Dec. 19, 1829)

Walker, Miss Elizabeth C. married to Mr. John B. Carson.

Walker, Mr. Leroy P. of Huntsville, Ala. married on Tuesday 21st inst. by the Rev. Dr. Edgar to Miss Elizabeth Hudnell of Mississippi.
Nashville Republican (Thurs., June 23, 1836)

Walker, Miss Judith married to Mr. Martin Turner.
National Banner (March 31, 1826)

Walker, Mr. Joseph married in Maury County to Miss Mary Hines.
National Banner & Nashville Whig (Mon., Aug. 8, 1831)

Walker, John W. Esq. of the house of J. W. Walker & Edwards, Nashville. Married at Springfield, Ten. on Tuesday 1st inst. by Rev. Benjamin Rawls to Miss Martha Washington Cheatham daughter of the late Gen. Richard Cheatham of Springfield.
Nashville Whig (Sat., Sept. 5, 1846)

Walker, John W. of Nashville married in Florence, Ala. on 19th Jan. to Miss Sarah A. Gray of Florence, Jan. 26, 1837)
Nashville Republican (Thurs., Jan. 26, 1837)

Walker, Mr. John F. married at New Echota to Miss Nancy Watie of Ougilogee.
National Banner (Sat., May 9, 1829)

Walker, Mr. John married in Smith County on the 18th inst. to Miss Prudence Archer.
National Banner & Nashville Daily Advertiser (Fri., Jan. 27, 1832)

Walker, Dr. Joel of Hickman County Speaker of the Senate of Tennessee married Miss Mary Motheral of Williamson by the Rev. Mr. Hume of Tuesday evening last.
National Banner & Nashville Whig (Fri., April 23, 1830)

Walker, Dr. J. M. married in Nashville on Thursday evening 20th inst. by the Rev. Mr. Edgar to Miss Mary McLemore eldest daughter of John C. McLemore Esq. all of Nashville.
National Banner & Nashville Daily Advertiser (Fri., Feb. 21, 1834)

Walker, Miss Janet married to Mr. Wyatt Collier.

Walker, Dr. James H. of Haywood County to Miss Isabella J. Meredith at Denmark.
National Banner & Nashville Whig (Wed., April 27, 1831)

Walker, Dr. James H. of Haywood County married to Miss Isabella Meridith in Madison County.
Nashville Republican & State Gazette (Thurs., April 28, 1831)

Walker, Mr. James merchant married on Thursday evening last to Miss Mary Norvell both of this town, Nashville.
Nashville Whig (Aug. 11, 1823)

Walker, Mr. James married in Williamson County to Miss Sally Phelps.
National Banner & Nashville Whig (Mon., April 13, 1835)

Walker, Mr. Isaac of South Florence married in Tuscumbia, Ala. to Miss Maria Winter daughter of Major W. H. Winter.
National Banner & Nashville Daily Advertiser (Mon., July 15, 1833)

Walker, Henry C. Esq. married in Memphis to Miss Margaret B. Trigg daughter of John Trigg Esq.
Nashville Whig (Thurs., June 25, 1846)

Walker, Miss Gabriella N. married to Mr. Nelson J. Maynard.

Wallace, Mr. Campbell, Knox County married to Miss Susan E. Lyon daughter of Capt. Wm. Lyon.
National Banner & Nashville Whig (Mon., June 13, 1831)

Wallace, Mr. Edward R. married in Huntsville on the 15th inst. by the Rev. John Allen to Miss Virginia Ann Penn.
Nashville Whig (Sat., Dec. 24, 1842)

Wallace, Mr. J. B. of New Orleans married on the 22nd ult. near Columbia by the Rev. Mr. Scott to Miss Ann Jane Todd daughter of Christopher Todd, Esq. of Maury County.
Nashville Whig (Wed., Aug. 4, 1841)

Wallace, James B. Esq. of Alabama married on Thursday evening last to Miss Caroline C. Craddock daughter of Mr. P. Craddock of this town, Nashville.
Nashville Whig (July 28, 1823)

Wallace, Mr. James H. married in Fayette County, Ky. to Miss Eliza Ann Bosworth.
National Banner & Nashville Whig (Sat., Nov. 17, 1827)

Wallace, Mr. John married at Chillicothe O. to Miss Maria Snyder.
National Banner (Jan. 27, 1826)

Wallace, Mr. Joseph married in Lincoln County to Miss Mary Harlan.
Dec. 30, Sat. 1826

Wallace, Major Joseph W. E. married at Port Gibson to Miss Harriet H. Holt.
National Banner (March 3, 1826)

Wallace, Miss Margaret A. married to Mr. James Browning.

Wallace, Miss Mary Jane married to Mr. Thomas Jefferson Brown.

Wallace, Miss Mary Jane married to Mr. Robert Donnel.

Wallace, Miss Nancy G. married to Mr. W. L. Berry.

Wallace, Mr. Oliver married in Jefferson County to Miss Thankful Harris on the 5 inst.
Knoxville Gazette (Fri., Feb. 27, 1795)

Wallace, Miss Polly married to Mr. John McClellan.

Wallace, Mr. William married on the 13th by the Rev. Mr. Howell to Miss Mary Ann Barry daughter of John G. Barry all of Nashville.
National Banner & Nashville Whig (Wed., Dec. 14, 1836)

Wallard, Mr. John married in Maury County to Miss Mary M. Turnage.
National Banner & Nashville Whig (Mon., Aug. 8, 1831)

Waller, Joseph married in Williamson County to Miss Nancy T. C. Dotson.
The Western Weekly Review - Franklin, Tenn. (Fri., Dec. 14, 1832)

Waller, Miss Lucinda married to Dr. J. Parrott.

Wallis, Miss Harriet C. married to Mr. Samuel D. M'Cullough.

Wallis, Mr. Jackson married in Rutherford County to Miss Mary Bradley daughter of Maj. John Bradley.
National Banner (Sat., Sept. 12, 1829)

Wallis, Mr. L. D. of Tuscumbia, Ala. married on Tuesday evening 18th by the Rev. C. P. Reed to Miss Eliza Smith daughter of the Rev. James Smith of Nashville.
Nashville Whig (Wed., Sept. 19, 1838)

Walls, Miss Mary Ann married to Mr. Henry F. Buesley.

Walls, Miss Nancy married to Mr. George W. Staton.

Walsh, Dr. Baker of Cairo, in Wilson County married Miss Jane T. Robertson.
National Banner & Nashville Whig (Fri., Feb. 19, 1830)

Walsh, Mr. Henry C. married in this town on Tuesday to Miss Ann M'Connell.
National Banner & Nashville Whig (Sat., June 20, 1828)

Walsh, Mr. Simon W. married near Baton Rouge to Miss Martha Hickey.
National Banner & Nashville Whig (Sat., April 14, 1827)

Walters, Mr. Obadiah married in Grainger County to Miss Nelly Powell.
National Banner (Sat., July 4, 1829)

Walton, Miss Barbara Ann married to Mr. A. M. M'Lean.

Walton, Miss Lavenia married to Mr. Edward Stratton.

Walton, Miss Mary married to Mr. Champion E. Smith.

Walton, Miss Mary O. married to Dr. A. G. Vaughn.

Walton, Miss Mary T. married to Mr. James Porter.

Walton, Miss Sebella married to Mr. Eli McKoin.

Walton, Mr. Timothy of this state married in Granville County, N. Caroline on the 27th ult. to Miss Mary Taylor daughter of John Taylor, Esq.
The Nashville Whig (Sept. 29th, 1817)

Walton, Col. William married on the 8th by the Rev. John W. Hall to Miss Jane M. Tyree both of Sumner County.
Nashville Republican (Tues., March 15, 1836)

Wampler, Miss Mary married to Mr. John Hull.

Wantland, Mr. Samuel married in Maury County to Miss Ann Alderson.
National Banner & Nashville Whig (Sat., March 8, 1828)

Wantland, Miss Susan married to Mr. Charles D. Crofford.

Warbriden, Miss Narcissa married to Mr. Robert Landman.

Ward, Mr. A. of Nashville married in Lincoln County, Ky. to Miss Mary Jane Mumford.
National Banner & Nashville Whig (Sat., May 19, 1827)

Ward, Mr. Albert G. married on Tuesday evening the 23d inst. to Miss Maria J. Baker.
Nashville Republican (Sat., Feb. 27, 1836)

Ward, Miss Arietta J. married to Edward H. Green, Esq.

Ward, Mr. David C. married in Smith County to Miss Mary Moore.
National Banner (March 31, 1826)

Ward, Mr. Edward married at Louisville, Ky. to Miss Eliza Oldham.
National Banner & Nashville Whig (Wed., Oct. 12, 1831)

Ward, Mr. Gideon married in Henry County to Miss Eleanor Gunter.
National Banner & Nashville Daily Advertiser (Wed., Jan. 18, 1832)

Ward, Mr. Hasen married in Wilson County by the Rev. Joshua Lester to
Miss Milly Johnson.
National Banner & Nashville Whig (Sat., Dec. 1, 1827)

Ward, Mr. John C. married in Madison County, Ala. to Miss Sally H.
Clark.
National Banner (Sat., April 25, 1829)

Ward, Mr. John H. of Ala. married on Wednesday the 26th by the Rev.
Dr. Davis to Miss Ann S. Reed of Nashville.
The Union (Thurs., July 27, 1837)

Ward, Mr. John Nelson married on Tuesday the 6th inst. by Rev. R. B. C.
Howell D.D. to Miss Eliza Ellen Norton all of Nashville.
Nashville Whig (Thurs., Aug. 8, 1844)

Ward, Mr. Littleton L. of Carroll County married in Belfast, Gibson
County to Miss Elizabeth Mitchell.
National Banner & Nashville Whig (Mon., Sept. 26, 1831)

Ward, Miss Margaret Louisa married to Dr. George W. White.

Ward, Miss Maria J. married to Dr. J. Fowlkes.

Ward, Miss Mary married to Mr. Douglas Ferris.

Ward, Miss M. J. C. married to Rev. A. H. Kerr.

Ward, Miss Sophia married to Mr. John M. Stokes.

Wardell, Miss Clara A. married to Mr. William Cooper.

Ware, Mr. John married in Madison County, Ala. to Miss Mary T. Key.
National Banner & Nashville Whig (Thurs., Aug. 19, 1830)

Ware, Mr. Wm. married in Crhistian County, Ky. to Miss Alphia G. J.
Clark.
National Banner & Nashville Daily Advertiser (Tues., Feb. 5, 1833)

Warfield, Miss Mary Jane married to Mr. Cassius M. Clay.

Warfield, Rev. Wm. married in Todd County to Miss Joyce Deagued.
National Banner & Nashville Whig (Mon., April 18, 1831)

Warford, Mr. Miles married at Meridianville, Ala. to Miss Elizabeth
Bell.
National Banner & Nashville Whig (Sat., Jan. 17, 1829)

Warmack, Mr. Edward married in Davidson County to Miss Jemimah Hackney
on 13th inst.
Nashville Republican & State Gazette (Thurs., March 27, 1834)

Warmack, Mr. Richard married by J. C. Bowers Esq. to Miss Elizabeth
A. Bryan.
Nashville Republican & State Gazette (Tues., Oct. 1, 1833)

Warner, Edward W. of Philadelphia married in Nashville by the Rev.
J. T. Edgar D.D. to Mary L. Berryhill daughter of Wm. M. Berryhill
Esq. of Nashville.
National Banner & Nashville Whig (Wed., Nov. 26, 1834)

Warner, Mr. J. L. married in Sumner County on the 12th inst. to Miss
Elizabeth Cartwright.
National Banner (Sat., May 30,1829)

Warner, Mr. Reuben T. married in Sumner County on the 14th by the Rev. Mr. H. W. Hunt to Miss Sophia G. Moss.
National Banner (Sat., May 30, 1829)

Warner, Col. Richard married in Bedford County to Miss Lucy Brown.
National Banner & Nashville Whig (Sat., Dec. 23, 1826)

Warner, Mr. S. A. Esq. married in Weakley County on the 12th inst. by Rev. Mr. Dunn to Miss Martha A. Mosley.
National Banner & Nashville Whig (Sat., Aug. 30, 1828)

Warnick, Mr. W. married in Henry County to Miss Pricilla Price.
National Banner & Nashville Daily Advertiser (Thurs., March 20, 1834)

Warner, Mr. Samuel married near Lexington, Ky. to Miss Sarah Ann Smith.
National Banner & Nashville Daily Advertiser (Tues., March 11, 1834)

Watson, Samuel Esq. of Nashville, Ten. married Miss Charlotte Morton Fountan, Mass.
Nashville Republican (Tues., Sept. 15, 1835)

Warner, Maj. Samuel A. married in Weakley County to Miss Martha Ann Mosely.
National Banner & Nashville Whig (Sat., Sept. 13, 1828)

Warner, Mr. William S. of Nashville married on New Year's Day to Miss Sarah Wood.
Nashville Republican (Sat., Jan. 3, 1835)

Warneck, Mr. Henry D. married in Knox County to Miss Acenith Chapman.
National Banner & Nashville Whig (Sat., Nov. 1, 1828)

Warr, Miss Martha married to Mr. Root Page.

Warren, Burrel married in Williamson County to Miss Mary Bedford.
The Western Weekly Review - Franklin, Ten. (Fri., Dec. 14, 1832)

Warren, Miss Fanny married to Mr. Wm. Taylor.

Warren, Miss Francis married to James Stewart.

Warren, Mr. Jesse married in Nashville on Thursday 9th inst. by the Rev. J. B. McFerrin to Miss Frances Ann Pride.
Nashville Whig (Fri., Sept. 10, 1841)

Warren, Mr. John married in Smith County to Miss Charlotte Carter.
National Banner & Nashville Daily Advertiser (Fri., Feb. 24, 1832)

Warren, Miss Lydia W. married to Rev. Andrew Herren Jr.

Warren, Nancy married to Jas. Pate.

Warren, Mr. P. G. publisher of the Courier married at Murfreesborough on 6th inst. by the Rev. German Baker to Miss Elizabeth Pylass.
National Banner & Nashville Daily Advertiser (Fri., Dec. 14, 1832)

Warren, Sarah O. N. married to Zebulon L. Sledge.

Warren, Miss Susan H. married to Mr. Ben C. Allen.

Warren, Mr. William married in Williamson County to Miss Lucy Bazzell.
The Western Weekly Review - Franklin, Tenn. (Fri., Dec. 2, 1831)

Warson, Miss America married to Mr. E. W. Lester.

Warwich, Miss Marinda married to Mr. R. C. McAlpin, Esq.

Wash, Robert Esq. one of the Judges of Supreme Court married at St. Louis to Mrs. Berry daughter of Maj. William Christy.
National Banner (May 27, 1826)

Washington, Miss Amanda married to Major Washington Ryburn.

Washington, Miss Emily married to Mr. Waller Lewis.

Washington, Mr. Geo. of Frankford married in Bourbon County, Ky. to Miss Gabriella Augusta Hawkins.
National Banner & Nashville Whig (Sat., May 19, 1827)

Washington, Dr. Henry F. of Rodney, Miss. married Miss Caroline M. Anderson Hopkinsville, Ky.
Nashville Republican & State Gazette (Tues., Dec. 24, 1833)

Washington, Miss Jane married to Mr. D. Walker.

Washington, Miss Keturak M. married to Mr. John Rowen.

Washington, Miss Martha Ann married to Mr. William C. Goodlett.

Washington, Miss Mary married to Mr. John Thompson.

Washington, Mrs. Susan married to Mr. William Spackman.

Washington, Thomas Esq. of Nashville married on Tuesday evening last to Mrs. Mary Osborne.
National Banner & Nashville Whig (Mon., Jan. 10, 1831)

Wason, Miss Emmaline married to Mr. John Pollock.

Wasson, Miss Sarah married to Mr. Marmon Spence.

Waterhouse, Mr. Blackstone at Tuscaloosa, Ala. married Miss Susan S. Lewin.
National Banner & Nashville Whig (Fri., March 26, 1830)

Waterhouse, Miss Mira married to Dr. Gideon B. Thompson.

Waterhouse, Col. Richard G. married to Miss Mary Lane.

Waters, Miss Catherine married to Mr. Thomas S. Shannon.

Waters, Doctor John married on Thursday evening last by the Rev. William Hume to Mrs. Eunice Flint all of this town.
Nashville Whig (May 10, 1824)

Waters, Dr. John married on the 21st inst. at the residence of John M. Bass Esq. to Miss Anna Rawlings all of Nashville.
Nashville Whig (Thurs., Oct. 22, 1846)

Waters, Mr. Jos. married at Russellville, Ky. to Miss Sarah Duncan.
National Banner & Nashville Daily Advertiser (Mon., Sept. 9, 1833)

Waters, Miss Lydia married to Dr. Felix Robertson.

Waters, Miss Mary Ann married to Mr. Allen Purvis.

Waters, Mr. Nelson married in Clarksville, Ten. to Mrs. Caldwell.
National Banner & Nashville Daily Advertiser (Sat., April 28, 1832)

Waters, Thomas H. Esq. married at Lexington, Ky. to Miss Caroline V. Higgins.
National Banner & Nashville Whig (Sat., June 14, 1828)

Waters, Mr. Thomas J. of Ala. married in this town on the 2nd inst. by the Rev. Mr. Hume to Miss Susan Smith.
National Banner & Nashville Whig (Sat., May 17, 1828)

Waters, Mr. William married in Henry County to Miss Marietta Swift.
National Banner & Nashville Whig (Mon., Nov. 1, 1830)

Wathall, Miss Louisa Ann married to Capt. Richard B. Phillips.

Watie, Miss Nancy married to Mr. John F. Walker.

Watkins, Miss Agnes married to Dr. William P. Sayles.

Watkins, Mr. Albert J. married in Huntsville, Ala. to Miss Maria
Louisa Clifton.
National Banner & Nashville Daily Advertiser (Wed., Aug. 21, 1833)

Watkins, Miss Betsy married to Philip Angling.

Watkins, Claiborn, Esq. of Abingdon married in Washington County,
Virginia on the 15th ult. to Miss Elizabeth Craig.
Knoxville Gazette (Thurs., June 5, 1794)

Watson, Mr. Cyrus L. married in Edwardsville, Ill. to Miss Mary W.
M'Kee.
National Banner (May 27, 1826)

Watkins, Miss Henriatta E. married to Mr. Albert C. Franklin.

Watkins, Miss Irean married to Mr. Benjamin Cox.

Watkins, Mr. James of Sumner County married on Thursday 5th inst. to
Miss Sarah W. Pugh of Davidson County.
National Banner & Nashville Whig (Mon., Feb. 23, 1835)

Watkins, Mr. James married in Blount County to Miss Elizabeth Roup.
National Banner & Nashville Daily Advertiser (Mon., Feb. 27, 1832)

Watkins, Mr. Jones married in Henry County to Miss Elizabeth Radford.
National Banner & Nashville Daily Advertiser (Tues., Aug. 7, 1832)

Watkins, Mr. Lorezo married in Sumner County to Miss Pamela Tally.
National Banner & Nashville Daily Advertiser (Thurs., Feb. 14, 1833)

Watkins, Miss Mary D. married to Mr. Jas. M. Patterson.

Watkins, Miss Mary Elizabeth married to Major Bolling Gordon.

Watkins, Miss Mary Jane married to Mr. C. H. Hinton.

Watkins, Dr. Miles S. of Huntsville married in Sumner County on the
15th by Rev. Mr. Hume to Dr. Miles S. Watkins of Huntsville to Miss
Sarah B. C. Shelby daughter of A. B. Shelby Esq.
National Banner (Sat., May 30, 1820)

Watkins, Miss Rebecca married to James Speers.

Watkins, Miss Sally married to Mr. John R. Robinson.

Watkins, Mr. Samuel J. married in Williamson County to Miss Martha Jane
Foster.
Nashville Whig (Sat., July 11, 1846)

Watkins, Miss Sarah married to Mr. Washington Foster.

Watkins, Stephen D. Esq. of Nashville married by the Rev. Mr. Elliott
to Miss Mary D. Baxter daughter of Robert Baxter Esq. of Montgomery
County.
Nashville Whig (Thurs., Dec. 22, 1842)

Watkins, Miss Susan A. married to Ephraim H. Foster, Jr.

Watkins, Mr. Thomas married in this County on Thursday Jan. 31st by Rev. Mr. Hume to Miss Pembroke Cartwright.
National Banner & Nashville Whig (Sat., Feb. 9, 1828)

Watkins, Thomas G. Capt. of Murfreesboro married in Rutherford County on the 12th inst. to Miss Mary Nelson daughter of Mr. Thomas Nelson.
The Nashville Whig & Tenn. Advertiser (March 21, 1818)

Watkins, Miss Virginia married to Thomas J. Foster, Esq.

Watkins, Mr. Wm. Jr. married in Madison County, Ala. to Miss Harriet Anderson.
National Banner & Nashville Whig (Sat., Dec. 30, 1826)

Watkins, Mr. William married in Williamson County to Miss Ritta Perkins.
The Western Weekly Review - Franklin, Tenn. (Fri., Dec. 2, 1831)

Watkins, Mr. William E. married on Tuesday evening last by Thomas Claiborne Esq. to Miss Matilda Hewett daughter of Robert Hewett of Davidson County.
The Nashville Gazette (Wed., Oct. 27. 1819)

Watkinson, Miss Nancy married to George Arnett.

Watmough, Hon. John G. married at Washington City to Miss Matilda Pleasanton.
Nashville Republican & State Gazette (Mon., Dec. 10, 1832)

Watson, Dr. of Williamson County married in Wilson County to Miss L. S. Brown.
National Banner & Nashville Whig (Wed., April 6, 1831)

Watson, Egbert R. Esq. one of the editors of the Charlottsville Advocate married at Charlottsville, Va. to Miss Mary Kelly Norris.
National Banner & Nashville Daily Advertiser (Fri., Sept. 20, 1833)

Watson, Miss Elizabeth married to Mr. Rigdon Wiggs.

Watson, Miss Emmeline married to Mr. John Pollock.

Watson, Doctor James married on Saturday the 15th inst. by John P. Erwin Esq. to Miss Mary M. Payzer daughter of Benjamin Payzer all of Nashville recently from England.
The Nashville Gazette (Sat., April 22, 1820)

Watson, Mr. James married in Williamson County, Ten. to Miss Nancy Andrews.
National Banner & Nashville Whig (Fri., Feb. 13, 1835)

Watson, Mr. Jeremiah married at Port Gibson, Miss to Miss Francis Lowry.
National Banner (March 3, 1826)

Watson, Mr. John married in Lincoln County, Ten. to Miss Launno Stewart.
National Banner & Nashville Whig (Mon., April 20, 1835)

Watson, Miss Mary Ann A. married to Mr. William B. Cook.

Watson, Miss Nancy J. married to Dr. John H. Marable.

Watson, Miss Rachael married to Mr. Sam'l T. Caughran.

Watson, Samuel Esq. of Nashville married in Taunton, Mass. to Miys Charlotte Morton daughter of Hon. Marcus Morton of Taunton.
National Banner & Nashville Whig (Mon., Sept. 14, 1835)

Watson, Mr. Thomas Jr. married on Thursday last to Miss Sally Smith daughter of Col. George Smith of Sumner County.
The Nashville Whig (Nov. 19, 1816)

Watson, Mr. Wm. married at Lexington, Ky. to Miss Elizabeth Cobb.
National Banner & Nashville Whig (Sat., Sept. 15, 1827)

Watterson, H. M. Esq. editor of the Shelbyville Western Freeman
married in Maury County to Miss T. Black.
National Banner & Nashville Daily Advertiser (Wed., June 20, 1832)

Watterson, Miss Louisa D. married to Capt. Andrew Maxwell.

Watts, Miss Frances married to Col. Joseph T. Haralson.

Watts, Mr. James married in Jessamine County, Kentucky to Miss Sally
Hulett.
National Banner (March 3, 1826)

Watwood, Miss Julia B. married to Mr. John R. Jackson.

Waxler, Mr. Benjamin married in Louisville, Ky. to Miss Charlotte
Hughes.
National Banner & Nashville Whig (Fri., March 13, 1835)

Wayland, Mr. Henry Jr. married near Jackson, Ark. on the 10th Jan.
by the Rev. David Orr to Miss Hetty English.
National Banner & Nashville Daily Advertiser (Fri., Feb. 8, 1833)

Wayne, Mr. Charles married at Cincinnati to Miss Sarah Ann Quinton.
National Banner & Nashville Whig (Sat., June 7, 1828)

Weagley, Mrs. Sarah married to Dr. John T. Cassel.

Weakley, Mr. James H. of Florence married at Huntsville, Ala. to Miss
Ellen M. Donegan.
National Banner & Nashville Whig (Thurs., Sept. 9, 1830)

Weakley, Miss Jane H. married to Mr. John L. Brown.

Weakley, Miss Margaret married to Dr. Charles Glasier.

Weakley, Miss Narcissa A. married to Maj. John P. Hickman.

Weakley, Miss Susan N. married to Mr. Thomas B. Trigg Esq.

Weakley, Mr. Tho's J. of Tenn. married in Christian County, Ky. to
Miss Elizabeth E. M'Carthy.
National Banner (June 3, 1826)

Wear, Capt. Robert married in Blount County to Miss Margaret Wilkinson.
National Banner & Nashville Whig (Mon., May 2, 1831)

Wear, Capt. Robert married Miss Margaret Wilkinson in Blount County.
National Banner & Nashville Whig (Mon., May 2, 1831)

Wear, Col. William Wallace of Davidson County married at Bolivar on
the 17th inst. by the Rev. H. C. Chisholm to Miss Francis E. Fort of
Hardeman County.
Nashville Whig (Mon., Feb. 22, 1841)

Weatherald, Mrs. Margaret married to Mr. Ambrose House.

Weatherford, Mr. John married in Smith County to Miss Matilda Dudley.
National Banner & Nashville Advertiser (Fri., Jan. 27, 1832)

Weatherly, Mr. David married in this County to Miss Sarah Wright.
Nashville Republican (Tues., Jan. 27, 1835)

Weatherly, Mr. David married in Maury County, Ten. to Miss Sarah
Wright.
National Banner & Nashville Whig (Mon., Jan. 26, 1835)

Weaver, Mr. Dempsey married on Tuesday the 16th inst. by the Rev.
R. B. C. Howell to Miss Mary D. Johnson daughter of Squire James Johnson.
Daily Republican Banner (Fri., April 16, 1839)

Weaver, Dempsey Esq. married in Nashville last evening by Rev. Mr.
Howell to Miss Mary D. Johnson daughter of James Johnson Esq.
Nashville Whig (Wed., April 17, 1839)

Weaver, Dempsy of the house of Johnson & Weaver married on Thursday
the 16th inst. by the Rev. P. P. Neeley to Miss Frances L. King
daughter of Thomas S. King all of Davidson County.
Nashville Whig (Tues., May 21, 1844)

Weaver, Miss Dolly married to Mr. Robert Covington.

Weaver, Miss Eleanor married to Mr. Rob. M'Clane.

Weaver, Miss Ellen Ann married to Mr. Thomas H. Johnson.

Weaver, Mr. George I. married in Huntsville, Ala. on the 29th Jan. to
Mrs. Martha H. M'Cartney.
National Banner & Nashville Daily Advertiser (Wed., Feb. 6, 1833)

Weaver, Mr. Henry married in New Orleans to Miss Madgelaine Robin.
National Banner & Nashville Whig (June 24, 1826)

Weaver, Mr. John C. married in Madison County, Ala. to Miss Ann Ford.
National Banner & Nashville Whig (Wed., Sept. 14, 1831)

Weaver, Miss Lucinda J. married to Mr. Pleasant W. Weaver.

Weaver, Miss Martha married to Mr. James Haley.

Weaver, Mr. Pleasant W. married in Madison County, Ala. to Mi-s
Lucinda J. Weaver.
National Banner & Nashville Whig (Fri., Jan. 9, 1835)

Weaver, Miss Polly married to Mr. Elijah Gillingwater.

Weaver, Miss Sally married to Mr. Jonathan Dobbs.

Weaver, Shadrock married in Williamson County to Miss Julia Ann Tucker.
The Western Weekly Review - Franklin, Tenn. (Fri., March 8, 1833)

Webb, Miss Amanda M. F. married to Mr. H. H. Holland.

Webb, Andrew married in Williamson County, Ten. to Elizabeth Woldridge.
National Banner & Nashville Whig (Wed., Dec. 17, 1834)

Webb, Miss Catherine married to Rev. Mr. Regan.

Webb, Miss Eliza married to Mr. John Meek.

Webb, Miss Elizabeth L. married to Mr. S. M. Webb.

Webb, Mr. Ezra married at Florence, Ala. to Miss Louisa Terross formerly
of Nashville.
National Banner (Feb. 10, 1826)

Webb, Miss Frances married to Mr. John R. Hampton.

Webb, Mr. George of Illinois married in Montgomery County, Tenn. to
Mrs. Emily Fauntleroy of Indiana.
National Banner & Nashville Daily Advertiser (Mon., July 8, 1833)

Webb, Capt. George M. married in Knoxville to Miss Nancy Callaway.
National Banner & Nashville Whig (Sat., Sept. 30, 1826)

Webb, Dr. Henry Y. married in Williamson Co., Ten. to Miss Martha J. Hughes.
National Banner & Nashville Daily Advertiser (Mon., June 9, 1834)

Webb, Miss Jane married to Mr. Benjamin D. Simmons.

Webb, Mr. Kindle married on Thursday evening last to Miss Mary Dougle both of Nashville.
The Nashville Gazette (Sat., June 10, 1820)

Webb, Mr. Mitchum married in Scott County, Ky. to Miss Susan Holmes.
National Banner (Feb. 10, 1826)

Webb, Mr. Northflet E. married in Nashville on the 25th inst. by the Rev. James Gwinn to Miss Caroline Malissa Clinard both of Nashville.
The Union (Thurs., Sept. 29, 1836)

Webb, Mr. S. M., Commission Merchant of Memphis, married in Williamson County, Tenn. on 8th inst. by the Rev. D. G. Doak to Miss Elizabeth L. Webb daughter of Dr. W. S. Webb.
The Politician & Weekly Nashville Whig (Wed., Sept. 15, 1847)

Webb, Mr. Thomas C. married on Monday morning the last by Rev. Howell to Miss Sophia P. Scovel all of Nashville.
The Christian Record (Sat., June 17, 1848)

Weber, Mr. Charles W. Esq. counsellor at law of Columbia married in Hickman County to Miss Dorothy Gordan.
National Banner (Sat., Aug. 22, 1829)

Webster, Mr. Benj. married in Fayette County, Ky. to Miss Rutha Webster.
National Banner (Sat., May 2, 1829)

Webster, Miss Caroline married to Mr. Benjamin Turner.

Webster, Hon. Daniel Senator in Congress from Mass. married Miss Caroline Leroy daughter of Hermann Leroy, Esq.
National Banner & Nashville Whig (Fri., Jan. 22, 1830)

Webster, Miss Emily L. married to Mr. Lemuel H. Duncan.

Webster, Miss Mary married to Col. J. P. Tate.

Webster, Miss Mary married to Mr. Gransford P. Smith.

Webster, Miss Rutha married to Mr. Benj. Webster.

Webster, Miss Sarah married to Mr. Joseph Masterson.

Webster, Miss Virginia married to Mr. Jones.

Weekes, Mr. G. D. married on the 16th inst. by Rev. James Marshall to Miss Margaret J. Hunter daughter of Isaac Hunter Esq. of Davidson County.
Nashville Whig (Tues., July 21, 1846)

Weems, Miss Margaret married to Mr. Alexander Sprowl.

Weigart, Mr. John married in Lincoln County, Ten. to Miss Millberry Ann Jones.
National Banner & Nashville Whig (Fri., June 10, 1836)

Weir, Miss Arminia married to Mr. Samuel H. Hansard.

Weir, Miss Frances married to Col. Willis W. Cherry.

Weir, Miss Jane married to Rev. John Tate.

Weir, Miss Jane married to Mr. Woodford Organ.

Weir, Miss Malvina married to Dr. James W. Lea.

Weir, Miss Margaret married to Mr. William A. Walker.

Weir, Col. Robert of Columbus, Mi. married in Nashville on the 10th inst. by Rev. O. B. Hays to Miss Sarah G. Sanders daughter of the late Dr. Sanders of Memphis.
Daily Republican Banner (Sat., Oct. 12, 1839)

Weir, Miss Telitha Emeline married to Mr. Thomas Douglass Hall.

Weisiger, Mr. Geo. of Tuscumbia married in Louisville, Ky. to Miss Amanthus Bullitt.
National Banner (Sat., June 6, 1829)

Weisiger, Miss Isabella married to Tho. S. Lindsey.

Welbborne, Miss Eliza Adeline married to Maj. William Ledbetter.

Welch, Miss Belinda married to Mr. James Lynn.

Welch, Miss Eliza married to Mr. Benjamin Rucker.

Welch, Mrs. Eliza married to Mr. Benjamin Rucker.

Welch, Miss Mary E. married to Mr. David L. Hope.

Welch, Mr. Nicholas married in Perry County, Ala. to Miss Cloe Lockett.
National Banner & Nashville Whig (Sat., July 8, 1826)

Weller, Mr. Christian married in Hopkinsville to Miss Julia Hetherington.
National Banner & Nashville Whig (Sat., Sept. 9, 1826)

Weller, Miss Elizabeth married to Mr. James Miller.

Wells, Mr. David of N. Orleans married Miss Ann M. Raney.
National Banner & Nashville Whig (Sat., Feb. 14, 1829)

Wells, Mr. Felix of West Tennessee married in Washington City to Miss Ann C. Barron daughter of Dr. W. Barron late of Prince George's Co., Va.
National Banner & Nashville Daily Advertiser (Mon., May 12, 1834)

Wells, Mr. Joshua H. married in this County on Monday 8th inst. by Rev. Mr. Graves to Miss Elizabeth Overton.
National Banner & Nashville Whig (Sat., Dec. 20, 1828)

Wells, Rev. Martin married in Arkansas County, Ark. to Miss Mary McLain.
National Banner & Nashville Whig (Fri., March 13, 1835)

Wells, Miss Mary married to Mr. G. C. Thorp.

Wells, Mr. Oliver married at Cincinnati to Miss Elizabeth Tudor.
National Banner & Nashville Whig (Sat., July 15, 1826)

Wells, Miss Rebecca married to Mr. Samuel Hale.

Wells, Hon. Robert W. Judge of the Federal Court for the District of Mo. married near Bowling Green, Ky. by Rev. James M. Pendleton to Miss Eliza W. Covington daughter of Gen. Covington of Ky.
Nashville Whig (Fri., July 17, 1840)

Wells, Mr. Samuel married in Mason County, Ky. to Miss Maria Wood.
National Banner (March 24, 1826)

Wells, Miss Sarah P. married to Mr. William B. Word.

Wells, Miss Susan P. married to Mr. James M. Goodrich.

Wells, Mr. Thomas of Nashville married on the 10th inst. by the Rev. Mr. Lecoq to Miss Elizabeth M. Garrett of Franklin.
Nashville Union, (Fri., Dec. 14, 1838)

Wells, Mr. William married in Knox County to Miss Mary Morefield.
National Banner & Nashville Whig (Mon., April 11, 1831)

Welsh, Mr. Patrick married at New Orleans to Miss Margaret L. Westbay.
National Banner & Nashville Whig (Sat., Feb. 23, 1828)

Welsh, Miss Theresa married to Mr. John O. Rourke.

Wentzell, Mr. Enoch E. married in Portland, Ky. to Miss Rossella Mungall.
National Banner & Nashville Whig (Sat., Sept. 16, 1826)

Werkley, Mr. Daniel married in this town on the 11th inst. by the Rev. Mr. Hume to Mrs. Elizabeth Miller.
Nashville Whig (May 31, 1824)

Wesbay, Mr. Samuel married in Cincinnati to Miss Lavina Alcocke.
National Banner & Nashville Whig (Sat., Jan. 10, 1829)

West, Miss Ann Virginia married to Mr. William Edwards.

West, Miss Arabella C. married to Mr. Quintus C. Atkinson.

West, Miss Arabella C. married to Mr. Quinton C. Atkinson.

West, Mr. Benjamin married in Jefferson County, Mi. to Miss Paulina Meng of Louisville, Ky.
National Banner (Sat., May 9, 1829)

West, Benj. A. of Kentucky married to Miss Elizabeth R. Cozart.
Nashville Republican & State Gazette (Thurs., April 21, 1831)

West, Miss Catherine A. married to James W. Conlan Esq.

West, Mr. Edward married in St. Clair County, Illinois to Miss Elizabeth Foxwell.
National Banner (May 27, 1826)

West, Miss Edy married to Mr. Joel Thacker.

West, Miss Elizabeth married to Mr. Baker W. Ayres.

West, Mr. Francis G. West married at Lexington, Ky. to Miss Nancy Williams.
National Banner & Nashville Whig (Sat., Feb. 23, 1828)

West, Miss George Ann married to W. M. Ellis Esq.

West, Miss Hannah married to Mr. Daniel H. McKinney.

West, Mr. Isaac married in Bedford County to Miss Sarah Murphree.
National Banner & Nashville Whig (Sat., Nov. 15, 1828)

West, Miss Jane married to Capt. Sterling M. Banner.

West, Miss Jane M. married to Raymond Augustin Bouch, Esq.

West, Mr. Joseph married in Sumner County to Miss Frances Dorris.
National Banner & Nashville Daily Advertiser (Tues., June 11, 1833)

West, Miss Mary married to Mr. Jesse L. Smith.

West, Miss Mary Ann Eliza married to Dr. Drew A. Outlaw.

West, Mr. Robert married in Sumner County on the 10th inst. to Miss Peggy Towell.
National Banner & Nashville Whig (Sat., Sept. 13, 1828)

West, Miss Sarah married to Mr. Henry T. Yeatman.

West, Mr. W. G., merchant of Nashville married on Thursday 17th inst. by Dr. W. H. Wharton to Miss Caroline C. Davis daughter of John Davis Esq. of Davidson County.
Nashville Whig (Tues., Nov. 22, 1842)

West, Mr. William H. H. married at Hopkinsville, Ky. to Miss Susan S. S. Long.
National Banner & Nashville Daily Advertiser (Mon., Aug. 5, 1833)

Westbay, Miss Margaret L. married to Mr. Patrick Welsh.

Westbrook, Mr. James married in Madison County to Miss Winefred Jordan.
National Banner & Nashville Whig (Wed., Sept. 7, 1831)

Westbrooks, Mr. J. R., Tutor in Union University, married in Hardeman County on the 3d inst. by Rev. Joseph H. Eaton to Miss Martha Ann Williams daughter of Mr. Robert F. Williams.
Nashville True Whig & Weekly Commercial Register (Fri., Sept. 13, 1850)

Westcoat, Miss Rachel P. married to Mr. Washington G. Halley.

Westervelt, Miss Frances married to Mr. R. A. Gannaway.

Westgate, Col. Thomas a Patriot of the Revolution, aged 83, married at Georgia Mills, New Jersey on the 14th July to Miss Susan Card, aged 14.
National Banner & Nashville Daily Advertiser (Tues., Sept. 10, 1833)

Westmoreland, Mr. F. A. married in Giles County to Miss Susan Tarpley.
Nashville Rebpulican & State Gazette (Thurs., May 1, 1834)

Westmoreland, Mr. Fisher A. married in Giles Co., T. to Mrs. Susan Tarpley.
National Banner & Nashville Daily Advertiser (Mon., May 12, 1834)

Westmoreland, Miss Harriet married to Mr. Nath. H. Marks.

Whalen, Mr. William married in Roane County to Miss Polly Britian.
National Banner & Nashville Daily Advertiser (Mon, June 3, 1833)

Whalon, Mrs. S. A. married to Mr. C. J. Jockers.

Wham, Miss Isabell married to Mr. Thomas Wyatt.

Wharton, Mr. of New Orleans married at Natchez, Mi. on the 25th of May to Mrs. Amanda Hoggatt of Ten.
Nashville Republican (Thurs., June 11, 1835)

Wharton, Mr. C. J. Fox of Nashville married to Miss Amanda E. Criddle in Williamson County on Thursday last.
Nashville Republican & State Gazette (Sat., Nov. 8, 1834)

Wharton, Mr. C. J. Fox of Nashville married in Williamson County on Thursday last by the Rev. Mr. Smith to Miss Amanda E. Criddle.
National Banner & Nashville Whig (Mon, Nov. 10, 1834)

Wharton, Miss Eliza Caroline married to Wm. White.

Wharton, Miss Eliza Jane married to Dr. Sydney Smith.

Wharton, Miss Eliza Jane married to Dr. Sidney Smith.

Wharton, Franklin Esq. married at cantonment Gibson, Arkansas to Miss
Mary Jane Baylor daughter of Dr. J. W. Baylor.
National Banner (March 10, 1826)

Wharton, Dr. John Overton married near Hagertown, Md. on the 9th ult.
to Miss Elizabeth Mason daughter of the late Hon. John Thompson Mason.
National Banner (Sat., May 2, 1829)

Wharton, Mr. Joseph P. Sen. of Wilson County married in Davidson County
on the 21st inst. to Miss Caroline C. Howett.
National Banner & Nashville Whig (Thurs., Sept. 23, 1830)

Wharton, Miss Martha A. married to Mr. Sterling H. Lester.

Wharton, Miss Martha M. married to Mr. John W. Love.

Wharton, Miss Sarah married to Maj. Thomas G. Green.

Wharton, Miss Susan S. married to Mr. Samuel Fain.

Wharton, Thomas J., Attorney at law, Jackson, Miss. married yesterday
morning by the Rev. Mr. Lapsley to Mary Edgar eldest daughter of the
Rev. J. T. Edgar.
National Banner & Nashville Whig (Fri., June 16, 1837)

Wharton, Miss Virginia married to Mr. Philip Schetter.

Wheat, Miss Salina Patten married to John Seay M. D.

Wheatcroft, Miss Mary married to Mr. E. Gerale.

Wheatley, Miss Salina M. married to Mr. Benj. H. Hopkins.

Wheatley Seth Esq., Attorney at law of Memphis, married on the 16th
inst. by the Rev. Dr. Edgar to Miss Mary Cook daughter of the Hon.
William A. Cook of Nashville.
Nashville Whig (Wed., April 17, 1839)

Wheaton, Dr. C. of Davidson County married Mrs. Jane Wheaton of
Davidson County, Sunday evening last.
Impartial Review & Cumberland Repository - published at Nashville.
(Sat., June 21, 1806)

Wheaton, Mrs. Jane married to Dr. C. Wheaton.

Wheeler, Miss Christiana married to Mr. Samuel Adams.

Wheeler, Miss Christiana married to Mr. Samuel Adams.

Wheeler, Miss Florilla C. married to John E. Wheeler, Esq.

Wheeler, Miss Harriet C. married to Mr. James C. Thatcher.

Wheeler, Mr. James married in August 1831 to Miss Mary Murry.
The Western Weekly Review - Franklin, Tenn. (Fri., Sept. 2, 1831)

Wheeler, Mr. John A. married in Campbell County to Miss Lucinda Johnson.
National Banner & Nashville Whig (Fri., Oct. 20, 1826)

Wheeler, Mr. John E. Esq. married at Knoxville to Miss Florilla C.
Wheeler.
National Banner (Sat., April 25, 1829)

Wheeler, Miss Kitty C. married to Rev. William Vannoy.

Wheeler, Miss Mary A. married to Mr. R. P. Bolling.

Wheeler, Miss Melinda E. married to William Cary Esq.

Wheeler, Mr. Peyton H. married in Madison County, Ala. to Miss Maria
Veitch.
National Banner & Nashville Whig (Mon., Sept. 5, 1831)

Wheeler, Mr. Wm. married in Roane County to Miss Huldah McElwee.
National Banner & Nashville Whig (Mon., Jan. 31, 1831)

Wheelwright, Miss Mary R. married to Mr. John Kealing.

Whetlock, Miss Ruth married to Mr. Samuel C. Wilson.

Whetlock, Miss Ruth married to Mr. Samuel C. Wilson.

Whirt, Miss Elizabeth Gamble married to Mr. Lewis M. Goldsborough.

Whistler, Mr. Charles of St. Louis married at Louisville, Ky. to Miss
Isabella Racine.
National Banner & Nashville Whig (Thurs., Sept. 2, 1830)

Whitaker, Mr. David married in Haywood County to Miss Mary Ann C.
Kavanaugh.
National Banner & Nashville Daily Advertiser (Wed., Feb. 8, 1832)

Whitaker, Miss Isabella married to Mr. James O'Hara.

Whitaker, Miss Margaret E. B. married to Dr. R. J. Waggoner.

Whitaker, Mr. Newton married on 25th inst. to Miss Frances Ann Wynn
Lincoln Co.
Nashville Republican (Thurs., Feb. 5, 1835)

Whitaker, Miss Perlina married to Mr. Charles Moore.

Whitby, Miss Martha married to William Pickering.

White, Dr. A. C. married on the 13th inst. by the Rev. Dr. Wharton
to Miss Eliza R. Fain daughter of the late Samuel Fain, Esq. all of
Nashville.
The Christian Record (Sat., April 17, 1847)

White, A. C. married on the 22nd inst. by the Rev. J. B. McFerrin to
Miss Mary Ann Ogden daughter of Rev. John W. Ogden both of this
vicinity.
Nashville Whig (Mon., Dec. 30, 1839)

White, Dr. A. C. married on the 13th inst. by the Rev. Dr. Wharton
to Miss Eliza R. Fain daughter of the late Samuel Fain Esq. all of
Nashville.
The Politician & Weekly Nashville Whig (Fri., April 16, 1847)

White, A. H. Esq. of Covington married in Tipton County on the 27th
ult. by the Rev. Dr. Cahpman to Miss Matilda Brown.
National Banner & Nashville Daily Advertiser (Wed., March 13, 1833)

White, Aaron Esq. of Sevier County married in Blount County to Miss
Lydia Davis.
National Banner & Nashville Daily Advertiser (Wed., May 8, 1833)

White, Mr. Abraham M. married in Williamson County to Miss Susan Parrish
National Banner & Nashville Whig (Sat., Sept. 16, 1826)

White, Hon. Albert S., U. S. Senator from Indiana married in Richmond,
Va. on the 25th inst. by Rev. Mr. Norwood to Harriet Randolph Third
daughter of Thomas Mann Randolph Esq. of Tuskahoe.
Nashville Whig (Tues., Feb. 7, 1843)

White, Miss Ann Maria married to Mr. Samuel Bigham.

White, Mr. Baker married in Maury County to Miss Winney White.
National Banner & Nashville Whig (Sat., Dec. 17, 1831)

White, Miss Betsey M. married to John N. Scott, Esq.

White, Col. Beverly W. married in Nashville last evening by the Rev.
Mr. Edgar to Miss Isabel Berryhill Anderson both of Nashville.
National Banner & Nashville Daily Advertiser (Fri., Nov. 1, 1833)

White, Col. Beverly W. married in Nashville to Miss Isabel Berryhill
Anderson.
Nashville Republican & State Gazette (Sat., Nov. 2, 1833)

White, Miss Catherine Louisa married to Mr. William T. White.

White, Miss Catherine Louisa married to Capt. Wm. F. White.

White, Miss Charlotte married to Mr. Howell Atkieson.

White, Danl. L. married in Williamson County, Ten. to Sarah Shepherd.
National Banner & Nashville Whig (Wed., Dec. 17, 1834)

White, Maj. E. A. of Lebanon married in Carthage on the 15th inst. to
Miss Barbara Bilbo of Carthage.
National Banner & Nashville Whig (Sat., May 26, 1827)

White, Miss Eleanor married to Mr. Robert V. Condon.

White, Miss Eliza married to Mr. Cuthbert Bullitt.

White, Mrs. Eliza H. C. married to Col. W. B. A. Ramsay.

White, Miss Eliza J. married to Mr. W. C. McClure.

White, Miss Eliza P. married to Mr. Thomas J. Goff.

White, Miss Elizabeth married to Mr. John H. Porter.

White, Miss Elizabeth married to Mr. Geo. M. White.

White, Miss Elizabeth married to Mr. Samuel M. Pugh.

White, Miss Frances married to Mr. Alexander Groves.

White, Miss Frances married to Mr. Alexander Groves.

White, Mr. Franklin of Smith County married Miss Martha Wright on
Thursday 27, Oct.
Nashville Republican (Tues., Nov. 10, 1835)

White, Mr. George married in Franklin, Ten. to Miss Maria Potts.
National Banner & Nashville Whig (Sat., April 12, 1827)

White, Mr. Geo. M. married in Williamson County to Miss Elizabeth
White.
National Banner & Nashville Whig (Fri., Jan. 9, 1835)

White, George M. Esq., Sheriff, married in Knoxville to Miss Sophia
Park.
National Banner & Nashville Whig (Sat., Dec. 15, 1827)

White, Dr. George W. of Spring Hill, Maury County, Ten. married on the
22nd inst. by Rev. Dr. Wm. H. Wharton of Nashville to Miss Margaret
Louisa Ward of Williamson County.
Nashville Whig (Tues., June 21, 1842)

White, George W. Esq. member of the Winchester Bar married in Winchester, Tennessee on 16th inst. by the Hon. Nathan Green Judge of the Supreme Court to Miss Mary A. Hutchins.
The Politician & Weekly Nashville Whig (Fri., Dec. 3, 1847)

White, Mr. George W. married in Lexington, Ky. to Miss Mary J. Bridewell.
National Banner & Nashville Whig (Sat., Jan. 12, 1828)

White, Miss Harriet married to Albert G. Sloo, Esq.

White, Mr. Hugh Jr. of Abingdon, Va. married at Lynchburg, Va. to Miss Ann Harrison Gordon.
National Banner & Nashville Daily Advertiser (Fri., Sept. 20, 1833)

White, Hugh L. Hon. of Tennessee married Mrs. Ann Peyton of Nashville.
Nashville Republican & State Gazette (Fri., Dec. 14, 1832)

White, Hon. Hugh L. Senator of Tenn. married at Washington City on the 29 ult. to Mrs. Ann Peyton.
National Banenr & Nashville Daily Advertiser (Fri., Dec. 14, 1832)

White, Miss Isabella married to William B. French, Esq.

White, Miss Isabella J. married to Mr. A. S. Waldin.

White, Miss Isabella R. married to Mr. Joseph F. Cayce.

White, Miss Isabella R. married to Mr. Joseph F. Cayce.

White, Mr. J. married in Louisville, Ky. to Miss Elizabeth Luby.
National Banner & Nashville Daily Advertiser (Thurs., June 19, 1834)

White, Mr. James married in Portsmouth on Tuesday evening 11th ult. by Elder D. Millard to Miss Clarissa L. Berry both of Portsmouth.
Daily Republican Banner (Fri., May 17, 1839)

White, Mr. James A. of Nashville married in Davidson County on 5th April by W. Hassell Hunt, Esq. to Miss Martha Hoobery.
Nashville Whig (Fri., April 6, 1838)

White, Mr. James A. of Nashville married in Davidson County on Thursday 5th April by W. Hasell Hunt, Esq. to Miss Martha Hooberry.
Nashville Union (Sat., April 7, 1838)

White, Mr. James J. B. of Mississippi married on the 26th July by the Rev. Dr. Edgar to Miss Rebecca Williams of Nashville.
National Banner & Nashville Whig (Fri., July 29, 1836)

White, James M. M. Esq. of Huntsville married in Knoxville to Miss Eliza H. Craighead.
National Banner & Nashville Whig (Sat., Sept. 30, 1826)

White, Mr. James R. of Shelbyville married on the 28th June by the Rev. James W. Allen to Miss Catharine M. Greer of Bedford County.
National Banner & Nashville Whig (Sat., July 14, 1827)

White, Miss Jane Eliza married to William W. Berry Esq.

White, Mr. John married in Maury County, Ten. to Miss Elizabeth Osborn.
National Banner & Nashville Whig (Fri., April 10, 1835)

White, John Esq. of Richmond, Ky. married to Miss Mary Humes married at Knoxville.
National Banner & Nashville Whig (Sat., July 15, 1826)

White, Joseph married in Williamson County to Miss Nancy Horseford.
The Western Weekly Review - Franklin, Ten. (Fri., Feb. 1, 1833)

White, Miss Lucy Caroline married to Dr. Joseph A. Bowman.

White, Miss Lydia married to Mr. James Glasgow.

White, Miss Margaret Ann married to Ebenezer Alexander, Esq.

White, Miss Margaret H. M. married to Mr. John M. Kirby.

White, Mrs. Maria married to Mr. John T. Minter.

White, Miss Martha married to Mr. Henderson Estes.

White, Miss Martha L. married to Mr. William Richards.

White, Miss Mary married to Mr. William Swan.

White, Miss Mary married to Rev. J. Y. Crawford.

White, Miss Mary L. married to Mr. Caleb H. Baker.

White, Miss Minerva H. married to Mr. B. F. Hardcastle.

White, Miss Nancy married to Zaccheus Wilson.

White, Miss Pamelia married to Nelson Lavender.

White, Miss Pamelia married to Nelson Lavender.

White, Miss Paulina married to Major Robert Beatie.

White, Miss Phebe E. married to Mr. Azchariah M. Murrell.

White, Miss Polly married to Mr. William Holt.

White, Mr. R. H. married in Rutherford County, Ten. to Miss M. A. F.
Nelson daughter of Daniel Nelson, Esq.
National Banner & Nashville Whig (Mon., Nov. 10, 1834)

White, Mr. R. H. formerly of Nashville married in Rutherford County
on Thursday 23d inst. to Miss M. A. F. Nelson.
Nashville Republican & State Gazette (Sat., Oct. 25, 1834)

White, Mr. Reuben married in Williamson County to Miss Sarah Wood.
The Western Weekly Review - Franklin, Ten. (Fri., Dec. 23, 1831)

White, Mr. Robert M. married in Rutherford County on 13th inst. by the
Rev. J. Allison to Miss Ann G. Barksdale daughter of Mr. Randolph
Barksdale.
Nashville Union (Thurs., March 22, 1838)

White, Mr. S. married in Williamson County to Miss Catharine Johnson.
The Western Weekly Review - Franklin, Ten. (Fri., Dec. 2, 1831)

White, Mr. S. married in Williamson County to Miss Catharine Johnson.
National Banner & Nashville Whig (Wed., Dec. 7, 1831)

White, Miss Sally married to Mr. Francis M'Namer.

White, Mr. Stephen married in August 1831 to Miss Catharine Johnson.
The Western Weekly Review - Franklin, Ten. (Fri., Sept. 2, 1831)

White, Miss Susan married to Mr. John McGoodwin.

White, Miss Unice W. married to Mr. P. M. Hughlett.

White, Wm. Esq. of this place married on Wednesday evening last, by Rev. Mr. Craighead to Miss Eliza Caroline Wharton eldest daughter of Geo. Wharton Esq. of this County.
The Nashville Whig & Tenn. Advertiser (Nov. 10, 1817)

White, Mr. William married at Louisville, Ky. to Miss Eliza Ann Thompson.
National Banner (Sat., April 18, 1829)

White, Capt. Wm. F. of Spottsylvania County, Va. married to Miss Catherine Louisa White.
Nashville Republican & State Gazette (Tues., Aug. 23, 1831)

White, William L. Esq. married in Nashville by the Rev. M. Hume, last evening to Miss Susan A. Brown daughter of Mr. Geo. Brown.
National Banner & Nashville Whig (Thurs., June 17, 1830)

White, Mr. William T. of Spotsylvania County, Va. married in Davidson County on Wednesday last by Rev. Mr. Weller to Miss Catherine Louisa White daughter of Gen. William White.
National Banner & Nashville Whig (Fri., Aug. 19, 1831)

White, Miss Winney married to Mr. Baker White.

Whitehead, Mr. Benjamin, aged 78, married in Montgomery County to Miss Sally Willis aged 58.
National Banner & Nashville Whig (Sat., Sept. 6, 1828)

Whitehead, Miss Frances married to Mr. Charles Smith.

Whitehead, Mr. John D. married on Thursday 19th inst. by John W. Billingsley to Miss Mary M. Boyd daughter of Dr. William Boyd all of Wilson County.
Daily Republican Banner (Fri., Sept. 27, 1839)

Whitehead, Robert married at Hanley on the 15th inst. to Margaret Oliver
National Banner & Nashville Whig (Mon., Oct. 20, 1834)

Whitenbarger, Mr. Christopher married in Blount County to Miss Polly Whitenbarger.
National Banner & Nashville Whig (Wed., Oct. 12, 1831)

Whitenbarger, Miss Polly married to Mr. Christopher Whitenbarger.

Whiteside, Mr. James M. married on the 10th inst. by the Rev. L. M. Woodson to Miss Samantha E. Carr all of Sumner County.
The Christian Record (Sat., Feb. 20, 1847)

Whiteside, Mr. John K., Engineer on the Nashville & Chattanooga Railroad married in Chattanooga on the 1st inst. by the Rev. Mr. Blackburn to Miss Adelaide Louisa Hooke eldest daughter of Judge R. M. Hooke all of Chattnooga.
Nashville True Whig & Weekly Commercial Register (Fri., Jan. 10, 1851)

Whiteside, Miss Tennessee married to Rev. Samuel Billingsley.

Whitesides, James A. of Jasper married in Grainger County to Miss Mary Massengill.
National Banner & Nashville Whig (Sat., Feb. 21, 1829)

Whitesides, Mr. Moses married in Madison County, Ill. to Miss Nancy Judy.
National Banner (May 27, 1826)

Whitfield, Miss Lucinda married to Mr. Smith Criddle.

Whitfield, Miss Sarah married to Doctor Daniel M'Phail.

Whitfield, Mr. Matthew married in Murfreesborough, Ten. to Miss Fanny Manahan.
National Banner & Nashville Daily Advertiser (Tues., Aug. 5, 1834)

Whitfield, Mr. Willy married in Montgomery County to Miss Mary Gibson.
National Banner & Nashville Whig (Sat., Sept. 13, 1828)

Whiting, Miss Mary L. married to Dr. D. Peyton Harmon.

Whiting, Dr. P. B. married at Tuscumbia, Ala. to Miss Elizabeth E. Winston.
National Banner & Nashville Daily Advertiser (Mon., June 3, 1833)

Whitington, Mrs. Nancy, married to Mr. Edward Harding.

Whitley, Miss Sally married to Mr. John Newman.

Whitlock, Mr. R. E. of Nashville married in Dixon on the 9th to Miss A. P. Bacon of Dixon.
National Banner & Nashville Whig (Mon., June 12, 1837)

Whitman, Mr. G. S. of the firm of McNairy Farman & Co. married on last evening at the Catholic Church by the Rt. Rev. Bishop Miles to Miss Emily M. Woods all of Nashville.
Nashville True Whig & Weekly Commercial Register (Fri., Feb. 14, 1851)

Whitmore, Mr. Oliver W. married at Mallett's Creek Washtemore County, Michigan to Miss Martha Merril.
National Banner & Nashville Whig (Sat., Dec. 23, 1826)

Whitney, Miss Harriett married to Mr. Phillip I. Seudder Esq.

Whitsitt, Miss Elizabeth married to Mr. W. W. Whitsitt.

Whitsitt, Miss Jane C. married to Col. John W. Hewgley.

Whitsitt, Mr. W. W. married at Memphis to Miss Elizabeth Whitsitt daughter of Mr. William Whitsitt.
National Banner & Nashville Daily Advertiser (Fri., Dec. 7, 1832)

Whitsitt, Mr. Wm. married on the 15th inst. at the residence of R. C. Foster Esq. to Miss Sally Slaughter.
The Nashville Whig & Tenn. Advertiser (Jan. 24, 1818)

Whitt, Mr. Anderson married in Jefferson County to Miss Sarah Palmer.
National Banner & Nashville Whig (Mon., Nov. 28, 1831)

Whittaker, Miss Celestia A. married to Mr. Elisha W. Harris.

Whittemore, Miss Nancy A. married to Mr. William H. Eason.

Whittingham, Mr. Charles married Miss Martha Starkey at Louisville, Ky.
National Banner & Nashville Whig (Fri., Jan. 22, 1830)

Whittington, Mrs. married to Mr. James Blount.

Whittington, Miss Jane married to Dr. Dorsey.

Whorton, Miss Ann E. married to Mr. Frank S. Buchanan.

Whyte, Miss Nancy married to Mr. Benjamin W. Bedford.

Whyte, Miss Phereby married to Mr. J. E. Craighead.

Wickliffe, Robert Esq. married at Lexington, Ky. to Mrs. Mary O. Russell.
National Banner & Nashville Whig (Sat., Oct. 28, 1826)

Wier, Mrs. Polly married to Mr. Andrew Shmidt.

Wier, Col. Robert of Columbus, Miss. married in Nashville on the 10th inst. by the Rev. O. B. Hays to Miss Sarah G. Sanders daughter of the late Doctor Sanders of Memphis.
Nashville Whig (Fri., Oct. 11, 1839)

Wiggington, Miss Elizabeth married to Mr. John M'Lane.

Wiggington, Miss Lucy married to Mr. Wm. P. Campbell.

Wiggington, Miss Susan B. married to Vivian B. Holmes Esq.

Wigginton, Miss Sarah Ann married to Mr. Henry W. Champion.

Wigginton, Miss Susan C. P. B. married to David W. M'Goodwin Esq.

Wiggonton, Miss Sarah Ann married to Mr. Henry W. Champion.

Wiggs, Mr. Rigdon married in Maury County to Miss Elizabeth Watson.
National Banner & Nashville Whig (Mon., Sept. 26, 1831)

Wilburn, Miss Mary married to Mr. Edmund W. Goodrich Jr.

Wilburn, Miss Mary married to Mr. Edmund W. Goodrich Jun.

Wilburn, Mr. William T. married in Louisville, Ky. to Miss Sarah O'Neal.
National Banner & Nashville Daily Advertiser (Fri., Sept. 7, 1832)

Wilcox, Mr. Bryant married to Miss Elizabeth Cook in Maury County.
National Banner & Nashville Whig (Fri., Feb. 12, 1830)

Wilcox, Mr. Charles G. married in Giles County to Miss Mary McDonald.
National Banner (Sat., April 18, 1829)

Wilder, Miss Electoria B. married to Mr. Gustavus U. Richards.

Wildie, Mr. Michael T. married in Russellville, Ky. to Miss Elizabeth Henby of Robinson County, Ten.
National Banner & Nashville Daily Advertiser (Tues., Dec. 17, 1833)

Wiley, Mr. John of Philadelphia married at Wheeling by the Rev. Mr. Wiley to Miss Sarah Stevenson of Shelbyville, Tenn.
National Banner & Nashville Whig (Sat., April 19, 1828)

Wiley, Mr. Thomas L. of Tuscaloosa, editor of the Alabama State Intelligencer married near Cahawba, Ala. to Miss Louis Perry.
National Banner & Nashville Whig (Mon., Oct. 4, 1830)

Wilgus, Mr. A. married in Russellville, Ky. to Mrs. Theodosia Wilgus.
National Banner (Jan. 13, 1826)

Wilkenson, Mr. Hansel T. married on the 12th inst. by Rev. J. B. McFerrin to Miss Martha Ann Buie all of Davidson County.
Nashville Whig (Fri., March 13, 1840)

Wilkerson, Mr. Daniel Smith County married to Miss Martha Saddler.
National Banner & Nashville Advertiser (Fri., Feb. 24, 1832)

Wilkerson, Mr. Edward C. married in Rutherford County to Miss Diana S. Mayfield.
National Banner & Nashville Daily Advertiser (Sat., Jan. 26, 1833)

Wilkerson, Miss Elizabeth married to Mr. Hezekiah Rochhold.

Wilkerson, Mr. Hubbard S. married in Rutherford County to Miss Adaline House.
National Banner & Nashville Daily Advertiser (Fri., Dec. 21, 1832)

Wilkerson, Mr. John M. married in this County on the 21st inst. to
Mrs. Charlotte Drake daughter of Mr. John Bosley.
National Banner (March 31, 1826)

Wilkerson, Judge of Mississippi married in Bardstown, Ky. on Thursday
evening last to Miss Eliza Crozier of Bardstown, Ky.
Nashville Whig (Wed., Jan. 9, 1839)

Wilkeson, Mr. Henry married at Pittsburgh to Miss Eliza Sophia Hunter.
National Banner & Nashville Advertiser (Sat., March 3, 1832)

Wilkins, Dr. Benjamin of Mississippi married Miss Sarah Brown Overton
in Montgomery County.
Nashville Republican & State Gazette (Wed., Oct. 3, 1832)

Wilkins, Dr. Benjamin married in Montgomery County to Miss Sarah Brown
Overton.
National Banner & Nashville Daily Advertiser (Wed., Oct. 3, 1832)

Wilkins, Mr. David of Madisonville, Ky. married on the 8th inst. in
Wilson County by the Rev. F. E. Pitts to Miss Indiana J. Hooper
daughter of John J. Hooper Esq.
The Politician & Weekly Nashville Whig (Fri., June 18, 1847)

Wilkins, Miss Martha married to Mr. Esau Beasley.

Wilkins, Miss Mary A. married to Mr. Hardin Burnley.

Wilkins, Miss Mary Jane married to Mr. John Thompson.

Wilkins, Miss Sarah married to Mr. William B. Duty.

Wilkinson, Miss Amelia married to Col. Lemuel Smith.

Wilkinson, Miss Clara Eliza married to George Wilson Esq.

Wilkinson, Miss Delila married to Mr. William Maxwell.

Wilkinson, Miss Eliza married to Mr. Lemuel Gay.

Wilkinson, Mr. Francis H. married in Giles County, Tennessee to Miss
Angeline Arguish.
National Banner & Nashville Whig (Thurs., June 19, 1834)

Wilkinson, H. T. Esq. married on the 19th inst. by the Rev. John
Morrow to Miss Edna H. Dozier all of Davidson County.
Nashville Whig (Tues., Nov. 24, 1846)

Wilkinson, Capt. Isaac married in Franklin County on the 12th inst. by
John W. Camden, Esq. to Miss Mary L. Willis daughter of Joseph Willis
Esq.
The Union (Sat., Nov. 21, 1835)

Wilkinson, Mr. James married on the 29th ult. by the Rev. A. L. P.
Green to Miss Lyda Jane Doughty all of Nashville.
Nashville Whig (Wed., May 1, 1839)

Wilkinson, Miss Margaret married to Capt. Robert Wear.

Wilkinson, Miss Mary married to Mr. Madison Riddle.

Wilkinson, Miss Nancy married to Dr. Langston Cooper.

Wilkinson, Miss Martha married to Micajar Autry Esq.

Wilkinson, Miss Matilda married to Mr. Reuben Johnson.

Wilkinson, Mr. Notley married in Fayetteville to Miss Peggy Richardson.
National Banner & Nashville Whig (Sat., July 8, 1826)

Wilkinson, Mrs. Sarah married to Mr. George A. Smith.

[Wilkison?], Mr. James married in Hardeman County to Miss Lucinda
Hanniss.
National Banner & Nashville Whig (July 28, 1827)

Wilks, Miss Unity married to Mr. Jeremiah Pruett.

Willett, Maj. Washington married in Washington Co., Ten. to Miss
Eliza Crookshank.
National Banner & Nashville Daily Advertiser (Tues., Aug. 19, 1834)

Willhite, Mr. William married in Franklin County, Tenn. on the 10th
inst. by John Thomas Slotter Esq. to Miss Elizabeth J. Little daughter
of Joseph Little Esq.
Nashville Whig (Sat., Sept. 19, 1846)

Willi, Mr. Samuel married in St. Louis to Miss Lucinda Musick.
National Banner & Nashville Whig (Sat., May 19, 1827)

William, Miss Cornelia married to Mr. Thos. W. Humes.

William, Miss Hannah H. married to Mr. James Ridley Jr.

Williams, Mrs. married to Mr. Robert Gift.

Williams, Dr. aged one hundred years married in Knoxville to Miss Nancy
Israel aged 17.
National Banner & Nashville Daily Advertiser (Tues., Aug. 19, 1834)

Williams, Mr. Alexander married in Knox County to Miss Fanny Bowman.
National Banner & Nashville Whig (Mon., Sept. 20, 1830)

Williams, Miss Amelia married to Mr. William T. Evans.

Williams, Miss Amelia Ann married to Mr. Hamilton M. Wright.

Williams, Miss Ann married to Maj. E. P. M'Neal.

Williams, Miss Ann married to Mr. John Wilson.

Williams, Miss Ann married to Maj. Ezekiel P. McNeal.

Williams, Miss Arabella married to Mr. Daniel A. Johnston.

Williams, Mr. Augustus of Brassoria Province of Texas married to Miss
Hellen Love Jeffreys of Carroll County, Tenn. on Thursday May 24 by
the Rev. David Weir.
National Banner & Nashville Advertiser (Wed., June 6, 1832)

Williams, B. W. Esq. of Hardeman County married on Wednesday 25th inst.
by Rev. Doct. Weakly to Mrs. Eliza Perkins daughter of Samuel Perkins
Esq. of Williamson Co.
Nashville Whig (Mon., Dec. 30, 1839)

Williams, B. W. of Hardeman County married on Wednesday 25th inst.
by the Rev. Dr. Weakley to Miss Eliza Perkins daughter of Samuel
Perkins of Williamson County.
Daily Republican Banner (Wed., Jan. 1, 1840)

Williams, Mr. Benjamin W. married in this County on the 20th ult. to
Miss Susan L. Battle.
National Banner & Nashville Whig (Sat., Jan. 3, 1829)

Williams, Miss Burchet married to Mr. John C. Stark.

Williams, Miss Catherine married to Mr. T. L. Marshall.

Williams, Miss Catherine S. married to Mr. Samuel M. Creswell.

Williams, Miss Charlotte married to Richard D. Starr.

Williams, Mr. Christopher C. married in this town by the Rev. Mr. Hume to Miss Jane E. Nichols.
National Banner & Nashville Whig (Sat., April 28, 1827)

Williams, Miss Cornelia married to Mr. Thomas W. Hume.

Williams, Mr. Daniel married in Williamson County to Miss Sarah E. Hill.
The Western Weekly Review - Franklin, Tenn. (Fri., Dec. 2, 1831)

Williams, Dr. Daniel O. late of Jackson County, Tenn. married on the 31st in Wilkinson County, Mis. to Miss Mary Jane Lacy.
National Banner & Nashville Whig (Sat., Aug. 25, 1827)

Williams, Mr. David of the house of Vaulx & Williams married in Nashville last evening 5th inst. to Miss Priscilla Shelby second daughter of Dr. John Shelby.
National Banner & Nashville Whig (Fri., May 6, 1831)

Williams, Mr. Dudley married in Henderson County to Miss Susan McClerkin
National Banner & Nashville Whig (Fri., March 6, 1835)

Williams, Mr. Elisha of Rutherford married in Davidson County to Miss Ridley.
National Banner & Nashville Whig (Mon., Nov. 14, 1831)

Williams, Miss Eliza married to Mr. John Matlock.

Williams, Miss Eliza N. married to Mr. Evander M'Iver.

Williams, Miss Elizabeth married to Mr. Burrell H. Peefles.

Williams, Miss Elizabeth married to Mr. Young Edwards.

Williams, Miss Elizabeth married to Mr. Elisha Timmons.

Williams, Miss Elizabeth F. married to Mr. William Lamb.

Williams, Miss Ellen married to Mr. David Cusick.

Williams, Miss Emily E. married to Thomas E. Peebles.

Williams, Mr. Etheldred of this place, Nashville, married Miss Frances A. Martin of Robertson County married on Saturday the 28th of May by Rev. Thomas Gun.
Whig (June 20, 1815)

Williams, E. J. of Conn. married at New Orleans to Miss Susan Aurelia Macon.
National Banner & Nashville Daily Advertiser (Fri., May 16, 1834)

Williams, Miss Fanny E. married to Dr. John Walker Percy.

Williams, Miss Fanny E. married to Thomas C. Trimble, Esq.

Williams, Miss Frances married to Mr. William B. Collins.

Williams, Frank of New Orleans married Miss Jane Catherine Brown on Tuesday the 1st instant, December 1st, 1857 by Rev. Dr. Edgar daughter of the late Morgan W. Brown.
Nashville Daily Gazette (Dec. 4, 1857)

Williams, Miss Hannah H. married to Mr. James Ridley Jr.

Williams, Miss Harriet married to Alexander De Bodisco.

Williams, Mr. H. L. married in Hardeman County to Miss Lucina Moore.
National Banner & Nashville Daily Advertiser (Wed., Feb. 8, 1832)

Williams, Mr. Jacob of Nashville married at Pulaski on Friday the 6th
inst. to Miss Henrietta Pollock.
National Banner & Nashville Daily Advertiser (Thurs., April 12, 1832)

Williams, Mr. James M. married at Memphis to Miss Margaret Vanhook.
National Banner & Nashville Advertiser (Feb. 15, 1832)

Williams, Mr. James M. married in Bedford County to Miss Martha Claxton
National Banner & Nashville Daily Advertiser (Mon., Dec. 31, 1832)

Williams, Miss Jane married to Mr. Moses E. Farmer.

Williams, Miss Jane W. married to George B. Brown Esq.

Williams, Mr. Jarvis printer married in Polk County to Miss Martha
Caneaster.
Nashville Whig (Tues., July 14, 1846)

Williams, Mr. John married in Monroe County to Miss Nancy Harrison.
National Banner & Nashville Whig (Fri., Sept. 9, 1831)

Williams, Mr. John S. married in Memphis to Miss Frances S. Lawrence
all of Memphis.
Nashville Whig (Tues., April 21, 1846)

Williams, Mr. John W. married on the 5th inst. by the Rev. Dr. Edgar
to Miss Elizabeth Boyd eldest daughter of the late Joseph Boyd, Esq.
of Nashville.
The Christian Record (Sat., Jan. 9, 1847)

Williams, Johnson D. married in Williamson County to Nancy L. Reader.
The Western Weekly Review - Franklin, Tenn. (Fri., Feb. 10, 1832)

Williams, Hon. Joseph L. Representative in Congress from the district
married in Raleigh, North Caroline on Tuesday 31st May by Rev. Dr.
Mason to Miss Malinda R. Williams daughter of the late Gen. Robert
Williams.
Nashville Whig (Tues., June 21, 1842)

Williams, Josiah married Miss Margaret Philips on Thursday last, Dec.
15, 1814 daughter of Joseph Philips Esq. by Rev. Mr. White all of this
County, Davidson.
Nashville Whig (Tues., Dec. 20, 1814)

Williams, Miss Levina married to Mr. Gardner Frierson.

Williams, Miss Lucretia married to Mr.C. B. M'Lean.

Williams, Miss Lucy married to Mr. Isaac Johnson.

Williams, Mr. L. J. married in Todd County, Ky. to Miss Malora Wright.
National Banner & Nashville Whig (Sat., July 14, 1827)

Williams, Miss Madaline M. married to Mr. A. D. McCracken.

Williams, Miss Malinda R. married to Hon. Joseph L. Williams.

Williams, Miss Margaret married to Major John D. Fleming.

Williams, Miss Maria married to Capt. Benjamin Talbot.

Williams, Miss Martha married to Mr. Philip G. Tucker.

Williams, Miss Martha Ann married to Mr. J. R. Westbrooks.

Williams, Miss Martha A. married to Mr. Hudson H. Kidd.

Williams, Miss Martha C. married to Mr. Jesse Bledsoe.

Williams, Miss Martha S. married to Mr. John B. Roberts.

Williams, Miss Martha V. married to Mr. Henry W. Bayliss.

Williams, Miss Mary married to Mr. Dewitt M'Nutt Esq.

Williams, Miss Mary married to Dewitt M'Nutt Esq.

Williams, Mrs. Mary A. married to Mr. Charles H. Conger.

Williams, Miss Mary A. married to Mr. John J. Garner.

Williams, Miss Mary Jane married to Maj. R. C. McNairy.

Williams, Miss Melbrey H. married to Orville Ewing Esq.

Williams, Mr. Morris P. married in Williamson County to Miss Nancy P.
Neal.
The Western Weekly Review - Franklin, Tenn. (Fri., Aug. 3, 1832)

Williams, Miss Nancy married to Mr. John Dyche.

Williams, Miss Nancy married to Mr. James Howell.

Williams, Miss Nancy married to Mr. Simon L. Morgan.

Williams, Miss Nancy married to Mr. Frances G. West.

Williams, Miss Nancy A. married to Mr. Joseph W. Comfort.

Williams, Miss N. M. S. married to Dr. E. P. Lipscomb.

Williams, Mr. O. D. of Jackson County married on the 14th inst. by the
Rev. Mr. Anderson of Rutherford County to Miss Coerella Isaacs of
Winchester daughter of the late Judge Isaacs of Winchester.
The Union (Sat., Sept. 30, 1837)

Williams, Mrs. Penelope married to Colonel Daniel Fisher.

Williams, Miss Penelope married to Jordan Stokes Esq.

Williams, Miss Polly married to Mr. Andrew Simpson.

Williams, Miss Polly married to Mr. B. B. Glisson.

Williams, Miss Polly married to Mr. Harman Bishop.

Williams, Miss Polly married to Mr. Andrew Simpson.

Williams, Mr. Reason married in Fleming County, Ky. to Miss Jane
Bauchanan.
National Banner & Nashville Whig (Sat., Jan. 20, 1827)

Williams, Miss Rebecca married to Mr. John Robinson.

Williams, Miss Rebecca married to Mr. James J. B. White.

Williams, Miss Rebecca L. married to Mr. John T. Deaderick.

Williams, Miss Rebecca P. married to Edwin H. Ewing Esq.

Williams, Mr. Richard C. of Davidson married in Fayette County to Miss
Attelia Alice Goodloe.
National Banner & Nashville Daily Advertiser (Thurs., Jan. 17, 1833)

Williams, Richard S. Esq. of Nashville married in Adams County, Miss. to Miss Agnes W. Hoggatt.
National Banner & Nashville Whig (Sat., Feb. 21, 1829)

Williams, Robert N. Esq. attorney at law married on the 23rd inst. by the Rev. Robert A. Lapsley to Miss Mary Paralee Ensley daughter of Enoch Ensley Esq. of Davidson County.
Nashville Whig (Sat., July 27, 1844)

Williams, Col. R. W. of Tallahassee married at Washington to Miss Rebecca Branch daughter of the Hon. John Branch of N. C.
National Banner & Nashville Whig (Fri., May 6, 1831)

Williams, Miss Sarah married to Rev. Thomas Stringfield.

Williams, Miss Sarah married to Mr. William J. Nowlen.

Williams, Miss Sarah married to Maj. John W. Childress.

Williams, Rev. S. M. married in Covington to Miss Mary R. Chapman.
National Banner & Nashville Daily Advertiser (Wed., Jan. 11, 1832)

Williams, Mr. Thomas, aged 17 married at Union Vale, N. J. to Miss Bulah Barnes aged 14.
National Banner & Nashville Daily Advertiser (Thurs., Sept. 12, 1833)

Williams, Mr. William married in Montgomery County to Miss Mary Hatcher.
National Banner & Nashville Whig (Sat., Jan. 3, 1829)

Williams, Mr. William A. married in Williamson County to Miss Mary Ann Howlett both of this County.
National Banner & Nashville (Tues., March 10, 1830)

Williams, Mr. William H. married at Louisville, Ky. to Miss Susannah M'Dade.
National Banner & Nashville Whig (Thurs., Sept. 2, 1830)

Williams, Mr. Willis married in Montgomery County to Miss Penelope Brunson.
National Banner & Nashville Advertiser (Sat., Feb. 11, 1832)

Williams, Miss Zarina married to Beverly R. McKennie.

Williamson, Mr. Alexander Esq. of Fayette County married on Thursday Oct. 3 at Columbia, Tenn. by Rev. Joseph Sherman to Miss Ann Brown second daughter of the late Dr. Thomas Brown.
Nashville Whig (Tues., Oct. 10, 1843)

Williamson, Miss Ann married to Mr. Robert Ellis.

Williamson, Miss Averille married to Mr. James Mangrum.

Williamson, Mr. Benjamin married on Tuesday the 15th inst. to Miss Elizabeth Harris all of Davidson County.
The Nashville Gazette (Sat., Feb. 20, 1820)

Williamson, Capt. Benjamin W. of Franklin, Ten. married in Halifax, North Carolina on the 5th of January to Miss Eliza J. Hamblin.
National Banner & Nashville Whig (Fri., Feb. 19, 1830)

Williamson, Dr. Francis A. of Louisiana married in Lexington, Ky. to Miss Ann Eliza Gatewood.
National Banner & Nashville Advertiser (Mon., April 2, 1832)

Williamson, Capt. George married Miss Edney Dejournett daughter of Mr. James Dejournett in Rutherford County.
National Banner & Nashville Whig (Fri., Jan. 22, 1830)

Williamson, Miss Harriet married to Mr. George Dismukes.

Williamson, Miss Jane married to Mr. Joseph Pott.

Williamson, Mr. John S. of this town married on Thursday evening last to Miss Nancy Phillips daughter of Mr. Benjamin Phillips of this County.
The Nashville Whig (Aug. 27, 1816)

Williamson, Miss Lucy married to Capt. F. P. Wood.

Williamson, Mrs. Lucy married to Capt. Fleming P. Wood.

Williamson, Miss Margaret E. married to Mr. Alexander H. Cromwell.

Williamson, Martha A. married to H. S. Creechlow.

Williamson, Miss Martha A. R. married to Mr. Benjamin H. Logan.

Williamson, Miss Mildred married to Calvin Jones Esq.

Williamson, Mr. Perry B. married in Montgomery to Miss Sarah Niplett.
Nashville Union (Mon., Dec. 2, 1839)

Williamson, Col. R. M. married near Jackson, Mi. to Mrs. Eliza Ann Breckenridge.
National Banner & Nashville Whig (Wed., Jan. 21, 1835)

Williamson, Mr. Robert S. married in Logan County, Ky. to Miss Elizabeth Hardy daughter of Mr. Solomon Hardy.
National Banner & Nashville Whig (Wed., Feb. 4, 1835)

Williamson, Miss Sarah married to Henry Eelbeck.

Williamson, Miss Sarah Jane married to Capt. E. S. Tappan.

Williamson, Rev. S. M. married in Covington to Miss Mary R. Chapman.

Williamson, Mr. William L. married at Jackson to Miss Sarah T. Jeffreys.
National Banner & Nashville Daily Advertiser (Wed., March 21, 1832)

Willieford, Mr. Britian married in Maury County, Ten. to Miss Jane Dugger.
National Banner & Nashville Whig (Fri., April 10, 1835)

Williford, Mr. W. married in Henry County to Miss Eliza Hutchins.
National Banner & Nashville Daily Advertiser (Thurs., March 20, 1834)

Willingham, Mr. Philip married in Bedford County to Miss Frances Brown.
National Banner & Nashville Daily Advertiser (Mon., April 7, 1834)

Willis, Mr. Abel M. married at Louisville, Ky. to Miss Martha Kelly.
National Banner & Nashville Whig (Sat., May 12, 1827)

Willis, Mr. Alexander married in Franklin County, Ten. on the 12th inst. to Miss Delany Dennison.
The Western Weekly Review - Franklin, Tenn. (Fri., June 15, 1832)

Willis, Mr. E. F. of Kirkmansville, Tenn. married at Florence, Ala. to Miss Eliza Asher.
National Banner & Nashville Whig (Fri., Jan. 14, 1831)

Willis, Miss Frances A. married to Mr. Thomas M. Harrell.

Willis, Miss Jane married to Mr. James B. Wood.

Willis, Mr. John married in Nashville on Wednesday evening 28th inst.

by the Rev. Mr. Whitsett to Mrs. Julia Hawkins.
National Banner & Nashville Whig (Thurs., July 29, 1830)

Willis, Mr. Josias married at Natchez to Miss Emily Layborne.
National Banner & Nashville Whig (Sat., Jan. 27, 1827)

Willis, Miss Martha married to Mr. Elias Underwood.

Wilson, J. W. married in Williamson County, Ten. to Frances Dowdy.
National Banner & Nashville Daily Advertiser (Mon., Aug. 26, 1833)

Wilson, Mr. Joseph H. B. married in Henry County, Ten. since the first
of Jan. to Miss Catherine Erwin.
National Banner & Nashville Whig (Fri., Feb. 13, 1835)

Wilson, Mr. Joseph F. married in Williamson County to Miss Nancy Baucom
National Banner & Nashville Whig (Wed., Dec. 7, 1831)

Wilson, Mr. Joseph T. married on June 25th by Joseph Jarrell, Esq. to
Miss Mary Ann Faircloth all of Davidson County.
Nashville True Whig & Weekly Commercial Register (Fri., July 5, 1850)

Wilson, Josiah married in Wilson County to Miss Mary Cobble.
The Western Weekly Review - Franklin, Tenn. (Fri., Dec. 14, 1832)

Wilson, Miss Lavinia married to David Barrow, Esq.

Wilson, Miss Lavinia married to David Barrow, Esq.

Wilson, Mr. Lemuel A. married in Franklin to Miss Nancy Taylor
National Banner (May 10, 1826)

Wilson, Miss Louisa A. married to Mr. J. D. Knight.

Wilson, Miss Margaret M. married to Mr. William M. Smith.

Wilson, Miss Margaret married to Col. William E. Owen.

Wilson, Miss Margaret F. married to Mr. Thomas J. Hough.

Wilson, Miss Mary married to Mr. John B. Hensley.

Wilson, Miss Mary married to Rev. Joseph R. Callaway.

Wilson, Miss Mary married to Mr. David S. Dirickson.

Wilson, Miss Mary E. married to Mr. William H. Pope.

Wilson, Miss Mary S. married to Mr. David S. Dirickson.

Wilson, Miss Matilda G. married to Mr. John K. Edmundson.

Wilson, Matthew married in Williamson County to Miss Elizabeth Russell.
The Western Weekly Review - Franklin, Ten. (Fri., Dec. 14, 1832)

Wilson, Miss Nancy S. married to Mr. John M'Clung.

Wilson, Mr. Oliver H. of Nashville married to Miss Sarah Green of
Nashville on Thursday evening.
Nashville Republican & State Gazette (Sat., Dec. 25, 1830)

Wilson, Dr. Paca of Randolph married in Haywood County to Miss Virginia
T. Estes.
National Banner & Nashville Whig (Wed., Oct. 5, 1831)

Wilson, Mr. Peter married in Louisville, Ky. to Miss Martha Scott.
National Banner & Nashville Daily Advertiser (Mon., July 28, 1834)

Wilson, Mr. Pleasant married near Cairo to Miss Sarah Stone.
National Banner & Nashville Whig (Sat., Jan. 6, 1827)

Wilson, Pleasant N. Esq. married at Tuscaloosa, Ala. to Miss
Catherine L. Drish.
National Banner & Nashville Whig (Fri., Aug. 19, 1831)

Wilson, R. married in Williamson County to Miss Nancy Haley.
The Western Weekly Review - Franklin, Tenn. (Fri., March 8, 1833)

Wilson, Mr. Robert married in Nashville to Miss Matilda Thornhill on
the 6th inst by the Rev. Mr. Hume.
National Banner & Nashville Advertiser (Sat., Dec. 8, 1832)

Wilson, Robert married in Williamson County to Miss Nancy Haley.
The Western Weekly Review - Franklin, Ten. (Fri., Feb. 1, 1833)

Wilson, Miss S. C. married to Hon. Samuel P. Carson.

Wilson, Capt. Samuel Cumberland County, Ky. to Miss Elizabeth Hughlett
Overton County on 15 ult.
Impartial Review & Cumberland Repository - published at Nashville
(Thurs., Sept. 3, 1807)

Wilson, Mr. Samuel married Miss Rosa Bateman.
National Banner & Nashville Whig (Fri., March 6, 1835)

Wilson, Mr. Samuel C. married in Williamson County to Miss Ruth
Whitlock.
National Banner & Nashville Daily Advertiser (Tues., July 3, 1832)

Wilson, Miss Sarah married to Dr. J. S. Mitchell.

Wilson, Mrs. Sarah married to Genl. Hugh C. Armstrong.

Wilson, Miss Sarah G. married to Mr. J. Williamson Butler.

Wilson, Miss Selina married to Dr. Alexander Hall.

Wilson, Miss Susan D. married to Mr. William Perkins.

Wilson, Mr. Thomas W. married in Williamson County to Miss Mary Banks.
National Banner & Nashville Daily Advertiser (Thurs., May 1, 1834)

Wilson, Miss Vesta L. married to Mr. Ross B. Edmundson.

Wilson, Miss Violet married to Mr. William Brooks.

Wilson, Mr. William married at Huntsville, Ala. to Miss Amenda M.
Rice.
National Banner & Nashville Whig (Thurs., Sept. 9, 1830)

Wilson, Mr. William married in Lexington, Ky. to Miss Susan Clark.
National Banner & Nashville Daily Advertiser (Wed., Aug. 14, 1833)

Wilson, Capt. William S. married in Louisville, Ky. to Miss Narcissa
Pepin. daughter of Mr. V. Pepin.
National Banner & Nashville Whig (Fri., July 29, 1831)

Wilson, Mr. Zaccheus married in Sept. 1831 to Miss Nancy White.
The Western Weekly Review - Franklin, Ten. (Fri., Sept. 2, 1831)

Wimberly, Miss Dorothy married to Mr. Whitmell Fort.

Wimberly, Mr. Joseph married in Henry County to Miss Nelly Lee.
National Banner & Nashville Daily Advertiser (Wed., Jan. 18, 1832)

Wimberly, Miss Susan married to Mr. John Pimberton.

Wimer, Mr. John married in St. Louis, Mo. to Miss Abagail Wise.
National Banner & Nashville Daily Advertiser (Mon., May 12, 1834)

Winchester, Miss Ann married to Mr. Samuel M'Daniel.

Winchester, Miss E. T. married to Mr. R. B. Johnson.

Winchester, Miss Lydia married to Mr. W. S. McDaniel.

Winchester, Valerius P. Esq. of Gallatin married in Nashville on
Wednesday 23d inst. by the Rev. Dr. Lindsley to Miss Samuella Price of
Nashville.
National Banner & Nashville Daily Advertiser (Mon., Oct. 28, 1833)

Winder, Miss Caroline E. married to Col. John McGavock.

Winder, Mr. V. P. of Natchez married at Winchester, Franklin County
on the 7th inst. to Miss Martha A. F. Grundy daughter of Felix Grundy
Esq.
National Banner & Nashville Whig (Sat., Dec. 20, 1828)

Windham, Mr. Irwin married at Huntsville, Ala. to Miss Ann Badlun.
National Banner & Nashville Whig (Sat., April 14, 1827)

Windle, Miss Juliet married to Mr. Steaphin Cantreal.

Wingfield, Mr. Albert married to Miss Salina Mays in Maury County.
National Banner & Nashville Whig (Fri., Feb. 12, 1830)

Wingfield, Miss L. A. of Columbia, Tenn. married on Wednesday the 26th
inst. by the Rev. R. A. Lapsley to Mr. May S. Orton of Nashville.
Nashville Whig (Thurs., Aug. 27, 1846)

Wingfield, Miss Mary married to Chesley P. Bynum, Esq.

Winne, Albert H. Esq. married in Lebanon on Thursday evening the 23d
inst. to Miss M. Marshall daughter of Mr. David Marshall of this place.
Nashville Whig (Jan. 29, 1823)

Winn, Miss Eliza married to Hon. Powhatan Ellis.

Winn, Mrs. Emma M. married to James N. T. Richardson Esq.

Winn, Mr. Joel of Henderson County, Ten. married Miss Sarah Herron
of Madison County.
National Banner & Nashville Daily Advertiser (Fri., Sept. 20, 1833)

Winn, Miss Maraha J. married to Mr. Samuel Atchison Esq.

Winn, Miss Mary Louise married to Gen. Richard G. Dunlap.

Winn, Mr. Owen D. married in Fayette County, Ky. to Miss Amanda Robinson.
National Banner & Nashville Whig (Sat., Dec. 23, 1826)

Winn, Mr. Philip married in Davidson County to Miss Joanna Wilhelmena
Howser
Nashville Republican (Tues., July 14, 1835)

Winn, Richard, Esq. Attorney at law of Alexandria formerly of Nashville
married on 24th ult. to Miss Emma Maria Overton daughter of Gen.
Walter H. Overton of Louisiana.
National Banner & Nashville Daily Advertiser (Mon., March 4, 1833)

Winns, Mr. W. G. of the firm Winns, Wall & Co. merchant married in
Dover, Ten. on the 10th inst. by Jno. Richards Esq. to Miss Sarah C.
Atkins all of Dover.
Daily Republican Banner (Fri., Sept. 14, 1838)

Winser, Mr. Robert married in Logan County, Ky. to Miss Sally Parish.
National Banner & Nashville Daily Advertiser (Mon., Oct. 1, 1832)

Winsett, Mr. Robert married in Bedford County to Miss Nancy Schooler
Nashville Republican & State Gazette (Wed., Dec. 5, 1832)

Winstead, Miss Mary married to Mr. E. B. Staggs.

Winston, Mr. Edmond married in Fayette County, Ten. to Miss Martha
A. W. Cocke.
National Banner & Nashville Whig (Sat., March 8, 1828)

Winston, Miss Elizabeth E. married to Dr. P. B. Whiting.

Winston, Miss Minarva married to Mr. Wimer Paine.

Winston, Thomas B. Esq. of Nashville, Tenn. married on the 26th inst.
in N. Orleans by the Rev. T. Clapp to Miss Margaret Jane Shall daughter
of Geo. Shall Esq. formerly of Nashville.
Nashville Republican (Sat., July 9, 1836)

Winston, Mr. Thomas J. married on the 1st of the present instant by
the Rev. Ralph Cushman to Miss Elvira Jones of Christian County, Ky.
Nashville Whig (May 14, 1823)

Winter, Miss Ann J. married at Tuscumbia, Ala. to Mr. D. S. Goodloe Jr.

Winter, Miss Catherine F. married to Mr. Benjamin S. Ricks.

Winter, Miss Elizabeth married to Mr. Henry S. Foote Esq.

Winter, Miss Maria married to Mr. Isaac Walker.

Winters, Mr. Geo. W. married in Maury County to Martha Henderson.
National Banner & Nashville Advertiser (Thurs., April 5, 1832)

Wintersteen, Mr. Nicholas married in Pickaway County, O. to Miss Mary
Dolbee.
National Banner & Nashville Whig (Sat., Sept. 15, 1827)

Winton, Miss Dolly married to Rev. John Grant.

Wirkham, Mr. William married in Henry County, Ten. since the first of
Jan. to Miss Alice Parker.
National Banner & Nashville Whig (Fri., Feb. 13, 1835)

Wirt, Miss Elizabeth Gamble married to Lewis M. Goldsborough.

Wirt, Miss L. married to Mr. W. H. Montgomery.

Wisdom, Mr. Francis N. married in Williamson County to Miss Cynthia
M. Brown.
Nashville Whig (Tues., March 31, 1846)

Wisdom, William S. married in Purdy, Ten. to Miss Jane Anderson.
National Banner & Nashville Daily Advertiser (Wed., Aug. 21, 1833)

Wise, Miss Abagail married to Mr. John Wimer.

Wise, Henry A. Esq. of Virginia married on Thursday the 23rd inst.
by Rev. O. Jennings to Miss Ann E. Jennings.
National Banner & Nashville Whig (Sat., Oct. 25, 1828)

Wise, Mr. James married in Nashville last evening to Miss Frances
G. Fisher.
National Banner & Nashville Whig (Wed., April 13, 1831)

Wiseman, Miss Sarah M. married to Mr. Jno. H. Turner.

Wetherill, Mr. John married in this town on Sat. last to Miss Virginia Foster.
National Banner & Nashville Whig (Sat., Oct. 11, 1828)

Witherspoon, A. D. of Elkton married in Elkton, Ky. on the 27th to Miss Letitia H. Park of Nashville.
National Banner & Nashville Whig (Wed., July 19, 1837)

Witherspoon, Miss Parthena married to Mr. Rawliegh Dotson.

Witherspoon, Miss Rachel married to Mr. David Taylor.

Witherspoon, Thomas Esq. married in Paris, Ky. to Mrs. Sarah W. Lapsley.
National Banner & Nashville Whig (Sat., Nov. 22, 1828)

Witherspoon, Mr. Winfrey married in Rutherford County to Miss Mary F. Orr.
National Banner & Nashville Whig (Sat., Feb. 17, 1827)

Withrow, Mr. William married in Madison County, Ala. to Miss Mary Ann Morris.
National Banner & Nashville Whig (Mon., Oct. 31, 1831)

Witt, Mr. Anderson married in Jefferson County to Miss Sarah Palmer.
National Banner & Nashville Whig (Mon., Nov. 28, 1831)

Witt, Mr. Caleb E. married in Logan County, Ky. to Miss Elizabeth Hopkins.
National Banner & Nashville Whig (Sat., Aug. 18, 1827)

Witt, Mr. Joseph married in Jefferson County to Miss Cynthia Lawrence.
National Banner & Nashville Whig (Fri., Jan. 14, 1831)

Woldridge, Elizabeth married to Andrew Webb.

Wolf, Capt. Henry of Nashville married in Caldwell County, Ky. on Thursday evening Sept. 23 to Miss Julia A. Harman.
National Banner & Nashville Whig (Thurs., Sept. 30, 1830)

Wollard, Mr. John married in Maury County to Miss Mary M. Turnage.
National Banner & Nashville Whig (Mon., Aug. 8, 1831)

Womas, Miss Mary F. married to Robert Reams.

Womack, Miss Judith B. married to N. Courtney.

Womack, Miss Sarah B. married to Mr. A. M. Kelly.

Wood, Miss Cindrella married to Mr. James Wood.

Wood, Mr. David married in Mercer County, Ky. to Miss Cerinda Step.
National Banner & Nashville Whig (Wed., Jan. 19, 1831)

Wood, Miss Della married to Capt. William M'Call.

Wood, Miss Eliza A. married to James F. Ruffin Esq.

Wood,, Elizabeth married to Elum Lewis.

Wood, Miss Elizabeth W. married to Mr. Thomas F. Smith.

Wood, Capt. Fleming P. merchant of Nashville married in Wilson County by Rev. John Bradford to Mrs. Lucy Williamson.
Nashville Republican (Tues., Jan. 31st 1837)

Wood, Miss Harriet married to Mr. Stith Harrison Esq.

Wood, Mr. James married in Russellville, Ky. to Miss Cindrella Wood.
National Banner & Nashville Whig (Sat., Sept. 9, 1826)

Wood, Mr. James Jr. married on the 31st inst. by the Rev. Dr. Edgar to Miss Elizabeth S. Crockett daughter of Mr. George Crockett of the Mansion House of Nashville.
The Union (Sat., Sept. 2, 1837)

Wood, Mr. James B. married in Madison County to Miss Jane Willis.
National Banner & Nashville Whig (Sat., May 24, 1828)

Wood, Maj. Jonathan married in Jefferson County to Miss Margaret H. Inman.
National Banner & Nashville Whig (Sat., Feb. 24, 1827)

Wood, Miss Judy married to Capt. Charles Ivey.

Wood, Kesiah married in Williamson County to Alanson Oslin.
The Western Weekly Review - Franklin, Ten. (Fri., Feb. 10, 1832)

Wood, Mr. Larkin F. of Nashville married on the 13th ult. by the Rev. Mr. Peck to Miss Eliza Echols daughter of Col. Wm. E. of Madison Co., Ala.
Nashville Whig (Aug. 2, 1824)

Wood, Miss Malinda married to Mr. Harvey Gray.

Wood, Miss Margaret B. married to Col. B. S. Tappan.

Wood, Miss Maria married to Mr. Samuel Wells.

Wood, Miss Matilda married to Mr. Harvey Gray.

Wood, Mr. Miles of Weakley County, Tenn. married on Thursday the 21st inst. by the Rev. Moses T. Spann to Miss Feriby Kendall of Henry County, Tenn.
Nashville Republican (Tues., Feb. 2, 1836)

Wood, Miss Nancy married to Mr. John N. Coffman.

Wood, Miss Nancy married to Mr. William Hendrex.

Wood, Miss Sarah married to Mr. William S. Warner.

Wood, Miss Sarah married to Mr. Rewben White.

Wood, Miss Sarah married to Mr. Ebenzer Jenkins.

Wood, Miss Sarah married to Mr. William S. Warrner.

Wood, Miss Sarah R. married to Mr. John G. Stewart.

Wood, Mr. William married in Logan County, Ky. to Mr. William Wood to Miss Virginia Bernard.
National Banner (March 31, 1826)

Wood, Mr. William married on the 21st inst. by the Rev. Dr. Edgar to Miss Elizabeth J. Clark all of Nashville.
Nashville Whig (Sat., May 23, 1846)

Wood, Mr. William H. married in Hardeman County, Ten. to Miss Benigna Polk daughter of the late Colonel Ezekiel Polk.
National Banner & Nashville Daily Advertiser (Fri., Aug. 15, 1834)

Woodall, Mr. W. married in Maury County to Jane Hodge.
National Banner & Nashville Advertiser (Thurs., April 5, 1832)

Woodall, Mr. Wiley married in Little Rock, Ark. to Mrs. Rebecca Massengill.
National Banner & Nashville Whig (Fri., April 10, 1835)

Woodfin, Miss Maria married to Mr. Richard Puryear.

Woodfin, Mr. Moses married in Henry County to Miss Margaret Rodgers.
National Banner & Nashville Whig (July 28, 1827)

Woodfin, Mr. Ryland H. married in Nashville on last Thursday by the
Rev. Mr. Green to Miss Henrietta Baily.
National Banner & Nashville Whig (Mon., Sept. 8, 1835)

Woodfolk, Col. William W. of Jackson County, Tenn. married on the
11th ult. by the Rev. Mr. Howell to Miss Ellen Horton daughter of
Mr. Jos. W. Horton Esq. of Nashville.
Nashville Republican (Sat., June 3, 1837)

Woodruff, Mr. Charles E. of Nashville married on Monday evening the
28th by the Rev. James Tompkins to Miss Elizabeth Patton of Wilson
County.
Nashville Whig (Tues., Sept. 5, 1843)

Woodruff, Mr. D. married Tuscaloosa to Miss Eliza Bell.
National Banner (Sat., Nov. 21, 1829)

Woodruff, Miss Eliza married to Mr. Andrew Anderson.

Woodruff, Miss Mariah married to Mr. John Bowman.

Woodruff, Mr. W. W. of Louisiana married in Williamson County to Miss
Mary A. Hamilton.
National Banner & Nashville Whig (Wed., Jan. 21, 1835)

Woods, Miss married to Capt. Jonathan Haynes.

Woods, Miss Agnes married to Mr. Charles C. Trabue.

Woods, Miss Agnes Adine married to Mr. W. Courtney.

Woods, Maj. Archibald of Jackson County, Ala. married in Franklin
County, Ten. on the 15th inst. to Miss Sally G. Caperton daughter of
Mr. Hugh Caperton.
National Banner & Nashville Whig (Mon., June 21, 1830)

Woods, Miss Delila married to Mr. John Alexander.

Woods, Miss Emily M. married to Mr. G. S. Whitman.

Woods, Miss Esther married to Mr. D. Kieth.

Woods, Mr. James formerly of Philadelphia married on the 31st Aug.
by the Rev. T. J. Edgar to Miss Elizabeth S. Crockett daughter of
George Crockett Esq. Mansion House, Nashville.
Daily Republican Banner (Fri., Sept. 8, 1837)

Woods, James Esq. of Nashville married on the 20th inst. at the resi-
dence of Mrs. Porter in Davidson County by the Rev. Dr. Edgar to Miss
Penelope Porter second daughter of the late Mr. Alexander Porter.
The Christian Record (Sat., April 24, 1847)

Woods, Mr. James A. of Westwood married on Tuesday last by the Rev.
Mr. Lapsley to Miss Elizabeth M. Campbell daughter of James Campbell
Esq. of Nashville.
Nashville Whig (Thurs., March 30, 1843)

Woods, Mr. John married in Weakley County to Miss Caroline E. Carr
daughter of Benj. Carr of Rutherford County.
National Banner & Nashville Whig (Sat., Oct. 6, 1827)

Woods, Mr. Joseph L. married in St. Louis to Miss Jane Clegg.
National Banner & Nashville Whig (Wed., June 8, 1831)

Woods, Miss Lovey Worthy married to Mr. Wm. Eaton.

Woods, Miss Lucy Ann married to Mr. Dabney M. Lipscomb.

Woods, Miss Margaret F. married to Mr. Edward Smith Handy.

Woods, Miss Martha married to Mr. Richard Arnett.

Woods, Mr. Robert K. merchant of St. Louis married on the 20th inst.
by Rev. Dr. Edgar to Miss Susan E. Berry daughter of Dr. Berry of
Nashville.
Nashville Whig (Fri., Oct. 22, 1841)

Woods, Miss Robina married to Mr. William B. Armestead.

Woods, Theora Jane married to Edward Smith Handey Esq.

Woodside, Miss Lucinda B. married to Mr. Sampson Lee.

Woodside, Mr. William married in Henry County to Miss Sally Lee.
National Banner & Nashville Daily Advertiser (Sat., Oct. 13, 1832)

Woodson, Mr. J. Wisley of Christian County, Ky. married on Sunday
morning the 27th inst. by the Rev. Dr. Wharton to Mary J. Dibrell
daughter of E. Dibrell Esq. of Nashville.
Nashville Whig (Tues., Sept. 29, 1846)

Woodson, Rev. Lewis W. married in Sumner County to Miss Lucinda Hannah.
National Banner (Sat., Nov. 14, 1829)

Woodson, Miss Martha A. married to Dr. John L. Bryan.

Woodson, William Esq. married in Davidson County to Miss Tennessee
Lowe.
National Banner & Nashville Whig (Sat., Dec. 10, 1831)

Woodward, Miss Ann Haven married to John Gross.

Woodward, Mr. Clement married in Huntsville, Ala. to Miss Martha Ann
Martin.
National Banner & Nashville Daily Advertiser (Wed., Oct. 3, 1832)

Woodward, Mr. Edward L. of Jasper married Miss Malinda J. Francis
daughter of Miller Francis, Esq.
National Banner & Nashville Advertiser (Mon., Dec. 10, 1832)

Woodward, Mrs. Mary Ann married to M. C. Goodlett.

Woodward, Mr. William married in Montgomery County to Miss Elizabeth
Henry.
National Banner & Nashville Whig (Sat., Dec. 27, 1828)

Wooldridge, Miss Judith married to Mr. James Trabue.

Woolen, Mr. Edward married in Vandalia, Ill. to Miss Nancy Stark.
National Banner & Nashville Whig (June 24, 1826)

Wooley, Miss Rhoda married to Mr. James Dunham.

Woolfolk, Miss married to Mr. Tandy.

Woolfolk, Mr. Madison married at Frankford, Ky. to Miss Elizabeth
Phillips.
National Banner (April 7, 1826)

Woolford, Miss Mary Ann married to Mr. William B. Hewlett.

Woollard, Miss Sarah married to Mr. Moses G. Bennett.

Wooten, Mr. William married in Smith County to Miss Lydia Kerley.
National Banner & Nashville Daily Advertiser (Fri., March 23, 1832)

Word, Mr. William B. married in Nashville last evening by the Rev.
Mr. Weller to Miss Sarah P. Wells.
National Banner & Nashville Daily Advertiser (Fri., Jan. 27, 1832)

Work, Miss Emily married to Mr. Robert Cully.

Work, Mr. John married in Davidson County, Tenn. to Miss Ellen Jones.
National Banner & Nashville Whig (Wed., Nov. 12, 1834)

Work, Mr. Joseph merchant of Bowling Green, Ky. married in Warren
County, Ky. at the residence of Col. William Marshall to Miss Sarah
D. Farmer.
National Banner & Nashville Whig (Wed., Feb. 25, 1835)

Workman, Mary married to Mr. Charles Headache, Esq.

Wormas, Miss Ann Jane married to Mr. J. W. Dickson.

Wormack, Miss Mary married to Mr. Joseph Pigg.

Wormley, Miss Eleanor married to Mr. Samuel P. Walker.

Wormley, Miss Jane B. married to Mr. Gladin Gorin.

Wornel, Miss Eliza married to Mr. Edward M'Nabb.

Wort, Mr. John married in Hardeman County to Miss Carolina Polk.
National Banner & Nashville Whig (Sat., Feb. 7, 1829)

Wortham, Miss married to Mr. William Dickson.

Wortham, Capt. James married in Shelbyville to Miss Catherine Camron.
National Banner & Nashville Daily Advertiser (Sat., Oct. 6, 1832)

Wortham, Dr. John P. married in Columbia by the Rev. Mr. Madden to
Miss Susan Voorhies daughter of Peter J. Voorhies, Esq.
National Banner & Nashville Whig (Fri., Aug. 19, 1831)

Worthington, Mr. Isaac of Mississippi married at Lexington, Ky. to
Miss Margaret Higgins youngest daughter of Richard Higgins,
Esq.
National Banner & Nashville Whig (Mon., Nov. 1, 1830)

Worthington, John F. Esq. married in Mercer County, Ky. to Miss Ann
Slaughter.
National Banner & Nashville Whig (Sat., Feb. 17, 1827)

Worthington, Miss Keturak M. married to Mr. John Rowen.

Wozencraft, Oliver M. late Lieut. in the Highlanders married on 23d
by the Rev. Mr. Pitts to Miss Lemiza A. Ramsey daughter of William
Ramsey Esq. all of Davidson County.
Nashville Republican (Thurs., March 2, 1837)

Wozencraft, Oliver M. late Lieut. in the Highlanders married on Thursday 23d ult. by the Rev. Mr. Pitts to Miss Lemiza A. Ramsey
daughter of Mr. William Ramsey all of Davidson County.
National Banner & Nashville Whig (Fri., March 3, 1837)

Wrenn, Miss Susan married to Mr. Hardy Petty.

Wrigglesworth, Miss Sarah married to Robert C. Thompson, Esq.

Wright, Mr. Aaron married in Nashville on May 31st by the Rev. Mr. Gayle
to Miss Margaret J. Thomas.
National Banner & Nashville Daily Advertiser (Sat., June 2, 1832)

Wright, Archibald Esq. married in Pulaski to Miss Elizabeth Eldridge daughter of the late Dr. Elisha Eldridge of Pulaski.
Nashville Republican (Sat., June 10, 1837)

Wright, Mr. Benjamin married in Maury County to Miss Chloe Yarborough.
National Banner & Nashville Whig (Fri., Dec. 10, 1830)

Wright, Miss Eliza Sterling married to Mr. Jos. C. Frye.

Wright, Miss Elizabeth married to Mr. John Cahoe

Wright, Miss Eveline married to Mr. Thomas M. Draper.

Wright, Mr. Hamilton M. of New Orleans married on the 8th inst. by Rev. Bishop Otey to Miss Amelia Ann Williams daughter of Capt. John Williams of Nashville.
National Banner & Nashville Whig (Mon., Sept. 12, 1836)

Wright, Mr. Isaac married in Blount County to Miss Susan Brown.
National Banner & Nashville Daily Advertiser (Wed., May 8, 1833)

Wright, Mr. James married on Tuesday the 22nd inst. to Miss Emeline Gleaves all of Nashville.
Daily Republican Banner (Thurs., Jan. 24, 1839)

Wright, Mr. James C. married in Henry County to Miss Nicy Hudson.
National Banner & Nashville Daily Advertiser (Fri., Jan. 27, 1832)

Wright, Miss Jane married to Mr. Thomas J. Black.

Wright, Mr. John married in this County to Miss Alethea Mumford.
National Banner (May 4, 1826)

Wright, Col. Jno. N. of Cottonport married on Sunday the 8th inst. by H. Owen Esq. to Miss Julia Ann Bibb of Davidson County.
The Western Weekly Review - Franklin, Tenn. (Fri., Jan. 13, 1832)

Wright, Judgematical of Westmoreland County, Va. married on Tuesday the 18th of Dec. by the Rev. Thomas C. Bracton to Miss Lucy Pursle of Richmond County.
National Banner & Nashville Whig(Mon., Jan. 5, 1835)

Wright, Miss Louise P. married to Mr. A. P. Eakin.

Wright, Miss Lydia married to Mr. Leonard Brown.

Wright, Miss Malora married to Mr. L. J. Williams.

Wright, Miss Martha married to Mr. B. G. Mitchell.

Wright, Miss Martha married to Mr. Franklin White.

Wright, Miss Mary married to Mr. John Davis.

Wright, Miss Mary Ann married to Mr. Smith Thomas.

Wright, Miss Mary married to Mr. Samuel Prather.

Wright, Mr. Moses married in Lauderdale County, Ala. to Miss Ann Wilson.
National Banner (April 21, 1826)

Wright, Miss Nancy married to Mr. John H. Hudson.

Wright, Miss Nancy married to Mr. Robert Brady.

Wright, Miss Narcissa A. L. married to C. C. Abernathy.

Wright, Miss Patience married to Mr. Nicholas Edington.

Wright, Mrs. Sally married to Mr. Jesse L. Page.

Wright, Mr. Samuel B. married in Tsucaloosa to Mrs. Mary Evans.
National Banner & Nashville Whig (Sat., March 1, 1828)

Wright, Miss Sarah married to Mr. Ambrose B. Gilbert.

Wright, Miss Sarah married to Mr. David Weatherly.

Wright, Miss Susan F. married to Mr. C. C. Saunders.

Wright, Mr. Thorton married in Henry County, Tenn. to Miss Abenica
Stone.
National Banner & Nashville Whig (Fri., March 6, 1835)

Wright, Mr. W. P. married in Logan County, Ky. to Miss Sarah Ragsdale.
National Banner (Feb. 3, 1826)

Wurts, Miss Maria married to Mr. John Muir.

Wyatt, Mr. Thomas married in Lincoln County to Miss Isabell Wham.
National Banner & Nashville Whig (Sat., Nov. 17, 1827)

Wyatt, Capt. Peter married at Montgomery, Ala. to Mary A. E. Mock.
National Banner (June 10, 1826)

Wyche, Miss Rebecca Ann married to Mr. William H. Wyche.

Wyllie, George A. Esq. of Virginia married in Sumner County to Miss
Elizabeth Elliott daughter of Col. Geo. Elliott.
National Banner & Nashville Whig (Mon., Jan. 3, 1831)

Wyly, Miss married to Mr. Jacob Russell.

Wynn, Miss Catherine G. married to Mr. William Wynn.

Wynn, Miss Cynthia married to Mr. A. G. Donoho.

Wynn, Miss Frances Ann married to Mr. Newton Whitaker.

Wynn, Mr. William married in Henderson County to Miss Catherine G. Wynn
National Banner (Sat., Nov. 7, 1829)

Wynne, Mr. Absalem G. (Alanson G.) married in Lebanon to Miss Martha
Hunt daughter of Dr. Thomas Hunt.
National Banner & Nashville Whig (Mon., Oct. 4, 1830)

Wynne, Doctor Augustus C. of New Orleans married on the 5th inst. by
Rev. Dr. Howell to Miss Laura J. Raworth eldest daughter of E. A.
Raworth Esq. of Nashville.
Nashville True Whig & Weekly Commercial Register (Fri., April 12, 1850)

Wynne, Miss Mary married to Mr. Thomas B. Herron.

Wynne, Miss Matilda C. married to Mr. Thomas H. Cannon.

Yager, Mr. Churchhill married in Lincoln County, Ky. to Miss Susan Stone.
National Banner & Nashville Whig (Sat., Jan. 6, 1827)

Yancy, Mr. William married in Maury County to Miss Ann Lusk daughter of Mr. Samuel Lusk.
National Banner (Sat., Nov. 21, 1829)

Yandle, Mr. William of Natchez, Mississippi married at Bardstown, Ky. on 2nd Sept. to Miss Catherine Ann Patterson of Bardstown, Ky.
Daily Republican Banner (Wed., Sept. 18, 1839)

Yarborough, Mr. Charles married in Henderson County to Miss Sarah B. Anderson daughter of Garland Anderson Esq.
National Banner (Sat., Sept. 19, 1829)

Yarborough, Miss Nancy married to Mr. Aaron Clements.

Yarbro, Miss Penelope married to Mr. Terrill.

Yarbrough, Mr. Benjamin married in Henry County, Tenn. to Miss Rhoda Nash.
National Banner & Nashville Daily Advertiser (Mon., May 28, 1832)

Yarbrough, Miss Chloe married to Mr. Benjamin Wright.

Yarbrough, Miss Eliza Ann married to Mr. Wm. N. Holmes.

Yardy, Capt. Thomas married in Rutherford County to Miss Mary Cox.
National Banner (Sat., Nov. 21, 1829)

Yarnell, Miss Eliza B. married to Mr. William H. Howard.

Yates, Miss Diana married to Samuel Adams.

Yates, John married in Williamson County to Nancy A. Jorman.
National Banner & Nashville Daily Advertiser (Mon., March 26, 1832)

Yates, Miss Maria married to Mr. Benj. Holland.

Yates, Mr. Perser married in Henry County to Miss Nancy Rodery.
National Banner & Nashville Daily Advertiser (Fri., April 12, 1833)

Yates, Mr. William of Carrellton, Ill. late of Clarksville married in Montgomery County, Ten. to Miss Frances Hinton daughter of John Hinton Esq.
National Banner & Nashville Whig (Fri., May 1, 1835)

Yearger, Miss Sarah M. married to Mr. Lewis M. Grigg.

Yearger, Miss Sarah M. married to Mr. Lewis M. Grigg.

Yeatman, Miss Emma married to Col. Thompson T. Player.

Yell, Arch'd, Judge of the Supreme Court of Arkansas married at Jackson County, Ark. on the 7th by Rev. Mr. Lee to Mrs. Maria Ficklin relict of the late Thompson H. Ficklin, Esq.
Nashville Republican (Sat., July 30, 1836)

Yell, Mr. James Jr. married in Bedford County to Miss A. P. Young daughter of James Young Esq.
National Banner & Nashville Daily Advertiser (Thurs., July 12, 1832)

Yell, Miss Jane C. married to Mr. Thomas J. Purdy.

Yerger, Mr. Cornelius married in Washington County, Ten. to Miss Salina Hoss daughter of Mr. Abraham Hoss all of Washington County.
National Banner & Nashville Whig (Fri., Jan. 9, 1835)

Yerger, Mr. John K. married in Giels County on the 10th inst. by Rev. H. H. Brown to Miss Ann Eliza Jones daughter of Mr. Richard H. Jones of Davidson County.
National Banner (Sat., Sept. 19, 1827)

Yerger, Mr. John K. merchant of Pulaski, Ten. married on the 23d ult. by the Rev. Robert Paine President of LaGrange College to Miss Erexine H. Pernell of Greene County, Ala.
National Banner & Nashville Whig (Mon., April 24, 1837)

Yerger, J. S. Esq. Attorney at law of Nashville married in Smith County to Miss Mary Bowen daughter of the late John H. Bowen Esq.of Smith.
National Banner & Nashville Daily Advertiser (Mon., Dec. 23, 1833)

Yerger,, J. S. Esq. of Nashville married in Smith County to Miss Mary Bowen.
Nashville Republican & State Gazette (Tues., Dec. 24, 1833)

Yerger, William married on Tuesday 23d inst. by the Rev. J. T. Edgar to Miss Malvina Rucks daughter of James Rucks of Nashville.
The Union (Sat., May 27, 1837)

Yerger, William Esq. Attorney at law of Jackson married in Nashville, Tenn. to Miss Malvina Rucks daughter of James Rucks Esq.
National Banner & Nashville Whig (Mon., May 29, 1837)

Yeargin, Miss Mary S. married to Thomas Sims.

Yeargin, Miss Mary w. married to Thomas Sims.

Yearout, Miss Lydia married to Mr. Adam Thomas.

Yearout, Miss Sarah married to Mr. David Caldwell.

Yeatman, Mr. Henry T. merchant married in Nashville Dec. 8th by the Rev. J. T. Edgar, D. D. to Miss Sarah West daughter of Mr. John B. West of Nashville.
National Banner & Nashville Whig (Fri., Dec. 12, 1834)

Yeatman, Mr. James E. Esq. of Nashville, Tenn. married in Ballemore on the 28th ult. to Miss Angelica Charlotte Thompson daughter of J. P. Thompson Esq. of Alexandria, D. C.
Daily Republican Banner (Sat., Oct. 20, 1838)

Yeatman, James E. Esq. of Nashville married in Baltimore, Sept. 28 to Miss Angelica Charlotte Thompson daughter of J. P. Thompson Esq. of Alexandria D. C.
Nashville Whig (Wed., Oct. 24, 1838)

Yeatman, Mrs. Jane married to Hon. John Bell.

Yeatman, Mr. Thomas merchant of this place married on the 11th inst. by the Rev. Mr. Hume to Miss Jane Erwin daughter of Colonel Andrew Erwin of Augusta, Georgia.
The Nashville Whig (Sept. 15, 1817)

Yeatman, Mr. William T. of the house of Misses J. & R. Yeatman married at White Cottage on Monday the 27th inst. by the Rev. Dr. Edgar to Miss Amelia Erwin daughter of John P. Erwin Esq.
Nashville Whig (Wed., Aug. 29, 1838)

Yeatman, Mr. William T. of the house of Messrs. J. & R. Yeatman & Co. married at White Cottage on 27th inst. by the Rev. Dr. Edgar to Miss Amelia Erwin third daughter of John Erwin Esq.
Daily Republican Banner (Wed., Aug. 29, 1838)

Yieser, Miss Margaret married to Mr. Augustine W. Pinhead.

Yoakum, Miss Louisa M. married to Dr. Benjamin M. Bayless.

Yoast, Miss Mary married to Mr. Duke Howell.

Yo-give-se married at the Valley Towns by the Rev. E. Jones 12th April 1830 to Gub-n-ne-da.
National Banner & Nashville Whig (Mon., July 26, 1830)

Yookum, Lieut, Anderson K. married in Roane County to Miss Evelina Cannon.
National Banner & Nashville Daily Advertiser (Fri., March 1, 1833)

York, Edward, Esq. of New Orleans married in Lauderdale County, Ala. to Miss Sarah Hanna.
National Banner & Nashville Whig (Mon., June 27, 1831)

Yorke, Miss Sarah married to Andrew Jackson Jun Esq.

Yorke, Mr. William married in Cincinnati, O. to Miss Mary Ann Murphy.
National Banner & Nashville Daily Advertiser (Thurs., June 19, 1834)

Younce, Mr. Samuel married at Louisville, Ky. to Miss Jane Kincade.
National Banner (Sat., June 6, 1829)

Young, Miss A. P. married to Mr. James Yell Jr.

Young, Rev. Acton of Bedford County married at Bethesda, Williamson County on 30th ulto. by the Rev. Henry C. Horton to Miss Elizabeth P. Lavender.
Nashville Whig (Sat., Sept. 3, 1842)

Young, Miss Ann E. married to Mr. W. J. Anderson.

Young, Miss Ann E. married to Mr. W. J. Anderson.

Young, Miss Eliza married to Mr. Joseph Melward.

Young, Miss Eliza Ann married to Mr. William Lynch.

Young, Miss Elizabeth married to Mr. Henry Allen.

Young, Miss E. M. married to Mr. Moses Hoge.

Young, Mr. Jacob married in Athens to Mrs. Patsey Hogue.
National Banner & Nashville Whig (Wed., Dec. 1, 1830)

Young, James M. D. of Jackson married in Nashville on the 15th inst. by the Rev. Mr. Hume to Miss Rebecca R. Hogg daughter of Dr. Sam Hogg.
National Banner & Nashville Daily Advertiser (Fri., March 16, 1832)

Young, Capt. John married on Thursday evening last by the Rev. Mr. Blackburn to Miss Caroline Sommerville daughter of Jno. Sommerville.
The Nashville Whig & Tenn. Advertiser (Oct. 20, 1817)

Young, Mr. John C. married in Lincoln County, Ten. to Miss Ara C. Caruthers.
National Banner & Nashville Whig (Mon., April 20, 1835)

Young, Rev. John C. married in Fayette County, Ky. to Miss Frances A. Breckenridge daughter of the late Joseph Cabell Breckenridge.
National Banner (Sat., Nov. 28, 1829)

Young, Miss Julia C. married to Mr. John Baird.

Young, Lucy married to Alexr R. Clark.

Young, Miss Martha married to Mr. Thomas Bovard.

Young, Miss Mary married to Dr. Benjamin Gray.

Young, Miss Mary married to Mr. Wm. Giles.

Young, Miss Nancy married to Rev. John Munger.

Young, Mrs. Nancy married to R. Higgins, Esq.

Young, Miss Patricia S. married to Mr. Andrew J. Smith.

Young, Miss Piety H. married to William Greenfield, Esq.

Young, Miss Sarah married to Mr. Hezekiah Faris.

Young, Miss Sarah married to Mr. Sowell Newson.

Young, Mr. William married in Bedford County to Miss Eliza C. Hooser.
Nashville Whig (Tues., March 24, 1846)

Young, Miss Winniford Y. married to Mr. John Violett.

Younger, Miss Icephena married to Mr. Andrew Finley.

Younger, Mr. James married in Maury County, Ten. to Miss Margaret
Hinson.
National Banner & Nashville Whig (Wed., March 4, 1835)

Younger, Mr. James married in Maury County to Miss Margaret Hinson on
the 19th ult.
Nashville Republican (Thurs., March 5, 1835)

Younger, Mr. John M. married in Williamson County to Miss Mary E. Church.
Nashville Whig (Tues., March 31, 1846)

Youngman, Mr. David married in Williamson County on Thursday evening
the 4th inst. to Miss Nancy M'Mahon.
National Banner & Nashville Daily Advertiser (Mon., April 8, 1833)

Youngman, Mr. David married on Thursday evening 4th inst. by the Rev.
Dr. Hardin to Miss Nancy M'Mahon.
The Western Weekly Review - Franklin, Tenn. (Fri., April 5, 1833)

Yowel, Joel Esq. married in Lincoln County to Mrs. Nancy Butler.
National Banner & Nashville Whig (Sat., Aug. 19, 1826)

Ziverly, Miss Mary married to Mr. John M. Donnahoo.

Zollicofer, Capt. Frederick married Miss Elizabeth P. Love in Maury
County.
National Banner & Nashville Whig (Fri., Jan. 22, 1830)